June 12–14, 2013
Amsterdam, The Netherlands

**Association for
Computing Machinery**

Advancing Computing as a Science & Profession

SACMAT'13

Proceedings of the 18th ACM

Symposium on Access Control Models and Technologies

Sponsored by:

ACM SACMAT

Supported by:

Università degli Studi di Padova & ASU

**Association for
Computing Machinery**

Advancing Computing as a Science & Profession

The Association for Computing Machinery
2 Penn Plaza, Suite 701
New York, New York 10121-0701

ISBN: 978-1-4503-1950-8 (Digital)

ISBN: 978-1-4503-2284-3 (Print)

Additional copies may be ordered prepaid from:

ACM Order Department
PO Box 30777
New York, NY 10087-0777, USA

Phone: 1-800-342-6626 (USA and Canada)
+1-212-626-0500 (Global)
Fax: +1-212-944-1318
E-mail: acmhelp@acm.org
Hours of Operation: 8:30 am – 4:30 pm ET

Printed in the USA

Foreword

It is our great pleasure to welcome you to the *18th ACM Symposium on Access Control Models and Technologies (SACMAT 2013)*. This year's symposium continues its tradition of being the premier forum for presentation of research results on leading edge issues of access control, including models, systems, applications, and theory.

62 papers have been submitted from a variety of countries around the world. Submissions were anonymous; each paper has been reviewed by at least three reviewers who are experts in the field. Extensive online discussions took place to make the selections for the symposium. The program committee finally accepted 19 papers that cover a variety of topics, including Privacy & Compliance, Policy Management & Enforcement, Systems & Information Flow, Policy Analysis, and Applications. The program again contains two demo sessions with 8 demos covering topics such as secure benchmarking in the cloud, sticky policies for mobile devices or secure Big Data Analytics. In addition, the program includes a panel on the granularity of access control models and their effect on policies, management and lifecycle as well as two keynote talks by Dr. Florian Kerschbaum and Prof. Dr. Ahmad Reza-Sadeghi. We hope that these proceedings will serve as a valuable reference for security researchers and developers.

Putting together SACMAT 2013 was a team effort. First of all, we would like to thank the authors for submitting to the symposium, the keynote speakers for graciously accepting our invitation, the demo presenters and panelists for contributing to the program. We are grateful to the program committee members and external reviewers for their efforts in reviewing the papers and their engagement in online discussions during the review process. Special thanks go to Ian Molloy and Mahesh Tripunitara (Panels Chairs), Axel Kern (Demonstrations Chair), Dongwan Shin (Webmaster), Lujo Bauer (Publicity Chair) and Mohamed Shehab (Proceedings Chair) for their help in organizing and publicizing the symposium. We also thank the members of the steering committee and especially its chair, Gail-Joon Ahn, for providing valuable advice and support. Many thanks also go to the local arrangements chair, Asia Slowinska.

We would like to thank our sponsor, ACM SIGSAC, for their continued support of this symposium. We would also like to acknowledge the University of Padua and Vrije Universiteit Amsterdam for supporting the organization of the conference.

We hope that you will find this program interesting and that the symposium will provide you with a valuable opportunity to share ideas with other researchers and practitioners from institutions around the world.

Mauro Conti
SACMAT '13 General Chair
University of Padua, Italy

Andreas Schaad
SACMAT'13 Program Chair
SAP Labs, Germany

Jaideep Vaidya
SACMAT'13 Program Chair
Rutgers University, USA

Table of Contents

Keynote Address
Session Chair: Jaideep Vaidya *(Rutgers University)*

Session 1: Privacy & Compliance
Session Chair: Vijayalakshmi Atluri *(NSF and Rutgers University)*

Session 2: Policy Management & Enforcement
Session Chair: Adam Lee *(University of Pittsburgh)*

Panel
Session Chair: Ian Molloy *(IBM Research)*

Keynote Address
Session Chair: Andreas Schaad *(SAP Labs)*

Session 3: Systems & Information Flow

Session Chair: Jason Crampton *(Royal Holloway, University of London)*

Session 4: Policy Analysis

Session Chair: Gail-Joon Ahn *(Arizona State University)*

Demo Session I

Session Chair: Axel Kern *(Beta Systems AG)*

Session 5: Applications

Session Chair: Murat Kantarcioglu *(University of Texas at Dallas)*

Demo Session II
Session Chair: Mahesh Tripunitara *(University of Waterloo)*

2013 ACM Symposium on Access Control Models and Technologies

General Chair: Mauro Conti *(University of Padua, Italy)*

Program Chairs: Jaideep Vaidya *(Rutgers University, USA)*
Andreas Schaad *(SAP AG, Germany)*

Panels Chairs: Ian Molloy *(IBM, USA)*
Mahesh Tripunitara *(University of Waterloo, Canada)*

Demonstrations Chair: Axel Kern *(Beta Systems Software AG, Germany)*

Proceedings Chair: Mohamed Shehab *(University of North Carolina at Charlotte, USA)*

Local Arrangements Chair: Asia Slowinska *(Vrije Universiteit Amsterdam, The Netherlands)*

Publicity Chair: Lujo Bauer *(Carnegie Mellon University, USA)*

Treasurer: Basit Shafiq *(Lahore University of Management Sciences, Pakistan)*

Webmaster: Dongwan Shin *(New Mexico Tech, USA)*

Steering Committee Chair: Gail-Joon Ahn *(Arizona State University, USA)*

Steering Committee: Axel Kern *(Beta Systems Software AG, Germany)*
Bhavani Thuraisingham *(University of Texas at Dallas, USA)*
Indrakshi Ray *(Colorado State University, USA)*
Ninghui Li *(Purdue University, USA)*
James Joshi *(University of Pittsburgh, USA)*

Program Committee: Jaime Acosta *(Army Research Laboratory, USA)*
Gail-Joon Ahn *(Arizona State University, USA)*
Vijay Atluri *(Rutgers University, USA)*
Lujo Bauer *(Carnegie Mellon University, USA)*
Elisa Bertino *(Purdue University, USA)*
Ruth Breu *(University of Innsbruck, Austria)*
Barbara Carminati *(University of Insubria, Italy)*
Jason Crampton *(Royal Holloway, University of London, UK)*
Elena Ferrari *(University of Insubria at Como, Italy)*
Philip Fong *(University of Calgary, Canada)*
Hongxin Hu *(Delaware State University, USA)*
Michael Huth *(Imperial College, UK)*
Trent Jaeger *(Pennsylvania State University, USA)*

Subreviewers: Jyothsna Rachapalli *(University of Texas at Dallas, USA)*
Sabrina De Capitani Di Vimercati *(University of Milan, Italy)*
Qun Ni *(Purdue University, USA)*
Machigar Ongtang *(Stony Brook University, USA)*
Divya Muthkumaran *(Pennsylvania State University, USA)*
Ping Yang *(Stony Brook University, USA)*
Xinyang Ge *(Pennsylvania State University, USA)*
Gerhard Hancke *(Royal Holloway, University of London, UK)*
Matthias Gander *(University of Innsbruck, Austria)*
Basel Katt *(University of Innsbruck, Austria)*
Nathalie Baracaldo *(University of Pittsburgh, USA)*
Christian Sillaber *(University of Innsbruck, Austria)*
Nicholas Farnan *(University of Pittsburgh, USA)*
Huseyin Ulusoy *(University of Texas at Dallas, USA)*
Erman Pattuk *(University of Texas at Dallas, USA)*
Nirupama Talele *(Pennsylvania State University, USA)*
Lianshan Sun *(University of Texas at San Antonio, USA)*
Pietro Colombo *(University of Insubria at Como, Italy)*
Thomas Trojer *(University of Innsbruck, Austria)*
Cuneyt Gurcan Akcora *(University of Insubria at Como, Italy)*
Lei Jin *(University of Pittsburgh, USA)*
Prachi Kumari *(Technische Universität München, Germany)*
Chris Gates *(Purdue University, USA)*
Zhongyuan Xu *(Stony Brook University, USA)*
Vaibhav Khadilkar *(University of Texas at Dallas, USA)*
Haining Chen *(Purdue University, USA)*
Hassan Takabi *(University of Pittsburgh, USA)*
William Garrison *(University of Pittsburgh, USA)*
Hayawardh Vijayakumar *(Pennsylvania State University, USA)*
Michele Guglielmi *(University of Insubria at Como, Italy)*
Dang Nguyen *(University of Texas at San Antonio, USA)*
Johan Oudinet *(Technische Universität München, Germany)*
Philipp Zech *(University of Innsbruck, Austria)*
Yuqiong Sun *(Pennsylvania State University, USA)*
James Alderman *(Royal Holloway, University of London, UK)*

SACMAT 2013 Sponsor & Supporters

Sponsor:

Supporters:

UNIVERSITÀ
DEGLI STUDI
DI PADOVA

Mobile Security and Privacy:
The Quest for the Mighty Access Control

Ahmad-Reza Sadeghi
CASED/System Security Lab, Technische Universität Darmstadt, Germany
Intel Collaborative Research Institute for Secure Computing (ICRI-SC) at TU-Darmstadt, Germany
Fraunhofer Institute for Secure Information Technology (SIT) Darmstadt, Germany
ahmad.sadeghi@trust.cased.de

ABSTRACT

Mobile smart devices are changing our lives and are the emerging dominant computing platform for end-users. Mobile applications (apps) provide flexible access to critical services such as online banking, health records, enterprise applications, or social networks. The increasing computing and storage capabilities, new interfaces such as near field communication technology (NFC) or integration of hardware-based secure execution environments as well as rich context sensing capabilities have turned these devices to enablers for many useful (and fancy) applications. In particular, we consider two emerging trends with high commercial interest: smart devices as access tokens (e.g., in conjunction with NFC), and smart devices as powerful sensors for context-aware access control to resources. We elaborate on the functional, security, and privacy challenges to realizing these applications in practice. To tackle these challenges (and depending on the underlying use-case) we clearly need security and privacy protecting measures at different system abstraction layers (applications, operating system, and hardware) and we may need them simultaneously.

Although mobile operating systems have been designed with security in mind from their infancy, they fail to resist sophisticated attacks as shown recently. We observe diverse attack vectors from application-level privilege escalation attacks and sensory malware [5, 9] to runtime attacks that hijack the execution flow of apps, in particular the recently proposed just-in-time return-oriented programming attack technique [7] which circumvents fine-grained address space layout randomization. Moreover, runtime attacks can be leveraged to compromise the underlying operating system through kernel based attacks (e.g., root exploits) allowing an attacker to get full control over the mobile device.

In the recent years, researchers have presented many proposals to enhance the security and privacy at different abstraction layers with the strong focus on the Android operating system for obvious reasons (open-source and popularity). Investigating the large body of literature on Android security we observe that almost all proposals for security extensions to Android constitute mandatory access control (MAC) mechanisms that are tailored to the specific semantics of the addressed problem, for instance, establishing fine-grained access control to the user's private data or protecting the platform integrity.

Moreover, these solutions consider protection mechanisms that operate only at a specific system abstraction layer, i.e., either at the middleware (and/or application) layer, or at the kernel-layer. In addition, security and privacy policy management itself would need to be made more context-aware and user-centric [4].

We elaborate on security solutions (including our work) that aim to mitigate attacks at application-level including control flow integrity (CFI) [1, 3] against runtime attacks on mobile devices, and discuss their trade-offs. We then present a generic security architecture – inspired by concepts of the Flask architecture [8] – for the Android OS which covers mandatory access control (MAC) on both the kernel- and middleware layers. It aims to serve as a flexible and effective ecosystem to instantiate different security solutions. Moreover, it aims at enforcing sensing- and context-based policies, e.g., using sensed contexts and their security-relevant properties to grant and deny access to device resources dynamically [2], in a truly context-aware manner. We then discuss further challenges in particular for deployment in practice.

Last but not least we leave the question open, how mighty the access control mechanisms should be on mobile smart devices to have an appropriate and reasonable trade-off of security, privacy and usability in practice.

Categories and Subject Descriptors

D.4.6 [**Operating Systems**]: Security and Protection— *Access Controls*

General Terms

Security

Keywords

access control; mobile security

Bio

Ahmad-Reza Sadeghi is a full professor of Computer Science at Technische Universität Darmstadt. He is the Director of the System Security Lab at the Center for Advanced Security Research Darmstadt (CASED) and Scientific Director of Fraunhofer Institute for Secure Information Technology (SIT). Since January 2012 he is also the Director of the Intel Collaborative Research Institute for Secure Computing (ICRI-SC) at TU-Darmstadt, Germany. He received his PhD in Computer Science with the focus

on privacy protecting cryptographic protocols and systems
from the University of Saarland in Saarbrücken, Germany.
Prior to academia, he worked in Research and Development
of Telecommunications enterprises, amongst others Ericsson
Telecommunications. He has been leading and involved in
a variety of national and international research and development projects on design and implementation of trustworthy computing platforms and trusted computing, security
in hardware, cryptographic privacy protecting systems, and
cryptographic compilers (in particular for practical secure
computation). He has been continuously contributing to
the IT-Security research community and serving as general
or program chair as well as program committee member of
many conferences and workshops in information security and
privacy. He is on the Editorial Board of the ACM Transactions on Information and System Security. Prof. Sadeghi
has been awarded with the renowned German prize "Karl
Heinz Beckurts" for his research on Trusted and Trustworthy
Computing technology and its transfer to industrial practice.
The award honors excellent scientific achievements with high
impact on industrial innovations in Germany. Further, his
group received the second prize of the German IT Security
Competition Award 2010.

1. REFERENCES

[1] Martín Abadi, Mihai Budiu, Úlfar Erlingsson, and Jay
    Ligatti. Control-flow integrity principles,
    implementations, and applications. In *ACM
    Transactions on Information and Systems Security*,
    13(1), 2009.
[2] Sven Bugiel, Stephan Heuser, and Ahmad-Reza
    Sadeghi. Towards a Framework for Android Security
    Modules: Extending SE Android Type Enforcement to
    Android Middleware *Technical Report
    TUD-CS-2012-0231*, 2012.
[3] Lucas Davi, Alexandra Dmitrienko, Manuel Egele,
    Thomas Fischer, Thorsten Holz, Ralf Hund, Stefan
    Nürnberger, and Ahmad-Reza Sadeghi. MoCFI: A
    framework to mitigate control-flow attacks on
    smartphones. In *Symposium on Network and
    Distributed System Security (NDSS)*, 2012.
[4] Aditi Gupta, Markus Miettinen, N. Asokan, and Marcin
    Nagy. Intuitive security policy configuration in mobile
    devices using context profiling. In *ASE International
    Conference on Social Computing (SocialCom)*, 2012.
[5] Philip Marquardt, Arunabh Verma, Henry Carter, and
    Patrick Traynor. (sp)iphone: decoding vibrations from
    nearby keyboards using mobile phone accelerometers.
    In *ACM Conference on Computer and Communications
    Security (CCS)*, 2011.
[6] S. Smalley and R. Craig. Security Enhanced (SE)
    Android: Bringing flexible MAC to Android. In
    *Symposium on Network and Distributed System
    Security (NDSS)*, 2013.
[7] Kevin Z. Snow, Lucas Davi, Alexandra Dmitrienko,
    Christopher Liebchen, Fabian Monrose, and
    Ahmad-Reza Sadeghi. Just-in-time code reuse: On the
    effectiveness of fine-grained address space layout
    randomization. In *IEEE Symposium on Security and
    Privacy*, 2013.
[8] Ray Spencer, Stephen Smalley, Peter Loscocco, Mike
    Hibler, David Andersen, and Jay Lepreau. The Flask
    Security Architecture: System Support for Diverse
    Security Policies. In *USENIX Security Symposium*,
    2013.
[9] Robert Templeman, Zahid Rahman, David Crandall,
    and Apu Kapadia. PlaceRaider: Virtual Theft in
    Physical Spaces with Smartphones. In *Symposium on
    Network and Distributed System Security (NDSS)*, 2013.

Privacy Promises That Can Be Kept: A Policy Analysis Method with Application to the HIPAA Privacy Rule

Omar Chowdhury‡, Andreas Gampe‡, Jianwei Niu‡, Jeffery von Ronne‡,
Jared Bennatt‡, Anupam Datta§, Limin Jia§

CS Department, The University of Texas at San Antonio‡ CyLab, ECE Department, Carnegie Mellon University§
{ochowdhu, agampe, niu, vonronne, jbennatt}@cs.utsa.edu ‡   {danupam, liminjia}@cmu.edu §

ABSTRACT

Organizations collect personal information from individuals to carry out their business functions. Federal privacy regulations, such as the Health Insurance Portability and Accountability Act (*HIPAA*), mandate how this collected information can be shared by the organizations. It is thus incumbent upon the organizations to have means to check compliance with the applicable regulations. Prior work by Barth *et al.* introduces two notions of *compliance*, weak compliance (*WC*) and strong compliance (*SC*). WC ensures that present requirements of the policy can be met whereas SC also ensures obligations can be met. An action is compliant with a privacy policy if it is both weakly and strongly compliant. However, their definitions of compliance are restricted to only propositional linear temporal logic (*pLTL*), which cannot feasibly specify HIPAA. To this end, we present a policy specification language based on a restricted subset of first order temporal logic (*FOTL*) which can capture the privacy requirements of HIPAA. We then formally specify WC and SC for policies of our form. We prove that checking WC is feasible whereas checking SC is undecidable. We then formally specify the property WC entails SC, denoted by Δ, which requires that each weakly compliant action is also strongly compliant. To check whether an action is compliant with such a policy, it is sufficient to only check whether the action is weakly compliant with that policy. We also prove that when a policy ℘ has the Δ-property, the present requirements of the policy reduce to the safety requirements imposed by ℘. We then develop a sound, semi-automated technique for checking whether practical policies have the Δ-property. We finally use HIPAA as a case study to demonstrate the efficacy of our policy analysis technique.

Categories and Subject Descriptors

K.4.1 [**Computers and Society**]: Public Policy Issues—*Privacy, Regulation*; F.4.1 [**Mathematical Logic and Formal Languages**]: Mathematical Logic—*Temporal logic*

Keywords

Privacy Policy, HIPAA, Policy Analysis, Obligations

1. INTRODUCTION

Our society is becoming increasingly dependent on computer information systems for the proper management of personal data. Medical records, financial data, and personal information collected from users are just a few examples. Organizations are required to store and share such information in a manner that conforms to specific privacy policies, which are mandated by custom, sound business practice, contract, and, often, by law. Examples of privacy policies that carry the force of law include the Health Insurance Portability and Accountability Act (HIPAA) [33], the Gramm-Leach-Bliley Act (GLBA) [3], Sarbanes-Oxley Act (SOX) [51]. Violations of these federal regulations can bring down heavy financial penalties on the organizations. For instance, Cignet Health Center was fined $1.3 million for violating §164.524 of HIPAA [10] which *obligates* the covered entity (hospital) to give patients access to their medical records when the patients request for it. It is thus important for the organizations to check compliance with applicable regulations.

Several frameworks have been proposed for specifying and analyzing privacy policies [4, 11, 13, 12, 45, 41, 21, 28, 19, 15, 22, 38]. Specifically, Barth *et al.* [11], present a framework, Contextual Integrity (*CI*), for specifying privacy regulations like HIPAA. They also introduce two notions of *compliance*, weak compliance (*WC*) and strong compliance (*SC*). WC ensures that all actions are compliant with the *present requirements* of the policy whereas SC ensures that *obligatory (future) requirements* incurred due to performing an action, will be consistent with the present conditions of the policy [20]. Consider the privacy rule from §164.502(e)(1)(i) of HIPAA which states that a covered entity (hospital) can disclose a patient's protected health information (*PHI*) to the covered entity's business associate if the covered entity has received a satisfactory assurance from the business associate ensuring that the business associate will protect the patient's *PHI*. According to this rule, covered entity receiving the satisfactory assurance from its business associate is a present condition imposed by the policy rule. An example of an obligatory requirement can be found in §164.524 of HIPAA discussed above. Requiring the covered entity to give access to the *PHI* to the patient is an example of an obligatory requirement. We prove that checking WC is feasible whereas checking SC is undecidable. Current work in this area [13, 28, 41, 4, 19, 22], while checking compliance, only considers WC without taking SC into account.

In the current work, we aim to verify the Δ-property of privacy policies. If a policy ℘ can be shown to have the Δ-property, to check whether an action is in compliance with

$\wp$, it suffices to only check whether that action is weakly compliant with $\wp$. For this, we introduce a specification language expressive enough to encode the HIPAA Privacy Policy. We formally specify WC and SC for our language. Barth *et al.*'s definitions of compliance (WC and SC) are not sufficient as they are restricted to only propositional linear temporal logic ($pLTL$) which cannot be feasibly used for specifying privacy regulations like HIPAA. We then present a sound, semi-automated technique to verify whether a privacy policy written in our specification language satisfies the Δ-property. To show the efficacy of our policy analysis technique, we formally verify that our encoding of HIPAA satisfies the Δ-property. This implies that whether an action is in compliance with the HIPAA Privacy Policy can be checked efficiently by checking WC only. Note that although the Δ-property has been introduced before [11], we are the first to present feasible techniques to decide whether a policy has the Δ-property and apply it to a practical privacy policy like HIPAA.

We now detail our technical contributions. We present a privacy policy specification language based on a restricted subset of first order temporal logic (FOTL). We demonstrate the expressive power of our language by encoding all 84 disclosure-related clauses of HIPAA [1]. We then formally specify what it means for an action to be weakly compliant and strongly compliant with FOTL policies of our form. We also prove that WC can be checked in PSPACE in the policy size provided the policy satisfies a constraint (*mode restriction* [28, 29]) whereas checking SC is undecidable. While the complexity of checking WC is in PSPACE, research [28, 13] has shown that it can be checked efficiently in practice.

To mitigate the undecidability of SC, we formally specify the property WC entails SC (denoted by Δ) [11] of a privacy policy. Prior work presents a semantic definition and a decision procedure for checking the Δ-property restricted to only pLTL policies. A policy has the Δ-property if every weakly compliant action is also strongly compliant. The Δ-property can be checked once statically before the policy is deployed. Given a FOTL policy $\wp$, we syntactically generate a first order CTL* with linear past (denoted by FO-CTL*$_{lp}$) [39] formula $\delta(\wp)$ from $\wp$. We prove that $\delta(\wp)$ is satisfied in the *most permissive model* $\mathbb{M}_\wp$ if and only if $\wp$ has the Δ-property. The most permissive model with respect to a policy $\wp$ (denoted by $\mathbb{M}_\wp$) is the model in which at each step one action from all the possible actions referred to by $\wp$, is non-deterministically chosen to be performed. However, model checking a FO-CTL*$_{lp}$ formula with respect to $\mathbb{M}_\wp$ is undecidable.

While checking the Δ-property for a FOTL policy is in general undecidable, this result is not discouraging as we can develop a sound, semi-automated technique with which we can check the Δ-property for practical privacy policies like HIPAA efficiently. We prove that there are exactly two cases in which the Δ-property can be violated (Theorem 8). In the first case, taking an action might cause the system to transition to a bad state from which there is no weakly compliant infinite extensions of the current finite trace. In the second case, the policy allows to incur an obligation which is not consistent with the present requirements imposed by the policy [20]. We prove that for policies written in our specification language, the former violation case cannot happen. Thus, it is sufficient to consider the second violation case only (Corollary 11). We then present a sound and complete *privacy policy slicing algorithm* which decomposes the original policy analysis problem into multiple smaller policy analysis problems by slicing the policy with respect to one obligation at a time assuming obligations do not interact with each other.

Finally, we use HIPAA as a case study to show the efficacy of our analysis techniques. We first show that the HIPAA policy $\wp_H$ is trivially *satisfiable*. HIPAA does not restrict transmission of any message that does not contain *PHI* of an individual. One can thus satisfy the HIPAA Privacy Policy by only sending messages not containing any *PHI*. Thus, from Corollary 11, it follows that $\wp_H$ can violate the Δ-property only through allowing a weakly compliant action to incur unsatisfiable obligations. We then slice $\wp_H$ with respect to two different obligations from HIPAA. The size of the sliced policies in both cases is only 5% of $\wp_H$, which is a significant reduction of the policy size to be considered. We then develop a small model theorem [25] for $\wp_H$ which reduces the problem of checking the Δ-property with infinite carrier sets to checking the Δ-property for finite carrier sets. A small model theorem for the complete language remains an open question. We then formally verify that the two sliced HIPAA policies have the Δ-property. While there is currently no tool support for model checking CTL*$_{lp}$, which we leave as future work, we utilize the approach of Barth *et al.* [11] which is applicable in this case.

Organization. Section 2 briefly overviews FOTL. We introduce our privacy policy specification language in section 3. In section 4, we formalize what it means for an action to be compliant with a privacy policy. Our main technical contribution is in section 5 where we present a sound, semi-automated technique by which we can verify the Δ-property of a privacy policy. In section 6, we demonstrate how to use our techniques for HIPAA. Related work is discussed in section 7. Section 8 discusses open problems, future work, and concludes the paper.

2. BACKGROUND ON FOTL

Linear temporal logic (LTL) [48] characterizes the behavior of reactive systems in terms of *traces* (σ), infinite sequences of states and/or events. LTL abstracts the explicit notion of time and only reasons about a relative temporal ordering of events. Our privacy policy language is a many-sorted, first-order linear temporal logic (FOTL) [24]. We briefly summarize FOTL here.

FOTL generalizes pLTL in the same way that first-order logic generalizes propositional logic. Along with boolean connectives (*e.g.*, $\land, \lor$, *etc.*), predicates, function symbols, and quantifiers, FOTL formulas can additionally contain unary and binary temporal operators where the operand(s) are FOTL sub-formula(s). Temporal operators can be classified as future and past. *Future Operators.* Henceforth: $\Box\phi$ says that ϕ holds in all future states. Eventually: $\Diamond\phi$ says that ϕ holds in some future state. Tomorrow: $\bigcirc\phi$ holds when the formula ϕ is true in the next step. Until: $\phi_1 \mathbin{U} \phi_2$ is true in the current state if ϕ_2 holds true in some future state (including the current one) and the formula ϕ_1 holds in all the states from the current state to the state before ϕ_2 holds. *Past Operators.* Historically: $\boxminus\phi$ says that ϕ held in all previous states. Once: $\diamondminus\phi$ says that ϕ held in some previous state. Yesterday: $\ominus\phi$ holds true when the formula ϕ held true in the previous state. Since: $\phi_1 \mathbin{S} \phi_2$ says that ϕ_2 held at some point in the past, and since then ϕ_1 has

$$\wp ::= \square \Big(\forall p_1, p_2, q : P. \forall m : M. \forall t : T. \forall u : U.$$
$$\text{send}(p_1, p_2, m) \wedge \text{contains}(m, q, t) \wedge \text{for-purpose}(m, u)$$
$$\rightarrow \Big(\bigvee_i \phi_i^+ \Big) \wedge \Big(\bigwedge_j \phi_j^- \Big) \Big)$$

Figure 1: Forms of our privacy policy ($\wp$)

held in every state. Note that the $\mathcal{S}$ operator can be used to represent the $\boxminus$ and $\diamondsuit$ operator.

A *logical environment* η maps each variable to a value in the carrier set according to the variable's sort. A formula ϕ is satisfied by a trace σ at an index i under η, denoted by $\sigma, i, \eta \models \phi$, can be defined inductively on the structure of ϕ. One says that σ satisfies ϕ, written $\sigma \models \phi$, if and only if for any η, we have $\sigma, 0, \eta \models \phi$. We use $\sigma_1 \cdot \sigma_2$ to denote the concatenation of two traces in which σ_1 is a finite trace whereas σ_2 is an infinite trace.

3. POLICY SPECIFICATION LANGUAGE

In this section, we introduce our privacy policy specification language. Our policy specification language is a restricted subset of first-order linear temporal logic (FOTL). It is inspired by the specification language, Contextual Integrity (CI), proposed by Barth *et al.* [11]. The specific differences between our language and CI are discussed in Section 7. We demonstrate the adequacy of our specification language by expressing all disclosure-related clauses of the HIPAA Privacy Rule [33] in it [1]. Note that we cannot express obligation deadlines in our language. Although enhancing our specification language to express obligation deadlines [37, 9] is plausible, we do not take obligation deadlines into account in our policy analysis. This is further discussed in section 8.

Top-level Policy. The form of our privacy policies is shown in Figure 1. We use $\wp$ to denote such policies. The sorts are $P, T, M, R,$ and U (denoting agents, attributes, messages, roles, and purposes) with associated carriers $\mathcal{P}, \mathcal{T}, \mathcal{M}, \mathcal{R},$ and $\mathcal{U}$, respectively. The variables $p_1, p_2,$ and q are of sort P, t is of sort T, m is of sort M, and u is of sort U.

The privacy policies we consider (*e.g.*, HIPAA) mandate transmission of messages between different parties. A communication action is denoted by $\text{send}(p_1, p_2, m)$, in which p_1 is the sender, p_2 is the receiver, and m is the message being sent. Each message contains a set of agent, attribute pairs, $content(m) \subseteq \mathcal{P} \times \mathcal{T}$. The predicate $\text{contains}(m, q, t)$ holds if message m contains attribute t of subject q. A *knowledge state* κ is a subset of $\mathcal{P} \times \mathcal{P} \times \mathcal{T}$. If $(p, q, t) \in \kappa$, this means p knows the value of attribute t of agent q. For example, Alice knows Bob's height. A transition between knowledge states occurs when a message is transmitted, as the attributes contained in the message become known to the recipient. We use $\text{inrole}(p, \hat{r})$ to specify that the principal p is in role $\hat{r}$, in which $\hat{r}$ is a constant of sort R. For instance, $\text{inrole}(p, psychiatrist)$ holds when the principal p is in the role psychiatrist. We also allow role hierarchies and consider them as input to the system. For instance, the role *psychiatrist* is a specialization of the role *doctor*. The predicate $\text{for-purpose}(m, u)$ holds true when the message m is sent for the purpose u (*e.g.*, payment). We use the predicate $\text{in}(t, \hat{t})$ to specify that the attribute t can be calculated from the attribute $\hat{t}$, in which $\hat{t}$ is a constant (*e.g.*, procedure) of sort T. For instance, the zip code can be calculated from a postal address. Finally, the predicate $\text{purpose}(u, \hat{u})$ holds when the purpose u has the value $\hat{u}$, in which $\hat{u}$ is a constant (*e.g.*, payment) of sort U.

Our policies consist of two kinds of norms of transmission, *positive norms* and *negative norms*. Positive norms can be thought of *allowing* policy rules whereas negative norms can be thought of *denying* policy rules. A positive norm (ϕ_i^+) allows a message transmission *if* the condition associated with it holds. On the contrary, a negative norm (ϕ_j^-) allows a message transmission *only if* the condition associated with it is satisfied. An action is thus allowed by the policy if it satisfies at least one of the positive norms and all the negative norms. Finally, the policy of Figure 1 has the following intuitive meaning. For all senders p_1, for all receivers p_2, for all subjects of the information q, for all messages m, for all message attributes t, for all purposes u, p_1 can send a message to p_2 about q's attribute t for purpose u if it satisfies at least one of the positive norms and all the negative norms.

Syntax of Norms. The form of the policy norms are shown in Figure 2. The formula meta-variables in the norms (*i.e.*, ψ, β, and χ) correspond to syntactic categories introduced below in Figure 3. Exception formulas $\psi_{exception}$ have the same form as ψ. In the norms (see Figure 2), the non-temporal formulas $\mathbb{C}_{\text{sender}}$, $\mathbb{C}_{\text{receiver}}$, and $\mathbb{C}_{\text{subject}}$ impose constraints on the role of the sender, receiver, and subject, respectively. Formulas $\mathbb{C}_{\text{sender}}$, $\mathbb{C}_{\text{receiver}}$, and $\mathbb{C}_{\text{subject}}$ are boolean combinations of atomic formulas of the form $\text{inrole}(p, \hat{r})$. In the same vein, the non-temporal formulas $\mathbb{C}_{\text{attribute}}$ and $\mathbb{C}_{\text{purpose}}$ intuitively impose restrictions on the message attributes and the purposes of the message transmission. Formulas $\mathbb{C}_{\text{attribute}}$ and $\mathbb{C}_{\text{purpose}}$ are boolean combinations of atomic formulas of the form $\text{in}(t, \hat{t})$ and $\text{purpose}(u, \hat{u})$, respectively. The formula $\mathbb{C} = \mathbb{C}_{\text{sender}} \wedge \mathbb{C}_{\text{receiver}} \wedge \mathbb{C}_{\text{subject}} \wedge \mathbb{C}_{\text{attribute}} \wedge \mathbb{C}_{\text{purpose}}$ can be viewed as specifying the target send event to which this norm applies to.

Positive Norm, ϕ_i^+ : $\quad (\mathbb{C} \wedge \psi \wedge \beta) \vee \psi_{exception}$
Negative Norm, ϕ_j^- : $\quad \mathbb{C} \wedge \psi \rightarrow (\chi \vee \psi_{exception})$
where $\mathbb{C} = \mathbb{C}_{\text{sender}} \wedge \mathbb{C}_{\text{receiver}} \wedge \mathbb{C}_{\text{subject}} \wedge \mathbb{C}_{\text{attribute}} \wedge \mathbb{C}_{\text{purpose}}$

Figure 2: Norms of transmission

(Atomic Formulas) $\gamma ::= R(\vec{x}) \mid true$
(Non-temporal Formulas) $\mu ::= \gamma \mid \mu \wedge \mu \mid \mu \vee \mu \mid \exists \vec{x} : \tau. \mu \mid$
$\quad \forall \vec{x} : \tau. (\mu_1(\vec{x}) \rightarrow \mu_2(\vec{x}))$
(Pure Past Formulas) $\psi ::= \mu \mid \psi \wedge \psi \mid \neg \psi \mid \psi \mathcal{S} \psi \mid \exists \vec{x} : \tau. \psi$
$\quad \mid \forall \vec{x} : \tau. (\mu_1(\vec{x}) \rightarrow \mu_2(\vec{x}))$
(Obligation Formulas) $\beta ::= \diamondsuit \mu \mid \beta \wedge \beta$
(Mixed Formulas) $\chi ::= \beta \mid \psi \mid \psi \wedge \beta \mid \psi \rightarrow \beta$

Figure 3: Meta-variables of the privacy policy.

We have already discussed some pre-defined predicates of our language (*e.g.*, inrole, *etc.*). We allow additional predicates denoted by $R(\vec{x})$ (see Figure 3) in which $\vec{x}$ denotes its arguments. Each element of $\vec{x}$ is a constant or a variable. We envision these predicates to be regulation-specific.

Restrictions. We now discuss the different constraints we impose in our specification language and their implications. Note, in particular, the limited way in which future temporal operators are used. Aside from the $\square$ at the outer-most level, the only future sub-formulas are of the form given by β and $\diamondsuit$ can be applied only to positive, non-temporal formulas. This is the key to our ability to syntactically extract the past and future requirements from the policy formula. It also enables us to define weak compliance (*WC*) gracefully in section 4. More precisely, we do not allow formulas expressing *general liveness properties* ($\square \diamondsuit q$). Instead we allow formulas expressing *response properties* [43]. Response properties have the general form $\Box(p \rightarrow \Diamond q)$, in which p is a pure-past formula and q is a non-temporal formula. The formula $\Box(p \rightarrow \Diamond q)$ intuitively requires every p to be followed by a q. Among the past temporal operators, we do not allow the $\ominus$ operator. As we shall show in section 5, a policy containing the $\ominus$ operator can fail to satisfy the Δ-property. We also do not allow function symbols in our specification language.

Example norms from HIPAA. A positive norm (shown below) can be found in §164.502(d)(1) of HIPAA. It states that a covered entity can send an individual's protected health information (PHI) to its business associate for creating de-identified (or, anonymized) information.

$$\begin{pmatrix} \text{inrole}(p_1, \textit{covered-entity}) \wedge \text{inrole}(p_2, \textit{business-associate}) \\ \wedge \text{inrole}(q, \textit{individual}) \end{pmatrix} \wedge$$
$$\text{in}(t, PHI) \wedge$$
$$\text{purpose}(u, \textit{creating-deidentified-info}) \wedge$$
$$\text{businessAssociateOf}(p2, p1)$$

A negative norm (shown below) can be found in §164.508(a)(2) of HIPAA. It specifies that a covered entity must obtain an authorization before disclosing an individual's psychotherapy notes.

$$\text{inrole}(p_1, \textit{covered-entity}) \wedge \text{inrole}(q, \textit{individual}) \wedge$$
$$\text{in}(t, \textit{psych-notes}) \longrightarrow$$
$$\exists m_2 : M. \Diamond(\text{send}(q, p_1, m_2)) \wedge$$
$$\quad \text{satisfiesAllValidAuthReqs}(m_2, p_1, p_2, q, t, u) \wedge$$
$$\quad \neg\text{violatesValidAuthReqs}(m_2, p_1, p_2, q, t, u))$$

4. PRIVACY POLICY COMPLIANCE

We now formally specify what it means for an action to be compliant with a privacy policy. Privacy policies $\wp$ can impose *present requirements* (which includes past requirements) and also *obligatory (future) requirements*. Recall the clause §164.502(e)(1)(i) of HIPAA discussed in Section 1. Obtaining the satisfactory assurance from the business associate is a present requirement of that clause. An obligatory requirement can be found in §160.310 of HIPAA, which requires the covered entity to provide PHI of an individual to the secretary for compliance investigation, if she has requested for the information. The covered entity's action of providing access to the individual's PHI to the secretary for compliance investigation is an obligatory requirement.

To this end, for checking compliance with policies $\wp$ it is helpful to separate the concerns of checking compliance with present and obligatory requirements. The syntactic restrictions in our policy language allow us to extract a formula that expresses the present requirements imposed by the policy. We can determine whether a contemplated action is in compliance with the present requirements of a policy by looking only at the current history. We call a contemplated action *weakly compliant* with respect to a policy when it is consistent with the present requirements of that policy. However, the present requirements do not give any assurance about whether the obligatory requirements can be met and can restrict an entity from performing its pending obligations. To this end, we use *strong compliance* [11], which formalizes the notion that a contemplated action will neither prevent pending obligatory requirements to be met nor incur any unsatisfiable obligatory requirements. An action is compliant with a privacy policy if it is both weakly compliant and strongly compliant. We will show that for our privacy policy language, checking whether an action is weakly compliant with a policy is feasible whereas checking whether that action is strong compliant with the policy is undecidable.

4.1 Weak Compliance (WC)

For formally specifying what it means for an action to be weakly compliant with $\wp$, we use the formula $weak(\wp)$.
$weak(\wp)$: $weak(\wp)$ denotes the formula derived from $\wp$ by replacing future sub-formulas (sub-formulas of the form $\Diamond\mu$) with logical *true* and removing the outermost $\Box$. Due to the syntactic manipulation, the formula obtained only contains past temporal operators and expresses the present requirements of $\wp$.

DEFINITION 1 (WEAK COMPLIANCE (WC)). *Given a policy $\wp$, a finite trace σ, and a contemplated action a, a is* weakly compliant *with respect to σ and $\wp$ if for all environments η, we have $\sigma \cdot s, |\sigma|, \eta \models \Box weak(\wp)$ where state $s \models a$.*

Although we have formally defined $\models$ only in terms of infinite traces (see Section 2), the usage of $\models$ for finite σ here is well defined because $weak(\wp)$ is a pure-past formula: $\sigma \cdot s, |\sigma|, \eta \models \Box weak(\wp)$ depends only on the states in σ and the state s.

Consider the HIPAA privacy rule in §164.508(a)(2) which states that a covered entity can disclose an individual's psychotherapy notes if he received the authorization from the individual. Now, if the covered entity discloses an individual's *psych-notes* without the authorization from the individual, then the action will not be weakly compliant with respect to the policy rule in §164.508(a)(2) as it violates the present requirement of obtaining an authorization.

Complexity of WC. For checking WC with respect to a policy $\wp$, we have to check whether a finite trace (including the current contemplated action) satisfies the formula $weak(\wp)$ in every point in that trace. Note that $weak(\wp)$ is a pure-past FOTL formula with quantifiers. Garg *et al.* [28, 29] present *mode restriction*, which ensures that quantifiers can be expressed as finite conjunctions or disjunctions. This enables an algorithm with PSPACE complexity that can check whether a finite trace satisfies a first-order logic policy. The authors [28] also show that mode restriction is still practical as the HIPAA privacy rules satisfy it. Note that their language is a proper superset of our language fragment used to express $weak(\wp)$. We can thus translate $weak(\wp)$ into their language, and if it passes mode checking, use their algorithm to check WC for $\wp$. Basin *et al.* [13] also present an algorithm for checking WC for a language similar to ours.

THEOREM 2. *Given a policy $\wp$, WC can be checked in PSPACE in the size of $\wp$ if $weak(\wp)$ satisfies the mode restriction.*

For brevity, we do not present proofs for our theorems. Proofs of all theorems appear in the technical report [2].

4.2 Strong Compliance (SC)

When we check weak compliance, we ensure that the present requirements of the policy are met. However, there can be a situation where the obligatory requirements are not consistent with the present requirements of the policy [20]. Strong compliance (SC) [11] ensures that this is not the case.

A contemplated action is strongly compliant with a policy $\wp$ if the current history (including the current action) can be extended to an infinite trace such that the concatenation of the finite trace and the infinite extension satisfies $\wp$. Intuitively, a strongly compliant action neither incurs an obligation that cannot be met nor prevents any pending obligations to be met. We can formally define strong compliance in the following way.

DEFINITION 3 (STRONG COMPLIANCE (SC)). *Given a finite history σ'_f and a contemplated action a where state $s \models a$ and $\sigma_f = \sigma'_f \cdot s$, the action a is strongly compliant with the privacy policy $\wp$ if there is an infinite extension σ_i of the current history σ_f such that $\sigma_f \cdot \sigma_i \models \wp$.*

Complexity of SC. Checking SC requires deciding whether the incurred future requirements (non-monadic FOTL formula) of an action are satisfiable. However, checking the satisfiability of non-monadic FOTL formulas is undecidable [34]. As a result, we have the following theorem.

THEOREM 4. *Given a policy $\wp$, a finite history σ, and a contemplated action a, to check whether action a is strongly compliant with respect to the policy $\wp$ is undecidable.*

5. PRIVACY POLICY ANALYSIS

We now formally specify the property *weak compliance entails strong compliance* (denoted by Δ) [11]. A policy has the Δ-property if every weakly compliant action is also strongly compliant. To check whether an action is compliant with such a policy, it suffices to just check whether the action is weakly compliant with that policy. We believe well-written policies should have this property. We also show that when a policy $\wp$ has the Δ-property, the present conditions of $\wp$, denoted by $weak(\wp)$, express the safety property (see Appendix A) imposed by $\wp$.

For a given privacy policy $\wp$, we syntactically construct a first order CTL* with linear past (denoted by FO-CTL*$_{lp}$) [39] formula $\delta(\wp)$ from $\wp$. We prove that *the most permissible model* (denoted by $\mathbb{M}_\wp$) of a policy $\wp$ satisfies $\delta(\wp)$ if and only if $\wp$ has the Δ-property (section 5.1). The most permissive model $\mathbb{M}_\wp$ of a policy $\wp$ is the model in which at each step one action from all the possible actions referred by $\wp$, is non-deterministically chosen to be performed. Considering $\mathbb{M}_\wp$ of a policy $\wp$ is reasonable because, if $\wp$ does not have the Δ-property in the $\mathbb{M}_\wp$ then $\wp$ is not well-formed. When a policy can incur obligations that cannot be met even in the most permissive model then it is unlikely that those obligations can be met in other models. Model checking a FO-CTL*$_{lp}$ specification with respect to a given model is undecidable. Thus, in section 5.2, we develop a sound, semi-automated technique that can feasibly decide in many practical cases whether a policy has the Δ-property.

5.1 The WC Entails SC Property (Δ-property)

As the Δ-property is a statically analyzable property of the policy, it enables offloading all complexity of checking this property to before the policy is actually deployed. We can then use more expensive decision methods that would not be feasible if we were to check it at runtime.

A policy satisfies the Δ-property if for any weakly compliant finite trace (history), there exists an infinite extension of the finite trace such that the concatenation of the finite trace and the infinite extension satisfies the policy. We call a finite trace *weakly compliant finite trace* if each of the actions of that finite trace is weakly compliant with the policy. Formally, for a given environment η, a finite trace (σ_f) is weakly compliant with respect to the policy $\wp$ if the following holds: $\sigma_f, |\sigma_f| - 1, \eta \models \boxminus weak(\wp)$. We now formally specify what it means for a privacy policy $\wp$ to have the Δ-property.

DEFINITION 5 (Δ-PROPERTY). *A policy $\wp$ has the Δ-property if and only if for any environment η and for any history (finite trace) σ_f that satisfies $\sigma_f, |\sigma_f| - 1, \eta \models \boxminus weak(\wp)$, there exists an infinite trace (extension) σ_i such that $\sigma_f \cdot \sigma_i \models \wp$.*

We now construct from a policy $\wp$ a formula $\delta(\wp)$ in the logic FO-CTL*$_{lp}$ [39] that is satisfied by the *most permissible model* ($\mathbb{M}_\wp$) of the policy (denoted by $\mathbb{M}_\wp \models \delta(\wp)$) if and only if $\wp$ has the Δ-property. The formula $\delta(\wp)$ is defined in Figure 4. The formula states that, given a finite weakly compliant history, it is possible to extend the finite history to an infinite one in which all the pending obligations are discharged while maintaining WC. To the best of our knowledge, we are the first to give a specification of the Δ-property within a formal logic. This formalization is an important first step toward being able to identify policies which have the Δ-property.

$$\delta(\wp) ::= \mathcal{A}\square \left(\begin{array}{l} (\boxminus weak(\wp)) \longrightarrow \\ E \left(\bigwedge_{\langle \lambda, \gamma \rangle \in \alpha(\wp)} \forall p_1, p_2, q : P. \forall m : M. \forall t : T. \forall u : U. \\ ((\neg \gamma \, \mathcal{S} \, \lambda) \rightarrow \Diamond \gamma) \wedge \square \, weak(\wp) \right) \end{array} \right)$$

Figure 4: FO-CTL*$_{lp}$ formulation of the Δ-property

The function α in the formula $\delta(\wp)$ takes as input a privacy policy $\wp$ and returns all possible $\langle \lambda, \gamma \rangle$ pairs in $\wp$. In a $\langle \lambda, \gamma \rangle$ pair, λ characterizes a condition, which, when true, incurs the obligation γ according to the policy $\wp$. The function α works on the norm level of the policy $\wp$ and syntactically extracts all the $\langle \lambda, \gamma \rangle$ pairs. The complete definition of function α is shown in appendix C.

The following theorem states that a policy $\wp$ has the Δ-property if and only if $\mathbb{M}_\wp \models \delta(\wp)$.

THEOREM 6. *Given a policy $\wp$, $\wp$ has the Δ-property if and only if $\mathbb{M}_\wp \models \delta(\wp)$.*

Sufficient and Necessary Condition for Δ-property. There are two cases in which an action that is weakly compliant with a policy $\wp$ is not strongly compliant with $\wp$. The first case occurs when taking a weakly compliant action can lead to a state from which it is not possible to take an unbounded number of weakly-compliant valid transitions (no infinite weakly complaint extension). We call a policy which does **not** allow this case, an *incrementally satisfiable policy*.

DEFINITION 7 (INCREMENTALLY SATISFIABLE). *A pure past FOTL formula ϕ is incrementally satisfiable if for any given finite trace σ and for any logical environment η, $\sigma, |\sigma| - 1, \eta \models \boxminus \phi$ implies that there exists an infinite trace $\hat{\sigma}$ such that $\sigma \cdot \hat{\sigma} \models \square \phi$.*

The second case in which a weakly compliant action for $\wp$ is not strongly compliant for $\wp$ is when that action incurs a future obligation which cannot be met. Theorem 8 states that these two cases are necessary and sufficient.

THEOREM 8. *A policy $\wp$ has the Δ-property if and only if $weak(\wp)$ is incrementally satisfiable and no weakly compliant action of $\wp$ incurs any unsatisfiable future obligations.*

We will now give an example for each violation case. First, consider the simple example policy in Figure 5, denoted by $\wp_1$. For brevity, we consider a pLTL policy in which A, B, and H are actions. We also assume at each step only one action can happen. An action is allowed by $\wp_1$ if it satisfies one of the positive norms and all the negative norms. Consider the finite trace BAH. Here, B is allowed as it satisfies the second positive norm and also satisfies all the negative norms. The same is true for A as it satisfies the first positive norm requiring that there is a B before an A and additionally it satisfies all the negative norms. The same goes for action H. However, after H no more actions are allowed to take place. A cannot take place as it would violate the first negative norm requiring H has not happened before. The same goes for B as it violates the second negative norm. Finally, H cannot happen as an H has happened already, which would in turn violate the third negative norm. The action H leads to a bad state from which it is not possible to take an unbounded number of weakly compliant transitions. Thus, $\wp_1$ is not incrementally satisfiable. The action that leads to a bad state is H, which although weakly compliant for $\wp_1$, is not strongly compliant with respect to $\wp_1$.

We use the policy in Figure 6 (denoted by $\wp_2$) to demonstrate the second violation case. We assume that at each step only one action can happen. Let us consider the finite trace $DCBA$. Each of the actions of the trace is weakly compliant with respect to $\wp_2$. The action A, however, incurs the obligation F. Note that the last positive norm allows F under the condition that action C has not happened before. However, for the above finite trace this is not the case. As a result, the obligation of taking action F cannot be discharged in a compliant fashion. Thus, the action A, although weakly compliant for $\wp_2$, is not strongly compliant with respect to $\wp_2$.

Negative Norms :	Positive Norms :
$A \rightarrow \neg(\diamondsuit H)$	$A \wedge \diamondsuit B \wedge \diamondsuit C$
$B \rightarrow \neg(\diamondsuit H)$	$B \wedge \diamondsuit C \wedge \diamondsuit D$
$H \rightarrow \ominus(\neg(\diamondsuit H))$	$C \wedge \diamondsuit D$
Positive Norms :	D
$A \wedge \diamondsuit B$	$F \wedge (\neg(\diamondsuit C))$
B	**Negative Norms :**
H	$A \rightarrow \diamondsuit F$

Figure 5: Violation (1)   **Figure 6: Violation (2)**

We now prove that the violation case 1 cannot happen for our forms of policies $\wp$ when they are satisfiable. A satisfiable policy $\wp$ that does not have the $\ominus$ operator is incrementally verifiable. This is stated in the following theorem.

THEOREM 9. *A closed, pure-past, and satisfiable policy $\wp$ without the $\ominus$ temporal operator, is incrementally satisfiable.*

Privacy policies of our form ($\wp$) do not allow the $\ominus$ temporal operator, which yields the following two corollaries.

COROLLARY 10. *For a given privacy policy $\wp$, $weak(\wp)$ is incrementally satisfiable if $weak(\wp)$ is satisfiable.*

This follows by Theorem 9, as $weak(\wp)$ is closed, has no future operators, and does not allow the $\ominus$ temporal operator.

COROLLARY 11. *A satisfiable privacy policy $\wp$ satisfies Δ-property if and only if no weakly compliant action of $\wp$ incurs any unsatisfiable future obligations.*

Corollary 11 follows from Theorem 8 and Corollary 10.

Given a policy $\wp$, $weak(\wp)$ denotes the present conditions imposed by $\wp$. Note that when $\wp$ has the Δ-property, $weak(\wp)$ denotes the safety property (see Appendix A) imposed by $\wp$.

THEOREM 12. *For a given privacy policy $\wp$ with the Δ-property, $weak(\wp)$ expresses the strongest safety property that contains the property expressed by $\wp$.*

We have proved that a privacy policy $\wp$ has the Δ-property if and only if $\mathbb{M}_\wp \models \delta(\wp)$. However, model checking a specification written in FO-CTL*$_{lp}$ with respect to a model is undecidable. The complexity of model checking a propositional CTL*$_{lp}$ formula with respect to a model is in EXPSPACE [39] in the formula length. Thus, for a pLTL policy we can check whether the policy has the Δ-property in exponential space in the policy size. As our privacy policy is in FOTL, we cannot directly use this technique to check the Δ-property.

5.2 Analysis Technique for Checking the Δ-property

We now present our sound, semi-automated analysis technique to check whether a policy $\wp$ has the Δ-property. Our analysis technique consists of the following three steps.

1. Privacy policy slicing.
2. Developing a small model theorem [25].
3. pLTL policy analysis.

By Corollary 11, a policy $\wp$ can violate the Δ-property only if $\wp$ allows a weakly compliant action to incur an unsatisfiable obligation. When obligations do not interact with each other, we can analyze permissibility of each of the obligations independently. To this end, we introduce *privacy policy slicing* which decomposes the policy to a sub-policy which only contains the norms that can potentially influence the permissibility of the obligation in question (step 1). In practice, the sliced policy is significantly smaller but deciding whether it has the Δ-property is still undecidable.

The next step (step 2) of our analysis addresses the undecidability of the sub-policies obtained from the previous step. Step 2 requires developing a small model theorem [25]. It proves that finite elements of the carriers of the policy are sufficient to simulate all possible behaviors necessary to prove the Δ-property of the policy. Then we can rewrite the universal and the existential quantifiers as finite conjunctions and disjunctions, obtaining a pLTL policy which can be analyzed. We show a template of the small model theorem which must be instantiated for specific policy analysis problem instance and whose proof is necessary to check whether a policy has the Δ-property. We want to emphasize that step 2 will be specific for each policy analysis instance.

Finally, we analyze the pLTL policy $\wp$ (step 3). We obtain a CTL*$_{lp}$ formula from $\wp$ (see Figure 4). We then model check $\mathbb{M}_\wp$ with respect to the CTL*$_{lp}$ specification. If $\mathbb{M}_\wp$ satisfies the CTL*$_{lp}$ specification then we can say that $\wp$ has the Δ-property. Note that while there are known algorithms for CTL*$_{lp}$ model checking, *e.g.*, Kupferman *et al.* [39], there exists no tool support for this. Currently, we rely on the approach proposed by Barth *et al.* [11]. Their algorithm begins by building a *tableau* [44] (with Büchi accepting condition [16]) from the pLTL formula representing the privacy policy. Then it checks to see whether all the reachable states from the *initial states* can reach a strongly connected component containing at least an *accepting state*. If this is the case, then the privacy policy specified in pLTL has the Δ-property. Note that the size of the tableau is exponential in the pLTL policy formula length. Thus, their algorithm has the complexity of EXPSPACE in the policy formula length.

5.2.1 *Privacy Policy Slicing*

For our policy analysis, the privacy policy size is a bottleneck. As it turns out, our policy specification language allows us to use a divide-and-conquer approach for verification. Without loss of generality, we assume that one send event occurs in a single state. The benefit of decomposition is that for a single obligation, potentially not all norms of the policy are necessary for analysis, reducing the policy size to be analyzed. Based on this, we introduce *privacy policy slicing* analogous to *program slicing* [54]. Slicing decomposes the privacy policy with respect to an obligation. The requirements of privacy policy slicing, which make it interesting for our analysis, are the following: (A) The slicing preserves the Δ-property of the original policy with respect to the slicing criterion. (B) The analysis results on the sliced policies can be composed to verify that the Δ-property holds for the original policy.

Slicing a privacy policy with respect to a slicing criterion collects all the norms of a policy which the said criterion depends on. The *slicing criterion* (P) is a non-temporal formula and it represents a set of send events. P has the following form: send(p_1, p_2, m)$\wedge$contains(m, q, t)$\wedge$for-purpose(m, u) $\wedge \mathbb{C}_{\text{sender}} \wedge \mathbb{C}_{\text{receiver}} \wedge \mathbb{C}_{\text{subject}} \wedge \mathbb{C}_{\text{attribute}} \wedge \mathbb{C}_{\text{purpose}}$. Note that one or more conjuncts can be missing in P when they are trivially true. Before precisely defining privacy policy slicing, we introduce some key notions first.

Types of send Events. We distinguish between three types of send actions: *regulatory*, *conditional*, and *obligatory*. We base our distinction on where they appear in the policy.

A send event, which has the form of a slicing criterion P, is called *conditional* with respect to a norm if it appears as a sub-formula in one of the following places: (1) In ψ or $\psi_{exception}$ portion of the positive norms. (2) In ψ portion of the negative norms' antecedent. (3) In ψ portion of χ in the negative norms' consequent. (4) In $\psi_{exception}$ portion of χ in the negative norms' consequent. A send event is called *obligatory* with respect to a norm if it appears as a sub-formula in one of the following places: (1) In β portion of the positive norms. (2) In β portion of χ in the negative norm's consequent. A send event is called *regulatory* with respect to a norm if it is the target send event that the norms refers to (or, applies to). An example of the regulatory send event is given in appendix B.

Consistency. We say a send event Q_1 is *consistent* with another send event Q_2 if all constraints (*e.g.*, $\mathbb{C}_{\text{sender}}$, *etc.*) in Q_1 are consistent with the constraints in Q_2. Q_1 and Q_2 have the same form as P and can contain free variables. One way to differentiate between the different send events are the constraints (*i.e.*, constraints on the sender role, *etc.*) on their free variables. Consistency is necessary for two reasons: first, Q_1 and Q_2 can contain free variables, which might not match the naming convention of each other, and second, it is admissible that one constraint subsumes another. For addressing the first issue, we rename the constraints to follow the same naming convention. We then formalize consistency (denoted by $\rightsquigarrow$) in the following way.

- inrole($p, \hat{r}$) $\rightsquigarrow$ inrole($p, \bar{r}$) if and only if $\hat{r} = \bar{r}$, $\hat{r}$ is a specialization of $\bar{r}$, or $\bar{r}$ is a specialization of $\hat{r}$. For instance, inrole(p, doctor) $\rightsquigarrow$ inrole(p, psychiatrist).

- in($t, \hat{t}$) $\rightsquigarrow$ in($t, \bar{t}$) if and only if $\hat{t} = \bar{t}$ or there exists an attribute t_1 such that t_1 can be calculated from both $\hat{t}$ and $\bar{t}$. For instance, in(t, PHI) $\rightsquigarrow$ in($t, psych\text{-}notes$) as the attribute "*diagnosis*" can be calculated from both PHI (protected health information) and *psych-notes*.

- purpose($u, \hat{u}$) $\rightsquigarrow$ purpose($u, \bar{u}$) when $\hat{u} = \bar{u}$.

- $\mathbb{C}_i^x \rightsquigarrow \mathbb{C}_i^y$ if and only if there exists an atomic formula a_x of $\mathbb{C}_i^x$ that is consistent with an atomic formula a_y of $\mathbb{C}_i^y$, where $i \in \{$sender, receiver, subject, attribute, purpose$\}$. For instance, (inrole(p_1, doctor) $\wedge$ inrole(p_1, resident)) is consistent with (inrole(p_1, psychiatrist) $\vee$ inrole(p_1, secretary)) as inrole(p_1, doctor) $\rightsquigarrow$ inrole(p_1, psychiatrist).

We assume that an empty constraint is consistent with any constraint. We can now inductively check whether two send events are consistent.

Dependency. The next notion we need for defining privacy policy slicing is called the norm *dependencies*.

A norm ϕ_1 *positively depends* on norm ϕ_2, if one of the conditional sends of ϕ_1 is *consistent* with the regulatory send of ϕ_2. Intuitively, this represents that ϕ_2 can influence one of the conditional sends of ϕ_1. A norm ϕ_1 *negatively depends* on norm ϕ_2, if one of the obligatory sends of ϕ_1 is consistent with the regulatory send of ϕ_2. Roughly, this represents that ϕ_2 can influence one of the obligatory sends of ϕ_1. A norm ϕ_1 has an *anti-dependency* on norm ϕ_2, if the regulating send of ϕ_1 is consistent with the regulatory send of ϕ_2. This signifies that both norms ϕ_1 and ϕ_2 allow the same send event based on possibly different conditions.

We say norm ϕ_1 *depends* on norm ϕ_2 if ϕ_1 has either a positive-, negative-, or anti-dependency on ϕ_2.

We can now precisely define privacy policy slicing.

DEFINITION 13 (SLICE OF A PRIVACY POLICY). *Given a privacy policy $\wp$ with the norm set ϕ, a slicing criterion P, $\wp_{s(P)}$ with the norm set $\phi_{s(P)}$ is a slice of $\wp$ with respect to P if it satisfies the following.*

1. *$\phi_{s(P)} \subseteq \phi$.*
2. *$\phi_P \subseteq \phi_{s(P)}$ where ϕ_P represents the set of all norms where P appears as an obligatory send.*
3. *$\phi^* \subseteq \phi_{s(P)}$ where ϕ^* is the transitive closure of the dependence relation on ϕ_P.*

These definitions of slicing, dependency, and consistency were carefully chosen so that the privacy policy slicing satisfies the requirements (A) and (B) mentioned above. To show that the slicing procedure satisfies both the requirements (A) and (B), we have the following theorems. The first (Theorem 14) formalizes the requirement that the slicing procedure preserves the Δ-property of the original policy with respect to the slicing criterion.

THEOREM 14. *For a policy $\wp$ and a slicing criterion P, the resulting sliced policy $\wp_{s(P)}$ satisfies the following. For any possible finite trace σ_f, any state s, and environment η where $\sigma_f, |\sigma_f|-1, \eta \models \boxminus weak(\wp)$, $\sigma_f, |\sigma_f|-1, \eta \models \boxminus weak(\wp_s)$, and $s, \eta \models P$, there exists an infinite extension σ_i such that $\sigma_f \cdot s \cdot \sigma_i \models \wp_{s(P)}$, if and only if there exists an infinite extension σ_j such that $\sigma_f \cdot s \cdot \sigma_j \models \wp$.*

The next theorem (Theorem 15) precisely formalizes the requirement that the results of the decomposed policies can be composed together to get the result of the original policy. Recall that we use obligations as our slicing criterion.

THEOREM 15. *For a policy $\wp$, if for all obligations P in $\wp$, $\mathbb{M}_{\wp_{s(P)}} \models \delta(\wp_{s(P)})$ where $\wp_{s(P)}$ is the slice of $\wp$ with respect to P, then $\mathbb{M}_\wp \models \delta(\wp)$.*

The slicing procedure generates the transitive closure by computing dependency in a lazy, by-need fashion. This algorithm is trivially correct, since it follows our theoretical development above. The algorithm is presented in appendix D.

5.2.2 Small Model Theorem (SMT)

Our policies are specified in a restricted subset of FOTL which is not a decidable fragment of full FOTL [34]. The fragment we consider can have more than one free variable for subformulas of form $\psi_1 \, \mathcal{S} \, \psi_2$ (non-*monadic*) [34]. On the contrary, pLTL is decidable. A small model theorem (or, a finite model theorem) [25] will establish that any *behavior of interest* of a policy in our specification language with infinite carriers can be captured with a small, finite amount of elements from each carrier. The behavior of interest in our case is the behavior necessary to prove the Δ-property of a policy. For example, the full infinite carrier $\mathcal{P}$ of principals might be able to be simulated with a finite amount of representatives, *e.g.*, just one person for each role. In that case, we can rewrite the FOTL policy to a pLTL policy by replacing universal quantifiers with finite conjunctions and existential quantifiers with finite disjunctions, where the quantified variables are instantiated with all carrier elements. By the theorem, the resulting propositional policy will capture all the behaviors, necessary to prove the property we are interested in, as the original FOTL policy. That means checking the pLTL policy will suffice.

It is not clear whether there exists a small model theorem for all privacy policies specified in our language. This is what results in the incompleteness in our technique. This means that small model theorems must be derived for specific policy instances and specific properties of it (*e.g.*, consistency, Δ-property, *etc.*). Moreover, developing such a small model theorem requires domain specific knowledge, invariants, and abstractions. For instance in HIPAA, whether a covered entity (hospital) can share a patient's (p_a) PHI is not dependent on covered entity's interactions with another patient (p_b) where $p_a \neq p_b$. As we will show in section 6, it is possible to develop small model theorems for the sliced HIPAA policies we are interested in. The small model theorem necessary for proving the Δ-property of a policy $\wp$ written in our specification language will have the following general form. The Theorem 16 in section 6 is a concrete example of the following small model theorem template.

Template of Small Model Theorem. A given policy $\wp$ has the Δ-property for every carrier set $\overrightarrow{\mathbb{C}} = \langle \mathbb{C}_1, \mathbb{C}_2, \ldots \rangle$ if and only if there exists a small, finite carrier set $\overrightarrow{\mathbb{C}_S} = \langle \mathbb{C}_{s1}, \mathbb{C}_{s2}, \ldots \rangle$ for which $\wp$ has the Δ-property.

6. HIPAA: A CASE STUDY

In this section, we demonstrate the adequacy of our policy analysis techniques by using HIPAA as a case study.

Specification of HIPAA. We have specified all 84 disclosure related clauses in our language [1]. We considered the HIPAA privacy rule in Subpart E of CFR §164. We have 66 positive norms and 8 negative norms. We cannot fully express access related rules found in §164.524 which ensure that an individual gets access to its own PHI. However, this clause is not related to disclosure of individually identifiable information (PHI). We consider the following sections of HIPAA: §164.502, §164.506, §164.508, §164.510, §164.512, §164.514, and simplified versions of §164.524 and §160.310.

Satisfiability of HIPAA. Any message that does not contain any individually identifiable information or is initiated by the patient or the environment (except business associates of the covered entity), is not regulated by the HIPAA privacy policy (denoted by $\wp_H$). Thus, messages not containing any PHI are trivially allowed by $\wp_H$. This kind of send events would falsify the contains predicate in the antecedent of $\wp_H$ making the implication trivially true. We can thus create an infinite trace, in each step of which, a message of the above kind is transmitted. Such a trace would trivially satisfy $\wp_H$.

Incremental satisfiability of HIPAA. In our policy language, we do not allow the $\ominus$ operator. Moreover, $\wp_H$ is trivially satisfiable as discussed just above. By Corollary 10, it follows that $weak(\wp_H)$ is incrementally satisfiable.

Policy slicing algorithm implementation. Note that obligations do not interact with each other in HIPAA and also HIPAA is trivially satisfiable. Thus, the only way $\wp_H$ can violate the Δ-property is through a weakly compliant action incurring unsatisfiable obligations. We have implemented our slicing algorithm using C++. The complexity of the algorithm is linear in the size of the policy norms and the number of send events that appear in the norms. We have sliced $\wp_H$ with respect to real obligations from HIPAA (§160.310, §164.524). The sliced policy contains 68 norms out of total 74 norms. The algorithm runs in 480 milliseconds in the worst case on an Intel Core i7 1.73 GHz machine with 4GB of RAM running Ubuntu 12.04.

Making the slicing procedure more precise. To preserve soundness, the dependence relations we define over-approximate the most-precise dependence relations. This is due to the fact that our dependence relation does not take into account the condition of the norms (when the condition is not a send event). However, it is not apparent how to incorporate conditions while defining our dependence relation. One way to get around it is human intervention while checking whether a norm is consistent to a send event. We have implemented our policy slicing algorithm with human intervention support and sliced $\wp_H$ with the obligations in §160.310 and §164.524 of HIPAA. The policy rule in §164.524 states: when an individual requests for access to her own PHI, the covered entity is obligated to give access to the individual. Our sliced policy in both cases has 4 norms (1 positive and 3 negative norm) out of total 74 norms (see Figure 7). This is a significant reduction in the size of the norms. We also sliced $\wp_H$ with respect to a synthetic obligation (*Synthetic-1*). To this end, we add an additional negative norm to $\wp_H$ that obligates a covered entity to provide access to an individual's parents to the individual's PHI when the parents request for it. The sliced policy has 1 positive norm and 6 negative norms out of total 75 norms.

Small Model Theorem. In the previous section, we have shown the general template of the small model theorem necessary for verifying whether a policy has the Δ-property. We now show a concrete small model theorem. To this end, we first impose some restrictions which enable us to develop a concrete small model theorem of a sliced HIPAA policy.

The first restriction we impose is to disallow the $\neq$ operator or any predicate simulating it. Thus, the policy cannot distinguish between two elements of the carrier. Consequently, we cannot specify in the policy that two individuals are different. The sliced HIPAA policies we consider satisfy this restriction. Moreover, we remove the message sort ($\mathcal{M}$) and also remove the predicates `contains` and `for-purpose`. We enhance the send predicate to have the signature $\mathcal{P} \times \mathcal{P} \times \mathcal{P} \times \mathcal{T} \times \mathcal{U}$. Now, the predicate $send(p_1, p_2, m, q, t, u)$ holds when p_1 sends a message to p_2 about q's attribute t for purpose u. Removing the message sort prevents us from specifying that a message con-

$(\S \mathbf{160.310})$: $\text{inrole}(p_1, secretary) \wedge \text{inrole}(p_2, covered\text{-}entity) \wedge \text{inrole}(q, individual) \wedge \text{purpose}(u, compliance\text{-}investigation) \wedge$

$\quad\quad \text{request}(p_1, p_2, q, PHI) \longrightarrow \Diamond(\exists m_1 : M.(\text{send}(p_2, p_1, m_1) \wedge \text{contains}(m_1, q, PHI) \wedge \text{for-purpose}(m_1, compliance\text{-}investigation)))$

$(\S \mathbf{164.502(a)(2)(ii)})$: $\text{inrole}(p_1, covered\text{-}entity) \wedge \text{inrole}(p_2, secretary) \wedge$

$\quad\quad\quad\quad\quad\quad \text{inrole}(q, individual) \wedge \text{in}(t, PHI) \wedge \text{purpose}(u, compliance\text{-}investigation)$

$(\S \mathbf{164.502(b)})$: $\text{inrole}(p_1, covered\text{-}entity) \wedge \text{inrole}(q, individual) \wedge \text{in}(t, PHI) \longrightarrow \text{believesMinimumNecessaryForPurpose}(p_1, p_2, q, t, u)$

$\quad\quad \vee (\text{inrole}(p_1, covered\text{-}entity) \wedge \text{inrole}(p_2, secretary) \wedge \text{inrole}(q, individual) \wedge \text{in}(t, PHI) \wedge \text{purpose}(u, compliance\text{-}investigation))$

$(\S \mathbf{164.508(a)(2)})$: $\text{inrole}(p_1, covered\text{-}entity) \wedge \text{inrole}(q, individual) \wedge \text{in}(t, psych\text{-}notes) \to \text{obtainedAuthorization}(p_1, p_2, q, t, u)$

Figure 7: Sliced HIPAA policy ($\wp_{H_P}$) norms with respect to the obligation in §160.310 of HIPAA.

tains multiple attributes of multiple individuals or is sent for multiple purposes. This is not as restricting as it sounds, at least for the slices of HIPAA we consider. Assume a set of send events, each for a message with a single attribute and for a single purpose. If all events are allowed, then the send of a single message that combines all the other messages' contents is allowed by the sliced policies. Now, we provide intuitions behind developing a small model theorem for the HIPAA policy sliced with respect to the obligation in §160.310 (Figure 7), denoted by $\wp_{H_P}$.

The number of attributes in the $\wp_{H_P}$ is finite and they are *PHI* and *psych-notes* (in short, *PSN*). Each of *PHI* and *PSN* can be viewed as a set of attributes where $PHI, PSN \subseteq \mathcal{T}$, $PSN \subset PHI$ and $\mathcal{T}$ is the carrier of attributes. Thus, if we consider any attribute $t \in \mathcal{T}$, one of the following would hold: $t \in \mathcal{T} \setminus (PHI \cup PSN)$, $t \in (PHI \setminus PSN)$, or $t \in (PHI \cap PSN)$. Thus, we consider three attributes, t_1, t_2, and t_3 such that $t_1 \in (PHI \cap PSN)$, $t_2 \in (PHI \setminus PSN)$, and $t_3 \in \mathcal{T} \setminus (PHI \cup PSN)$. These three attributes can simulate all possible attributes referred to by $\wp_{H_P}$. The only purpose present in the $\wp_{H_P}$ is *compliance-investigation*. We thus consider two purposes in the system u_1 and u_2 where u_1 is the purpose *compliance-investigation* and u_2 refers to a purpose which is something other than *compliance-investigation*. These two purposes capture all the possible purposes referred by $\wp_{H_P}$. For the principal sort, we consider one principal for each role in $\wp_{H_P}$ and one additional principal not having any roles. The roles in $\wp_{H_P}$ are: covered entity, secretary, and individual. Considering one individual from each role is sound as $\wp_{H_P}$ cannot differentiate between two principals. We actually could have considered only two principals, one acting in all the roles and another not in any role. For clarity, we consider principals of different roles are different. Having multiple principals in each role does not change the result of the Δ-property holding, as these 4 principals can simulate all possible behaviors. We have the following small model theorem for $\wp_{H_P}$.

THEOREM 16. *The policy $\wp_{H_P}$ has the Δ-property for infinite carriers of sorts $\mathcal{P}$, $\mathcal{T}$, and $\mathcal{U}$ if and only if $\wp_{H_P}$ has the Δ-property for finite carriers $\hat{\mathcal{P}}$, $\hat{\mathcal{T}}$, and $\hat{\mathcal{U}}$ in which $|\hat{\mathcal{P}}| = 4$, $|\hat{\mathcal{T}}| = 3$, and $|\hat{\mathcal{U}}| = 2$.*

Obligation	Norms in the slice	Automata generation time (s)	Graph analysis time (ms)	Analysis results
§160.310	4	3	2	Passed
Synthetic-1	6	98	16	Passed
Synthetic-2	6	324	31	Failed
§164.524	4	22	5	Passed

Table 1: Policy analysis result (HIPAA)

Policy Analysis Results. We slice $\wp_H$ with respect to 2 obligations in HIPAA (§160.310, §164.524) and 1 synthetic

obligation (Synthetic-1). Once we have the small model theorem, we convert the FOTL sliced policy to a pLTL policy. Once we have the pLTL policy, we follow the approach proposed by Barth *et al.* [11], as discussed before. We convert each of the sliced pLTL policies to a tableau (with Büchi accepting condition) using the GOAL automata generation tool [53], then check whether all the reachable states can reach a strongly connected component with an accepting state in it. The experimental results are presented in Table 1. We verify that for the two obligations in HIPAA, the Δ-property holds for the sliced policies.

Observation. While verifying the sliced policy with respect to the synthetic obligation, we observed something interesting. Investigating the regulations manually led us to believe that the policy sliced with respect to the synthetic obligation (Synthetic-1) should **not** satisfy the Δ-property. However, our experimental result seems to differ. Upon close inspection, we figured out that the result is due to how HIPAA is specified. Specifically, rule §164.502(g)(3)(ii)(b) states that a covered entity cannot share an individual's *PHI* if it is forbidden by some law. In our specification of HIPAA, we keep the room that even though an action is now forbidden by some law, the law might change, and allow the forbidden action later. When we changed our specification in such a way that laws cannot change (*Synthetic-2*), then we got the desired result of the Δ-property not holding.

Discussion. There are two more occurrences of obligations in HIPAA (§164.512(c)(2) and §164.502(b)) which require sending privacy notices to the patient. We consider that privacy notices do not contain any *PHI* of the patient. Thus, those obligations are trivially allowed. However, in the case that notices contain *PHI* of the patient, then the corresponding slice of the policy is similar to the slice of §164.524.

Counter Example. When a policy violates the Δ-property, we can traverse the tableau to find a path to the violating node. This path corresponds to a finite trace showing the violation of the Δ-property. This counter example (expressed as a finite trace) can help the policy author to rewrite the policy to satisfy the Δ-property.

7. RELATED WORK

May *et al.* [45], based on the extension of the HRU model [30], present a formalism, called Privacy APIs, to encode HIPAA. They only consider §164.506 of the 2000 and 2003 version of HIPAA. They convert their formalism into the specification language of the SPIN model checker [35] and check whether it satisfies some desired invariants.

Ni *et al.* [46] present a family of models named P-RBAC (Privacy-aware Role Based Access Control) that extends the traditional RBAC [26] to support specification of practical but complex privacy policies. Their model can specify conditions, purposes, obligations, *etc.*, which are necessary for privacy policy specification. However, it is not apparent whether HIPAA can be encoded in their language due to absence of examples of such encodings.

Lam *et al.* [41] propose a privacy policy specification language called pLogic based on Datalog. They can only encode §164.502, §164.506, and §164.508 of HIPAA in pLogic. pLogic cannot specify any kinds of temporal conditions. Our specification language is richer than pLogic. Lam *et al.* [40] later developed a small model theorem for pLogic.

Recall that our specification language is inspired by CI [11]. We now discuss the distinctions between our language and CI. We allow future operators only in specific places. However, this is not the case for CI. It allows arbitrary nesting of future and past temporal operators. In such a case, separating past and future requirements from a FOTL formula is not trivial [27]. Additionally, in CI, one cannot express the purpose of the transmission and other conditions in HIPAA as they only have a fixed set of pre-defined predicates. In light of CI [11, 12], DeYoung *et al.* [21] propose an expressive policy specification language, PrivacyLFP. We adopted some of their improvements over CI (*e.g.*, purpose, subjected belief, *etc.*) but left out others that were not relevant for HIPAA (fixed point operators). The goal of their work is developing a specification language of HIPAA whereas our work focuses on static policy analysis of privacy policies like HIPAA. Garg *et al.* [28] propose an expressive, first-order logic-based privacy policy specification language. HIPAA can be completely encoded in their specification language. They present an auditing algorithm that incrementally inspects the system log against a policy and detects violations. Their approach only considers WC. Our work on the contrary presents a sound, semi-automated technique for verifying the Δ-property of a policy. Once verified, one can use their auditing algorithm to check WC. In the same vein, Basin *et al.* [13, 14] present a monitoring algorithm for policies written in metric first-order temporal logic. Their monitoring algorithm can be also used to check WC for a policy. Chowdhury *et al.* [17] propose extensions of XACML [55] for specifying HIPAA. In their work, they assume all the obligatory actions are authorized. Moreover, their approach can only check WC. Havelund and Roşu [31, 32, 50] propose a dynamic programming approach for monitoring pLTL formula which can be used for checking WC of pLTL policies. Krukow *et al.* [38] provide an algorithm which can be used to check WC of very restrictive FOTL policies.

Several work[36, 49, 18] have addressed permissibility of user obligations in context of access control policies. They introduce a property *"accountability"* of the access control policy and authorization state which ensures that all the incurred obligations be authorized. The accountability property has to be maintained as an invariant of the system whereas the Δ-property is a statically checkable property of the privacy policy which one needs to check once for a policy. Dougherty *et al.* [23] present an expressive obligation model and present analysis technique to approximate obligations for monitoring. The goal of our work is to provide static guarantee of a privacy policy's well-formedness and is thus complementary to [23].

8. CONCLUSION

In this paper, we propose a privacy policy specification language which is expressive enough to capture HIPAA. We then formally specify two different notions of privacy policy compliance (WC and SC). We show that although deciding WC is feasible, checking SC is undecidable. We then formally specify the Δ-property. To check compliance of an action with a privacy policy satisfying the Δ-property, it suffices to only check whether the action is weakly compliant with the policy. The Δ-property can be checked statically before the policy is deployed. While checking the Δ-property for a policy is undecidable, we have developed a sound, semi-automated technique, which we show is adequate for checking the Δ-property for our formalization of the HIPAA Privacy Policy.

Open Problems & Future Work. Our final policy analysis step requires model checking the propositional CTL^*_{lp} formula with respect to $\mathbb{M}_{\wp}$. There are currently no such tools which can model check a propositional CTL^*_{lp} specification against a given model. In an on-going work, we are developing a model checker following [39]. For preliminary results and to show feasibility we currently rely on the approach of Barth *et al.* [11].

LTL abstracts away the explicit notion of time and only reasons about relative orderings of different events. Although the obligations in HIPAA have explicit deadlines, our specification language cannot express explicit deadlines. An extension covering deadlines is plausible (see [13]). However, extending the policy analysis is not trivial, due to the fact that propositional branching time logic with explicit time is undecidable [8]. In HIPAA, deadlines appear only in the context of obligations. Our analysis of a policy without obligation deadlines is extendable to policies, which only have deadlines on obligations. Consider a policy with the following two rules. (1) When a patient's parents request to access the patient's *PHI*, then the doctor is obligated to give the patient's parents access to the *PHI*. (2) The doctor can disclose a patient's *PHI* to anybody if the patient gave an authorization to do so. Now according to our analysis this policy has the Δ-property as the incurred obligation of the doctor (from rule 1) can be fulfilled if the doctor received a patient's authorization (rule 2). Now let us add a deadline of 10 days for the doctor's obligation. Even with the deadline, it is possible for the doctor to discharge the obligation in 10 days if the patient sends the authorization in 10 days.

Currently we verify the Δ-property for a simplified version of the obligation in §164.524 of HIPAA. We plan to verify it for the general obligation in §164.524. We also want to explore techniques to check whether specific models of the system satisfy the Δ-property. We also would like to apply our policy analysis techniques to other regulations like GLBA [3], SOX [51], *etc.*

Additional Authors

William H. Winsborough contributed in this research until he passed away in August, 2011.

Acknowledgement

This material is based upon work supported by the National Science Foundation under Grant No. CNS-0964710 and by the Department of Health & Human Services under Grant No. HHS 90TR0003/01. The authors thank Ninghui Li, Keith Irwin, Murillo Pontual, Deepak Garg, Sruthi Bandhakavi, and the anonymous reviewers for their helpful suggestions. The authors also thank the team members of the GOAL tool [53].

9. REFERENCES

[1] HIPAA ENCODING.
http://galadriel.cs.utsa.edu/~ochowdhu/HIPAA-POLICY/.

[2] Privacy Promises That Can Be Kept: A Static Policy Analysis Method with Application to the HIPAA Privacy Rules. Technical Report CS-TR-2013-004. UT San Antonio.

[3] Senate banking committee, Gramm-Leach-Bliley Act, 1999. Public Law 106-102.

[4] Enterprise privacy authorization language (EPAL) version 1.2, Nov. 2003.
http://www.zurich.ibm.com/pri/projects/epal.html.

[5] M. W. Alford and *et al.*, editors. *Distributed Systems: Methods and Tools for Specification '85*, LNCS.

[6] B. Alpern and F. B. Schneider. Defining liveness. *Information Processing Letters*, 21(4):181–185, Oct. 1985.

[7] B. Alpern and F. B. Schneider. Recognizing safety and liveness. *Distributed Computing*, 2:117–126, 1987.

[8] R. Alur. *Techniques for automatic verification of real-time systems*. PhD thesis, Stanford, CA, 1992.

[9] R. Alur and T. Henzinger. Logics and models of real time: A survey. In *Real-Time: Theory in Practice*, Lecture Notes in Computer Science. 1992.

[10] amednews.com. Clinics fined $4.3 million for hipaa violations, 2011. Available at *http://www.ama-assn.org/amednews/2011/03/07/bisb0307.htm*.

[11] A. Barth, A. Datta, J. C. Mitchell, and H. Nissenbaum. Privacy and contextual integrity: Framework and applications. *IEEE Symposium on Security and Privacy.*

[12] A. Barth, J. Mitchell, A. Datta, and S. Sundaram. Privacy and utility in business processes. In *IEEE CSF '07.*

[13] D. Basin, F. Klaedtke, and S. Müller. Monitoring security policies with metric first-order temporal logic. In *ACM SACMAT '10.*

[14] D. A. Basin, F. Klaedtke, S. Marinovic, and E. Zalinescu. Monitoring compliance policies over incomplete and disagreeing logs. In *RV*, 2012.

[15] T. Breaux and A. Antón. Analyzing regulatory rules for privacy and security requirements. *IEEE TSE '08.*

[16] J. R. Büchi. On a decision method in restricted second order arithmetic. In *Proceedings of LMPS'60*, 1962.

[17] O. Chowdhury, H. Chen, J. Niu, N. Li, and E. Bertino. On xacml's adequacy to specify and to enforce hipaa. In *HealthSec'12.*

[18] O. Chowdhury, M. Pontual, W. H. Winsborough, T. Yu, K. Irwin, and J. Niu. Ensuring Authorization Privileges for Cascading User Obligations. In *ACM SACMAT '12.*

[19] D. Damianou, N. Dulay, E. Lupu, and M. Sloman. The Ponder Policy Specification Language. In *IEEE POLICY '01.*

[20] F. Dederichs and R. Weber. Safety and liveness from a methodological point of view. *Information Processing Letters*, 1990.

[21] H. DeYoung, D. Garg, L. Jia, D. Kaynar, and A. Datta. Experiences in the logical specification of the hipaa and glba privacy laws. In *ACM WPES '10.*

[22] N. Dinesh, A. Joshi, I. Lee, and O. Sokolsky. Checking traces for regulatory conformance. In *RV '08.*

[23] D. J. Dougherty, K. Fisler, and S. Krishnamurthi. Obligations and their interaction with programs. In *Proceedings of ESORICS 2007*, pages 375–389.

[24] E. A. Emerson. Handbook of theoretical computer science. chapter Temporal and modal logic, pages 995–1072. 1990.

[25] E. A. Emerson and K. S. Namjoshi. Reasoning about rings. In *POPL '95*, 1995.

[26] D. F. Ferraiolo, R. S. Sandhu, S. Gavrila, D. R. Kuhn, and R. Chandramouli. Proposed NIST standard for role-based access control. *ACM TISSEC '01.*

[27] D. Gabbay. The imperative future. chapter : The declarative past and imperative future, pages 35–67. John Wiley & Sons, Inc., New York, NY, USA, 1996.

[28] D. Garg, L. Jia, and A. Datta. Policy auditing over incomplete logs: theory, implementation and applications. In *ACM CCS '11.*

[29] D. Garg, L. Jia, and A. Datta. A logical method for policy enforcement over evolving audit logs. *CoRR*, abs/1102.2521, 2011.

[30] M. A. Harrison, W. L. Ruzzo, and J. D. Ullman. Protection in operating systems. *CACM '76.*

[31] K. Havelund and G. Roşu. Efficient monitoring of safety properties. *Int. J. Softw. Tools Technol. Transf., '04.*

[32] K. Havelund and G. Rosu. Synthesizing monitors for safety properties. In *TACAS' 02.*

[33] Health Resources and Services Administration. Health insurance portability and accountability act, 1996. Public Law 104-191.

[34] I. M. Hodkinson, F. Wolter, and M. Zakharyaschev. Decidable fragment of first-order temporal logics. *Ann. Pure Appl. Logic '00.*

[35] G. J. Holzmann. The model checker SPIN. *TSE '97.*

[36] K. Irwin, T. Yu, and W. H. Winsborough. On the modeling and analysis of obligations. In *Proceedings of the 13th ACM conference on Computer and communications security*, pages 134–143, New York, NY, USA, 2006. ACM.

[37] R. Koymans. Specifying real-time properties with metric temporal logic. *Real-Time Syst.*, 1990.

[38] K. Krukow, M. Nielsen, and V. Sassone. A logical framework for history-based access control and reputation systems. *J. Comput. Secur.*, 16(1):63–101, 2008.

[39] O. Kupferman, A. Pnueli, and M. Y. Vardi. Once and for all. *J. Comput. Syst. Sci. '12.*

[40] P. E. Lam, J. C. Mitchell, A. Scedrov, S. Sundaram, and F. Wang. Declarative privacy policy: finite models and attribute-based encryption. In *ACM IHI '12.*

[41] P. E. Lam, J. C. Mitchell, and S. Sundaram. A Formalization of HIPAA for a Medical Messaging System. In *TrustBus '09.*

[42] L. Lamport. Proving the correctness of multiprocess programs. *IEEE TSE'77.*

[43] Z. Manna and A. Pnueli. The anchored version of the temporal framework. In *REX Workshop '88.*

[44] Z. Manna and A. Pnueli. *Temporal verification of reactive systems: safety.* Springer-Verlag New York, Inc., New York, NY, USA, 1995.

[45] M. J. May, C. A. Gunter, and I. Lee. Privacy APIs: Access control techniques to analyze and verify legal privacy policies. In *IEEE CSFW '06.*

[46] Q. Ni, A. Trombetta, E. Bertino, and J. Lobo. Privacy -aware role based access control. In *ACM SACMAT '07.*

[47] S. Owicki and L. Lamport. Proving liveness properties of concurrent programs. *ACM TOPLAS '82.*

[48] A. Pnueli. The temporal logic of programs. In *Proceedings of the 18th IEEE Symposium on Foundations of Computer Science*, volume 526, pages 46–67, 1977.

[49] M. Pontual, O. Chowdhury, W. H. Winsborough, T. Yu, and K. Irwin. On the management of user obligations. SACMAT '11, New York, NY, USA. ACM.

[50] G. Roşu and K. Havelund. Synthesizing dynamic programming algorithms from linear temporal logic formulae. Technical report, 2001.

[51] Securities and Exchange Commission. Sarbanes-oxley act, 2002. Public Law 107-204.

[52] A. P. Sistla. Safety, liveness and fairness in temporal logic. *Formal Aspects of Computing*, 6:495–511, 1994.

[53] Y.-K. Tsay, M.-H. Tsai, J.-S. Chang, and Y.-W. Chang. Büchi store : An open repository of büchi automata. In *TACAS '11.*

[54] M. Weiser. Program slicing. In *ICSE '81.*

[55] XACML TC. Oasis extensible access control markup language (xacml).

APPENDIX

A. SAFETY AND LIVENESS PROPERTIES.

A temporal property is a set of traces. We can divide temporal properties into mainly two categories, safety [42, 5] and liveness [6]. Such a classification of properties can enable choosing the right proof methodology for proving correctness. For instance, methods based on global invariants can be used to prove safety properties whereas methods based on proof lattices or well-founded induction [47] can be used to prove liveness properties.

A safety property asserts that something bad never happens. For instance, a doctor cannot share a patient's information without receiving an authorization from the patient. Liveness properties on the contrary asserts that something good eventually happens. For instance, if a patient requests for accessing her own information, the doctor should provide her access eventually. LTL formulas can express both safety and liveness properties. Furthermore, Alpern and Schneider [7] have shown that any LTL formula can be written as conjunctions of safety and liveness properties. A past only LTL formula can express only safety properties whereas future only LTL formula can express both safety and liveness properties [52]. We now formally define what it means for a property to be safety property or a liveness property.

DEFINITION 17 (SAFETY PROPERTY). *A property P is a safety property if the following holds: $\forall \sigma : \sigma \in S^{\omega} : (\sigma \models P \iff (\forall i : i \geq 0 : (\exists \beta : \beta \in S^{\omega} : \sigma[\ldots i] \cdot \beta \models P)))$. Here, S^{ω} represents the set of infinite sequences, each element of which, is an element of the state set S. Moreover, $\sigma[\ldots i]$ represents the finite prefix of length $i+1$ of σ.*

DEFINITION 18 (LIVENESS PROPERTY [7]). *A property P is a liveness property if the following holds: $\forall \alpha : \alpha \in S^{*} : (\exists \beta : \beta \in S^{\omega} : \alpha \cdot \beta \models P)$. Here, S^{*} represents the set of finite sequences, each element of which, is an element of the state set S.*

B. EXAMPLE OF REGULATORY SEND

Consider the following negative norm:

inrole(p_1, *covered-entity*)$\wedge$inrole(q, *individual*)$\wedge$in(t, PHI)
$\to$ believesMinimumNecessaryForPurpose(p_1, p_2, q, t, u)

The regulated send of the above negative norm is:

send(p_1, p_2, m) $\wedge$ contains(m, q, t) $\wedge$ for-purpose(m, u) $\wedge$
inrole(p_1, *covered-entity*) $\wedge$ inrole(q, *individual*) $\wedge$ in(t, PHI)

C. DEFINITION OF THE α FUNCTION

Our positive norms have the form: $(\mathbb{C} \wedge \psi \wedge \beta) \vee \psi_{exception}$. For such a positive norm where β is not trivially true, α function would return the following $\langle \lambda, \gamma \rangle$ pair: $\langle (\mathbb{C} \wedge \psi \wedge \neg(\psi_{exception}) \wedge \bigwedge_j \hat{\phi}_j^-, \beta \rangle$ in which $\bigwedge_j \hat{\phi}_j^-$ is the conjunction of all the modified negative norms. The modified negative norms are same as the original negative norms except that they do not have any future temporal operators in them (modified ones).

The form of our negative norms are as follows: $\mathbb{C} \wedge \psi \to \chi \vee \psi_{exception}$. In the negative norms, χ can have one of the following forms: (1) β, (2) ψ_1, (3) $\psi_1 \wedge \beta$, and (4) $\psi_1 \to \beta$. When χ has form (2) then there are no obligations in that norms. For rest of them, let us consider β is not trivially true. For a negative norm ϕ_j^- whose χ is of form case (1), α function would return the following $\langle \lambda, \gamma \rangle$ pair: $\langle \mathbb{C} \wedge \psi \wedge \neg(\psi_{exception}) \wedge \bigwedge_{k \neq j} \hat{\phi}_k^- \wedge \bigvee_i \hat{\phi}_i^+, \beta \rangle$ in

which $\hat{\phi}_k^-$ and $\hat{\phi}_i^+$ respectively, represents modified negative and positive norms. When the χ has the form (3) or (4), the function α would return the following $\langle \lambda, \gamma \rangle$ pair: $\langle \mathbb{C} \wedge \psi \wedge \neg(\psi_{exception}) \wedge \psi_1 \wedge \bigwedge_{k \neq j} \hat{\phi}_k^- \wedge \bigvee_i \hat{\phi}_i^+, \beta \rangle$.

D. SLICING ALGORITHM

In this section, we present the algorithm for calculating the slice of a privacy policy $\wp$ based on a slicing criterion P. It additionally takes as input the role hierarchy and the attribute computation rules necessary for determining consistency. The slicing procedure calculates the transitive closure of the dependence relation in a lazy, by-need fashion.

Algorithm 1 is the main procedure. It takes as input a privacy policy (represented by the set of norms) and an obligatory send event which is used as the slicing criterion, the role hierarchy, the attribute computation rules and returns another sub-policy which influences the obligatory send P. Algorithm 2 is a utility procedure used by algorithm 1. The procedure AddSend takes as input a send event of form P and checks to see whether the send event has been processed before. If the send has not been processed before, the procedure adds it to the queue UnderprocessingSends and also to the map ProcessedSends so that it is not processed again.

Algorithm 1 Slice(Φ, P)

Input: A privacy policy represented as a set of norms Φ and a slicing criterion P.
Output: returns a sub-policy of the input policy represented as a set of norms Φ_r.
1: /* **We assume the following variables to be global** */
2: Φ_r = empty
3: Queue UnderprocessingSends = empty
4: Map ProcessedSends = ProcessedNorms =empty
5: Initialize(P)
6: **while** UnderprocessingSends$\neq$empty **do**
7:    Send Q = UnderprocessingSends.dequeue() ;
8:    **for all** $\phi \in \Phi$ **do**
9:      **if** $\phi \notin$ProcessedNorms **then**
10:       **if** ϕ is of form $(R \wedge \psi \wedge \beta) \vee \psi_{exception}$ and $R \rightsquigarrow Q$ **then**
11:         $\Phi_r = \Phi_r \cup \phi$ /* **add** ϕ **to the result** */
12:         Insert ϕ to the map processedNorms
13:         **for all** Send $x \in \psi \vee x \in \psi_{exception} \vee x \in \beta$ **do**
14:           AddSend(x)
15:       **if** ϕ is of form $R \wedge \psi \to \chi \vee \psi_{exception}$ and $R \rightsquigarrow Q$ **then**
16:         $\Phi_r = \Phi_r \cup \phi$ /* **add** ϕ **to the result** */
17:         Insert ϕ to the map processedNorms
18:         **for all** Send $x \in \psi \vee x \in \psi_{exception} \vee x \in \chi$ **do**
19:           AddSend(x)

Algorithm 2 Initialize(Q)

Input: A send event Q (non-temporal formula)
1: **for all** $\phi \in \Phi$ **do**
2:    **if** $\phi \notin$ProcessedNorms **then**
3:      **if** ϕ is of form $(R \wedge \psi \wedge \beta) \vee \psi_{exception}$ and Q appears as an obligatory send in β **then**
4:        $\Phi_r = \Phi_r \cup \phi$, Insert ϕ to the map processedNorms
5:        AddSend(R)
6:        **for all** Send $x \in \psi \vee x \in \psi_{exception} \vee x \in \beta$ **do**
7:          AddSend(x)
8:      **if** ϕ is of form $R \wedge \psi \to \chi \vee \psi_{exception}$ and Q appears as an obligatory send in χ **then**
9:        $\Phi_r = \Phi_r \cup \phi$, Insert ϕ to the map processedNorms
10:        AddSend(R)
11:        **for all** Send $x \in \psi \vee x \in \psi_{exception} \vee x \in \chi$ **do**
12:          AddSend(x)

Combining Social Authentication and Untrusted Clouds for Private Location Sharing

Andrew K. Adams
Pittsburgh Supercomputing Center
University of Pittsburgh
akadams@psc.edu

Adam J. Lee
University of Pittsburgh
adamlee@cs.pitt.edu

ABSTRACT

Recently, many location-sharing services (LSSs) have emerged that share data collected using mobile devices. However, research has shown that many users are uncomfortable with LSS operators managing their location histories, and that the ease with which contextual data can be shared with unintended audiences can lead to regrets that sometimes outweigh the benefits of these systems. In an effort to address these issues, we have developed SLS: a secure location sharing system that combines location-limited channels, multi-channel key establishment, and untrusted cloud storage to hide user locations from LSS operators while also limiting unintended audience sharing. In addition to describing the key agreement and location-sharing protocols used by SLS, we discuss an iOS implementation of SLS that enables location sharing at tunable granularity through an intuitive policy interface on the user's mobile device.

Categories and Subject Descriptors

C.2.0 [**Computer-Communication Networks**]: General—*Security and protection*; C.2.2 [**Computer-Communication Networks**]: Network Protocols—*Applications*; K.6.5 [**Management Of Computing And Information Systems**]: Security and Protection—*Authentication*

General Terms

Security

Keywords

Key Management; Location Tracking; Presence Systems; Privacy; Security

1. INTRODUCTION

Over the last several years, location- and presence-sharing systems have received considerable attention from both researchers [6, 8, 18, 21, 22, 28] and in practice [12, 14, 16, 17]. The recent explosion in mobile computing and social networking has led to deployment of a wide range of location-sharing systems (LSSs), both

stand-alone in nature (e.g., Google Latitude [17], FourSquare [14], or Glympse [16]) as well as integrated with other social networking platforms (e.g., Facebook places [12], Twitter, or Yelp). These types of systems allow a user to share her geographic location with her social contacts either as a first-class data object or as support for other content (e.g., attaching one's location to restaurant review). This sharing can be done in a near seamless manner, particularly when the LSS is embedded within a larger social platform.

Despite their popularity, LSSs are not without their own security and privacy problems. By their very design, these systems have the implicit shortcoming that sharing one's location with social contacts *requires* sharing this location with the LSS operator as well. This can lead to undesirable profiling of users by third parties, or increase users' exposure risk in the event of an LSS compromise. In addition, it is has been shown that social networks in general [29] and LSSs in particular [22] can sometimes lead to situations in which users experience regrets after (over)sharing information. This is often the result of the so-called *unintended audience* problem, in which data is shared with individuals other than those with whom the subject intended to share. This may manifest as a result of a location being automatically attached to content posted on a social network, accidental sharing of a location with a user's entire set of contacts instead of a restricted subset, or posting a location that contradicts other statements made by the user [22].

The latter problem is symptomatic of both LSS and access control complexity. For instance, it is well-known that users social networks have many more contacts than they interact with on a day-to-day basis: a 2011 poll of 1,954 British citizens found that the average person had 476 Facebook friends, but only 152 contacts in their cellular phone [31]. Furthermore, research studies have shown that users frequently make mistakes when authoring even basic access control policies in commodity systems [4, 11, 23]. As such, it is clear that accidents and misconfigurations can lead to oversharing in large social networks. On the other hand, the problem of required sharing with LSS operators is one of economic incentives: the ability to study user habits and carry out targeted advertising provides revenue for operators of the systems.

An interesting observation, however, is that current generation smartphones are capable of helping mitigate both of the above types of concerns. Given the 3G/4G connectivity of these devices and the open APIs to cloud storage-as-a-service (SaaS) providers like Amazon S3 [1], it is possible for mobile applications to explicitly manage a user's published location history. Furthermore, smartphones store rich information about a users' close contacts (e.g., email addresses, phone numbers) and have access to multiple channels of communication (e.g., WiFi, 3G/4G, Bluetooth, SMS). As a result, it is possible to develop robust key exchange protocols—e.g., based on multiple distinct avenues of communication and historical context, or by leveraging location-limited channels—that allow location data to be selectively encrypted prior to upload, thereby preventing snooping attack by the SaaS provider and limiting incidences of over-sharing.

In this paper, we describe *Secure Location Sharing* (SLS), a decentralized LSS that leverages the above observations to limit the over-exposure of user location data without relying on trusted infrastructure. Specifically, SLS allows users to set up secure location sharing with selected contacts by pairing devices in one of two ways. Users who happen to be physically co-located can use location-limited visual channels to pair devices (similar to [20]). Users who are located apart from one another can instead leverage multiple communication channels (e.g., email and SMS) along with contextual question/answer protocols to help prevent man-in-the-middle (MitM) attacks during device pairing. Keys established during this pairing process are then used to aid in securely sharing a user's location at a tunable granularity (e.g., GPS coordinate, city-level, etc.) via untrusted SaaS services. In exploring SLS, we make the following contributions:

1. We demonstrate the first decentralized LSS that is capable of providing flexible and secure location sharing over untrusted infrastructure. Unlike existing approaches to securing social networks (e.g., X-pire! [2]) our work does not involve abuse of existing social network APIs, but rather builds secure and flexible sharing into the real-life social networks managed by users' smartphones.

2. We propose an alternate economic model for LSSs, in which the users providing their location to others pay for the storage used to host their data.[1] This removes the economic incentives driving traditional LSS providers to view user location histories, and further reduces the risk of accidental over-exposure due to LSS compromise.

3. SLS limits the unintended audience sharing problem by requiring explicit device pairing between providers and consumers of location sharing. By leveraging multi-channel and/or location-limited pairing protocols, this setup procedure is robust against even very strong adversaries with control over large portions of the network environment.

4. We develop an iOS application as a proof-of-concept implementation of SLS. This demonstrates both the efficiency of our approach, as well as the simplicity of interfaces needed to manage the secure device pairing aspects of SLS.

The rest of this paper is organized as follows. In Section 2, we discuss related work, and briefly explain the problems associated with canonical location-sharing or presence system. We discuss our goals, properties and principals of our system in Section 3. In Section 4 we present our framework and implementation for secure location sharing. Section 5 re-examines our design, evaluates the performance and security of the system, and explores our directions for future work. We present our conclusions in Section 6.

2. RELATED WORK

Google Latitude [17], FourSquare [14], Facebook Places [12], and Glympse [16] are examples of LSSs that operate by having users upload their location data to the service, such that others (i.e.,

consumers) can access the location data. Current strategies for addressing privacy issues in LSSs are typically based on obfuscating the location data or anonymizing the provider; the efficiency of these techniques are discussed in, e.g., [26,27]. In [24], the authors address oversharing in LSSs by providing users with interactive feedback about the number of users accessing their location, and the frequency of these accesses. Our work deviates from prior work by (i) preventing the LSS from viewing a user's location data, and (ii) by ensuring that a user has full control over *who* she chooses to share her location data with and *how* she intends for her location to be consumed.

The protection and secrecy of a user's data contained in the cloud is the focus of DataLocker [9], which is a collection of tools that enable a provider to encrypt data prior to uploading the data to the cloud. Our model does this precisely with location data, however, our model is not tied to any specific cloud entity. Moreover, we do not generically encrypt location data: policy dictates the precision with which data is presented to the consumers, and how it is protected in the cloud. Instead of protecting data, X-Pire! [2] attempts to *decay* data (ostensibly images, but the technique could be applied to location data) by associating a key to an image; when the key expires the X-pire! aware server refuses to serve the data. Similarly, Vanish [15] decays data by altering links to the data stored within a DHT. Although our model does not address the decaying of data, it could benefit from techniques like these in the future.

Several papers present advanced key management protocols that make use of smart phone technology [7, 13, 19, 20]. McCune et al. describe the protocol, *Seeing-is-Believing (SiB)* [20], in which the camera in users' smart phones capture 2D barcodes—these 2D barcodes are used as commitments for exchanging public keys. Our key management protocol relies heavily on the concepts and ideas introduced presented in this work. SafeSlinger [13] is a protocol and framework designed to exchange public keys between smart phones; this is precisely one of the tasks that our key management protocol is designed to accomplish; our work diverges from [13] by (i) using the *location-limited* channel between pairing smart phones to fully exchange asymmetric keys, and (ii) by leveraging what we refer to as a *file-store deposit* (a pointer to a dropbox) to assist in symmetric key management. Accelerometer data from two smart phones is used in [19] and [7] to aid in authentication for secure pairing. Mayrhofer et al. [19] employ a strategy of shaking two phone simultaneously to generate a *movement limited* channel, while BUMP [7] uses the accelerometer *and* location data between to bumping smart phones. Again, our work differs from pairing protocols based on movement limited channels, by operating over location-limited and multichannel communication channels.

Multichannel security protocols, as surveyed in [30], are ways to mitigate against MitM attacks by using multiple communication channels, e.g., radio, visual and 1-bit on/off or toggle buttons, during authentication. The idea is that a malicious eavesdropper cannot eavesdrop on all channels. We use an instantiation of this idea in the variant of our pairing protocol based on historical, multiple open-lines of communication.

Limitations of Prior Work. As alluded to in Section 1 and Section 2, LSS have significant privacy issues, and in fact the primary issue was exposed in [5]. In this study, it was shown that that users are uncomfortable with a service controlling access to their location data. Techniques have been introduced to mitigate users' privacy issue concerns, e.g., data can be diffused, or aggregated, but all of these reduce the utility of the data. This is especially troubling if the providers' intentions are for their data to be consumed at a high precision by a specific user, or one or more groups

---

[1]Note, however, that some SaaS providers provide lower-tier service that is sufficient for SLS at little to no cost to the user (e.g., http://aws.amazon.com/free/).

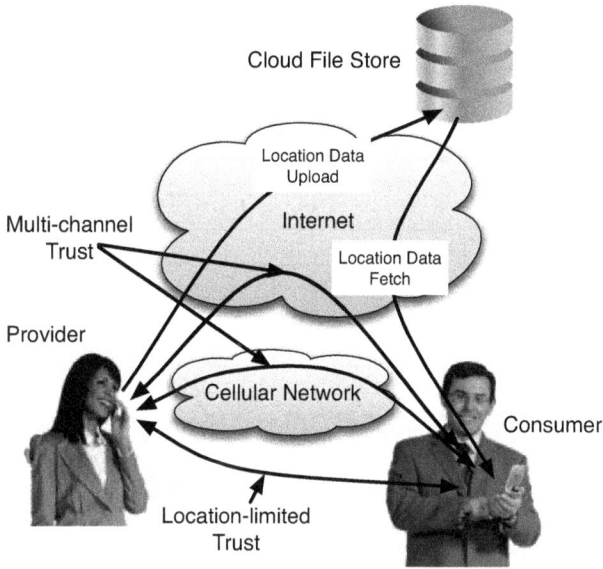

Figure 1: SLS Architecture Overview.

Architecture Overview. Figure 1 presents a high-level view of the SLS system. Users in the system can be divided into two classes: *providers* and *consumers*. Providers share their location with others, while consumers retrieve the locations of others; a user can act as both a provider and a consumer. We assume that all users have smartphones, as well as (perhaps self-signed) asymmetric key pairs. Providers' smartphones must be able to detect their current location, e.g., via GPS or cellular/WiFi localization. Secure location sharing is enabled by shared, symmetric keys. The sharing of these symmetric keys is facilitated by asymmetric keys exchanged during a device pairing protocol. SLS provides two pairing protocols to exchange asymmetric keys: one based upon in-person communication over location-limited channels, and another that leverages multi-channel communication for situations in which in-person exchange is not possible. To pair devices using location-limited channels, users' smartphones must have the ability to read and decode QR codes. To pair devices using multiple, historical open-lines of communication, users' smartphones must have both network access (e.g., via WiFi), as well as the ability to send and receive SMS messages. Although the multi-channel based pairing protocol requires that principals have previously communicated, there is no such restriction within the location-limited pairing protocol. Encrypted location data is shared through the use of a *SaaS service* (e.g., Amazon S3) contracted by the provider. Note, although one can currently find SaaS services that are free, our model assumes an associated cost to use the service. We require that the SaaS service allow any user to download data posted to the provider's account. We do not require all providers to use the same SaaS service.

Adversary Model. In this paper, we make the following assumptions. We first assume that user smartphones are free of malware, as this would immediately make user locations available to the adversary through the smartphone API. We assume that all network communications are subject to read, replay, reorder, and modification by a Dolev-Yao style adversary [10]. Finally, we assume that the SaaS providers used are honest-but-curious in nature. That is, we assume that they will correctly execute the GET and PUT operations provided by their APIs, but may try to derive provider locations by inspecting the data that they host. In this work, we do not address DoS/DDoS attacks against SaaS providers as a means of thwarting location sharing.

4. SECURE LOCATION SHARING

We now describe the design of the Secure Location Sharing (SLS) framework. We first describe how multiple granularities of location data are encrypted and managed by the provider (Section 4.1). Then, we describe two protocols for pairing provider and consumer devices to enable secure retrieval of provider locations from SaaS services (Sections 4.2–4.3). Next, we discuss the policy controls available to providers within SLS (Section 4.4). Finally, we describe our iOS implementation of SLS (Section 4.5).

4.1 Location Sharing

In SLS, a provider's smartphones is responsible for capturing her location data using, e.g., WiFi/cellular localization or GPS. Each location sample collected by SLS is represented as a four-tuple containing a location coordinate, an estimate of the provider's speed of travel, the providers bearing/heading, and a timestamp indicating when the sample was collected. In total, each location sample collected by SLS requires approximately 200 bytes to store. Given that a provider may wish to share her location at multiple granularities, the sample collected by SLS is generalized to each desired

of users. A secondary issue that arose in the study is that many users are uncomfortable knowing that *anyone* can see their location information, i.e., once the location data is uploaded to the LSS the user forfeits control over the data.

Although not novel, the combination of symmetric and asymmetric cryptography can help address both of these concerns: i.e., providers encrypt their location data prior to uploading it to a LSS, and then must distribute the decryption key(s) to enable retrieval by authorized consumers. However, this key management process can be a heavy burden. McCune et al. and Farb et al. [13, 20] observe that smart phones are fast becoming ubiquitous and are exceptionally portable and, as such, are usually available during vis-a-vis interactions. This makes smartphones an ideal platform for bootstrapping the exchange of cryptographic keys through the location-limited channels that can exist between two parties. We further observe that current smart phones possess the technology to perform key management efficiently and fully over location-limited channels, but only lack the protocols and framework to achieve this. SafeSlinger [13] is architected to rely on Internet connectivity to/from a server to aid in the key exchange protocol (i.e., SafeSlinger only uses the location-limited channel between the pairing smart phones for initializing the key exchange, and then for confirmation). This has the obvious disadvantages of requiring (i) that the server be available at all times, and (ii) that the exchange occurs in an environment that possesses network connectivity. We argue that both of these requirements are unnecessary to exchange asymmetric keys in a close, vis-a-vis setting that leverages location-limited channels, while using current smart phone technology.

3. SYSTEM DESIGN

The SLS system was designed with two main goals in mind: (i) enabling tunable and private location sharing with limited contacts, and (ii) limiting end-user location over exposure. We now overview our system architecture and describe the threat model within which we expect SLS to be used.

granularity or precision prior to upload (e.g., exact, neighborhood, county, or state precision). These (perhaps generalized) provider locations are shared with consumers via an (untrusted) SaaS service contracted by the provider. As such, location data must be cryptographically protected prior to upload. To accomplish this, the provider generates one symmetric key for each granularity level at which her data is to be shared, and then CBC encrypts each sample prior to upload.

Encrypted location samples are thus unreadable to the SaaS service, with whom the user is under no obligation to share her location (unlike in a traditional LSS). We note, however, that there is economic incentive for the SaaS service to correctly house the data, regardless what the data's contents are: users are not bound to a particular SaaS service and can simply migrate their data should the SaaS service misbehave. Further, providers also have complete control over the amount of information shared: they may post only a single "current" location (e.g., by overwriting a single location sample), or instead maintain a history of location samples (e.g., by storing a sliding window of n location samples). In SLS, we refer to these two operational modes as *update* and *history*, respectively. Finally, consumers are under no obligation to create accounts with an LSS, as all data is pulled from SaaS providers by SLS using HTTP GET requests made to world-readable URLs.

Of course, the reliance of SLS on symmetric keys to protect provider location data raises two issues. First, it must be possible for providers and consumers to securely authenticate one another and exchange the cryptographic material needed to retrieve location data at the desired level of granularity. To this end, we present protocols for device pairing based on location-limited and multi-channel protocols in Sections 4.2 and 4.3, respectively. Second, it must be both possible and efficient for the provider to alter the list of consumers with whom she shares information and the granularity at which this information is shared, which are challenges that are addressed in Sections 4.2 and 4.4.

4.2 Location-Limited Pairing

In-person interactions are an ideal setting for device pairing and key exchange. These interactions present the users engaging in the pairing protocol with an opportunity to physically identify the owner of the device with which they are attempting to establish a secure channel, as well as enable the use of location limited (e.g., visual [20]) channels to exchange data. The combination of human-to-human authentication and device-to-device communication that is difficult to intercept results in *demonstrative identification* [3] of the participants in location-limited device pairing protocols. SLS utilizes the traits of visual, location-limited channels, and extends the concepts presented in SiB [20] when pairing devices to aid in symmetric key management.

Figure 2 illustrates our location-limited device pairing protocol, which we call *Communionable Trust (CT)*. This protocol makes use of human-to-human audio and visual communication, as well as device-to-device visual communication using on-board cameras and Quick Response (QR) codes. The first step of this protocol is the real-world identification and authentication of the humans who wish to pair devices to facilitate location sharing via SLS. After the human participants have agreed to pair devices, the remainder of the protocol focuses on the exchange of public key information between provider and consumer, and exchanging metadata that enables the sharing of both symmetric keys and location data.

In Step 2 of the protocol, the consumer generates a QR code that contains her public key (K_C) as well as a device identity token (ID_C) used to associate her device with her real-world identity, as managed by the provider's smartphone. Figure 3 shows a QR code

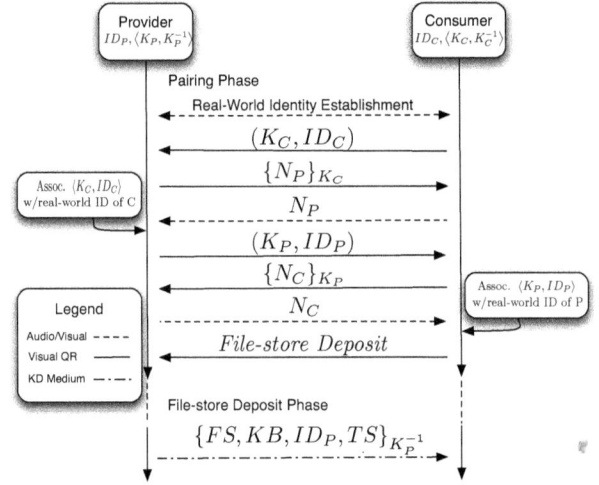

Figure 2: Communionable Trust Protocol.

containing a 1024-bit RSA public key and it's associated identity token.[2] The provider scans this code with his phone, and recovers K_C and ID_C. He then generates a random challenge nonce, N_P, encrypts N_P using K_C, and generates a QR code containing the resulting ciphertext (Step 3). The consumer scans this QR code, decrypts the resulting ciphertext, and verbally communicates the nonce value to the provider (Step 4). After verifying this exchange, the provider associates K_C and ID_C with the consumer's contact information in his smartphone.

This process is then mirrored in Steps 5, 6, and 7 of the communionable trust protocol, which provides the consumer with the providers public key (K_P) and identity token (ID_P).

In the final step of the Pairing Phase, the consumer QR-encodes their *file-store deposit*—a description of an out-of-band channel over which the consumer wishes to be notified of the provider's SaaS store—and presents it for the provider to scan. This message is sent unencrypted due to the location-limited nature of the visual channel used by this protocol. The use of this consumer-specified "drop box" allows the provider to inform the consumer asynchronously (e.g., via SMS) if they change SaaS providers at a later date, and thus obviates the need to re-execute the CT protocol.

File-store Deposit Phase. The final message of the communionable trust protocol handles the distribution of metadata that enables the consumer to retrieve location samples uploaded by the provider. This message is sent over the channel identified in Step 8 of the communionable trust protocol, and is a four-tuple of values containing a URI for the file store at which the provider's location data will be hosted (FS), a URI at which the consumer can access her shared key bundle (KB), the provider's identity token (ID_P), and a timestamp (TS). The entire message is then signed by the provider to ensure authenticity. After using TS and K_P (which is associated with ID_P by the consumer) to validate the freshness and authenticity of this message, FS and KB provide the consumer with all of the information that is needed to securely access the provider's location data.

---

[2] We note that version 40 QR codes can encode approximately 1500 bytes of data, which is more than sufficient for exchanging even 2048-bit public keys.

Figure 3: QR-encoded 1024-bit RSA public key (with associated identity token).

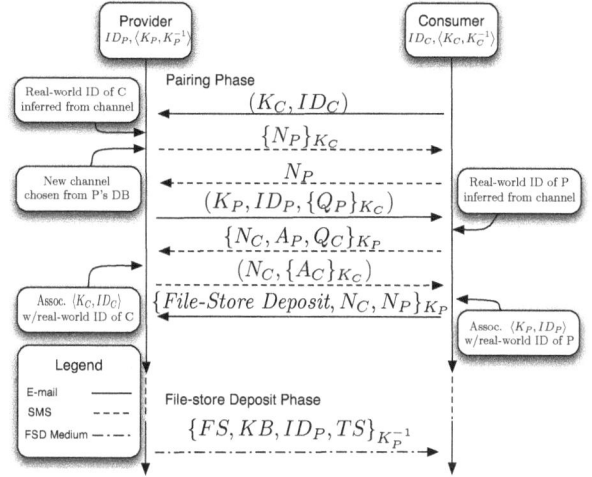

Figure 4: Historical Communication Channels Protocol.

The key bundle URI, KB, provides the consumer with a pointer to an encrypted key bundle stored on the provider's SaaS service. This key bundle is a (*key*, *version*, *signature*) three-tuple that is encrypted using the consumer's public key (K_C). The *key* field of this tuple contains the current symmetric key corresponding to the precision level with which the consumer is permitted to access the provider's location, the *version* field indicates the version of this key, and the *signature* field is a hash of the key and version fields encrypted with provider's private key (K_P^{-1}). Key versions are used to facilitate location retrieval as keys change in response to changes in provider access controls (see Section 4.4). The level of indirection added by the key bundle—as opposed to directly transferring keys as part of the CT protocol—eliminates the need for direct communication between the provider and consumer upon every policy change. After recovering their key bundle, the consumer can easily retrieve provider locations from the file store URI, FS, and decrypt this data.

4.3 Multi-channel Pairing

It is unreasonable to assume that users of SLS will always have the ability to physically co-locate during the device pairing process. As such, we also describe a pairing protocol that can be used by individuals who are not within close proximity. As such protocols can be vulnerable to MitM attacks, we make use of multiple *historical, open-lines of communication* associated with principals on their smart phones (e.g., email address, phone number, or instant messaging account). In this context, *historical* refers to pre-existing contacts, and *open-lines of communication* implies that the principals have communicated with the preexisting contact over those multiple channels. This combination of properties gives providers (resp. consumers) higher assurance that the identity of the consumer (resp. provider) is correct, since (i) existing contact information is used to bootstrap the communication process and (ii) an active attacker would need to control multiple communication channels to subvert the protocol. Our *Historical Communication Channels (HCC)* protocol is described in Figure 4.

HCC is initiated in the first step of the Pairing Phase by the consumer, who sends their public key (K_C) and device identity token (ID_C) used to associate her device with her real-world identity

(which is established through previous contact as managed by the provider's smartphone). This message is sent to the provider over an existing communication channel (e.g., a known email address), signified using a solid line in Figure 4. Upon receiving K_C and ID_C, the provider generates a random challenge nonce N_P, encrypts N_P using K_C, and sends $\{N_P\}_{K_C}$ to the consumer via a *different* historical, open-line of communication that the provider has previously associated with the consumer (e.g., via SMS), which is denoted by a dashed line in Figure 4. The consumer decrypts the ciphertext and returns N_P back to the provider over *HCC Secondary* (Step 3). At this point in the protocol, the provider is confident that the consumer has access to the private key associated with the public key received in Step 1.

However, the provider does *not* yet have a high level of confidence that the consumer is indeed whom the provider believes they are (e.g., someone other than the consumer could have stolen the consumer's smart phone). Hence, the provider generates a *secret question* (Q_P) that, within reason, only she and the consumer should know the answer to; e.g., *"Who was the away team at the last hockey game that we attended together?"*. Q_P is encrypted with K_C and is sent to the consumer along with K_P and ID_P over the primary channel (Step 4). The consumer generates (i) the answer (A_P) to Q_P, (ii) her own random nonce N_C, and (iii) her own *secret question* (Q_C). All three are encrypted with K_P and sent to the provider via *HCC Secondary* (Step 5). If, after decrypting the resulting ciphertext, A_P is correct the provider sends N_C and her answer (A_C) encrypted with K_C via *HCC Secondary* (Step 6). After verifying A_C, the consumer encrypts their file-store deposit (*File-Store Deposit*), N_P and N_C with K_P and sends them via *HCC Primary* (Step 7).

Finally, similar to the CT protocol, the provider assigns the consumer's precision level and the File-store Deposit Phase begins (see Section 4.2 and 4.4). We note that the HCC protocol should be terminated if either (i) a principal receives a *secret question* via SLS without first initiating or receiving a public key from the same principal over a different channel, or (ii) the response to a participant's secret question is incorrect.

4.4 Policy Control

As alluded to in the Section 4.2, after learning the consumer's public key and file-store deposit (either through CT or HCC), the provider must associate the consumer with the precision level at which they are authorized to view the provider's data. All consumers that are assigned the same precision level by a provider are considered to be in the same group and, thus, all have access to a single symmetric key protecting location disclosures made at this precision level. As a result, the symmetric key associated with a particular precision level may need to be updated as the group of users who have access to that precision level changes over time.

To provide the highest level of security for the provider's location data—i.e., preserving forward- and backward-secrecy—these shared symmetric keys should be changed whenever a consumer is *added* to a precision group or *removed* from a precision group. The former case ensures that new consumers cannot access old data, while the latter ensures that former consumers cannot access new data. Altering the symmetric key for a particular precision level requires creating a new symmetric key, encrypting key bundles for each user authorized at this precision level, and depositing the bundles on the provider's file store. After asynchronously retrieving these new key bundles, authorized consumers can again access the providers data. While shared symmetric key update is non-trivial, our evaluation (Section 5.1) shows that the overheads associated with this process in practice are minimal. We note that it is not necessary for the provider to re-pair their device with consumers via CT or HCC, as the asymmetric keys use for key management are *not* affected by a consumer's change in precision level.

We recognize that our LSS model prevents the enforcement of certain policies found in existing LSSs; e.g., policies that enable location sharing only when two parties are within a certain physical proximity, or policies that place access count limits on individual users. LSSs that can implement proximity-based policies are able to do so because they have access to the location data of all their users, and can thus determine the distance between two users. Since our goal is to prevent the LSS from acquiring this information, this type of policy can not easily be enforced in SLS. Enforcing constraints on access frequency is also enabled via LSS intervention, which is contrary to our assumed sharing model. We do note, however, that the ability to enforce these types of policies would be a worthwhile addition to SLS. However, we defer the exploration and development of techniques for achieving these goals to future work.

4.5 Implementation

SLS was implemented as an iOS iPhone application. It was installed on an iPhone 4s, and the location-sharing and CT pairing protocol were evaluated via the IPhone 4s and an iPhone simulator (modified to behave as if it could *scan* the iPhone 4s' public keys).

Precision Levels. Our SLS implementation collects and stores provider locations as GPS coordinates, and provides four precision levels at which a these locations can be shared. The precision levels supported are *exact*, *neighborhood*, *state*, and *none*. Support for the neighborhood and state sharing levels is provided by masking lower-order bits in the exact GPS coordinates stored within SLS.

Management Interface. The utility and usability of a security system's policy interface is crucial to its successful use: the ability to clearly indicate *who* can access an individual's data *at what precision* is key. We approached this in SLS by presenting the provider with a clean, simple display that consists of a list of principals (i.e., smartphone-managed identities associated with each consumer), and the precision-level at which each consumers have been authorized (see Figure 5). The precision level can easily be changed

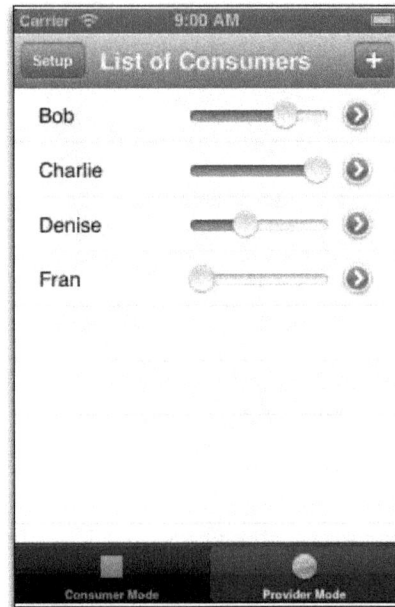

Figure 5: List of Alice's Consumers in SLS.

by the provider by adjusting a slider within this interface. Additionally, a *detail view* icon at the end of each row allows the provider to immediately review the consumer's information, resend the consumer's shared key bundle URL, or delete the consumer.

New consumers can easily be added when the provider taps the [+] button in the upper-right corner of the *List of Consumers* view (see Figure 5). This presents the provider (or the consumer, when they navigate into their respective *Add Provider* screen) with a choice of either the location-limited, CT-based key pairing protocol, or the HCC pairing protocol to exchange public keys and the consumer's file-store deposit.

Figure 6 shows several steps of the CT device pairing process, as executed by the provider and consumer. In the first step, the provider (Alice) has entered the consumer's identity (Bob), and Bob has done the same for Alice. When both tap the QR-code button, SLS will present both the provider and consumer with the task list associated with device pairing in CT (Step 2). The provider and consumer will iterate through the steps, synchronizing when QR images are printed and scanned, or during challenge/responses—these steps have been omitted from the Figure for clarity. In Step 7, the provider taps the button to scan the consumer's file-store deposit as a QR code, and Step 8 shows the consumer's screen after displaying their file-store deposit QR code to the provider.

SaaS Support. Our current implementation of SLS supports the use of Amazon's S3 services as a cloud file-store.[3] The period at which SLS updates GPS coordinates and then uploads the location data is configurable by the provider.[4] For simplicity, our imple-

---

[3]An example file-store URL using Amazon's S3 service is: `https://s3.amazonaws.com/id-precision-hash/ locationdata.b64`, where `id-precision-hash` is a hash of the provider's identity token and the precision level assigned to this location data.

[4]iOS has two settings for location gathering, the first operates using a *distance filter* to determine when a new location update should occur, the second is a *power-saving* mode, in which a location update

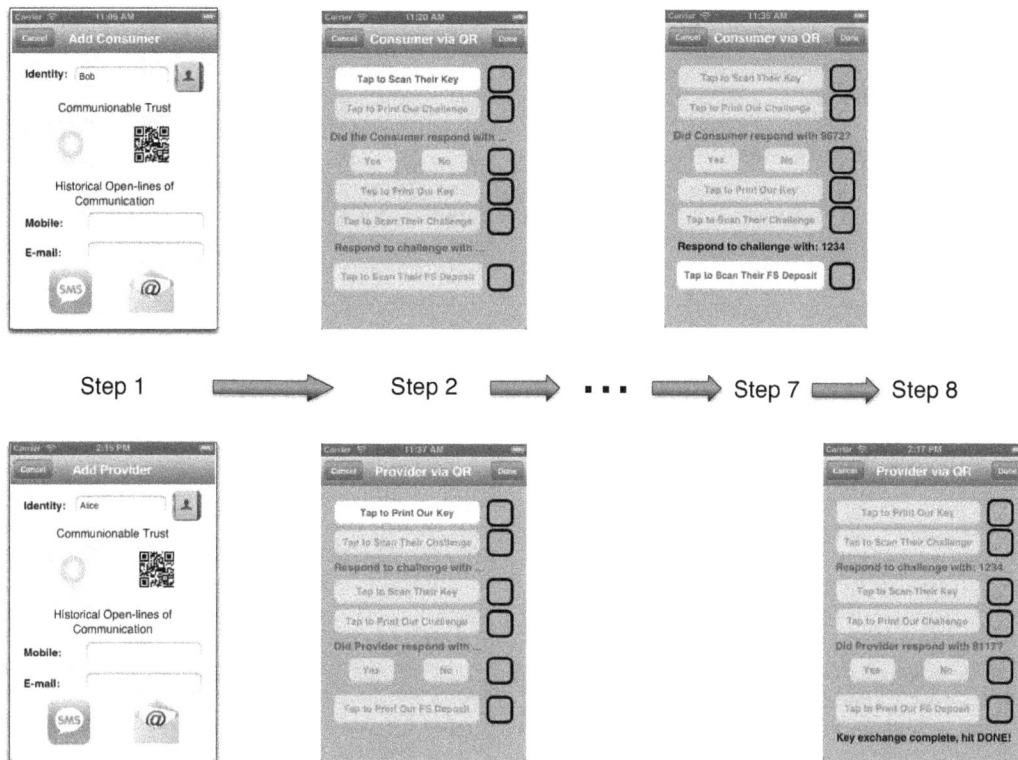

Figure 6: Screenshots of Communionable Trust protocol implemented in SLS. Steps 1, 2 and 7 are shown for the provider, and Steps 1, 2, and 8 are shown for the consumer.

mentation used the iOS Core Library API to serialize the location data that was gathered for the provider, with the resulting serialized location objects being $1KB$ in size. Although these objects are larger than those that could be produced by a custom serializer, the encryption and transmission overheads associated with these larger objects are not significant on the iPhone 4s.

Amazon S3 is also used to store encrypted key bundles for the consumers associated with a given producer. Whenever a consumer is added or a consumer's precision level is changed, the shared keys (for all precision-levels involved) are regenerated, new key bundles are generated and uploaded to the provider's S3 store, and all future location samples are encrypted using the new key. Upon detecting a key version mismatch, the SLS application used by a consumer automatically fetches the new key bundle from S3. The new key can then be used to decrypt more recent location updates, which may be stored in either *update* or *history* mode. To support history mode, updates are stored in a log file referred to as the *history log*, which contains an entry for each location data update in the window. The entries consist of the location data, time stamp and a signature over a hash of the two components. Thus, a consumer can check the history log to fetch any updates they may have missed, as their periodicity can be set differently than the providers.

Map View. The consumer's initial view displays their providers' positions on a map (see Figure 7). If the provider is operating in history mode, in which a log of location data updates is being kept in their file-store, the consumer can view the provider's location as a path. Since the location data stored on S3 also contains the bear-

Figure 7: Consumer's view of a provider walking up the street.

---

only occurs during a "significant" location change. Both modes are supported in our implementation.

ing of the provider (in addition to the location coordinate), SLS can plot the provider's location using the entire history that it can obtain. This resulting view is a trail of footprints corresponding to the provider's path along the map. Tapping on a provider's footprints displays the provider's name and a *details disclosure* button, which leads to that provider's detailed information view.

5. DISCUSSION

We developed a system for enhancing user privacy during location sharing by adopting and extending previous work in device pairing, and tapping into the ubiquity and availability of cloud services. Our system was architected to be both scalable and secure, while also preserving providers' sharing policies and affording utility to consumers. We now discuss both the performance of our SLS implementation, and assurance provided by our pairing protocols.

5.1 Performance Evaluation

In evaluating the runtime overheads of SLS, we break our analysis into four phases: the device pairing phase, the file-store deposit phase, location data upload by providers, and location data download by consumers. To evaluate the communionable trust protocol (Section 4.2), we carried out 15 pairings using our iOS implementation of SLS and found the average time required for this process was 110 seconds. Although this pairing process takes longer than, e.g., Bluetooth device pairing, the overheads are reasonable given the human effort required by this protocol (i.e., scanning QR codes). We did not evaluate the time required by the historical communication channels protocol (Section 4.3) as this protocol was designed to be run asynchronously over multiple higher latency channels (e.g., email and SMS).

After devices are paired using either the CT or HCC protocol, the provider sends the consumer a digitally signed message that includes URIs that are to be used to retrieve the consumer's key bundle and the provider's location data. This data can only be sent after the provider has indicated the precision level with which the consumer may access his information, and is returned to the consumer over a communication channel identified in the final message of the pairing phase of the CT or HCC protocol (i.e., the file-store deposit message). The overhead associated with this phase is linear in the number of consumers, but is only a one time cost, as this only occurs once per consumer (or in the wake of the rare event of the provider changing cloud services). In our iOS implementation of SLS, the generation of the signature on this message took $98ms$ on average over 15 runs

A consumer that is tracking n providers must retrieve n encrypted location samples from up to n different SaaS providers. The frequency with which this process occurs is a parameter that can be set within our implementation by the consumer. We measured the average time required to execute the `HTTP GET` command required to obtain a provider's encrypted location sample and execute the symmetric key decryption of this sample. When using Amazon S3 as SaaS provider, this process took approximately $40ms$ per provider.

On the other hand, the cost incurred by the provider during uploads is constant: an encrypted location sample must be uploaded at each of the p precision levels used by the provider's policy. The provider can choose the periodicity that new GPS coordinates are produced, so the constant time cost can be applied once per day, or several times per minute (depending on how fast the smart phone is moving and how fast it can generate new GPS coordinates). In our iOS implementation, encrypting and uploading location samples at three precision levels over 15 runs took on average, $3.7s$, with a standard deviation of $1.8s$.

5.2 Security Analysis

The SLS system was designed with two main goals in mind: (i) enabling tunable and private location sharing with limited contacts, and (ii) limiting end-user location over exposure. This is achieved by storing encrypted location samples on SaaS servers contracted by the provider, and leveraging location-limited or multi-channel pairing protocols to facilitate the key management required by this approach. We now informally analyze the security afforded by the protocols developed in this paper.

Location-limited Pairing Protocol. The communionable trust protocol described in Section 4.2 provides principals with high assurance regarding the secure handling of location data. In particular, the face-to-face nature of this protocol allows the human device owners to authenticate each other in the most natural sense. As a result, the public keys exchanged and validated using this protocol are intrinsically tied to the real-world participants in the protocol, since anyone attempting to launch a MitM attack would be quite conspicuous—we refer the reader to the security analysis in [20] for a thorough examination of attacks against this type of channel, as well as comparisons against other channels (e.g., audio, infrared, physical contact, etc.). For this reason, the principal's public key and identity exchanged via CT are made available to other applications outside of SLS.[5] Assuming that the consumer keeps her private key a secret, the public key obtained during this process enables the provider to safely transmit symmetric keys needed to recover his location to the consumer without exposing his location to unauthorized individuals (including the SaaS provider).

Multi-Channel Pairing Protocol. In settings where the provider and consumer are not physically located together, obtaining the assurance level of the communionable trust protocol is difficult. The protocol in Section 4.3 attempts to overcome the lack of physical proximity in three ways. First, it leverages *historical* communication channels managed by each user's smartphone to increase assurance in the identity of the party being communicated with, thereby reducing the likelihood of accidental sharing with inappropriate parties. Second, the HCC protocol makes use of *multiple* communication channels to decrease the likelihood of a successful MitM attack against the protocol. In examining Figure 4, we can see that an adversary with access to *only* the e-mail channel has the ability to inject public keys into the protocol, but cannot complete the validation process for these keys. Likewise, an adversary with access to *only* the SMS channel can cause parties in the protocol to reject valid public keys, but cannot inject their own public keys.

While this protocol cannot protect against a MitM attack when the adversary has access to both channels used by the protocol, as long as the implementation ensures that both channels are indeed distinct (e.g., WiFi + SMS, as opposed to 3G/4G + SMS) the cost to mount such an attack would be prohibitive to most. A more realistic attack vector against cell phones would be a physical attack, i.e., the attacker steals the smartphone of the consumer (resp. provider). However, the third protection mechanism in HCC does allow it to protect against this attack. Specifically, each party is required to answer a contextual "secret question" (i.e., Q_P and Q_C in Figure 4) proposed by the other party prior to finalizing the pairing process and enabling location sharing. Unless the individual possessing the stolen smartphone has intimate knowledge of the relationship between the provider and consumer, they would be unable to answer this type of question and, thus, the protocol would fail.

---

[5] iOS provides for this by using a shared or public group within the key-chain.

Although this question-and-answer mechanism is useful, it is not perfect. Moreover, although the protocol requires that the implementation leverage distinct communication channels, the mechanisms used to ensure the channels are distinct could themselves be attacked, i.e., an attacker could try to trick the implementation to use multiple channels that he controls. For these reason, we encourage principals to *upgrade* their public keys exchanged via HCC with CT, whenever the opportunity presents itself.

Shared Key Management. The shared or symmetric key management scheme employed by SLS provides three assurances to its users, including; the assurance that only a provider can upload new key material to the cloud file-store, the assurance that the location data can *not* be accessed by anyone without the appropriate shared key, and the assurance that exposure of the identities of the provider's consumers is mitigated within the cloud file-store. The first assurance is ensured by the act of encrypting the shared key bundle with the consumer's public key, while including a version and signature, i.e., an adversary can *not* alter the contents of the bundle as it is signed. The adversary could replay (or overwrite) an older shared key bundle, however, as the version of the key is included in the bundle the consumer will know that the current shared key bundle is incorrect.

Since the shared key bundles are encrypted with the consumers' public keys, and the uploaded location data is encrypted with the shared keys contained within those bundles, the provider is assured that only those consumers possessing the appropriate shared key will be able to view the provider's location data. Granted, a consumer could make the symmetric key accessible to non-authorized users, however, we note that this is the bane of *all* shared key security systems, and its mitigation is outside the scope of this paper.

Finally, exposure of the consumers' identities is mitigated through the use of the file-store deposit. Specifically, the provider can use any unique token to identify a consumer's shared key bundle, as the location of the shared key bundle is delivered to the consumer out-of-band via the file-store deposit. Admittedly, the cloud service will know how many consumer a provider has, and possibly how many precision levels are in use by the provider (by examining the contents of the history log, if in use). Thus, in order for the cloud service to uniquely identify a consumer, they'll have to rely on properties of the HTTP connection during the fetch (e.g., IP address, HTTP message headers).

5.3 Beyond Location Sharing

Interestingly, although our system was designed to share location data, there is no reason that the protocols and framework constituting SLS could not be adopted for other types of data (e.g., documents, pictures, music, or videos). That being said, we do not envision these SLS-like services replacing forums like Flickr or YouTube, which have proven to be de-facto file stores for widely sharing information. However, these SLS-like services could be useful for providing secure hosting for information that is to be shared with a more limited audience.

5.4 Future Work

The most pertinent area of future work involves conducting a user study to assess the utility and ease-of-use of our SLS implementation. Although this paper focused on the correctness and feasibility of a system like SLS, ensuring that the system is indeed usable is also quite important. A user study of our prototype iOS implementation could help answer questions about the usability of the policy interface built into the application, as well as about the ability of users to manage their privacy using SLS. Insights from exit surveys conducted with participants in such a study could also help guide the design of more intuitive sharing interfaces, and protections that might help further limit unintended audience sharing (e.g., short-term sharing settings, etc.).

Another area that we intend to pursue is the development of more advanced and cooperative policy controls.For example, consider a provider that only feels comfortable sharing her location data with consumers in the same region. We believe that this could be accomplished, for example, if the pair had mutual sharing configured between them (i.e., both acted as providers and consumers), and secure function evaluation was leveraged to decide when the distance between the two principals crossed some threshold (at which point SLS would operate normally). Although such advanced controls are likely possible, making these controls both intuitive for the user and efficient for the device to execute could prove to be challenging in practice.

Another intriguing extension of SLS's key management protocols would be implementing support for a type of key escrow for emergency response. Specifically, the symmetric key used in encrypting high-precision location data could not only be encrypted with the consumers' public keys, but also broken into *shares*, to be distributed to emergency respondents using a threshold scheme (e.g., [25]). For example, consider a 2-of-n threshold scheme in which key shares are distributed to the local police force for the provider's municipality, the state police, and the security contractor used by the provider's employer. In this case, for instance, the provider's employer could cooperate with the local authorities in the event that the provider was missing long enough for the employer to file a missing persons report. Further developing these sorts of policy-based extensions to SLS could prove to be an interesting area of study.

6. CONCLUSIONS

location-sharing systems (LSSs) have high utility, but recent research has shown that (i) many users are wary of sharing detailed trace information with LSS operators and (ii) the large social networks with which LSSs are often integrated make it all too easy to accidentally share location data with unintended audiences. In this paper, we make inroads to the above problems by developing SLS, a framework for private location sharing that combines the use of social authentication protocols based upon location-limited or multi-channel protocols, with user-contracted cloud SaaS providers to facilitate secure data storage and location sharing. In particular, our device pairing protocols leverage the smaller social networks managed by user smartphones to provide a high degree of assurance in the identities of the individuals with which sharing is to occur. The asymmetric keys exchanged during this process can then be used to distributed shared symmetric keys that protect a location provider's sensitive location information from unauthorized viewers, including the cloud service used to host the data. Our iOS prototype implementation of SLS shows that the overheads associated with this form of key management are reasonable.

Although the information sharing model developed in this paper was developed to facilitate secure location sharing based upon an individual's real-world social contacts, we believe that our techniques have application beyond location sharing. In particular, the combination of device pairing with high identity assurance and third-party storage that is used by SLS can be used to facilitate the sharing of many types of information currently shared using existing social networks (e.g., photos, etc.) without requiring implicit trust in the operators of these social networks.

Acknowledgements. This research was supported in part by the National Science Foundation under awards CNS–0964295 and CNS–1017229.

7. REFERENCES

[1] Amazon s3. https://s3.amazonaws.com/.

[2] J. Backes, M. Backes, M. Dürmuth, S. Gerling, and S. Lorenz. X-pire! - a digital expiration date for images in social networks. *CoRR*, abs/1112.2649, 2011.

[3] D. Balfanz, D. K. Smetters, P. Stewart, and H. C. Wong. Talking To Strangers : Authentication in Ad-Hoc Wireless Networks. In *ISOC Network and Distributed Systems Security Symposium (NDSS)*, 2002.

[4] L. Bauer, L. F. Cranor, R. W. Reeder, M. K. Reiter, and K. Vaniea. Real life challenges in access-control management. In *CHI 2009: Conference on Human Factors in Computing Systems*, pages 899–908, April 2009.

[5] J. T. Biehl, E. Rieffel, and A. J. Lee. When privacy and utility are in harmony: Towards better design of presence technologies. *Personal and Ubiquitous Computing*, 2012.

[6] J. T. Biehl, E. G. Rieffel, and A. J. Lee. When privacy and utility are in harmony: towards better design of presence technologies. *Personal and Ubiquitous Computing*, 17(3):503–518, 2013.

[7] Bump. http://bu.mp/.

[8] Y. Cai and T. Xu. Design, analysis, and implementation of a large-scale real-time location-based information sharing system. *Proceeding of the 6th international conference on Mobile systems applications and services MobiSys 08*, page 106, 2008.

[9] Datalocker. http://www.appsense.com/labs/data-locker.

[10] D. Dolev and A. C. Yao. On the security of public key protocols. In *Proceedings of the 22nd Annual Symposium on Foundations of Computer Science*, SFCS '81, pages 350–357, Washington, DC, USA, 1981. IEEE Computer Society.

[11] S. Egelman, A. Oates, and S. Krishnamurthi. Oops, i did it again: mitigating repeated access control errors on facebook. In *CHI 2011: Conference on Human Factors in Computing Systems*, pages 2295–2304, 2011.

[12] Facebook places. http://www.facebook.com/about/location?_fb_noscript=1.

[13] M. Farb, M. Burman, G. Singh, C. Jon, and M. A. Perrig. Safeslinger: An easy-to-use and secure approach for human trust establishment. http://www.cmu.edu/homepage/computing/2012/winter/safeslinger.shtml.

[14] Foursquare. https://foursquare.com/.

[15] R. Geambasu, T. Kohno, A. Levy, and H. M. Levy. Vanish: Increasing data privacy with self-destructing data. In *Proc. of the 18th USENIX Security Symposium*, 2009.

[16] Glympse. http://www.glympse.com/.

[17] Google latitude. https://www.google.com/latitude/.

[18] J. Lindqvist, J. Cranshaw, J. Wiese, J. Hong, and J. Zimmerman. I âĂŹ m the mayor of my house : Examining why people use foursquare - a social-driven location sharing application. *Design*, 54(6):2409–2418, 2011.

[19] R. Mayrhofer and H. Gellersen. Shake Well Before Use: Intuitive and Secure Pairing of Mobile Devices. *IEEE Transactions on Mobile Computing*, 8(6):792–806, June 2009.

[20] J. McCune, A. Perrig, and M. Reiter. Seeing-Is-Believing: Using Camera Phones for Human-Verifiable Authentication. In *IEEE Symposium on Security and Privacy*, pages 110–124. IEEE, 2005.

[21] B. Palanisamy and L. Liu. Mobimix: Protecting location privacy with mix-zones over road networks. *Data Engineering, International Conference on*, 0:494–505, 2011.

[22] S. Patil, G. Norcie, A. Kapadia, and A. J. Lee. Reasons, rewards, regrets: Privacy considerations in location sharing as an interactive practice. In *Symposium on Usable Privacy and Security (SOUPS)*, July 2012.

[23] R. W. Reeder, L. Bauer, L. F. Cranor, M. K. Reiter, K. Bacon, K. How, and H. Strong. Expandable grids for visualizing and authoring computer security policies. In *CHI 2008: Conference on Human Factors in Computing Systems*, pages 1473–1482, 2008.

[24] R. Schlegel, A. Kapadia, and A. J. Lee. Eyeing your exposure: quantifying and controlling information sharing for improved privacy. In *Proceedings of the Seventh Symposium on Usable Privacy and Security*, SOUPS '11, pages 14:1–14:14, New York, NY, USA, 2011. ACM.

[25] A. Shamir. How to share a secret. *Commun. ACM*, 22(11):612–613, 1979.

[26] R. Shokri, G. Theodorakopoulos, G. Danezis, J.-P. Hubaux, and J.-Y. Le Boudec. Quantifying Location Privacy: The Case of Sporadic Location Exposure. In *The 11th Privacy Enhancing Technologies Symposium (PETS)*, 2011.

[27] R. Shokri, G. Theodorakopoulos, J.-Y. Le Boudec, and J.-P. Hubaux. Quantifying Location Privacy. In *2011 Ieee Symposium On Security And Privacy (Sp 2011)*, IEEE Symposium on Security and Privacy, pages 247–262. Ieee Computer Soc Press, Customer Service Center, Po Box 3014, 10662 Los Vaqueros Circle, Los Alamitos, Ca 90720-1264 Usa, 2011.

[28] J. Y. Tsai, P. Kelley, P. Drielsma, L. F. Cranor, J. Hong, and N. Sadeh. Who's viewed you?: the impact of feedback in a mobile location-sharing application. In *Proceedings of the SIGCHI Conference on Human Factors in Computing Systems*, CHI '09, pages 2003–2012, New York, NY, USA, 2009. ACM.

[29] Y. Wang, S. Komanduri, P. Leon, G. Norcie, A. Acquisti, and L. Cranor. I regretted the minute i pressed share: A qualitative study of regrets on facebook. In *Symposium on Usable Privacy and Security (SOUPS)*, 2011.

[30] F. L. Wong and F. Stajano. Related Work in Multichannel Security Protocols. *IEEE Pervasive Computing*, 6(4):31–39, 2007.

[31] www.MyVoucherCodes.co.uk. Average brit has 476 facebook friends compared to 152 mobile phone contacts, 2011.

Private Data Warehouse Queries

Xun Yi
School of Engineering and
Science
Victoria University
Melbourne, VIC 8001,
Australia
xun.yi@vu.edu.au

Russell Paulet
School of Engineering and
Science
Victoria University
Melbourne, VIC 8001,
Australia
russell.paulet@vu.edu.au

Elisa Bertino
Department of Computer
Science
Purdue University
West Lafayette, IN 47907,
USA
bertino@purdue.edu

Guandong Xu
Advanced Analytics Institute
University of Technology,
Sydney
Broadway NSW 2007,
Australia
guandong.xu@uts.edu.au

ABSTRACT

Publicly accessible data warehouses are an indispensable resource for data analysis. But they also pose a significant risk to the privacy of the clients, since a data warehouse operator may follow the client's queries and infer what the client is interested in. Private Information Retrieval (PIR) techniques allow the client to retrieve a cell from a data warehouse without revealing to the operator which cell is retrieved. However, PIR cannot be used to hide OLAP operations performed by the client, which may disclose the client's interest. This paper presents a solution for private data warehouse queries on the basis of the Boneh-Goh-Nissim cryptosystem which allows one to evaluate any multi-variate polynomial of total degree 2 on ciphertexts. By our solution, the client can perform OLAP operations on the data warehouse and retrieve one (or more) cell without revealing any information about which cell is selected. Furthermore, our solution supports some types of statistical analysis on data warehouse, such as regression and variance analysis, without revealing the client's interest. Our solution ensures both the server's security and the client's security.

Categories and Subject Descriptors

H.2 [**Database Management**]: Security, integrity, and protection; H.2.7 [**Database Administration**]: Data warehouse and repository

General Terms

Security

Keywords

Data warehouse, OLAP, privacy, homomorphic encryption

1. INTRODUCTION

Data warehousing provides tools for business executives to systematically organise, understand, and use their data to make strategic decisions. A large number of organizations have found that data warehouses are valuable in today's competitive, fast-evolving world. In the last several years, many firms have spent millions of dollars in building enterprise-wide data warehouse. Many people feel that with competition mounting in every industry, data warehouse is the latest must-have marketing weapon - a way to keep customers by learning more about their needs [16].

A data warehouse is a **subject - oriented**, **integrated**, **time - variant** and **non - volatile** collection of data in support of management's decision making process [17]. Data warehouses are built on a multidimensional data model. This model views data in the form of a data cube. A data cube, defined by dimensions and measures, allows data to be viewed in multiple dimensions. In general, dimensions are the entities with respect to which we want to keep records. For example, a sales data warehouse may keep records of the store's sales with respect to dimensions - time, location and product. Measures are the quantities by which we want to analyse relationships between dimensions. Examples of measures for a sales data warehouse include the sales amount, the number of units sold, and the average sales amount.

In the multidimensional model, data is organised into multiple dimensions, where each dimension has multiple-levels of abstraction defined by a concept hierarchy. A concept hierarchy defines a sequence of mapping from a set of low-level concepts to high-level, more general concepts. The concept hierarchy for locations could be street, city, state, and country. This organisation provides clients with the flexibility to view data from different perspectives. A number of online analytical processing (OLAP) operations exist to materialise these different views, supporting interactive querying and analysis of the data at hand. Typical OLAP operations include: **roll-up** (aggregation by climbing up a concept hierarchy); **drill-down** (the reverse of roll-up); **slice** (a selection on one dimension, resulting in a sub-cube); **dice** (a selection on two or more dimensions, resulting in a sub-cube); **pivot** (rotating the data axes in view in order to provide an alternative presentation of the data).

Queries to the data warehouse are based on a star-net model, which consists of radial lines emanating from a central point, where each line represents a concept hierarchy of a dimension. These represent the granularities available for use by OLAP operations such as drill-down and roll-up.

In order to query the data warehouse, a user usually first requests the server to perform OLAP operations and then sends back a cell. An important issue in this simple process is represented by the privacy of the user query as a user query may reveal to the server business sensitive information about the user. For example, for a stock exchange data warehouse, the user may be an investor, who queries the data warehouse for the trend of a certain stock. He may wish to keep private the identity of the stock he is interested in. For a pharmaceutical data warehouse, the user may be a laboratory, which would like to keep private the active principles it wants to use. To protect his privacy, the user accessing a data warehouse may therefore want to perform OLAP operations and retrieve a cell without revealing any information about which cell he is interested in.

A trivial solution to the above private data warehouse query problem is for the user to download the entire data warehouse and then locally perform OLAP operations and retrieve the cell of interest. This solution is not suitable if the owner of the data warehouse wishes to make profit through data warehouse services (for example, a health care data warehouse). Usually, the user is interested in only a part of the data warehouse. Purchasing the entire data warehouse may not be an economic way to the user.

Private Information Retrieval (PIR) protocols, such as [8], do not fully address the private data warehouse query problem. A PIR protocol allows a user to retrieve a record from a database without the owner of that database being able to determine which record was selected with communication cost less than the database size. By using PIR, a user can retrieve a cell (a record) from a data warehouse (a database) without revealing any information about which cell is retrieved. However, the user cannot hide his OLAP operations to the server when he requests the server to perform the operations. These operations may reveal the user's interest. For example, when the user requests the server to perform a slice operation with respect to a location, the server can learn the user's interest in the location. It is a challenge to assure the user's privacy when performing OLAP operations.

In this paper, we give a solution for private data warehouse queries on the basis of the Boneh-Goh-Nissim cryptosystem [4]. Our basic idea is to allow the data warehouse owner to encrypt its data warehouse and distribute the encrypted data warehouse to the user who wishes to perform private data warehouse queries. The user can perform any OLAP operations on the encrypted data warehouse locally without revealing his interest. When the user wishes to decrypt a cell of the encrypted data warehouse, the user and the server run a Private Cell Retrieval (PCR) protocol jointly to decrypt the cell without revealing to the server which cell is retrieved. Assume that the serve charges the client per query, our solution allows the user to perform some statistical analysis, such as regression and variance analysis, on the encrypted data warehouse with the lowest cost.

Unlike operational databases, data warehouse is non-volatile. The data in the data warehouse is never over-written or deleted - once committed; the data is static, read-only, and retained for future reporting. It is feasible to allow the data warehouse owner to distribute the encrypted data warehouse to potential users only once and later let the users download new added data online if any.

Our solution ensures both the server's security in the sense that the server, for billing purpose, releases to the user only a data per query, and the client's security in the sense that the client does not reveal any information about his queries to the server. We have implemented our solution on an example of data warehouse and experiments have shown that our solution is practical for private data warehouse queries.

The rest of the paper is organized as follows. Related work is surveyed in Section 2. We define our model and described our solution in Section 3. The security and performance analysis is carried out in Section 4. Experiment results are shown in Section 5. Conclusions are drawn in the last section.

2. RELATED WORK

Private Information Retrieval (PIR) was firstly introduced by Chor, Goldreich, Kushilevitz, and Sudan in 1995 [8]. In their paper, they proposed a set of schemes to implement PIR through replicated databases, which provide users with information-theoretic security as long as some of the database relicas do not collude against the user. Since then, a lot of research on PIR has been done. We classify the results as follows [2, 29].

- *Theoretical Private Information Retrieval*

  "Theoretical" stands for the fact, that the user privacy is assumed to be unbreakable independently from the computational power of a cheater. Chor et al. proved, that any theoretical PIR solution has a communication with a lower bound equal to the database size [8]. Thus they relax the problem setting. They assume that there are several (instead of one) database servers, which do not communicate among each other, with the same data. This assumption makes the non-trivial theoretical PIR feasible. The basic idea is to send several queries to several databases. The queries are constructed in such a way, that they give no information to the servers about the record that user is interested in. But using the answers from the queries, the user can construct the desired record. There is also a case considered, when up to t of the servers are allowed to cooperate against the user.

  Ambainis [1] improved the results of Chor et al. [8], which led to the following non-trivial theoretical PIR solutions: (1) A k database scheme (i.e., a scheme with k identical databases non-communicating to each other), for any constant $k \geq 2$, with communication complexity $O(N^{1/(2k-1)})$; (2) A $\Theta(\log N)$ database scheme with communication complexity $O(log^2 N \cdot loglog N)$, where N is the size of the database. Further research on theoretical PIR appears in [18, 19, 20, 3].

- *Computational Private Information Retrieval*

  In order to get better communication complexity, another assumption was weakened by Chor and Gilboa [7]. "Computational" means that the database servers are presumed to be computationally bounded, i.e., under an appropriate intractability assumption, the database cannot gain information about which data element was selected by the user. For every $\epsilon > 0$, Chor and Gilboa [7] presented two computational PIR schemes with complexity $O(N^\epsilon)$.

  In the first paper on PIR [8] it was proven, that the theoretical PIR problem has no non-trivial solutions for the case of single database. Surprisingly, the substitution of an information-theoretic security with an intractability assumption achieves a non-trivial PIR protocol for single database schema [22]. Its communication complexity is $O(N^\epsilon)$ for any $\epsilon > 0$. They use an intractability assumption, described in [15]. The basic approach is to encrypt a query in such a way, that the server still can process it using special algorithms. However, the server recognizes neither the clear-text query nor the result.

The result can be decrypted only by the user. This was the first single-database protocol, where designer considers and provides database privacy. Using another intractability assumption, Cachin et al. [5] demonstrated a single database computational PIR protocol that has poly-logarithmic communication. This is an improvement in comparing to polynomial communication complexity in [22]. This result looks particular effective, because the user has to send a minimum $\log N$ bits just to address the bit he wants to retrieve in the database. A scheme with better result appears in [6, 23, 24, 12].

- *Symmetrical Private Information Retrieval*

  Symmetrical PIR is a PIR problem, where the privacy of the database is considered, i.e., a symmetrical PIR protocol must prevent the user from learning more than one record of the database during a session. Clearly, symmetrical privacy (database privacy) is a very important property for practical applications, since an efficient billing is only then possible. A symmetrical PIR protocol for single server was first proposed in [21], and for several servers it was considered in [14]. Other symmetrical PIR were later proposed in [27, 26].

In addition, Private Block Retrieval (PBR) is a natural extension of PIR in which, instead of retrieving only a single bit, the user retrieves a d-bit block that begins at an index i. PBR techniques are important for making PIR practical. Theoretic PBR was introduced in [8]. A practical PBR scheme for a single database was given by Gentry and Ramzan [12]. The security of this scheme is based on a simple variant of the Φ-hiding number-theoretic assumption by Cachin, Micali and Stadler [5]. This scheme has communication complexity $O(k+d)$ only, where $k \geq \log N$ is a security parameter that depends on the database size N and d is the bit-length of the retrieved database block.

Current PIR or PBR protocols can be only used for Private Cell Retrieval (PCR) in private data warehouse queries. They are unable to support private OLAP operations.

3. PRIVATE DATA WAREHOUSE QUERIES

3.1 Our Model

We consider a data cube D with n dimensions $y_1, y_2, \cdots y_n$ and m measures $x_1, x_2, \cdots, x_m$, denoted as

$$D = (x_1, x_2, \cdots, x_m)_{y_1, y_2, \cdots, y_n}.$$

We assume that the data cube is provided by a server S and used by clients. The server S wishes to make a profit by providing data warehouse services to clients. The clients wish to learn some knowledge from D through OLAP operations on D without revealing their interests to S.

First of all, on input a security parameter k, the server S generates its public/private key pair $\{PK, SK\}$, encrypts the data cube D into $E(D)$ with the public key PK, where the values of all measure attributes are encrypted, but the values of all dimension attributes are in plaintexts. The encrypted data cube $E(D)$ can be then released to clients.

A client C can either download the encrypted data cube $E(D)$ from the server's Web site or request the server to send a CD of the encrypted data cube by post. It happens only once because the data warehouse is non-volatile. For new data added into the data cube, we allow the users to download it online. The client can then perform any OLAP operation on the encrypted data cube $E(D)$ locally.

Remark In many cases, the "client" is actually an organization that then has no problem in downloading and storing the encrypted data warehouse $E(D)$ and performing OLAP operations on $E(D)$.

In order to retrieve a cell from the data cube D after several OLAP operations on $E(D)$ (i.e., to decrypt a ciphertext C from the encrypted data cube $E(D)$ after several OLAP operations on $E(D)$), the server S and the client C runs a Private Cell Retrieval (PCR) protocol, composed of three algorithms as follows.

(1) Query Generation (QG): Takes as input the public key PK of the server S, the ciphertext C, which is an encryption of either a measure value or a function of several measure values, (the client) outputs a query Q and a secret s, denoted as $(Q, s) = \mathsf{QG}(C, PK)$.

(2) Response Generation (RG): Takes as input the query Q and the private key SK of the server S, (the server) outputs a response R, denoted as $R = \mathsf{RG}(Q, SK)$.

(3) Response Retrieval (RR): Takes as input the public key PK of the server S, the response R and the secret s of the client, (the client) outputs a plaintext x, denoted as $x = \mathsf{RR}(R, PK, s)$.

A PCR protocol can be illustrated as in Fig. 1 and is correct if, for any security parameter k, for any ciphertext C, $Decrypt(C, SK) = \mathsf{RR}(R, PK, s)$ holds, where $(Q, s) = \mathsf{QG}(C, PK)$ and $R = \mathsf{RG}(Q, SK)$.

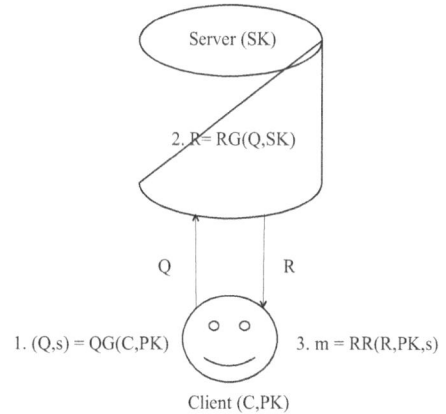

Figure 1: Private Cell Retrieval

The security of the PCR protocol involves the server's security and the client's security. Intuitively, the serve S wishes to release only one measure value to the client C each time when the client sends a query. Meanwhile, the client C does not wish to reveal to the server which cell is retrieved.

Formally, the server's security can be can be defined with a game as follows.

Given a data cube D and the public key PK of the server, consider the following game between an adversary (the client) $\mathcal{A}$, and a challenger $\mathcal{C}$. The game consists of the following steps:

(1) Given the public key PK of the server, the adversary $\mathcal{A}$ chooses two different values m_1, m_2 of two measure attributes and sends them to $\mathcal{C}$.

(2) The challenger $\mathcal{C}$ chooses a random bit $b \in \{0, 1\}$, and encrypts m_b to obtain $C_b = Encrypt(m_b, PK)$, and then sends C_b back to $\mathcal{A}$.

(3) The adversary $\mathcal{A}$ can experiment with the code of C_b in an arbitrary non-black-box way, and finally outputs $b' \in \{0, 1\}$.

The adversary wins the game if $b' = b$ and loses otherwise. We define the adversary $\mathcal{A}$'s advantage in this game to be

$$\mathsf{Adv}_{\mathcal{A}}(k) = |\mathsf{Pr}(b' = b) - 1/2|.$$

Definition 1 (Server's Security Definition). In a PCR protocol, the data warehouse server has semantic security if for any probabilistic polynomial time (PPT) adversary $\mathcal{A}$, we have that $\mathsf{Adv}_{\mathcal{A}}(k)$ is a negligible function, where the probability is taken over coin-tosses of the challenger and the adversary.

Remark. Server's security ensures that the client cannot decrypt any ciphertext in the encrypted data cube $E(D)$ without the help of the server.

Next, we formally define the client's security with a game as follows.

Give an encrypted data cube $E(D)$ and the public/private key pair (PK, SK) of the server, consider the following game between an adversary (the server) $\mathcal{A}$, and a challenger $\mathcal{C}$. The game consists of the following steps:

(1) Given the public/private key pair (PK, SK) of the server, the adversary $\mathcal{A}$ chooses two different ciphertexts C_1 and C_2, and then sends them to the challenger $\mathcal{C}$.

(2) The challenger $\mathcal{C}$ chooses a random bit $b \in \{0, 1\}$, and executes the Query Generation (QG) to obtain $(Q_b, s_b) = \mathsf{QG}(C_b, PK)$, where s_b is the secret of the challenger $\mathcal{C}$, and then sends Q_b back to $\mathcal{A}$.

(3) The adversary $\mathcal{A}$ can experiment with the code of Q_b in an arbitrary non-black-box way, and finally outputs $b' \in \{0, 1\}$.

The adversary wins the game if $b' = b$ and loses otherwise. We define the adversary $\mathcal{A}$'s advantage in this game to be

$$\mathsf{Adv}_{\mathcal{A}}(k) = |\mathsf{Pr}(b' = b) - 1/2|.$$

Definition 2 (Client's Security Definition). In a PCR protocol, the client has semantic security if for any probabilistic polynomial time (PPT) adversary $\mathcal{A}$, we have that $\mathsf{Adv}_{\mathcal{A}}(k)$ is a negligible function, where the probability is taken over coin-tosses of the challenger and the adversary.

Remark. Client's security ensures that the server cannot tell what information the client has retrieved from the data cube $E(D)$.

3.2 Private Cell Retrieval

Based on our model, we give a construction of a PCR protocol which allows the client to retrieve a measure value in a cell without revealing the measure and cell attributes to the server.

Our protocol is built on the BGN homomorphic encryption scheme [4] (please refer to Appendix). The data server S generates and publishes its public key $PK = \{N, \mathbb{G}, \mathbb{G}_1, e, g, h_1, e(g, g)^{q_1}\}$, and keeps its private key $SK = \{q_1\}$ secret.

Remark: Slightly different from the BGN scheme, we replace h with h_1 in the public key (please refer to Appendix) and include $e(g, g)^{q_1}$ as a public parameter. It does not affect the security of the BGN scheme because the discrete logarithm problem of determining the private key q_1 from $e(g, g)^{q_1}$ is hard, where q_1 is large prime. We publish $e(g, g)^{q_1}$ so that the client $\mathcal{C}$ can obtain the decryption privately (please refer to Algorithm 4).

Before releasing the data cube to clients, the data warehouse server S runs the Initialisation algorithm to encrypt the data cube D to $E(D)$, as described in Algorithm 1.

After obtaining the encrypted data cube $E(D)$, if a client $\mathcal{C}$ wishes to retrieve a measure value in a cell, in other words, to decrypt a ciphertext C in a cell, the client $\mathcal{C}$ and the server S run our Private Cell Retrieval protocol, composed of three algorithms, Query Generation (QG), Response Generation (RG), and Response Retrieval (RR), as described in Algorithms 2-4.

Algorithm 1 Initialisation (Server)

Input: $D = (x_1, x_2, \cdots, x_m)_{y_1, y_2, \cdots, y_n}, PK$
Output: $E(D) = (E(x_1), E(x_2), \cdots, E(x_m))_{y_1, y_2, \cdots, y_n}$
1: Let $E(D) = D$
2: For each measure value $x = (x_i)_{y_1, y_2, \cdots, y_m}$, where $1 \leq i \leq m$ and $(y_1, y_2, \cdots, y_m) \in DD$ (dimension domain) .
3: Pick a random integer r from $\{1, 2, \cdots, N\}$
4: Compute $z = Encrypt(x, PK) = g^x h^r$ and replace $(x_i)_{y_1, y_2, \cdots, y_n}$ with z, denoted as $(E(x_i))_{y_1, y_2, \cdots, y_n}$.
5: **return** $E(D)$

Algorithm 2 Query Generation QG (Client)

Input: C, PK
Output: Q, s
1: Pick two random integers s, r from $\{1, 2, \cdots, N\}$
2: If $C \in \mathbb{G}$, compute $Q = e(C, g)e(g, g)^s h_1^r$
3: If $C \in \mathbb{G}_1$, compute $Q = Ce(g, g)^s h_1^r$
4: **return** (Q, s)

Algorithm 3 Response Generation RG (Server)

Input: $Q \in \mathbb{G}_1, SK = q_1$
Output: R
1: Compute $R = Q^{SK}$
2: **return** R

Algorithm 4 Response Retrieval RR (Client)

Input: R, PK, s
Output: m
1: Compute $R' = R/(e(g, g)^{q_1})^s$
2: Compute $m = \log_{e(g,g)^{q_1}} R'$ with Porland's lambda method [25].
3: **return** m

Theorem 1 (Correctness) Our PCR protocol is correct. In other words, for any security parameter k, for any ciphertext C,

$$Decrypt(C, SK) = \mathsf{RR}(R, PK, s)$$

holds, where $(Q, s) = \mathsf{QG}(C, PK)$ and $R = \mathsf{RG}(Q, SK)$.

Proof In case of the ciphertext $C \in \mathbb{G}$, we assume that $C = g^{m'} h^{r'}$. With reference to Appendix, we have $Decrypt(C, SK) =$

m'. In addition,

$$
\begin{aligned}
R &= \mathsf{RG}(Q, SK) = Q^{SK} \\
&= (e(C, g)e(g, g)^s h_1^r)^{q_1} \\
&= e(g^{m'} h^{r'}, g)^{q_1} e(g, g)^{q_1 s} h_1^{q_1 r} \\
&= e(g^{q_1 m'} h^{q_1 r'}, g) e(g, g)^{q_1 s} h_1^{q_1 r} \\
&= (e(g, g)^{q_1})^{m'} e(g, g)^{q_1 s}
\end{aligned}
$$

In case of the ciphertext $C \in \mathbb{G}_1$, we assume that $C = e(g, g)^{m'} h_1^{r'}$. With reference to Appendix, we have $Decrypt(C, SK) = m'$. In addition,

$$
\begin{aligned}
R &= \mathsf{RG}(Q, SK) = Q^{SK} \\
&= (Ce(g, g)^s h_1^r)^{q_1} \\
&= (e(g, g)^{q_1})^{m'} e(g, g)^{q_1 s} h_1^{q_1 (r + r')} \\
&= (e(g, g)^{q_1})^{m'} e(g, g)^{q_1 s}
\end{aligned}
$$

Therefore, $R' = R/e(g, g)^{q_1 s} = (e(g, g)^{q_1})^{m'}$ and we have $m = \log_{e(g,g)^{q_1}} R' = m'$, i.e., $Decrypt(C, SK) = \mathsf{RR}(R, PK, s)$. The theorem is proved. $\triangle$

3.3   Private OLAP Operations

Typical OLAP operations include roll-up (performing aggregation by climbing up a concept hierarchy), drill-down (the reverse of roll-up), slice (performing a selection on one dimension, resulting in a sub-cube), dice (performing a selection on two or more dimensions, resulting in a sub-cube), and pivot (rotating the data axes in view in order to provide an alternative presentation of the data).

After obtaining the encrypted data cube $E(D)$, a client $\mathcal{C}$ can perform drill-down, slice, dice or pivot operation on $E(D)$ as he does on the original data cube D because the dimension values in $E(D)$ are in plain. It is obvious that the sub-cube obtained by slice, dice or pivot operation on the encrypted data cube $E(D)$ takes a form of encryption of the sub-cube obtained by the same operation on the original data cube D.

For a roll-up operation on $E(D)$, without loss of generality, we consider summarising a measure x_i along the j-th dimension from a concept $y_j \in \{a_1, a_2, ...\}$ to a higher concept $Y_j \in \{A_1, A_2, ...\}$, where for any a_s, there is A_t such that $a_s \in A_t$. Our roll-up operation on $E(D)$ is described in Algorithm 5.

Algorithm 5 Roll-Up (Client)

Input: $E(D) = (E(x_1), E(x_2), \cdots, E(x_m))_{y_1, \cdots, y_j, \cdots, y_n}, PK,$ $\{A_1, A_2, ...\}$
Output: $E(D)^* = (E(x_1), E(x_2), \cdots, E(x_m))_{y_1, \cdots, Y_j, \cdots, y_n}$
1: Let $E(D)^* = (E(0), E(0), \cdots, E(0))_{y_1, \cdots, Y_j, \cdots, y_n}$
2: For each encrypted measure value $x = (E(x_i))_{y_1, \cdots, y_j, \cdots, y_m}$ in $E(D)$, where $1 \le i \le m$ and $y_j \in \{a_1, a_2, \cdots\}$
3: If $y_j = a_s \in A_t$ and $X = (E(x_i))_{y_1, \cdots, Y_j, \cdots, y_n}$ in $E(D)^*$ where $Y_j = A_t$, let $Z = xX$ and replace X with Z in the cell $(y_1, \cdots, Y_j, \cdots, y_n)$ of $E(D)^*$.
4: **return** $E(D)^*$

Theorem 2 In Algorithm 5, given $1 \le i \le m$, let

$$
X_{A_t} = E(x_i)_{(y_1, \cdots, Y_j, \cdots, y_n)}
$$

where $Y_j = A_t$ and $x_{a_s} = (x_i)_{(y_1, \cdots, y_j, \cdots, y_n)}$ where $y_j = a_s$, then $Decrypt(X_{A_t}, SK) = \sum_{a_s \in A_t} x_{a_s}$.

Proof According to Algorithm 5, we have

$$
X_{A_t} = \prod_{a_s \in A_t} E(x_{a_s}).
$$

Due to the homomorphic property of the BGN cryptosystem, we obtain

$$
X_{A_t} = E(\sum_{a_s \in A_t} x_{a_s}).
$$

Therefore,

$$
Decrypt(X_{A_t}, SK) = \sum_{a_s \in A_t} x_{a_s}
$$

The theorem is proved. $\triangle$

Theorem 2 ensures that our roll-up operation on the encrypted data cube is correct.

3.4   Private Statistical Analysis

Our data cube is encrypted by the BGN cryptosystem. As shown in Appendix, the BGN cryptosystem has an additive homomorphism. In addition, the bilinear map allows for one multiplication on encrypted values. As a result, the BGN cryptosystem supports arbitrary additions and one multiplication (followed by arbitrary additions) on encrypted data. This property in turn allows the evaluation of multi-variate polynomials of total degree 2 on encrypted values.

In view of this, we are able to perform those statistical analyses on the data cube in private, which involves the evaluation of multi-variate polynomials of total degree 2 on encrypted values, e.g., regression and variance analysis.

Remark. Most practical homomorphic cryptosystems, such as RSA [32], ElGamal [11], Goldwasser-Micali [15], Damgard-Jurik [9] and Paillier [30] schemes, provide only one homomorphism, either addition, multiplication, or XOR. They cannot be used to evaluate multi-variate polynomials of total degree 2 on encrypted values. Some statistical analysis requires to compute multi-variate polynomials of total degree 2. Although fully homomorphic encryption techniques [13, 33, 10] can be used to evaluate multi-variate polynomials of any degree, the state-of-the-art is still impractical in applications because the ciphertext size and computation time increase sharply as one increases the security level. So far, the BGN cryptosystem [4] is the only practical encryption scheme which can evaluate multi-variate polynomials of total degree 2 on encrypted values. This is why we choose the BGN cryptosystem as our underlying encryption scheme.

Let $f(x_1, x_2, \cdots, x_\ell)$ be a ℓ-variate polynomial of total degree 2. For a purpose of statistical analysis, a user wishes to compute $f(a_1, a_2, \cdots, a_\ell)$ in private, where $a_1, a_2, \cdots, a_\ell$ are measure values in the data cube D. Given the encrypted data cube $E(D)$, the user obtains the encryptions of $a_1, a_2, \cdots, a_\ell$, denoted as $E(a_1), E(a_2), \cdots, E(a_\ell)$ and runs Algorithm 6.

Algorithm 6 Private Evaluation (Client, Server)

Input: $f, E(a_1), E(a_2), \cdots, E(a_\ell), PK$
Output: $f(a_1, a_2, \cdots, a_\ell)$
1: Client computes $C = f(E(a_1), E(a_2), \cdots, E(a_\ell))$
2: Client and Server run Algorithms 2-4
3: Client obtains $m = RR(R, PK, s)$
4: **return** m

Theorem 3 In Algorithm 6, $m = f(a_1, a_2, \cdots, a_\ell)$.

Proof Because the BGN cryptosystem allows the evaluation of multivariate polynomials of total degree 2 on encrypted values and the degree of the function f is less than 2, we have that

$$C = f(E(a_1), E(a_2), \cdots, E(a_\ell)) = E(f(a_1, a_2, \cdots, a_\ell)).$$

Based on Theorem 1, we have that

$$m = Decrypt(C, SK) = f(a_1, a_2, \cdots, a_\ell).$$

The theorem is proved. $\triangle$

Theorem 3 ensures that our private evaluation is correct.

4. SECURITY AND PERFORMANCE ANALYSIS

4.1 Security Analysis

In this section, we analyse the security of our Private Cell Retrieval protocol (PCR) in terms of the server's security and the client's security defined in Section IV. We consider the server's security at first.

In our scenario, the server wishes to make profit through data warehouse services. The business model is most likely that the server charges the client per query. In other word, the server reveals one measure value only in each client query. In order to prevent the client from knowing all data in the data warehouse without paying queries, the server encrypts the data warehouse with the BGN cryptosystem [4], where the decryption key is known the server only.

The security of the BGN cryptosystem is built on the subgroup decision problem: With reference to Appendix, let $k \in \mathbb{Z}^+$ and let $(q_1, q_2, \mathbb{G}, \mathbb{G}_1, e)$ be a tuple produced by $KeyGen(k)$ where $N = q_1 q_2$. Given $(N, \mathbb{G}, \mathbb{G}_1, e)$ and an element $x \in \mathbb{G}$, output 1 if the order of x is q_1 and output 0 otherwise; that is, without knowing the factorization of the group order N, decide if an element x is in a subgroup of $\mathbb{G}$.

We say that $KeyGen(k)$ satisfies the subgroup decision assumption if for any polynomial time algorithm $\mathcal{A}$, the advantage of $\mathcal{A}$ in solving the subgroup decision problem,

$$|Pr(\mathcal{A}(N, \mathbb{G}, \mathbb{G}_1, e, x) = 0) - Pr(\mathcal{A}(N, \mathbb{G}, \mathbb{G}_1, e, x) = 1)|,$$

is a negligible function in k.

In [4], it has been shown that the BGN scheme is semantically secure if $KeyGen(k)$ satisfies the subgroup decision assumption.

Theorem 4 If $KeyGen(k)$ satisfies the subgroup decision assumption in the BGN scheme, the server in our Private Cell Retrieval (PCR) protocol has the semantic security.

Proof Please refer to [4] for the proof that the BGN scheme is semantic security if $KeyGen(k)$ satisfies the subgroup decision assumption.

Slightly different from the BGN scheme, we replace h with h_1 in the public key and include $e(g,g)^{q_1}$ as a public parameter. Because $h_1 = e(g,h)$, the replacement does not affect the security of the BGN scheme. In addition, it is hard to determine q_1 from $e(g,g)^{q_1}$ because the discrete logarithm is hard, and $e(g,g)^{q_1}$ does not help to solve the subgroup decision problem at all, i.e., to decide if $x^{q_1} = 1$ given an element x. Therefore, the definition for the server's security is the same as the semantic security of the BGN scheme and the theorem is proved. $\triangle$

Next, we analyse the client's security. Based on the definition of client's security, we consider the following game:

(1) Given the public/private key pair (PK, SK) of the BGN cryptosystem, the adversary $\mathcal{A}$ chooses two different ciphertexts C_1 and C_2, and then sends them to the challenger $\mathcal{C}$.

(2) The challenger $\mathcal{C}$ chooses a random bit $b \in \{0, 1\}$, and executes the Query Generation (QG) to obtain $(Q_b, s_b) = QG(C_b, PK)$. According to Algorithm 2, if $C \in \mathbb{G}$,

$$Q_b = e(C_b, g)e(g,g)^{s_b}h_1^{r_b};$$

if $C \in \mathbb{G}_1$,

$$Q_b = C_b e(g,g)^{s_b}h_1^{r_b},$$

where s_b, r_b are randomly chosen from $\{1, 2, \cdots, N-1\}$ and known to the challenger $\mathcal{C}$. Then Q_b is sent back to $\mathcal{A}$.

(3) The adversary $\mathcal{A}$ can experiment with the code of Q_b in an arbitrary non-black-box way, and finally outputs $b' \in \{0, 1\}$.

Theorem 5 The client in our Private Cell Retrieval (PCR) protocol has the semantic security.

Proof In Step 2 of the above game, the ciphertext C_b is blinded by random $e(g,g)^{s_b}h_1^{r_b}$. Without knowledge of random s_b, r_b, the adversary $\mathcal{A}$ cannot tell which ciphertext is blinded even if $\mathcal{A}$ can apply the decryption key SK on C_b in Step 3 to obtain $R_b = e(g,g)^{q_1 m_b} e(g,g)^{q_1 s_b}$ where $m_b = Decrypt(C_b, SK)$. In view of this, the adversary $\mathcal{A}$'s advantage in this game $(\mathsf{Adv}_{\mathcal{A}}(k) = |\mathsf{Pr}(b' = b) - 1/2|)$ is negligible. Therefore, the theorem is proved. $\triangle$

Remark. In Algorithm 2, if $C \in \mathbb{G}$, the client generates the query Q in $\mathbb{G}$ by letting $Q = Cg^s h^r$ where s, r are randomly chosen from $\{1, 2, \cdots, N-1\}$ and sends the query Q to the server. But this may leak to the server the client's intention, such that retrieving a cell or performing statistical analysis. Therefore, in order to keep the client's intention private, the client has to generate the query Q in $\mathbb{G}_1$ no matter whether $C \in \mathbb{G}$ or $C \in \mathbb{G}_1$ as in Algorithm 2.

4.2 Performance Analysis

The core of our solution is our Private Cell Retrieval (PCR) protocol, composed of Query Generation, Response Generation and Response Retrieval. Before the client and the server can run the PCR protocol, the server is required to encrypt the whole data warehouse D in Algorithm 1 and distribute it to the client. This initialisation costs $O(|D|)$ computation complexity and $O(|D|)$ communication complexity in the server, and $O(|D|)$ communication complexity in the client. This initialisation happens only once. Then the client and the server can run our PCR protocol any number of times.

In the query generation (Algorithm 2) of our PCR protocol, the client generates a query (Q, s) with at most two exponentiations in $\mathbb{G}_1$ and one pairing, and sends a group element of $\mathbb{G}_1$ to the server.

In the response generation (Algorithm 3), the server receives a group member of $\mathbb{G}_1$ and generates a response R with one exponentiation in $\mathbb{G}_1$ and then replies a group element of $\mathbb{G}_1$ to the client.

In the response retrieval (Algorithm 4), after receiving a group element of $\mathbb{G}_1$, the main time of the client is spent on determining the discrete logarithm $m = \log_{e(g,g)^{q_1}} R'$ with Porland's lambda method [25]. The computation complexity of Porland's lambda method is $\sqrt{T}$ where T is the upbound of m.

Computation of exponentiations and pairings and communications of group elements of $\mathbb{G}_1$ can be very fast. Thus, the main running time of our PCR protocol is $O(\sqrt{T})$. If T is around 2^{32}, the computation complexity is around $2^{16} = 65536$.

Next, we analyse the performance of private OLAP operations. The computation complexity for the client to perform drill-down, slice, dice, drill-down or pivot operation on the encrypted data cube is the same as that of the same operation on the original data cube. In Algorithm 5, assume that the domain for the dimension y_j includes λ different values, then the computation complexity of the roll-up operation is $O(\lambda)$ group multiplications, which can be done very quickly.

At last, we analyse the performance of our private statistical analysis. In Algorithm 6, to evaluate a ℓ-variate polynomial $f(x_1, x_2, \cdots, x_\ell)$ of total degree 2 at a point $(a_1, a_2, \cdots, a_\ell)$, the client and the server need jointly to run our PCR protocol once. For this evaluation, the client and the server can also run our PCR protocol ℓ times to retrieve $a_1, a_2, \cdots, a_\ell$ at first and then the client computes $f(a_1, a_2, \cdots, a_\ell)$ locally. Assume that the upbound of x_i (where $1 \leq i \leq \ell$) is T, then the upbound of $f(x_1, x_2, \cdots, x_\ell)$ is about T^2. In this case, the main running time of Algorithm 6 is about $O(T)$ while the main running time of ℓ PCR protocols is about $O(\ell\sqrt{T})$, usually less than $O(T)$. However, the client in Algorithm 6 needs to pay once while running ℓ PCR protocols needs to pay ℓ times. Therefore, our private statistical analysis Algorithm 6 has the lowest cost.

To balance the cost and the running time for private statistical analysis, the client may retrieve a part of $(a_1, a_2, \cdots, a_\ell)$ and then run Algorithm 6. The cost and running time are inversely proportional. We can see that if the client wishes to perform statistical analysis on the data warehouse with less cost, he has to spend more time to get the result. If the client wishes to perform statistical analysis on the data warehouse with less time, he has to pay more to get the result.

To the best of our knowledge, our solution is only one to provide private OLAP operations. In our solution, our private cell retrieval (PCR) protocol is essentially a private information retrieval (PIR) protocol. Unlike existing PIR protocols, such as [21, 5, 12], our PCR protocol needs to communicate the encrypted data warehouse in the initialisation to enable private OLAP operations. This happens only once. Without considering the initialisation, the performance comparison of our PCR protocol with some single database PIR protocols are listed in TABLE 1.

Table 1: Performance Comparison

Protocols	Comm. Complexity	Comp. Complexity
KO[21]	$O(\lvert D \rvert^\epsilon)$ any $\epsilon > 0$	client $O(\lvert D \rvert^\epsilon)$ server $O(\lvert D \rvert / 2)$
CMS[5]	$O(\log^8 \lvert D \rvert)$	client $O(\log \lvert D \rvert)$ server $O(\lvert D \rvert / 2)$
GR[12] $(N = \prod_i p_i^{e_i})$	$O(\log^2 \lvert D \rvert)$	client $O(\sum_i e_i (\log N + \sqrt{p_i})$[31]) server $O(\lvert D \rvert / 2)$
Our PCR	$O(1)$	client $O(\sqrt{T})$ server $O(1)$

From TABLE 1, we can see that our PCR protocol is more efficient than other single database PIR protocols in terms of communication if we do not consider the initialisation. In addition, only our solution supports private OLAP operations.

Compared with a centralised data warehouse which supports OLAP operations, our solution has two advantages as follows:

- A centralised data warehouse cannot protect the privacy of OLAP operations required by the client even if PIR may be used to prevent the server from knowing the final cell retrieved by the client. Our solution can protect the privacy of

both OLAP operations performed by the client and the final cell retrieved by the client.

- A centralised data warehouse is inefficient when multiple clients concurrently perform OLAP operations in the server and run PIR with the server. Our solution is distributed and the client can perform OLAP operations in his local computer and only run our efficient PCR with the server.

Remark. We should point out that our solution may not be suitable for operational databases which need to update their data frequently. This will require our solution to run initialisation many times and leads the performance of our solution worse than others. Our solution is in particular suitable for data warehouse where the data is non-volatile. In this scenario, our solution needs to run initialisation only once.

5. EXPERIMENTAL EVALUATION

In order to evaluate the practice of our solution, we have done some experiments on the Oracle global data warehouse example[1], which has four dimensions, Channel, ShipTo, Product and Time, and a units fact table storing three measures, units, sales and cost. The date cube keeps 9 years sale history data and contains about 300,000 cells. Our experiment is executed on a desktop machine with a Intel Core i7-2600 processor, which has a clock speed of 3.40GHz, and 16GB of RAM, and we use SQL and C programming language.

First of all, we implemented the BGN cryptosystem [4], in which the elliptic curve structures $\mathbb{G}, \mathbb{G}_1$ and associated bilinear pairing e are provided by the Pairing Based Cryptography (PBC) library[2]. For the public/private key pair (PK, SK) where $PK = \{N, \mathbb{G}, \mathbb{G}_1, e, g, h_1, e(g,g)^{q_1}\}$, $N = q_1 q_2$, $h_1 = e(g, u^{q_2})$ and $SK = \{q_1\}$, we use the values in Table 2.

In our setting, we choose the two primes q_1 and q_2, each has roughly 512 bits in length, so that it is impossible to factorize N according to the current computing technology.

Based on the BGN cryptosystem, we encrypt all measure values in the units fact table. This initialisation takes about 5 hours. The size of the original data cube is 45 Mbytes while the size of the encrypted data cube becomes 850 Mbytes.

Remark In practice, a data warehouse is a very sparse multi-dimensional data set. In this case, the size of the encrypted data cube can be significantly reduced because only the measures with values need to be encrypted.

Based on the encrypted data cube $E(D)$, we have done four experiments described in what follows. The goal of these experiments is to determine the actual times required by various OLAP operations, from the most simple, that is, retrieving a single cell, to the most complex ones, such as performing regression analysis and variance analysis.

Experiment 1 (Private Cell Retrieval) Consider the ciphertext C in Table 3 which is the encrypted value of a cell the user wants to retrieve. To do so, the client generates a query $(Q, s) = QG(C, PK)$ with values of Q and s shown in Table 3, and sends Q to the server. The server generates a response $R = RG(Q, SK)$ as shown in Table 3 and turns R to the client.

The client computes $m = RR(R, PK, s)$ with Porland's lambda method, where $m = 3346$.

---

[1]http://www.oracle.com/technetwork/database/options/olap/global-11g-readme-082667.html

[2]http://crypto.stanford.edu/pbc/

Table 2: Setting

Para.	Values
q_1	210754186407604102310925188159859071072187549 727704467965310206936564933603873461196303262 642786480951780132666506364093582465543068449 71313514949562360857
q_2	127707578650528883113295334590981718968728937 878725402284946055541062874329871667476514811 389292826651236287717409754447822015620351794 49188842497114643083
N	269149068365773261841824041671333984122651229 207631208954991210415522316622671277634208088 843014413860367743186861524577200017371584463 927286387273029973442850457450263045480185806 500527854730802543879971807379459036648210795 717878207455901709230864575970688020145718885 793966526448525040987835358478405002131
g	[385415833869521041078389458073469223213315262 760669641124899551348857051123127875141089007 714527824427443188616396621912530181137147121 870447696068628604002854494442009563963141580 756926191397532999397829406565934259561055970 554703419949372001563073197258958319877077753 216741702156041831655844141890780432157126,7 480911976241807747934632097048398180200105998 822744599035552243464272721936069407066922848 681186534355607954535020561134603030182187722 681209428254633017341515467050549483142767178 688953392003318854120308972805480677016226334 643239789167325213173963299635951154235542201 237755220067092164079566743266180947221]
u	[903551131917073490336503216710648192334117 91 554488948056631073957107032184057077540247156 969053761302738958171477136366680144692611719 400895154756559355801930222886350399605246802 012080359890355376422384293752890166573180008 042710290122021244649546918197580253304536519 279950176817945174866553861242002236175118,91 234402775643178015354290188903324675733841740 787776314525487458132229222432297506474819321 295819916644881701149670224771561523459777244 699718715893247838335015592417414766946680054 568360496527404452082429881562821921617122620 787126291583946026460700670166393134322784351 346342103872802765111089380627867938185]

Table 3: Experiment 1

Para.	Values
C	[215222387384615254578042475926030982390823920 387850637503254337743640053800801528894647710 460931004202066956644782011121982503522391733 769483799342744110217483812004451801026036675 028687897707670405079381650737148867828535797 412610493107345524676804397627280852017191294 849308280713904839422012086503989541407513 803401062802803611669710650042637313843290526 205704651819069769663874847208344009914491314 498017794637941714616376720513725601967496618 671574197331105775429251809783142282868934923 403194455486949263780893751731609669875213865 342483211597115040375577714048719922339756050 150435462595411512244945603617747945032903,90]
Q	[137242154510796490730330164718410557669461844 558647225102057747528895940287210185840417789 685426671341811953351361076137849250939701896 715951186934072866629376091534352595084355161 200516460359669392541441176267004702827276086 210005073428754033710283210773178651345538052 214834584548541975741014889339971816170893,6 789190810624682660133959786034535199713803350 404803984144005758221566298342064505940659232 352014684692147165371779033874095272799194779 069288966002726386439683760159063612504080920 926714514025566061803064930982113032440254855 005080117332252350700330304815649593087828358 526837137059231442270972333540099866782]
s	188857674807555849528532796096897013926314903 570009472779352231629993166112778876777630402 393044880461058951359315772953414254388265799 018043444401815792645824517581283228316321701 047479133908428806317280841136455777666483401 759509633043124148231096623706520495844956120 643045136913607186633855095825607139394
R	[333243658719658408065982005629568505613085996 021403060183417149618139008163841174822239463 350827804843399577119545830922465717860990783 838226442733915537510654088764947302123115753 348294421103565260537624676507874759043352 212103371943683688353291709453168918442266250 865883638219437764600010671859246570929590,66 793981002937657883003772969898511586042127405 070794625849013710789773587940207846147752840 791701441913128264545400920126504391119435655 804859002976782405306798948607938220165139491 772181244832765171489970171197466768678129027 664013605467300628414621290211719800812523241 481892911105514786006870381361360003652]

The total running time of this cell retrieval operation performed using our PCR protocol is about 1.14 seconds.

Experiment 2 (Private OLAP operations) Given the encrypted data warehouse, the client performs a slice operation implemented by the following SQL query:

CREATE VIEW Catalogues AS
SELECT ShipTo, Product, Time, units, sales, cost
FROM units_fact_table
WHERE Channel="CAT"

where "CAT" stands for Catalogues. The resulting Catalogues view is a 3-dimension subcube, from which the client further performs a slice operation implemented by the following SQL query,

CREATE VIEW Mouse AS
SELECT ShipTo, Time, units, sales, cost
FROM Catalogues
WHERE Product="MOUSE"

The resulting Mouse view is a 2-dimension subcube, from which the client further performs a roll-up operation along the ShipTo dimension from customer to all (i.e., aggregating three measures units, sales and cost for all customers), and then a roll-up operation along the time dimension from month to year (i.e., aggregating three measures units, sales and cost from months into years), with Algorithm 5 implemented by the C programming language.

At last, the client obtains a subcube with only the Time dimension Time, which takes values in the set $\{0, 1, \cdots, 9\}$.

The total running time for the above sequential OLAP operations is less than 3 minutes.

Remark We can speed up our roll-up operation by parallel computation. For example, if we allocate the task for the roll-up operation to multiple computers and run 5 computers in parallel, the total running time for the above experiment can be reduced from 3 minutes to 36 seconds.

Experiment 3 (Private Regression Analysis) The sequence of the OLAP operations in Experiment 2 restricts and shapes the data warehouse so that it is ready for a regression analysis, by which the client would like to investigate the relationship between the number of sold mouse units and the time.

Consider the 1-dimension subcube that resulted from the sequential OLAP operations in Experiment 2, and assume that the units measure takes values $E(Y_1), E(Y_2), \cdots, E(Y_n)$ in years $X_1, X_2, \cdots, X_n$, respectively.

A simple regression analysis is to determine b_0 and b_1 in the linear equation $Y_i = b_0 + b_1 X_i$, where the formulas for the least squares estimates are

$$
\begin{aligned}
b_1 &= \frac{\sum_{i=1}^{n}(X_i - \overline{X})(Y_i - \overline{Y})}{\sum_{i=1}^{n}(X_i - \overline{X})^2} \\
b_0 &= \overline{Y} - b_1\overline{X}
\end{aligned}
$$

where $\overline{X} = \frac{\sum_{i=1}^{n} X_i}{n}$ and $\overline{Y} = \frac{\sum_{i=1}^{n} Y_i}{n}$.

Given $X_1, X_2, \cdots, X_n$ and $E(Y_1), E(Y_2), \cdots, E(Y_n)$, to compute b_0, b_1, the client gets $\prod_{i=1}^{n} E(Y_i) = E(\sum_{i=1}^{n} Y_i)$ decrypted by our PCR protocol and then computes $\overline{X}$ and $\overline{Y}$. Next, let $[\overline{X}], [\overline{Y}]$ be the round results of $\overline{X}, \overline{Y}$ (note that the number of sold units is positive integer), and let

$$
Z = \prod_{i=1}^{n}(E(Y_i)/E([\overline{Y}]))^{X_i - [\overline{X}]}.
$$

Based on the homomorphic property of the BGN cryptosystem, we have that

$$
\begin{aligned}
Z &= \prod_{i=1}^{n}(E(Y_i - [\overline{Y}]))^{X_i - [\overline{X}]} \\
&= \prod_{i=1}^{n} E((X_i - [\overline{X}])(Y_i - [\overline{Y}])) \\
&= E(\sum_{i=1}^{n}(X_i - [\overline{X}])(Y_i - [\overline{Y}])) \\
&= E(b_1 \sum_{i=1}^{n}(X_i - [\overline{X}])^2)
\end{aligned}
$$

Then the client gets Z decrypted by our PCR protocol and then computes $b_1 = Decrypt(Z, SK)/\sum_{i=1}^{n}(X_i - [\overline{X}])^2$ and $b_0 = \overline{Y} - b_1\overline{X}$.

By the above private regression analysis, we obtain the linear equation

$$
Y = 9407.33 - 658.08X.
$$

This result is very close to the actual linear equation $Y = 9407.67 - 658.08X$ obtained by performing the regression analysis on the plain data warehouse. In addition, our private regression analysis needs two decryptions only.

Remark. The difference between two linear equations is due to the round operation.

Experiment 4 (Private Variance Analysis) Consider the 1-dimension subcube that resulted from the sequential OLAP operations in Experiment 2, i.e., $X_1, X_2, \cdots, X_n$ (years) and $E(Y_1), E(Y_2), \cdots, E(Y_n)$ (encrypted units), and suppose that the client would like to compute the variance for units measure in private.

The variance v^2 can be computed as follows:

$$
\begin{aligned}
v^2 &= \frac{\sum_{i=1}^{n}(Y_i - \overline{Y})^2}{n} \\
&= \frac{\sum_{i=1}^{n}(nY_i - n\overline{Y})^2}{n^3} \\
&= \frac{\sum_{i=1}^{n}(nY_i - \sum_{j=1}^{n} Y_j)^2}{n^3}
\end{aligned}
$$

From $E(Y_1), E(Y_2), \cdots, E(Y_n)$, the client can obtain $E(nY_i - \sum_{j=1}^{n} Y_j) = E(Y_i)^n / \prod_{j=1}^{n} E(Y_j)$. Let

$$
Z = e(E(nY_i - \sum_{j=1}^{n} Y_j), E(nY_i - \sum_{j=1}^{n} Y_j)),
$$

where e denotes the pairing operation (please refer to Appendix). Based on the homomorphic property of the BGN cryptosystem, we have

$$
\begin{aligned}
Z &= \prod_{i=1}^{n} e(E(nY_i - \sum_{j=1}^{n} Y_j), E(nY_i - \sum_{j=1}^{n} Y_j)) \\
&= \prod_{i=1}^{n} \mathcal{E}((nY_i - \sum_{j=1}^{n} Y_j)^2) \\
&= \mathcal{E}(\sum_{i=1}^{n}(nY_i - \sum_{j=1}^{n} Y_j)^2)
\end{aligned}
$$

where $\mathcal{E}$ denotes the BGN encryption over $\mathbb{G}_1$ (please refer to Appendix).

Next, the client gets Z decrypted by our PCR protocol and computes $v^2 = Decrypt(Z, SK)/n^3$.

By the above private variance computation, the client obtains the variance $v^2 = 3212337.56$ for units measure with only one decryption. This result is the same as the actual variance by performing the variance analysis on the plain data warehouse.

Remark. If our underlying encryption scheme were the ElGamal scheme [11] or Paillier scheme [30] instead of the BGN scheme [4], the private variance analysis in Experiment 4 would have needed 9 decryptions instead of 1 decryption.

6. CONCLUSION

In this paper, we have presented a solution for private data warehouse queries. Our solution allows the client to perform OLAP operations, such as roll-up, drill-down, dice, slice, pivot, and then retrieve a cell from the resulted data warehouse without revealing to the server what operations are performed and what cell is retrieved. In particular, our solution allows the client to perform some statistical analysis on the data warehouse with the lowest cost if the server charges the client per query.

Our solution provides not only the client's security but also the server's security. Performance analysis and experiments have shown that our solution is practical for private data warehouse queries.

So far, our solution only allows the client to privately perform statistical analyses which can be algebraically expressed as a polynomial of degree at most 2 on the data warehouse, such as regression and variance analysis. Our future work will extend our solution so that the client can privately perform statistical analyses which cannot be algebraically expressed as a polynomial, such as min, max and count.

7. REFERENCES

[1] A. Ambainis. Upper bound on the communication complexity of private information retrieval. In *Proc. 24th International Colloquium on Automata, Languages and Programming*, pp. 401-407, 1997.

[2] D. Asonov. Private information retrieval - an overview and current trends. In *Proc. ECDPvA Workshop, Informatik'01*, 2001.

[3] A. Beimel and Y. Ishai. Information-theoretic private information retrieval: a unified construction. In *Proc. 28th International Colloquium on Automata, Languages and Programming*, pp. 912-926, 2001.

[4] D. Boneh, E. Goh and K. Nissim. Evaluating 2-DNF formulas on ciphertexts. In *Proc. TCC'05*, pp. 325-341, 2005.

[5] C. Cachin, S. Micali and M. Stadler. Computational private information retrieval with polylogarithm communication. In *Proc. EUROCRYPT'99*, pp. 402-414, 1999.

[6] Y. Chang. Single database private information retrieval with logarithmic communication. In *Proc. 9th Australasian Conference on Information Security and Privacy*, pp. 50-61, 2004.

[7] B. Chor and N. Gilboa. Computational private information retrieval. In *Proc. 29th ACM Symposium on the Theory of Computing*, pp. 304-313,1997.

[8] B. Chor, O. Goldreich, E. Kushilevitz, and M. Sudan. Private information retrieval. In *Proc. 36th IEEE Symposium on Foundations of Computer Science*, pp.41-51, 1995.

[9] I. Damgard and M. Jurik. A Generalisation, a simplification and some applications of Paillier's probabilistic public-key system. In *Proc. PKC'01*, pages 119-136, 2001.

[10] M. Dijk, C. Gentry, S. Halevi and V. Vaikuntanathan. Fully homomorphic encryption over the integers. In *Proc. EUROCRYPT'10*, pages 24-43, 2010.

[11] T. ElGamal. A public-key cryptosystem and a signature scheme based on discrete logarithms. *IEEE Transactions on Information Theory*, 31 (4): 469ÃŘ472, 1985.

[12] C. Gentry and Z. Ramzan. Single-database private information retrieval with constant communication rate. In *Proc. 31th International Colloquium on Automata, Languages and Programming*, pp. 803-815, 2005.

[13] C. Gentry. Fully homomorphic encryption using ideal lattices. In *Proc. STOC'09*, pages 169-178, 2009.

[14] Y. Gentner, Y. Ishai, E. Kushilevitz and T. Malkin. Protecting data privacy in private information retrieval schemes. In *Proc. 30th ACM Symposium on Theory of Computing*, pp. 151-160, 1998.

[15] S. Goldwasser S. and Micali (1984) Probabilistic encryption, Journal of Computer and System Science, 28(2), pp. 270-299.

[16] J. Han and M. Kamber, *Data Mining: Concepts and Techniques*. 2nd Edition. Morgan Kaufmann Publishers, 2006.

[17] W. H. Inmon, *Building the Data Warehouse*. John Wiley & Sons, 1996.

[18] Y. Ishai and E. Kushilevitz. Improved upper bounds on information theoretic private information retrieval. In *Proc. 31st ACM Symposium on the Theory of Computing*, pp. 79-88, 1999.

[19] T. Itoh. Efficient private information retrieval. *IEICE Trans. Fund. Electron. Communi. Comput. Sci.* E. 82-A(1), pp. 11-20, 1999.

[20] T. Itoh. On lower bounds for the communication complexity of private information retrieval. *IEICE Trans. Fund. Electron. Communi. Comput. Sci.* E. 84-A(1), pp. 157-164, 2001.

[21] E. Kushilevitz and R. Ostrovsky. Replication is not needed: single database, computational private information retrieval. In *Proc. 38th IEEE Symposium on Foundations of Computer Science*, pp. 364-373, 1997.

[22] E. Kushilevitz and R. Ostrovsky. One-way trapdoor permutations are sufficient for non-trivial single-server private information retrieval. In *Proc. EUROCRYPT'00*, pp. 104-121, 2000.

[23] H. Lipmaa. An oblivious transfer protocol with log-squared communication. In *Proc. 8th International Conference on Information Security*, pp. 314-328, 2005.

[24] H. Lipmaa. First CPIR protocol with data-dependent computation. In *Proc. ICISC'09*, pages 193-210, 2009.

[25] A. Menezes, P. van Oorchot and S. Vanstone, *Handbook of Applied Cryptography*. CRC Press, 1997.

[26] S. K. Mishra and P. Sarkar. Symmetrically private information retrieval. In *Proc. INDOCRYPT'00*, pp. 225-236, 2000.

[27] M. Naor and B. Pinkas. Oblivious transfer and polynomial evaluation. In *Proc. 31th ACM Symposium on Theory of Computing*, pp. 245-254, 1999.

[28] T. Okamoto and S. Uchiyama. A new public-key cryptosystem as secure as factoring. In *Proc. EUROCRYPT'98*, 1998.

[29] R. Ostrovsky and W. E. Skeith III. A survey of single-database PIR: techniques and applications. In *Proc. PKC'07*, pages 393-411, 2007.

[30] P. Paillier. Public key cryptosystems based on composite

degree residue classes. In *Proc. EUROCRYPT'99*, pages 223-238, 1999.

[31] S. Pohlig and M. Hellman. An improved algorithm for computing logarithms over GF(p) and its cryptographic significance. *IEEE Transactions on Information Theory*, 24(1): 106-110, 1978.

[32] R. Rivest, A. Shamir and L. Adleman. A method for obtaining digital signatures and public-key cryptosystems. *Communications of the ACM*, 21 (2): 120ÄŘ126, 1978.

[33] N. Smart and F. Vercauteren. Fully homomorphic encryption with relatively small key and ciphertext sizes. In *Proc. PKC'10*, pages 420-443, 2010.

APPENDIX

A. BONEH-GOH-NISSIM CRYPTOSYSTEM

We introduce the Boneh-Goh-Nissim cryptosystem [4] in this section.

A.1 Bilinear Group

We use the following notations:

1. $\mathbb{G}$ and $\mathbb{G}_1$ are two (multiplicative) cyclic groups of finite order n.

2. g is a generator of $\mathbb{G}$.

3. e is a bilinear map $e : \mathbb{G} \times \mathbb{G} \to \mathbb{G}_1$. In other words, for all $u, v \in \mathbb{G}$ and $a, b \in \mathbb{Z}$, we have $e(u^a, v^b) = e(u,v)^{ab}$. We also require that $e(g,g)$ is a generator of $\mathbb{G}_1$.

We sat that $\mathbb{G}$ is a bilinear group if a group $\mathbb{G}_1$ and a bilinear map as above exist.

A.2 Boneh-Goh-Nissim Encryption Scheme

Boneh-Goh-Nissim encryption scheme, BGN scheme by brevity, resembles the Paillier [30] and the Okamoto-Uchiyama [28] encryption schemes. The three algorithms making up the scheme are described as follows:

A.2.1 Key Generation $KeyGen(k)$

Given a secure parameter $k \in \mathbb{Z}^+$, run $KeyGen(k)$ to obtain a tuple $(q_1, q_2, \mathbb{G}, \mathbb{G}_1, e)$. Let $N = q_1 q_2$. Pick up two random generators g, u from $\mathbb{G}$ and set $h = u^{q_2}$. Then h is a random generator of the subgroup of $\mathbb{G}$ of order q_1. The public key is $PK = \{N, \mathbb{G}, \mathbb{G}_1, e, g, h\}$. The private key $SK = q_1$.

A.2.2 Encryption $Encrypt(m, PK)$

Assume the message space consists of integers in the set $\{0, 1, \cdots, T\}$ with $T < q_2$. We encrypt bits in which case $T = 1$. To encrypt a message m using the public key PK, pick a random r from $\{1, 2, \cdots, N\}$ and compute

$$C = g^m h^r \in \mathbb{G} \qquad (1)$$

Output C as the ciphertext.

A.2.3 Decryption $Decrypt(C, SK)$

To decrypt a ciphertext C using the private key $SK = q_1$, observe that

$$C^{q_1} = (g^m h^r)^{q_1} = (g^{q_1})^m$$

To recover the message m, it suffices to compute the discrete logarithm of C^{q_1} to the base g^{q_1}. Since $0 \le m \le T$, this takes expected time $O(\sqrt{T})$ using Polland's lambda method [25].

A.3 Homomorphic Properties

The BGN scheme is clearly additively homomorphic. Let $PK = \{N, \mathbb{G}, \mathbb{G}_1, e, g, h\}$ be a public key. Given two ciphertexts $C_1, C_2 \in \mathbb{G}$ of messages $m_1, m_2 \in \{0, 1, \cdots, T\}$ respectively, anyone can create a uniformly distributed encryption of $m_1 + m_2 (mod\ N)$ by computing the product $C = C_1 C_2 h^r$ for a random r in $\{1, 2, \cdots, N - 1\}$.

More importantly, anyone can multiply two encrypted messages once using the bilinear map. Let $g_1 = e(g,g)$ and $h_1 = e(g,h)$, then g_1 is of order N and h_1 is of order q_1. There is some (unknown) $\alpha \in \mathbb{Z}$ such that $h = g^{\alpha q_2}$. Suppose that we are given two ciphertexts $C_1 = g^{m_1} h^{r_1} \in \mathbb{G}$ and $C_2 = g^{m_2} h^{r_2} \in \mathbb{G}$. To build an encryption of the product $m_1 m_2 (mod\ N)$, (1) pick a random $r \in \mathbb{Z}_N$, and (2) let $C = e(C_1, C_2) h_1^r \in \mathbb{G}_1$. Then

$$
\begin{aligned}
C &= e(C_1, C_2) h_1^r \\
&= e(g^{m_1} h^{r_1}, g^{m_2} h^{r_2}) h_1^r \\
&= e(g^{m_1 + \alpha q_2 r_1}, g^{m_2 + \alpha q_2 r_2}) h_1^r \\
&= e(g,g)^{(m_1 + \alpha q_2 r_1)(m_2 + \alpha q_2 r_2)} h_1^r \\
&= e(g,g)^{m_1 m_2 + \alpha q_2 (m_1 r_2 + m_2 r_1 + \alpha q_2 r_1 r_2)} h_1^r \\
&= e(g,g)^{m_1 m_2} h_1^{r + m_1 r_2 + m_2 r_1 + \alpha q_2 r_1 r_2}
\end{aligned}
$$

where $r + m_1 r_2 + m_2 r_1 + \alpha q_2 r_1 r_2$ is distributed uniformly in $\mathbb{Z}_N$. Thus C is a uniformly distributed encryption of $m_1 m_2 (mod\ N)$, but in $\mathbb{G}_1$ rather than $\mathbb{G}$. We note that the BGN scheme is still additively homomorphic in $\mathbb{G}_1$.

Evolving Role Definitions Through Permission Invocation Patterns

Wen Zhang
EECS Dept.
Vanderbilt University
Nashville, TN, USA
wen.zhang.1@vanderbilt.edu

You Chen
Biomedical Informatics Dept.
Vanderbilt University
Nashville, TN, USA
you.chen@vanderbilt.edu

Carl A. Gunter
Dept. of Computer Science
University of Illinois
Urbana, IL, USA
cgunter@illinois.edu

David Liebovitz
Dept. of Medicine
Northwestern University
Chicago, IL, USA
davidl@northwestern.edu

Bradley Malin
Biomedical Informatics Dept.
Vanderbilt University
Nashville, TN, USA
b.malin@vanderbilt.edu

ABSTRACT

In role-based access control (RBAC), roles are traditionally defined as sets of permissions. Roles specified by administrators may be inaccurate, however, such that data mining methods have been proposed to learn roles from actual permission utilization. These methods minimize variation from an information theoretic perspective, but they neglect the expert knowledge of administrators. In this paper, we propose a strategy to enable a controlled evolution of RBAC based on utilization. To accomplish this goal, we extend a subset enumeration framework to search candidate roles for an RBAC model that addresses an objective function which balances administrator beliefs and permission utilization. The rate of role evolution is controlled by an administrator-specified parameter.

To assess effectiveness, we perform an empirical analysis using simulations, as well as a real world dataset from an electronic medical record system (EMR) in use at a large academic medical center (over 8000 users, 140 roles, and 140 permissions). We compare the results with several state-of-the-art role mining algorithms using 1) an outlier detection method on the new roles to evaluate the homogeneity of their behavior and 2) a set-based similarity measure between the original and new roles. The results illustrate our method is comparable to the state-of-the-art, but allows for a range of RBAC models which tradeoff user behavior and administrator expectations. For instance, in the EMR dataset, we find the resulting RBAC model contains 22% outliers and a distance of 0.02 to the original RBAC model when the system is biased toward administrator belief, and 13% outliers and a distance of 0.26 to the original RBAC model when biased toward permission utilization.

Categories and Subject Descriptors

D.4.6 [**Operating Systems**]: Security and Protection—*Access Control*; H.2.8 [**Database Management**]: Database Applications—*Data mining*

General Terms

Security, Algorithms

Keywords

Audit logs, role-based access control, role mining

1. INTRODUCTION

Role-based access control (RBAC) is a framework that has been adopted widely for managing the rights of users in information systems [16]. It was designed to simplify the allocation of access rights by mapping users to a set of roles, each of which is associated with a set of permissions. Beyond the specification of rights, RBAC can be employed for intrusion detection purposes [1, 25]. For instance, the actions of a user can be compared to those of the users associated with the same role to determine if deviation from expected behavior has transpired. Thus, roles which consist of users with relatively similar behavior are desirable for detecting and preventing insider threats [14].

The process of defining roles, which is often referred to as role engineering [5], is a notoriously challenging problem. In general, role engineering approaches have fallen into two camps: i) *top-down* and ii) *bottom-up*. In the top-down setting, organizational experts (or system administrators) model the workflows associated with an enterprise, which are subsequently decomposed into tasks and roles [17, 20]. Bottom-up approaches (e.g., [18, 23]), on the other hand, discover roles by leveraging information that already exists in the system. Many of these approaches (e.g., [18, 22, 23, 26]) propose roles based on patterns in existing user-permission assignments.

There are benefits and drawbacks to each camp. Top-down approaches, for instance, are based on expert reasoning, in-depth interviews, and tend to reflect organizational expectations [21]. However, these approaches often result in high costs to an enterprise [17] because they require a substantial amount of time to document the workflows which exist. They may also be subject to the problem of informant inaccuracy [7] and, thus, access control models which are incomplete or contain errors [12]. By contrast, bottom-up approaches enable an RBAC system to be derived automatically, such that their cost is significantly lower than their top-down counterparts. Yet, there is no guarantee that users in the same role, as defined by their permissions, will exhibit similar behavior.

Historically, role engineering strategies have treated these camps independently, but we believe there is merit in combining them into a more comprehensive role engineering framework. Consider, while it may be that expert-specified RBAC configurations are not entirely representative of an enterprise, it is unlikely that such information is completely uninformed. As such, the goal of this paper is to propose a role engineering approach that evolves roles in a manner that balances 1) the desire to retain an existing RBAC configuration with 2) the need to assign users with similar behavior into common roles.

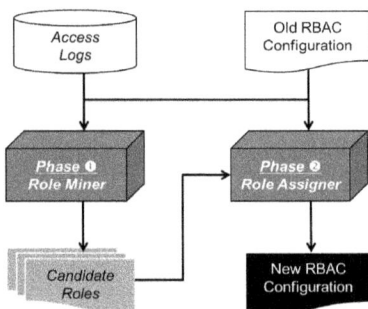

Figure 1: An architectural overview of DDRE algorithm

From a high-level, our evolution strategy, which we call the Data Driven Role Evolution (DDRE) algorithm, consists of mainly two phases as shown in Figure 1. In the first phase, we mine a set of candidate roles, which are selected to optimize an objective function that balances distance from the original roles with behaviorial similarity in the form of permission invocation in access logs. In the second phase, each user is assigned to roles according to a criterion that mitigates redundancy in the access control model. There are several primary contributions of this paper, including:

- **A new objective function for the role mining problem.** We devise an objective that balances the administrator's belief with the evidence in existing access logs. The function is parameterized, such that a user can bias the resulting RBAC configurations toward belief or evidence as deemed desirable.

- **A hybrid role engineering algorithm.** We propose a new role engineering algorithm that builds on a subset enumeration technique employed in previous role engineering strategies. Our algorithm evolves existing RBAC configurations into new configurations which are are more effective at addressing administrators' beliefs and permission utilization goals than current role engineering strategies.

- **A multi-objective empirical evaluation.** To evaluate the resulting RBAC configurations, we compare our algorithm with state-of-the-art role mining techniques using a real dataset derived from a large electronic medical record system, as well as a controlled synthetic dataset. The results show that our role evolution algorithm can, unlike previous methods, produce a range of RBAC configurations in comparison to previous methods. Moreover, we show the resulting configurations follow the expected bias of the algorithm and indicate utilization patterns exist in the real dataset.

The remainder of this paper is organized as follows. Section 2 reviews the foundations upon which our method is built, including the role mining problem, access logs, distance measures, and outlier detection methods. Section 3 then describes our role evolution algorithm. Section 4 presents the experiments performed to evaluate our approach. Section 5 provides a survey of related work in role engineering and role mining. Finally, Section 6 concludes the paper and suggests next steps for extending this work.

2. PRELIMINARIES

In this section, we review several topics that inform the development of our role revision method. This section begins with a formalization of a generalized version of the role mining problem. Next, we provide a description of access logs as they are utilized in our method. Then, we introduce a formalization of the objective function invoked in our variation of the role mining problem. Finally, this section concludes with a description of one-class support vector machines, an effective outlier detection algorithm, which we employ as a measure of the quality of RBAC configurations.

2.1 Generalized Role Mining Problem

We begin with a generalized perspective of the role mining problem, which will be refined to model the problems studied in this work.

Definition: [*Generalized Role Mining Problem*] Let $t = \langle U, P, UPA \rangle$ denote an access control configuration, where $U = \{u_1, u_2, \ldots, u_m\}$ is a set of users, $P = \{p_1, p_2, \ldots, p_n\}$ is a set of permissions, and UPA is an $m \times n$ Boolean matrix indicating the mapping between U and P.

The goal of the *Generalized Role Mining Problem* is to find an RBAC configuration $c = \langle U, P, R, URA, RPA \rangle$[1], subject to $UPA = URA \otimes RPA$, such that an objective function $f()$ is optimized. In the configuration, $R = \{r_1, r_2, \ldots, r_k\}$ is a set of roles, URA is an $m \times k$ Boolean matrix indicating the mapping between U and R, and RPA is a $k \times n$ Boolean matrix indicating the mapping between R and P.[2] □

The matrices in Figures 2(b) and (c) depict an example of an RBAC configuration. It can be seen there are six users, seven permissions, and two roles.

Given a role r_l, we can readily extract the corresponding users and associated permissions. In this paper, we use $\mathbb{P}_l^{(c)} = \{p_x \mid RPA_{lx} = 1\}$ to denote the set of permissions assigned to r_l, and $\mathbb{U}_l^{(c)} = \{u_y \mid URA_{yl} = 1\}$ to denote the set

---

[1] In this paper, we only consider the $RBAC_0$ model (i.e., we do not consider role hierarchies or constraints).

[2] $x = a \otimes b$ denotes the Boolean matrix product, in which an element is defined as $x_{ij} = \vee_k(a_{ik} \wedge b_{kj})$.

	p_1	p_2	p_3	p_4	p_5	p_6	p_7
u_1	116	485	151	402	249		
u_2	181	797	21	58	33		
u_3	199	819	77	196	91		
u_4			29	81	44	402	174
u_5			108	278	161	530	215
u_6			25	62	31	334	118

(a) *UPIM*

	r_1	r_2
u_1	1	0
u_2	1	0
u_3	1	0
u_4	0	1
u_5	0	1
u_6	0	1

(b) *URA*

	p_1	p_2	p_3	p_4	p_5	p_6	p_7
r_1	1	1	1	1	1	0	0
r_2	0	0	1	1	1	1	1

(c) *RPA*

Figure 2: An example of a user-permission invocation matrix (*UPIM*) and an RBAC configuration (*URA* and *RPA*).

of users under r_l in the RBAC configuration c. When appropriate, we adopt the standard convention of representing a role as its corresponding set of permissions. For example, $\gamma = \{p_1, p_2\}$ represents a role possessing two permissions. In general, all users whose permission set is the superset of γ automatically obtain this role. There are, however, exceptions to this role that will be introduced in Section 3.

Various objective functions have been proposed for the role mining problem. Certain functions are based on the size of R [23], while others use variations of structural complexity [26]. With regard to the latter, objective functions have been based on the size of R and the total number of elements in *URA* and/or *RPA*. In this paper, we define the objective function from the perspective of i) user behavior similarity and ii) distance to the initial RBAC configuration.

2.2 Access Log

In this work, an access log is represented as an $m \times n$ user-permission invocation matrix *UPIM*. We use ω_{ij} to denote the number of times user u_i invoked permission p_j. Figure 2(a) depicts the *UPIM* that corresponds to the RBAC configuration in Figures 2(b) and (c). To mitigate bias which may occur from working with the raw frequency counts, we preprocess *UPIM* through a row-wise normalization (i.e., all numbers are divided by their rowsum) to represent *UPIM* as a set of user-specific probability distributions.

To measure the homogeneity of a role, we need to extract the corresponding access records from *UPIM*. This is accomplished through the application of a projection matrix.

Definition: [*Projection Matrix*] Given an RBAC configuration c and user-permission invocation matrix *UPIM*, the *projection matrix* M_{r_l} for role r_l is an $p \times q$ matrix, where $p = |\mathbb{U}_l^{(c)}|$ and $q = |\mathbb{P}_l^{(c)}|$. Each row (column) of M_{r_l} represents a user (permission) associated with r_l. Let β_{ij} be defined as an element of M_{r_l} as follows. If the ith user in $\mathbb{U}_l^{(c)}$ is u_f in U, and the jth permission in $\mathbb{P}_l^{(c)}$ is p_g in P, then $\beta_{ij} = \omega_{fg}$. □

2.3 Objective Function

To balance existing beliefs in roles with actual user behavior, we propose a new objective function for the role mining problem, which is based on two goals. The first goal is to enable each role to possess high homogeneity in the rate at which permissions are accessed. The second goal is to ensure the new and pre-existing RBAC are "near" one another. We use functions $h()$ and $j()$ to measure the first and second goal, respectively, and define the objective function as:

$$f(c_{new}) = \alpha \cdot h(c_{new}) + (1 - \alpha) \cdot j(c_{old}, c_{new}) \qquad (1)$$

where c_{new} is the RBAC configuration proposed by a role mining algorithm, c_{old} is the existing RBAC configuration, and α is a real value between 0 and 1 to bias the system from $h()$ to $j()$. The following subsections provide details regarding how the functions $h()$ and $j()$ are computed.

2.3.1 RBAC homogeneity

In this section, we formally introduce the notion of homogeneity, which will be applied to characterize the similarity of the users in a role.

Definition: [*Homogeneity*] Given an RBAC configuration $c = \langle U, P, R, URA, RPA \rangle$ and a user-permission matrix *UPIM*, the *role homogeneity* of r_l is:

$$\mathsf{ho}(r_l) = m^{-1} \sum_{i=1}^{m} (1 - \mathsf{cosine}(\mathbf{x}_i, \mathbf{c}_l)), \qquad (2)$$

where m is the number of row vectors in M_{r_l}, $\mathbf{x}_i$ is the ith row vector of M_{r_l}, $\mathbf{c}_l$ is the mean vector of all row vectors in M_{r_l}, and $\mathsf{cosine}(\mathbf{a}, \mathbf{b})$ is the cosine similarity $\frac{\mathbf{a} \bullet \mathbf{b}}{|\mathbf{a}||\mathbf{b}|}$.

The *RBAC homogeneity* of c is then defined as:

$$h(c) = |R|^{-1} \sum_{r_l \in R} \mathsf{ho}(r_l) \qquad (3)$$

□

Role and RBAC homogeneity (Equations 2 and 3) have a natural geometric interpretation. Consider, if a role consists of a set of highly similar users, then the vectors representing the behaviors of these users will form a relatively compact cluster in $\mathbb{R}^k$ (where k is the dimensionality of the vectors) and the degree of the angle between each vector and the mean of the cluster, measured by $1 - \mathsf{cosine}(\mathbf{x}_i, \mathbf{c}_l)$, will tend to be small. Conversely, if the users in a role exhibit highly diverse behavior, then the cluster will tend to have a long diameter and the degree of the angle will be large.

2.3.2 Distance Between RBAC Configurations

In order to measure how far a new RBAC configuration has migrated from the initial configuration, we introduce a set-based similarity measure. First, we define the distance between two roles.

Definition: [*Role Distance*] Let γ_i and δ_j be roles in RBAC configurations c_1 and c_2, respectively. The *role distance* between the roles is defined as:

$$\mathsf{jac}(\gamma_i, \delta_j) = 1 - \frac{|(\mathbb{P}_i^{(c_1)} \times \mathbb{U}_i^{(c_1)}) \cap (\mathbb{P}_j^{(c_2)} \times \mathbb{U}_j^{(c_2)})|}{|(\mathbb{P}_i^{(c_1)} \times \mathbb{U}_i^{(c_1)}) \cup (\mathbb{P}_j^{(c_2)} \times \mathbb{U}_j^{(c_2)})|} \qquad (4)$$

where $A \times B$ is the Cartesian product of sets A and B. □

In our setting, a role corresponds to the Cartesian product of its associated set of permissions and set of users. This enables the comparison of two roles to be performed in the joint space of permissions and users. Thus, our definition corresponds to the Jaccard distance, a widely used measure for the comparison of two sets [9].

We leverage the distance between roles to define the distance between a role and a role set.

Definition: [*Role Set Distance*] The *role set distance* from role γ to role set R is the minimum distance to any role in the set:

$$\mathsf{minjac}(\gamma, R) = \min_{\delta \in R} \mathsf{jac}(\gamma, \delta) \qquad (5)$$

□

Finally, we can define the distance from one RBAC configuration to another.

Definition: [*RBAC Distance*] Let c_i and c_j be RBAC configurations. The *RBAC distance* from c_i to c_j is:

$$j(c_i, c_j) = |R_i|^{-1} \sum_{\gamma \in R_i} \mathsf{minjac}(\gamma, R_j) \qquad (6)$$

where R_i and R_j are the role sets of c_i and c_j, respectively.
□

2.3.3 Quality of a Role

We further use the metrics above to define a heuristic function that computes a score for a role γ. This function, which we call the *role score rs*, is defined as:

$$\mathsf{rs}(\gamma) = \alpha \cdot \mathsf{ho}(\gamma) + (1 - \alpha) \cdot \mathsf{minjac}(\gamma, R), \qquad (7)$$

where α is as defined in Equation 1 and R is the role set of c_{old} in Equation 1. This function will be leveraged to guide our role evolution algorithm (described in Section 3).

2.4 One-Class SVM

To evaluate the homogeneity of the resulting roles, we employ an outlier detection algorithm. The selection of this strategy is based on the hypothesis that the more homogeneous a role is, the smaller the number of outlying users it will contain. In this paper, we use a one-class support vector machine (SVM) [19] to detect outlying users for each role. SVMs have been reported as comparable, and often superior, to other anomaly detection methods in various settings [11], including intrusion detection [6].

One-class SVMs can be applied to learn a region that contains only the training set, which is expected to be typical data for a class. Any data point in a test set that falls out of the region will be predicted as an anomaly. Theoretically, the goal of SVM in this scenario is to find a hyperplane $\mathbf{w} \in F$ that separates the training set from the origin with the maximum margin. This can be formalized as an optimization problem as follows:

$$\min_{\mathbf{w} \in F, \xi \in \mathbb{R}^l, \rho \in \mathbb{R}} \frac{1}{2} \|\mathbf{w}\|^2 + \frac{1}{v \cdot l} \sum_i \xi_i - \rho, \qquad (8)$$
$$subject\ to\ (\mathbf{w} \cdot \Phi(\mathbf{x}_i)) \geq \rho - \xi_i, \xi_i \geq 0$$

where ξ_i are non-zero slack variables to be penalized in the objective function. When values for $\mathbf{w}$ and ρ can be found which solve the optimization function, the majority of the training set satisfies $\mathsf{sgn}(\mathbf{w} \cdot \Phi(\mathbf{x}_i)) \geq \rho$, while the regularization term $\|\mathbf{w}\|$ remains small. The parameter v determines the tradeoff between these two goals. With $\mathbf{w}$ and ρ, we have a decision function $f(\mathbf{x}) = \mathsf{sgn}(\mathbf{w} \cdot \Phi(\mathbf{x}) - \rho)$ to determine if an new instance $\mathbf{x}$ is anomalous.

In this work, we specifically use one-class SVMs with an RBF kernel, as defined in Equation 9:

$$K(\mathbf{x}_i, \mathbf{x}_j) = \mathsf{exp}(-g \cdot \|\mathbf{x}_i - \mathbf{x}_j\|^2) \qquad (9)$$

The parameters g in Equation 9 and v in Equation 8 are key factors that influence the performance of one-class SVMs. We utilize a grid search technique to find values for g and v that enable a robust SVM [10].

For evaluation, for each role r_l, we split the row vectors of a projection matrix into a training set and a test set. We perform gird search on the training set to obtain g and v, which are then applied to train and test a one-class SVM. The proportion of outlying users identified by the one-class SVM is applied to measure the homogeneity of the role.

3. ROLE EVOLUTION BY PERMISSION UTILIZATION

This section begins by formally defining the *Role Evolution By Permission Utilization* (REPU) problem.

Definition: [*REPU Problem*] Given an existing RBAC configuration $c = \langle U, P, R, URA, RPA \rangle$, a user-permission assignment UPA ($UPA = URA \otimes RPA$) and a user-permission invocation matrix $UPIM$, $REPU$ is to find a new RBAC configuration $c^* = \langle U, P, R^*, URA^*, RPA^* \rangle$ subject to $UPA = URA^* \otimes RPA^*$, such that the objective function $f(c^*) = \alpha \cdot h(c^*) + (1 - \alpha) \cdot j(c^*, c)$ is minimized. □

The role mining problem has been shown to be NP-complete [23]. The REPU problem is a variation on role mining and can be reduced to this problem, making it NP-complete as well. Thus, we propose a heuristic-based search strategy based on a two-phase process as defined below.

3.1 Algorithm Description

To address the REPU problem, we designed the *Data-Driven Role Evolution* (DDRE) algorithm. Here we provide a walkthrough of the process and refer the reader to Algorithm 1 for specific details. The two phases of the algorithm are: i) candidate role generation and ii) role assignment.

3.1.1 Candidate Role Generation

The first phase begins with a set of *unit roles UR*, such that there is one permission per role and no roles have the same permission (i.e., a one-to-one mapping of permissions and unit roles). Next, UR is copied to a candidate role set CR. The algorithm then iterates until a termination condition is satisfied. Each iteration begins by instantiating a set of new roles into an empty pool DP, which is based on a pairwise union for all roles in CR. For example, the union of $\{p_x\}$ and $\{p_y\}$ yields $\{p_x, p_y\}$.

The roles in DP are sorted by their quality scores (defined in Section 2.3.3), such that DP serves as a priority queue, where the best role is at the top. The algorithm then proceeds through the queue, by moving a role from the top of DP to CR and flipping the 1's in the user-permissions assignment UPA_{temp} that are covered by the role to 0's. This process continues until every element in UPA_{temp} is set to 0. The algorithm then reiterates.

3.1.2 Role Assignment

Once CR is stable or the max number of iterations is reached (i.e., the termination condition), the algorithm enters the second phase of role assignment, the details of which are in Algorithm 3. The goal of this phase is to ensure that each user is assigned to non-redundant roles. By default, any user whose permission set is a superset of one role will automatically obtain this role. This would result in redundancy and an increasing unnecessary complexity in the system. For example, consider a set of users assigned to roles $\gamma = \{p_1, p_2, p_3\}$ and $\mu = \{p_1, p_2\}$. The latter role μ is redundant because the affiliated users can accomplish their task using only the γ role. Thus μ could be removed for the sake of succinctness.

Algorithm 1 Data-Driven Role Evolution

Input: $c = \langle U, P, R, URA, RPA \rangle, UPIM, \alpha, maxTimes$
Output: $c^* = \langle U, P, R^*, URA^*, RPA^* \rangle$
1: $t \leftarrow 0, DP \leftarrow \varnothing, CR \leftarrow \varnothing, CR_{old} \leftarrow \varnothing, UR \leftarrow \varnothing, UPA = URA \otimes RPA, UPA_{temp} = UPA$
2: **for** each $p_i \in P$ **do**
3: $\quad UR \leftarrow UR \cup \{\{p_i\}\}$
4: **end for**
5: $CR \leftarrow UR$
6: **while** $|CR_{old} - CR| > 0$ && $t{+}{+} \leq maxTimes$ **do**
7: $\quad DP \leftarrow \varnothing$
8: $\quad$ **for** each $\mu_i \in CR$ **do**
9: $\quad\quad$ **for** each $\mu_j \in CR$ **do**
10: $\quad\quad\quad DP \leftarrow DP \cup \{\mu_i \cup \mu_j\}$
11: $\quad\quad$ **end for**
12: $\quad$ **end for**
13: $\quad CR_{old} \leftarrow CR, CR \leftarrow \varnothing$
14: $\quad$ Sort($DP, UPIM, c, \alpha$){Sort roles in DP according to their quality score. See Algorithm 2 for details.}
15: $\quad$ **for** each $\gamma_i \in DP$ **do**
16: $\quad\quad$ **if** every element in UPM_{temp} is 0 **then**
17: $\quad\quad\quad$ break
18: $\quad\quad$ **end if**
19: $\quad\quad$ **if** γ_i cannot cover any 1's in UPA_{temp} **then**
20: $\quad\quad\quad$ continue
21: $\quad\quad$ **end if**
22: $\quad\quad CR \leftarrow CR \cup \gamma_i$
23: $\quad\quad$ change all 1's in UPA_{temp} covered by γ_i to 0's
24: $\quad$ **end for**
25: **end while**
26: $\{R^*, URA^*\} = RoleAssignment(U, P, UPA, CR)$
27: Initialize a $p \times n$ Boolean matrix RPA^* with all elements equal to zero, where $p = |R^*|$ and $n = |P|$.
28: **for** each $\mu_i' \in R^*$ **do**
29: $\quad$ **for** each $p_j \in P$ **do**
30: $\quad\quad$ **if** $p_j \in \mu_i'$ **then**
31: $\quad\quad\quad RPA_{ij}^* = 1$
32: $\quad\quad$ **end if**
33: $\quad$ **end for**
34: **end for**
35: **return** $c^* = \langle U, P, R^*, URA^*, RPA^* \rangle$

Algorithm 2 Sort()

Input: $DP, UPIM, \alpha, c = \langle U, P, R, URA, RPA \rangle$
1: Initialize an array of real value, $score[]$, which has the same size as DP
2: **for** each $\gamma_i \in DP$ **do**
3: $\quad score[i] = rs(\gamma_i)$
4: **end for**
5: Sort DP in ascending order according to $score[]$
6: **return**

The problem of winnowing the system down to a minimal set of roles for each user is similar to the set cover problem: given a user who possesses a set of permissions $PMS_i = \{p_{i_1}, p_{i_2}, \ldots, p_{i_k}\}$ and a set of roles $ROLES_i = \{\gamma_1, \gamma_2, \ldots, \gamma_l\}$ whose elements are all subsets of PMS_i, identify the smallest number of roles in $ROLES_i$ whose union equals PMS_i. It has already been shown that this problem is NP-complete [8]. Given the complexity of the problem, we adopt an approximation algorithm [3] to resolve the prob-

---

Algorithm 3 RoleAssignment()

Input: U, P, UPA, CR
Output: URA, R
1: $R \leftarrow \varnothing, m = |U|$
2: **for** each $u_i \in U$ **do**
3: $\quad PMS_i \leftarrow \{p_j | \forall p_j \in P, UPA_{ij} = 1\}, ROLES_i \leftarrow \varnothing$
4: $\quad$ **while** $PMS_i \neq \varnothing$ **do**
5: $\quad\quad$ Select role μ_k from CR, such that $\mu_k \subseteq PMS_i$ and $|PMS_i \cap \mu_k|$ is maximized.
6: $\quad\quad PMS_i \leftarrow PMS_i - \mu_k, ROLES_i \leftarrow ROLES_i \cup \{\mu_k\}$
7: $\quad$ **end while**
8: $\quad R \leftarrow R \cup ROLES_i$
9: **end for**
10: Re-index the roles in R using integers 1 to $h = |R|$, such that $R = \{\mu_1', \mu_2', \ldots, \mu_h'\}$
11: Construct $m \times h$ Boolean matrix URA, such that if $\mu_j' \in ROLES_i$, $URA_{ij} = 1$, otherwise $URA_{ij} = 0$
12: **return** R, URA

---

lem, as shown in Algorithm 3. At each iteration, we select the role in $ROLES_i$ with the largest number of permissions in common with PMS_i. The role is added to R_i and the permissions which were in common with PMS_i are removed from further consideration. This procedure repeats until no elements exist in PMS_i.

Finally, roles in R_i are assigned to user i. After assigning roles for each user, we obtain a final role set R^* and a user-role assignment URA^*. Specifically, we generate a role-permission assignment RPA^* from the permission sets of the roles. Thus, a new RBAC configuration $c^* = \langle U, P, R^*, URA^*, RPA^* \rangle$ is returned.

3.2 An example

In this section, we use the RBAC configuration and $UPIM$ in Figure 2 with $\alpha = 1$ to illustrate how the DDRE algorithm works in detail.[3]

UPA and RPA indicate there are two roles and six users. The roles are represented by permission sets $\{p_1, p_2, p_3, p_4, p_5\}$ and $\{p_3, p_4, p_5, p_6, p_7\}$. For this example, we create a set of ideal roles as the optimal solution, from which we design a series of generative models to construct $UPIM$. This set contains three roles, which correspond to $\{p_1, p_2\}$, $\{p_3, p_4, p_5\}$ and $\{p_6, p_7\}$. The generative model for each of the roles follows a fixed distribution, which for this example is set to $\{0.2, 0.8\}$, $\{0.2, 0.5, 0.3\}$, and $\{0.7, 0.3\}$, respectively. This means, for instance, that for an arbitrary user u_k associated with the first role, $UPIM_{k1}:UPIM_{k2}$ is 1:4.

First, the algorithm initializes the system with a set of unit-roles: $\{\{p_1\}, \{p_2\}, \{p_3\}, \{p_4\}, \{p_5\}, \{p_6\}, \{p_7\}\}$. Next, the algorithm performs a pairwise combination of the unit-roles to derive a pool DP of the form $\{\{p_1, p_2\}, \{p_1, p_3\}, \ldots, \{p_6, p_7\}\}$. From this pool, four roles, $\{p_1, p_2\}$, $\{p_3, p_4\}$, $\{p_6, p_7\}$, and $\{p_4, p_5\}$, are selected for the next round of pairwise combination because they comprise the top four positions of the pool and are able to recover the UPA. When this set of roles is combined, it updates the pool to become $\{\{p_1, p_2\}, \{p_3, p_4\}, \{p_4, p_5\}, \{p_6, p_7\}, \{p_1, p_2, p_3, p_4\}, \{p_1, p_2, p_4, p_5\}, \{p_3, p_4, p_5\}, \{p_4, p_5, p_6, p_7\}\}$.

---

[3] $\alpha = 1$ implies the algorithm is completely biased to generate a set of roles with high homogeneity in user behavior (i.e., it ignores the structure of the original roles).

At this point, we select another four roles, $\{p_1, p_2\}$, $\{p_3, p_4\}$, $\{p_6, p_7\}$ and $\{p_3, p_4, p_5\}$, from the pool because they comprise the top four positions in the pool and are able to recover the UPA. Again, these roles are combined to update the pool to become $\{\{p_1, p_2\}, \{p_3, p_4\}, \{p_3, p_4, p_5\}, \{p_6, p_7\}, \{p_1, p_2, p_3, p_4\}, \{p_1, p_2, p_3, p_4, p_5\}, \{p_3, p_4, p_6, p_7\}, \{p_3, p_4, p_5, p_6, p_7\}\}$. At this point, roles in the top four positions of the pool, $\{p_1, p_2\}$, $\{p_3, p_4\}$, $\{p_6, p_7\}$ and $\{p_3, p_4, p_5\}$, are selected to constitute the candidate role set. Since the candidate role set is the same as the previous round, this phase of the DDRE algorithm terminates and returns this candidate role set.

Next, the roles $\{p_3, p_4\}$ are redundant in the presence of $\{p_3, p_4, p_5\}$, so they are discarded in the second phase.

Finally, the remaining three roles $\{p_1, p_2\}$, $\{p_3, p_4, p_5\}$, and $\{p_6, p_7\}$ constitute the role set in RBAC configuration as a solution, which are the same as the three ideal roles alluded to earlier.

4. EXPERIMENTS

We investigated the performance of the DDRE algorithm on both synthetic and real world datasets. In the process, we varied α to characterize how the resulting RBAC configuration changes. Additionally, we compared DDRE with several related role mining algorithms, including the minimal perturbation role mining algorithm [24] and role mining with latent Dirichlet allocation (LDA) [13]. We defer the description of these methods to the Related Work (Section 5).

Table 1: Statistics for the EMR access log.

	Users	Job Titles	Reasons	Accesses
Total #	8095	140	143	1,138,555

4.1 Description of Datasets

4.1.1 Electronic Medical Record Roles & Access Logs

The real world dataset was extracted from three consecutive months of access logs from the Cerner Corporation's PowerChart electronic medical record (EMR) system in use at Northwestern Memorial Hospital, which is an 854 bed primary teaching affiliate of Northwestern University. All clinicians retrieve clinical context and enter inpatient notes and orders using the system. Each entry of the log contains information about a distinct access made to the EMR, including user-id, patient-id, time, job title of the user, reason for the access, type of service, and location where the access transpired.

Table 1 depicts summary statistics for the access logs. Although the EMR is not based on RBAC, the reason is an option selected when a chart is accessed by the user during a patient's hospitalization and the options available are tied to the job title of the user. As a result, we believe it is reasonable to utilize the reasons as privileges and job titles as roles in the system. Table 2 shows how we acquire an RBAC configuration $c = \langle U, P, R, URA, RPA \rangle$ and a user-permission invocation matrix $UPIM$ from the access log.

4.1.2 Synthetic Roles & Access Logs

To allow for replication of our study and comparison to the EMR dataset, we created a synthetic dataset which consists of an RBAC configuration $c' = \langle U', P', R', URA', $

Table 2: A summary of how the RBAC configuration and $UPIM$ are derived from the EMR access logs.

Feature	Derivation Process
U	*The set of users in the access logs.*
R	*The set of job titles in the access logs.*
P	*The union of reason sets available to each job title in R.*
URA	$\lvert U \rvert \times \lvert R \rvert$ *Boolean matrix. If the ith user and j^{th} job title (role) co-occur in one entry of the access log, $URA_{ij} = 1$; otherwise $URA_{ij} = 0$.*
RPA	$\lvert R \rvert \times \lvert P \rvert$ *Boolean matrix. If the jth reason (permission) belongs to the reason set available to i^{th} job title (role), $RPA_{ij} = 1$; otherwise $RPA_{ij} = 0$.*
$UPIM$	$\lvert U \rvert \times \lvert P \rvert$ *real value matrix. If the ith user and j^{th} reason (permission) co-occur in the same entry of the access log t times, then $UPIM_{ij} = t$.*

$RPA' \rangle$ and a corresponding $UPIM$. As in the example in Section 3.2, there are several ideal roles, each of which has a corresponding probability distribution over its affiliated permissions.

To enable a clean analysis, there is no overlap in the permission sets of these roles. We merge the permission sets of several ideal roles to realize an *actual* role in the RBAC system. For each user under one actual role, we utilize the ideal roles hiding in the actual role to generate its corresponding vector in $UPIM$, where the numbers corresponding to one ideal role need to follow the probability distribution of this ideal role. For instance, we can merge two ideal roles $\{p_1, p_2, p_3\}$ and $\{p_4, p_5, p_6\}$ whose distributions are $\{0.2, 0.3, 0.5\}$ and $\{0.1, 0.7, 0.2\}$, respectively, to create an actual role $\{p_1, p_2, p_3, p_4, p_5, p_6\}$. The rates of permissions invoked by each user u_i assigned to this role need to be consistent with the distributions of both ideal roles, which means $UPIM_{i1} : UPIM_{i2} : UPIM_{i3} = 2:3:5$ and $UPIM_{i4} : UPIM_{i5} : UPIM_{i6} = 1:7:2$. The $UPIM$ matrix is constructed by performing this procedure for each user. A more detailed example is reported in the Appendix.

For this study, we created 10 ideal roles, and use 10 actual roles, which are derived by merging different sets of the ideal roles as R'. We synthesize 20 users per role (i.e., 200 users in total) as U'. For each actual role, the ideal roles used for merging are randomly selected from the 10 ideal roles. Since the actual roles are represented by permission sets, RPA' is derived accordingly. In addition, we derive P' by uniting the permission sets of all actual roles. Thus, a synthetic RBAC c' is successfully constructed.

4.2 Evaluation Measures

We use two measures to assess the quality of the resulting RBAC system.

RBAC Evolution Distance: This measure characterizes the distance between the old and new RBAC configurations. It directly corresponds to Equation 6.

Outlier Rate: This measure characterizes the homogeneity of users' behavior in the resulting roles. For this measure, we use the rate at which users are predicted to be outliers in the system. The outlier rate is computed as follows. For each role r_l, we perform outlier detection on the corresponding projection matrix M_{r_l} using one-class SVM.[4] To do so, the row vectors in M_{r_l} are split into three equally-sized partitions $\{part_1, part_2, part_3\}$. We pick one partition as the test set, and the remaining two partitions as training

---

[4] All SVM calculations were performed in *libsvm* [2].

and validation sets for a one-class SVM. After we obtain a one-class SVM model, we perform the outlier detection on the test set. All vectors classified as negatives are designated as outliers. This process is performed in three-fold cross-validation (i.e., three times with a different test set), so that each row vector in M_{r_l} is evaluated. The outlier rate of a role r_l is computed as:

$$or_l = \frac{\sum_{i=1}^{3}(\# \ of \ outliers \ in \ part_i)}{\# \ of \ row \ vectors \ in \ M_{r_l}} \quad (10)$$

Finally, the outliers from each role are consolidated to calculate the outlier rate for the entire RBAC system:

$$oor = \frac{\sum_i or_i \cdot n_i}{\sum_i n_i} \quad (11)$$

where n_i is the number of users who are members of role r_i.

Detecting the outlier rate is a more intuitive and straightforward way to measure the homogeneity of the entire RBAC system[5] because the two concepts are strongly related. As proof, Figure 3 shows the relationship for both the EMR and synthetic datasets, where each point is derived from the RBAC configuration from the DDRE algorithm over a range of α values. The correlation coefficient (r^2) for a linear regression was found to be 0.912 and 0.837 for the EMR and synthetic datasets, respectively. Thus, we conclude that the outlier rate is positively correlated with RBAC homogeneity and use it to measure the homogeneity of the system in the following evaluation.

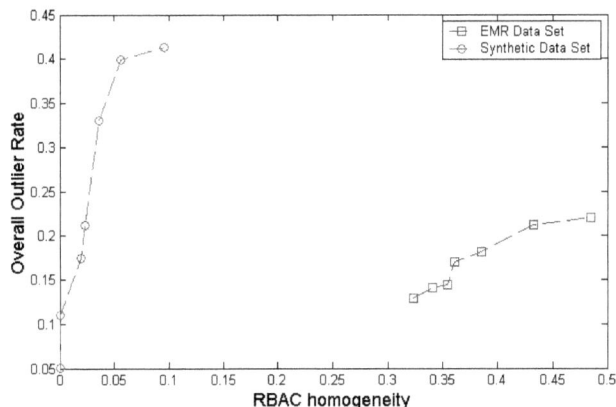

Figure 3: Relationship between RBAC homogeneity and outlier rate.

4.3 Results

4.3.1 Assessing the Tradeoff

All of the following experiments were run on an Intel Core i5 2.40GHz CPU with 4G memory and a Windows XP operating system. We ran the DDRE algorithm with a range of

---

[5]The RBAC homogeneity in Definition 3 could be replaced with the outlier rate. However, RBAC homogeneity has significantly lower time complexity ($O(mn)$, where m is the number of roles which ever exist in DP of Algorithm 1, n is the average number of users contained by each role) and can be computed in a feasible amount of time on a commodity server. By contrast, the outlier rate requires computation on the order of ($O(mn^2)$).

α values to assess its efficiency. Table 3 shows the time consumed by the algorithm on the EMR dataset. The longest time was 21.7 minutes, which shows the algorithm can terminate in a practical amount of time. Moreover, the runtime is directly correlated with α.

Next, we investigated how the RBAC configuration yielded by DDRE changes with α. Figure 4 summarizes this result, where the number near each point in the curves of DDRE corresponds to the value of α used to generate the corresponding RBAC configuration. In this figure, it can be seen that when α biases the system towards behavior, the overall outlier rate is low, whereas the distance between the old RBAC configuration and the resulting RBAC configuration is large. On the contrary, when α is biased towards the distance to old RBAC configuration, the overall outlier rate is high, while the distance between the two RBAC configurations is significantly smaller. In particular, we find that the outlier rate corresponding to $\alpha = 1$ is 41.1% and 87.7% lower than that corresponding to $\alpha = 0$ on the EMR and synthetic datasets, respectively. The Jaccard distance between the two RBAC configurations when $\alpha = 0$ is 90.9% and 100% lower than that corresponding to $\alpha = 1$ on the EMR and synthetic datasets, respectively. This observation indicates that we can obtain an almost identical RBAC configuration to the initial one when $\alpha = 0$. These results suggest that the DDRE algorithm is effective.

Table 3: Runtime of the DDRE algorithm.

α	1	0.97	0.93	0.9	0.8	0.7	0
Runtime(min)	21.7	15.5	12.7	12.5	10.4	7.3	6.4

We also note that the EMR dataset yields a much smaller range of outlier rates and Jaccard distances than the synthetic dataset. We hypothesized that this is because each actual role in the synthetic dataset is composed of more ideal roles than the actual roles in the EMR dataset. For instance, imagine there is an actual role composed of m ideal roles. When we compute the distance from one ideal role to the actual role, a larger m means the ideal role has permission set with a smaller size. This will result in a smaller numerator in Equation 4 and, thus, will yield a larger value for $j()$. Moreover, the ideal role exhibits a strong pattern as a single role, but the more ideal roles that aggregate into an actual role, the faster their patterns are diluted. This leads to a significant increase in outlier detection. By studying the original roles (actual roles) and the resulting roles (ideal roles) yielded by the DDRE algorithm with $\alpha = 1$, we find that each original role in the EMR dataset possesses 1.5 roles on average in the corresponding resulting role set. By contrast, each original role in the synthetic dataset possesses 5.4 roles on average in the corresponding resulting role set. We believe this finding validates our hypothesis.

Figure 4 also depicts the results of the minimal perturbation role mining (RM-MP) and role mining with LDA (RM-LDA) algorithms.[6] The number near each point of the RM-MP curve corresponds to the value of w that controls the balance between the number of roles generated and the *Roles_Roles Distance*, a set-based distance between new role set and old role set (D in the objective function in [24]). It can be seen that the curves for RM-MP have the same

---

[6]Following the strategy in [13], the number of topics (i.e.,roles) specified for the LDA is $\sqrt{|U|}$.

tendency as that generated through DDRE. This is an intuitive and expected finding. Consider, when w is biased towards the number of generated roles, the algorithm will prefer the roles with larger size to those that are closer to original roles. This can lead to low homogeneity and large distances to the original roles. In addition, we notice that RM-MP yields curves that are close to those from DDRE, however, DDRE has a broader range of solutions, which can be observed by observed at the points when α approaches the boundary cases of 0 and 1. This indicates DDRE can yield better results when α be biased toward either sole objective. The result of RM-LDA on the EMR dataset shows it yields an overall outlier rate that is comparable to the results of DDRE when biased towards permission utilization, however, the RBAC it generated is significantly different than the original RBAC. The result of RM-LDA on the synthetic dataset is in the neighboring region of that of DDRE, but it is easy to find a solution from the curve of DDRE that has both a lower RBAC distance and a lower outlier rate than RM-LDA.

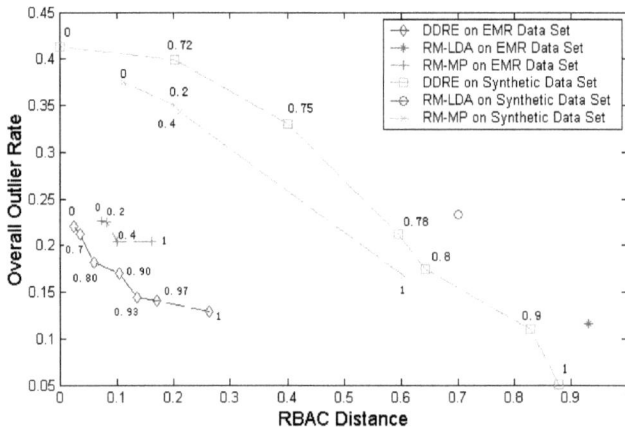

Figure 4: Summary of the tradeoff between the distance of old and new RBAC configurations (i.e., RBAC distance) and the rate of outlying behavior for the EMR and synthetic datasets.

4.3.2 Influence of SVM Training on Outliers

Next, we investigated how the results of one-class SVM are influenced with respect to the v parameter.[7] This experiment is performed to determine if there exist patterns in the EMR dataset or if our results are based on random effects. As mentioned earlier, v controls the tradeoff between the fraction of training instances falling into the learned region and the value of the regularization term. As v increases, less instances in the training set will fall into the learned region. So, if the entire dataset follows a pattern, the test set will be distributed in approximately the same region as the training set even though v is decreasing. Otherwise, due to the high diversity of the support vectors, the test set will likely be located in a different region.

To perform this portion of our analysis, we created two uncontrolled versions of *UPIM* for the two data sets used

---

[7]The paratmeter g is determined by the grid search method and is not investigated.

earlier by assigning a random value to $UPIM_{ij}$ that was originally $UPA_{ij} = 1$. The uncontrolled version of *UPIM* is used for simulating the access log without any pattern. We then employed one-class SVM to compute the accuracy (calculated by $1 - $ oor) for the RBAC configurations with the real and uncontrolled *UPIM* matrices for the EMR dataset (called EMR and EMR$_{UN}$) and synthetic dataset (called SYN and SYN$_{UN}$). It is expected that the accuracy on the uncontrolled dataset will decrease more quickly than the controlled dataset.

Table 4: Role prediction accuracy as a function of v.

	v =0.16	v=0.21	v=0.26	v=0.31	v=0.36
EMR$_{UN}$	79.48%	75.48%	71.08%	66.25%	61.93%
EMR	82.48%	77.35%	75.10%	71.51%	67.02%
SYN$_{UN}$	78.10%	72.00%	66.59%	60.75%	54.93%
SYN	77.18%	73.82%	68.73%	64.18%	58.91%

Table 4 shows the accuracy of one-class SVM with different v on the resulting RBAC configurations. Here it can be seen that the accuracy of SYN$_{UN}$ decreases by 29.67%, while the accuracy on SYN decreases by 23.67%. By performing a proportion test, the latter accuracy decrease rate is slower than the former one with 90% confidence. This observation confirms our suspicion. We further note that the accuracy on EMR$_{UN}$ decreases by 22.08%, while the accuracy on EMR decreases by 18.74%, and the difference between them is also proven statistically significant with 90% confidence by the proportion test, which suggests permission invocation patterns exist in the real EMR dataset.

4.3.3 Statistics of Generated Roles

Finally, Figures 5 and 6 provide summary statistics of the roles generated when DDRE is applied to the EMR dataset. In Figure 5, each circle (x, y) represents one role γ. x is calculated by minjac(γ, R) (see Equation 5), where R is the role set of the original RBAC, while y is the outlier rate (see Equation 10) detected for this role. From Figure 5, it can be seen there is a major difference between the distributions of roles yielded by the algorithm with α set to 1 and 0.

Moreover, we show the marginal distributions of minjac(γ, R) and the outlier rate under different α in Figure 6. The histogram in Figure 6(a) demonstrates that the roles generated by $\alpha = 1$ tend to have less outlying users than the roles generated by $\alpha = 0$. By contrast, the histogram in Figure 6(b) demonstrates that the roles generated by $\alpha = 0$ tend to be closer to the role set in the original RBAC than the roles generated by $\alpha = 1$. These observations further validate the effectiveness of the DDRE algorithm.

5. RELATED WORK

The concept of role engineering was first proposed by Coyne [5]. As mentioned earlier, the process of role engineering can be grossly categorized into top-down and bottom-up strategies. There have been various approaches proposed for top-down approaches (e.g., [20, 17, 15]), but given the time-consuming and costly nature of this approach, it has limited adoption in real settings [17].

Thus, over the past decade, there has been a growing interest in bottom-up approaches, which enables role engineering to be automated with significantly lower cost. Here, we highlight several approaches that are conceptually similar to our work in that they iteratively build larger permission sets

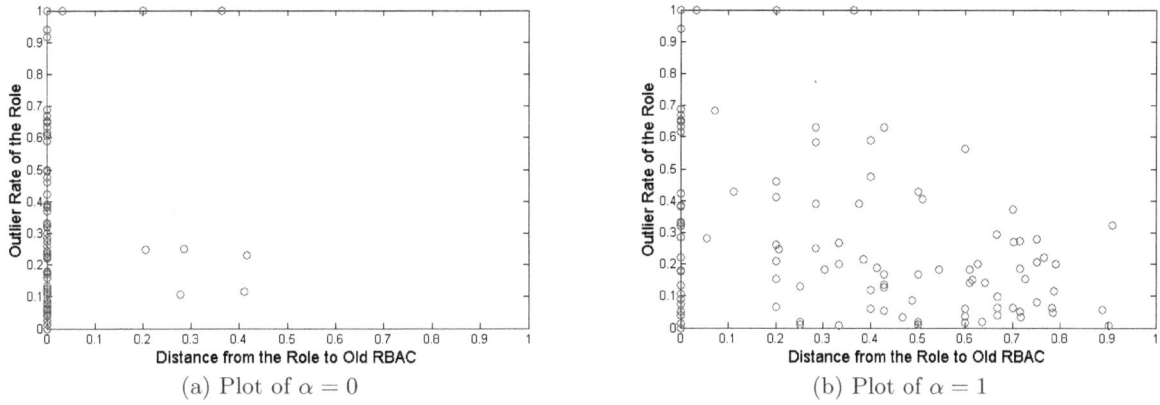

(a) Plot of $\alpha = 0$ (b) Plot of $\alpha = 1$

Figure 5: Plots of roles denoted by corresponding distance to old RBAC and outlier rate

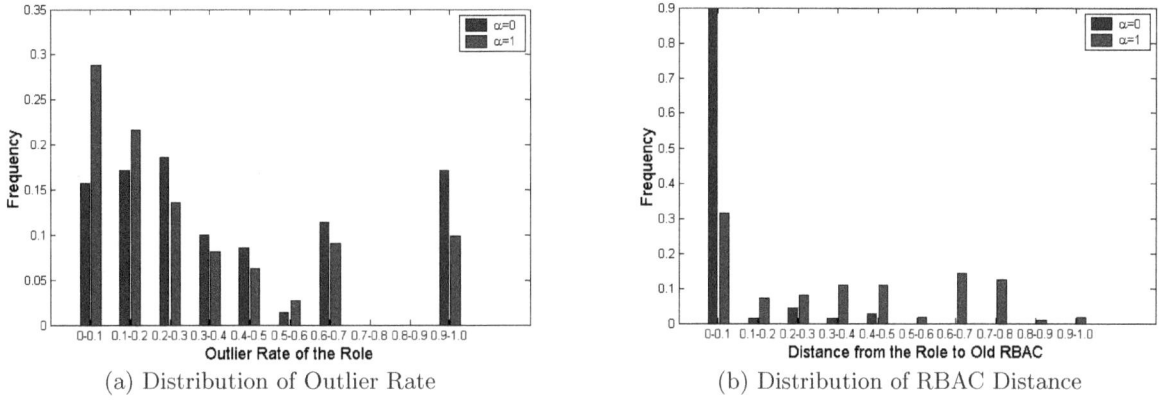

(a) Distribution of Outlier Rate   (b) Distribution of RBAC Distance

Figure 6: Frequency distributions of (a) outlier and (b) distance rates under $\alpha = 0$ and $\alpha = 1$

for roles. In [23], the goal is to minimize the number of roles and permissions per role. It was shown that this problem is computationally challenging and so a greedy heuristic-driven algorithm was proposed. The algorithm consists of two phases: in the first phase, *FastMiner* [22] produces a set of candidate roles by intersecting each pair of permission sets of users, and then, in the second phase, candidates with the greatest ability to cover the *UPA* (i.e., 1's in the matrix) are selected until coverage is complete. Alternatively, [18] proposes the ORCA algorithm, which generates roles by performing a hierarchical clustering on permission sets. In this process, the quality of a cluster (role) corresponds to the number of users associated with it. [26] use graphs to represent the relations among users, roles, and permissions, and then employs graph optimization to solve the role mining problem. The process begins with a set of possible roles, which is composed of the permission sets of all users. Next, pairs of roles are iteratively selected and are split or merged, to gain the largest improvement on the optimization measure of the resulting graph. While these strategies propose roles, they do not attempt to maximize homogeneity and minimize the distance to an existing set of roles. [4] proposes a role engineering method that leverages organizational information to generate a set of roles with clear business meaning. The method first partitions the data set

(user-permission assignment) according to certain appropriate business information (e.g. organization unit). Next, they adopt a divide-and-conquer approach that is to perform role mining on each subset. This approach may produce a RBAC configuration that is close to that built by administrators or experts due to the use of business information that is often used in top-down role engineering. However, like other role mining algorithms, it does not leverage information in access logs, such that roles with high homogeneity could not be searched.

There have been several approaches proposed which attempt to revise roles and leverage permission utilization patterns (which we empirically compared to in the previous section). [24] defines the minimal perturbation role mining problem, whose objective is to find a set of roles that has both small distance to the original roles and a small number of roles in total. The objective function is defined as $f(R) = w \cdot k + (1 - w) \cdot k \cdot D$, where k is the number of roles, D is the distance between old and new role sets, and w is a parameter used to control the balance between k and D. In this method, a role is constantly selected from the candidate role sets produced by *FastMiner* [22] according to its value on a heuristic function $f(r) = w \cdot a + (1 - w) \cdot a \cdot d$, where a is the remaining 1's in *UPA* covered by this role and d is the distance between this role and the original role set. The selection process terminates when UPA is covered by the selected roles. However, this work is limited in that it neither takes the users' behavior into consideration, nor does it measure the similarity of RBAC configurations. Rather, it only uses the similarity between two role sets. By contrast, [13] takes user behavior into consideration and proposes a simulated annealing approach to mine URA and RPA with the usage of privileges. This approach begins with a random initialization of URA and RPA, which is derived from the probability distribution of users over roles, and the probability distribution of roles over permissions calculated by the LDA model learned from the access log. It then iteratively decides if a new pair of URA and RPA matrices would be accepted to replace the old ones by a λ-distance (a measure of how well they explain the usage of permissions). For simplicity, the resulting URA and RPA does not necessarily have to be consistent with the original UPA. Thus, this work is significantly different than ours in that the resulting RBAC configuration is not necessarily subject to $UPA = URA \otimes RPA$.

6. DISCUSSION AND CONCLUSIONS

This paper proposed a novel role engineering algorithm that enables a controlled evolution of an RBAC configuration based on the utilization of permissions (as documented in access logs). We devised an objective function that balances an administrator's beliefs and actual permission utilization, and defined a role mining problem for finding an RBAC configuration that optimizes this objective. To solve this problem, we proposed a two-phase algorithm. In the first phase, a heuristic function related to the objective is applied to propose a set of candidate roles. In the second phase, each user is assigned roles in the candidate role set to minimize redundancy in role definitions. We then performed an empirical analysis with real and simulated datasets to show that our algorithm can generate appropriate RBAC configurations for various biases of the two competing goals of the objective function.

There are several limitations to our strategy, however, which we highlight to provide a roadmap for future work. First, our strategy is based on permission utilization patterns in an atemporal fashion. This is a simplification of the access logs and neglects that the order in which permissions are invoked may be correlated. Second, our approach is predicated on the hypothesis that there is only one pattern (in the form of a distribution of permission rates) associated with the underlying roles. Yet, it is possible there could be multiple patterns. We plan to extend our strategy to determine when such a situation arises and tease apart these patterns into distinct roles.

7. ACKNOWLEDGEMENTS

This research was supported by grants CCF-0424422 and CNS-0964063 from the National Science Foundation (NSF), R01-LM010207 from the National Institutes of Health (NIH), and HHS-90TR0003/01 from the Office of the National Coordinator for Health Information Technology at the Department of Health and Human Services (HHS). Its contents are solely the responsibility of the authors and do not necessarily represent the official views of the HHS, NIH, or NSF. The authors also thank Nathan Sisterson for supplying the dataset used in this study, Ian Molloy of IBM Research for discussing the specification of the parameters for the simulated annealing algorithm for LDA and Jaideep Vaidya of Rutgers University for discussing the implementation of FastMiner.

8. REFERENCES

[1] E. Bertino, A. Kamra, E. Terzi, and A. Vakali. Intrusion detection in RBAC-administered databases. In *Proceedings of the 21st ACSAC*, pages 170–182, 2003.

[2] C.-C. Chang and C.-J. Lin. LIBSVM: A library for support vector machines. *ACM Transactions on Intelligent Systems and Technology*, 2:27, 2011.

[3] V. Chvatal. A greedy heuristic for the set-covering problem. *Mathematics of Operations Research*, 4:233–235, 1979.

[4] A. Colantonio, R. D. Pietro, A. Ocello, and N. V. Verde. A new role mining framework to elicit business roles and to mitigate enterprise risk. *Decision Support Systems*, 50:715–731, 2011.

[5] E. J. Coyne. Role engineering. In *Proceedings of the 1st ACM Workshop on Role-Based Access Control*, 1995.

[6] E. Eskin, A. Arnold, M. Prerau, L. Portnoy, and S. Stolfo. A geometric framework for unsupervised anomaly detection: Detecting intrusions in unlabeled data. In *Proceedings of Applications of Data Mining in Computer Security*, pages 78–100. Kluwer, 2002.

[7] L. Freeman, A. Romney, and S. Freeman. Cognitive structure and informant accuracy. *American Anthropologist*, 89:310–325, 1987.

[8] M. R. Garey and D. S. Johnson. *Computers and Intractability; A Guide to the Theory of NP-Completeness*. W.H. Freeman and Company, New York, NY, 1990.

[9] T. H. Haveliwala, A. Gionis, D. Klein, and P. Indyk. Evaluating strategies for similarity search on the web. In *Proceedings of the 11th International Conference on the World Wide Web*, pages 432–442, 2002.

[10] C. W. Hsu, C. C. Chang, and C. J. Lin. A practical guide to support vector classification. Technical report, Dept. of Computer Science and Information Engineering, National Taiwan University, Taipei, Taiwan, 2003.

[11] L. M. Manevitz and M. Yousef. One-class SVMs for document classification. *The Journal of Machine Learning Research*, 2:139–154, 2002.

[12] S. Mehrotra, C. Butts, D. V. Kalashnikov, N. Venkatasubramanian, R. Rao, and et al. Project RESCUE: challenges in responding to the unexpected. In *Proceedings of SPIE*, volume 5304, pages 179–192, 2004.

[13] I. Molloy, Y. Park, and S. Chari. Generative models for access control policies: applications to role mining over logs with attribution. In *Proceedings of the 17th ACM Symposium on Access Control Models and Technologies*, pages 45–56, 2012.

[14] J. Park and J. Giorgano. Role-based profile analysis for scalable and accurate insider-anomaly detection. In *Proceedings of the 25th IEEE International Performance, Computing, and Communications Conference*, pages 470–476, 2006.

[15] H. Roeckle, G. Schimpf, and R. Weidinger. Process-oriented approach for role-finding to implement role-based security administration in a large industrial organization. In *Proceedings of the 5th ACM Workshop on Role-Based Access Control*, pages 103–110, 2000.

[16] R. Sandhu, E. Coyne, H. Feinstein, and C. Youman. Role-based access control models. *IEEE Computer*, 29:38–47, 1996.

[17] A. Schaad, J. Moffett, and J. Jacob. The role-based access control system of a european bank: a case study and discussion. In *Proceedings of the 6th ACM Symposium on Access Control Models and Technologies*, pages 3–9, 2001.

[18] J. Schlegelmilch and U. Steffens. Role mining with ORCA. In *Proceedings of the 10th ACM Symposium on Access Control Models and Technologies*, pages 168–176, 2005.

[19] B. Scholkopf, J. Platt, J. Shawe-Taylor, A. Smola, and R. Williamson. Estimating the support of a high-dimensional distribution. *Neural Computation*, 13(7):1443–1471, 2001.

[20] D. Shin, G. Ahn, S. Cho, and S. Jin. On modeling system-centric information for role engineering. In *Proceedings of the 8th ACM Symposium on Access Control Models and Technologies*, pages 169–178, 2003.

[21] M. Strembeck. Scenario-driven role engineering. *IEEE Security and Privacy Magazine*, 8:28–35, 2010.

[22] J. Vaidya and V. Atluri. Roleminer: mining roles using subset enumeration. In *Proceedings of the 13th ACM Conference on Computer and Communications Security*, pages 144–153, 2006.

[23] J. Vaidya, V. Atluri, and Q. Guo. The role mining problem: A formal perspective. *ACM Transactions on Information and System Security*, 13:27, 2010.

[24] J. Vaidya, V. Atluri, Q. Guo, and N. Adam. Migrating to optimal RBAC with minimal perturbation. In *Proceedings of the 13th ACM symposium on Access Control Models and Technologies*, pages 11–20, 2008.

[25] G. Wu, S. Osborn, and X. Jin. Database intrusion detection using role profiling with role hierarchy. In *Proceedings of the 6th VLDB Workshop on Secure Data Management*, pages 33–48, 2009.

[26] D. Zhang and T. E. K. Ramamohanarao. Role engineering using graph optimisation. In *Proceedings of the 10th ACM Symposium on Access Control Models and Technologies*, pages 139–144, 2007.

APPENDIX

A. SYNTHETIC DATA SET GENERATION

We use the ideal roles in example of Figure 2 in this section. These roles are $r_1 = \{p_1, p_2\}$, $r_2 = \{p_3, p_4, p_5\}$ and $r_3 = \{p_6, p_7\}$ and their probability distributions are $\{0.2, 0.8\}$, $\{0.2, 0.5, 0.3\}$, and $\{0.7, 0.3\}$, respectively. When synthesizing the actual role γ_i, we first select a random set of ideal roles (i.e., each role has a 0.5 probability of being selected). Next, we merge all roles in the set to form γ_i. For instance, r_1 and r_2 are selected, then $\gamma_i = \{p_1, p_2, p_6, p_7\}$.

Then, we simulate users for the γ_i. Let us use u_j as an example. The row vector corresponding to u_j in $UPIM$ needs to be consistent with the probability distributions associated with r_1 and r_3. When we try to assign values to $UPIM_{j1}$ and $UPIM_{j2}$ (which correspond to r_1), we need to ensure that $UPIM_{j1} : UPIM_{j2} = 1 : 4$. To finish the assignment, we first generate a random integer (e.g., 100), and repeat the following procedure 100 times: we add one to $UPIM_{j1}$ with probability 0.2 and if we fail to add to $UPIM_{j1}$, we add one to $UPIM_{j2}$. Similarly, we assign values to $UPIM_{j6}$ and $UPIM_{j7}$. For $UPIM_{jk}$ where $k = 3, 4, 5$, the value is set to 0 because the role associated with u_j does not contain p_k.

Ensuring Continuous Compliance Through Reconciling Policy With Usage

Suresh Chari, Ian Molloy, Youngja Park, Wilfried Teiken
IBM T.J. Watson Research
Yorktown Heights, NY
{schari,molloyim,young_park,wteiken}@us.ibm.com

ABSTRACT

Organizations rarely define formal security properties or policies for their access control systems, often choosing to *react* to changing needs. This paper addresses the problem of reconciling entitlement usage with configured policies for multiple objectives: policy optimization and risk mitigation. Policies should remain up-to-date, maintaining least privilege, and using unambiguous constructs that reduce administrative stress.

We describe a number of algorithms and heuristics, validated on real-world data, to address various aspects of reconciling access control policies with security audit logs. The first set of algorithms track and correlate which policy items enable which actions, using which we can identify over privileged entitlements, redundant policy items that may not be correctly revoked by administrators, rarely used entitlements, and overly permissive entitlements. They can help reduce administrative errors and general operational risk. The second body of work compares user groups defined in the policy with roles generated from the actual usage patterns, from which we derive quality and security measures for policy groups. Finally, we track policy changes through assignments and revocations and test precursors for such changes (e.g., a failed request before an assignment). Broadly speaking, this body of work presents different facets of continuous compliance to see if the enforced security policy and the resulting usage is consistent with a common intended security goal.

Categories and Subject Descriptors

D.4.6 [**Operating Systems**]: Security and Protection—*Access Controls*; K.6.4 [**Management of Computing and Information Systems**]: System Management—*Management audit*

General Terms

Experimentation, Management, Measurement, Security, Verification

Keywords

compliance, auditing, access control, log analysis

1. INTRODUCTION

Risk mitigation in organizations crucially depends on verifying *compliance*, i.e., verifying that, at any given time, the usage of permissions granted to users by the enforced security policy is consistent with the high level security goals that the organization is trying to meet. Bishop et al. [5] highlights a typical layering of security policies in organizations which complicates the task of establishing compliance.

In their terminology, the *Oracle* security policy corresponds to the high level security policy that the organization is trying to meet. This includes non-machine encodable parameters, such as hidden subject's *intent*. Not all *Oracle* policies are enforceable [19]. The *Feasible* policy level represents the subset that can be defined, encoded, and enforced. For example, the oracle policy can deny access for the purpose of memorizing information leaking it, while the feasible policy cannot. The *Feasible* policy must be evaluated by some policy decision point (PDP) and enforced by the policy enforcement point (PEP). The types of policies the PDP can evaluate depend on the access control model it uses, and the expressive power of models can vary, where some models are strictly more powerful than others, or two models may be incomparable [22]. To capture these subtleties, we introduce the *Model* policy layer as a subset of the *Feasible* policies that represents a partial order of enforceable policy models.

The *Configured* Policy is what is currently configured in the security framework (given the access control model) and the *Enforced* or *Used* policy is the policy that is actually being enforced and reflected in the usage of the permissions. Bishop et al. argue that a number of security vulnerabilities and breaches occur because of the mismatch in these policy layers.

The goal of this work is to define techniques to verify and minimize the distance between policy layers, i.e., the *Used* policy closely implements the *Oracle* policy by comparing the *Used* and *Model* layers directly. To verify *compliance*, our tools and techniques need to be combined with reasoning that the *Model* policy correctly approximates the intended high level policy. We can do this inductively as follows: initially we verify through automated analysis and reasoning that the *Configured* policy is consistent with the *Model* policy. After this, we continuously verify that:

- Usage is consistent with the *Configured* policy

- The policy constructs, e.g., the policy rules, relationships between subjects and permissions, and capabilities or ACLs, are consistently invoked by the user population to grant access, ensuring the constructs are still valid and required. Further, it is desirable that the frequency or patterns with which the constructs are used is consistent with the policy over time.

Together, these steps are the evidence that our methodology provides that the usage of permissions is *compliant* with the *Model* and hence the intended high level policy. In this paper, we will define the process of verifying continuous compliance as the process of verifying these two properties above at each instance in time.

Verifying the *continuous compliance* of usage to the intended policy has many distinct benefits to the security administrator. Foremost is the general reduction in operational risk due to the assurance that the usage is consistent with the intended policy. Security policy is verified to be fresh and up-to-date, accurately reflecting the current needs and behaviors of users and maintaining least privilege. A number of the analytic techniques we describe also reduce the ambiguity in policies by verifying that policy entries are not redundant or overly-expressive. This simplifies the administration of policies and reduces assignment errors made by administrators when assigning and revoking assignments.

The data we use for validation comes from a z/OS mainframe system where the security subsystem RACF (Resource Access Control Facility) sets security policy and controls access to resources. The policy model implemented by RACF is based on users, groups, subgroups, and assignment of permissions to these entities (see details in Section 3). In this paper, we are concerned primarily with dataset resources which correspond loosely to files and directories. The techniques we develop for these will be fairly generic and apply to many other systems where there is a natural hierarchy in the resources. We describe the following analytic models and techniques:

- *Policy analysis and analytics* We analyze policy entries to identify redundant assignments[1] and track policy changes such as revocations and assignments. The analytics then identify potential assignment and revocation errors in policies throughout their lifecycle.

- *Correlation of policy with logs* These analytics correlate the permission usage logs with the *Configured* policy, allowing us to directly measure and reduce violations of least privilege.

- *Correlating implicit and explicit groups and roles* Natural profile usage creates patterns that define common user roles and tasks. We use generative models [15] to correlate mined roles with policy groups. This measures group definitions for relevance and potentially meaning to administrators, at which point changes can be suggested and the risk of administrative errors reduced. If initially stabilized, this key analytic establishes the inductive step of whether the usage reflects the high level goals.

- *Tracking policy changes from logs* We introduce analytics to track changes to the *Configured* policies from the usage logs. Changed requests, or changes in logged policy rules, implicitly indicate policy changes and can be precursors for future changes. This is important when the granularity of policy changes is coarse, e.g., daily. By analyzing the types of changes (e.g., changes to profiles versus revoked profiles) and the net result (e.g., revoked access versus maintaining access to resources), we can detect potential errors.

For this work, we omit analysis that is specific to z/OS and RACF, and focus on policy and log analysis that we believe are applicable to a wide variety of platforms. We will discuss the generality of our analytics in more detail in Section 7. We present a number of tools and techniques that accomplish concrete tasks in policy administration which we believe is applicable across a wide range of data sets. Our work is the first to address the notion of automated tools for verifying *continuous compliance* of usage of permissions to the intended high level policy. We have validated these analytic models on about a years worth of usage data on the z/OS mainframe system and about a month's worth of daily record of the policy that is configured on this system. Our results yield good results on this data set and can identify when the usage drifts from the *Configured* policy (and the intended policy). Our measurement based approach is in contrast to other approaches which rely on formally proving that the *Configured* policy satisfies desirable properties.

2. PROBLEM SCOPE AND APPROACH

In this section, we outline our approach for ensuring compliance and provide metrics to measure how much the usage patterns of a user population (the subjects the policy applies to) have deviated from policy. While it is impossible for us to definitively know the intent of the subjects or policy administrators and to prove compliance (see Bishop et al. [5]), we believe these definitions and measures are useful for indicating when policy and usage are inconsistent.

When an access control policy does not adequately reflect the needs of the users, the organization is at risk. In this work, we are concerned with two types of risk to an organization: *operational* and *administrative*.

DEFINITION 1. Operational risk *is an adverse outcome or harm that is the result of failed processes or other activity. Such risks could be the result of misuse or abuse of privileges, intentional or otherwise.*

For example, an error in a program may misuse a user's privileges to cause harm that was not intended[2]. A standard way to limit operational risk is to enforce the principle of least privilege. In the policy hierarchy, this is a discrepancy between the configured layer with the intent and environment.

Our analysis identifies unused or rarely used privileges, overly permissive privileges, and over privileged group definitions as examples of operational risk. In many scenarios, operational risk may be the result of administrative errors, which, we argue, represents a separate category of risk.

DEFINITION 2. Administrative risk *is an adverse outcome or harm caused by a discrepancy between an administrator's intention and the policy specification. Such risk*

---

[1]Two or more assignments granting an overlapping set of rights.

[2]For example, a confused deputy.

may be the result of a misinterpretation or an oversight of the policy language or policy model.

Administrative risk occurs when the changes to the model layer are inconsistent with the feasible or intended policy layers. For example, imagine there are two policy rules that grant a user access to a resource, and an administrator revokes only one. The user still retains access, though the administrator believes the access has been revoked. Other types of errors could be misinterpreting group semantics, e.g., inverting the semantics of subgroup-supergroup relationships. We use these notions of risk to define compliance:

DEFINITION 3. *We consider resource usage and policy are in* compliance *of each other if the usage indicates that the policy is enforcing least privilege, and policy changes are unambiguous.*

While this is a very high-level definition, it is difficult to produce a more concrete definition without an oracle into the intent of the users and administrators. To address this gap, we define several concrete measures intended to "get to the heart" of the notion of risk and compliance.

2.1 Approach

Prior work on compliance verification has focused on formally proving that the security policy satisfies certain desirable properties [10], chosen to reflect the intent of the high level security policy. In contrast, our approach is to effectively measure the usage of the permissions granted to users to verify that the policy is enforcing the notion of least privilege. We believe that our approach is significantly easier to adopt than the formalism-based approaches which often require complex proofs every time the policy is changed even slightly. On the other hand, a measurement-based approach needs to ensure that we are comprehensively measuring indicators for compliance, and there is no formal proof that this is indeed the case. This section outlines the broad contours of our approach.

We use a few conventions throughout the paper. When referring to a policy, we use the term *group* for a set of users and permissions and reserve the term *role* for latent constructs extracted from usage logs. The term *policy profile* refers to a specific item, rule, construct, entitlement, or permission in the security policy which assigns a set of resources to a user/group.

We monitor the security policy and usage to ensure the following:

- **Identifying redundant policy profiles**: Through multiple policy provisioning actions (e.g., multiple group assignments), users may be authorized to the same set of resources through multiple profiles. When all resources identified by a profile are also identified by another profile assigned to the same users or groups, the profile is redundant and can be removed. This is especially useful when we consider revocations. To revoke correctly, we must remove all profiles which cover the revoked permission, and redundant profiles could result in the user still retaining these privileges.

- **Eliminating unused profiles**: This is a simple analytic aimed at ensuring that there are no authorizations granted in the policy but not used for a while.

Unused profiles generate incremental operational risk and, in most cases, reflect permissions that are not revoked. While there are permissions *only* used occasionally and, thus, will be unused for long periods of time, we err on the side of caution. Of course, we can adapt the analytic based on feedback and adapt to seasonal usage.

- **Detecting too generic policy profiles**: In most systems, a single policy profile authorizes multiple resources through the use of wildcards or inheritance. Based on usage over some time period, we can measure if there are policy profiles whose authorizations are too general. Profiles which are too generic clearly violate the definition of least privilege.

- **Reconciling latent roles in usage with policy**: Recently Molloy et al. [15] introduce the notion of generative models of roles which reflect the way in permissions are used by users. The roles uncovered by these algorithms reflect definitions that match the usage. Our key analytic to measure compliance is to compare groups defined in the policy with the roles uncovered from usage. This detects if the policy group definitions are still relevant. Assuming that we start with a policy in which all groups are relevant and match high level intent, this analytic measures if the usage continues to match the groups (and intent). From the roles mined from usage, we measure the following:

  1. For each group in the policy, we measure if there is a corresponding mined role, i.e., the role covering the same permissions. In reality, we measure if the policy group is statistically close to the mined roles.

  2. For groups which don't match roles, we determine if these cover some combination of the roles defined by usage. This uncovers groups in policies defined for convenience as combinations of other groups.

  3. We compare user-group assignments in the policy with the user-role assignments identified in the mined models to measure if the groups are still being authorized to the right set of users.

This group of analytics measures the continued relevance of the group definitions.

- **Discovering over-provisioned groups**: This measures, from the usage logs, if the policy assigns too many profiles to groups, i.e., many permissions assigned to groups are not used.

While we can never know the true intent of the policy designer, we believe our approach allows us to narrow down a policy to enable just the actions that are necessary, enforcing least privilege and reducing ambiguity in policy to reduce administrative risk. Many of these techniques seek to identify profiles that go unused or underutilized and narrow their scope to clearly converge on a least-privileged policy. Reducing policy redundancies limits the number of policy profiles an administrator must reason about to make policy change. This clearly reduces their cognitive load, cutting the time required to make decisions and the complexities of policy evaluation order, precedence, etc., that impact proper understanding of policy items [12]. Finally, by matching groups with roles, we gain confidence that the group structures still define semantically meaningful constructs.

2.2 Definitions

We use the following definitions in the paper.

DEFINITION 4. *A policy profile is α-consistent with usage, if α percentage of the total granted authorizations have been used within a given time window. We may write (α, t, t')-consistent to make the time window $[t, t']$ explicit.*

A policy profile may be an individual permission that grants access to multiple resources (for example, granting access to a database that grants access to the individual tables and columns), or a group permission that aggregate multiple individual permissions.

DEFINITION 5. *A profile is* unused *in the time window $[t, t']$, if no user attempts to perform an action that requires evaluating the profile during the time period $[t, t']$.*

Note that an unused profile may be applicable to a request made in $[t, t']$, but there exists a more specific profile that is evaluated instead.

DEFINITION 6. *A profile is α-generic, if α percentage of the resources it protects are never accessed by a user. One might say a profile is* too generic *if α exceeds a threshold ϵ.*

DEFINITION 7. *A group is β-over privileged, if it contains profiles not used by more than β percentage of the group members.*

DEFINITION 8. *A profile p is* applicable *to a request r, if $p(r)$ returns a decision.*

DEFINITION 9. *Given a policy P and a profile item p, we define that an administrative revocation has* ambiguous intent *if for all requests r that p is applicable to, $p(r) \equiv P(r) \equiv P \setminus \{p\}(r)$, and similarly* redundant *for an assignment $p(r) \equiv P(r) \equiv P \cup \{p\}(r)$.*

3. DATA FOR ANALYSIS

We have extensively validated our proposed analytics and present results taken from a z/OS sysplex. z/OS is a modern mainframe operating system that supports legacy functionality with modern UNIX certification. z/OS contains a wide range of security services, including firewalls, open cryptographic plug-ins, PKI services, etc. In this work, we will focus on the Resource Access Control Facility (RACF) security subsystem, which manages users, groups, and other authorizations, and the System Management Facility (SMF) which logs security sensitive events for later auditing.

We provide a *very* brief overview of key RACF details necessary to understand our analysis, and how our analytics may be applied to other systems. While some of the presented analytics exploit specifics of the RACF systems, broadly, all the analytics and the underlying models will generalize to other systems, especially those where the resources can be organized into a hierarchy.

While z/OS supports a wide variety of access control models, including multilevel security and digital certificates, they are not used on our sample system, and we focus on the more traditional user and group based security policies. RACF manages the access control policy through what are known as *profiles*. A profile can be assigned at the user, group, or system level (similar to user, group, and other in Unix systems), and is used to protect any resource, such as datasets, terminals, or commands. There are two types of profiles, *discrete* and *generic*. A discrete profile protects a single resource, while a generic profile can protect one or more resources, including resources not yet created.

A dataset in z/OS is represented as a period-delimited path. Discrete profiles explicitly reference the full dataset name, e.g., `A.B.C.DATA`, while generic profiles can leverage the following wildcards:

- `%` : a single character, e.g., `A.B.C.%ATA` matches the above

- `*` : more than one character, but not the period, e.g., `A.B.C.*` matches the above, but `A.B.*` does not

- `**` : more than one character including the period, e.g., `A.B.**` matches the above

In all instances, the high-level qualifiers cannot contain wildcards, i.e., `**.DATA` is not valid.

While the nuances of these profiles may be specific to z/OS, assigning users to resources at multiple levels is common in many systems. For example, in a DBMS, a user may be assigned privileges to the entire database (the MySQL privilege `ALL`), a specific table, column, or even row (by defining view). Many operating systems have privileged user accounts such as `root`, and groups such as `wheel`, that are granted additional privileges. Profiles can be assigned directly to users, to groups, or to the system (the profile `**`).

Audit logs on z/OS are handled by the SMF system. The Security Server writes Type 80 SMF records for security sensitive operations, including authorized and unauthorized access attempts to RACF-protected resources. The information contained in each SMF 80 record depends on the type (the user action), but, in general, contains information necessary to perform auditing, including timestamp, user and group identification, resource and profile accessed. For more information on z/OS, see IBM's documentation [1–3]. One unique feature of RACF is that if an action is authorized by multiple profiles, the log records which specific profile was actually used to authorize. We use this property in our analysis but note that they can be generalized to other systems where this information is not available.

In this work, due to space limitations, we will focus on a user's access to datasets. We have collected SMF records for over one year (currently, 420+ days), and have daily snapshots of the RACF policy for the last 40+ days.

3.1 Characteristics of z/OS RACF Data

This section presents statistics of the dataset and its characteristics which are then be explored in later sections.

User and Group Membership

As mentioned, RACF security policies are based on profiles applied to users and groups. Further, RACF allows for the definition of a group hierarchy to reduce the complexity of the policy. The groups belonging to the terminal nodes in the group hierarchy can be assigned users (members). Table 1 describes basic statistics about the number of users,

Number of users	9,925
Number of groups	1,536
Number of groups with user assignment	307
Min. number of members	1
Max. number of members	5,001
Mean number of members	36.7
Median number of members	2

Table 1: Statistics of User-Group Membership. Only about 20% of the groups have assigned members, and the number of members in a group is relatively small (mean = 36.7 and median = 2).

Avg. number of paths per user to the root node	1.14
Avg. depth of user-group hierarchy	3.02
Maximum depth	9

Table 2: Statistics of the Group Hierarchy

groups and user-group assignments, and Table 2 shows statistical properties of the group hierarchy.

Profile Hierarchy

z/OS profiles can be either discrete or generic with wildcard symbols %, *, and **. We can define a natural hierarchy on profiles by saying that a profile p_1 "belongs to" profile p_2, if the profile p_2 is more general than p_1. For instance, a discrete profile A.B.C belongs to a more generic profile A.B.% which belongs to A.B.*, etc., resulting in a hierarchical relationship (A.B.C $\to$ A.B.% $\to$ A.B.*). Note that a profile can belong to multiple parents, and the profiles can form a lattice and are not constrained to a tree. For instance, A.B.% belongs to both A.B.* and A.%.%, but A.B.* $\not\to$ A.%.% and A.%.% $\not\to$ A.B.*.

Table 3 describes the hierarchy structure of the z/OS dataset profiles. We note that most profiles (92%) appear independently (i.e., singletons), and only 176 profiles have hierarchical relationships with other profiles.

Number of total unique profiles	2,674
Number of singletons[1]	2,455
Number of terminal nodes[2]	177
Number of root nodes	36
Number of intermediate nodes	6

Table 3: Statistics of the z/OS dataset profile hierarchy. (1) Singletons denote the profiles with no sub-profiles nor super-profiles. (2) Terminal nodes specify the most specific profiles.

Profile Assignment

Users can be assigned profiles directly or through the groups they belong to. Figure 1 shows the histogram of user profile assignment, i.e., how many profiles are assigned to each user. In our test system, about half of the users (53%) are assigned only one profile, while most of the remaining users are assigned around 500 different profiles. The average user is assigned about 217 policies. Another interesting characteristic of our policy is that about 96% of the assigned profiles are group profiles, i.e., assigned to a group as opposed to individual users.

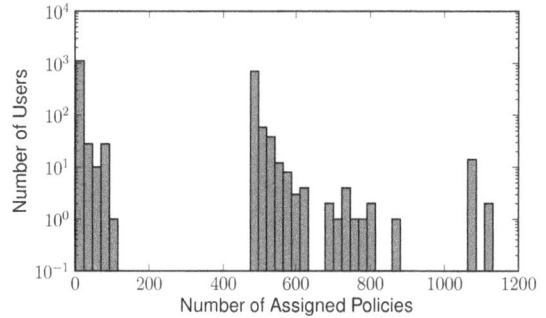

Figure 1: Histogram of User Profile Assignment

4. POLICY ANALYTICS

This section describes analytics aimed at validating the *Configured Policy* and are designed to uncover inconsistent or non-optimal profiles in the policy and policy profiles which are redundant in that the authorizations in these profiles are covered by other profiles. These analytics can be used to eliminate policy errors and over-provisioning, and ensure the policy is more manageable, all of which collectively reduces the operational risk discussed in Definition 1.

4.1 Identifying Redundant Assignments

Redundant profile authorities occur when a user is assigned two profiles where one profile subsumes the other, making the more specific authority redundant. We define a profile subsumption relation as in the following.

DEFINITION 10. *A profile p_1 subsumes profile p_2 if p_1 appears in a path from the root to p_2 in the policy hierarchy.*

For instance, profile C.*.** subsumes C.D.E.*.**, and V.** subsume V.*.F*.** respectively. In these examples, C.D.E.*.** and V.*.F*.** are redundant policies, as all permissions the two profiles authorize can be granted by their subsuming profiles. These redundant profiles are unnecessary and only increase the complexity and maintenance burden of the policy (Definition 2). Further, having redundant policy profiles can lead to errors when assignments are removed. When a permission assignment is removed from a user, all subsumed policies should be evaluated and the administrator notified of possible omissions.

To detect redundant profile assignments, we collect all assigned entitlements for a user, and check if there are any two entitles in which one subsumes the other. Profile subsumption relationship can be efficiently detected using the policy hierarchy described in Section 3.1, and, thus, this analytic can be applied to any policy domain where the resources are hierarchically organized and policy is inherited.

Table 4 summarizes the results of profile redundancy analysis. In our policy data, more than 45% of the dataset users are assigned redundant profiles. Further, we note that users with redundant entitlements tend to be more entitled (482 entitlements on average) than users with no redundant entitlements (1.8 entitlements on average).

Figure 2 depicts a summary of the redundancy rate of the users with redundant entitlements, which ranges from 1% to 69%. While the rate for most users is below 10%, 28 users have higher than 50% redundancy rate.

	w/ Redundancy	w/o Redundancy
Number of users	903 (44.7%)	1,116 (55.3%)
Avg. entitlements	482.2	1.8
Med. entitlements	487	1
Max. entitlements	1,130	46

Table 4: Comparison of number of entitlements owned by users with and without redundancies.

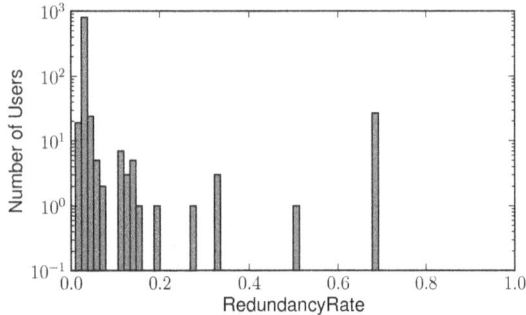

Figure 2: The ratio of redundant entitlements for users with redundant entitlements

As we can see, a high fraction of users are assigned with redundant entitlements, and, the redundancy rate is quite high. This clearly indicates that security administrators may not perform redundancy checks when a user is assigned multiple entitlements, since manual verification of entitlement redundancy is infeasible given the number of entitlements and users. We describe other analytics in this paper where we correlate a user's configured policy with a user's actual access patterns, and identify which profiles, among the redundant profiles, control resources that the user actually uses the most. Combined with that analytic, we can generate an optimal set of profiles for the user without redundant profile assignments.

4.2 Tracking Policy Changes

User entitlements change over time, as new entitlements can be assigned or existing entitlements get revoked. In this section, we introduce the analytics to monitor how policy assignments change over time. In particular, we address the following two questions.

- Are users mostly granted new entitlements, or are policy assignments often revoked?

- When a policy assignment is revoked, are all the redundant policies also revoked?

The failure in the latter case indicates incomplete revocations. The policy hierarchy (Section 3.1) enables automatic identification of incomplete revocations in a straightforward manner. When a profile is removed for a user, we retrieve all the subsuming policies from the hierarchy, and check if they are still authorized for the user.

We measured these policy changes with two sets of policies – a set over a short time period and the other over a longer time period. The short term policy set consist of 35 snapshots of the z/OS policies over 35 days, and the long term policy set include two snapshots of the polices which

	Short Term	Long Term
Num. of added users	2	64
Num. of removed users	0	298
Num. of users with new entitlements	12	247
Total num. of new entitlements	52	7,962
Num. of users with revoked policies	0	1,144
Total num. of revoked policies	0	4,739
Num. of incomplete revocation	0	1

Table 5: Policy changes over time

are about one year apart. Table 5 summarizes the changes in the two policy sets.

As we can see in the Table, policy revocations do not occur in a short time period, as expected, but do occur often in a long time period. Further, we detected one incomplete revocation from the second policy set. Policy W.G.H was revoked for a user, but the user was still granted with W.*.**.

4.3 Inferring Policy Changes from Logs

While an analysis of the policy alone can indicate when policy changes are made, access control logs can provide subtleties not present in the policy change logs. For example, if a policy rule changes, how does that impact the actual usage of the users? In this section we search for administrative actions that are ambiguous and redundant as defined in Def. 9.

We track access control decisions to datasets across time to detect changes in the policy and measure how the changes may impact the end users. Later, we will extend this analysis to use allowed or denied user actions as a precursor to policy changes. This analysis will allow us to test the practice of Saltzer and Schroeder's principle of least privilege [18]. Saltzer and Schroeder argue that a least privileged user, combined with fail-safe defaults, e.g., default deny, lead to increased security. In such a policy, an error would be quickly detected and corrected when a user was denied access, while an incorrect allow may take time to discover.

To accomplish this, we analyze the SMF records to produce a temporally ordered list of user requests and note several key details. First, we note the decision, e.g., SUCCESS or INSAUTH (insufficient authorization), which indicates when a privilege was allowed or denied. Any change in the decision correlates with a grant or revoke operation. Next, we note the RACF profile used to handle the request[3], even when the access control decision does not change. Because RACF uses (and records) the most specific profile[4], we can make inference on the types of policy changes that occurred. When a more specific profile is used (e.g., for an allow), one can argue the administrator is reaffirming the user's access to those resources (albeit including a potentially *redundant* assignment), while a more generic profile indicates the user's profile was revoked. If the decision does not change, then the administrative intent was *ambiguous*.

After analyzing over 128+M log lines of dataset access requests, we find a relatively small number of requests whose decisions change over time. In total we observed twenty requests with changed decisions: sixteen of the requests represent new profiles assigned to users, while four were re-

---

[3] As noted the SMF records contain the policy profile which authorized the action

[4] The least general, or discrete, profile that matches the request.

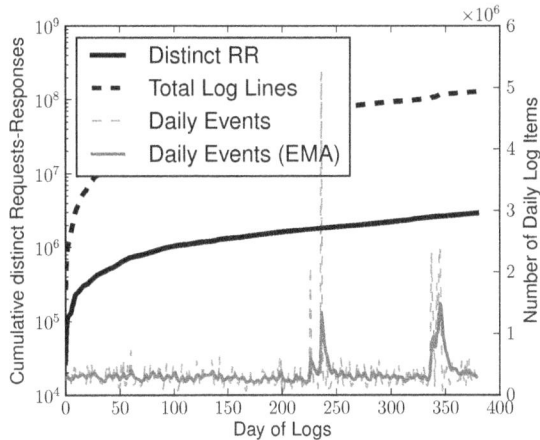

Figure 3: Cumulative number of distinct request-responses from the SMF records and the number of SMF ACCESS records per day.

	S→S	W→S	W→I	I→I	S→I
More Specific	1	8	0	1	0
More General	0	0	4	5	4

Table 6: Profile changes and decisions to and from: success(S); warning(W); and insufficient authorization(I). Note, a more general change represents a revocation, and a more specific is an assignment.

vocations. All four revocations were for the same profile and access to the same dataset. Users were revoked the I.A.J.* profile granting READ access, and the I.A.*.* profile assigned to the users did not grant READ access.

Next we analyze any requests where the most specific profile recorded in the SMF logs changes. There are twenty-three such instances (minus the above four revocations). We summarize our results in Table 6. In total, 10 changes were to more specific profiles, while 13 were to more general. Next, we note that, of the nine changes that resulted in the access control decision remaining SUCCESS, all were changes to more specific profiles, indicating an explicit decision to grant the privileges. Because all revocations result in IN-SAUTH, we do not find any ambiguous policy changes. We do find two redundant assignments, and eight that remove a warning, and could also be considered redundant (the prior request returned a warning, but access was still granted).

Finally, we test a hypothesis that access control decisions in the SMF records may not change because the resources are short lived, temporary, or the users only access them a small number of times over a short duration. For each request, decision, and profile tuple, we note that first and last timestamp seen for a contiguous block. For example, if a decisions switches from INSAUTH, to SUCCESS, and back to INSAUTH, we will have three disjoint time periods. Next, we plot the length of the lifespan of the requests, last time minus first time, in Figure 4 as a series of three histograms. On the top, we plot the entire range, while, in the remaining plots, we limit to resources active for at most one day, and five minutes. What we can clearly observe is most resources are active for a very short time period, fewer than

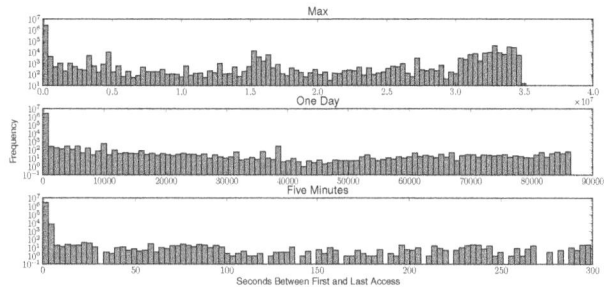

Figure 4: Lifespan of a dataset

ten seconds. We also observe there is an increase in the long tail distribution of around 400 days, the total duration of the data collected. This indicates there are two types of datasets and requests: those to temporary files, and those to long term datasets.

5. CORRELATING USAGE AND POLICY

While Section 4 discussed various analytics which analyzed policies *statically*, in this section, we propose analytics for dynamically monitoring the use of the policy, and how policy elements are used to authorize various actions. These analytics provide insights on how policies are actually being used, if the use conforms to the goal of the policy, and if the policy is optimal to meet the users' requirements and the security goal.

5.1 Policy Usage Statistics

The first analytic is to simply count which policy profiles are relevant, i.e., actually authorize specific actions. We correlated our RACF policy with 14.2 million access logs over 43 day period. The characteristics of the policy is shown in Table 3, and the statistics of the policy usage is shown in Table 7. The analysis shows that only a small portion (22.4%) of polices are being used, and, surprisingly, the usage rates of the intermediate node policies and the root node policies (i.e., not the most specific profiles) are higher than terminal node policies and singleton nodes (i.e., most specific profiles). The overall percentage of unused profiles during the time period is 78% (Definition 5).

	Num. Used Policies	Usage Rate
Total number	599	22.4%
Singletons	511	20.8%
Terminal nodes	70	39.5%
Root nodes	13	36%
Intermediate nodes	5	83.3%

Table 7: The usage statistics of z/OS dataset policy by correlating the policy with 14 million access logs.

5.2 Over-privileged Users

A policy profile is considered to be an over-assignment for a user if the user never or rarely uses the profile, and a user is considered an over-privileged user if the user owns many over-assignments. It is infeasible for the security administrators to predict possible over-assignments beforehand, and, thus, there can be a large number of unintended over-privileged users, resulting in a suboptimal policy.

Over-privileged users can be discovered by correlating access logs and the policy, and, here, we report the result of the monitoring user policy usages in the 43 days of access logs. Surprisingly, 93% of all the users accessed none of their assigned policies during the time period, and 6% of the users used only half of their assigned policies. This result shows that 99% of users did not actually use more than half of the assigned profiles during the time period. This result needs to be confirmed with a longer period of logs to draw a conclusive insight. However, it illustrates that a large number of over-privileged users can exist.

5.3 Overly Permissive Entitlements

Another analytic we have explored is that of an overly permissive policy assignment. Such assignments can occur in two ways. The first case is through overly permissive groups. Consider the permissions assigned to a group that are actually used by very few users. These are overly permissive groups, and the policies assigned to the group becomes overly permissive assignments to other users in the group.

The second case arises through overly generic profiles. Specifying access control policy at each individual resource level makes the size of the policy unmanageably large. Thus, most of the policies are represented as generic profiles using wildcard symbols such as % and * to cover multiple resources. While more generic profiles reduce the number of profiles and thus decrease the maintenance burden for security administrators, these generic profiles become overly permissive and increase the security vulnerability.

5.3.1 Over-Privileged Groups

Overly permissive groups are the groups of which many members rarely use the permissions granted to the group (Definition 7). A user who does not use any of the group policies or uses only few policies may be over-provisioned, and the policy with these over-provisioned users violates the principle of least privilege [20].

We monitor how often each member of a group executes the policies assigned through the group. Our analysis with z/OS RACF and the 14 million SMF logs show that a relatively small percentage of members use their group policies, and a small fraction of the group policies used by the members. Figure 5 shows the percentage of group members and the percentage of group policies for each group that were found in the SMF logs.

There are 44 unique groups that were assigned group policies. Out of the 44 groups, policies assigned to only 16 groups (i.e., 36% of the groups) were ever used. As we can see from the figure, 36% of the groups were never used, and, on average, only 19% of the members of a group have used the group policies. We can notice that there are two outliers in the policy usage with 100% usage rate. We note that the two groups are assigned only 1 policy each.

5.3.2 Overly Permissive Profiles

The second case of overly permissive entitlements is due to overly generic profiles. Since z/OS RACF policy items can be generic, we can reconcile the expressiveness of the resource specified in the policy with the actual resource to which access was granted. We detect overly permissive generic profiles by examining all the resources accessed by the profiles, and by generating the most specific generic profile name that covers all the accessed resources in a bottom-

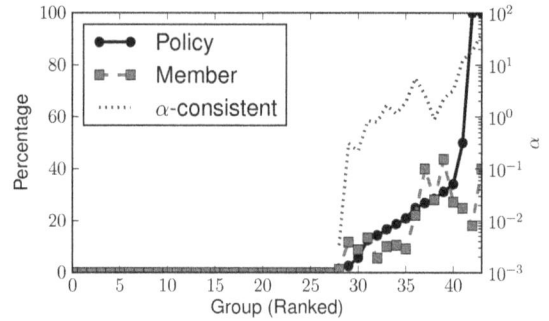

Figure 5: The percentage of group members and profiles used in resource accesses. The dotted line shows a hypothetical usage rate to make the policy α-consistent (Definition 4).

Defined Policy	Total Accesses	Unique Resources	Proposed Policy
K.*.**	3,410,708	1	K.B.TEST
Q.**	383,794	1	Q.PROD
R.P.**	24,398	24,398	R.P.%02*
L.**	57,576	15,000	L.U.OPEN*
M.**	318	19	M.T.*
N.S.O*.**	120	11	N.S.O%%

Table 8: Samples of overly permissive profiles, and the more specific profile names generated dynamically by analyzing accessed resources

up way. If the defined profile is much more generic than the generated profile name, then the policy is considered overly permissive. When access logs over a long time period are available, these dynamically generated profile names can be very reliable, and can be used to rewrite the overly permissive profiles with a lower scope.

Our analysis shows most of the defined profiles are unnecessarily permissive. Table 8 shows some examples of overly permissive profiles, and the proposed profiles generated by analyzing the accessed resources by the profiles. Note that K.*.** is used over 3 million times but accessed only one resource. On the other hand, the profile L.** was used to grant 15,000 different resources. However, the resources can be represented in a much more specific profile as proposed by our system. Note that our analytic simply compares the expressiveness of the policy item with the least generic policy which cover all the *observed* actions. We do not have information about the actual resources which are present in the system, so we can not quantify the degree of the resources that are never accessed by the user (Definition 6). However, the examples in Table 8 illustrate that many profiles are overly generic.

6. POLICY GROUPS AND ROLES

Our key analytic for verifying if the *Configured* policy is consistent with its *Enforced* or *Used* policy is to validate if the group definitions in the policy (i.e., *explicit* roles) are currently relevant and reflect the actual roles the group members assume (i.e., *implicit* roles). Users' actual roles can be inferred from logs of the permissions usage, using role mining techniques [8,15]. This section presents analytic methods to test if the policy groups correspond to actually assumed roles. If the mined roles differ significantly from the defined groups, this indicates the policy's group definition is, perhaps, no longer relevant and we could assert that the usage is not compliant.

6.1 Role Mining

We apply generative role modeling approach described in [15] to discover the implicit roles from users' access patterns. Molloy et al. apply Latent Dirichlet Allocation (LDA) [6],to mine roles from access logs. The technique attempts to explain how the observations (i.e., use of entitlements) were generated given certain hidden parameters (i.e., roles) in the following way.

Each user is modeled as a finite mixture over underlying set of roles, and each role is, in turn, modeled as a distribution over profiles. LDA assumes the following generative process in which a user u is created:

1. For each user $u \in U$, a distribution over roles is sampled from a Dirichlet distribution, $\theta \sim Dir(\alpha)$.

2. For each profile p used by a user, select a role, z, according to the distribution, $Multinomial(\theta)$.

3. Finally, a profile is chosen from a multinomial probability distributions over profiles conditioned on the role, $p(p|z, \beta)$.

The role mining system produces two probability distributions—a probability distribution over the roles for each user, and a distribution over profiles for each role.

For the remainder of this section we're using the set of distribution vectors for various models m: $\Phi_m = \{\phi_{m,r} \mid r \in R_m\}$ where each $\phi_{m,r}$ is one probability distribution for a role r out of the set or roles R_m for the model m; we do use the discrete roles from [15].

6.2 Consistency of Mined Roles

Before we compare the roles mined from logs with the groups in policy, we must first convince ourselves that the roles obtained are consistent over time. To validate this, we generate generative models from access logs across different periods in time and evaluate how similar these models are.

Using the SMF logs collected over a year, we first partition them into four equal size periods (each representing 3 months of access logs). We apply the generative role mining models and discover the roles for each period. The number of mined roles in the experiments was set to 50 to reflect the number of the defined groups in the policy. Because the role mining algorithm is probabilistic, the algorithm may produce different results each run due to inherent random sampling from distributions. Therefore, we extract 10 different models for each period, resulting in a total of 40 models.

Let Φ_m be the probability distribution of the mined roles over permissions for a model m. We will use Φ_{pq} to denote the probability distribution for the p-th model generated from the q-th period ($1 \leq p \leq 10$ and $1 \leq q \leq 4$ in this experiment). For validation, we compare the models within each period as well the models for different time periods.

DEFINITION 11. *An* Optimal Role Mapping *is the mapping of all roles in a model m onto the roles of model m' (i.e., a permutation π over the role indexes) so that the aggregate*

Period	1	2	3	4	All
1	0.165	0.189	0.240	0.272	0.234
2		0.116	0.225	0.251	0.219
3			0.180	0.250	0.239
4				0.158	0.259
All					0.219

Table 9: Average aggregated RMSE for comparison of models from different periods

root-mean-square error (RMSE) for a vector-wise comparison is minimized:

$$\sum_{i=1}^{k} \mathrm{RMSE}(\phi_{m,i}, \phi_{m',\pi(i)}) \mid \phi_{m,i} \in \Phi_m \wedge \phi_{m',\pi(i)} \in \Phi_{m'}.$$

DEFINITION 12. *The* distance *between models m and m' ($D(\Phi_m, \Phi_{m'})$) is the aggregate RMSE for a vector-wise comparison given an optimal role mapping between m and m'.*

Table 9 shows model comparison results. Each entry shows the average model distance when comparing all models within the appropriate periods (i.e., the average across all $D(\Phi_{pq}, \Phi_{p'q'})$, where $pq \neq p'q'$ for the period numbers q and q' according to the row and column in the table).

The comparisons indicate that the models overall are fairly stable (i.e., the average RMSE for any two roles is 0.004 as each model contains 50 roles). Additionally the results for the various subsets are consistent with the intuition reflecting people perform the same roles in a short time period and gradually shift to different roles, as the average model similarity within a period is higher than the similarity between models from different periods. The further apart the time periods of compared models are the more the similarity degrades, this again seems intuitive since job roles and processes within the organization shift over time.

6.3 Comparison of Defined Groups and Mined Roles

After ensuring that the mined roles are stable, we compare the mined roles to the groups defined in the policy. This helps measure if the defined groups are relevant; i.e., do the mined roles and the profile distributions they represent match the way the profiles are linked to groups. We compare groups and roles by comparing probability distributions representing the expected activity (i.e., the distribution across the exercised profiles) for both groups and roles. For roles, we can extract the probability distribution for the i-th model for the q-th period from the LDA model $\Phi_{iq} = \{\phi_{iq,r} \mid r \in R_{iq}\}$.

For groups, we create the probability distribution based on the usage information from the audit logs. For each logged resource access for a user, we determine the list of groups that may grant the user access to this resource. The audit logs contain the profile granting access, so this is done by finding all groups the user is assigned to that are linked to the used profile. All accesses are aggregated per group, resulting in a vector describing how often a profile was used to grant access to a resource. The aggregation aligned to the time periods used to create the LDA models, resulting in four aggregate profile usage count vectors per group. These aggregate usage counts are normalized to obtain the probability distribution over the profiles for each group. Thus

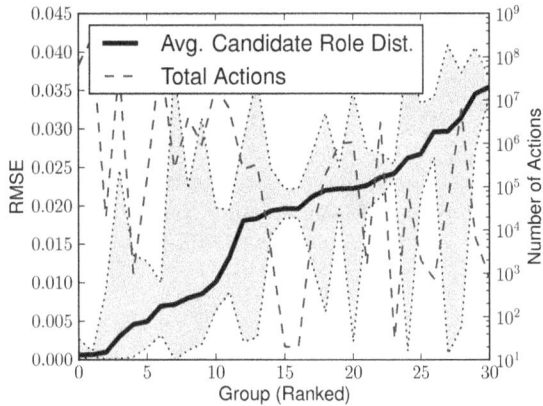

Figure 6: Average candidate role distance. The shaded region denoted the min-max region.

we have a set probability distributions $\phi_{g,q}$, where g is the group id and q is the period number ($1 \leq q \leq 4$). Each one of these probability distributions can now be compared to all the roles for all models in the same period q (i.e., all $\phi_{iq,r} \mid 1 \leq i \leq 10 \wedge r \in R_{iq}$).

DEFINITION 13. *Candidate role* $c(\phi_{g,q}, \Phi_{iq})$ *for a group probability distribution and a model for the same time period is the role r minimizing* RMSE($\phi_{g,q}, \phi_{iq,r}$). *Candidate role distance is the RMSE between the candidate role and the model probability distribution for the corresponding period.*

Candidate roles represent the most likely matching mined role for a group. Candidate role distance allows us to estimate if a group has a properly matching role. The goal is to define a threshold to determine if a candidate role is likely to be the mined equivalent of the defined group.

DEFINITION 14. *Candidate role set for a group g is the set of all candidate roles for all probability distributions for the group and their corresponding models:*

$$C(g) = \{c(\phi_{g,q}, \Phi_{iq}) \mid 1 \leq q \leq 4 \wedge 1 \leq i \leq 10\}$$

Candidate role sets represent the possible matches for a group across multiple time periods multiple iterations of the role mining. By examining candidate role sets, we can determine if a group is consistently matched (or unmatched).

Figure 6 shows statistics for candidate role sets for each group. For each candidate set the average (black line), minimal and maximal (shaded area) values for the candidate role distance for all roles in $C(g)$ are plotted. Some groups show small candidate role distances across the candidate role set (e.g., groups 1 and 2), some have both similar and distant roles in the candidate set (e.g., group 25), and some have no candidate roles with small distances for any model (e.g., groups 23 and 31). For the remainder of the paper, we will use 0.01 as the threshold, and only candidate roles with a distance lower than the threshold will be considered *valid*.

Table 10 shows how many of the candidate roles are considered *valid*. It also shows the total number of accesses found in the audit logs for the group. Most of the groups that do not have matching roles are *rarely* used, so a statistical analytic like LDA can't reliably detect them in the

Group	avg. RMSE	valid candidates	access count
1	0.000609	40	132137560
7	0.006962	40	205468320
11	0.010120	30	40771820
20	0.022250	0	1987240
23	0.023730	0	6032320
25	0.026200	4	175040
31	0.035356	0	1480

Table 10: Number of valid candidate roles and group prevalence

the data set. The exception to this are groups 20 and 23 having a significant number of access in the audit logs but not matching any roles.

Detailed investigation of roles 20 and 23 shows that almost all members of the group are also assigned to another group (11 and 7 respectively) that subsumes the heavily used profiles from role 20 and 23, while the profiles that are unique to groups 20 and 23 are rarely exercised. This indicates a questionable overlap of profiles between the two groups that may require some adjustments in the profile design. Group 25 is used moderately often, but not consistently across the one year of audit logs we processed. As a result, in the phases with heavier use, it is matched to some degree, but, in the phases with very low usage, it is not matched at all.

Our analysis confirms our initial hypothesis about the relationship between groups and roles:

- Groups that are *frequently used* and *consistent with usage* are clearly identified by our analytics based on our chosen threshold parameters. While this analytic easily generalizes across other data sets, we expect that the actual thresholds will vary across datasets and can be obtained with some experimentation.

- Groups that are *frequently used* but identified as *inconsistent with use* show high overlaps with other groups in terms of use and should probably be re-engineered to better match the actual use. Once the correct adjustments to the group design are determined we can evaluate if further analytics can be used to support the redesign process based on best practices created in cooperation with the administrators.

- There are a small number of groups which are *rarely* used and are a poor match with the mined roles. The relevance of these groups must be hand-validated via administrator feedback. We expect similar behavior in other data sets since the statistical models can not determine infrequently assumed roles.

From this validation, we conclude that this is a powerful analytic which can be used to validate the relevance of policy defined groups.

7. GENERALITY OF DATA AND ANALYSIS TO XACML

For this work, we omit analysis that is specific to z/OS and RACF, and focus on policy and log analysis that we believe are applicable to a wide variety of platforms. The key constructs from RACF we rely on are groups, general and discrete profiles, and their hierarchical relationships, both implicit and explicit. We believe the presented analysis is general and can be applied to a variety of access control models and contexts. Specifically, the above analytics can be applied to other access control models or adapted in the following contexts:

- **Models grouping subjects, objects, or permissions** Groups are common in many access control systems and models and are closely related to roles in RBAC for the types of analysis performed here. Such constructs are found in many operating systems (e.g., Windows and Linux), database management systems (e.g., DB2 and Oracle), and identity management systems (e.g., Tivoli Identity Manager). In attribute-based systems, such as XACML, the group memberships can be implicitly defined using `subject` of a `rule target` (rather, we can interpret the `subject` constructs as group definitions). In fact, throughout much of this work, the term profile as used in RACF can be replaced with `rule` or `policy` / `policyset` in XACML.

- **Hierarchical and partial orders of resources and policy rules** Generic profiles and hierarchical relationships are implicit in many systems. For example, in a database management system, users can be granted authorization at the database, table, column, and row level. This type of relationship is quite natural in XACML where the target resource is defined over the set of attributes. Given the attribute-based structure of an XACML target (both the subject and resource), the same partial orders and groups can be implicitly defined for XACML policies as with RACF. We can thus apply the redundant, over-provisioned, and too generic (over-permissive) analytics on an XACML policy with little modification.

- **Policies combining rules** In this work, we assumed rules are applied in "most specific first" order, but any of the XACML policy combining rules can be applied. In fact, the analysis presented here may be especially useful for XACML policies given the often counter-intuitive interpretation of policy combining rules that may be misinterpreted in practice, leading to administrative policy errors [12]. Note that, in this work, we do not go into details about possible return types (such as warnings), and our work does not extend to obligations in XACML.

8. RELATED WORK

Most related work on "reconciling" policy focuses on a body of work seeking to combine multiple policies into one and ensuring all sub-policies are being enforced. For example, McDaniel at al. [13] study the problem of reconciling two-or-more policies and detecting conflicts and resolution. Rao et al. [16] investigate how to integrate XACML policies while Li et al. [12] discuss more flexible models for combining multiple sub-policies in XACML. These are different problems from the one we investigate here. While there may be parallels between combining policies and sub-policies and redundant and overlapping profiles as seen in z/OS, we do not investigate them in this work. On the other hand, when referencing access control audit logs, log reconciliation typically refers to the process of combining logs from distributed systems with integrity [11].

There is a large body of work on role mining, much of which addresses the issue of errors and policy misconfigurations in the input data [14, 15, 21]. We leverage many of the techniques from [15], which performs role mining and detects policy over-assignments by mining logs. We view many of these techniques as complimentary to ours. While most work on role mining only has an input access control policy, we explicitly correlate policy with logs.

A closely related area of work to ours is break-glass systems—constrained ways to override access control policies [4, 7]. In such systems, a user is provided with the ability to disable the standard protections for increased logging, and, in theory, an ex post facto audit. Such audits will typically investigate the *intent* of the request and seek to fill the gap between feasible and oracle layers postmortem [17]. Garg et al. [9] present a method for verifying the actions in an audit log adhere to a policy implemented in first-order logic. Their work is similar to previous approaches to validate compliance with a policy, but assume a policy is correct and static. To our knowledge, this is the first work that focuses on verifying a policy from audit logs to reduce operational and administrative risk.

9. CONCLUSION

In this paper, we proposed a new approach to verify the enforcement of security policies and the usage of permissions meets desired high level goals. Rather than focus on using formalisms to prove desirable properties of the policy, its enforcement, and usage, we propose an analytics based method which attempts to ensure that the usage of permissions is consistent with the configured policy and that the configured policy is following the principle of least privilege.

We have proposed a number of analytic techniques to achieve this goal. The key analytic is to ensure that the group definitions in the policy correspond to actual roles mined from usage. This analytic measures the relevance of the role definitions as configured in the policy. We also propose a number of other techniques geared toward ensuring the configured policy satisfies least-privilege. These include identifying that are: redundant; unused; overly generic; and over provisioned groups.

We believe our approach allows us to narrow a policy to enable just the actions that are necessary, enforcing least privilege and reducing ambiguity to reduce administrative risk. We believe our tools are far easier for a security administrator to use than a formal methods based approach. On the other side, our analytic techniques are far more sophisticated than typical compliance monitoring products which can, at best, only enforce simple compliance conditions.

10. REFERENCES

[1] Security Server (RACF) Introduction. Technical Report GC28-1912-06, IBM Corporation, Sept. 1999.

[2] z/OS V1R12.0 Security Server RACF Macros and Interfaces. Technical Report SA22-7682-14, IBM Corporation, June 2010.

[3] z/OS V1R12.0 Security Server RACF Messages and Codes. Technical Report SA22-7686-14, IBM Corporation, June 2010.

[4] J. Alqatawna, E. Rissanen, and B. S. Firozabadi. Overriding of Access Control in XACML. In *Proceedings*, pages 87–95, 2007.

[5] M. Bishop, S. Engle, S. Peisert, S. Whalen, and C. Gates. We Have Met the Enemy and He is Us. In *NSPW '08: Proceedings of the 2008 workshop on New security paradigms*, 2008.

[6] D. Blei, A. Ng, and M. Jordan. Latent dirichlet allocation. *J. Mach. Learning Research*, 3, 2003.

[7] A. D. Brucker and H. Petritsch. Extending access control models with break-glass. In *the 14th ACM symposium*, pages 197–206, New York, New York, USA, 2009. New York, NY, USA, ACM Press.

[8] M. Frank, A. Streich, D. Basin, and J. Buhmann. A probabilistic approach to hybrid role mining. In *CCS*, 2009.

[9] D. Garg, L. Jia, and A. Datta. A Logical Method for Policy Enforcement over Evolving Audit Logs. *Arxiv preprint arXiv:1102.3176*, cs.LO, Feb. 2011.

[10] M. A. Harrison, W. L. Ruzzo, and J. D. Ullman. Protection in Operating Systems. *Communications of the ACM*, 19(8):461–471, 1976.

[11] J. H. Huh and J. Lyle. Trustworthy Log Reconciliation for Distributed Virtual Organisations. In *rd.springer.com*, pages 169–182. Springer Berlin Heidelberg, Berlin, Heidelberg, 2009.

[12] N. Li, Q. Wang, W. Qardaji, E. Bertino, P. Rao, J. Lobo, and D. Lin. Access control policy combining: theory meets practice. *SACMAT '09: Proceedings of the 14th ACM symposium on Access control models and technologies*, June 2009.

[13] P. McDaniel and A. Prakash. Methods and limitations of security policy reconciliation. *ACM Transactions on Information and System Security*, 9(3):259–291, Aug. 2006.

[14] I. Molloy, N. Li, J. Lobo, Y. A. Qi, and L. Dickens. Mining Roles with Noisy Data. In *SACMAT'10*, 2010.

[15] I. Molloy, Y. Park, and S. N. Chari. Generative models for access control policies: Applications to role mining over logs with attribution. In *Proceedings of the 17th ACM Symposium on Access Control Models and Technologies*, SACMAT '12, 2012.

[16] P. Rao, D. Lin, E. Bertino, N. Li, and J. Lobo. An algebra for fine-grained integration of XACML policies. *SACMAT '09: Proceedings of the 14th ACM symposium on Access control models and technologies*, June 2009.

[17] L. Rostad and O. Edsberg. A Study of Access Control Requirements for Healthcare Systems Based on Audit Trails from Access Logs. In *Proceedings*, pages 175–186. Washington, DC, USA, 2006.

[18] J. H. Saltzer and M. D. Schroeder. The Protection of Information in Computer Systems. *Proceedings of the IEEE*, 63(9):1278–1308, 1975.

[19] F. B. Schneider. Enforceable security policies. *Transactions on Information and System Security (TISSEC*, 3(1), Feb. 2000.

[20] F. B. Schneider. Least privilege and more. *IEEE Security and Privacy*, 1(5):55–59, 2003.

[21] A. P. Streich, M. Frank, D. Basin, and J. M. Buhmann. Multi-assignment clustering for Boolean data. In *Proceedings of the 26th Annual International Conference on Machine Learning*, pages 969–976. New York, NY, USA, 2009.

[22] M. V. Tripunitara and N. Li. A Theory for Comparing the Expressive Power of Access Control Models. *Journal of Computer Security*, 15:231–272.

Least-Restrictive Enforcement of the Chinese Wall Security Policy

Alireza Sharifi
a9sharif@uwaterloo.ca

Mahesh V. Tripunitara
tripunit@uwaterloo.ca

ECE, University of Waterloo, Canada

ABSTRACT

The Chinese Wall security policy states that information from objects that are to be confidential from one another should not flow to a subject. It addresses conflict of interest, and was first articulated in the well-cited work of Brewer and Nash, which proposes also an enforcement mechanism for the policy. Work subsequent to theirs has observed that their enforcement mechanism is overly restrictive – authorization states in which the policy is not violated may be rendered unreachable. We present two sets of novel results in this context. In one, we present an enforcement mechanism for the policy that is simple and efficient, and least-restrictive – an authorization state is reachable if and only if it does not violate the policy. In our enforcement mechanism, the actions of a subject can constrain the prospective actions of another, a trade-off that we show every enforcement mechanism that is least-restrictive must incur. Our other set of results is that the enforcement mechanism of Brewer-Nash is even more restrictive than previous work establishes. Specifically, we show: (1) what is called the *-rule is overspecified in that one of its sub-rules implies the other, and, (2) if a subject is authorized to write to an object that contains confidential information, then all objects that contain confidential information must belong to the same conflict of interest class. Our work sheds new light on what is generally considered to be important work in information security.

Categories and Subject Descriptors

D.4.6 [**Operating Systems**]: Security and Protection—*Access controls*; K.6.5 [**Management of Computing and Information Systems**]: Security and Protection—*Unauthorized access*

General Terms

Security

Keywords

Chinese Wall, Security Policy, Enforcement

1. INTRODUCTION

The Chinese Wall security policy [6] relates to conflict of interest a subject may have over two pieces of information. The policy states that information from two objects that are to be confidential from one another should not flow to a subject. Conflict of interest is recognized as important in several settings – legal, financial and governmental [7], and technical, including in the emergent area of cloud-computing [4, 22, 24].

We address an issue at the foundations of the policy — its enforcement. We begin with some discussions on the policy itself. To our knowledge, the policy was first articulated in information security research by Brewer and Nash [6]. Their work is cited extensively in the research literature [20], and included in popular books on information security [3, 5, 11].

In articulating the Chinese Wall security policy, Brewer-Nash adopt an abstraction for the authorization state of systems in which the policy is relevant. We show an example in Figure 1. A system comprises objects and subjects; the former is a passive container of information, and the latter actively accesses objects. There are only two kinds of access, read and write. When a subject reads an object, information flows from the object to the subject. When a subject writes an object, information flows from the subject to the object. Apart from such direct flows of information, there can be indirect flows of information. In Figure 1 for example, the subject s_2 read object o_6, and later wrote o_4; therefore, information has flowed from o_6 to o_4.

Each object belongs to a Company Dataset, and Company Datasets are grouped into Conflict of Interest classes. An object that contains confidential information is called an unsanitized object. If two unsanitized objects belong to different Company Datasets within the same Conflict of Interest class, then, for the Chinese Wall security policy to be maintained, information from both those objects should not flow to a subject. An exception is a distinguished Conflict of Interest class for what are called sanitized objects. Such objects do not contain confidential information at the start, and therefore data that is initially contained in them is allowed to flow freely.

In Figure 1 for example, there are three Conflict of Interest classes, one of which is for sanitized objects. Objects o_3 and o_4 belong to the same Company Dataset within a Conflict of Interest class, and are therefore not in conflict. The objects o_2 and o_3 that belong to different Company Datasets that are in different Conflict of Interest classes are also not in conflict. The objects o_3 and o_5 that belong to different Company Datasets within the same Conflict of Interest class are in conflict and therefore we need to guard against data flow from those two objects that may be in violation of the policy.

Apart from articulating the policy, Brewer-Nash propose an enforcement mechanism for it. Their enforcement mechanism comprises two rules, the simple security rule and the *-rule [6]. A rule

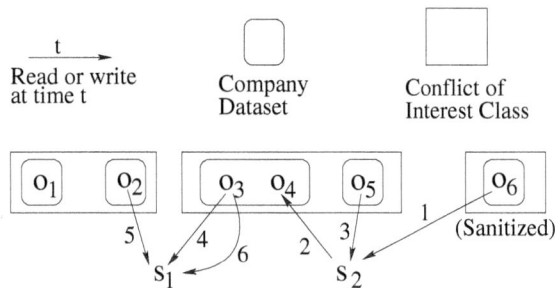

Figure 1: An authorization state with two subjects and six objects. As the legend expresses, boxes with sharp corners are Conflict of Interest classes and boxes with rounded corners are Company Datasets. An arrow indicates read or write at a particular time. The Conflict of Interest class to the far right, and the Company Dataset within it, contain sanitized objects only.

is a precondition on the authorization state of the system that must be satisfied before access is granted to a subject.

The simple security rule is: "Access is only granted if the object requested (a) is in the same Company Dataset as an object already accessed by that subject, or, (b) belongs to an entirely different Conflict of Interest Class." "Access" means read or write. The *-rule is: "Write access is only permitted if (a) access is permitted by the simple security rule, and, (b) no object can be read which is in a different Company Dataset to the one for which write access is requested and contains unsanitized information."

In Figure 1, for example, if the subject s_1 attempts to read o_1, it is disallowed by the simple security rule as o_1 belongs to the same Conflict of Interest class as another object, o_2, that it has already read. If it attempts to read o_2 or o_3 again, it is allowed to do so by the simple security rule. The subject s_1 is disallowed from writing any object by the *-rule because it is allowed to read both o_2 and o_3, which are in different Company Datasets.

We point out, however, that if s_1 is allowed to write to o_2 or o_3, no violation of the policy results. This is an example of the restrictiveness of the Brewer-Nash enforcement mechanism. While the enforcement mechanism (simple-security and *-rules) is sufficient to preclude conflict of interest, it is not necessary.

We point out also that in Figure 1, the *-rule of Brewer-Nash disallows s_2 from writing to o_4. No flow of information to a subject from objects that are in conflict results from such an action by s_2. However, such a write results in information flow from o_5 to o_4, which are in conflict. It is unclear whether Brewer-Nash intend for this to be a violation of the policy. We address it as well, as some subsequent work appears to adopt this as a policy violation. (We call it an "object violation" of the policy, as opposed to a "subject violation" — see Definition 2 in Section 2.2.)

Work subsequent to Brewer-Nash has pointed out that their enforcement mechanism can be highly restrictive. Specifically, Kessler [13] and Sandhu [17, 18] establish the following two properties:

P_1: A subject that has read objects from two or more Company Datasets cannot write to any object.

P_2: A subject that has read objects from exactly one Company Dataset can write to that Dataset only.

Our work We address the following questions that, to our knowledge, have not been addressed previously. Can we articulate a notion of least-restrictive enforcement for the Chinese Wall security policy? If so, does there exist an enforcement mechanism that is least-restrictive? What are the trade-offs it incurs?

We answer the above questions by first proposing a notion of least-restrictive enforcement: under such enforcement, an authorization state is reachable if and only if it does not violate the policy. We then propose an enforcement mechanism and show that it is least-restrictive. We identify that the trade-off we incur regards the independence of the actions of a subject from another. That is, the read or write actions of a subject can constrain prospective read or write actions of another subject. We then show that this trade-off in inherent to least-restrictive enforcement — any enforcement mechanism that is least-restrictive must incur this trade-off.

Separately, we show that the Brewer-Nash enforcement mechanism is even more restrictive than previous work establishes. We establish two new results. (1) The second sub-rule of the *-rule implies the simple security rule (the first sub-rule of the *-rule). (2) If a subject is authorized to write to an unsanitized object, then all unsanitized objects must belong to the same Conflict of Interest class.

Our work not only provides a least-restrictive enforcement mechanism of the Chinese Wall security policy that incurs only the trade-off it must, but also sheds new light on Brewer-Nash, which is generally considered to be important work in information security.

Layout The remainder of this paper is organized as follows. In the next section, we discuss a graph-based formalism to represent the authorization state and express the Chinese Wall security policy precisely. In Section 3, we characterize an enforcement mechanism. In Section 4, we present our enforcement mechanism, and establish its soundness, efficiency and least-restriction properties. We also show that any enforcement mechanism that is least-restrictive must incur the same trade-off that our enforcement mechanism does. We present new results on the Brewer-Nash enforcement mechanism in Section 5. In that section, we discuss also Bishop's [5] description of the Brewer-Nash enforcement mechanism and establish that it is different from the original enforcement mechanism of Brewer-Nash. We discuss related work in Section 6, and conclude with Section 7.

2. A FORMALISM AND THE CHINESE WALL SECURITY POLICY

We seek to carefully distinguish policy from enforcement mechanism. In this section, we articulate the policy precisely. As the Chinese Wall security policy pertains to accesses subjects have made to objects, we adopt a graph-based formalism for what we call authorization states that capture such accesses.

We first describe our graph-based formalism in Section 2.1. Then, in Section 2.2 we express the Chinese Wall security policy, and in Section 2.3, we discuss ways in which an authorization state can change. (Henceforth, we sometimes simply say "state" for "authorization state," and "policy" for "Chinese Wall security policy.")

2.1 Authorization State

An authorization state is a tuple $\langle D, \delta, C, G \rangle$, where $G = \langle V, exists, E \rangle$ is a graph, and:

- D is a finite set of company datasets $\{D_{[s]}, D_1, \ldots, D_k\}$. The Dataset $D_{[s]}$ is the one reserved for sanitized objects. All other Datasets contain unsanitized objects.

- $V = S \cup O$ is the set of vertices which represent the subjects and objects. We assume that $S \cap O = \emptyset$, and:

  - $S = \{s_1, s_2, \ldots\}$ is a countably infinite set of subjects. These are all the subjects that can possibly exist.

We use the term "subject," rather than "user" or "principal" intentionally. Sandhu [17, 18] points out some confusion in Brewer-Nash on this issue. We adopt the mindset from his work. A subject may be created and destroyed, and is an agent of a user; for example, an operating system process.

  – $O = \{o_1, o_2, \ldots\}$ is a countably infinite set of objects. These are all the objects that can possibly exist.

- The function $exists\colon V \longrightarrow \{0, 1\}$ associates each vertex with a bit that indicates whether it exists. We assume that in any given state, only finitely many subjects and objects exist.

One may wonder why we model subjects and objects in this manner, and not simply have only those subjects and objects that exist as vertices in an authorization state. The reason is that, as we discuss in Section 2.3, subjects and objects that exist can be destroyed later. Even after a subject or object is destroyed, it can be part of an information flow that leads to a violation of the Chinese Wall security policy (see the discussion after Definition 2 in Section 2.2). Consequently, we keep track of all subjects and objects that can possibly exist, and annotate the ones that exist using the $exists$ function.

- The function $\delta\colon O \longrightarrow D$ maps an object to a Company Dataset.

- The function $C\colon D \times D \longrightarrow \{0, 1\}$ identifies Conflict of Interest. That is, $C(D_i, D_j) = 1$ if and only if $D_i \neq D_j$, $D_i \neq D_{[s]}$, $D_j \neq D_{[s]}$ and D_i and D_j are in conflict (i.e., in the same Conflict of Interest class).

It may seem that we could simply partition D into Conflict of Interest classes instead of specifying the function C. We choose this approach to address Lin's generalization [15] to the Brewer-Nash characterization of Conflict of Interest classes. Lin's work points out that the Brewer-Nash characterization requires the Conflict of Interest relation to be transitive, when in practice, it does not have to be. In our case, the relation $\{\langle D_i, D_j \rangle : C(D_i, D_j) = 1\}$ is irreflexive, symmetric and not necessarily transitive.

- $E \subseteq V \times V \times \mathbb{Z}^+$ is the set of edges, where $\mathbb{Z}^+$ is the set of positive integers. Each $\langle v_1, v_2, t \rangle \in E$ represents an access that occurred at time t. If $v_1 \in S$, then $v_2 \in O$, and the access was a write. If $v_1 \in O$, then $v_2 \in S$, and the access was a read.

We can represent the system in Figure 1 using our formalism. In the graph, we would have $|D| = 5$, and $C(D_i, D_j)$ would correspond to the Conflict of Interest classes shown in the figure. For example, $C(\delta(o_1), \delta(o_2)) = 1$, but $C(\delta(o_3), \delta(o_4)) = 0$. The vertices for which $exists = 1$ are those shown in the figure, and the only edges that exist are those between vertices that exist.

2.2 The Chinese Wall Security Policy

In this section, we first introduce the notion of an information flow in a state, which is a kind of path in the graph. We then characterize the Chinese Wall security policy.

DEFINITION 1 (INFORMATION FLOW). *In an authorization state (a graph) G, an information flow from vertex v_1 to v_n, denoted $v_1 \rightsquigarrow v_n$, is a path with edges $\langle v_1, v_2, t_{1,2} \rangle$, $\langle v_2, v_3, t_{2,3} \rangle$, $\ldots$, $\langle v_{n-1}, v_n, t_{n-1,n} \rangle$ such that $t_{1,2} \leq t_{2,3} \leq \ldots \leq t_{n-1,n}$.*

For example, in the state that corresponds to Figure 1, $o_6 \rightarrow s_2 \rightarrow o_4$ is an information flow. Subjects and objects alternate in a path that is an information flow; i.e., information can flow between two objects only via a subject, and information can flow between two subjects only via an object.

Brewer and Nash [6] express the Chinese Wall security policy as, "[Subjects] are only allowed access to information that is not held to conflict with any other information that they already possess." We express this in our graph-based formalism as follows. As we discuss in Section 1, we capture also the policy for flows between objects.

DEFINITION 2 (CHINESE WALL SECURITY POLICY). *The Chinese Wall security policy is said to be satisfied for subjects in a state if there exists no pair of information flows, $o_1 \rightsquigarrow s$ and $o_2 \rightsquigarrow s$ such that $s \in S$, $o_1, o_2 \in O$, and, $C(\delta(o_1), \delta(o_2)) = 1$. The policy is said to be satisfied for objects if there exists no pair of information flows, $o_1 \rightsquigarrow o$ (or $o_1 = o$) and $o_2 \rightsquigarrow o$ (or $o_2 = o$) such that $o, o_1, o_2 \in O$, and, $C(\delta(o_1), \delta(o_2)) = 1$.*

If the policy is not satisfied for subjects in a state, then we say that there is a *subject-violation* of the policy in the state. If the policy is not satisfied for objects, then we say that there is an *object-violation* of the policy. As an example, the Chinese Wall security policy is satisfied for both subjects and objects in the state that corresponds to Figure 1. However, if s_2 writes to o_4 at time 7, we have an object-violation from the flow $o_5 \rightsquigarrow o_4$. If s_1 reads o_1, there is a subject-violation from the flows $o_1 \rightsquigarrow s_1$ and $o_2 \rightsquigarrow s_1$.

We point out that for our definitions above, a violation can be caused by a flow in which there is a subject or object that has been destroyed. This is reasonable: even if an object is destroyed, for example, if a subject has previously read that object, we need to consider that flow of information in any future determination of a violation of the policy.

We point out also that subject- and object-violations are mutually exclusive in that one is neither a necessary nor a sufficient condition for the other to exist. However, if an object-violation exists, then there exists a read action by one of a particular set of subjects that causes a subject-violation. Similarly, if a subject-violation exists, then there exists a write action by one of a particular set of subjects that causes an object-violation.

2.3 Changes to the Authorization State

Of course, the Chinese Wall policy is interesting only if we consider changes to the authorization state as actions are performed. The only part of the state that can change is the graph, G. Within G, the only possible changes are to $exists$, and the set of edges E. The former happens when a subject or object is created or destroyed, and the latter when a subject reads or writes an object. Edges can only be added, and never removed, because an edge represents a read or write action, which cannot be revoked once it is performed.

Brewer-Nash explicitly consider only the actions read and write, and not the creation and destruction of subjects and objects. However, their rules for creation and destruction are straightforward to intuit (see Section 5). Also, some of the work subsequent to theirs such as that of Sandhu [17, 18] considers creation and destruction of subjects and objects explicitly.

In each of the following, we denote as G the current state, and as G_{new} the state that results from the change.

- A subject or object may be created. If $\alpha \in S \cup O$ is the subject/object that is created, $exists(\alpha) = 0$ in G (α does not already exist in G). The only difference between G and G_{new} is that in the latter, $exists(\alpha) = 1$.

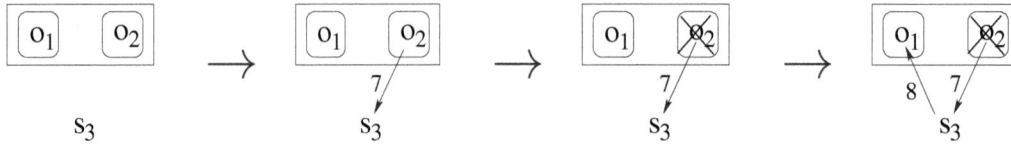

Figure 2: Changes to the authorization state starting at the state in Figure 1. We show only the Conflict of Interest class that contains o_1 and o_2. In the state to the far left, the subject s_3 is created. In the next state, s_3 reads o_2. In the next state, o_2 is destroyed. In the final state to the far right, s_3 writes to o_1 causing an object-violation. All these states are reachable from the state in Figure 1.

In the context of enforcement in the next section, we make the additional assumption that once a subject or object is destroyed, it cannot be recreated. We defer a discussion on this to the next section.

- A subject or object may be destroyed. If $\alpha \in S \cup O$ is destroyed, $exists(\alpha) = 1$ in G, and $exists(\alpha) = 0$ in G_{new}. That is the only difference between G and G_{new}.

- A subject may read or write an object. Suppose $s \in S$ is a subject that reads or writes $o \in O$. Then, in G, $exists(s) = exists(o) = 1$; that is, both s and o exist in G. The only difference between G and G_{new} is that an edge that corresponds to the action additionally exists in G_{new}, with a timestamp that corresponds to the time the action occurs.

We assume that time is discretized, and only one action occurs at a time. The latter assumption is needed for clarity of exposition only. We can allow multiple actions at the same time without affecting any of our contributions. Our use of "$\leq$" in relating the time-stamps $t_{1,2}, t_{2,3}, \ldots, t_{n-1,n}$ in Definition 1 accounts for this. If only one action is allowed to happen at a time, then we can change that to "$<$."

DEFINITION 3 (REACHABLE STATE). *Given two states σ_1 and σ_n, we say that σ_n is reachable from σ_1 if and only if either $\sigma_1 = \sigma_n$, or there exists a state σ_{n-1} that is reachable from σ_1 and σ_n results from a state-change to σ_{n-1}.*

In Figure 2, we show examples of reachable states starting at the state in Figure 1. One may ask why we have chosen state-changes at the above granularity. Why not allow, for example, multiple subjects to be created in a single state-change? The granularity is important for reads and writes only. That is, from the standpoint of enforcing the Chinese Wall security policy, a read and a write must each constitute a state-change, and is atomic. The reason, as we discuss in the next section, is that we may need to prevent a particular read or write from happening to ensure that the policy is met in all reachable states.

We point out that the simple security and *-rules of Brewer-Nash are articulated with exactly such a granularity of state-changes in mind for reads and writes. As for the other state-changes (creation and destruction of subjects and objects), the granularity is unimportant. That is, we can allow multiple subjects and objects to be created and destroyed simultaneously without affecting any of our contributions. The reason is that those state-changes by themselves cannot cause the satisfaction of the policy to be affected.

3. ENFORCEMENT

We now consider enforcement of the Chinese Wall security policy. Enforcement is the process by which we allow or disallow a prospective change to the authorization state. An enforcement mechanism specifies, given a particular state, which changes are allowed. We define it more precisely below.

In the context of the Chinese Wall security policy, an attempt to create or destroy a subject or object always succeeds, so long as the subject/object being created has not been created before, and the subject/object being destroyed exists. The reason, as we discuss in the previous section, is that those state-changes do not affect satisfaction of the policy. Any conditions on such actions is beyond the scope of the policy. Of course, an enforcement mechanism may want to keep track of which subjects/objects exist. The main focus of an enforcement mechanism is whether an attempt by a subject that exists to read or write an object that exists is allowed.

DEFINITION 4 (ENFORCEMENT MECHANISM). *An* enforcement mechanism *is an algorithm that either allows or denies a request for a state-change (creation, destruction, read and write). Some persistent data that we call* enforcement state *may be consulted and updated by the algorithm.*

We have kept the above definition somewhat informal. We could, instead, have defined an enforcement mechanism by characterizing it as a particular kind of automaton, as is done in some prior work on access enforcement (see, for example, [14, 19]). We have adopted the above definition for clarity of exposition but without compromising rigor or correctness.

Enforcement state The enforcement state "shadows" a corresponding authorization state. Indeed, an enforcement state could be exactly the corresponding authorization state. However, that would not correspond to an efficient enforcement mechanism. The reason is that we would then be maintaining data even for subjects and objects that do not exist — that size can be unbounded in the number of subjects and objects that exist.

It is reasonable that the size of the enforcement state is a non-constant (e.g., linear) function of the number of subjects and objects that exist because in any realistic system, some data is associated with something that exists to indicate that it exists.

An example A simple example of an enforcement mechanism is one that maintains, as the enforcement state, a set of subjects and objects that exist, allows the creation of any subject or object that does not already exist, allows any subject that exists to write any object that exists, and disallows all reads. When a subject or object is created, it is added to the set that is the enforcement state, and when a subject or object is destroyed, it is removed from the set.

Such an enforcement mechanism is time and space efficient — the enforcement state is linear in the number of subjects and objects that exist, and the algorithms are each at worst linear-time in the number of subjects and objects that exist. It also ensures that the Chinese Wall security policy is always met. However, it is highly restrictive as a consequence of disallowing any attempt to read. Large numbers of states that do not violate the Chinese Wall security policy are precluded from being reached.

Least-restrictive enforcement This leads us to our notion of a least-restrictive enforcement mechanism, and axes for trade-offs other than restrictiveness. We define the former in this section, and discuss the latter in the next section. Before we define what it means for an enforcement mechanism to be least-restrictive, we define the notion of an empty authorization state.

DEFINITION 5 (EMPTY AUTHORIZATION STATE). *An empty authorization state is a graph as characterized in Section 2.1 in which for all $v \in V$, exists$(v) = 0$ and $E = \emptyset$.*

An empty state can be seen as characterizing a system at the start. No subjects or objects have been created yet, and nothing has been accessed. We discuss why we need it after our following definition on least restrictive enforcement.

DEFINITION 6 (LEAST-RESTRICTIVE). *Let σ_0 be the empty state. Let $\sigma_0 \rightarrow \sigma_1 \rightarrow \ldots \rightarrow \sigma_n$ be a sequence of states such that σ_{i+1} is reachable from σ_i via a state-change. Let σ_n be such that the Chinese Wall security policy is satisfied in it. An enforcement mechanism is said to be least-restrictive if it allows σ_n to be reached from σ_0 via some sequence of state-changes.*

The above definition of a least-restrictive enforcement mechanism captures our intent that every state that does not violate conflict of interest should be reachable from σ_0. The reason we insist that the start state of any sequence we consider is the empty state σ_0 is because we want the particular enforcement mechanism under consideration to be used from the start of the system. An enforcement mechanism maintains an enforcement state as we specify in Definition 4. We expect that the enforcement state that corresponds to σ_0 for any enforcement mechanism is empty. If we allow a sequence of state-changes to begin at some arbitrary authorization state, we would have to allow a particular enforcement mechanism to initialize its enforcement state to be consistent with that start state. We simply require the start state to be σ_0 instead.

In the above definition, it may seem interesting that we do not require the intermediate states $\sigma_1, \ldots, \sigma_{n-1}$ to also satisfy the policy. The reason is captured by the following lemma.

LEMMA 1. *Let $\sigma_0 \rightarrow \sigma_1 \rightarrow \ldots \rightarrow \sigma_n$ be a sequence of authorization states each reachable from the previous by a state-change, where σ_0 is the empty state. Let σ_k for $k \in [0, n]$ violate the Chinese Wall security policy. Then, each of the states $\sigma_{k+1}, \ldots, \sigma_n$ violates the policy as well.*

PROOF. Let some state σ_i where $i \in [k+1, n]$, not violate the policy when some prior state σ_k does. We use induction on $i - k$. For the base case, $i = k + 1$. We do a case-analysis on the state-change $\sigma_k \rightarrow \sigma_{k+1}$ and produce a contradiction for each case in a straightforward manner. If the state-change is the creation of a subject or object, then this cannot affect the violation of the policy that exists in σ_k. We observe similarly that the destruction of a subject or object, or a read or write action by a subject on an object do not affect the policy violation that exists in σ_k.

We adopt the induction assumption that for $i = k+m-1$, where $m \geq 1$, all the states $\sigma_k, \ldots, \sigma_i$ violate conflict of interest. For the step, we adopt $i = k + m$, and perform a case-analysis similar to that for the base case above for the state-change $\sigma_{i-1} \rightarrow \sigma_i$ and produce a contradiction. ☐

As a consequence of the above lemma, in Definition 6, given that σ_n satisfies the Chinese Wall security policy, we know that each of the prior states $\sigma_0, \sigma_1, \ldots, \sigma_{n-1}$ satisfies it as well. Furthermore, we are able to assert the following lemma that states that if a state

σ satisfies the policy, then an enforcement mechanism that is least-restrictive allows *every* possible sequence of states that reaches σ from the empty state. (We recognize that we could have simply defined "least-restrictive" to be this. However, we argue that ours is a better enforcement mechanism — adopt the notion that appears weaker as the definition, and then assert this stronger result as a lemma.)

LEMMA 2. *Let $\mathcal{A}$ be a least-restrictive enforcement mechanism for the Chinese Wall security policy. Let the policy be satisfied in the state σ_n and let $\Psi = \sigma_0 \rightarrow \ldots \rightarrow \sigma_n$, where σ_0 is the empty state, be some sequence of states via which σ_n is reached. Then, $\mathcal{A}$ allows the sequence Ψ to occur.*

PROOF. The policy is satisfied for any σ_k in Ψ. Therefore, σ_k is reachable under $\mathcal{A}$. Induction on k completes the proof. ☐

3.1 Axes for Trade-offs

While the main focus of this paper is least-restrictive enforcement, we recognize that an enforcement mechanism that is least-restrictive should not be unduly poor in other properties of interest such as time- and space-efficiency. Indeed, in Section 4.2, we ask along what axis we (need to) trade-off to achieve least-restriction.

Example For example, it is possible to conceive an enforcement mechanism that is least-restrictive that maintains as its enforcement state the authorization state (the graph). The enforcement mechanism would work as follows. If there is an attempt by a subject to read or write, we simply simulate that action by changing the graph as though the attempt is allowed — that is, we add the corresponding edge to the graph. We then run a graph-search algorithm similar to Floyd-Warshall's [9, 23] to determine whether the policy is violated in the new graph. Such an algorithm would correctly tell us whether the policy is violated or not because information flow demonstrates optimal substructure similar to shortest-paths in graphs — a sub-path of an information flow is an information flow.

If we discover that the policy is violated in the new graph, we disallow the request and retain the current authorization state as our enforcement state. If it is not, we allow it and adopt the new state as the enforcement state. It is possible to show that this enforcement mechanism is indeed least-restrictive. (We omit a proof in this paper.) However, as we discuss in the previous section, it is inefficient from the standpoint of space and time. The space is unbounded in the number of subjects and objects that exist. And this in turn causes an algorithm such as Floyd-Warshall's [9, 23] to be inefficient, as it is polynomial-time in the input graph.

The axes we consider

- *Soundness* – we want an enforcement mechanism to be sound — an attempt to read or write is denied if it would cause a violation of the policy. This captures the basic security property that we need to maintain.

- *Time- and Space-efficiency* – we would want an enforcement mechanism to be time- and space-efficient. By space, we mean what we call enforcement state, and any other auxiliary space used by an algorithm in the enforcement mechanism.

- *Least-restriction* – we would want an enforcement mechanism to be least-restrictive in the authorization states it allows to be reached.

- *Independence of subjects* – an issue with which prior work [13] deals is whether the prospective actions of a subject can be constrained by the actions of other subjects. This can be

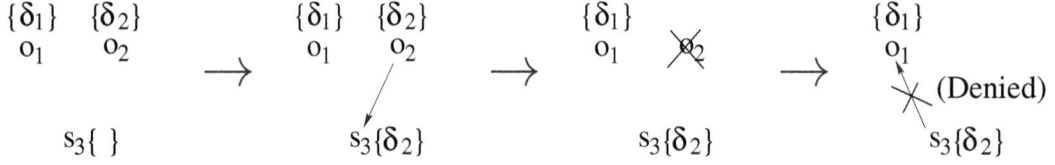

$$
\begin{array}{ccccccc}
\{\delta_1\} & \{\delta_2\} & & \{\delta_1\} & \{\delta_2\} & & \{\delta_1\} \\
o_1 & o_2 & \rightarrow & o_1 & o_2 & \rightarrow & o_1 \quad \cancel{o_2} & \rightarrow & o_1 \\
& & & & & & & & \text{(Denied)} \\
s_3\{\ \} & & & s_3\{\delta_2\} & & & s_3\{\delta_2\} & & s_3\{\delta_2\}
\end{array}
$$

Figure 3: Our enforcement algorithm for the state-changes from Figure 2. We denote $\delta(o_1) = \delta_1$ and $\delta(o_2) = \delta_2$. The enforcement state that corresponds to each subject and object is shown in "{ }." The figure to the far left indicates that no information from any Company Dataset other than the one to which each belongs has flowed into o_1 and o_2. As s_3 is created in that state, the set that corresponds to it is empty. The write by s_3 in the final state is denied because the "if" condition in WRITE evaluates to true.

deemed undesirable. We make this notion of independence of subjects more precise in the following definition so we can articulate Theorem 3 in Section 4.3. That theorem asserts that it is impossible to achieve least-restriction without trading-off independence of subjects.

DEFINITION 7 (INDEPENDENCE OF SUBJECTS). *Let σ_0 be the empty state and $\mathcal{A}$ be an enforcement mechanism. Starting at σ_0, suppose $\Psi_a = \langle \psi_1, \psi_2, \ldots, \psi_n \rangle$ is a sequence of state-changes that is allowed by $\mathcal{A}$, but the state-change ψ_{n+1} that is the read or write by a subject s on some object is not allowed by $\mathcal{A}$ immediately after Ψ_a. Let Ψ_b be a subsequence of Ψ_a that we get by removing one or more read and write actions of a subject $s' \neq s$ such that $\mathcal{A}$ allows ψ_{n+1} immediately after Ψ_b. Then we say that under $\mathcal{A}$, the actions of a subject are not independent of the actions of other subjects. If no such pair $\langle \Psi_a, \Psi_b \rangle$ exists, then we say that under $\mathcal{A}$, the actions of a subject are independent.*

We point out that our above definition has similarities to non-interference [1, 2].

- *Access to sanitized objects* – given that the intent of sanitized objects is to contain public information, it is desirable that subjects are able to read such objects freely so long as there has been no flow of information into a sanitized object from an unsanitized object.

- *Transitivity of the conflict of interest relation* – as Lin [15] points out, the conflict of interest relation is not necessarily transitive, and therefore an enforcement mechanism should not assume that it is.

4. OUR APPROACH

In this section, we present our enforcement mechanism and show that it is least-restrictive. We discuss also how well it does along the other axes for trade-offs that we discuss in the previous section.

Enforcement state The enforcement state in our approach, $\mathcal{V}$, is a set of sets. We maintain a set for every subject and object that exists; that is, has been created and not destroyed. Let $\Delta_v \in \mathcal{V}$ be associated with $v \in S \cup O$ where $exists(v) = 1$. Then $\Delta_v \subseteq D$, where D is the set of Company Datasets (see Section 2.1). $\mathcal{V}$ is initialized to $\emptyset$.

Algorithm Our enforcement algorithm is conceptually simple. When information flows from v_1 to v_2 via a read or write, our approach propagates some "control data" as well — the set of Com-

pany Datasets with which v_1 is associated. We present the algorithm as a set of sub-routines, each corresponding to the kind of state-change that is attempted.

CREATE (v)
    if $\exists \Delta_v \in \mathcal{V}$ **then** Error
    if $v \in O$ **then** $\Delta_v \leftarrow \{\delta(v)\}$ **else** $\Delta_v \leftarrow \emptyset$
    $\mathcal{V} \leftarrow \mathcal{V} \cup \Delta_v$

DESTROY (v)
    $\mathcal{V} \leftarrow \mathcal{V} - \Delta_v$

READ (s, o)
    if $\exists d_i, d_j$ with $\{d_i, d_j\} \subseteq \Delta_s \cup \Delta_o$ and $C(d_i, d_j) = 1$
    then deny
    else $\Delta_s \leftarrow \Delta_s \cup \Delta_o$; allow

WRITE (s, o)
    if $\exists d_i, d_j$ with $\{d_i, d_j\} \subseteq \Delta_s \cup \Delta_o$ and $C(d_i, d_j) = 1$
    then deny
    else $\Delta_o \leftarrow \Delta_s \cup \Delta_o$; allow

When a subject or object v is created, CREATE initializes a set Δ_v and adds it to the enforcement state, $\mathcal{V}$. Δ_v is set to $\emptyset$ if v is a subject, and the Company Dataset to which v belongs if v is an object. When a subject or object is destroyed, DESTROY removes the set that corresponds to it from the enforcement state, $\mathcal{V}$.

When a subject s attempts to read or write an object o, it may be denied by the corresponding "if" condition, which examines $\Delta_s \cup \Delta_o$ for the existence of company datasets that are in conflict. If a read by s of o succeeds, then Δ_s is updated, and if a write succeeds, then Δ_o is updated.

The "if" condition in READ above is needed only if we wish to prevent subject-violations. The "if" condition in WRITE is needed only if we wish to prevent object-violations. If, for example, we seek to prevent subject-violations only and not object-violations, then we can remove the "if" condition in WRITE (thereby allowing all write requests), and only update Δ_o as specified under "else" in WRITE.

The conceptual simplicity of our approach ensures its efficiency, and belies its power. In the next three sections, we discuss how our approach performs along each axis from Section 3.1. In particular, in Section 4.2 we show that it is least-restrictive, and in Section 4.3 we show that any enforcement mechanism that is least-restrictive must incur the same trade-off that our enforcement mechanism does. In Section 4.4, we address the question as to whether ours is the only possible enforcement mechanism to enforcing the Chinese Wall security policy that is least-restrictive.

4.1 Soundness

The soundness of our enforcement mechanism is based on the following lemma regarding the set Δ_v that corresponds to a vertex v in the enforcement state $\mathcal{V}$ in our enforcement mechanism.

LEMMA 3. *Let $\sigma_0 \to \sigma_1 \to \ldots \to \sigma_n$ be an authorization state-change sequence that is allowed by our enforcement mechanism. Let $v_1 \rightsquigarrow v_2$ be an information flow in σ_n where $v_1 \in O$ and $exists(v_2) = 1$. Then, in the enforcement state, $\mathcal{V}$, that corresponds to σ_n, (1) $\exists \Delta_{v_2} \in \mathcal{V}$, and, (2) $\delta(v_1) \in \Delta_{v_2}$.*

PROOF. For (1), we observe that Δ_{v_2} is created and added to $\mathcal{V}$ in CREATE, and is removed in DESTROY only. Therefore, given that v_2 is created, but not destroyed in the sequence $\sigma_0 \to \ldots \to \sigma_n$, we know (1) is true. For (2), we use induction on n.

For the base cases with $n = 0$ and $n = 1$, the assertion is trivially true as there is no information flow in either σ_0 or σ_1 — there are no vertices in σ_0, and at most one vertex in σ_1. For the step, we assume that the assertion is true for all n between 0 and k. We consider the case that $n = k + 1$, and perform a case-analysis on the state-change $\sigma_k \to \sigma_{k+1}$.

If the state-change is a creation or destruction of a subject or object, no new information flows are added to σ_k, and we rely directly on the induction assumption for the proof. Consider the case that the state-change is a read by subject s on object o. Then, the only new information flows that are added are into s. We observe also that the only component of the enforcement state that changes in READ is Δ_s. Consider an information flow $v \rightsquigarrow s$, for some $v \in O$, in σ_{n+1} that does not exist in σ_n. As the only new edge in E is from o to s, there must have existed an information flow $v \rightsquigarrow o$ in σ_n. By the induction assumption, in the enforcement state that corresponds to σ_n, $\delta(v) \in \Delta_o$. The component Δ_o does not change between σ_n and σ_{n+1}, and in READ, we perform $\Delta_s \leftarrow \Delta_s \cup \Delta_o$, and therefore $\delta(v) \in \Delta_s$ in the enforcement state that corresponds to σ_{n+1}, as desired.

The proof for the case that the state-change $\sigma_n \to \sigma_{n+1}$ is a write by s to o is identical to the above. □

THEOREM 1 (SOUNDNESS). *Let $\sigma_0 \to \sigma_1 \to \ldots \to \sigma_n$ be an authorization state-change sequence that is allowed by our enforcement mechanism such that σ_n satisfies the Chinese Wall security policy. Let $\sigma_n \to \sigma_{n+1}$ be a state-change such that the policy is violated in σ_{n+1}. Then our enforcement mechanism disallows the sequence $\sigma_0 \to \sigma_1 \to \ldots \to \sigma_n \to \sigma_{n+1}$.*

The full proof for subjection-violations is in Appendix A. The proof for object-violations is analogous. The intuition behind the proof is that we have only two cases: one of the intermediate state-changes $\sigma_i \to \sigma_{i+1}$ is denied, or the state-change $\sigma_n \to \sigma_{n+1}$ is denied. The former implies that the sequence is disallowed. For the latter, we assume that the state-change is a read by s on o which is allowed, but there are flows $o_1 \rightsquigarrow s, o_2 \rightsquigarrow s$ that cause a subject-violation in σ_{n+1}. We then derive a contradiction. To do this, we show that we have only two possibilities for the enforcement state, $\mathcal{V}$, in σ_n. Either $\{\delta(o_1), \delta(o_2)\} \subseteq \Delta_o$, or one of $\delta(o_1)$ and $\delta(o_2)$ is in Δ_s and the other is in Δ_o. Then, the "if" condition in READ evaluates to false, thereby contradicting our claim that the state-change is allowed.

4.2 Least-Restriction

In this section, we show that our enforcement mechanism is least-restrictive.

LEMMA 4. *Let $\sigma_0 \to \sigma_1 \to \ldots \to \sigma_n$ be a sequence of authorization states that is allowed by our enforcement mechanism. In*

the enforcement state that corresponds to σ_n, suppose $d_i \in \Delta_v$ for $v \in V$. Then, either $v \in O$ and $d_i = \delta(v)$, or there exists some $o \in O$ with $\delta(o) = d_i$ and an information flow $o \rightsquigarrow v$ in σ_n.

PROOF. We use induction on $n \geq 1$. For the base case, $n = 1$, we know that the state-change $\sigma_0 \to \sigma_1$ is the creation of a subject or object. If a subject s is created, then the enforcement state $\mathcal{V} = \{\Delta_s\}$ where $\Delta_s = \emptyset$, and the assertion is trivially true. If an object o is created, then there is only one entry $d_i \in \Delta_o$ where $d_i = \delta(o)$, and the assertion is true. For the step, we make the induction assumption that the assertion is true for all sequences with $n \leq k$. For the case that $n = k + 1$, we do a case-analysis on the kind of state-change $\sigma_k \to \sigma_{k+1}$. We adopt the notation $\mathcal{V}_j$ for the enforcement state that corresponds to the state σ_j.

If the state-change is the creation of a subject, then $d_i \in \Delta_v$ in $\mathcal{V}_{k+1}$ implies $d_i \in \Delta_v$ in $\mathcal{V}_k$, and we rely directly on the induction assumption for the proof. If it is the creation of an object o, then only $\delta(o) \in \Delta_o$ is a new entry in any Δ_v between $\mathcal{V}_k$ and $\mathcal{V}_{k+1}$. In this case, with the induction assumption, we have the proof. If it is read by subject s on object o, only Δ_s changes between $\mathcal{V}_k$ and $\mathcal{V}_{k+1}$. For all others, the induction assumption provides the proof. Let d_i be a new entry in Δ_s. Then, we know that $d_i \in \Delta_o$ in $\mathcal{V}_k$. By the induction assumption, either $d_i = \delta(o)$, or there is information flow $o' \rightsquigarrow o$ in σ_k where $\delta(o') = d_i$. The addition of the edge from o to s into E results in information flows $o \rightsquigarrow s$ and $o' \rightsquigarrow s$, and hence the proof. The proof for the case that the state-change is a write is similar to the one for read. □

LEMMA 5. *Let $\sigma_0 \to \sigma_1 \to \ldots \to \sigma_n$ be a sequence of authorization states that is allowed by our enforcement mechanism. Let $\sigma_n \to \sigma_{n+1}$ be a state-change that is denied by our enforcement mechanism. If the state-change from σ_n to σ_{n+1} is a read, then allowing σ_{n+1} results in a subject-violation of the Chinese Wall security policy. If the state-change from σ_n to σ_{n+1} is a write, then allowing σ_{n+1} results in an object-violation of the Chinese Wall security policy.*

PROOF. We present the proof for the case that the state-change from σ_n to σ_{n+1} is a read. The proof for the case that it is a write is analogous.

By Theorem 1, we know that σ_n does not violate the policy. Let the state-change $\sigma_n \to \sigma_{n+1}$ be an attempt by a subject s to read an object o for which the "if" condition in READ evaluates to true. Let d_i, d_j be a pair that causes the "if" condition to evaluate to true. One of the following two cases is true for the enforcement state that corresponds to σ_n. (1) $d_i \in \Delta_s$ and $d_j \in \Delta_o$, or, (2) $\{d_i, d_j\} \subseteq \Delta_o$. We point out that the case $\{d_i, d_j\} \subseteq \Delta_s$ in the enforcement state that corresponds to σ_n cannot happen. The reason is that if that is the case, then there exist information flows $o_1 \rightsquigarrow s$ and $o_2 \rightsquigarrow s$ in σ_n with $\delta(o_1) = d_i$ and $\delta(o_2) = d_j$. This is a violation of the policy, and by Theorem 1, this cannot happen.

If case (1) is true, then by Lemma 4, there exists $o_1 \in O$ such that $d_i = \delta(o_1)$ and the information flow $o_1 \rightsquigarrow s$ exists in σ_n. Also, there exists o_2 such that $d_j = \delta(o_2)$ and either $o_2 = o$ or there exists information flow $o_2 \rightsquigarrow o$ in σ_n. The addition of the edge from o to s would result in information flows $o_1 \rightsquigarrow s$ and $o_2 \rightsquigarrow s$, which results in a subject-violation.

In case (2), we know from Lemma 4 that there exist $o_1, o_2 \in O$ such that there exist information flows $o_1 \rightsquigarrow o$ and $o_2 \rightsquigarrow o$ in σ_n, or one of o_1, o_2 is the same as o. Thus, the addition of the edge from o to s to E results in information flows $o_1 \rightsquigarrow s$ and $o_2 \rightsquigarrow s$ which results in a subject-violation. □

THEOREM 2 (LEAST-RESTRICTION). *A sequence of authorization states $\sigma_0 \to \sigma_1 \to \ldots \to \sigma_n$ is allowed by our en-*

forcement mechanism if and only if σ_n does not violate conflict of interest.

PROOF. The "only if" part is exactly Theorem 1. The "if" part is exactly Lemma 5. □

4.3 Other Axes

In the previous sections, we show that our enforcement mechanism is sound and least-restrictive. In this section, we discuss how our enforcement mechanism does along the other axes from Section 3.1.

Time-efficiency Our enforcement mechanism is constant in the number of objects and subjects that exist. It is polynomial (at worst quadratic) in the number of company datasets, which we can think of as constant in the number of subjects and objects that exist.

Space-efficiency The size of the enforcement state is $O(|V_{exists}| \times |D|)$, where V_{exists} is the set of subjects and objects that exist, and D is the set of company datasets. If we assume that the number of company datasets is constant, then the space we need is linear in the number of subjects and objects that exist.

Independence of subjects In our enforcement mechanism, the actions of a subject can constrain the actions of another subject. This can be seen as a limitation of our enforcement mechanism. However, as we express in Theorem 3 below, this is unavoidable for any enforcement mechanism that is least-restrictive. It may be possible to characterize the "degree" of independence of subjects; this is beyond the scope of our work.

THEOREM 3. *Let $\mathcal{A}$ be an enforcement mechanism. If $\mathcal{A}$ is least-restrictive, then subjects are not independent. That is, the actions of a subject can constrain the prospective actions of other subjects.*

The proof for the above theorem is in Appendix A.

Access to sanitized objects Our enforcement mechanism places no restrictions on access to sanitized objects so long as those objects are not used as conduits to a policy violation.

Transitivity of the conflict of interest relation The conflict of interest relation does not have to be transitive in our enforcement mechanism.

4.4 Uniqueness of Our Enforcement Mechanism

One may ask whether ours is the only possible enforcement mechanism that is least-restrictive. While we are unable to prove such a strong result, we assert in the following theorem that any enforcement mechanism that is least-restrictive must deny *some* attempt by a subject to read an object to prevent subject-violations, and some attempt by a subject to write an object to prevent object-violations. This validates our design choice of mediating read attempts to prevent subject-violations, and mediating write attempts to prevent object-violations.

THEOREM 4. *Let $\mathcal{A}$ be an enforcement mechanism for the Chinese Wall security policy that is least-restrictive. Then $\mathcal{A}$ must deny some attempt by a subject to read an object to prevent subject-violations, and must deny some attempt by a subject to write to an object to prevent object-violations.*

The proof for the case that we deny a read to prevent subject-violations is in Appendix A. The proof for denying a write to prevent object-violations is analogous.

5. THE BREWER-NASH APPROACH

In this section, we present new results on the Brewer-Nash enforcement mechanism. We identify the enforcement state that their approach needs to maintain, and express the simple security and ∗-rules, and the corresponding rules for read and write as algorithms.

Enforcement state We can directly infer the enforcement state that needs to be maintained from the simple-security and ∗-rules. To assess whether the simple-security rule is met when a subject s requests access to an object o, we need to know whether an object from $\delta(o)$ has already been accessed, and whether given any $o' \in O$ already accessed by s, $C(\delta(o'), \delta(o)) = 0$. In addition, for the ∗-rule, we need to know whether the Company Dataset for any object that can be read by s is different from $\delta(o)$.

Consequently, these rules can be applied if we maintain: (a) for each subject that exists, the set of Company Datasets of objects it has already accessed (read or written), and, (b) the set of objects that exist. (For (a), we can alternately maintain the set of Company Datasets from which no object has been accessed by each subject.)

As for our enforcement mechanism, we represent the enforcement state as $\mathcal{V}$, which comprises sets $\Delta_s \subseteq D$ of Company Datasets, where the subscript s is the subject with whom Δ_s is associated.

Algorithm We now present the algorithm for the Brewer-Nash enforcement mechanism as sub-routines for read and write attempts, READ-BN and WRITE-BN, respectively. We omit the ones for creation and destruction — those involve straightforward updates to the enforcement state, similar to our enforcement mechanism. We present the simple-security and ∗-rules as sub-routines invoked by READ-BN and WRITE-BN. (We number the lines of SIMPLE-SECURITY and ∗ below as we need to refer to them in our proofs in the next section.)

SIMPLE-SECURITY(s, o)

1 **if** $\delta(o) \in \Delta_s$ **then return** true
2 **else if** $\exists o'$ with $\delta(o') \in \Delta_s$ *and* $C(\delta(o), \delta(o')) = 1$ **then return** false
3 **else return** true

∗(s, o)

1 **if** *SIMPLE-SECURITY$(s, o) = false$* **then return** false
2 **else if** $\exists o'$ with *SIMPLE-SECURITY$(s, o') = true$*, $\delta(o) \neq \delta(o')$, *and* $\delta(o') \neq D_{[s]}$ **then return** false
3 **else return** true

READ-BN(s, o)

   if *exists(o) and SIMPLE-SECURITY(s, o)* **then**
      $\Delta_s \leftarrow \Delta_s \cup \{\delta(o)\}$; allow
   else deny

WRITE-BN(s, o)

   if *exists(o) and ∗(s, o)* **then**
      $\Delta_s \leftarrow \Delta_s \cup \{\delta(o)\}$; allow
   else deny

Evaluation The Brewer-Nash enforcement mechanism is sound — if a request is allowed, we are guaranteed that the policy is not violated in the subsequent state.

The enforcement mechanism is not least-restrictive. For example, as we mention in Section 1, the authorization state that corresponds to Figure 1 is not reachable under Brewer-Nash even though it does not violate the Chinese Wall security policy. The subject s_2

would have been denied the ability to write to o_4 having previously read o_5.

Although the original exposition of Brewer-Nash [6] assumes that the conflict of interest relation is transitive, there is nothing in their enforcement mechanism that requires this, as is demonstrated above by our exposition.

Under Brewer-Nash, subjects are independent; that is, the actions of a subject do not constrain the prospective actions of another subject. (By Theorem 3 in Section 4.3, this is another way to intuit that Brewer-Nash is not least-restrictive.) It is space-efficient — we maintain only $O(|S_{exists}| \cdot |D| + |O_{exists}|)$ amount of space, where S_{exists} and O_{exists} are the sets of subjects and objects that exist, respectively. It is less time-efficient than our enforcement mechanism, but still polynomial-time in the number of objects that exist. The algorithm SIMPLE-SECURITY, and therefore READ-BN, runs in time $O(|O_{exists}| \cdot |D|)$, and $*$, and therefore WRITE-BN, runs in time $O(|O_{exists}|^2 \cdot |D|)$.

5.1 New Properties

In this section, we present new properties of the Brewer-Nash enforcement mechanism. Theorem 5 expresses that the enforcement mechanism is even more restrictive than previous work suggests [13, 17, 18]. Theorem 6 expresses that the $*$-rule is overstated.

THEOREM 5. *Suppose there exists a subject s and an unsanitized object o such that s is allowed to write to o under Brewer-Nash. Then, there is exactly one Conflict of Interest class to which all unsanitized objects belong.*

PROOF. We can restate the theorem as the following: suppose there exists $s \in S$ and $o_1 \in O$ such that WRITE-BN$(s, o_1) =$ allow. Then for any $o_2 \in O$ with $exists(o_2) = 1$, $\delta(o_2) \neq D_{[s]}$ and $\delta(o_2) \neq \delta(o_1)$, we have $C(\delta(o_1), \delta(o_2)) = 1$.

Suppose, as in the premise, WRITE-BN$(s, o_1) =$ allow. This means that $*(s, o_1) =$ true. Therefore, $*(s, o_1)$ returns in Line 3 of that routine. Now consider any other $o_2 \in O$ with $exists(o_2) = 1$, $\delta(o_2) \neq \delta(o_1)$ and $\delta(o_2) \neq D_{[s]}$. We need to show that $C(\delta(o_2), \delta(o_1)) = 1$.

Suppose, for the purpose of contradiction, that $C(\delta(o_2), \delta(o_1)) = 0$. We have two cases: (a) READ-BN(s, o_2) returns allow, or, (b) READ-BN(s, o_2) returns disallow. In case (a), we have the following contradiction. We know that $*(s, o_1) =$ true, yet, the condition in Line 2 of $*(s, o_1)$ evaluates to true for $o' = o_2$. The reason is that SIMPLE-SECURITY(s, o_2) has to return true for READ-BN(s, o_2) to be allow.

In case (b), we know that SIMPLE-SECURITY$(s, o_2) =$ false. Therefore, there is some o_3 that serves as the o' in Line 2 of SIMPLE-SECURITY(s, o_2). We now consider the following sub-cases. (i) $o_3 = o_1$. This results in a contradiction because by Line 2 of SIMPLE-SECURITY(s, o_2), $C(\delta(o_3), \delta(o_2)) = 1$, but we have assumed that $C(\delta(o_1), \delta(o_2)) = 0$. (ii) $o_3 \neq o_1$, but $\delta(o_3) = \delta(o_1)$. This results in the same contradiction as (i). And finally, (iii) $o_3 \neq o_1$ and $\delta(o_3) \neq \delta(o_1)$. Now, because o_3 serves as the o' in Line 2 of SIMPLE-SECURITY(s, o_2), we know that $\delta(o_3) \in \Delta_s$. This means that READ-BN$(s, o_3) =$ allow. Now consider an invocation of $*(s, o_1)$. The "if" condition in Line 2 evaluates to true for $o' = o_3$, and the invocation returns false. But this contradicts the assumption that WRITE-BN(s, o_1) returns allow. $\square$

Before we present the next theorem, we restate the $*$-rule. "Write access is only permitted if (a) access is permitted by the simple security rule, and, (b) no object can be read which is in a different Company Dataset to the one for which write access is requested and contains unsanitized information."

THEOREM 6. *If a subject s and object o satisfy subrule (b) of the $*$-rule of Brewer-Nash, then they satisfy subrule (a) (the simple-security rule).*

PROOF. We can restate the theorem as follows: let $s \in S$ and $o \in O$. Assume that $\nexists o'$ such that READ-BN$(s, o') =$ allow, $\delta(o) \neq \delta(o')$ and $\delta(o') \neq D_{[s]}$. Then, SIMPLE-SECURITY$(s, o) =$ true.

Given our assumption, we know that for all $o' \neq o$, at least one of the following is true. (a) READ-BN$(s, o') =$ deny, (b) $\delta(o') = \delta(o)$, or, (c) $\delta(o') = D_{[s]}$. For the purpose of contradiction, assume that SIMPLE-SECURITY$(s, o) =$ false. This means that the "if" condition in Line 2 of SIMPLE-SECURITY(s, o) evaluates to true. That is, there exists some o'' that serves as the o' in Line 2. Specifically, $\delta(o'') \in \Delta_s$.

Such an o'' cannot serve as o' in (c) above, as then, $C(\delta(o''), \delta(o)) = 0$. Suppose it serves as the o' in (b) above. Then, SIMPLE-SECURITY$(s, o) =$ true from Line 1; a contradiction. Finally, suppose o'' serves as the o' in (a) above. But, in the last sentence of the previous paragraph, we asserted that $\delta(o'') \in \Delta_s$. Therefore, READ-BN$(s, o'') =$ allow, a contradiction. $\square$

5.2 Bishop's Rendition [5]

Bishop [5] reproduces the work of Brewer and Nash in his popular book on computer security. However, perhaps for brevity of exposition, he treats sanitized objects differently. In Bishop's rendition, D, the set of Company Datasets does not contain the special Dataset $D_{[s]}$ for sanitized objects, but only a Dataset for each company, $D_1, \ldots, D_k$. Every object also has what one can think of as a one-bit labelling function, $l: O \longrightarrow \{u, \overline{u}\}$, which indicates whether it is unsanitized or sanitized. The simple security rule is amended to the following.

SIMPLE-SECURITY-BISHOP(s, o)
  if $l(o) = \overline{u}$ **then return** true
  else return SIMPLE-SECURITY(s, o)

This somewhat subtle difference in expressing the simple-security rule has fairly significant consequences. A system that adopts SIMPLE-SECURITY-BISHOP instead of SIMPLE-SECURITY does not behave as it would under the Brewer-Nash rules. Specifically, Theorem 6 is no longer necessarily true.

We can show this with a counterexample. Suppose we have a subject s and two objects o_1 and o_2. The objects belong to different Company Datasets, D_1 and D_2, respectively. The two Company Datasets are in conflict; i.e., $C(D_1, D_2) = 1$. The object o_1 is sanitized, and o_2 is unsanitized. The subject s has read the object o_1 at time t.

We observe that SIMPLE-SECURITY-BISHOP(s, o_2) is false. The reason is that the "if" condition in Line 2 of SIMPLE-SECURITY, which is invoked by SIMPLE-SECURITY-BISHOP, is met for $o' = o_1$, and therefore it returns false in Line 2. However, subrule (b) of the $*$-rule is trivially true. Consequently, satisfaction of subrule (b) of the $*$-rule does not imply satisfaction of subrule (a) in Bishop's rendition, which is what Theorem 6 asserts about Brewer-Nash.

This suggests something good about Bishop's enforcement mechanism when compared to the Brewer-Nash enforcement mechanism: the $*$-rule is not overstated. However, a closer examination of our counterexample shows a somewhat peculiar behaviour by the system. Suppose s has not yet read o_1. Then, s is allowed to read o_2. And, s may later read o_1 as well, because $l(o_1) = \overline{u}$ and therefore SIMPLE-SECURITY-BISHOP is always true for it. In other words, the order in which s reads sanitized and unsanitized objects matters. This is not the case with the Brewer-Nash enforcement mechanism.

6. RELATED WORK

There is a large body of work that pertains to the Chinese Wall security policy [20]. A comprehensive discussion is beyond the scope of our paper. Our work pertains to enforcement of the policy. As such, it is most closely related to the original work of Brewer and Nash [6], and the subsequent work of Lin [15], Kessler [13] and Sandhu [17, 18]. We discuss those pieces of work first, and then sample other work. We have discussed the work of Brewer and Nash [6] extensively in this paper, and therefore do not discuss it any further.

The work of Lin [15] points out that Brewer-Nash assumes that the conflict of interest relation is transitive, but it does not have to be. We have adopted his generalization in this work.

The work of Kessler [13] makes observations about how restrictive the Brewer-Nash enforcement mechanism can be (see Section 1). That work then proposes an alternate enforcement mechanism that is purportedly less restrictive. It does not consider the notion of least-restrictive enforcement.

Furthermore, Kessler [13] precludes two subjects from being able to write to the same object. Specifically, once a subject writes to an object, no other subject can write to the same object. We point out that two subjects could read and write a single object only, and thereby not violate the Chinese Wall security policy.

This is an aspect with which Kessler's approach cannot be said to be less restrictive than Brewer-Nash. That is, there exist authorization states that satisfy the Chinese Wall security policy that are unreachable under Kessler's approach that are reachable under Brewer-Nash. And, there exist other authorization states that satisfy the policy that are unreachable under Brewer-Nash that are reachable under Kessler's approach.

Sandhu's work [17, 18] also observes that the Brewer-Nash enforcement mechanism is restrictive (see Section 1). It also points out some confusion in the work of Brewer and Nash [6] regarding subjects, as opposed to users and principals. We have incorporated Sandhu's mindset in our work. Sandhu's work [17, 18] also refutes an assertion of Brewer and Nash [6] that the Chinese Wall security policy cannot be encoded in a lattice. That work proposes a construction, which we can perceive as an enforcement mechanism for the policy.

In Sandhu's enforcement mechanism, every object and subject is associated with a label from a lattice. The enforcement mechanism then simply uses the "no read up" and "no write down" rules that is customary for lattice-based access control systems. In Sandhu's enforcement mechanism, subjects are independent, and this immediately tells us that the enforcement mechanism is not least-restrictive (see Theorem 3 in Section 4.3). Furthermore, as a subject is bound to a label in the lattice, if an object belongs to only one Company Dataset (as is the case in the original specification of Brewer and Nash [6]), a subject that can read objects from two Company Datasets cannot write to any object. The reason is that such a subject must be at least one level above all objects in the lattice, and by the "no write down" rule, it cannot write any object. (We discuss below, however, that Sandhu's work [17, 18] proposes the generalization that an object can be labelled with multiple Company Datasets from different Conflict of Interest classes.) We point out also that Sandhu's enforcement mechanism requires the Conflict of Interest relation to be transitive.

We now sample other work on the Chinese Wall security policy with which our work is not related closely. Our intent is to give a somewhat broad overview of the kinds of work related to the Chinese Wall security policy that exists.

There has been work on realizing the Chinese Wall security policy in specific contexts. Recent work [22, 24] proposes the application of the policy to cloud computing environments. Tsai et al. [22] propose to use the Chinese Wall security policy to resist particular kinds of attacks in the context of cloud-computing, such as what they call an inter-Virtual Machine (VM) attack. They give an algorithm based on graph-coloring to assign VMs that do not belong to the same Conflict of Interest class to the same physical machine, and then use the Brewer-Nash enforcement mechanism to prevent such attacks. Wu et al. [24] propose to use the Brewer-Nash enforcement mechanism as an Infrastructure-as-a-Service (IaaS) in cloud-computing environments, and provide an implementation. Similar earlier work on applying the Chinese Wall security policy to specific contexts are those of Loscocco and Smalley [16], Jajodia et al. [12], and Edjlali et al. [8].

Other work, such as that of Atluri et al. [4] and Sobel and Alves-Foss [21] generalizes the Brewer-Nash policy. The work of Sandhu [17, 18] also proposes the generalization that objects be allowed to be associated with multiple Company Datasets from different Conflict of Interest classes. Such generalizations are certainly interesting, but are beyond the scope of this work. We consider only the original setup of Brewer and Nash [6], and leave dealing with such generalizations for future work.

Finally, there is work that attempts to reconcile or model the simple-security and ∗-rules of Brewer-Nash within it. An example of such work is that of Fong [10]. Such work is relevant to enforcement. However, it does not consider the issues our work addresses — that of least-restrictive enforcement of the policy.

7. CONCLUSION

We have addressed enforcement of the Chinese Wall security policy. Specifically, we have proposed a notion of least-restrictive enforcement of the policy, devised an enforcement mechanism and shown that it is least-restrictive. Our enforcement mechanism is simple, sound and efficient. Our enforcement mechanism mediates read attempts only to prevent subject-violations, and write attempts only to prevent object-violations.

We have precisely identified the trade-off our enforcement mechanism incurs in achieving least-restriction. The actions of a subject may constrain the prospective actions of other subjects, a property that we call (lack of) independence of subjects. We have established the somewhat strong result that *any* enforcement mechanism to enforcing the Chinese Wall security policy that is least-restrictive must incur this trade-off.

We have then established two new results for the Brewer-Nash enforcement mechanism to enforcement [6]. We have shown that it is more restrictive than previous work points out. We have shown that if a subject is allowed to write to an object, then all objects must belong to the same Conflict of Interest class. We have shown also that the so-called ∗-rule that is part of the Brewer-Nash enforcement mechanism to enforcement is overstated in that one of its sub-rules implies the other. We have also investigated the rendition of the Brewer-Nash enforcement mechanism in Bishop's work [5], and shown that it is not equivalent to the Brewer-Nash enforcement mechanism.

In summary, our work establishes new results, and thereby sheds new light on what is generally considered to be important work in information security.

In our discussion on related work, we observe that subsequent enforcement mechanisms of Kessler [13] and Sandhu [17, 18] are also restrictive in their own ways, and not least-restrictive.

We see applications of our enforcement mechanism as the most promising future work. Specifically, we seek to investigate the problems in cloud-computing that prior work such as those of Tsai et al. [22] and Wu et al. [24] have proposed, and ask whether the least-restriction that our enforcement mechanism provides is useful and meaningful in those contexts.

Another direction of future work is to investigate extensions that have been proposed to the policy in work such as those of Atluri et al. [4] and ask how we can extend our enforcement mechanism to deal with such extensions. We seek also to rigorously establish that other enforcement mechanisms such as those of Kessler [13] and Sandhu [17, 18] are indeed incomparable to the Brewer-Nash enforcement mechanism from the standpoint of reachable authorization states.

8. REFERENCES

[1] J. A. and Meseguer J. Goguen. Security policies and security models. In *Proceedings of the 1982 IEEE Symposium on Security and Privacy*, pages 11–20, 1982.

[2] J. A. and Meseguer J. Goguen. Unwinding and inference control. In *Proceedings of the 1984 IEEE Symposium on Security and Privacy*, pages 75–86, 1984.

[3] Ross Anderson. *Security Engineering – A Guide to Building Dependable Distributed Systems*. Wiley, 2008.

[4] Vijayalakshmi Atluri, Soon Ae Chun, and Pietro Mazzoleni. A chinese wall security model for decentralized workflow systems. In *Proceedings of the 8th ACM conference on Computer and Communications Security*, CCS '01, pages 48–57, New York, NY, USA, 2001. ACM.

[5] Matt Bishop. *Computer Security: Art and Science*. Addison-Wesley Professional, Boston, MA, 2003.

[6] D.F.C. Brewer and M.J. Nash. The chinese wall security policy. In *Proceedings of the IEEE Symposium on Security and Privacy*, pages 206–214, may 1989.

[7] Michael Davis and Andrew Stark, editors. *Conflict of Interest in the Professions*. Oxford University Press, USA, October 2001.

[8] Guy Edjlali, Anurag Acharya, and Vipin Chaudhary. History-based access control for mobile code. In *Proceedings of the 5th ACM conference on Computer and communications security*, CCS '98, pages 38–48, New York, NY, USA, 1998. ACM.

[9] Robert W. Floyd. Algorithm 97: Shortest path. *Commun. ACM*, 5(6):345–, June 1962.

[10] P.W.L. Fong. Access control by tracking shallow execution history. In *Proceedings of the 2004 IEEE Symposium on Security and Privacy*, pages 43–55, may 2004.

[11] Dieter Gollmann. *Computer Security (3. ed.)*. Wiley, 2011.

[12] Sushil Jajodia, Pierangela Samarati, V. S. Subrahmanian, and Eliza Bertino. A unified framework for enforcing multiple access control policies. In *Proceedings of the 1997 ACM SIGMOD international conference on Management of data*, SIGMOD '97, pages 474–485, New York, NY, USA, 1997. ACM.

[13] Volker Kessler. On the chinese wall model. In *Proceedings of the European Symposium on Research in Computer Security*, ESORICS, pages 41–54, 1992.

[14] Jay Ligatti, Lujo Bauer, and David Walker. Run-time enforcement of nonsafety policies. *ACM Trans. Inf. Syst. Secur.*, 12(3):19:1–19:41, January 2009.

[15] T.Y. Lin. Chinese wall security policy-an aggressive model. In *Proceedings of the Fifth Annual Computer Security Applications Conference*, ACSAC, pages 282–289, dec 1989.

[16] Peter Loscocco and Stephen Smalley. Integrating flexible support for security policies into the linux operating system.

[17] In *USENIX Annual Technical Conference, FREENIX Track*, pages 29–42, 2001.

[17] Ravi S. Sandhu. Lattice-based enforcement of chinese walls. *Computers & Security*, 11(8):753–763, 1992.

[18] Ravi S. Sandhu. A lattice interpretation of the chinese wall policy. In *Proceedings of the 15th National Computer Security Conference*, NISSC, pages 221–235, October 1992.

[19] Fred B. Schneider. Enforceable security policies. *ACM Trans. Inf. Syst. Secur.*, 3(1):30–50, February 2000.

[20] Google Scholar. The chinese wall security policy – brewer and nash, citation count, September 2012. http://scholar.google.ca/scholar?hl=en&q=the+chinese+wall+security+policy&btnG=&as_sdt=1%2C5&as_sdtp=.

[21] Ann E. Kelley Sobel and Jim Alves-Foss. A trace-based model of the chinese wall security policy. In *Proceedings of the 22nd National Information Systems Security Conference*, NISSC, 1999.

[22] Tien-Hao Tsai, Yen-Chung Chen, Hsiu-Chuan Huang, Pei-Ming Huang, Kuo-Sen Chou, and Kuo-Sen Chou. A practical chinese wall security model in cloud computing. In *Network Operations and Management Symposium (APNOMS)*, pages 1–4, 2011.

[23] Stephen Warshall. A theorem on boolean matrices. *J. ACM*, 9(1):11–12, January 1962.

[24] Ruoyu Wu, Gail-Joon Ahn, Hongxin Hu, and M. Singhal. Information flow control in cloud computing. In *Proceedings of the 6th International Conference on Collaborative Computing: Networking, Applications and Worksharing (CollaborateCom)*, pages 1–7, October 2010.

APPENDIX

A. PROOFS FOR THEOREMS 1, 3 AND 4

PROOF FOR THEOREM 1. (For subject-violation.)

We have only two cases. (1) one of the state-changes $\sigma_i \rightarrow \sigma_{i+1}$ for $i \in [0, n-1]$ is disallowed by our enforcement mechanism. In this case, we are done as the sequence is disallowed by our enforcement mechanism. (2) all of the state-changes $\sigma_i \rightarrow \sigma_{i+1}$ for $i \in [0, n-1]$ are allowed by our enforcement mechanism. In this case, we need to show that $\sigma_n \rightarrow \sigma_{n+1}$ is disallowed by our enforcement mechanism. As the policy is violated in σ_{n+1} but not σ_n, we know that the state-change $\sigma_n \rightarrow \sigma_{n+1}$ is a read by some subject s on some object o, and all causes for the policy being violated in σ_{n+1} are pairs of paths that terminate at s.

Assume, for the purpose of contradiction, that our enforcement mechanism allows the state-change, and in σ_{n+1} we have the two information flows $o_1 \rightsquigarrow s$ and $o_2 \rightsquigarrow s$ with $C(\delta(o_1), \delta(o_2)) = 1$. As our enforcement mechanism allows the state-change, we know that the "if" condition in READ evaluates to false.

We claim that there are only two possibilities in the enforcement state that corresponds to σ_n. Either (a) $\{\delta(o_1), \delta(o_2)\} \subseteq \Delta_o$. Or, (b) one of $\delta(o_1)$ or $\delta(o_2)$ is in Δ_s, and the other is in Δ_o. If we are able to prove this claim, then we have the desired contradiction, as the "if" condition in READ would evaluate to true when s attempts to read o.

To prove the claim, we first observe that we have only one of the following two possibilities. Either one of the information flows $o_1 \rightsquigarrow s$ or $o_2 \rightsquigarrow s$ is in σ_n, or neither is. We point out that both information flows cannot be in σ_n as then σ_n contains a subject-violation, which contradicts our assumption. In the former case, assume without loss of generality that $o_1 \rightsquigarrow s$ is in σ_n. Then, by

Lemma 3, $\delta(o_1) \in \Delta_s$ in the enforcement state that corresponds to σ_n. The only edge added to E between σ_n and σ_{n+1} is from o to s. As we have a new path $o_2 \rightsquigarrow s$ in σ_{n+1}, we must have $o_2 \rightsquigarrow o$ or $o_2 = o$ in σ_n. By Lemma 3 (for the case that $o_2 \rightsquigarrow o$) and how CREATE works for objects (for the case that $o_2 = o$), $\delta(o_2) \in \Delta_o$ in the enforcement state that corresponds to σ_n. This corresponds to Case (b) above.

In the latter case that neither $o_1 \rightsquigarrow s$ and $o_2 \rightsquigarrow s$ is in σ_n, both paths are created newly in σ_{n+1} by the addition of the edge from o to s in E. Therefore, in σ_n, $o_1 \rightsquigarrow o$ and $o_2 \rightsquigarrow o$, and by Lemma 3, in the enforcement state that corresponds to σ_n, $\{\delta(o_1), \delta(o_2)\} \subseteq \Delta_o$. This is Case (a) above. $\quad\square$

PROOF FOR THEOREM 3. To establish the theorem, we provide a counterexample to the opposite assertion. In the context of Definition 7 from Section 3.1, the sequence Ψ_a is the creation of subjects s_1, s_2 and objects o_1, o_2, o_3 with $C(o_1, o_2) = 1$ and $C(o_1, o_3) = C(o_2, o_3) = 0$. This is followed by a read of o_1 by s_1, write of o_3 by s_1 and read of o_2 by s_2. We point out that the authorization state that results (starting at σ_0) does not violate conflict of interest, and therefore is reachable under $\mathcal{A}$. As Ψ_b, we pick the subsequence of Ψ_a without any of the read and write actions of s_1. The subsequent action we want to execute is a read of o_3 by s_2. $\mathcal{A}$ does not allow this action after Ψ_a as it causes a conflict of interest violation:

$o_1 \rightsquigarrow s_2$ and $o_2 \rightsquigarrow s_2$. But it allows this action after Ψ_b, as the resulting state does not violate conflict of interest. $\quad\square$

PROOF FOR THEOREM 4. We present a proof for denying a read to prevent subject-violations.

Assume otherwise, for the purpose of contradiction. That is, $\mathcal{A}$ does not deny any attempt to read. Let $\sigma_0 \rightarrow \ldots \rightarrow \sigma_n$ be a sequence of states each reachable from the previous by a state-change such that we have a subject-violation in σ_n, but not in any of the prior states. We make two observations: (1) in σ_n, all information flows because of which the policy is violated are into a particular subject s, and, (2) the state-change $\sigma_{n-1} \rightarrow \sigma_n$ must be a read by s that causes there to exist information flows of the form $o_1 \rightsquigarrow s$, $o_2 \rightsquigarrow s, \ldots, o_m \rightsquigarrow s$ such that $m \geq 2$ and $C(\delta(o_i), \delta(o_j)) = 1$ for all $i, j \in [1, m], i \neq j$. To prevent such a sequence of states from occurring without denying any read in the sequence, either (a) the creation of a subject or object, or, (b) the write by a subject s' on an object o' must be denied. Let the state-change $\sigma_{k-1} \rightarrow \sigma_k$ be such a state-change that is denied. Then, by (2) above, $k < n$, because the state-change $\sigma_{n-1} \rightarrow \sigma_n$ is a read. Therefore, by (1) above, the sequence $\sigma_0 \rightarrow \ldots \rightarrow \sigma_k$ contains only those states that do not contain a subject-violation. As that sequence is precluded by $\mathcal{A}$, this contradicts the assumption that $\mathcal{A}$ is least-restrictive. $\quad\square$

Constraint Expressions and Workflow Satisfiability

Jason Crampton
Royal Holloway
University of London
United Kingdom
jason.crampton@rhul.ac.uk

Gregory Gutin
Royal Holloway
University of London
United Kingdom
g.gutin@rhul.ac.uk

ABSTRACT

A workflow specification defines a set of steps and the order in which those steps must be executed. Security requirements and business rules may impose constraints on which users are permitted to perform those steps. A workflow specification is said to be satisfiable if there exists an assignment of authorized users to workflow steps that satisfies all the constraints. An algorithm for determining whether such an assignment exists is important, both as a static analysis tool for workflow specifications, and for the construction of runtime reference monitors for workflow management systems. We develop new methods for determining workflow satisfiability based on the concept of constraint expressions, which were introduced recently by Khan and Fong. These methods are surprising versatile, enabling us to develop algorithms for, and determine the complexity of, a number of different problems related to workflow satisfiability.

Categories and Subject Descriptors

D4.6 [**Operating Systems**]: Security and Protection—*Access controls*; F2.2 [**Analysis of Algorithms and Problem Complexity**]: Nonnumerical Algorithms and Problems; H2.0 [**Database Management**]: General—*Security, integrity and protection*

General Terms

Algorithms, Security, Theory

Keywords

authorization constraints, workflow satisfiability, parameterized complexity

1. INTRODUCTION

It is increasingly common for organizations to computerize their business and management processes. The coordination of the tasks or steps that comprise a computerized business process is managed by a workflow management system (or business process management system). Typically, the execution of these steps will be triggered by a human user, or a software agent acting under the control of a human user, and the execution of each step will be restricted to some set of authorized users.

A workflow is defined by the steps that comprise a business process and the order in which those steps should be performed. Moreover, it is often the case that some form of access control, often role-based, should be applied to limit the execution of steps to authorized users. In addition, many workflows require controls on the users that perform groups of steps. The concept of a Chinese wall, for example, limits the set of steps that any one user can perform [9], as does separation-of-duty, which is a central part of the role-based access control model [1]. Hence, it is important that workflow management systems implement security controls that enforce authorization rules and business rules, in order to comply with statutory requirements or best practice [6]. It is these "security-aware" workflows that will be the focus of the remainder of this paper.

A simple, illustrative example for purchase order processing [10] is shown in Figure 1. In the first step of the workflow, the purchase order is created and approved (and then dispatched to the supplier). The supplier will submit an invoice for the goods ordered, which is processed by the create payment step. When the supplier delivers the goods, a goods received note (GRN) must be signed and countersigned. Only then may the payment be approved and sent to the supplier. Note that a workflow specification need not be linear: the processing of the GRN and of the invoice can occur in parallel, for example.

In addition to defining the order in which steps must be performed, the workflow specification includes rules to prevent fraudulent use of the purchase order processing system. In our example, these rules restrict the users that can perform pairs of steps in the workflow: the same user may not sign and countersign the GRN, for example.

It is apparent that it may be impossible to find an assignment of authorized users to workflow steps such that all constraints are satisfied. In this case, we say that the workflow specification is *unsatisfiable*. The WORKFLOW SATISFIABILITY PROBLEM (WSP) is known to be NP-hard, even when the set of constraints only includes constraints that have a relatively simple structure (and that would arise regularly in practice).[1]

---

[1]In particular, the GRAPH k-COLORABILITY problem can be reduced to a special case of WSP in which the workflow specification only includes separation-of-duty constraints [21].

(a) Ordering on steps

(b) Constraints

s_1	create purchase order
s_2	approve purchase order
s_3	sign GRN
s_4	create payment
s_5	countersign GRN
s_6	approve payment
$\neq$	different users must perform steps
$=$	same user must perform steps

(c) Legend

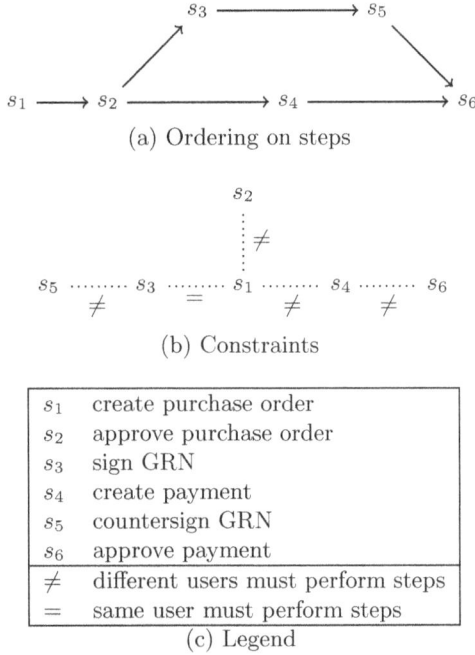

Figure 1: A simple constrained workflow for purchase order processing

The rules described above can be encoded using constraints [10], the rules being enforced if and only if the constraints are satisfied. More complex constraints, in which restrictions are placed on the users who execute sets of steps can also be defined [3, 12, 21], can encode more complex business requirements. (We describe these constraints in more detail in Section 2.1.) A considerable body of work now exists on the satisfiability of workflow specifications that include such constraints [6, 12, 21].

In this paper, we use constraint expressions to solve WSP. Constraint expressions were introduced by Khan and Fong in their work on workflow feasibility [16]. However, the potential of constraint expressions was not fully realized. In this paper, we show how constraint expressions can be used to solve WSP and a number of related problems.

We also introduce a set of operators for combining workflows. This allows us to model workflows in which the execution of steps is determined at execution time, which we will call *conditional workflows*. Our model enables us to formulate the satisfiability problem for conditional workflows, which we solve using constraint expressions. To our knowledge, these are the first results on conditional workflows.

The main contributions of this paper are:

- to generalize the results of Wang and Li on the fixed parameter tractability of WSP (Section 3);

- to introduce a language for workflow composition (Section 4);

- to establish new results on the satisfiability of conditional workflows (Section 4);

- to demonstrate how a problem studied by Armando *et al.* [3] and a problem introduced by Crampton [10] can be solved using constraint expressions (Section 5).

In the next section we provide relevant background material. In Section 3–5, we describe our results. The proofs of our results can be found in the appendix, with the exception of the proof of Theorem 5. We conclude with a summary of our contributions, a discussion of related work, and our plans for future work.

2. BACKGROUND

In this section, we introduce our notation and definitions, derived from earlier work [10, 21], and then define the workflow satisfiability problem. In order to make the paper self-contained, we also provide a short overview of parameterized complexity and summarize a number of useful results from the literature.

2.1 The Workflow Satisfiability Problem

A directed acyclic graph $G = (V, E)$ is defined by a set of nodes V and a set of edges $E \subseteq V \times V$. The reflexive, transitive closure of a directed acyclic graph defines a partial order, where $v \leqslant w$ if and only if there is a path from v to w in G. If $(V, \leqslant)$ is a partially ordered set, then we write $v \parallel w$ if v and w are incomparable; that is, $v \not\leqslant w$ and $w \not\leqslant v$. We may write $v \geqslant w$ whenever $w \leqslant v$. We may also write $v < w$ whenever $v \leqslant w$ and $v \neq w$. Finally, we will write $[n]$ to denote $\{1, \ldots, n\}$.

DEFINITION 1. *A* workflow specification *is defined by a directed, acyclic graph* $G = (S, E)$, *where S is a set of steps and $E \subseteq S \times S$. Given a workflow specification (S, E) and a set of users U, an* authorization policy *for a workflow specification is a relation $A \subseteq S \times U$. A* workflow authorization schema *is a tuple (G, U, A), where $G = (S, E)$ is a workflow specification and A is an authorization policy.*

We will use the representations of a workflow specification as a partial order and a DAG interchangeably. The workflow specification describes a sequence of steps and the order in which they must be performed when the workflow is executed, each such execution being called a *workflow instance*. If $s < s'$ then s must be performed before s' in every instance of the workflow; if $s \parallel s'$ then s and s' may be performed in either order. User u is authorized to perform step s only if $(s, u) \in A$.[2] We assume that for every step $s \in S$ there exists some user $u \in U$ such that $(s, u) \in A$.

DEFINITION 2. *Let $((S, E), U, A)$ be a workflow authorization schema. A* plan *is a function $\pi : S \to U$. A plan π is* authorized *for $((S, E), U, A)$ if $(s, \pi(s)) \in A$ for all $s \in S$.*

DEFINITION 3. *A* workflow constraint *has the form (ρ, S_1, S_2), where $S_1, S_2 \subseteq S$ and $\rho \subseteq U \times U$. A* constrained workflow authorization schema *is a tuple $((S, E), U, A, C)$, where C is a set of workflow constraints.*

---

[2] In practice, the set of authorized step-user pairs, A, will not be defined explicitly. Instead, A will be inferred from other access control data structures. In particular, R^2BAC – the role-and-relation-based access control model of Wang and Li [21] – introduces a set of roles R, a user-role relation $UR \subseteq U \times R$ and a role-step relation $SA \subseteq R \times S$ from which it is possible to derive the steps for which users are authorized. For all common access control policies (including R^2BAC), it is straightforward to derive A. We prefer to use A in order to simplify the exposition.

DEFINITION 4. *A plan $\pi : S \rightarrow U$ satisfies a workflow constraint (ρ, S_1, S_2) if there exist $s_1 \in S_1$ and $s_2 \in S_2$ such that $(\pi(s_1), \pi(s_2)) \in \rho$. Given a constrained workflow authorization schema $((S, E), U, A, C)$, a plan π is valid if it is authorized and it satisfies all constraints in C.*

We write $\Delta \subseteq U \times U$ to denote the diagonal relation $\{(u, u) : u \in U\}$ and Δ^c to denote its complement $\{(u, u) : (u, u) \notin \Delta\}$. Thus, the constraint on steps s_1 and s_2 in Figure 1 would be written as $(\Delta^c, \{s_1\}, \{s_2\})$.

We may now define the workflow satisfiability problem, as defined by Wang and Li [21].

WORKFLOW SATISFIABILITY PROBLEM (WSP)

Input: A constrained workflow authorization schema $((S, E), U, A, C)$

Output: A valid plan $\pi : S \rightarrow U$ or an answer that there exists no valid plan

---

We now discuss constraints in more detail, including the type of business rules we can encode using our constraints and compare them to constraints in the literature. Our definition of workflow constraint is more general than similar definitions used when studying WSP. Crampton defined constraints in which S_1 and S_2 are singleton sets: we will refer to constraints of this form as *Type 1* constraints; for brevity we will write (ρ, s_1, s_2) for the Type 1 constraint $(\rho, \{s_1\}, \{s_2\})$. Wang and Li defined constraints in which at least one of S_1 and S_2 is a singleton set: we will refer to constraints of this form as *Type 2* constraints and we will write (ρ, s_1, S_2) in preference to $(\rho, \{s_1\}, S_2)$. Constraints in which S_1 and S_2 are arbitrary sets will be called *Type 3* constraints.

We say that two constraints γ and γ' are *equivalent* if a plan π satisfies γ if and only if it satisfies γ'. The Type 2 constraint (ρ, s_1, S_2) is equivalent to (ρ, S_2, s_1) if ρ is symmetric, in which case we will write (ρ, s_1, S_2) in preference to (ρ, S_2, s_1).

It is worth pointing out that Type 1 constraints can express requirements of the form described in Section 1, where we wish to restrict the combinations of users that perform pairs of steps. The plan π satisfies constraint (Δ, s, s'), for example, if the same user is assigned to both steps by π, and satisfies constraint (Δ^c, s, s') if different users are assigned to s and s'. In other words, these represent, respectively, binding-of-duty and separation-of-duty constraints. Abusing notation in the interests of readability, we will replace Δ and Δ^c by $=$ and $\neq$, respectively.

Type 2 constraints provide greater flexibility, although Wang and Li, who introduced these constraints, do not provide a use case for which such a constraint would be needed. However, there are forms of separation-of-duty requirements that are most naturally encoded using Type 3 constraints. Consider, for example, the requirement that a set of steps $S' \subseteq S$ must not all be performed by the same user [2]. We may encode this as the constraint $(\neq, S', S')$, which is satisfied by a plan π only if there exists two steps in S' that are allocated to different users by π.

Henceforth, we will write $\mathrm{WSP}(\rho_1, \ldots, \rho_t)$ to denote a special case of WSP in which all constraints have the form (ρ_i, S', S'') for some $\rho_i \in \{\rho_1, \ldots, \rho_t\}$ and for some $S', S'' \subseteq S$. We will write $\mathrm{WSP}_i(\rho_1, \ldots, \rho_t)$ to denote a special case of $\mathrm{WSP}(\rho_1, \ldots, \rho_t)$, in which there are no constraints of Type j for $j > i$. Thus, $\mathrm{WSP}_1(=, \neq)$, for example,

indicates an instance of WSP in which all constraints have the form $(=, s_1, s_2)$ or $(\neq, s_1, s_2)$ for some $s_1, s_2 \in S$.

We will write c, n and k to denote the number of constraints, users and steps, respectively, in an instance of WSP. We will analyze the complexity of the workflow satisfiability problem in terms of these parameters.

Note that definition of WSP given above does not make any reference to the ordering on the set of steps. The original definition, as formulated by Crampton [10], included constraints that were sensitive to the order in which steps were executed. If $s \parallel s'$, we may define two different constraints (ρ, s, s') and (ρ', s', s), the first of which must be satisfied if s is performed before s', while the second must be satisfied if s' is performed before s. To facilitate direct comparison with the work of Wang and Li on WSP, we defer the analysis of Crampton's version of the problem until Section 5.

2.2 Applications of WSP

There are a number of different execution models for workflow systems. In some systems, a tasklist is created when a workflow is instantiated. The tasklist is simply a valid plan for the worfklow instance, allocating users to specific steps in the workflow instance. In other systems, the workflow system maintains a pool of ready steps for each worfklow instance. We say a step is *ready* in a workflow instance if all its immediate predecessor steps have been executed. The workflow system may allocate ready steps to users; alternatively users may select steps to perform from the pool. In both cases, the system must ensure both that the user is authorized and that allowing the user to perform the step does not prevent the remaining steps in the workflow instance from completing.

For systems that create tasklists, it is sufficient to know that the workflow specification is satisfiable. Thus, an algorithm for deciding WSP is an important static analysis tool for such systems. However, such an algorithm will only need to be executed when the workflow specification is created or when it changes. The fact that the problem is NP-hard means that it is important to find as efficient an algorithm as possible.

For other systems, however, the algorithm will need to be run repeatedly: every time a user is allocated to a step. Note that the decision whether to allow a user to execute a step in a partially completed workflow instance can be determined by solving an instance of WSP. Specifically, suppose $W = ((S, E), U, A, C)$ is a workflow specification, some subset S' of steps have been performed in some instance of W, and the system needs to decide whether to allow u' to perform s'. Thus we have a partial plan $\pi : S' \rightarrow U$. We then construct a new workflow instance $W' = ((S, E), U, A', C)$, where $(s, u) \in A'$ if and only if one of the following conditions holds: (i) $s \in S'$ and $u = \pi(s)$ (ii) $s = s'$ and $u = u'$ (iii) $s \notin S' \cup \{s'\}$ and $(u, s) \in A$. Clearly, the workflow instance is satisfiable (when u' performs s') if and only if W' is satisfiable. Assuming that these checks should incur as little delay as possible, particularly in the case when users select steps in real time [17], it becomes even more important to find an algorithm that can decide WSP as efficiently as possible.

The definition of workflow satisfiability given above assumes that the set of users and the authorization relation are given. This notion of satisfiability is appropriate when the workflow schema is designed "in-house". A number of large information technology companies develop business process systems which are then configured by the end users of those systems. Part of that configuration includes the assignment of users to steps in workflow schemas. The developer of such a schema may wish to be assured that the schema is satisfiable for some set of users and some authorization relation, since the schema is of no practical use if no such user set and authorization relation exist. The desired assurance can be provided by solving an instance of WSP in which there are k users, each of which is authorized for all steps. The developer may also determine the minimum number of users required for a workflow schema to be satisfiable. The minimum number must be between 1 and k and, using a binary search, can be determined by examining $\lceil \log_2 k \rceil$ instances of WSP.

2.3 Parameterized Complexity

A naïve approach to solving WSP would consider every possible assignment of users to steps in the workflow. There are n^k such assignments if there are n users and k steps, so an algorithm of this form would have complexity $O(cn^k)$, where c is the number of constraints. Moreover, Wang and Li showed that WSP is NP-hard, by reducing GRAPH k-COLORABILITY to WSP($\neq$) [21, Lemma 3]. In short, WSP is hard to solve in general. The importance of finding an efficient algorithm for solving WSP led Wang and Li to look at the problem from the perspective of parameterized complexity [21].

Suppose we have an algorithm that solves an NP-hard problem in time $O(f(k)n^d)$, where n denotes the size of the input to the problem, k is some (small) parameter of the problem, f is some function in k only, and d is some constant (independent of k and n). Then we say the algorithm is a *fixed-parameter tractable* (FPT) algorithm. If a problem can be solved using an FPT algorithm then we say that it is an *FPT problem* and that it belongs to the class FPT [13, 18].

Wang and Li showed, using an elementary argument, that WSP$_2$($\neq$) is FPT and can be solved in time $O(k^{k+1}N)$, where N is the size of the entire input to the problem [21, Lemma 8]. They also showed that WSP$_2$($\neq$, =) is FPT [21, Theorem 9], using a rather more complex approach: specifically, they constructed an algorithm that runs in time $O(k^{k+1}(k-1)^{k2^{k-1}}N)$; it follows that WSP$_2$(=, $\neq$) is FPT. One of the contributions of this paper is to describe a new method for solving WSP$_3$(=, $\neq$) (that can also be used to solve WSP$_2$(=, $\neq$)), thus generalizing Wang and Li's result.

3. SOLVING WSP USING CONSTRAINT EXPRESSIONS

In this section, we show how to extend the elementary methods used by Wang and Li to obtain results for WSP$_2$(=, $\neq$) and WSP$_3$(=, $\neq$). Informally, our results make use of two observations:

- A construction used by Crampton *et al.* [11] can be used to transform an instance of WSP$_1$(=, $\neq$) into an equivalent instance of WSP$_1$($\neq$) in time polynomial in the numbers of constraints, steps and users.

- We can transform an instance of WSP$_i$(=, $\neq$) into multiple instances of WSP$_1$(=, $\neq$), the number of instances being dependent only on the number of steps.

We use constraint expressions [16] to represent workflow constraints and to reason about multiple constraints and the relationships between different types of constraints.

3.1 Reducing WSP$_1$(=, $\neq$) to WSP$_1$($\neq$)

The basic idea is to merge all steps that are related by constraints of the form $(=, s_1, s_2)$ for $s_1, s_2 \in S$. More formally, consider an instance $\mathcal{I}$ of WSP$_1$(=, $\neq$), given by a workflow $((S, E), U, A, C)$.

(1) Construct a graph H with vertices S, in which $s', s'' \in S$ are adjacent if C includes a constraint $(=, s', s'')$.

(2) If there is a connected component of H that contains both s' and s'' and C contains a constraint $(\neq, s', s'')$ then $\mathcal{I}$ is unsatisfiable, so we may assume there is no such connected component.

(3) For each connected component T of H,

(a) replace all steps of T in S by a "superstep" t;

(b) for each superstep t, authorize user u for t if and only if u was authorized (by A) for all steps in t

(c) for each such superstep t, merge all constraints for steps in t.

Clearly, we now have an instance of WSP$_1$($\neq$), perhaps with fewer steps and a modified authorization relation, that is satisfiable if and only if $\mathcal{I}$ is satisfiable. For ease of reference, we will refer to the procedure described above as the *WSP$_1$ constraint reduction method*. The reduction can be performed in time $O(kc + kn)$, where c is the number of constraints: step (1) takes time $O(k + c)$; step (3) performs at most k merges; each merge takes $O(k + c + n)$ time (since we need to merge vertices, and update constraints and the authorization relation for the new vertex set);[3] finally, if $k \leqslant c$ we have $O(k(k + c + n) = O(k(c + n))$, and if $c \leqslant k$ then we perform no more than c merges in time $O(c(k + c + n)) = O(ck + cn) = O(ck + kn)$.

3.2 Constraint Expressions

To understand the intuition behind our approach, consider a workflow $W = ((S, E), U, A, \{(\rho, S', S'')\})$, which defines an instance of WSP$_3$(ρ). By definition, a plan π satisfies the constraint (ρ, S', S'') if there exist $s' \in S'$ and $s'' \in S''$ such that $(\pi(s'), \pi(s'')) \in \rho$. In other words, we could decide the satisfiability of W by considering the satisfiability of multiple instances of WSP$_1$: specifically, for each pair $(s', s'') \in S' \times S''$, we consider the satisfiability of the workflow $((S, E), U, A, \{(\rho, s', s'')\})$; if any one of these instances is satisfiable, then so is W. On the other hand, a plan satisfies a workflow $W = ((S, E), U, A, \{\gamma_1, \gamma_2\})$, for constraints γ_1 and γ_2, if and only if π satisfies workflows $((S, E), U, A, \{\gamma_1\})$ and $((S, E), U, A, \{\gamma_2\})$.

More formally, given a set of steps S, we define a *constraint expression* recursively:

- (ρ, s_1, s_2) is a (*primitive*) constraint expression;

- if γ and γ' are constraint expressions, then $\gamma \wedge \gamma'$ and $\gamma \vee \gamma'$ are constraint expressions.

A plan π satisfies constraint expression:

---

[3]We can check step (2) when we merge constraints in step 3(c).

- $\gamma \wedge \gamma'$ if and only if π satisfies γ and γ'; and

- $\gamma \vee \gamma'$ if and only if π satisfies γ or γ'.

3.3 Reducing $\text{WSP}(\rho_1, \ldots \rho_t)$ to $\text{WSP}_1(\rho_1, \ldots, \rho_t)$

We now express workflow specifications using constraint expressions, rather than sets of constraints. A constraint (ρ, S', S''), $\rho \in \{\rho_1, \ldots, \rho_t\}$, is equivalent to a constraint expression $\bigvee_{s' \in S', s'' \in S''} (\rho, s', s'')$, so every constraint can be written as the disjunction of primitive constraints. Moreover, the set of constraints $\{\Gamma_1, \ldots, \Gamma_c\}$, where each Γ_i is a disjunction of primitive constraint expressions, is equivalent to the constraint expression $\Gamma_1 \wedge \cdots \wedge \Gamma_c$.

In other words, we can reduce the problem of determining the satisfiability of $((S, E), U, A, C)$ to the problem of determining the satisfiability of a workflow of the form

$$((S, E), U, A, \Gamma_1 \wedge \cdots \wedge \Gamma_c),$$

where $c = |C|$; each *clause* $\Gamma_i = (\rho, S_i', S_i'')$ has the form $\gamma_{i,1} \vee \cdots \vee \gamma_{i,m(i)}$, with $m(i) = |S_i'| \cdot |S_i''|$; and each *literal* $\gamma_{i,j}$ has the form (ρ, s', s'') for some $s' \in S_i'$ and $s'' \in S_i''$. In other words, we can represent any instance of $\text{WSP}_3(=, \neq)$ as a workflow containing a constraint expression in "conjunctive normal form" in which each of the "literals" is a primitive constraint (which corresponds to a single Type 1 constraint). Moreover, each literal is positive.

3.4 Solving $\text{WSP}(=, \neq)$

Given a constraint expression $\Gamma_1 \wedge \cdots \wedge \Gamma_c$, it is easy to see that if we can find a plan π for some constraint expression of the form $\gamma_1 \wedge \cdots \wedge \gamma_c$, with $\gamma_i \in \Gamma_i$, then π is a plan for C. This is because such a plan satisfies at least one literal in each clause Γ_i, thereby causing each Γ_i to be satisfied; and C is satisfied if each clause is satisfied. Conversely, if π is a plan for C then it is a plan for $\Gamma_1 \wedge \cdots \wedge \Gamma_c$ and there exists a workflow expression of the form $\gamma_1 \wedge \cdots \wedge \gamma_c$ for which π is a plan. In other words, π is a plan for C if and only if it is a plan for $\gamma_1 \wedge \cdots \wedge \gamma_c$ for some $\gamma_i \in \Gamma_i$, where γ_i is a Type 1 constraint and $\gamma_1 \wedge \cdots \wedge \gamma_c$ represents the constraint set $\{\gamma_1, \ldots, \gamma_c\}$. We call $\gamma_1 \wedge \cdots \wedge \gamma_c$ a *simple constraint expression*. That is, we have reduced the satisfiability of an instance of $\text{WSP}_3(=, \neq)$ to determining the satisfiability of *one or more* instances of $\text{WSP}_1(=, \neq)$. The number of instances is equal to $\prod_{i=1}^{c} |\Gamma_i|$, where $|\Gamma_i|$ denotes the number of literals (primitive constraint expressions) in Γ_i. Our strategy for solving an instance of $\text{WSP}_3(=, \neq)$, therefore, is to try to determine the satisfiability of these related instances of $\text{WSP}_1(=, \neq)$.

THEOREM 5. $\text{WSP}_2(=, \neq)$ and $\text{WSP}_3(=, \neq)$ can be decided in time

$$O((k-1)^c(c(k-1)^k + kn)) \quad and \quad O\left(k^{2c}(c(k-1)^k + kn)\right),$$

respectively, where c is the number of constraints in the workflow instance.

PROOF. We first consider an instance of $\text{WSP}_1(=, \neq)$, to which we apply the WSP_1 constraint reduction to obtain an instance of $\text{WSP}_1(\neq)$. As any step with at least k authorized users can be assigned a user that has not been assigned to any other step, we may focus on the allocation of users to steps having fewer than k authorized users.

We consider each possible plan in turn and for each plan we check whether every constraint is satisfied. There are no

more than $(k-1)^k$ plans to check—since each of the steps has at most $k-1$ authorized users and there are no more than k steps—and each constraint contains two steps, so the time taken to solve $\text{WSP}_1(\neq)$ is $O(c(k-1)^k)$ and the time taken to solve $\text{WSP}_1(\neq, =)$ is $O(c(k-1)^k + kn)$.

Now suppose we are given an instance of $\text{WSP}(=, \neq)$. Then we can determine its satisfiability by considering the satisfiability of multiple instances of $\text{WSP}_1(=, \neq)$, each instance containing c constraints. We now determine the number of instances of $\text{WSP}_1(=, \neq)$ that need to be considered in the worst case.

For a Type 2 constraint (ρ, s, S'), we may assume that $s \notin S'$: for $(=, s, S')$, if $s \in S'$, then the constraint is satisfied by every plan and the constraint is redundant; for $(\neq, s, S')$, if $s \in S'$, then the constraint is equivalent to $(\neq, s, S' \setminus \{s\})$. Hence, each Type 2 constraint (ρ, s, S') gives rise to $|S'|$ literals in a clause with $|S'| < k$. So we have c clauses, each of which contains no more than $k-1$ literals.

Type 1 constraints are equivalent to clauses with a single literal. Hence, for an instance of $\text{WSP}_2(=, \neq)$ there are no more than $(k-1)^c$ simple constraint expressions and so there are no more than $(k-1)^c$ instances of $\text{WSP}_1(=, \neq)$ to check, which can be done in time $O((k-1)^c(c(k-1)^k + kn + kc)) = O((k-1)^c(c(k-1)^k + kn))$.

Each Type 3 constraint (ρ, S', S'') yields a clause containing fewer than $|S'| \cdot |S''| \leqslant k^2$ literals (which is greater than the number of clauses that can be obtained from a Type 1 or Type 2 constraint). Hence, there are no more than $O(k^{2c})$ simple constraint expressions and $\text{WSP}_3(\neq, =)$ can be decided in time $O(k^{2c}(c(k-1)^k + kn + kc)) = (k^{2c}(c(k-1)^k + kn))$. □

COROLLARY 6. $\text{WSP}_2(=, \neq)$ and $\text{WSP}_3(=, \neq)$ are FPT.

3.5 Kernelization of WSP

Formally, a *parameterized problem* P can be represented as a relation $P \subseteq \Sigma^* \times \mathbb{N}$ over a finite alphabet Σ. The second component is call the *parameter* of the problem. In particular, WSP is a parameterized problem with parameter k, the number of steps. We denote the size of a problem instance $(\mathcal{I}, k)$ by $|\mathcal{I}| + k$.

DEFINITION 7. *Given a parameterized problem P, a kernelization of P is an algorithm that maps an instance $(\mathcal{I}, k)$ to an instance $(\mathcal{I}', k')$ in time polynomial in $|\mathcal{I}| + k$ such that (i) $(\mathcal{I}, k) \in P$ if and only if $(\mathcal{I}', k') \in P$, and (ii) $k' + |\mathcal{I}'| \leqslant g(k)$ for some function g; $(\mathcal{I}', k')$ is the kernel and g is the size of the kernel. If $g(k) = k^{O(1)}$, then we say $(\mathcal{I}', k')$ is a polynomial-size kernel.*

A kernelization provides a form of preprocessing aimed at compressing the given instance of the problem. Polynomial-size kernels are particularly useful in practice as they often allow us to reduce the size of the input of the problem under consideration to an equivalent problem with an input of significantly smaller size.

Crampton *et al.* recently established that $\text{WSP}_1(=, \neq)$ has a polynomial-size kernel [11, §6]. In the case of $\text{WSP}_1(=, \neq)$, we can reduce the problem to one containing at most k users [11, Theorem 6.5]. Crampton *el al.* also showed that $\text{WSP}_2(=, \neq)$ (and hence $\text{WSP}_3(=, \neq)$) does not have a polynomial-size kernel, so there is no efficient preprocessing step for such instances of WSP. However, our results in this paper show we can reduce an instance of $\text{WSP}(=, \neq)$

to at most k^{2c} instances of $\text{WSP}_1(\neq)$ and then solve each instance by first computing a (polynomial-size) kernel. The proof of Corollary 6 asserts that $c \leqslant 4^k$, although we would expect c to be linear or quadratic in the number of steps in practice. This approach is similar to those that use so-called *Turing kernels* (see [19], for example).

3.6 Negative Constraint Expressions

We could extend the syntax for constraint expressions to include negation. In other words, if γ is a constraint expression, then $\neg\gamma$ is a constraint expression. A plan π satisfies $\neg\gamma$ if and only if π violates γ. A plan π satisfies the constraint $\neg(=, S_1, S_2)$, for example, if and only for all $s_i \in S_i$, $(\pi(s_1), \pi(s_2)) \notin \Delta$; that is, if and only if for all $s_i \in S_i$, $\pi(s_1) \neq \pi(s_2)$.[4] Thus, we can encode any instance of $\text{WSP}(=, \neq)$ using only constraints of the form $(=, s_1, s_2)$ if we allow the use of negation. Note, however, this means that the method for solving $\text{WSP}(=, \neq)$ described in Section 3.4 no longer works, because we may have negative literals in our conjunctive normal form expressions.

However, we can determine the satisfiability of the constraint expression using any SAT solver. A satisfying assignment returned by the SAT solver provides a "template" for a valid plan: if the variable $(=, s_1, s_2)$ is set to true, then our plan must assign the same user to s_1 and s_2. This induces a partition of the set of steps into blocks, each of which must be executed by a different user. Hence, each satisfying assignment of the constraint expression gives rise to an instance of $\text{WSP}_1(\neq)$ in which each "step" is a block of steps in the original problem instance. We can solve this instance in time $O(\binom{k}{2}(b-1)^b)$, where $b \leqslant k$ is the number of blocks, since there are at most $\binom{k}{2}$ constraints of the form $(=, s_1, s_2)$. If b is small relative to k, then this may prove to be a very efficient way of solving the original instance of $\text{WSP}(=, \neq)$. However, we may need to consider $2^{\binom{k}{2}}$ satisfying assignments. In future work we hope to explore whether the additional expressive power of negative constraint expressions allows us to encode business rules of practical relevance. Further experimental work, investigating which strategies for solving WSP work best in practice, is required.

4. CONDITIONAL WORKFLOWS

In some situations, we may wish to have conditional branching in a workflow specification, sometimes known as *OR-forks* [20] or *exclusive gateways* [22]. In our workflow system for purchase order processing, for example, we may require that only orders with a value exceeding some threshold amount need to be signed for twice. Informally, we can represent this extended specification by the diagram shown in Figure 2, where s_3' represents a step for signing a goods received note on low-valued items. The nodes containing $\|$ and $\oplus$ are "orchestration" steps (or "gateways") at which no processing is performed: $\oplus$ indicates that exactly one of the two branches is executed, while $\|$ denotes that both branches must be executed.

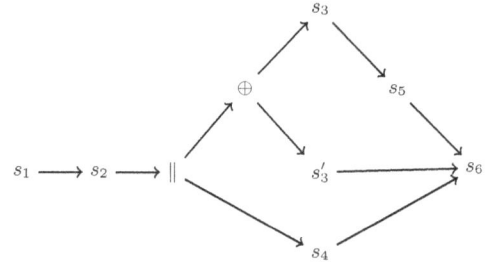

Figure 2: A workflow specification with conditional step execution

4.1 Workflow Composition

We now introduce a simple language for defining workflows. This language enables us to extend the definition of WSP to workflows containing OR-forks, but not to arbitrary workflow patterns.

We assume every workflow specification includes a start step and a finish step, which we will denote by α and ω, respectively, with subscripts where appropriate. These steps are *orchestration* steps: no processing is performed by these steps and no constraints are applied to their execution; they are used by the workflow management system solely to manage the initiation and completion of workflow instances. Given two workflow specifications $W_1 = (S_1, E_1)$ and $W_2 = (S_2, E_2)$, we may construct new workflow specifications using serial, parallel and xor composition, denoted by $W_1; W_2$, $W_1 \parallel W_2$ and $W_1 \oplus W_2$, respectively. We assume throughout that $S_1 \cap S_2 = \emptyset$. (If this were not the case with $s \in S_1 \cap S_2$, we could simply introduce subscripts or new labels to distinguish the two copies of s.)

For serial composition, all the steps in W_1 must be completed before the steps in W_2. Hence, the graph of $W_1; W_2$ is formed by taking the union of S_1 and S_2, the union of E_1 and E_2, and the addition of a single edge between ω_1 and α_2.

For parallel composition, the execution of the steps in W_1 and W_2 may be interleaved. Hence, the graph of $W_1 \parallel W_2$ is formed by taking the union of S_1 and S_2, the union of E_1 and E_2, the addition of new start and finish steps α_{par} and ω_{par}, and the addition of edges from α_{par} to α_1 and α_2 and from ω_1 and ω_2 to ω_{par}. This form of composition is sometimes known as an *AND-fork* [20] or a *parallel gateway* [22].[5]

In both serial and parallel composition, all steps in W_1 and W_2 are executed. In xor composition, either the steps in W_1 are executed or the steps in W_2, but not both. In other words, xor composition represents non-deterministic choice in a workflow specification. The graph of $W_1 \oplus W_2$ is formed by taking the union of S_1 and S_2, the union of E_1 and E_2, the addition of new start and finish steps α_{xor} and ω_{xor}, and the addition of edges from α_{xor} to α_1 and α_2 and from ω_1 and ω_2 to ω_{xor}.

Henceforth, we will assume that ω_1 followed by α_2 will be merged to form a single (orchestration) node ϵ. Similarly, we will assume that (i) α_{par} followed by α_1 and α_2 in serial composition will be merged to form a single node α_{par}; (ii) ω_{par} followed by ω_1 and ω_2 will be merged to form a

---

[4]This constraint is similar to the separation of duty constraints described by Basin *et al.* [7] and the universal constraints described by Wang and Li [21]. Of course, we can represent this constraint as the set of Type 1 constraints $\{(\neq, s_1, s_2) : s_1 \in S_1, s_2 \in S_2\}$.

[5]The workflows that arise from serial and parallel composition have a lot in common with series-parallel graphs; see [5], for example, for further details.

single node ω_{par}; (iii) α_{xor} followed by α_1 and α_2 will be merged to form a single node α_{xor}; (iv) ω_{xor} followed by ω_1 and ω_2 will be merged to form a single node ω_{xor}.

Serial and parallel composition are illustrated in Figure 3. The structure of xor composition is identical to that for parallel composition so it is not shown.

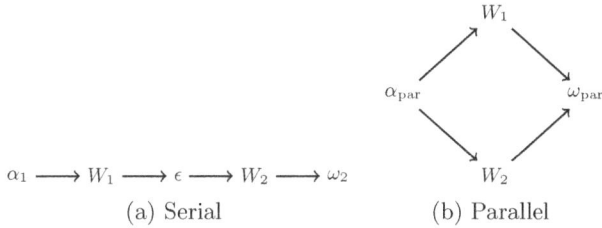

(a) Serial (b) Parallel

Figure 3: Workflow composition

4.2 Execution Sets

When we have conditional branching in a workflow, there exists more than one set of steps that could comprise a complete workflow instance. Formally, an *execution set* is defined recursively:

- for a workflow specification comprising a single step s, there is a single execution set $\{s\}$;

- if W_1 and W_2 are workflow specifications and S_1 and S_2 are execution sets for W_1 and W_2, respectively, then

  - $S_1 \cup S_2$ is an execution set for $W_1 \, ; W_2$,
  - $S_1 \cup S_2$ is an execution set for $W_1 \parallel W_2$,
  - S_1 and S_2 are execution sets for $W_1 \oplus W_2$.

In our running example, both $\{s_1, s_2, s_3, s_4, s_5, s_6\}$ and $\{s_1, s_2, s_3', s_4, s_6\}$ represent possible execution sets, with the second set representing a workflow instance in which the value of goods ordered is lower than the threshold requiring the GRN to be countersigned.[6]

4.3 Workflow Formulas and Trees

Clearly, each workflow step represents a workflow specification, in fact the simplest possible specification. Hence, we may represent the example workflow specification in Figure 2 as the *workflow formula*

$$(s_1 \, ; s_2) \, ; (((s_3 \, ; s_5) \oplus s_3') \parallel s_4) \, ; s_6.$$

Thus, we may also represent the workflow specification as a *workflow tree*, as illustrated in Figure 4.

The number of different possible execution sets is determined by the structure of the workflow formula. Specifically, let $\sharp(W)$ denote the number of possible execution sets for workflow W. For a workflow W comprising a single step, we have $\sharp(W) = 1$. In general, we have

$$\sharp(W_1 \, ; W_2) = \sharp(W_1 \parallel W_2) = \sharp(W_1) \cdot \sharp(W_2)$$
$$\sharp(W_1 \oplus W_2) = \sharp(W_1) + \sharp(W_2),$$

---

[6]The concept of an execution set is related to, but simpler than, the concept of an *execution history* [7]: for any execution set $\{s_1, \ldots, s_m\}$, an execution history is a set $\{(s_1, u_1), \ldots, (s_m, u_m)\}$ for some users $u_1, \ldots, u_m$. An execution history also has some similarity to our concept of a plan.

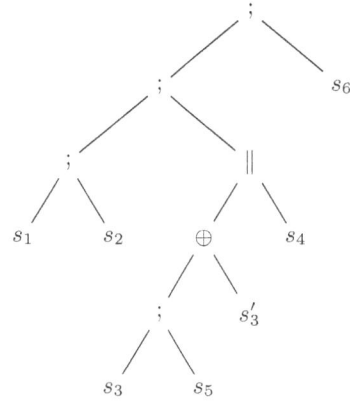

Figure 4: A workflow tree

where $\cdot$ denotes multiplication.

Using a post-order traversal of the workflow tree, we can compute the number of possible execution sets: we assign the value 1 to each leaf node; we compute the number of possible execution sets for each non-leaf node using the values assigned to its children and the appropriate formula for the operation associated with the node. The root node in the tree depicted in Figure 4 is assigned the value 2, for example.

We write $\flat(W)$ to denote the maximum number of steps in any possible execution set for a workflow specification W. Then

$$\flat(W_1 \, ; W_2) = \flat(W_1 \parallel W_2) = \flat(W_1) + \flat(W_2)$$
$$\flat(W_1 \oplus W_2) = \max\{\flat(W_1), \flat(W_2)\}.$$

Clearly, we can compute $\flat(W)$ from the workflow tree associated with W using a similar algorithm to the one described above for calculating $\sharp(W)$.

4.4 Constraints in Conditional Workflows

Let W_1 and W_2 be two workflow specifications with constraints C_1 and C_2, respectively. When we form $W_1 \, ; W_2$ or $W_1 \parallel W_2$, we include all constraints in C_1 and C_2. In addition, we may create new constraints, governing the execution of some steps in S_1 and some steps in S_2. However, we prohibit the addition of constraints in which all the steps are contained in either S_1 or S_2 (the assumption being that they would have been created earlier, if required). In other words, any constraint that is added when we form $W_1 \, ; W_2$ (or $W_1 \parallel W_2$) has the form (ρ, S', S''), where $S' \cup S'' \not\subseteq S_1$ and $S' \cup S'' \not\subseteq S_2$.

In contrast, since xor composition requires that we either perform the steps in S_1 or those in S_2, any constraint that includes steps from both S_1 and S_2 serves no purpose. Hence, we assume that we add no constraints when we form $W_1 \oplus W_2$.

4.5 Derived Deterministic Workflows

We say a workflow specification is *deterministic* if it has a single execution set (and *non-deterministic* otherwise). Each possible execution set in a non-deterministic workflow specification gives rise to a different, deterministic workflow specification. In particular, given a workflow specification $W = (S, E)$ with execution sets $\{S_1, \ldots, S_m\}$, we define

$W_i = (S_i, E_i)$, where

$$E_i \stackrel{\text{def}}{=} (S_i \times S_i) \cap E.$$

Then W_i is a (derived) deterministic workflow specification.

For a constrained workflow specification $W = ((S,E), A, C)$ with possible execution sets $\{S_1, \ldots, S_m\}$, we define $W_i = (S_i, E_i, A_i, C_i)$, where

$$A_i \stackrel{\text{def}}{=} (S_i \times U) \cap A,$$

and, for each $\gamma = (\rho, S_1, S_2) \in C$ such that $S_1 \cap S_i \neq \emptyset$ and $S_2 \cap S_i \neq \emptyset$,

$$\gamma_i \stackrel{\text{def}}{=} (\rho, S_1 \cap S_i, S_2 \cap S_i) \in C_i.$$

Each W_i is a deterministic, constrained workflow specification. Notice that when we form γ_i, $S_1 \cap S_i \neq \emptyset$ and $S_2 \cap S_i \neq \emptyset$: this follows by a simple induction on the structure of the workflow formula and the assumptions we make about the addition of constraints when we compose workflows (as described in Section 4.4).

Hence, we may model any non-deterministic workflow specification as a collection of deterministic workflow specifications. We may define the notion of *weakly satisfiable* and *strongly satisfiable* for a non-deterministic specification: the former holds if there exists a derived, deterministic workflow specification that is satisfiable; the latter holds if all derived, deterministic workflow specifications are satisfiable. In practice, it is likely that a workflow specification should be strongly satisfiable (otherwise there exist execution paths that can never complete).

PROPOSITION 8. *Let W be an instance of $WSP_1(=, \neq)$. Then we can determine whether W is weakly or strongly satisfiable in time $O(\sharp(W)(\flat(W)-1)^{\flat(W)})$.*

Note that we can extend this result to $WSP_3(=, \neq)$ as described in the proof of Theorem 5 (that is, using the reduction to multiple instances of $WSP_1(=, \neq)$, where the number of instances is $O(\flat(W)^2)$). The above result asserts that the complexity of checking whether a workflow is strongly satisfiable is determined by $\flat(W)$ and $\sharp(W)$. Crude upper bounds for these parameters are k and 2^k, both functions of k only. Thus, determining whether a conditional workflow is strongly satisfiable is FPT.

Of course, these bounds can be improved: the upper bound for $\flat(W)$ is only attained if no xor composition is used, in which case $\sharp(W) = 1$; conversely, introducing xor composition may reduce the maximum length, and using only xor composition reduces the number of derived specifications to k. The question is: What deployment of $k-1$ composition operators for k steps yields the worst-case complexity? We have the following result.

THEOREM 9. *Given k workflow steps, a workflow has no more than:*

- *$3^{k'}$ execution sets if $k = 3k'$;*

- *$4 \cdot 3^{k'-1}$ execution sets if $k = 3k' + 1$; and*

- *$2 \cdot 3^{k'}$ execution sets if $k = 3k' + 2$.*

REMARK 10. *The proof of the above result (see appendix) is constructive, in the sense that it tells us how to maximize*

the number of execution sets for a fixed set of k steps. Given k steps, we obtain a workflow with the greatest possible number of execution sets by taking the serial (or parallel) composition of sub-workflows $\oplus_2$ and $\oplus_3$, where $\oplus_i$ denotes the xor composition of i steps. More specifically, if $k = 3a$, we take the serial composition of a copies of $\oplus_3$; if $k = 3a + 1$, we take the serial composition of $a - 1$ copies of $\oplus_3$ and two copies of $\oplus_2$; and if $k = 3a + 2$, we take the serial composition of a copies of $\oplus_3$ and one copy of $\oplus_2$. We may conclude that $\flat(W)$ for such a workflow is no greater than $\lceil k/3 \rceil$.

REMARK 11. *Note that using xor composition reduces $\flat(W)$. And note that the exponential term in the complexity of solving $WSP_1(=, \neq)$ is determined by the number of steps in the workflow, for which an upper bound is $\flat(W)$ in the case of non-deterministic workflow specifications. For a fixed k, it follows from Theorem 9 that the worst-case complexity for $WSP_1(=, \neq)$ occurs for a workflow specification with a single execution set (of k steps).*

5. FURTHER APPLICATIONS

In this section, we study two problems from the literature and establish that they are fixed-parameter tractable. In both cases, we represent the problem as a workflow satisfiability problem using constraint expressions.

5.1 Ordered WSP

We note that the version of WSP considered so far in this paper makes no use of the order relation on the set of steps. This is a simplification introduced by Wang and Li [21]. In fact, the definition of workflow constraints by Crampton [10] prohibited constraints of the form (ρ, s, s') for $s > s'$. Moreover, a plan was required to specify an execution order for the steps in the workflow (in addition to the assignment of steps to users). This, in turn, means that Crampton's definition of constraint satisfaction (and hence of the workflow satisfiability problem) is more complex. More formally, we have the following definitions.

DEFINITION 12. *Let $\mathcal{W} = ((S, E), U, A, C)$ be a workflow comprising k steps. A tuple $(s_1, \ldots, s_k)$ is an execution schedule for $\mathcal{W}$ if $\{s_1, \ldots, s_k\} = S$ and, for all $1 \leqslant i < j \leqslant k$, $s_i \not\geqslant s_j$.[7] We say s_i precedes s_j in an execution schedule if $i < j$.*

For the workflow depicted in Figure 1, $(s_2, s_1, \ldots)$ is not an execution schedule, for example, but $(s_1, s_2, s_3, s_5, s_4, s_6)$ and $(s_1, s_2, s_3, s_4, s_5, s_6)$ are.

DEFINITION 13. *The (Type 1) constraint (ρ, s, s') is satisfied by execution schedule σ and plan π if one of the following holds: (i) s precedes s' in σ and $(\pi(s), \pi(s')) \in \rho$; (ii) s' precedes s in σ.*

The intuition here is that a constraint (ρ, s, s') is well-formed only if s could precede s' in the execution of some instance of the workflow (that is, either $s < s'$ or $s \parallel s'$). Moreover, if s does occur before s', then the execution of s' is constrained by ρ and the identity of the user that performed s. A modified version of WSP, based on the above definitions, is defined in the following way.

---

[7]In other words, an execution schedule is a *linear extension* or *topological sort* of $(S, \leqslant)$.

ORDERED WSP (OWSP)

  Input: A constrained workflow authorization schema
  $((S, E), U, A, C)$.

  Output: TRUE if there exists an execution schedule σ
  and a plan π that satisfy all constraints in C,
  and FALSE otherwise.

Note that it may not be possible to find a valid plan π for a particular execution schedule σ. Conversely, there may be a plan π for which there exist schedules σ and σ' such that (σ, π) satisfies all constraints but (σ', π) does not. Consider, for example, a plan π that is valid for our purchase order workflow such that $\pi(s_3) = \pi(s_4)$. If we add the constraint $(\neq, s_3, s_4)$, then π is valid for any execution schedule in which s_4 precedes s_3 and invalid otherwise.

The above example also shows there exist workflows for which a plan π is not a solution to WSP, but for which (σ, π) is a solution to OWSP for certain choices of σ. Crampton introduced the notion of a *well-formed workflow*, which has the following property: for all $s_i \parallel s_j$, $(\rho, s_i, s_j) \in C$ if and only if $(\tilde{\rho}, s_j, s_i) \in C$, where $\tilde{\rho}$ is defined to be $\{(u, u') \in U \times U : (u', u) \in \rho\}$. To ensure that the workflow in the above example is well-formed, we would add the constraint $(\neq, s_4, s_3)$ to C. It is easy to see that OWSP for well-formed workflows and WSP are essentially equivalent, since a valid plan for one execution schedule will be a valid plan for any execution schedule [10, Lemma 9].

Nevertheless, there will be business processes that cannot be represented using a well-formed workflow schema. In the purchase order example illustrated in Figure 1, for example, it would be quite reasonable to impose constraints on s_3 and s_4 that would mean the resulting workflow schema was not well-formed. Suppose, for example, that $\sim$ is an equivalence relation on U, where $u \sim u'$ if and only if u and u' belong to the same department. Then the constraints $(\approx, s_3, s_4)$ and $(\neq, s_4, s_3)$ require that if s_3 (the sign GRN step) is performed before s_4 (the create payment step), then the user that performs s_4 must be in a different department from the user that performs s_3; whereas if the steps are performed in the reverse order, we only require the users to be different (since the more commercially sensitive step has been performed first in this case).

Note that OWSP is only defined for Type 1 constraints (see Definition 13). Wang and Li showed that WSP is W[1]-hard [13] for arbitrary constraint relations (even if only Type 1 constraints) are used [21]. Moreover, any instance of WSP defines an instance of OWSP. Thus, OWSP is W[1]-hard. However, there is a strong connection between WSP and OWSP.

PROPOSITION 14. $OWSP_1(\rho_1, \ldots, \rho_t)$ *is FPT if* $WSP_1(\rho_1, \ldots, \rho_t)$ *is.*

A stronger notion of satisfiability for OWSP would require that there exists a plan for every execution schedule (as for conditional workflows). In this case, we simply require that every one of the $O(k!)$ derived instances of WSP is satisfiable. The worst-case complexity of determining "weak" and "strong" satisfiability for OWSP is, therefore, the same. Note that an instance of WSP is satisfiable if the corresponding instance of OWSP is strongly satisfiable.

5.2 Identifying Constraint Violation

Consider the following problem: *Given a constrained workflow specification $((S, E), U, A, C)$, does there exist a plan α such that $(s, \alpha(s)) \in A$ for all $s \in S$ and at least one constraint C that is not satisfied?* This question is of interest because if we know that no such plan exists, then we do not need a reference monitor: any allocation of (authorized) users to steps will satisfy all the constraints. This question has been studied by Armando and colleagues [2, 4] and solutions have been computed using model checkers. We answer this question by examining the satisfiability of the "negation" of the problem, rewritten using the language of constraint expressions.

THEOREM 15. *Determining whether there exists a plan that violates a workflow specification $((S, E), U, A, C)$, where all constraints have the form $(=, S_1, S_2)$ or $(\neq, S_1, S_2)$, is FPT.*

The approach described above can also be used to "prune" a workflow specification. Given a workflow specification $((S, E), U, A, C)$, we can identify, with the same (worst-case) time complexity, all constraints in C that can be violated. This enables us to remove any constraints that cannot be violated, leaving a workflow specification $((S, E, U, A, C')$, with $C' \subseteq C$. In Section 2.2, we identified situations in which we may be required to solve WSP for a workflow specification multiple times. Thus, reducing the set of constraints will reduce the complexity of subsequent attempts to determine the satisfiability of the workflow specification.

6. CONCLUDING REMARKS

In this paper, we have explored the use of constraint expressions as a means of translating different versions of the workflow satisfiability problem into one or more instances of $WSP_1(\neq)$. Constraint expressions provide a uniform way of representing the workflow satisfiability problem and related problems, such as WSP for conditional workflows (Section 4), ordered WSP and the identification of constraints that can be violated (Section 5). This, in turn, enables us to establish the complexity of solving these problems. We also believe our characterization of workflow composition, the representation of workflows as trees, and execution sets may be useful modeling tools for future research on authorization in workflow systems.

6.1 Related Work

Work on computing plans for workflows that must simultaneously satisfy authorization policies and constraints goes back to the seminal paper of Bertino *et al.* [8]. This work considered linear workflows and noted the existence of an exponential algorithm for computing valid plans. Crampton extended the model for workflows to partially ordered sets (equivalently, directed acyclic graphs) and to directed acyclic graphs with loops [10]. Wang and Li further extended this model to include Type 2 constraints [21].

Wang and Li first investigated the computational complexity and, significantly, the existence of fixed-parameter tractable algorithms for the workflow satisfiability problem [21]. One or their main results [21, Theorem 9] is very similar to the result we prove for $WSP_2(=, \neq)$ (Theorem 5), although our approach is more direct and generalizes to $WSP_3(=, \neq)$. Crampton *et al.* introduced a new method for solving the problem [12], which yields significantly better complexity bounds for $WSP_3(=, \neq)$. However, their methods only apply for certain kinds of constraints; indeed, it is not clear whether their approach extends to relations other than Δ, Δ^c and constraints using equivalence relations defined on the user set.

The use of constraint expressions to represent and reason about the complexity of the workflow satisfiability problem appears, therefore, to have some significant advantages, one specific advantage being its versatility, over existing approaches. Khan and Fong introduced the notion of a constraint expression to reason about the problem of workflow feasibility [16], which asks: Given a set of constraints and restrictions on admissible authorization policies, does there exist an authorization policy from which we can construct a valid plan? Their work was undertaken in the context of the relationship-based access control model [14], in which the "shape" of authorization policies is restricted, and does not explore fully the possibility of using constraints expressions to solve the "classical" workflow satisfiability problem.

It is widely accepted that it is useful to have conditional branching in workflow specifications [20, 22]. However, there is very little prior work on the workflow satisfiability problem, or its complexity, for conditional workflows. Khan's master's thesis includes work on existential satisfiability (what we have called weak satisfiability) and universal (strong) satisfiability [15, Chapter 8] but does not consider fixed parameter tractability.

6.2 Future Work

There are a number of opportunities for future work. Crampton *et al.* studied the workflow satisfiability problem in the presence of constraints specified using an equivalence relation $\sim$ defined on U [12]. The relation Δ may be viewed as an equivalence relation, in which each equivalence class is a single user. We would like to investigate whether our methods can be extended to solve $WSP(=, \neq, \sim, \not\sim)$, where $\sim$ is not equal to Δ. This is a non-trivial problem as we cannot use our trick of considering only those steps for which there are fewer than k authorized users. A second problem we would like to consider is the *optimal workflow-aware authorization administration problem*, which determines whether it is possible to modify the authorization relation, subject to some bound on the "cost" of the changes, when the workflow is unsatisfiable [7]. Finally, we would like (a) to remove the restriction that (S, E) is an acyclic graph, so that we can model sub-workflows that can be repeated, and (b) to include *inclusive gateways* [22], allowing for one or more sub-workflows to be executed. Both of these extensions can be readily modeled using execution sets (or multisets). If, for example, S_1 and S_2 are execution sets for W_1 and W_2, respectively, then S_1, S_2 and $S_1 \cup S_2$ are execution sets for $W_1 + W_2$, where $+$ indicates inclusive-or composition.

7. REFERENCES

[1] American National Standards Institute. *ANSI INCITS 359-2004 for Role Based Access Control*, 2004.

[2] A. Armando, E. Giunchiglia, and S. E. Ponta. Formal specification and automatic analysis of business processes under authorization constraints: An action-based approach. In S. Fischer-Hübner, C. Lambrinoudakis, and G. Pernul, editors, *TrustBus*, volume 5695 of *Lecture Notes in Computer Science*, pages 63–72. Springer, 2009.

[3] A. Armando and S. Ponta. Model checking of security-sensitive business processes. In P. Degano and J. D. Guttman, editors, *Formal Aspects in Security and Trust*, volume 5983 of *Lecture Notes in Computer Science*, pages 66–80. Springer, 2009.

[4] A. Armando and S. Ranise. Automated analysis of infinite state workflows with access control policies. In C. Meadows and M. C. F. Gago, editors, *STM*, volume 7170 of *Lecture Notes in Computer Science*, pages 157–174. Springer, 2011.

[5] J. Bang-Jensen and G. Gutin. *Digraphs: Theory, Algorithms and Applications*. Springer, 2nd edition, 2009.

[6] D. A. Basin, S. J. Burri, and G. Karjoth. Obstruction-free authorization enforcement: Aligning security with business objectives. In *CSF*, pages 99–113. IEEE Computer Society, 2011.

[7] D. A. Basin, S. J. Burri, and G. Karjoth. Optimal workflow-aware authorizations. In V. Atluri, J. Vaidya, A. Kern, and M. Kantarcioglu, editors, *SACMAT*, pages 93–102. ACM, 2012.

[8] E. Bertino, E. Ferrari, and V. Atluri. The specification and enforcement of authorization constraints in workflow management systems. *ACM Trans. Inf. Syst. Secur.*, 2(1):65–104, 1999.

[9] D. F. C. Brewer and M. J. Nash. The Chinese Wall security policy. In *IEEE Symposium on Security and Privacy*, pages 206–214. IEEE Computer Society, 1989.

[10] J. Crampton. A reference monitor for workflow systems with constrained task execution. In E. Ferrari and G.-J. Ahn, editors, *SACMAT*, pages 38–47. ACM, 2005.

[11] J. Crampton, G. Gutin, and A. Yeo. On the parameterized complexity and kernelization of the workflow satisfiability problem. *CoRR*, abs/1205.0852, 2012. http://arxiv.org/abs/1205.0852.

[12] J. Crampton, G. Gutin, and A. Yeo. On the parameterized complexity of the workflow satisfiability problem. In T. Yu, G. Danezis, and V. D. Gligor, editors, *ACM Conference on Computer and Communications Security*, pages 857–868. ACM, 2012.

[13] R. G. Downey and M. R. Fellows. *Parameterized Complexity*. Springer Verlag, 1999.

[14] P. W. L. Fong. Relationship-based access control: protection model and policy language. In R. S. Sandhu and E. Bertino, editors, *CODASPY*, pages 191–202. ACM, 2011.

[15] A. A. Khan. Satisfiability and feasibility in a relationship-based workflow authorization model. Master's thesis, University of Calgary, 2012.

[16] A. A. Khan and P. W. L. Fong. Satisfiability and feasibility in a relationship-based workflow authorization model. In S. Foresti, M. Yung, and F. Martinelli, editors, *ESORICS*, volume 7459 of *Lecture Notes in Computer Science*, pages 109–126. Springer, 2012.

[17] M. Kohler and A. Schaad. Proactive access control for business process-driven environments. In *ACSAC*, pages 153–162. IEEE Computer Society, 2008.

[18] R. Niedermeier. *Invitation to Fixed-Parameter Algorithms*. Oxford University Press, 2006.

[19] A. Schäfer, C. Komusiewicz, H. Moser, and R. Niedermeier. Parameterized computational complexity of finding small-diameter subgraphs. *Optimization Letters*, 6(5):883–891, 2012.

[20] W. M. P. van der Aalst, A. H. M. ter Hofstede, B. Kiepuszewski, and A. P. Barros. Workflow patterns. *Distributed and Parallel Databases*, 14(1):5–51, 2003.

[21] Q. Wang and N. Li. Satisfiability and resiliency in workflow authorization systems. *ACM Trans. Inf. Syst. Secur.*, 13(4):40, 2010.

[22] S. A. White and D. Miers. *BPMN Modeling and Reference Guide*. Future Strategies, Incorporated, 2008.

APPENDIX

A. PROOFS

PROOF OF COROLLARY 6. For $\text{WSP}_2(=,\neq)$, in the worst case, each constraint has the form (ρ, s, S'), with $s \notin S'$. Hence, the number of Type 2 constraints can be no greater than $k2^{k-1}$. It now follows from Theorem 5 that $\text{WSP}_2(=,\neq)$ is FPT. For $\text{WSP}_3(=,\neq)$, in the worst case, each constraint has the form (ρ, S', S''). Thus, noting that (ρ, S', S'') is equivalent for $\text{WSP}_3(=,\neq)$, the number of Type 3 constraints can be no greater than $2^k \cdot 2^k = 2^{2k}$, from which it follows that $\text{WSP}_3(=,\neq)$ is FPT. □

PROOF OF PROPOSITION 8. The result follows by noting that determining strong satisfiability requires us to check whether all $\sharp(W)$ derived instances of W are satisfiable, while determining weak satisfiability requires us to check whether at least one derived instance is satisfiable. The complexity, in the worst case, is the same. The complexity of checking a single instance is $(k'-1)^{k'}$, where k' is the number of steps in the derived instance. The result now follows. □

PROOF OF THEOREM 9. First observe that may disregard the $\|$ operator in computing an upper bound on $\sharp(W)$. To see this, note that the parallel operator requires, like the serial operator, that all steps in the sub-workflows are performed. In particular, an execution set for workflow $W_1 \| W_2$ has the form $S_1 \cup S_2$, where S_i is an execution set for workflow W_i.

Recall $\oplus_i$ represents the xor composition of i steps and $\sharp(\oplus_i ; \oplus_j) = \sharp(\oplus_j ; \oplus_i) = ij$.

We proceed by induction on k. For $k = 2$, we may construct

$$\oplus_1 ; \oplus_1 \quad \text{and} \quad \oplus_2,$$

thus the result holds for $k = 2$. For $k = 3$, we may construct three different workflows:

$$\oplus_1 ; \oplus_1 ; \oplus_1, \quad \oplus_1 ; \oplus_2, \quad \text{and} \quad \oplus_3,$$

thus the result holds for $k = 3$. Finally, for $k = 4$, we may construct

$$\oplus_1 ; \oplus_1 ; \oplus_1 ; \oplus_1, \quad \oplus_1 ; \oplus_1 ; \oplus_2, \quad \oplus_1 ; \oplus_3, \quad \oplus_2 ; \oplus_2 \quad \text{and} \quad \oplus_4,$$

thus the result holds for $k = 4$.

Now consider $k > 4$ steps and suppose the result holds for all workflows constructed from $k - 1$ or fewer steps. Then

for any split of k into workflows W_1 and W_2 comprising k_1 and k_2 steps, respectively, such that $k_1 + k_2 = k$, we may form $W_1 ; W_2$ or $W_1 \oplus W_2$. Clearly, for $k > 4$, $\sharp(W_1 ; W_2) > \sharp(W_1 \oplus W_2)$. Moreover, $\sharp(W_1 ; W_2) = \sharp(W_1) \cdot \sharp(W_2)$.

First consider the case $k = 3a$ and let $k_i = 3a_i + b_i$, $i = 1, 2$, with $b_i \in \{0, 1, 2\}$. We assume (without loss of generality) that $b_1 \leqslant b_2$. If $b_1 = b_2$, then k_1 and k_2 are divisible by 3 and $\sharp(W_i) \leqslant 3^{a_i}$ by the inductive hypothesis, whence

$$\sharp(W) = \sharp(W_1) \cdot \sharp(W_2) \leqslant 3^{a_1} \cdot 3^{a_2} = 3^a.$$

If $b_1 = 1$ and $b_2 = 2$, then we have $a_1 + a_2 = a - 1$ and

$$\sharp(W) = \sharp(W_1) \cdot \sharp(W_2) \leqslant 4 \cdot 3^{a_1 - 1} \cdot 2 \cdot 3^{a_2} = 8 \cdot 3^{a-2} < 3^a$$

and the result holds.

Now consider the case $k = 3a + 1$. If $b_1 = 0$, then $b_2 = 1$ and $a_1 + a_2 = a$. Hence, by the inductive hypothesis, we have

$$\sharp(W) \leqslant 3^{a_1} \cdot 4 \cdot 3^{a_2 - 1} = 4 \cdot 3^{a-1},$$

as required. If $b_1 = b_2$, then we have $b_i = 2$ and $a_1 + a_2 = a - 1$. Hence, by the inductive hypothesis, we have

$$\sharp(W) \leqslant 2 \cdot 3^{a_1} \cdot 2 \cdot 3^{a_2} = 4 \cdot 3^{a-1},$$

as required.

Finally, consider the case $k = 3a + 2$. If $b_1 = 0$, then $b_2 = 2$ and $a_1 + a_2 = a$. Hence, by the inductive hypothesis, we have

$$\sharp(W) \leqslant 3^{a_1} \cdot 2 \cdot 3^{a_2} = 2 \cdot 3^a,$$

as required. If $b_1 = b_2$, then $b_i = 1$ and $a_1 + a_2 = a$. Hence, we have

$$\sharp(W) \leqslant 16 \cdot 3^{a_1 + a_2 - 2} = \frac{16}{9} \cdot 3^a < 2 \cdot 3^a.$$

as required. □

PROOF OF PROPOSITION 14. An instance of OWSP_1 contains a set of constraints C and we may assume that C contains at least two constraints of the form (ρ_i, s, s') and (ρ_j, s', s) with $\rho_i \neq \tilde{\rho}_j$. (If no such constraints exist then $\text{OWSP}_1(\rho_1, \ldots, \rho_t)$ is identical to an instance of $\text{WSP}_1(\rho_1, \ldots, \rho_t)$.) Observe that the number of linear extensions of $(S, \leqslant)$ (and hence possible execution schedules) is determined only by k. Specifically, the number of linear extensions is no greater than $k!$. Note also that in any execution of the workflow, either s precedes s' or vice versa. Hence each linear extension allows us to discard either (ρ_i, s, s') or (ρ_j, s', s) (since exactly one of them will be irrelevant to the schedule defined by the linear extension), thus defining an instance of WSP that contains fewer constraints than the original problem. In other words, we may consider our instance of OWSP_1 to be the disjunction of $k!$ instances of WSP_1. If each instance of WSP_1 is FPT, we can solve each of these instances, thus solving the original instance of OWSP_1. □

PROOF OF THEOREM 15. A Type 1 constraint (ρ, s, s') is satisfied by a plan α if $(\alpha(s), \alpha(s')) \in \rho$ and is not satisfied ("violated") otherwise. In other words, (ρ, s, s') is violated by α if $(\alpha(s), \alpha(s')) \notin \rho$. Equivalently, a constraint (ρ, s, s') is violated iff $(\overline{\rho}, s, s')$ is satisfied, where

$$\overline{\rho} \stackrel{\text{def}}{=} \{(u, u') \in U \times U : (u, u') \notin \rho\}.$$

83

A Type 2 constraint (ρ, s, S'), $S' \subseteq S$ is violated if (ρ, s, s') is violated for all $s' \in S'$. In other words, (ρ, s, S') is violated iff the constraint expression

$$\bigwedge_{s' \in S'} (\overline{\rho}, s, s')$$

is satisfied. Similarly, a Type 3 constraint (ρ, S', S'') is violated iff the constraint expression

$$\bigwedge_{s' \in S', s'' \in S''} (\overline{\rho}, s', s'')$$

is satisfied. Finally a set of constraints $\{c_1, \ldots, c_t\}$ is violated if at least one c_i is violated. In other words, we can determine whether there exists a plan that violates a set of constraints by determining if there exists a plan α that satisfies a constraint expression in disjunctive normal form, where each clause is a conjunction of Type 1 constraints. We make the following observations.

- There are no more than c disjuncts, where c is the number of constraints in the original workflow specification.

- A Type 2 constraint, when rewritten in the above way, gives rise to a conjunction of no more than $k - 1$ Type 1 constraints, while a Type 3 constraint gives rise to no more than k^2 Type 1 constraints.

- There can be no more than $k2^k$ Type 2 constraints in a workflow specification and no more than 4^k Type 3 constraints.

- $\overline{\Delta}$ is Δ^c and $\overline{\Delta^c}$ is Δ.

- By Theorem 5, the time taken to solve $\mathrm{WSP}_1(\Delta, \Delta^c)$ (that is, $\mathrm{WSP}_1(=, \neq)$) is $O(c(k-1)^k + kn)$, where c is the number of constraints.

Therefore, there exists an FPT algorithm to determine whether there exists a plan π in which each user is authorized and a constraint that π does not satisfy, since we need only find a single disjunct that is true, and each disjunct represents a workflow specification containing only Type 1 constraints. The time taken to solve this new problem is $O(k2^{k-1}((k-1)^{k+1} + kn))$ for Type 2 constraints and $O(4^k(k(k-1)^{k+1} + kn))$ for Type 3 constraints. $\square$

Panel
On Granularity in Access Control

Organizer
Ian Molloy
IBM Research TJ Watson
molloyim@us.ibm.com

Volkmar Lotz
SAP Global Research
volkmar.lotz@sap.com

Casey Schaufler
Intel Open Source Technology
Center
casey.schaufler@intel.com

Organizer
Mahesh Tripunitara
University of Waterloo
tripunit@uwaterloo.ca

Martin Kuhlmann
Omada
mku@omada.net

Vijay Atluri
Rutgers University
atluri@rutgers.edu

ABSTRACT

This panel will address the following question.

> Does an increase in the granularity of access control systems produce a measurable reduction in risk and help meet the goals of the organization, or is the cost prohibitively high?

After decades of access control research, products, and practice, there has been a trend towards more complex access control policies and models that more finely restrict (or allow) access to resources. This allows policy administrators to more closely specify any high level abstract policy they may have in mind, or accurately enforce regulations such as HIPPA, SOX, or PCI. The end goal is to allow only those actions that are desirable in hindsight, or via an approach to which Bishop et al. [2] refer as the *Oracle Policy*.

As the expressive power of access control models can vary [4], an administrator may need a more powerful model to specify the high level policy they need for their particular application. It is not uncommon for new models to add new key-attributes, data-sources, features, or relations to provide a richer set of tools. This has resulted in an explosion of new one-off models in the literature, few of which make their way to real products or deployment.

To increase the expressive power of a model, increase its granularity, reduce the complexity of administration and to answer desirable security queries such as safety, a plethora of new concepts have been added to access control models. To name a few: groups and roles; hierarchies and constraints; parameterized permissions; exceptions; time and location of users and resources; relationships between subjects; attributes of subjects, objects, and actions; information flow; conflict of interest classes; obligations; trust, benefit, and risk; workflows; delegation; situational awareness and context; and so on. All of these constructs build to a meta-model, as Barker observes [1].

SACMAT'13, June 12–14, 2013, Amsterdam, The Netherlands.
ACM 978-1-4503-1950-8/13/06.

This granularity has resulted in many novel and useful findings, new algorithms, and challenging open research issues, but poses potential problems as well. With granularity often comes complexity which manifests itself in specifying policies, managing and maintaining policies over time, and auditing logs to ensure compliance.

This panel will discuss issues surrounding the problem of complexity in access control. From designing and specifying new models, designing enforcement mechanisms on real-world systems, policy lifecycle, and the role of analytics from automatically generating policies to auditing logs. So, is this complexity worth it? Does increasing the granularity produce a measurable reduction in the risk to sensitive resources and protect the goals of the organization or is the cost prohibitively high?

Can we ever truly specify a "correct" and "complete" policy, which may be too dynamic and require the interpretation of the courts to decide, especially when policies are intended to enforce ambiguous regulations. Finally, at what cost should we strive for a perfect, fine-grained policy? Should more resources be places on recovery from security breaches than on prevention? Should we be "going for mean time to repair equals zero rather than mean time between failure equals infinity" [3]?

Categories and Subject Descriptors

D.4.6 [**Operating Systems**]: Security and Protection—*Access Controls*

Keywords

Granularity, Security

1. PANELISTS

Volkmar Lotz.

Volkmar Lotz has more than 20 years experience in industrial research on Security and Software Engineering. He is heading the Security & Trust program of SAP Global Research, a group of 40 researchers investigating into applied research and innovative security solutions for modern software platforms, networked enterprises and Future Internet applications. The Security & Trust program defines and executes SAP's security research agenda in alignment with SAP's business strategy and global research trends. Volkmar's current research interests include Business Process Security, Service Security, Authorisation, Security Engineering, Formal Methods and Compliance. Volkmar has published numerous scientific papers in his area of interest and is regularly serving on Programme Committees of internationally renowned conferences. He has been supervising various European projects, including large-scale integrated projects. Volkmar holds a diploma in Computer Science from the University of Kaiserslautern.

Martin Kuhlmann.

Dr. Martin Kuhlmann is a Lead Solution Consultant within Omada. Martin has been active in the IT Security space for more than a decade and has been a frequent speaker and panelist at international conferences. As a consultant and strategist, he had a leading role in various integration projects for provisioning systems in large organizations. He specializes in Identity & Access Management and IT governance, risk & compliance. Martin published numerous journal articles and several scientific papers on Role-based access control (RBAC) and application security. In 1992, he completed his doctorate in mathematics from Bochum University, Germany.

Casey Schaufler.

Casey Schaufler has been working on operating systems since the 1970's, spending the bulk of that time on security in general and access controls in particular. In the Orange Book era was the architect of Silicon Graphics' Trusted Irix B1 system. In the Open Source era he created the Smack Linux security module, breaking the SELinux monopoly on advanced security methods in the Linux kernel. He has worked with mobile devices, embedded systems, personal workstations and supercomputers in a wide variety of market segments. Casey is currently working on support for multiple concurrent Linux security modules and security policy models for modern computer systems. He lives on the California coast, just south of San Francisco.

Casey is employed by the Intel Open Source Technology Center. He can be contacted at casey@schaufler-ca.com or casey.schaufler@intel.com.

Vijay Atluri.

Dr. Vijay Atluri received her B.Tech. in Electronics and Communications Engineering from Jawaharlal Nehru Technological University, Kakinada, India, M.Tech. in Electronics and Communications Engineering from Indian Institute of Technology, Kharagpur, India, and Ph.D. in Information Technology from George Mason University, USA. She is a Professor of Computer Information Systems in the MSIS Department, and research director for the Center for Information Management, Integration and Connectivity (CIMIC) at Rutgers University. She is currently a program director at the National Science Foundation in the Information & Intelligent Systems division.

Dr. Atluri's research interests include Information Security, Privacy, Databases, Workflow Management, Spatial Databases and Distributed Systems. Her research has been sponsored by NSF, DHS, DoD, NSA, ARO, NOAA, EPA, Lawrence Livermore National Laboratory, Hackensack Meadowlands Development Commission and SAP Research. She has published over 150 technical papers in such journals and conferences as the IEEE Transactions on Dependable and Secure Computing, IEEE Transactions on Knowledge and Data Engineering, ACM Transactions on Information Systems Security, The VLDB Journal, Distributed and Parallel Databases: An International Journal, IEEE Symposium on Security and Privacy, IEEE Conference on Data Engineering and ACM Conference on Computer and Communication Security. She is the co-author of the book, Multilevel Secure Transaction Processing, Kluwer Academic Publishers (1999). She served as a member of the Steering Committee for the ACM Special Interest Group on Security Audit (SIGSAC). She currently serves as the Vice-chair for SIGSAC and Chair of the IFIP WG11.3 Working Group on Data and Application Security. She served as the general chair for the 2004 and 2005 ACM Conference on Computer and Communications Security (CCS), co-general chair for the 2005 International Conference on Web Information Systems Engineering, member of the steering committee of the ACM Symposium on Access Control Models and Architectures (SACMAT), program chair for the 2003 CCS, 2008 IFIP WG11.3 Working Conference on Data and Application Security, and on the program committees of a number of conferences in the security and database areas. Currently she is on the editorial board of IEEE Transactions on Dependable and Secure Computing, Journal of Computer Security, International Journal on Digital Libraries and International Journal of Information and Computer Security. In the past, she served as the associate editor for the IEEE Transactions on Knowledge and Data Engineering. In 1996, she was the recipient of the National Science Foundation CAREER Award. In 1999, she received the Rutgers University Research Award for untenured faculty for outstanding research contributions. Dr. Atluri is a senior member of the IEEE Computer Society and member of the ACM.

2. REFERENCES

[1] S. Barker. The next 700 access control models or a unifying meta-model? In *SACMAT*, pages 187–196, 2009.

[2] M. Bishop, S. Engle, D. Frincke, C. Gates, F. Greitzer, S. Peisert, and S. Whalen. A risk management approach to the "insider threat". In C. W. Probst, J. Hunker, D. Gollmann, and M. Bishop, editors, *Insider Threats in Cyber Security*, volume 49 of *Advances in Information Security*, pages 115–137. Springer US, 2010.

[3] G. McGraw. Silver bullet speaks with Dan Geer. *Security Privacy, IEEE*, 4(4):10–13, 2006.

[4] M. V. Tripunitara and N. Li. A Theory for Comparing the Expressive Power of Access Control Models. *Journal of Computer Security*, 15:231–272, 2007.

Searching over Encrypted Data in Cloud Systems

Florian Kerschbaum
SAP Research
Karlsruhe, Germany
florian.kerschbaum@sap.com

ABSTRACT

Security is still a major inhibitor of cloud computing. When companies are testing cloud applications, e.g. for storage or databases, they use generated data for fear of data loss. Modern encrypted databases where the cryptographic key remains at the client provide a solution to this problem. Recent results in cryptography, such order-preserving encryption, and database systems [3] enable the practical use of these systems. We report on our pre-development efforts of implementing such an encrypted database in an in-memory, column store database [1]. We highlight some unsolved research challenges: such as access control, infrequent queries and security vs. performance query optimization. Challenges to key management in multi-user environments remain largely unsolved [2]. We give an overview of the architecture and performance benchmarks on our prototype which are very encouraging for practical adoption.

The talk is structured in three parts:

1. We will give *background* on the architecture of the cloud database. First, we present overviews of recent developments in cryptography, e.g., order-preserving encryption, searchable encryption, proxy re-encryption and somewhat homomorphic encryption. Second, we give an introduction to new in-memory, column-store database architectures including compression techniques such as order-preserving dictionaries and multi-core database operators.

2. We highlight some *research challenges*, such as access control, infrequent queries, security vs. performance trade-offs and key management. Particularly, in multi-user environments databases need to handle access control, as well as sophisticated key management. Furthermore, when using adjustable (onion) encryption selection queries can modify the (security) state of the database.

3. We report on some *initial pre-development results* in our research group. We implemented a prototype and can give some performance figures. Furthermore, we show our progress on some of the outlined challenges.

Categories and Subject Descriptors

C.2.4 [**Computer-Communication Networks**]: Distributed Systems—*Distributed databases*; D.4.6 [**Operating Systems**]: Security and Protection—*Cryptographic controls*

Keywords

Cloud, Database, Encryption

Short Biography

Florian Kerschbaum is a chief expert in the security research department at SAP in Karlsruhe, Germany. In the academic year 2011/12 he was on leave as the deputy professor for the chair of privacy and data security at Dresden University of Technology. His research interests center around security and privacy algorithms and protocols for the next-generation, cross-organizational business applications. He holds a Ph.D. in computer science from the Karlsruhe Institute of Technology, a master's degree from Purdue University, and a bachelor's degree from Berufsakademie Mannheim.

Acknowledgements

I would like to thank my colleagues Andreas Schaad, Axel Schröpfer and Mathias Kohler, Martin Härterich, Walter Tighzert, Patrick Grofig working with me on this exciting project. Also, I would like to give a special thanks to our former manager Stephan Fischer for initiating the project.

REFERENCES

[1] S. Hildenbrand, D. Kossmann, T. Sanamrad, C. Binnig, F. Färber, and J. Wöhler. Query processing on encrypted data in the cloud. *Department of Computer Science, Technical Report 735, ETH Zürich*, 2011.

[2] F. Kerschbaum. Collusion-resistant outsourcing of private set intersection. In *Proceedings of the 27th ACM Symposium On Applied Computing (SAC)*, 2012.

[3] R. Popa, C. Redfield, N. Zeldovich, and H. Balakrishnan. CryptDB: Protecting confidentiality with encrypted query processing. In *Proceedings of the 23rd ACM Symposium on Operating Systems Principles (SOSP)*, 2011.

Information Flow Control for Stream Processing in Clouds

Xing Xie
Computer Science
Department
Colorado State University
Fort Collins, CO 80523
xing@cs.colostate.edu

Indrakshi Ray
Computer Science
Department
Colorado State University
Fort Collins, CO 80523
iray@cs.colostate.edu

Raman Adaikkalavan
Computer and Information
Sciences
Indiana University South Bend
South Bend, IN 46634
raman@cs.iusb.edu

Rose Gamble
Tandy School of Computer
Science
The University of Tulsa
Tulsa, OK 74104
gamble@utulsa.edu

ABSTRACT

In the near future, clouds will provide situational monitoring services using streaming data. Examples of such services include health monitoring, stock market monitoring, shopping cart monitoring, and emergency control and threat management. Offering such services require securely processing data streams generated by multiple, possibly competing and/or complementing, organizations. Processing of data streams also should not cause any overt or covert leakage of information across organizations. We propose an information flow control model adapted from the Chinese Wall policy that can be used to protect against sensitive data disclosure. We propose architectures that are suitable for securely and efficiently processing streaming information belonging to different organizations. We discuss how performance can be further improved by sharing the processing of multiple queries. We demonstrate the feasibility of our approach by implementing a prototype of our system and show the overhead incurred due to the information flow constraints.

Categories and Subject Descriptors

K.6.5 [**Management of Computing and Information Systems**]: [Security and Protection]

Keywords

Chinese Wall Policy; Information Flow; Data Streams; Clouds

1. INTRODUCTION

Data Stream Management Systems (DSMSs) [1, 6, 9, 8, 14, 7, 16] are needed for situation monitoring applications that collect high-speed data, run continuous queries to process them, and compute results on-the-fly to detect events of interest. Consider

one potential situation monitoring application – collecting real-time streaming audit data to thwart various types of attacks in a cloud environment. Detecting such precursors to attacks may involve analyzing streaming audit data belonging to various, possibly competing and/or complementing, organizations. Consequently, it is important to protect such data from unauthorized disclosure and modification. Moreover, the processing of continuous queries should not cause leakage or modification of sensitive data. Towards this end, we redesign a DSMS such that it can process information generated in a multi-domain environment, each consisting of competing entities, in a secure manner.

Researchers have worked on secure data and query processing in the context of DSMSs. However, almost all of these works focus on providing access control to streaming data [20, 13, 22, 12, 21, 4, 5]. Controlling access is not enough to prevent security breaches in cloud computing applications where illegal information flow can occur across multiple domains. The existence of covert and overt channels can cause sensitive information to be illegally passed from one domain to another. We need to prevent unauthorized access but also ensure the absence of such illegal information flow. Towards this end, we propose an information flow control model adapted from the Chinese Wall policy [23] that can be used to provide secure processing of streaming data generated from multiple organizations.

A cloud contains a set of companies that offer services. In order to keep the cloud operational, it is important to detect security and performance problems in a timely manner. Thus, auditing live events streaming from the cloud is very essential. Services offered in a cloud can be competing or complementing. To detect attacks and performance issues, the cloud has to be audited as a whole, though the audit events may be generated by competing or complementing companies. Chinese Wall policy aims to protect disclosure of company sensitive information to potentially competing organizations, but does not deal with complementing organizations. In a cloud, companies are organized into various domains based on the types of services they provide. Each of these domains forms a conflict of interest (COI) class. Companies in the same COI class are in direct competition. We must aim to prevent leakage of a company's sensitive information to other organizations belonging to the same COI class. Companies that offer complementing services can be assigned a complementing interest (CI) class. Companies in the same COI class cannot be in the same CI. Companies belonging

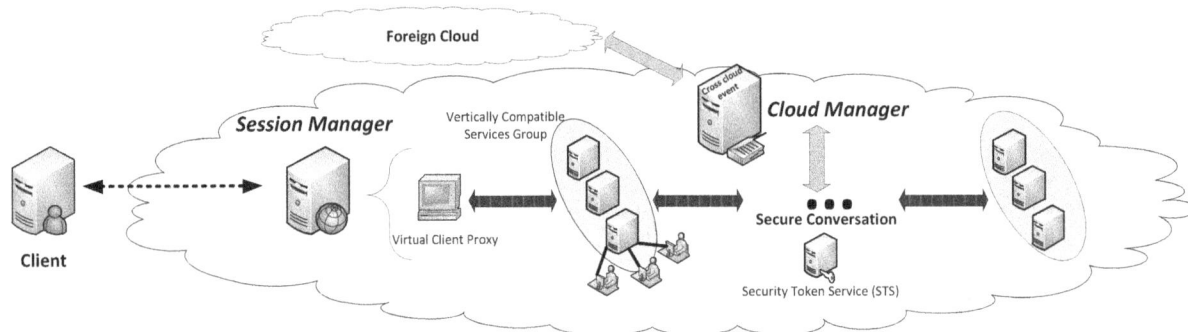

Figure 1: Multi-Tier Architecture of a Cloud

to the same CI have no such direct competition and do not require trusted entities to manage their information.

Streaming audit data generated by various organizations must be analyzed in real-time to detect the presence of various types of attacks. A company may want to audit its own data to detect malicious insider threats. Sometimes it may be needed to detect a denial-of-service attack for a particular type of service offered by companies in a COI class. On the other hand, detecting the delay between the service request and response may involve analyzing audit streams in a service chain invocation that has multiple companies belonging to some CI class. For each such case, it should be possible to detect the attack without causing a company's sensitive information from being leaked to its competitors.

Our goal in this paper is not to address potential security attacks in the cloud. We focus on how streaming data generated by various organizations can be processed in a secure manner so as to protect against unauthorized disclosure and modification. Our threat model is that processing units may contain unintentional bugs or trojan horses that cause information leakage. We also want protection from honest but curious users who want to know information that they are not authorized to access. We do not address denial-of-service attacks. We assume that the underlying infrastructure is trusted.

In this work, we start with identifying the access requirements and the information flow constraints for processing streaming audit data in a cloud computing environment. We adapt the Chinese Wall policy formulated by Sandhu [23] to formalize the information flow constraints in clouds. We demonstrate how cloud computing queries can be formulated and provide an architecture for executing such queries. We demonstrate how multiple queries can share their computation to improve performance and provide good resource utilization. We also implement a prototype to demonstrate the feasibility of our approach and show how the performance is impacted by the information flow constraints.

The rest of the paper is organized as follows. In Section 2, we present an architecture for processing continuous queries generated from the various tiers in the cloud. In Section 3, we present our information flow control model that formulates the rules for accessing data streams generated by various organizations in the cloud. In Section 4, we present some example queries that are executed in the cloud. In order to accelerate throughput, we show how continuous queries can be shared in Section 5. In Section 6, we discuss our prototype and show some performance results. In Section 7, we mention a few related work. In Section 8, we conclude the paper with pointers to future work.

2. CONTINUOUS QUERY PROCESSING ARCHITECTURE

In this section, we present our example application that motivates the need for secure stream processing in cloud computing environments. We have a service that aims to prevent and detect attacks in real-time in the cloud. Such a service provides warning about various types of attacks, often involving multiple organizations.

Figure 1 shows a multi tier architecture of the cloud adopted from [26]. Various types of auditing may take place in the cloud. The first level is the *company auditing tier*, not explicitly shown in Figure 1, that is represented by the users connected to some service. In this tier, the activities pertaining to an organization are analyzed in isolation. The next level is the *service auditing tier*, identified by shaded ellipses that contain sets of resources and services. Each shaded ellipse depicts vertically compatible services or resources; this implies the services or resources that can be functionally substituted for each other, possibly on demand. The *cloud auditing tier* is shown with connecting dark arrows, which depicts the internal communication within the cloud due to a service invocation chain.

Various types of audit streams must be captured to detect the different types of attacks that may take place in a cloud. The company auditing tier logs the activities of the various users in the organization. If the behavior of an authorized user does not follow his usual pattern, we can perform analysis to determine if the user's authentication information has been compromised. This tier is responsible for analyzing the audit streams of individual companies in isolation. Typically, at this layer, the audit streams generated by a single company are analyzed.

The service auditing tier logs information pertaining to the various companies who provide similar services. Session Manager at this tier can detect whether there is a denial-of-service attack targeted at a specific type of service. Session Manager analyzes audit streams generated from multiple competing organizations, so we need to protect against information leakage and corruption. In short, the Session Manager needs to analyze data from one or more companies belonging to the same COI class.

The cloud auditing tier collects audit information pertaining to a service invocation chain and is able to detect the presence of man-in-the-middle attack. Cloud Provider is responsible for analyzing audit streams from multiple organizations associated with service invocation chains, but the organizations may not have conflict of interest. Thus, at this tier, the audit streams from the companies belonging to one or more CI classes are analyzed.

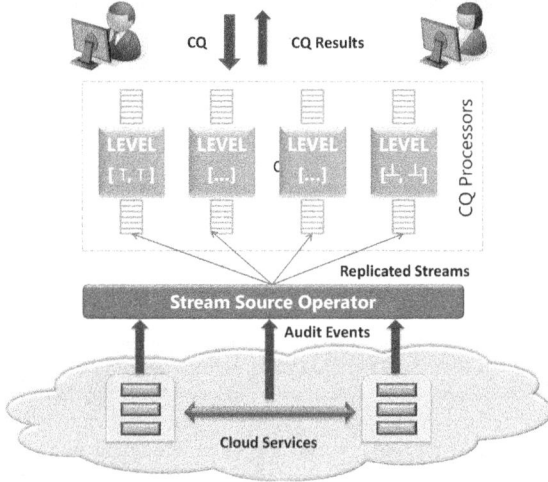

Figure 2: CQ Processing Architecture

In order to detect and warn against these attacks, continuous queries must be executed on the streaming data belonging to various organizations. Queries must be processed such that there are no overt or covert leakage of information across competing organizations. We assign security levels to categorize the various classes of data that are being generated and collected at the various tiers. The security level of the data determines who can access and modify it. In the next section, we discuss how security levels are assigned to various classes of data.

We propose the architecture shown in Figure 2 that provides a way to capture events from the cloud, monitor them, and trigger alerts. The architecture uses concepts based on cloud computing [26], data stream processing [16, 8, 6, 17], event processing [15, 3], Chinese wall security [23], replicated and trusted multilevel database management [2] and multilevel secure data stream management system [5].

As shown in Figure 2 there are several services offered in the cloud. Audit data generated by the services are sent to the DSMS. For this paper, we consider a centralized DSMS architecture. Compatible services are grouped and they interact based on client needs. Servers contain event detectors that monitor and detect occurrence of interesting events. The detectors sanitize and propagate the events to the data stream management system, which arrive at the stream source operator. This operator checks for the level of the incoming audit events and propagates them to the appropriate query processor's input queue. The query processor architecture is based on the replicated model, where there is a one-to-one correspondence between query processors and security levels. A query specified by a user at a particular level is executed by the query processor running at that level. Also a query processor at some level can only process data that it is authorized to view. After processing the query results are disseminated to authorized users via the output queues of queries. In addition to the query processors and stream source operator the data stream management system contains various other components (trusted and untrusted) as discussed in the implementation and experimental evaluation section.

3. INFORMATION FLOW MODEL

In the following, we present an information flow model for cloud applications to protect against improper leakage and disclosure. We provide an information flow model that is adapted from the lattice structure for Chinese Wall proposed by Sandhu [23].

We have a set of companies that provide services in the clouds. The companies are partitioned into conflict of interest classes based on the type of services they provide. Companies providing the same type of service are in direct competition with each other. Consequently, it is important to protect against disclosure of sensitive information to competing organizations. We begin by defining how the conflict of interest classes are represented.

DEFINITION 1. **[Conflict of Interest Class Representation:]** *The set of companies providing service to the cloud are partitioned into a set of n conflict of interest classes, which we denote by COI_1, COI_2, ..., and COI_n. Each conflict of interest class is represented as COI_i, where $1 \leq i \leq n$. Conflict of interest class COI_i consists of a set of m_i companies, where $m_i \geq 1$, that is $COI_i = \{1, 2, 3, \ldots, m_i\}$.*

On the other hand, a set of companies, who are not in competition with each other, may provide complementing services in the cloud. A single company can provide some service, and sometimes multiple companies may together offer a set of services. In the following, we define the notion of complementing interest (CI) class and show how it is represented.

DEFINITION 2. **[Complementing Interest Class Representation:]** *The set of companies providing complementing services is represented as an n-element vector $[i_1, i_2, \ldots, i_n]$, where $i_k \in COI_k \cup \{\perp\}$ and $1 \leq k \leq n$. $i_k = \perp$ signifies that the CI class does not contain services from any company in the conflict of interest class COI_k. $i_k \in COI_k$ indicates that the CI class contains services from the corresponding company in conflict of interest class COI_k. Our representation forbids multiple companies that are part of the same COI class from being assigned to the same complementing interest class.*

We next define the security structure of our model. Each data stream, as well as the individual tuples constituting it, is associated with a security level that captures its sensitivity. Security level associated with a data stream dictates which entities can access or modify it. Input data stream generated by an individual organization offering some service has a security level that captures the organizational information. Input streams may be processed by the DSMS to generate *derived streams*. Derived data streams may contain information about multiple companies, some of which are in the same COI class and others may belong to different COI classes. Before describing how to assign security levels to derived data streams, we show how security levels are represented.

DEFINITION 3. **[Security Level Representation:]** *A security level is represented as an n-element vector $[i_1, i_2, \ldots, i_n]$, where $i_j \in COI_j \cup \{\perp\} \cup \{T\}$ and $1 \leq j \leq n$. $i_j = \perp$ signifies that the data stream does not contain information from any company in COI_j; $i_j = T$ signifies that the data stream contains information from two or more companies belonging to COI_j; $i_j \in COI_j$ denotes that the data stream contains information from the corresponding company in COI_j.*

Consider the case where we have 3 COI classes, namely, COI_1, COI_2, and COI_3. COI_1, COI_2, and COI_3 have 5, 3, and 2 companies, respectively. The audit stream generated by Company 5 in COI_1 has a security level of $[5, \perp, \perp]$. Similarly, the audit stream generated by Company 2 in COI_3 has a security level $[\perp, \perp, 2]$. When audit streams generated from multiple companies are combined, the information contained in this derived stream has a higher security level. For example, audit stream having level $[5,\perp,2]$ contains information about Company 5 in COI_1 and Company 2 in COI_3. It is also possible for audit streams to have information from multiple companies belonging to the same COI class. For example, a security level of $[5,\perp,T]$ indicates that the data stream has information from Company 5 in COI_1, does not contain information from COI_2, and information about multiple companies in COI_3. We also have a level $[\perp,\perp,\perp]$ which we call *public* and that has no company specific information. The level $[T,T,T]$ correspond to level *trusted* and it contains information pertaining to multiple companies in each COI class and can be only accessed by trusted entities. We next define dominance relation between security levels.

DEFINITION 4. **[Dominance Relation:]** *Let* **L** *be the set of security levels, L_1 and L_2 be two security levels, where $L_1, L_2 \in$ **L**. We say security level L_1 is dominated by L_2, denoted by $L_1 \preceq L_2$, when the following conditions hold: $(\forall i_k = 1,2,\ldots,n)(L_1[i_k] = L_2[i_k] \lor L_1[i_k] = \perp \lor L_2[i_k] = T)$. For any two levels, L_p, $L_q \in$ **L**, if neither $L_p \preceq L_q$, nor $L_q \preceq L_p$, we say that L_p and L_q are incomparable.*

The dominance relation is reflexive, antisymmetric, and transitive. The level *public*, denoted by $[\perp,\perp,\perp]$, is dominated by all the other levels. Similarly, the level *trusted*, denoted by $[T,T,T]$, dominates all the other levels. Note that the dominance relation defines a lattice structure, where level *public* appears at the bottom and the level *trusted* appears at the top. Incomparable levels are not connected in this lattice structure. In our earlier example, level $[5,\perp,\perp]$ is dominated by $[5,\perp,2]$ and $[5,\perp,T]$. $[5,\perp,2]$ is dominated by $[5,\perp,T]$. That is, $[5,\perp,\perp] \preceq [5,\perp,2]$ and $[5,\perp,2] \preceq [5,\perp,T]$. $[5,\perp,\perp]$ and $[\perp,\perp,2]$ are incomparable.

Each data stream is associated with a security level. Each of the tuples constituting the data stream also has a security level assigned to it. Thus, the schema of the data stream has an attribute called level that captures the security level of tuples. The level attribute is generated automatically by the system and cannot be modified by the users. Note that, the security level of an individual tuple in a data stream is dominated by the level of the data stream. When a DSMS operation is executed on multiple input tuples, each having its own security level, an output tuple is produced. The security level of the output tuple is the least upper bound (LUB) of the security levels of the input tuples.

In our work, various types of queries are executed to detect security and performance problems. Each continuous query Q_i, submitted by a process, inherits the security level of the process. We require a query Q_i to obey the simple security property and the restricted $\star$-property of the Bell-Lapadula model [10].

1. Query Q_i with $L(Q_i) = C$ can read a data stream x only if $L(x) \preceq C$.
2. Query Q_i with $L(OP_i) = C$ can write a data stream x only if $L(x) = C$.

Note that, for our example, a process executing at level $[5,\perp,T]$ can execute streams belonging to Company 5 in COI_1 and all companies in COI_3 and also streams derived from them. Thus, the process is trusted w.r.t. COI_3, but not w.r.t. the other COI classes. Our information flow model thus provides a finer granularity of trust than provided by the earlier models. Our goal is to allow information flow only from the dominated levels to the dominating ones. All other information flow, either overtly or covertly, should be disallowed by our architecture.

4. QUERY PROCESSING IN CLOUD DSMS

In this section, first we discuss the different types of queries that can be executed on cloud audit data at the different tiers.

4.1 Cloud CQL Queries

Consider a simple application that tries to detect example denial-of-service attacks in the cloud. We have two conflict of interest classes denoted by COI_1 and COI_2. The constituent companies in each COI class is given by, $COI_1 = \{1,2\}$ and $COI_2 = \{A,B,C\}$. Examples of security levels in our configuration are $[\perp,\perp]$ (public knowledge), $[T,T]$ (completely trusted), $[1,\perp]$ (data from 1), $[\perp,T]$ (trusted w.r.t. COI_2), $[1,B]$ (data from 1 and B), $[1,T]$ (data from 1 in COI_1 and trusted w.r.t. COI_2). Continuous queries are executed at various tiers to detect performance delays and possibly denial-of-service (DoS) attacks. In any given tier, different types of DoS attacks may occur – some involving the data belonging to single organizations, others involving data belonging to multiple organizations. Thus, a tier can have query processors at different levels, each of which executes queries on data that it is authorized to view and modify.

We consider a single data stream, called MessageLog, that contains the audit stream data associated with message events, such as send and receive. MessageLog is obtained from SystemLog by filtering the events related to sending and receiving the messages. Note that, MessageLog in reality may contain many other fields, but we only deal with those that are pertinent to this example. The various attributes in MessageLog are serviceId, msgType, sender, receiver, timestamp, outcome. serviceId is a unique identifier associated with each service; msgType gives the type of message which is either send or receive; sender (receiver) gives the id of the organization sending (receiving) the message; timestamp is the time when the event (send or receive) occurred; outcome denotes success or failure of the event. In addition to these attributes, we have an attribute referred to as level that represents the security level of the tuple. The level attribute is assigned by the system and it cannot be modified by the user.

```
MessageLog(serviceId, msgType, sender, receiver,
                timestamp, outcome)
```

The queries are expressed using the CQL language [7]. We describe the various types of queries that can be executed at the various tiers.

4.1.1 Company Auditing Tier

In the company auditing tier, companies have access only to their own audit records.

In this section we give some sample queries that are executed by *Company1* to detect performance delays and DoS attacks. All the queries are executed at level $[1,\perp]$.

Query 1 (Q1)
Company1 requests service from *CompanyB*. It is trying to check the times when such message could be successfully delivered.

```
SELECT timestamp FROM MessageLog
    WHERE msgType = "send" AND outcome = "success"
        AND receiver = "CompanyB"
```

Query 2 (Q2)
Company1 requests service from *CompanyB*. It is trying to check the times when such message could not be successfully delivered.

```
SELECT timestamp FROM MessageLog
    WHERE msgType = "send" AND outcome = "failure"
        AND receiver = "CompanyB"
```

4.1.2 Service Auditing Tier

Service auditing tier receives log records from all the companies making use of some service. However, as the queries below demonstrate, not all the queries need to access all the data from the same COI class.

Query 3 (Q3): Level $[\perp, B]$
Log records received at the service auditing tier can be analyzed by the Session Manager to find out whether *CompanyB* is not available for some service.

```
SELECT timestamp FROM MessageLog
    WHERE msgType = "send" AND outcome = "failure"
        AND receiver = "CompanyB"
```

Query 4 (Q4): Level $[\perp, T]$
Session Manager may wish to find out whether all companies in COI_2 are target of some DoS attacks.

```
SELECT timestamp FROM MessageLog
    WHERE msgType = "send" AND outcome = "failure"
        AND receiver = "CompanyB" OR
        receiver = "CompanyA" OR
        receiver = "CompanyC"
```

4.1.3 Cloud Auditing Tier

Cloud auditing tier gets log records pertaining to all the services. However, the various queries will have different types of security requirements.

Query 5 (Q5): Level $[1, B]$
Cloud Provider may want to look at all records pertaining to `serviceId` 5 and measure the delays in order to detect possible man-in-the-middle attack. `serviceId` 5 involves *Company1* and *CompanyB*.

```
SELECT  MIN(timestamp), MAX(timestamp)
    FROM MessageLog [ROWS 100]
        WHERE outcome = "success" AND serviceId = "5"
```

Query 6 (Q6): Level $[1, B]$

Cloud Provider wants to find the delay encountered by *Company1* between sending the request and receiving the service from *CompanyB* for the last 100 tuples.

```
SELECT R.timestamp - S.timestamp  AS  delay
    FROM MessageLog R[Rows 100], MessageLog S[Rows 100]
    WHERE S.msgType = "send" AND S.outcome = "success"
    AND R.msgType = "receive" AND R.outcome = "success"
    AND R.receiver = "Company1" AND R.sender = "CompanyB"
    AND S.receiver = "CompanyB" AND S.sender = "Company1"
    AND S.serviceId = R.serviceId
```

Query 7 (Q7): Level $[T, T]$
Cloud Provider may want to find out the delay incurred in the different service invocation chains.

```
SELECT MIN(timestamp), MAX(timestamp)
    FROM MessageLog[ROWS 100]
        WHERE outcome = "success"
            GROUP BY serviceId
```

4.2 Execution of Cloud Queries

For each tier, we may have one or multiple query processors. In the Company Auditing Tier, we have a single query processor for analyzing each company data. Thus, *Company1* has a single query

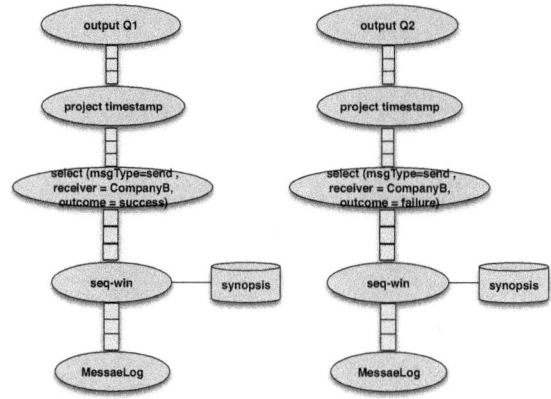

Figure 3: Operator Tree for Q_1 **and** Q_2

processor at level $[1, \perp]$. In the Service Auditing Tier, we may have one or more query processors running at different levels. In our examples, we can have a query processor at level $[\perp, B]$ and another one at $[\perp, T]$. Alternatively, we can use $[\perp, T]$ to process both the queries. Using $[\perp, T]$ to process the query at level $[\perp, B]$ comes at a cost: the query submitted at $[\perp, B]$ must be rewritten such that it can access only those tuples that it is authorized to view. Similarly, for the Cloud Auditing Tier, we may have a single query processor at level $[T, T]$ or two query processors: one at level $[1, B]$ and the other at $[T, T]$.

When a query has been submitted by a user, it must be rewritten to ensure that no unauthorized tuples are returned to the user. Our query rewriting algorithm modifies the algorithm in the following ways. Let Q_x be the original query submitted at level $L(Q_x)$. Let $selectCond(Q_x)$ and $window(Q_x)$ be the selection and window condition associated with the query. The query rewriting algorithm restricts the window to filter those tuples that the query is authorized to view; this is denoted by $|window(Q_x)|_{L_{Q_x}}$. Note that, all queries may not have a window operator. In such cases, the query rewriting algorithm adds a new security conjunct to the existing selection condition. This conjunct ensures that the tuples satisfying the query is dominated by the level of the query. The query rewriting algorithm is given below.

Algorithm 1: Secure Query Rewriting

INPUT: (Q_x)
OUTPUT: $OPT(Q'_x)$ representing the rewritten query
if $window(Q_x) \neq \{\}$ **then**
   | $window(Q_x) = |window(Q_x)|_{L(Q_x)}$
end
else
   | $selectCond(Q_x) = selectCond(Q_x) \cup (level \preceq L(Q_x))$
end

Let us consider *Q5* once again that is submitted at Level $[1, B]$.

```
SELECT  MIN(timestamp), MAX(timestamp)
    FROM MessageLog [ROWS 100]
        WHERE outcome = "success" AND serviceId = "5"
```

If this query is executed by the query processor at Level $[1, B]$, no rewriting is needed. However, if the query is executed at Level $[T, T]$, the query must be rewritten to ensure that it can view only authorized information. In such a case, the query is rewritten as follows:

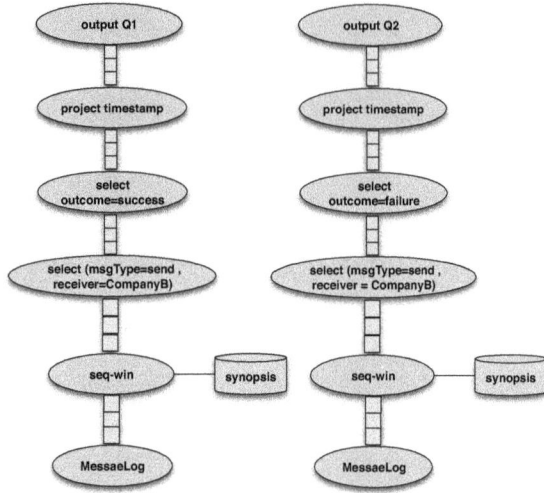

Figure 4: Overlapping Nodes Decomposed in Q_1 and Q_2

```
SELECT  MIN(timestamp), MAX(timestamp) FROM
 MessageLog [ROWS 100 WHERE Level DOMINATED BY [1,B]]
    WHERE outcome = "success" AND serviceId = "5"
```

Next, the secure queries are represented in the form of an operator tree. The formal definition of an operator tree appears below.

DEFINITION 5. **[Operator Tree:]** *An* operator tree *for a query Q_x, represented in the form of* OPT(Q_x), *consists of a set of nodes N_{Q_x} and a set of edges E_{Q_x}. Each internal node N_i corresponds to some operator in the query Q_x. Each edge (i, j) in this tree connecting node N_i to node N_j signifies that the output of node N_i is the input to node N_j. Each node N_i has a label that provides details about processing the corresponding operator. The name component of the label, denoted by $N_i.op$, specifies the type of the operator, such as,* select, project, join *and* average. *The parameter component of the label, represented by $N_i.parm$, denotes the set of conjuncts for the* select *operator or the set of attributes for the* project *operator. The synopsis component, denoted by $N_i.syn$, is needed for operators specified with windows that require a set of tuples to accumulate before processing can start, such as,* join, count, *and* sum. *The synopsis component has two attributes, namely, type and size, that specify the type of window (tuple-based, time-based) and its size. The input queue component of the label, denoted by $N_i.inputQueue$, lists the input streams needed by the operator. The output queue component, denoted by $N_i.outputQueue$, indicates the output streams produced by the operator that can be used by the vertices or sent as response to the user. The leaf nodes of the operator tree represent the source nodes for the data streams and the root nodes are the sink nodes receiving output.*

The operator trees for $Q1$ and $Q2$ are shown in Figure 3. Note that, an operator tree has all the information needed for processing the query.

5. QUERY SHARING

Typically, in a DSMS there can be several queries that are being executed concurrently. Query sharing will increase the efficiency of these queries and save resources such as CPU cycles and memory usage. Query sharing obviates the need for evaluating the same operator(s) multiple times if different queries need it. In such a case, the operator trees of different queries can be merged.

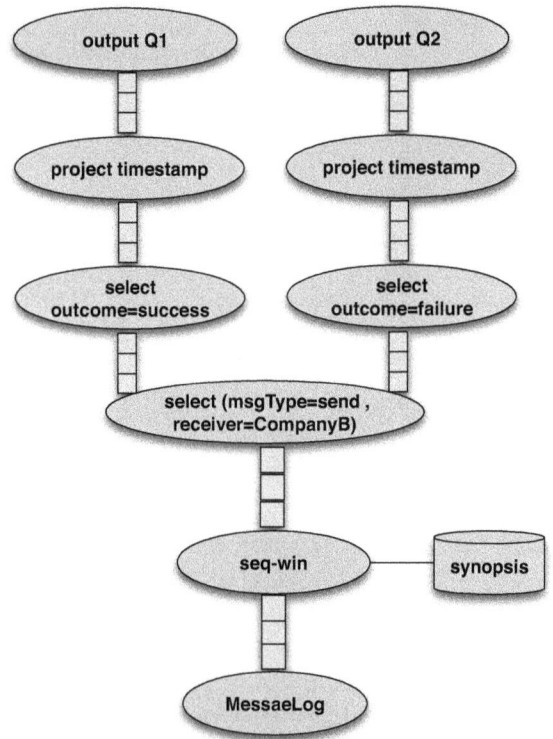

Figure 5: Merged Operator Trees of Q_1 and Q_2

We next formalize basic operations that are used for comparing the nodes belonging to different operator trees. Such operations are needed to evaluate whether sharing is possible or not between queries. We begin with the equivalence operator. If a pair of nodes belonging to different operator trees is equivalent, then only one node needs to be computed for evaluating the queries corresponding to these different operator trees.

DEFINITION 6. **[Equivalent Nodes:]** *Node $N_i \in N_{Q_x}$ is said to be* equivalent *to node $N_j \in N_{Q_y}$, denoted by $N_i \equiv N_j$, where N_i, N_j are in the operator trees OPT(Q_x), OPT(Q_y) respectively, if the following condition holds: $N_i.op = N_j.op \wedge N_i.parm = N_j.parm \wedge N_i.syn = N_j.syn \wedge N_i.inputQueue = N_j.inputQueue$*

In Figure 3, the *seq-win* operator nodes are equivalent in the two given operator trees. Two nodes may not be equivalent, but they may have common subexpressions; we may wish to process such subexpressions only once. For example, the *select* nodes in the two trees are not equivalent, but they have common subexpressions. This leads to the definition of *overlapping nodes*.

DEFINITION 7. **[Overlapping Nodes:]** *Node $N_i \in N_{Q_x}$ is said to be* overlapping *with node $N_j \in N_{Q_y}$, denoted by $N_i \equiv \bar{N}_j$, where N_i, N_j are in the operator trees OPT(Q_x), OPT(Q_y) respectively, if the following condition holds: $N_i.op = N_j.op \wedge Ni.op$ is non blocking operator, $\wedge N_i.parm \cap N_j.parm \neq \{\} \wedge N_i.inputQueue = N_j.inputQueue$*

Each of the overlapping nodes is decomposed into two nodes as follows.

DEFINITION 8. **[Decomposition of Overlapping Nodes:]** *Node N_i that overlaps with node N_j is decomposed into node N_k and N_i' as follows.*

94

1. $N_k.op = N_i.op$ and $N_i'.op = N_i.op$
2. $N_k.inputQueue = N_i.inputQueue$ and
   $N_i'.inputQueue = N_k.outputQueue$
3. $N_k.parm = N_i.parm \cap N_j.parm$ and
   $N_i'.parm = N_i.parm - N_k.parm$, if $N_i.op = select$
4. $N_k.parm = N_i.parm \cup N_j.parm$ and
   $N_i'.parm = N_i.parm$, if $N_i.op = project$

The *select* nodes in $Q1$ and $Q2$ are overlapping, so they are each decomposed into two nodes as shown in Figure 4.

If two operator trees have equivalent nodes, they are said to *overlap*. The formal definition appears below.

DEFINITION 9. **[Overlap of Operator Trees:]** *Two operator trees $OPT(Q_x)$ and $OPT(Q_y)$ are said to overlap if $OPT(Q_x) \not\equiv OPT(Q_y)$ and there exists a pair of nodes N_i and N_j where $N_i \in N_{Q_x}$ and $N_j \in N_{Q_y}$ such that $N_i \equiv N_j$.*

Algorithm 2: Merge Operator Trees
***
INPUT: $OPT(Q_x)$ and $OPT(Q_y)$
OUTPUT: $OPT(Q_{xy})$ representing the merged operator tree
Initialize $N_{Q_{xy}} = \{\}$
Initialize $E_{Q_{xy}} = \{\}$
foreach *node $N_i \in N_{Q_x}$* **do**
$\quad | \quad N_{Q_{xy}} = N_{Q_{xy}} \cup N_i$
end
foreach *edge $(i,j) \in E_{Q_x}$* **do**
$\quad | \quad E_{Q_{xy}} = E_{Q_{xy}} \cup edge\,(i,j)$
end
foreach *node $N_i \in N_{Q_y}$* **do**
$\quad$ **if** $\nexists N_j \in N_{Q_{xy}}$ *such that $N_i \equiv N_j$* **then**
$\quad \quad | \quad N_{Q_{xy}} = N_{Q_{xy}} \cup N_i$
$\quad$ **end**
end
foreach *edge $(i,j) \in E_{Q_y}$* **do**
$\quad$ **if** *edge $(i,j) \notin E_{Q_{xy}}$* **then**
$\quad \quad | \quad E_{Q_{xy}} = E_{Q_{xy}} \cup edge\,(i,j)$
$\quad$ **end**
end

When operator trees corresponding to two queries overlap, we can generate the merged operator tree using Algorithm 2. The merged operator tree signifies the processing of the partially shared queries. The two operator trees shown in Figure 4 can now be merged. The merged tree appears in Figure 5.

6. PROTOTYPE IMPLEMENTATION

We have developed the replicated CW-DSMS shown in Figure 6. This system is a modified version of the Stanford STREAM DSMS [6]. The CW-DSMS supports: (i) multi-user server with user authentication, (ii) replicated query processors executing at different security levels, (iii) a global trusted scheduler that schedules operators across all query processors, (iv) a global trusted interpretation unit that supports centralized query plan generation for all query processors, (v) trusted stream shepherd operator that takes trusted streams and outputs streams based on the security level of the query processor, (vi) security level aware windows, (vii) security level aware query operators i.e., modification to blocking operators (e.g., *join*, *average*) to create output tuples with appropriate level identification, and (viii) single security level input streams and tuples.

The *trusted command unit* shown in Figure 6 is responsible for handling client communication, authentication, and query processor instantiation. It accepts queries at different security levels. The *authentication module* performs user authentication and security level verification and assignment. The *query processor identifier (QPI) module* gets user's client ID, security level and query specifications from the authentication module. The QPI maintains the list of currently running query processors. The QPI first checks whether the user queries can be executed in one of the query processors by matching the incoming and existing security levels. If *Yes*, user's client ID as well as all the input queries are bound to that processor. If *No*, a new query processor is created at that level. This approach allows starting query processors on demand. The maximum number of query processors is bounded by the number of security levels supported. In addition, the trusted command unit still controls the query operations like commit and abort with the help of the QPI module.

The *trusted interpretation unit* is responsible for generating query plans and setting up the operators in the scheduler. This unit receives user and query information from the trusted command unit. It creates the physical and logical query plans. It sends the physical plans to the appropriate query processor based on the user's security level. The list of operators (also the physical plan) is sent to the trusted scheduler. The modified built-in interpretation components (*parser, semantic interpreter,* and *logical plan generator*) and the execution unit of the query processor handle CW security extensions.

As shown in Figure 6 the server has multiple *query processors* running at different security levels, but, only one trusted interpretation unit and trusted scheduler. Each query processor contains an input unit, execution unit, and output unit. The *input unit* can accept input streams from outside sources through the trusted stream shepherd unit. It can also accept the output streams produced from other queries processed by the same query processor. The *execution unit* is used by the server to execute physical plans continuously. This unit contains the physical operators and their corresponding algorithms. We have modified the window processing so that it can support conditions based on security levels. We have modified the aggregate and join operator algorithms to compute the least upper bound (LUB) of the input tuples and use that as the security level of the output tuples. For example, if an aggregate operation computes the maximum timestamp of three input tuples in levels $[\bot, A], [\bot, B]$ and $[\bot, C]$, the output tuple is in level $[\bot, T]$. On the other hand, all the operators are untrusted. The execution unit accepts the commands from the trusted scheduler and executes the corresponding operators. There is only one operator running at any point of time, since we have only one scheduler. The *output unit* sends the results back to users continuously.

The *trusted stream shepherd unit* handles all input streams. It contains the modified input operator (trusted stream shepherd operator) that handles the trusted streams in different security levels and sends it to the appropriate query processors.

In the vanilla STREAM prototype, the scheduler uses round robin algorithm to schedule operators. We have modified the scheduler so that it can handle scheduling of queries in more than one query processor. The scheduler maintains all executing query plan information shared by the trusted interpretation unit. When a query plan is received by the scheduler, operators in the plan are scheduled for execution from bottom to top order. The scheduler sends out commands (including plan id and operator id) to the appropriate query processor to start executing an operator. The operators execute at least once per scheduling round. When a new plan arrives at the scheduler, operators of that plan will be scheduled in

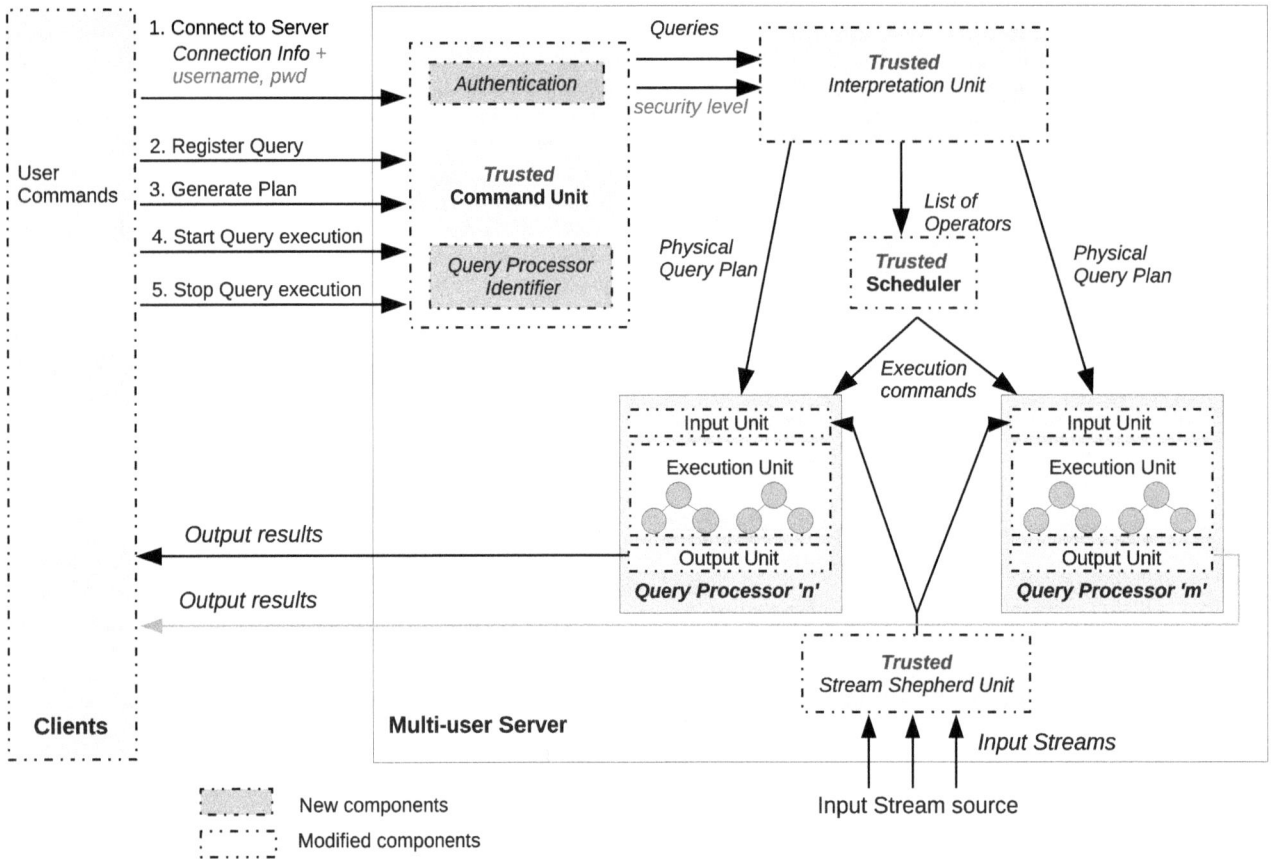

Figure 6: Prototype Architecture

the next execution round. Such mechanism prevents starvation of late coming queries, as each operator is scheduled every round. In every round, each operator processes a maximum of 170 data tuples before switching to other operators. The DSMS can process a maximum input 100,000 tuples per second. "First come first serve" strategy is used for executing the query plans. We adapt the round-robin method in our trusted scheduler which is able to schedule operators across all query processors.

6.1 Experiments

We conducted experiments in the prototype to compare the performance between the old vanilla DSMS and the redesigned CW-DSMS. The experiments were conducted in a system with Intel i7 Q820 1.73GHZ quad core processor, 6GB RAM, and Ubuntu 11.10 64 bit operating system. Except experiment 6 (join operation), for all other experiments, we used three different data sets with 2, 5, and 10 million tuples with a data input rate of 50,000 tuples per second. Each tuple is associated with a COI class in terms of $[x,0]$ or $[0,y]$, where x refers to company 1 or 2 and y can be one of the companies A, B, or C. 0 means the public knowledge $\perp$. For all experiments, the round robin method is used for operator scheduling. We ran each experiment five times and discarded the first two runs. The average execution time from the last three runs are shown

in Table 1. We measured the query execution time (the time taken from first tuple entering the first operator of the query plan and last tuple exiting the query) for the following experiments. We executed Queries Q1 through Q6 that we discussed in Section 4 for these experiments.

1. **Experiment 1: Company auditing Query 1 in level [1, $\perp$]**
   In order to maximize the difference in execution time, we used 100% selectivity (all tuples are in level [1, $\perp$]) on both the systems, so that no tuples are filtered by the select operator. As shown in Table 1 under Exp 1, the performance overhead due to security modification to the vanilla DSMS is negligible for all the data sets used, and it is between 0.003% and 0.025%.

2. **Experiment 2: Company auditing Query 2 in level [1, $\perp$]**
   In query 2, we used 50% selectivity. The performance overhead is again negligible, and is between 0.002% and 0.017%.

3. **Experiment 3: Service auditing Query 3 in level [$\perp$, B]**
   In the service auditing experiments 3 and 4, the input stream has tuples at 5 different levels: [1, $\perp$], [2, $\perp$], [$\perp$, A], [$\perp$, B] and [$\perp$, C]. Tuples in each level occupied 20% of the input stream. Since query 3 runs in level [$\perp$, B], only 20% tuples

Table 1: Performance Overhead of Chinese Wall Processing

	Data Size (tuples)	Average Execution Time (ms)		Overhead Due to CW-DSMS (in %)	Standard Deviation (ms)	
		Vanilla	CW-DSMS		Vanilla	CW-DSMS
Exp 1	2M	40031	40041	0.025%	2.52	2.52
	5M	100046	100055	0.009%	2.08	3.21
	10M	200057	200063	0.003%	3.21	2.52
Exp 2	2M	40032	40039	0.017%	2.52	1.53
	5M	100042	100049	0.007%	2.08	2.65
	10M	200052	200056	0.002%	3.51	3.51
Exp 3	2M	40030	40041	0.027%	2.89	1.73
	5M	100043	100057	0.014%	3.06	3.51
	10M	200054	200065	0.005%	2.08	3.06
Exp 4	2M	40044	40053	0.023%	3.51	2.65
	5M	100056	100065	0.009%	2.89	4.93
	10M	200062	200069	0.003%	1.53	2.52
Exp 5	2M	40047	40059	0.030%	2.52	3.51
	5M	100082	100099	0.018%	4.93	6.81
	10M	200094	200116	0.011%	4.58	6.24
Exp 6	100K	40532	40621	0.218%	11.36	30.35
	250K	100593	100726	0.132%	9.85	30.09
	500K	200628	200789	0.081%	14.47	33.86

from inputs should be processed by query 3. So in the vanilla system we must include the condition based on security level in the query:

```
Vanilla:
SELECT timestamp FROM MessageLog
WHERE msgType = "send" AND outcome = "failure"
AND receiver = "CompanyB" AND level = [0,B]

CW-DSMS [0,B]:
SELECT timestamp FROM MessageLog
WHERE msgType = "send" AND outcome = "failure"
AND receiver = "CompanyB"
```

In CW-DSMS, unqualified tuples i.e., tuples not in level [⊥, B], are filtered by the trusted stream shepherd operator due to the replicated architecture. The performance overhead is between 0.005% and 0.027% for all data sets used, which is again negligible.

4. **Experiment 4: Service auditing Query 4 in level [⊥, T]** Using the same input from experiment 3, the selectivity becomes 60% because level [⊥, T] is authorized to access inputs with levels [⊥, A], [⊥, B] and [⊥, C].

```
Vanilla:
SELECT timestamp FROM MessageLog
WHERE msgType = "send" AND outcome = "failure"
AND (receiver = "CompanyB" OR receiver = "CompanyA"
OR receiver = "CompanyC")
```

```
AND (level = [0,A] OR level = [0,B] OR level = [0,C])

CW-DSMS [0,T]:
SELECT timestamp FROM MessageLog
WHERE msgType = "send" AND outcome = "failure"
AND (receiver = "CompanyB" OR receiver = "CompanyA"
OR receiver = "CompanyC")
```

The query language of CW-DSMS uses simplified form because of the replicated architecture. As shown in Table 1, the performance overhead is between 0.003% and 0.023%.

5. **Experiment 5: Cloud auditing Query 5 in level [1, B]**: We studied the overhead caused by the extra least upper bound computations in CW-DSMS. The level of output tuple always reflects the highest possible level (COI class) of all the input tuples involved in the computation. Input tuples were either at [1,⊥] or [⊥,B]. To maximize the difference, we used 100% selectivity. The performance difference due to the LUB computation is between 0.011% and 0.030%.

6. **Experiment 6: Cloud auditing Query 6 in level [1, B]** In the join query, input stream R and S refer to the same input stream source MessageLog. We set up 50% selectivity for R and S respectively. To activate LUB computation on join, input tuples were kept at either [1, ⊥] or [⊥, B] and streamed in a random fashion.

Since join is an expensive operation, the input rate of 50,000 tuples used in the previous experiments caused an overload situation in both the systems. Thus, we reduced the data input rate to 2,500 tuples per second. Accordingly, the data sizes of the three input tuple sets were reduced to 100K, 250K, and 500K tuples, respectively. The performance overhead is between 0.081% and 0.218%, which is higher than the other experiments. On the other hand, the overhead is still considered negligible as it is within 0.218%.

Experiments Summary: As shown in Table 1 and discussed above, maximum overhead due to information flow constraints is 0.218% This demonstrates that the overhead due to addition of security constraints is negligble.

THEOREM 1. *The proposed architecture ensures information flow constraints.*

PROOF. Let Q be a query submitted by a process at level l that operates on the relations and streams in the DSMS. For each stream accessed by the query, the query rewriting operator takes into account the security level of the query and only provides the projection of the respective stream that the process is authorized to view. The query is then forwarded to the processor that executes in the same level as the query.

The query processor at level l can view only those input tuples whose levels are dominated by l and produce output streams at level l. Thus, during query processing overt information flow can only occur from levels dominated by level l to level l. In the proposed architecture, level l receives tuples from dominated levels and stores them at its own level. Thus, within the scope of our DSMS architecture there is no common storage that is shared across security levels. Thus, a dominating level cannot manipulate the common storage in our architecture to pass information to the dominated level. This ensures that there are no covert storage channels. The query processor at level l executes queries only in its allotted time slot as decided by the trusted scheduler which ensures that there are no timing channels. □

The above claim holds only when we consider the architecture in isolation. However, in real world this is never the case and it is possible for the underlying framework to have covert channels. For example, if the query processors at different levels are executing on the same server it is possible to have storage and/or timing channels.

7. RELATED WORK

In this section, we will discuss works from closely related areas: DSMS, DSMS security, and Chinese Wall policy.

Data Stream Management Systems (DSMSs): Most of the works carried out in DSMSs address various problems ranging from theoretical results to implementing comprehensive prototypes on how to handle data streams and produce near real-time response without affecting the quality of service. Some of the research prototypes include: Stanford STREAM Data Manager [8, 6], Aurora [9], Borealis [1, 17], and MavStream [19].

DSMS Sharing: In general DSMSs like STREAM [8, 6], Aurora [9], and Borealis [1, 17], queries issued by the same user at the same time can share the Seq-window operators and synopses. In STREAM system, base Seq-window operators are reused by queries on the identical streams. Instead building up sharing parts between plans, Aurora research focus on providing better execution scheduling of large number queries, by batching operators as atomic execution unit. In Borealis project, the information on input

data criteria from executing queries can be shared and modified by new incoming queries. Here the execution of operators will be the same but the input data criteria can be revised. Even though many approaches target on better QoS in terms of scheduling and revising, sharing execution and computation among queries submitted at different times by the same user or at the same time between different users are not supported in general DSMS. Besides common source Seq-windows like regular DSMSs, sharing intermediate computation results is a better way to make big performance achievement.

DSMS Security: There has been several recent works on securing DSMSs [20, 13, 22, 12, 21, 4] by providing role-based access control. Though these systems support secure processing they do not prevent illegal information flows. Punctuation-based enforcement of RBAC over data streams is proposed in [22]. Access control policies are transmitted every time using one or more security punctuations before the actual data tuple is transmitted. Query punctuations define the privileges for a CQ. Both punctuations are processed by a special filter operator (stream shield) that is part of the query plan. Secure shared continuous query processing is proposed in [4]. The authors present a three-stage framework to enforce access control without introducing special operators, rewriting query plans, or affecting QoS delivery mechanisms. Supporting role-based access control via query rewriting techniques is proposed in [13, 12]. To enforce access control policies, query plans are rewritten and policies are mapped to a set of map and filter operations. When a query is activated, the privileges of the query submitter are used to produce the resultant query plan. The architecture proposed in [20] uses a post-query filter to enforce stream level access control policies. The filter applies security policies after query processing but before a user receives the results from the DSMS. Designing DSMS taking into account multilevel security constraints has been addressed by researchers [5].

Chinese Wall Policy: Brewer and Nash [11] first demonstrated how the Chinese Wall policy can be used to prevent consultants from accessing information belonging to multiple companies in the same conflict of interest class. However, the authors did not distinguish between human users and subjects that are processes running on behalf of users. Consequently, the model proposed is very restrictive as it allows a consultant to work for one company only. Sandhu [23] improves upon this model by making a clear distinction between users, principals, and subjects, defines a lattice-based security structure, and shows how the Chinese Wall policy complies with the Bell-Lapadula model [10].

Chinese Wall and Cloud Computing: Wu et al. [25] show how the Chinese Wall policy can be used for information flow control in cloud computing. The authors enforce the policies at the Infrastructure-as-a-Service layer. The authors developed a prototype to demonstrate the feasibility of their approach. In our current work, we have adapted the Chinese Wall policy and demonstrated how stream data generated from the various organizations can be processed in a secure manner. Our work is addressed at the Software-as-a-Service level. Tsai et al. [24] discusses how the Chinese Wall policy can be used to prevent competing organizations virtual machines to be placed on the same physical machine. Graph coloring is used for allocating virtual machines to physical machines such that the Chinese Wall policies are satisfied and better utilization of cloud resources is achieved. Jaeger et al. [18] argue that covert channels are inevitable and propose the notion of risk information flows that captures both overt and covert flows across two security levels. Capturing both covert flows and overt flows in a unified framework allows one to reason about the risks associated with information leakage.

8. CONCLUSIONS AND FUTURE WORK

Data streams generated by various organizations in a cloud may need to be analyzed in real-time for detecting critical events of interest. Processing of such data streams should be done in a careful and controlled manner such that company sensitive information is not disclosed to competing organizations. We propose a secure information flow control model, adapted from the Chinese Wall policy, to be used for protecting sensitive company information. We also provide architectures for executing continuous queries, such that the information flow constraints are satisfied. We implemented a prototype to demonstrate the feasibility of our ideas.

A lot of work remains to be done. We have assumed that certain components are trusted. We have made similar assumptions about the underlying infrastructure. However, we have not explicitly stated our trust assumptions. We need to formally state and analyze these assumptions in view of real-world constraints in order to evaluate the security of our DSMS.

We plan to propose alternative architectures and do a comparative study to find out which approach is the most suitable for processing cloud streaming queries. We also plan to implement our query sharing ideas. Thus, when a new query is submitted, we need to check how plans for existing queries can be reused to improve the performance. Note that, such verification must be carried out dynamically. Towards this end, we plan to see how existing constraint solvers can be used to check for query equivalences. We also plan to evaluate the performance impact of dynamic plan generation and equivalence evaluation. We also plan to investigate more on how scheduling and load shedding can be done with information flow constraints.

9. ACKNOWLEDGEMENT

This material is based on research sponsored in part by the Air Force Office of Scientific Research (AFOSR), under agreement number FA-9550-09-1-0409.

10. REFERENCES

[1] D. J. Abadi, Y. Ahmad, M. Balazinska, U. Çetintemel, M. Cherniack, J. Hwang, W. Lindner, A. Maskey, A.Rasin, E.Ryvkina, N.Tatbul, Y.Xing, and S. B. Zdonik. The Design of the Borealis Stream Processing Engine. In *Proc. of the CIDR*, pages 277–289, 2005.

[2] M. D. Abrams, S. G. Jajodia, and H. J. Podell, editors. *Information Security: An Integrated Collection of Essays.* IEEE Computer Society Press, Los Alamitos, CA, USA, 1st edition, 1995.

[3] R. Adaikkalavan and S. Chakravarthy. SnoopIB: Interval-based Event Specification and Detection for Active Databases. *DKE*, 59(1):139–165, 2006.

[4] R. Adaikkalavan and T. Perez. Secure Shared Continuous Query Processing. In *Proc. of the ACM SAC (Data Streams Track)*, pages 1005–1011, Taiwan, 2011.

[5] R. Adaikkalavan, I. Ray, and X. Xie. Multilevel Secure Data Stream Processing. In *Proc. of the DBSec*, pages 122–137, 2011.

[6] A. Arasu, B. Babcock, S. Babu, J. Cieslewicz, M. Datar, K. Ito, R. Motwani, U. Srivastava, and J. Widom. Stream: The Stanford Data Stream Management System. Technical Report 2004-20, Stanford InfoLab, 2004.

[7] A. Arasu, S. Babu, and J. Widom. The CQL Continuous Query Language: Semantic Foundations and Query Execution. *VLDB Journal*, 15(2):121–142, 2006.

[8] B. Babcock, S. Babu, M. Datar, R. Motwani, and J. Widom. Models and Issues in Data Stream Systems. In *Proc. of the PODS*, pages 1–16, 2002.

[9] H. Balakrishnan, M. Balazinska, D. Carney, U. Çetintemel, M. Cherniack, C. Convey, E. Galvez, J. Salz, M. Stonebraker, N. Tatbul, R. Tibbetts, and S. B. Zdonik. Retrospective on Aurora. *VLDB Journal: Special Issue on Data Stream Processing*, 13(4):370–383, 2004.

[10] D. E. Bell and L. J. LaPadula. Secure Computer System: Unified Exposition and MULTICS Interpretation. Technical Report MTR-2997 Rev. 1 and ESD-TR-75-306, rev. 1, The MITRE Corporation, Bedford, MA 01730, 1976.

[11] D. F. C. Brewer and M. J. Nash. The Chinese Wall Security Policy. In *Proc. of the IEEE S & P*, pages 206–214, 1989.

[12] J. Cao, B. Carminati, E. Ferrari, and K. Tan. ACStream: Enforcing Access Control over Data Streams. In *Proc. of the ICDE*, pages 1495–1498, 2009.

[13] B. Carminati, E. Ferrari, and K. L. Tan. Enforcing Access Control over Data Streams. In *Proc. of the ACM SACMAT*, pages 21–30, 2007.

[14] D. Carney, U. Çetintemel, M. Cherniack, C. Convey, S. Lee, G. Seidman, M. Stonebraker, N. Tatbul, and S. B. Zdonik. Monitoring Streams - A New Class of Data Management Applications. In *Proc. of the VLDB*, pages 215–226, 2002.

[15] S. Chakravarthy and R. Adaikkalavan. Event and Streams: Harnessing and Unleashing Their Synergy. In *Proc. of the DEBS*, pages 1–12, 2008.

[16] S. Chakravarthy and Q. Jiang. *Stream Data Processing: A Quality of Service Perspective Modeling, Scheduling, Load Shedding, and Complex Event Processing.* Advances in Database Systems , Vol. 36. Springer, 2009.

[17] M. Cherniack, H. Balakrishnan, M. Balazinska, D. Carney, U. Çetintemel, Y. Xing, and S. B. Zdonik. Scalable distributed stream processing. In *Proc. of the CIDR*, 2003.

[18] T. Jaeger, R. Sailer, and Y. Sreenivasan. Managing the Risk of Covert Information Flows in Virtual Machine Systems. In *Proc. of the ACM SACMAT*, pages 81–90, 2007.

[19] Q. Jiang and S. Chakravarthy. Anatomy of a Data Stream Management System. In *ADBIS Research Communications*, 2006.

[20] W. Lindner and J. Meier. Securing the Borealis Data Stream Engine. In *IDEAS*, pages 137–147, 2006.

[21] R. V. Nehme, H. Lim, E. Bertino, and E. A. Rundensteiner. StreamShield: A Stream-Centric Approach towards Security and Privacy in Data Stream Environments. In *Proc. of the ACM SIGMOD*, pages 1027–1030, 2009.

[22] R. V. Nehme, E. A. Rundensteiner, and E. Bertino. A Security Punctuation Framework for Enforcing Access Control on Streaming Data. In *Proc. of the ICDE*, pages 406–415, 2008.

[23] R. Sandhu. Lattice-Based Enforcement of Chinese Walls. *Computers & Security*, 11(8):753–763, 1992.

[24] T. Tsai, Y. Chen, H. Huang, P. Huang, and K. Chou. A Practical Chinese Wall Security Model in Cloud Computing. In *Proc. of the APNOMS*, pages 1–4, 2011.

[25] R. Wu, G. Ahn, H. Hu, and M. Singhal. Information Flow Control in Cloud Computing. In *Proc. of the CollaborateCom*, pages 1–7, 2010.

[26] R. Xie and R. Gamble. A Tiered Strategy for Auditing in the Cloud. In *Proc. of IEEE CLOUD*, June 2012.

An Information Flow Control Meta-Model

Dennis Kafura, Denis Gracanin
Department of Computer Science
Virginia Tech
Blacksburg, VA USA
{kafura,gracanin}@cs.vt.edu

ABSTRACT

In this paper a meta-model for information flow control is defined using the foundation of Barker's access control meta-model. The purposes for defining this meta-model is to achieve a more principled understanding of information flow control, to compare information flow control and access control at an abstract level, and to explore how information flow control and access control might be composed to yield a rich new set of ideas and systems for controlling the dissemination of sensitive information. It is shown that it is possible to define a meta-model for information flow control, that such a model is more complex compared to the access control meta-model, and that the meta-models for information flow control and access control can be composed in a conceptually straightforward way.

Categories and Subject Descriptors

D.4.6 [**Security and Protection**]: Access controls, information flow controls.

General Terms

Security, Theory.

Keywords

Information flow control, access control meta-model, security, dissemination control, information security.

1. INTRODUCTION

Confidentiality, one of the three defining requirements of information security, means that information is only disclosed to properly authorized individuals [1]. Approaches to assuring confidentiality include access control, enforced by a reference monitor, encryption, enforced by key controls, and information flow, enforced by dynamic (re)labelling. Each of these approaches has proven valuable in a achieving some form of confidentiality.

Exploration of how to achieve confidentiality through access control has led to a wide variety of access control models [2]. These models have evolved to achieve increased expressiveness, stricter regulation, or improved functionality. Access control models have incorporated notions of roles [3, 4], teams [5], tasks [6], status [7], geographic location[8, 9], context [10, 11], privacy [12, 13], and obligations [14] among others.

The wide variety of access control models motivated Barker's definition of a meta-mode for access control [15, 16]. The meta-

model is an abstract description of access control from which specific access control policies or systems can be derived by specialization. Barker's meta-model idea (summarized later in the paper) has a number of theoretical and practical advantages. It:

- explicates the fundamental principles of access control,
- provides a common basis for specifying access control and understanding the relationship among different models,
- facilitates sharing of access control policy information across models, and
- creates a basis for developing policy languages with a solid semantic foundation.

Among these, the uses of a meta-model to reveal fundamental principles and to understand the relationships among alternative models are the most important in this paper.

We show how to use Barker's meta-model framework to construct an information flow control meta-model that has all of the above advantages with respect to information flow control that Barker's meta-model has with respect to access control. In addition, our meta-model allows two important questions to be addressed:

- What are the fundamental differences between information flow control and access control?
- How can combinations of information flow control and access control be better understood?

We provide some initial thoughts on answering these questions.

To further motivate this work we present two information flow examples. The first is a simple file sharing scenario. The second, taken from HiStar [17], involves realistic and complex information flow controls. The examples introduce well known information flow concepts and are used to illustrate the meta-model.

Figure 1 shows an information flow graph for a simple sharing system involving two principals, Alice and Bob, and three resources, A, B, and C. Each principal and resource has an annotation representing the sensitivity of information held by or known to the entity. These annotations are variously referred to as "classes" [18], "taints" [19, 20], "labels" [21, 22], or other similar terms. The term "label" is used here without implying any specific connection to how that term might be used in other information flow systems. In many cases, the label represents a "clearance" specifying the highest or a range of sensitivities with which the entity can be associated. The labels apply to both principals and resources. These labels are significant because the general goal of information flow control is to restrict the ways in which information may flow across different levels of sensitivity. For example, it might be desired that there cannot be a flow of information from a principal with a current label of *private* to a resource with a current label of *public*. The assignment of label may also be dynamic, changing with the operations that are performed. For example, a system might require a flow of information from a principal with a current label of *private* to a resource with a current label of *public* is allowed only if the resource's label is changed to *private*. The change in the resource's label may then prevent information from this newly labeled resource flowing to other principals whose labels are *public*.

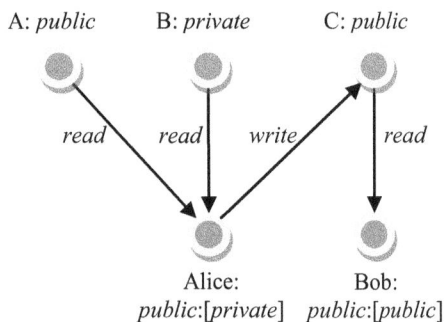

A: *public*   B: *private*   C: *public*

read   *read*   *write*   *read*

Alice: Bob:
public:[*private*]   *public*:[*public*]

Figure 1: A File Sharing Example

The arcs in Figure 1 are annotated by the names of actions. The annotation indicates an action that could cause the information flow. For example, the flow from a resource to a principal might be labeled with a "*read*" action to indicate that the flow could occur if the principal performed a read operation. We assume that each action causes either a flow from a resource to a principal (e.g., a process performs a "*read*" action on a file) or a flow from a principal to a resource (e.g., a process performs a "*write*" action on a file), but not both simultaneously.

As shown in Figure 1, the files and principals (Alice and Bob) have labels indicating the sensitivity level of their current state and, for principals, a "clearance" indicating the highest sensitivity level permitted for them. Files A and C hold public information while B holds private information. Information that is labeled *public* is viewed as less sensitive than information that is labeled *private*. Alice has a label indicating her current status as *public* and also a "clearance", shown as [*private*], meaning that she is able to be the target of an information flow that comes from a resource with the label *private*. Bob's label is interpreted to mean that his status is currently *public* and that he is able to be the target of an information flow that comes from a resource with the label *public* only since his clearance is [*public*].

A simple information flow control policy requires the system to operate so that Bob cannot receive private information. Enforcing such a policy means that information from a public source can flow to public or private targets but information from a private source cannot flow to a public target. Consider two scenarios.

Scenario 1: In this scenario Alice first reads from file A. This action is possible because a flow from a public resource to a principal that can receive either public or private conforms to the policy. In this case Alice's label remains unchanged. Alice can then write information to file C. This also conforms to the policy. Finally, Bob can read file C in conformance with the policy. Thus, information has flowed through Alice to Bob and this flow conforms to the policy.

Scenario 2: In this scenario Alice first read from file B. This action is possible because a flow from a private resource to a principal that can receive either public or private conforms to the policy. In this case Alice's label changes to *private*:[*private*], meaning that she currently holds private information which is allowed by her clearance. Alice may also read from file A at this

point because a flow from a public source to a private target is allowed. However, Alice cannot write to file C because this violates the information flow control policy (i.e., flows are disallowed from a private source to a public target).

Typically, the history-sensitive control possible with information flow control is not possible with access control alone. For example, an access control system that grants Alice and Bob the authorizations to perform the read and write operations shown in Figure 1 cannot differentiate between the two scenarios just described. In order to satisfy Scenario 1, Bob must have permission to read file C. In order to satisfy Scenario 2, Bob must not have permission to read file C.

The second example is from HiStar [17, 23]. The structure of an anti-virus system is shown in Figure 2. The anti-virus system has two parts, one part scans local data for known viruses and another part updates the set of viruses that are known. The scanner process reads user data and compares the data to the signatures of known viruses. The scanner reports to the user any detected infected data through a user output device. The signatures of known viruses are stored in a virus database. The scanner may also launch helper process to parse structured data and communicate with these helpers through files in the /tmp directory. The antivirus system also contains an update daemon that periodically updates its virus database to include virus signatures that it obtains over the network (e.g., from a networked repository maintained by a company or a user community). The update daemon reports over the network its current signatures and receives new signatures that it does not already have.

To perform its function the scanner must have read access to all user data (to perform the scanning) and to the virus database (to obtain the signatures involved in the scanning). To perform its function the update daemon must have read/write access to the network (to report its state and receive updates) and to the virus database (to examine and update its collection of virus signatures).

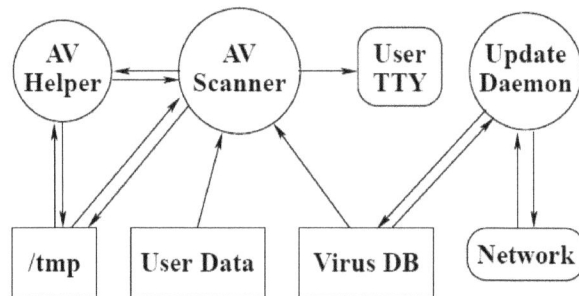

Figure 2: An Anti-virus Scanner

A security concern is the possibility that sensitive information may be compromised if the anti-virus system is malicious or is hijacked by an attacker. In such a case, the malicious scanner may look for "interesting" information (e.g., social security numbers, account numbers, passwords) in the user data and leak this information to the update daemon through a variety of channels. The update daemon will subsequently use its network access to export this information to the attacker. In [17] the authors identify a variety of system facilities that can be exploited to leak the information from the scanner to the update daemon. To prevent the compromise of information due to a malicious anti-virus system it is necessary to prevent the leakage of user data from the scanner to the update daemon through information flow controls.

The rest of this paper is organized as follows. In Section 2 Barker's access control meta-model is summarized. Only those parts of the meta-model needed for the development of the information flow control meta-model are described. Section 3 presents the information flow control meta-model. This section presents the core axiom as well as the relations for histories, levels, and clearances. Section 4 shows how the information flow control meta-model can be specialized to model the information flow controls for the file sharing system (Figure 1) and the HiStar virus scanner (Figure 2). The purpose of this specialization is to demonstrate that the information flow control meta-model is sufficiently robust to deal with complex information flow controls. The discussion in Section 5 focuses on comparing and combining information flow control with access control. It is shown here that the two meta-models are distinctly different but can be easily composed, at least conceptually. Related work is highlighted in Section 6. Conclusions and future work are given in Section 7.

2. ACCESS-CONTROL META-MODEL

In this section we summarize the key elements of Barker's access control meta-model. The purpose of this summary is to establish the definitions and ideas that will be extended in subsequent sections to model information flow.

The key elements of Barker's access control meta-model, M, are sets of constants, relations defined over the sets of constants, a rule language to specify access control policies in the meta-model, and a single core axiom.

The sets of constants are defined as follows by Barker:

- A countable set C of categories, where $c_0, c_1, \ldots$ are used to denote arbitrary category identifiers.

- A countable set P of principals, where $p_0, p_1, \ldots$ are used to identify principals.

- A countable set A of named atomic actions, where $a_0, a_1, \ldots$ are used to denote arbitrary action identifiers.

- A countable set R of resource identifiers, where $r_0, r_1, \ldots$ are used to denote arbitrary resources.

- A countable set E of event identifiers, $e_0, e_1, \ldots$ are used to denote arbitrary occurences.

Barker's model defines other sets (e.g., situational identifiers) which are not included in this description because they are not relevant to the main issue being addressed. Each principal in the set P may access a resource that is contained in the set R. The actions performed by principals are given by the set A. The principals and permissions, to be defined, are organized into categories. Significant occurrences during the execution of a system are captured in the set E.

Three relations are defined using the above sets. The first relation, PCA, defines how principals are organized into categories. Here, $PCA \subseteq P \times C$ where $(p, c) \in PCA$ iff a principal $p \in P$ is assigned to the category $c \in C$. The second relation is a ternary relation, $ARCA$, where $ARCA \subseteq A \times R \times C$ and $(a, r, c) \in ARCA$ iff the action $a \in A$ on resource $r \in R$ can be performed by principals assigned to the category $c \in C$. The pair (a, r) is referred to as a permission. Authorization are defined by another ternary relation, PAR, where $PAR \subseteq P \times A \times R$. In this case, $(p, a, r) \in PAR$ iff a principal $p \in P$ can perform the action $a \in A$ on the resource $r \in R$. In other words, the triple (p, a, r) means that principal p has the permission (a, r).

The formal definition of the rule language is not given here though examples below illustrate its syntax and semantics. The formal definition is given in Barker's paper [15].

The core axiom in Barker's meta-model is:

$$par(P, A, R) \leftarrow pca(P, C), contains(C, C'), arca(A, R, C')$$

where $contains(C, C')$ means that the set of principals related to $C' \in C$ is a subset of the principals related to $C \in C$.

The elements in the core axiom are depicted visually in Figure 3. The dotted line represents how an authorization is formed.

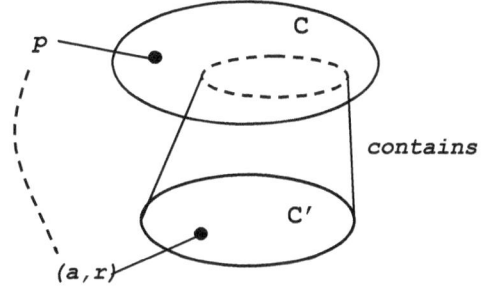

Figure 3: Access Control Meta-Model

This summary of Barker's model focuses on the core elements. Not included here are other aspects such as purposes and meta-policy identifiers used by Barker in defining a privacy model.

3. INFORMATION FLOW META-MODEL

In this section Barker's framework is used to define a meta-model for information flow control. Many of the definitions given for the access control meta-model will be reused. A key difference between access control and information flow control is that with information flow control principals and resources are annotated to indicate the sensitivity of the information they currently possess. The information flow control meta-model represents such annotations by a set of categories. The use of these categories does not extend, but only uses, the framework defined above. As noted by Barker, a principal or resource may be associated with multiple different categories.

We begin by focusing on how information flow control can be represented in a meta-model and later consider how information flow control and access control are related.

3.1 Core Axiom

Three key relations are defined to express the core axiom of the information flow control meta-model. These relations are presented first followed by a number of other relations that deal with the history dependent nature of information flow labels.

To define new relations a set of categories is defined as:

- A countable set L of label categories, where $l_0, l_1, \ldots$ are used to denote arbitrary label category identifiers.

Technically, there is no difference between C and L, they are both countable sets of categories. We introduce L to clarify when categories in the information flow control meta-model are meant.

The first two relations deal with the labeling of processes and resources. The first relation, PLA, expresses how principals are associated with labels. Here, $PLA \subseteq P \times L$ where $(p, l) \in$

$\mathcal{PLA}$ iff a principal $p \in \mathcal{P}$ is assigned to the label category $l \in \mathcal{L}$. The second relation expresses how resources are associated with labels. In this case, $\mathcal{RLA} \subseteq \mathcal{R} \times \mathcal{L}$ where $(r, l) \in \mathcal{RLA}$ iff a resource $r \in \mathcal{R}$ is assigned to the label category $l \in \mathcal{L}$.

The third relation deals with whether an information flow between two label categories is allowed. This relation is defined as $allowed \subseteq L \times A \times L$ where $(l, a, l') \in allowed$ iff a flow of information between label category l and label category l' caused by the action a is allowed.

The core axiom for the information flow meta-model can be stated as follows:

$$par(P, A, R) \leftarrow pla(P, L_P), rla(R, L_R), allowed(L_P, A, L_R)$$

The core axiom allows for two kinds of specialization. First, the *allowed* relation can be specialized to represent different policies regarding the information flows that may occur. Second, the label categories can be specialized to represent different classes of information (e.g., public vs. private) or different abilities that principals or resources have to access or store information (e.g., clearances). Examples of such specializations will be seen below.

The elements of the information flow core axiom are depicted visually in Figure 4. Comparing Figures 3 and 4 gives an immediate sense of the differences between access control and information flow control. These differences are discussed in Section 5.1.

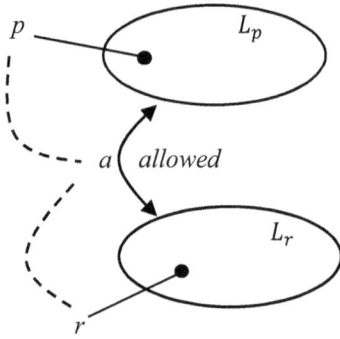

Figure 3: Information Flow Meta-model

The core axiom must be supplemented because the label currently associated with principals and resources may depend on previous information flows. For example, whether information flowing from a principal is public or private information may depend on the information previously allowed to flow into that principal. Capturing how the labeling of principals and resources changes involves reasoning over the history of operations. For this purpose the framework created by Barker for reasoning over the history of events in status-based access control [7] is used. While the approach is the same the presentation here simplifies the details of the history and uses names that are more suggestive in an information flow context.

The first step is to relate the $\mathcal{PLA}$ and $\mathcal{RLA}$ relations to time as follows:

$$pla(P, L) \leftarrow current\_time(T), plat(P, L, T),$$

$$rla(R, L) \leftarrow current\_time(T), rlat(R, L, T),$$

These relations are anchored in time by the initial assignment of principals and resources to classes of labels. This is defined as:

$$plat(P, L, 0) \leftarrow initial(P, L)$$

$$rlat(R, L, 0) \leftarrow initial(R, L)$$

where the *initial* relation is defined at the start of the system's execution.

For an information flow system the history consists of a time-ordered sequence of actions, each of which records a flow that was allowed at a given point in time. Specifically, it is assumed that the history is a time-ordered sequence of records each of which denotes an authorization that was granted. Authorizations that were requested but not granted need not (at least of the purposes here) be recorded. Each record is of the form $granted(P, L_P, A, R, L_R)$. The values in the granted record are those used in the core axiom.

The next step is to establish the direction of the information flow caused by performing an action recorded in the history. A *read* action, for example, induces an information flow from the resource being read to the principal performing the read action. Other actions with a similarly directed flow might be named query, select, input, receive accept, and the like. A *write* action induces an information flow from the principal performing the write action to the resource on which the action is performed. Other actions with a similarly directed flow might be named append, update, edit, send, delete, remove, add and the like. It is assumed here that actions cause only unidirectional flows. That is, no action can cause a flow from and into the same principal and the resource pair simultaneously. Actions that are seen as having a bidirectional flow must be modeled as two related but distinct unidirectional flows. For example, consider an operation causing an explicit flow from the resource to the principal and an implicit flow from the principal to the resource due to the mutation of the resource as a side effect of the operation. Such an operation can be accommodated in the model by representing it as two separate actions, one action causing the explicit flow from the resource to the principal and the other action causing the implicit flow from the principal to the resource through a mutation of the resource.

Two relations define the information flow direction. The *mutate* relation identifies those actions which induce an information flow from the principal to the resource. Here, $mutate \subseteq A$ where $a \in mutate$ iff the action a, when applied, causes the information flow just described. This relation is named to reflect the notion that flows from a principal to a resource alter the resource in some way. The *inspect* relation identifies those actions which induce an information flow from the resource to the principal. Here, $inspect \subseteq A$ where $a \in inspect$ iff the action a, when applied, causes the information flow from the resource to the principal. This relation is named to reflect the notion that flows from the resource leave the resource unchanged but some aspect of the principal may be altered by the inspection of the resource. Because of the assumption of unidirectional flows no action can be in both relations.

The label category for a principal is determined by the most recent prior operation performed by that principal. It is assumed that a principal is associated with at most one label category. The label category for a principal is defined in two cases:

$$plat(P, L_P, T) \leftarrow happens(granted(P, L_P, A, R, L_R), T'),$$
$$T' < T, mutate(A), last(P, T', T)$$

$$plat(P, L_P, T) \leftarrow happens(granted(P, L_P, A, R, L_R), T'),$$
$$T' < T, inspect(A), last(P, T', T),$$
$$combine(L_R, L_P, L)$$

The *happens* relation is the same as defined by Barker [7] where $happens(e, T)$ means that event e occurred at time T in the event history. In our case the events are the granting of an authorization.

The *last* relation means that no action involving P occurred in the time interval (T',T). This relation is not further defined here for space reasons although it is straightforward to do so.

The first form of the *plat* relation means that if the last action P was granted permission to performed involved a flow from P (to the resource) then P at the current time, T, is associated with the same label category with which it was associated at the time, T', of the last action. The second form means that if the last action that P was granted permission to perform involved a flow into P (from the resource) then P at the current time, T, is associated with a label category that is defined by a combination of the level categories with which P and R were associated at the time, T', of the most recent operation. The *combine* relation is one that must be specialized for each information flow system.

In a similar way, to know the level category with which a resource is associated it is sufficient to examine the most recent prior operation performed on that resource. It is assumed here that a resource is associated with at most one label category. The label category for a resource is defined in two cases:

$$rlat(R, L_R, T) \leftarrow happens(granted(P, L_P, A, R, L_R), T'),$$
$$T' < T, inspect(A), last(R, T', T)$$

$$rlat(R, L, T) \leftarrow happens(granted(P, L_P, A, R, L_R), T'),$$
$$T' < T, mutate(A), last(R, T', T),$$
$$combine(L_P, L_R, L)$$

The meaning of these two cases is analogous to those above for principals.

It should be noted that the *combine* relation produces a label that is the "current" label of the destination of the information flow. The *plat* relation determines the current label of a principal. In this case, *combine* is used when $inspect(A)$ holds which means that the information flow's destination is the principal. The *rlat* relation determines the current label of a resource. In this case, *combine* is used when $mutate(A)$ holds which means that the information flow's destination is the resource.

To summarize, the information flow control meta-model contains six relations that must be specialized for a particular system. These relations are:

- $initial(P, L)$ and $initial(R, L)$ specifying the initial assignment of principals and resources to label categories,
- $mutate(A)$ and $inspect(A)$ specifying the direction of the information flow based on the action performed,
- $allowed(L, A, L')$ specifying whether information can flow between an entity with label category L to an entity with label category L' due to action A, and
- $combine(L_{from}, L_{to}, L)$ specifying the label category L resulting from a flow from an entity whose label category is L_{from} to an entity whose label category is L_{to}.

The following section shows how to specialize these relations for specific systems.

3.2 Representing Levels and Clearances

The label categories can be specialized to represent different information flow systems. In this section a common structuring of label categories is presented both to illustrate one type of specialization and to create the framework for the examples presented in the next section.

One specialization of the label categories creates both *levels* and *clearances* that appear in many information flow control models.

The level indicates the degree of sensitivity of the information associated with a principal or resource at a given point in time. The level changes over time as information flows within the system. The clearance represents a limit on the sensitivity of information that could ever be associated with a principal or resource. Thus, the level may change but is limited by the clearance.

The levels and clearances can be modeled as specialized set of label categories as follows:

- A countable set *Levels* of categories, where $l_{v0}, l_{v1}, ...$ are used to denote arbitrary level identifiers.

- A countable set *Clearances* of categories, where $c_{l0}, c_{l1}, ...$ are used to denote arbitrary clearance identifiers.

Two relations establish the association of a given label category with a clearance category and with a level category. The first relation is defined as: $clearance \subseteq L \times Clearances$ where $(l, c_l) \in clearance$ iff the category $l \in L$ is associated with the clearance category $c_l \in Clearances$. The second relation is defined as: $level \subseteq L \times Levels$ where $(l, l_v) \in level$ iff the category $l \in L$ is associated with the level category $l_v \in Levels$.

Clearances and levels can be associated with principals as follows:

$$has\_clearance(P, C_l) \leftarrow pla(P, L), clearance(L, C_l)$$
$$has\_level(P, L_v) \leftarrow pla(P, L), level(L, L_v)$$

Similarly, clearances and levels can also be associated with resources:

$$has\_clearance(R, C_l) \leftarrow rla(R, L), level(L, C_l)$$
$$has\_level(R, L_v) \leftarrow rla(R, L), level(L, L_v)$$

The ease with which clearances and levels can be associated with both principals and resources is due to the symmetry of how each is associated with a label category. We note that it is more common to associate clearances with principals and not with resources. However, the simplicity and generality of allowing both argues against restricting clearances only to principals. Of course, a given system could make this restriction by defining the *rla* relation to be empty.

When clearances and levels are part of a model the *allowed* relation which is defined in terms of label categories and actions can be expressed in terms of level and clearance categories. The first step is to establish the direction of the information flow:

$$allowed(L_P, A, L_R) \leftarrow mutate(A), permitted(L_P, L_R)$$
$$allowed(L_P, A, L_R) \leftarrow inspect(A), permitted(L_R, L_P)$$

Here, $permitted \subseteq L \times L$ where $(l, l') \in permitted$ iff a flow of information from a source with label l to a destination with label l' is valid. The two cases where an information flow is allowed correspond to a flow from a principal to a resource that is permitted by their current labels, and a flow from a resource to a principal that is permitted by their current labels.

The *permitted* relation can be defined in terms of level categories and clearance categories as follows:

$$permitted(L_{from}, L_{to}) \leftarrow level(L_{from}, L), level(L_{to}, L'),$$
$$can\_flow(L, L')$$

$$permitted(L_{from}, L_{to}) \leftarrow level(L_{from}, L), level(L_{to}, L'),$$
$$not\ can\_flow(L, L'), clearance(L_{from}, L''),$$
$$can\_flow(L'', L')$$

$$permitted(L_{from}, L_{to}) \leftarrow level(L_{from}, L), level(L_{to}, L'),$$
$$not\ can\_flow(L, L'), clearance(L_{to}, L''),$$
$$can\_flow(L, L'')$$

The first case is when the level categories themselves allow a flow. For example, information from a source at the level *public* may flow into a destination also labeled as *public*. The second case is when the level of the source is insufficient to allow the flow but the source's clearance is sufficient to allow the flow. For example if the source has the level *public* and a clearance *private* this case would allow a flow to a destination that is labeled *private*. The third case is when the level of the destination is insufficient to allow the flow but the destination's clearance is sufficient to allow the flow. For example if the destination has a level *public* and a clearance *private* this case would allow a flow from a source that is labeled *private*. The *not* in the second and third cases is used to express the fact that the clearances should not be used unless necessary, that is, only in the cases where the first rule expressed in terms of levels cannot be applied.

The *can_flow* relation must be specialized for a particular system.

When levels and clearances are used the *combine* relation can be partially defined. As noted above the *combine* relation is used to determine the destination's label after an information flow. If the label of the destination of an information flow is L_D and the label of the source is L_S then the label of result, L'_D, of combining these labels can be expressed as:

$$combine(L_S, L_D, L'_D) \leftarrow clearance(L_D, C_D), clearance(L'_D, C_D),$$
$$level(L_D, V_D), level(L_S, V_S), level(L'_D, V),$$
$$join(V_S, V_D, V)$$

This definition means that the destination's clearance category is the same but its level category now reflects the influence of the information flow as determined by the *join* relation. The *join* is now the relation that must be specialized for a particular system.

4. SPECIALIZING THE META-MODEL
We now show how the two example information flow systems presented in Section 1 can be obtained by specializing the features of the information flow meta-model.

4.1 File Sharing
In this section the information flow control policy for the file sharing example shown in Figure 1 is presented. The principals, resources, and label categories are defined as:

$\mathcal{P} = \{Alice, Bob\}$

$\mathcal{R} = \{A, B, C\}$

$\mathcal{A} = \{read, write\}$

$\mathcal{L} = \{L_{Bob}, L_{Alice}, L_A, L_B, L_C\}$

$Clearances = \{public, private\}$
$Levels = \{public, private\}$

The directionality of flows is given by specifying these properties of operations:

$mutate(write), inspect(read)$

The initial assignment of labels is:

$initial(Alice, L_{Alice}), initial(Bob, L_{Bob})$

$initial(A, L_A), initial(B, L_B), initial(C, L_C)$

The level and clearance categories for principals are:

$level(L_{Bob}, public), level(L_{Alice}, public)$

$clearance(L_{Bob}, public), clearance(L_{Alice}, private)$

The level and clearance categories for resources are:

$level(L_A, public), level(L_B, private), level(L_C, public)$

$clearance(L_A, public), clearance(L_B, private),$
$clearance(L_C, public)$

The flows of information that can occur are:

$can\_flow(public, public), can\_flow(public, private),$

$can\_flow(private, private)$

Finally, levels are joined as follows:

$join(public, public, public),$

$join(private, private, private),$

$join(public, private, private),$

$join(private, public, private)$

We can follow in detail the two scenarios used in the introduction.

Scenario 1: Alice reads from A and writes to C followed by Bob reading from C. When Alice reads from A the core axiom determines that Alice has label L_{Alice} and A has the label L_A. Since *inspect(read)* holds, the flow from A to Alice is valid if *permitted*(L_A, L_{Alice}) holds. The first form of the *permitted* relation finds that the levels associated with L_{Alice} and L_A are both *public* as defined by their initial assignments since the history is empty. Since *can_flow(public, public)* holds, the read operation associated with the information flow is authorized.

In a similar way when Alice writes to C it is determined that Alice and C both have the level categories of *public*. In this case, the level for C is determined from the initial assignment (since no operation has been performed on C previously) while the level for Alice is determined by examining the history (since Alice has performed an operation previously). The last operation performed by Alice in the history is *granted*$(Alice, L_{Alice}, read, A, L_A)$. Because *inspect(read)* holds for this operation, Alice's current label category is the result of combining L_{Alice} and L_A. Because Alice is the destination of the information flow the *combine* relation determines that the combination is a label category whose associated clearance category is the same as that of L_{Alice} (namely *private*) and whose level category is the *join* of the level of L_{Alice} and the level of L_A, both of which are *public*. For this system the join yields *public*.

At this point the current label categories of Alice and A have been determined. Since *mutate(write)* holds the relation *permitted*(L_{Alice}, L_A) must be determined. The first form of the *permitted* relation succeeds since the level categories of Alice and A are *public* and for this system *can_flow(public, public)* is allowed. Thus, the write operation is allowed.

Lastly, Bob attempts to read from C. The evaluation of the core axiom will proceed largely as above to establish that Bob and C both have current level labels of *public*, that *inspect(read)* holds and that the *permitted* relation allows a flow from *public* to *public*. In determining these facts, Bob's initial label is used to determine that his current level category is *public*. The label for C is determined by examining the history. The last operation

106

performed on C in the history is the write operation performed by Alice: $granted(Alice, L_{Alice}, write, C, L_C)$. In this operation $mutate(write)$ holds so C's current label category, L, is the result of $combine(L_{Alice}, L_C, L)$. The resulting label has the clearance category of L_C, the destination, and a level category determined by joining the levels of Alice and C yielding the level category $public$. Finally, the read operation will be allowed because a flow from $public$ to $public$ is permitted.

Scenario 2: Alice reads from B, reads from A, and writes to C. The last of these operations will not be allowed. When Alice reads from B the core axiom will use the facts that Alice has the level category $public$ and B has the level category $private$. These categories are their initial assignments.

Because $inspect(read)$ holds the $permitted(L_B, L_{Alice})$ relation will be evaluated. The level categories for Alice ($public$) and B ($private$) mean that the can_flow relation between these level categories does not hold. However, the last of the three forms of the $permitted$ relation determines that Alice's clearance category is $private$, and that an information flow can flow from the category $private$ to the category $private$. It is important to recognize that the flow from B to Alice was only permitted because of Alice's clearance. This use effectively changes Alice's current label category.

Next Alice reads from A. At this point the core axiom determines that A has a level category of $public$ while Alice has a level category of $private$. Alice's level category is determined by examining the history. The last operation performed by Alice is $granted(Alice, L_{Alice}, read, B, L_B)$. Since $inspect(read)$ holds, Alice's level category is the result of combining $public$ and $private$ yielding $private$. Note that the effect of using Alice's clearance is now evident because Alice's current label category is now (and hereafter) $private$.

Because $inspect(read)$ holds the $permitted(L_A, L_{Alice})$ relation will be evaluated. For the level categories of file A ($public$) and Alice ($private$) the can_flow relation holds. Thus, Alice will be allowed to read A.

When Alice attempts to write to C the core axiom determines that the level category of Alice is $private$ (as shown above by examining the history), the level category of C is $public$, and $mutate(write)$ holds. However, none of the three forms of the permitted relation can be satisfied. The first form compares the level categories of Alice ($private$) and C ($public$), the second form compares the level category of Alice's clearance ($private$) to the level category of C ($public$), and the third form compares the level category of Alice ($private$) to the clearance level of C ($public$). However, none of these forms can be satisfied because $can\_flow(private, public)$ is not allowed. Thus, Alice will not be able to write to C as desired.

4.2 Modeling HiStar

The information flow control model in HiStar defines a label as a function from categories to taint levels. Note that the use in HiStar of the term "categories" is distinct from that term used in this paper to refer to the meta-model element. The meaning of the term should be clear from context.

The taint levels, denoted by small integers and two special symbols, and their ordering are given by the following:

$$* < 0 < 1 < 2 < 3 < \circledast$$

The $*$ and $\circledast$ symbols have significance in HiStar. The $*$ taint level on a category applies to principals and means that the principal owns the category. A label is a list of categories and the taint level for each category together with a default taint level for any category not explicitly specified. An example label is $L = \{w0, r3, 1\}$ which denotes a taint level of 0 in category w, a taint level of 3 in category r, and a default taint level of 1 for all other categories. The taint level in label L for category c is denoted as $L(c)$.

The general rule in HiStar is that information may not flow from a more source to a destination if the source is more tainted in any category than the destination. For example, if Alice has the label $L_{Alice} = \{1\}$ and a file has the label $L_{file} = \{c3, 1\}$ then information may not flow from the file to Alice. The flow is not allowed because in category c the file has the taint level of 3 which is higher than Alice's taint level for that category (which is 1 by default). In other words, $L_{Alice}(c) < L_{file}(c)$. HiStar denotes the label relationship, $\sqsubseteq$, as:

$$L_1 \sqsubseteq L_2 \ iff \ \forall c: L_1(c) \le L_2(c)$$

HiStar labels form a lattice under the partial order of the $\sqsubseteq$ relation. In the lattice the least upper bound, L, of two categories is written as $L = L_1 \sqcup L_2$ is the category defined as $L(c) = \max(L_1(c), L_2(c))$.

The owner of a category is considered as having unlimited privileges in that category. For mutate operations the ownership taint should be considered high so that an information flow to a destination is not precluded due to the destination's taint in the owned category. However, for inspect operations the ownership taint should be considered low so that an information flow from a source is not precluded due to the source's taint in the owned category. HiStar treats this dual nature of the ownership taint by considering the taint $*$ to be the ownership taint when it should be treated as a low and $\circledast$ when it should be considered high. The label notation is used to indicate which interpretation to use in a particular case. For example, if $L = \{a*, b \circledast, 1\}$ then $L^* = \{a*, b*, 1\}$ and $L^{\circledcirc} = \{a \circledast, b \circledast, 1\}$.

The HiStar rules for information flow can be stated as:

- P can inspect R only if $L_R \sqsubseteq L_P^{\circledcirc}$
- P can mutate R only if $L_P \sqsubseteq L_R \sqsubseteq L_P^{\circledcirc}$

The first rule is interpreted as meaning "no read up" while the second is interpreted as the "no write down". The sense of up and down is with respect to the lattice created by the labels.

The general representation of HiStar in the information flow meta-model is as follows. The principal and resource categories are defined as the six system resources in HiStar: entities that are threads or gates are principals while entities that are containers, devices, segments, or address spaces are resources. The (meta-model) label categories are the (HiStar) labels forming a lattice. The meta-model $allowed$ and $combine$ relations are specialized:

$$allowed(L_P, A, L_R) \leftarrow mutate(A), L_P \sqsubseteq L_R \sqsubseteq L_P^{\circledcirc}$$

$$allowed(L_P, A, L_R) \leftarrow inspect(A), L_R \sqsubseteq L_P^{\circledcirc}$$

$$combine(L_1, L_2, L) \leftarrow L = L_1 \sqcup L_2$$

The anti-virus scanner system with HiStar labels is shown in Figure 5. The specific initializations needed to complete the meta-model for the anti-virus scanner are then:

$$P = \{AVScanner, Helper, UpdateDaemon, wrap\}$$

$$R = \{tmp, UserData, VirusDB, Network, TTY\}$$

$$L = \{\{b_r *, v3, 1\}, \{b_w 0, b_r 3, 1\}, \{b_r *, v *, 1\}, \{1\}\}$$

$initial(AVScanner, \{b_r *, v3, 1\})$

$initial(Helper, \{b_r *, v3, 1\})$

$initial(UpdateDaemon, \{1\})$

$initial(wrap, \{b_r *, v *, 1\})$

$initial(tmp, \{b_r 3, v3, 1\})$

$initial(UserData, \{b_w 0, b_r 3, 1\})$

$initial(VirusDB, \{1\})$

$initial(Network, \{1\})$

$initial(TTY, \{1\})$

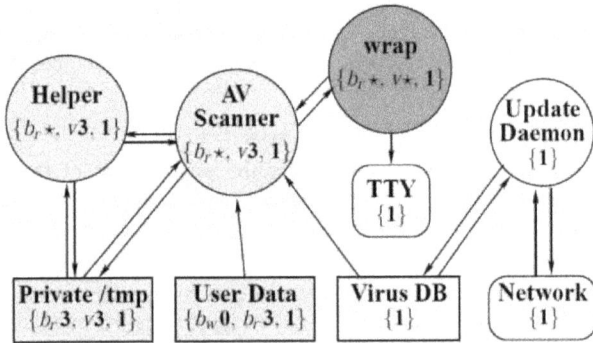

Figure 5: HiStar Labeling of Anti-Virus Scanner

5. DISCUSSION

In this section the features of access control and information flow control are compared and the possibility of combining these two forms of control is discussed.

5.1 Comparison

A number of interesting observations can be made about the differences between access control and information flow control based solely on an examination of their respective meta-models.

Explicit vs. Implicit Permissions. Access control and information flow control both address confidentiality but they do so in ways which have complementary limitations and abilities. With access control the permission are explicit and the information flows are implicit while in information flow control the permissions are implicit and the information flows are explicit. In general, access control makes precise statements about the specific operations which are permitted on specific resources as captured by the permission structure in Barker's meta-model. Information flow control makes precise statements about permitted flows of information as captured by the labels in the information flow control meta-model.

Event History. An important question is the role of a history of prior events in modeling access control and information flow control. Barker's initial access control model [15] did not incorporate a history. Interesting policies including mandatory access control could be represented by this meta-model. However, Barker's status-based access control [7] led to the introduction of a history to maintain "status" information. The use of a history would also seem to be needed in modeling access control systems with "mutable attributes" [24]. While the basic axiom of the information flow meta-model does not involve a history, reasoning over an event history is needed to represent even simple information flow control policies. Both the file sharing example and the HiStar example needed such a history to maintain the current labels associated with principals and resources. Further

study is needed to understand whether history-keeping differentiates different categories of policies and what it may imply about the fundamental distinctions between access control and information flow control.

Action Granularity. With access control the specific operation that is authorized is important while with information flow only the class of the operation is important (i.e., for action A whether $mutate(A)$ or $inspect(A)$ holds). The information flow model could be defined using only two actions: $mutate$ and $inspect$.

Containment. The *contains* relation is fundamental to the access control meta-model. This relation plays a key role in representing mandatory access control policies Barker shows that a variation of the Bell-LaPadula multi-level security (MLS) model [24] can be described as a specialization of the access control meta-model. In this case the *contains* relation is specialized to represent the levels of information sensitivity with the more sensitive category containing the less sensitive category. Containment provides for "read down" (alternatively, no "write down") permissions. In the information flow meta-model the *allowed* relation underpins the representation of mandatory access control. The allowed relation can express containment among categories but can also express more complex relationships as well. In this sense the information flow meta-model is more flexible. It is interesting to explore further the trade-offs between these two approaches. For example, the containment approach may be more "efficient" but less "expressive" than the alternative.

Complexity of Model. The information flow control meta-model formulation requires more machinery (i.e., more relations) than does the access control meta-model. This greater complexity is due to two causes: the relations for history keeping to determine the current labels of principles and resources, the relations for levels and clearances. The first of these causes does not have practical significance because the current label state can be maintained directly without the need for a history. The second cause is more fundamental but only occurs in situations where levels and clearances are needed. The HiStar example, for instance, did not require level and clearances.

Meta-model Relationships. There are problems that can be solved by both access control and information flow control. It was noted in the discussion of containment that both approaches could be used to model a form of mandatory access control. Interesting related questions are whether all policies can be represented in each meta-model and, if not, is one meta-model more powerful than the other. In the first case the two meta-models are "merely" different representational forms of the same phenomenon. This difference may still be practically significant because some policies could be more easily expressed in one model than the other. In the latter case, it is important to understand the limits of each model. If the meta-models are fundamentally different there might be some continuum whose ends are "pure" access control or information flow control policies and in between are policies that require some aspects of each.

5.2 Combined Control

Combining access control and information flow control could achieve confidentiality more completely than would be possible by either one alone. Prior work has explored this combination [25] while others have combined access control with non-discretionary (mandatory) control (e.g., [24, 26, 27]). This approach was modeled by Barker as described immediately above. Interesting questions concern the similarities, differences, and limitations among these approaches. The meta-models for access control and information flow control provide a basis for exploring these questions.

A first attempt to combine access control and information flow control in a principled way can be done using the core axioms of each meta-model. The core axioms are repeated here with $\mathcal{M}_{AC}$ referring to the access control meta-model and $\mathcal{M}_{IFC}$ referring to the information flow meta-model.

$\mathcal{M}_{AC}: par(P, A, R) \leftarrow pca(P, C), contains(C, C'), arca(A, R, C')$

$\mathcal{M}_{IFC}: par(P, A, R) \leftarrow pla(P, L_P), rla(R, L_R), allowed(L_P, A, L_R)$

A combined system is hypothesized to have a core axiom which is the direct combination:

$$\mathcal{M}_{AC+IFC}: \quad par(P, A, R) \leftarrow pca(P, C), contains(C, C'), \\ arca(A, R, C'), pla(P, L_P), rla(R, L_R), \\ allowed(L_P, A, L_R)$$

The surface reading of the meta-model for the combined system suggests that access controls could be directly overlaid on top of information flow control system, or the reverse. For example, it seems straightforward to imagine doing so for the file sharing system in Figure 1. A set of permissions could be defined to indicate exactly which files could be read or written by Alice and Bob. Use of the permissions would also be subject to information flow control. The permission given to Alice and Bob might not allow some information flows that would have been allowed if only the information flow controls were used. For example, if Alice were not given read permission to file A then part of the information flow in *Scenario 1* would not be permitted.

It is also possible to ask about the deeper integration of access and information flow controls. What relationship might there be between the access control categories (C and C') and the information flow categories (L_P and L_R)? Is it possible to have a unified set of categories that create a more compact model or capture some unrealized but fundamental connection between permissions and flows? Is there any interaction between the history-based reasoning needed for information flow control and the permissions in access control? Status based access control also uses history-based reasoning. Is this connection accidental or reflective of an intriguing new possibility for more expressive or powerful forms of confidentiality assurance?

6. RELATED WORK

As noted above, the information flow meta-model uses the framework established by Barker for access control [15]. This framework has proven to be adequate to apply to information flow control as well. The time-related reasoning was first by Barker in defining status-based access control [7] but was also used to define policies in the meta-model work. Additional meta-model elements were subsequently introduced by Barker to express personalized access control policies [16]. These extensions have not been used in the current paper. As future work (see below), we will explore how these additional model elements can be included in the information flow meta-model.

A meta-model approach was used for a different purpose by Staab and Mueller [28]. They defined MITRA, a meta-model to formalize and organize the information flow within and among agents who assess trust and reputation. At the top level, MITRA defines four consecutive sub-processes: observation, evaluation, fusion, and decision-making. In contrast to our work, MITRA focuses on trust and reputation while we focus on modeling regulatory mechanisms and policies. Similar to the work here, the goal of MITRA is to allow comparisons among concrete trust and reputation models and to identify new approaches to trust and reputation assessment.

Our work to define an information control meta-model is, of course, related to previous concrete information flow control models. The work in information flow control has a long history. A common theme in much of this work is the use of a lattice to model information categories as originally defined by Denning [18]. The lattice model has been used as a basis for work in language and system information flow control in languages, systems, and applications.

An extensive survey of language-based information-flow control issues is given in [29]. The body of work with language-oriented information flow control is represented by the work of Liskov and Meyer [21, 30]. JFlow and Jif use a decentralized label model in a language framework that allows privileges to be checked statically and authority to be used and checked dynamically.

The lattice model was also used in controlling operating system information flows in Asbestos [22, 31] and, as noted above, in HiStar [17, 23]. The label model described above used in HiStar is largely the label model defined in Asbestos. Asbestos also defines event processes. An event process abstracts the notion of a subset of a service process' data that belongs to a particular user. The Asbestos label restricts the privileges available to the service process when using the data for a particular user. Beyond the description of the HiStar label model given above, the HiStar kernel is based on containers, gates, threads, segments, quotas, and address spaces. The kernel design provides strict information flow control in accordance with the labeling of objects.

Information flow abstractions have also been created for application developers. The decentralized label model defined in [30] has been used in Laminar [32] to incorporate language and system support for building applications that can enforce information flow policies. A related effort developed information flow policies at the Infrastructure-as-a-Service layer in a cloud computing environment [33]. This approach uses a Chinese Wall policy to constrain information dissemination in the cloud.

Combining information flow control with access control has been explored in the context of information flow policy languages that incorporate role-based concepts. One example of this approach is Paralocks [34] which combines roles with flow locks to express policies regulating dissemination of information.

7. CONCLUSIONS AND FUTURE WORK

In this paper a meta-model for information flow control has been developed using the framework established by Barker for access control. This demonstrates the flexibility and generality of Barker's approach. The information flow meta-model was specialized to show that it could model file sharing systems that required levels and clearances. The specialization of the HiStar system demonstrated that the meta-model could also represent complex and realistic information flow control mechanisms.

The comparison of the access control and information flow control meta-models yielded a number of interest observations. In particular, the history-dependent nature of information flow control is seen as an inherent feature in contrast to access control. Also, the fact that some problems can be solved by either access control of information flow control suggests further exploration might yield a better understanding of the spectrum of possibilities for assuring confidentiality.

The potential for combining access control and information flow control was also seen. The combination would allow for explicit assignment of permission and for explicit regulation of information flows. Using either approach alone only allows one of these to be explicitly addressed. The hypothesis was raised that this could be conceptually accomplished by merging the core axioms of each. Such a merger raised several interesting questions about the possible relationship among the categories used in each and the role in the combined model of the history-dependent aspect of information flow control.

Our ongoing work will address five topics. First, specializations of the information flow meta-model will be created for other information flow systems (e.g., [30, 32]) to further demonstrate the expressiveness of the meta-model. Second, extensions to the information flow meta-model will be done. Following Barker's extensions for access control notions of purposes and privacy will be explored. Third, the combination of access and information flow control will be pursued. Problems that require the combination of both forms of control will be used to study the relationship between the categories needed for each form of control. Is it possible for these categories to be merged in some way? Does the combination suggest new structures for expressing the combined form of control? Fourth, proving that the information flow model possess important properties such as soundness and completeness. These fundamental properties assure a rigorous formal basis. Fifth, the relationship between access control and information flow control will be explored. A number of questions about this relationship were noted in this paper. The two meta-models provide a good starting point for beginning this exploration.

8. ACKNOWLEDGEMENTS

We would like to acknowledge the contributions of other members of our research group whose collaboration on issues of community-oriented privacy led us to consider the questions of how to model information flow policies in a fundamental way. We thank our colleagues Dr. Manuel Perez-Quinones and Dr. Andrea Kavanaugh.

9. REFERENCES

[1] M. Bishop, Computer Security: Art and Science. Boston, MA: Pearson Education, 2003.

[2] W. Tolone, G.-J. Ahn, T. Pai, and S.-P. Hong, "Access control in collaborative systems," ACM Computing Surveys, vol. 37, pp. 29-41, 2005.

[3] D. F. Ferraiolo and D. Kuhn, "Role Based Access Control," 15th National Computer Security Conference, 1992.

[4] D. F. Ferraiolo, R. Sandhu, S. Gavrila, D. R. Kuhn, and R. Chandramouli, "Proposed NIST standard for Rel-Based Access Control," ACM Transactions on Information and Systems Security, vol. 4, pp. 224-274, 2001.

[5] R. K. Thomas, "Team-based access control (TMAC): a primitive for applying role-based access controls in collaborative environments," Proceedings of the Second ACM Workshop on Role-Based Access Control, Fairfax, Virginia, United States, 1997.

[6] R. K. Thomas and R. S. Sandhu, "Task-Based Authorization Controls (TBAC): A Family of Models for Active and Enterprise-Oriented Authorization Management," Proceedings of the IFIP TC11 WG11.3 Eleventh International Conference on Database Securty XI: Status and Prospects, 1998.

[7] S. Barker, M. J. Sergot, and D. Wijesekera, "Status-Based Access Control," ACM Trans. Inf. Syst. Secur., vol. 12, pp. 1-47, 2008.

[8] E. Bertino, B. Catania, M. L. Damiani, and P. Perlasca, "GEO-RBAC: a spatially aware RBAC," Proceedings of the Tenth ACM Symposium on Access Control Models and Technologies, Stockholm, Sweden, 2005.

[9] S. M. Chandran and J. Joshi, "LoT-RBAC: A Location and Time-Based RBAC Model," Web Information Systems Engineering (WISE 2005), 2005.

[10] C. K. Georgiadis, I. Mavridis, G. Pangalos, and R. K. Thomas, "Flexible team-based access control using contexts," Proceedings of the Sixth ACM Symposium on Access Control Models and Technologies, Chantilly, Virginia, United States, 2001.

[11] J. H. Jafarian, and Amini, Morteza, "CAMAC: A Context-Aware Mandatory Access Control Model," ISeCure, The ISC International Journal of Information Security, vol. 1, pp. 35--54, 2009.

[12] Q. Ni, D. Lin, E. Bertino, and J. Lobo, "Conditional Privacy-Aware Role Based Access Control," 12th European Symposiun on Research in Computer Security (ESORICS 2007), Dresden, Germany, 2007.

[13] Q. Ni, A. Trombetta, E. Bertino, and J. Lobo, "Privacy-aware role based access control," Proceedings of the 12th ACM Symposium on Access Control Models and Technologies, Sophia Antipolis, France, 2007.

[14] Q. Ni, E. Bertino, and J. Lobo, "An obligation model bridging access control policies and privacy policies," Proceedings of the 13th ACM Symposium on Access Control Models and Technologies, Estes Park, CO, USA, 2008.

[15] S. Barker, "The next 700 access control models or a unifying meta-model?," Proceedings of the 14th ACM Symposium on Access Control Models and Technologies, Stresa, Italy, 2009.

[16] S. Barker, "Personalizing access control by generalizing access control," Proceedings of the 15th ACM Symposium on Access Control Models and Technologies, Pittsburgh, Pennsylvania, USA, 2010.

[17] N. Zeldovich, S. Boyd-Wickizer, E. Kohler, and D. Mazieres, "Making information flow explicit in HiStar," Proceedings of the 7th USENIX Symposium on Operating Systems Design and Implementation - Volume 7, Seattle, WA, 2006.

[18] D. E. Denning, "A lattice model of secure information flow," Communication of the ACM, vol. 19, pp. 236-243, 1976.

[19] W. Enck, P. Gilbert, B.-G. Chun, L. P. Cox, J. Jung, P. McDaniel, and A. N. Sheth, "TaintDroid: an information-flow tracking system for realtime privacy monitoring on smartphones," Proceedings of the 9th USENIX conference on Operating Systems Design and Implementation, Vancouver, BC, Canada, 2010.

[20] K. Hyung Chan, A. D. Keromytis, M. Covington, and R. Sahita, "Capturing Information Flow with Concatenated Dynamic Taint Analysis," in International Conference on Availability, Reliability and Security (ARES '09), 2009, pp. 355-362.

[21] A. C. Myers, "JFlow: practical mostly-static information flow control," Proceedings of the 26th ACM SIGPLAN-SIGACT Symposium on Principles of Programming Languages, San Antonio, Texas, United States, 1999.

[22] S. Vandebogart, P. Efstathopoulos, E. Kohler, M. Krohn, C. Frey, D. Ziegler, F. Kaashoek, R. Morris, and D. Mazieres, "Labels and event processes in the Asbestos operating system," ACM Transactions on Computer Systems, vol. 25, p. 11, 2007.

[23] N. Zeldovich, S. Boyd-Wickizer, and D. Mazieres, "Securing distributed systems with information flow control," Proceedings of the 5th USENIX Symposium on Networked Systems Design and Implementation, San Francisco, California, 2008.

[24] J. Park and R. Sandhu, "The UCONABC Usage Control Model," ACM Transactions on Information Systems Security, vol. 7, pp. 128-174, 2004.

[25] S. Ayed, N. Cuppens-Boulahia, and F. Cuppens, "An integrated model for access control and information flow requirements," Proceedings of the 12th Asian Computing Science Conference on Advances in Computer Science: Computer and Network Security, Doha, Qatar, 2007.

[26] V. Atluri, W.-K. Huang, and E. Bertino, "A semantic-based execution model for multilevel secure workflows," Journal on Computer Security, vol. 8, pp. 3-41, 2000.

[27] U.S. Department of Defense, "Trusted Computer System Evaluation Criteria ", 1985, pp. 116.

[28] E. Staab and G. Muller, "MITRA: A Meta-Model for Information Flow in Trust and Reputation Architectures," Computing Research Repository (CoRR), vol. abs/1207.0405, 2012 2012.

[29] A. Sabelfeld and A. C. Myers, "Language-based information-flow security," IEEE Journal on Selected Areas in Communications, vol. 21, pp. 5-19, January 2003 2003.

[30] A. C. Myers and B. Liskov, "Protecting privacy using the decentralized label model," ACM Transactions on Software Engingeering Methodology, vol. 9, pp. 410-442, 2000.

[31] P. Efstathopoulos, M. Krohn, S. VanDeBogart, C. Frey, D. Ziegler, E. Kohler, D. Mazieres, F. Kaashoek, and R. Morris, "Labels and event processes in the asbestos operating system," Proceedings of the twentieth ACM symposium on Operating systems principles, Brighton, United Kingdom, 2005.

[32] I. Roy, D. E. Porter, M. D. Bond, K. S. McKinley, and E. Witchel, "Laminar: practical fine-grained decentralized information flow control," Proceedings of the 2009 ACM SIGPLAN Conference on Programming Language Design and Implementation, Dublin, Ireland, 2009.

[33] R. Wu, G.-J. Ahn, H. Hu, and M. Singhal, "Information Flow Control in Cloud Computing," The Fifth International Workshop on Trusted Collaboration (TrustCol 2010), Chicago, IL, USA, 2010.

[34] N. Broberg and D. Sands, "Paralocks: role-based information flow control and beyond," Proceedings of the 37th annual ACM SIGPLAN-SIGACT Symposium on Principles of Programming Languages, Madrid, Spain, 2010.

HyXAC: a Hybrid Approach for XML Access Control

Manogna Thimma
Cerner Corporation
Kansas City, MO, USA
manogna.thimma@cerner.com

Tsam Kai Tsui
NIPR
Kansas City, MO, USA
ttsui@nipr.com

Bo Luo
EECS, University of Kansas,
Lawrence, KS, USA
bluo@ku.edu

ABSTRACT

While XML has been widely adopted for information sharing over the Internet, the need for efficient XML access control naturally arise. Various XML access control enforcement mechanisms have been proposed in the research community, such as view-based approaches and pre-processing approaches. Each category of solutions has its inherent advantages and disadvantages. For instance, view based approach provides high performance in query evaluation, but suffers from the view maintenance issues.

To remedy the problems, we propose a hybrid approach, namely HyXAC: Hybrid XML Access Control. HyXAC provides efficient access control and query processing by maximizing the utilization of available (but constrained) resources. HyXAC first uses the pre-processing approach as a baseline to process queries and define sub-views. In HyXAC, views are not defined in a per-role basis, instead, a sub-view is defined for each access control rule, and roles with identical rules would share the sub-view. Moreover, HyXAC dynamically allocates the available resources (memory and secondary storage) to materialize and cache sub-views to improve query performance. With intensive experiments, we have shown that HyXAC optimizes the usage of system resource, and improves the performance of query processing.

Categories and Subject Descriptors

H.2.7 [**Database Management**]: Database Administration

Keywords

Security, XML, Access control, View

1. INTRODUCTION

The eXtensible Markup Language (XML) has become very popular for information sharing in the Internet age. It was designed to store and transport semi-structured data. Due to the increased use of XML documents over the web, the need to secure these documents has increased. In a multi-user system, where the information is being shared across users who have different access rights, it is very important to implement a security model that gives controlled access to the authorized users. XML access control was introduced to suit this purpose. XML access control research could be roughly categorized into *access control models* and *access control enforcement mechanisms*. Access control models define how access control rules are specified (e.g. how to specify "who can access which information under what circumstances"), and how such rules should be enforced (e.g. how to handle conflict rules.) Meanwhile, enforcement mechanisms implement such access control rules for XML databases. Various access control models and enforcement mechanisms have been proposed in the research community. In this paper, we focus on XML access control enforcement.

There are different categories of enforcement mechanisms proposed in the literature [22], such as built-in approaches, the pre-processing approaches, view-based approaches, and postprocessing approaches. In particular, the view-based approaches, as the most conventional mechanism, create and manage views for every user/role by making a (virtual) copy of all the data that are accessible by the user/role. All the queries are evaluated on the views of the corresponding roles. The pre-processing approaches modify incoming user queries to new "safe" queries, which request only authorized data. Such queries can then be evaluated on the XML document without any further security protection. Post processing approaches evaluate all the queries from the user on the database and get "unsafe" results. Once the results are obtained, they are pruned to discard unauthorized nodes. While all these approaches are secure, each category has its own advantages and disadvantages. In particular, the view-based approaches are considered the fastest for query processing (with materialized views) because queries are answered by smaller documents (views). However, view maintenance becomes an issue – it is non-trivial to maintain and synchronize a large number of views. On the other hand, the pre-processing approaches introduce minimum overhead for access control enforcement. However, queries are still evaluated against the original XML documents – query processing could be slow when the documents are large, especially when caching or indexing is not well supported in the XML DBMS. To the best of our knowledge, there is no approach that tries to utilize multiple XML access control enforcement mechanisms to provide a hybrid solution, which combines the advantages of mechanisms from different categories.

In this paper, we introduce a hybrid approach for XML access control, namely HyXAC, which combines pre-processing and view-based approaches to provide secure and efficient query processing, as well as maximize the utility of available resources. The HyXAC approach first adopts the pre-processing approach (in particular, the QFilter approach [23, 24]) as the baseline to process the queries. Unlike conventional view-based approaches that construct a view for each role, HyXAC defines a sub-view for every positive access control rule (or a set of rules). A query accepted by a positive access control rule is evaluated on the corresponding sub-view. Fine-grained view management also allows sub-views to be shared across multiple roles. This eliminates the need for maintaining a view for every role, thus reducing the number of views in the DBMS. Moreover, HyXAC enables dynamic allocation of resources for materializing and caching sub-views. Based on a cost-benefit analysis, dynamic view management is introduced to achieve optimal query performance for the available resource.

The main contributions of this paper are: (1) we introduce an XML access control enforcement mechanism that exploits the advantages of both pre-processing and view-based mechanisms. (2) We are the first to propose fine-grained views that are defined for each access control rule or a set of access control rules, instead of a user/role. It becomes possible for various roles to share fine-grained views, thus reduces the redundancy of data storage and also improves query performance. (3) We further introduce a cost-benefit model for fine-grained view materialization. The dynamic view management approach maximizes the utilization of available resources to obtain best query performance.

The rest of this paper is organized as follows. The background and related works are discussed in Section 2. We present our hybrid XML access control enforcement mechanism in Section 3, and the dynamic view management technique in Section 4. We show the experimental results Section 5, and then conclude the paper.

2. BACKGROUND

2.1 Related Work

The eXtensible Markup Language (XML) is a metalanguage that could be used to define customized markup languages [8]. Due to its flexibility and descriptive power, XML becomes the *de facto* standard for information sharing over the Internet. Meanwhile, the need for access control naturally arises as the XML model gets very popular for data management. In the literature, XML access control research could be roughly categorized into *access control modeling* and *enforcement mechanisms*.

An access control model defines how access control policies are specified. Some of the earlier access control models that are widely recognized are: discretionary access control (DAC), mandatory access control (MAC), and role based access control (RBAC). An introduction of legacy database access control practices could be found at [33]. In the literature, most of the XML access control approaches adopt the RBAC [34] or attribute based access control [3] to specify the users. Meanwhile, fine-grained access control is employed so that accessibility is defined at the node level. In pioneer works in XML access control, such as [4, 5], an access request is defined as a triple: the subject, the object and the access modality, which specifies whether the sub-

ject is requesting a read or a modify access. In addition to the authorization model for XML, [18] presents an XML access control language that integrates authorization; confidentiality etc. [11] defines a 5-tuple ACR where the type is L, R, LW (local weak), or RW (recursive weak). [31] proposes a different rule-function-based access control model to improve scalability and performance.

The access control enforcement mechanism implements access control models. As we have introduced, existing XML access control enforcement mechanisms could be categorized as: engine-level, view-based, pre-processing, and postprocessing. Engine-level (a.k.a. run-time) mechanisms [39, 10, 40, 15] attach an *accessibility list* to each node in the XML tree, and check the list during query processing to return only accessible nodes. Engine-level approaches require modifications to XML engine kernels and also introduces extra storage and query processing overhead. They are currently not adopted in commercial XML engines. On the other hand, view based approaches [3, 11, 37] create a separate copy of data for every role. Each view contains all the nodes that can be accessed by the role. When the user queries, the view related to that user is loaded and the queries are answered over the view. Views are relatively small (compared to the original document), and are faster to load into memory. Query processing is also faster when queries are evaluated on a much smaller XML tree. Materialized views have been employed to improve XML query performance (e.g. [38, 1]). However, as the number of views increases, excessive storage overhead is required to store the views, and it becomes difficult to maintain and update these views. In particular, although many of the roles may have similar access control rules, the views are not shared, and hence increase redundancy of the data being stored in the views.

Another important category is pre-processing approaches, including virtual view approaches. They check the queries against access control rules before evaluating them in the XML engine. Only safe queries are evaluated, while unsafe queries are either rejected or rewritten. The static analysis approach [27, 28] creates automata for queries, access control rules and the XML schema, and compares the automata to decide if a query is accepted or denied. Meanwhile, the security-view approaches [12, 19, 14] publish a schema (DTD) that only contains accessible portion of the XML document for users to write queries. User queries on the security view are then translated to equivalent queries on the original XML document and evaluated in the XML engine. QFilter [23] is another pre-processing mechanism that uses NFA structures developed from access control rules to check queries and decide if they are accepted or denied. If a query is neither completely accepted nor rejected, QFilter rewrites it to a *safe query* that only yield accessible data. Since HyXAC employs QFilter as the baseline, we will introduce more details of this approach in the next subsection. Moreover, other mechanisms in this category include: access condition table [29], secure query rewrite [26], policy matching tree [30], etc. The pre-processing approaches pass safe queries to the XML engine, therefore, no additional security check is necessary. This feature allows such approaches to be adopted by any XML engine without requiring additional changes to the query processor.

Last but not least, postprocessing approaches (e.g. [7]) evaluate the original queries against the entire XML document to get unsafe answers. A postprocessing mechanism is employed to take access control rules and prune all the access-denied nodes from the results. This approach could be useful for streaming XML data or subscription services.

2.2 Preliminaries

2.2.1 Access control model

XML access control modeling is not the focus of this paper, hence, we adopt a relatively simple access control model used in [24]. In this model, every access control rule (ACR) consists of a 4-tuple:

$$R = \{subject, object, action, sign\}$$

where the *subject* denotes the role who is authorized (or denied) to access the data; the *object* is a set of XML nodes to be accessed; the *action* is the operation that can be performed on the object by the given subject (ex: read, write, update etc.); and the *sign* specifies whether the action can be performed on the object or not (ex: +, −: "+" specifies "access granted" and "−"specifies "access denied"). The "−" takes precedence, when there is a conflict between rules concerning the same node/set of nodes. When there is no explicitly defined rule for a node then the access to that node is denied. In this model, the object is specified using XPath [2]. XPath is a query language used for selecting nodes in a XML document. A more powerful XML query language, XQuery [6], also uses XPath to access data. In this paper, like in many other XML access control enforcement mechanisms [24, 27], we use a subset of XPath that includes child ("/") and descendent-or-self ("//") axes, wildcards ("*"), and predicates ("[]"). As an example, the following rule:

$$R_1 = \{assistant, //person/name, read, +\}$$

defines that "users of the **assistant** role are allowed to read the `<name>` child of `<person>` nodes".

2.2.2 The QFilter approach

Our HyXAC approach uses the QFilter for query pre-processing. Hence, we briefly introduce the QFilter approach. QFilter is an NFA-based implementation for XML access control. It first reads access control rules (*ACR*) as input, builds an NFA structure using the *ACR* to represent the XPath expressions that are defined as valid (i.e. access granted) by the *ACR*. For an incoming query Q, it is processed over the NFA to obtain one of three possible results: (1) the query is accepted as is – all of the requested nodes are accessible to the user; (2) the query is denied – none of the requested nodes is accessible to the user; and (3) the query is rewritten into a safe query Q' – some of the requested nodes are inaccessible to the user, and the new query does not request those nodes. In case (1) and (3), the output query is transmitted to the underlying XML engine to be evaluated. Let us look at an example:

Example 1: We use the popular XMark DTD and document [35], which simulates an online auction scenario. The XMark document stores item information, auction (open and closed) information as well as user information. The "Assistant" (AS) role has the following access control rules defined:

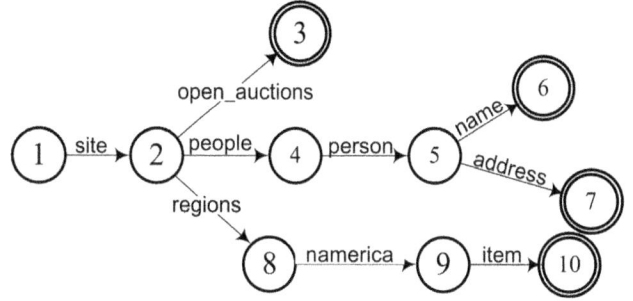

Figure 1: Example of QFilter.

```
R1: {AS, /site/open_auctions, read, +}
R2: {AS, /site/people/person/name, read, +}
R3: {AS, /site/people/person/address, read, +}
R4: {AS, /site/regions/namerica/item, read, +}
```

The corresponding QFilter NFA is shown in Figure 1. The accept states of the QFilter correspond to positive rules. For instance, accept state 3 corresponds to rule R1.

A new query "/site/open_auctions/interval" will be accepted at state 3[1]. Another query "/site/regions/*/item" will be rewritten into "/site/regions/namerica/item", which only requests for accessible nodes. □

For more details of the QFilter approach, please refer to [23, 24]. Moreover, it has been extended to handle multi-user scenarios in [21, 20]. Please note that although HyXAC employs QFilter for query pre-processing and sub-view definition, the concepts and mechanisms for fine-grained views, sub-view sharing and dynamic view management are all original contributions of HyXAC.

3. HYXAC: HYBRID XML ACCESS CONTROL

Conceptually, the HyXAC model is introduced in two stages. In the first stage, we add fine-grained view management to NFA-based access control enforcement, to create sub-views for distinct access control rules, and allow sub-views to be shared among roles. In the second stage, the views are dynamically materialized and cached, to get maximum query evaluation performance for limited resources.

3.1 The HyXAC framework

In this section, we introduce our new model named Hybrid XML Access Control (HyXAC). HyXAC is a hybrid model produced by the combination of a pre-processing approach (QFilter) and the view based approach.

The QFilter used in our approach is similar to the QFilter described in the previous section. For now, we only consider positive access control rules. First, a set of access control rules are used to construct the NFA structure of QFilter. When an access control rule is added, the last XPath step from the XPath will result an accept state to be added to the NFA. For instance, in Figure 1, state 6 is created and set to be an accept state, when QFilter construction process reaches the XPath step "/name". Therefore, every accept

---

[1]The *recursive* semantics is employed in the 4-tuple model – granting access to a node inherently grants access to the entire subtree. For more details, please refer to [24].

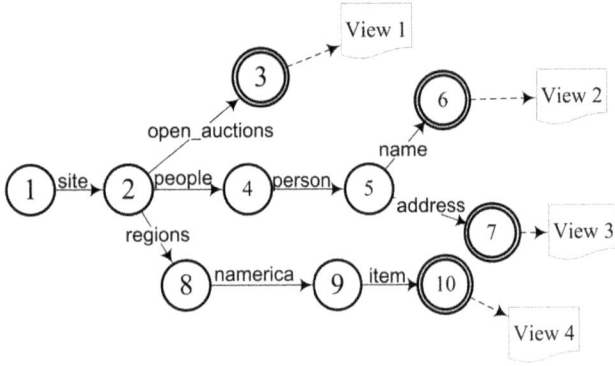

Figure 2: Example of sub-views in HyXAC.

state in the NFA corresponds to one access control rule. In HyXAC, we introduce fine-grained view management. That is, we create a sub-view for this rule, which stores the *object* node(s) of the access control rule, i.e., the subtree rooting at the XPath in the object field of the rule. However, this sub-view is not necessarily materialized. In each accept state of the NFA, the ID and status of the corresponding view is stored.

During query processing, each query is first processed in the NFA exactly the same as the QFilter approach [24]. When the last token from the query reaches an accept state in the NFA, it implies that the query, or a re-written query, is accepted by the QFilter. This query could be answered by the raw XML document, without yielding any inaccessible data. However, when the corresponding sub-view is materialized, we can exploit the view to answer the query, for better query evaluation performance.

Example 2: Let us revisit Example 1 in the previous section. If we employ HyXAC in this scenario, 4 sub-views will be created for the "Assistant" role, as shown in Figure 2. For instance, View 1 stores the subtree for "/site/open_auctions". Meanwhile, State 3 stores the ID of the view (View 1), as well as the status of the view: materialized, or cached in memory.

The query "//person[@pid='18']/name" will be accepted at State 6. If view 2 is materialized, we can answer the query using the view, which is smaller to load into memory and manipulate.

3.2 View sharing

In the conventional view-based access control enforcement mechanisms, a view is created for every role. In the above example, all four sub-views will be merged into one view, which will be used to answer queries from role "AS". However, many of the roles would have overlaps in access control rules, hence, there is a lot of redundant data across all the views.

To handle multiple roles, Multi-Role QFilter (MRQ) has been introduced in [21]. In MRQ, rules from all roles are put together to create one NFA, in which every state is attached with an access-list and an accept-list.

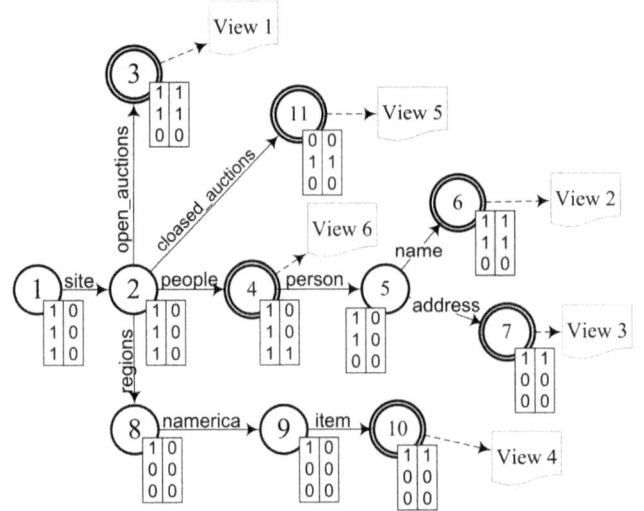

Figure 3: Example of multiple roles in HyXAC.

Example 3: We add two roles: Auction Manager (AM) and User Manager (UM), to the scenario in Example 1, with the following access control rules[2]:

```
R5: {AM, /site/open_auctions, read, +}
R6: {AM, /site/closed_auctions, read, +}
R7: {AM, /site/people/person/name, read, +}
R8: {UM, /site/people/person, read, +}
```

The MRQ for all three roles are shown in Figure 3. In particular, each state is attached with an access list and an accept list. For instance, the lists for State 4 indicate that this state is accessible to queries from all three roles, but only accept queries from role "UM". In HyXAC, 6 sub-views are created for the accept states (i.e. rules). Please note that View 6 actually contains Views 2 and 3, so that we may not need to materialize the descendent views if View 6 is materialized. We will discuss this issue later. □

The redundant storage of data is one of the drawbacks of the view-based approaches. Creating a view for every accept state (i.e. every distinct access control rule) rather than creating one for every role, answers the problem of redundant storage. Roles having identical access control rules would share accept states in the MRQ, and hence share the sub-views. For instance, if we employ conventional view-based approaches for the roles in Example 3, three views will be created, as shown in Figure 4. More duplicate data will be observed when we have more roles.

In practice, if the sub-views are materialized, they could be used to answer queries, for better query evaluation performance. In particular, fine-grained views are relatively smaller than conventional views, so that they are even faster to load into memory. In the next section, we will discuss how to select a subset of views to materialize to maximize the performance with limited resource. Before we move to sub-view management, we discuss some practical issues in HyXAC.

---

[2]QFilter supports wildcards and predicates, hence, they are also supported in HyXAC. For the simplicity of the illustrations, we only included simple path expressions in our examples.

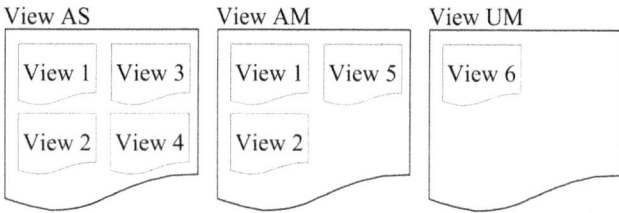

Figure 4: Conventional views for the three roles in Example 3.

3.3 Discussions

Handling negative rules. So far, we only considered positive rules – rules that grant access to a set of nodes. In [24], a separate NFA is constructed for negative rules – all the output from the positive NFA are processed in the negative NFA, and the results are connected by a *deep except* operator. In HyXAC, negative rules could be handled in two different ways: (1) same as [24], or (2) with views.

1. As introduced in [24], a separate NFA could be generated to capture negative rules. Queries accepted by the positive NFA are further processed by the negative NFA, and a "deep-except" operator is used to connect the outputs from two NFAs. The result query could be directly answered by the sub-view that is constructed from the positive rule. However, this solution is less efficient since: (1). the views are larger than the need to be, since inaccessible XML nodes are included; and 2. evaluation for queries with the deep-except operator could be slow, since recursion is needed.

2. Another approach is to remove inaccessible XML nodes from sub-views, so that queries (w/o deep-except) answered by the sub-view would not yield any inaccessible data. Consider that access is forbidden by default, negative rules are only used to revoke access to a subset of nodes that have been granted access by positive rules. Hence, each positive rule may correspond to some negative rules, while "dangling negative rules" could be ignored, since the object nodes are inaccessible to the user by default. In HyXAC, each view is created from a positive rule (or a set of positive rules), hence, we can remove the nodes identified by the corresponding negative rules from the view. In this way, when queries reach the accept state and are to be answered by the view, there will be no need to go through the negative NFA, since the view only contains authorized data.

Example 4: Let us revisit Examples 1 and 3. Assume that a negative rule is added for the role Assistant:

R9: {AS, /site/regions/*/item/payment, read, -}

The rule says that AS cannot read the `<payment>` child of the `<item>` nodes. With the negative rule, View 4 will be updated to eliminate all `<payment>` nodes. Next, a user of the AS role issues the following query:

/site/regions/namerica/item[quantity>15]

The query will be accepted (as is) by the positive NFA (shown in Figure 3) at state 10. In conventional solutions [24], the query need to further go through the negative NFA and the output will be appended to the original query with a *deep-except* operator, which is computationally more expensive. With HyXAC, View 4 could be materialized, and the

accepted query from positive NFA will be directly answered the View 4. □

As we can see, in HyXAC, negative rules could be handled by the sub-views, to provide better flexibility and efficiency.

Contained views and combined views. For access control rules from different roles, the nodes referred in the object fields could have parent-child or ancestor-descendent relationships. Therefore, the corresponding views may contain each other. As shown in Example 3, the object in R8 is the ancestor of the objects in R2, R3 and R7. Hence, view 6 would contain views 2 and 3. In this case, we may choose to (1) drop views 2 and 3, and use view 6 to answer queries from States 6 and 7 (note that this will not jeopardize security since the queries generated by QFilter are safe). (2) Keep all three views. It is up to the database administrator to pick an option. In particular, approach (2) requires additional storage, but provides better query evaluation performance for queries from States 6 and 7.

Meanwhile, we may also choose to combine fine-grained views, if we observe that the accept list for the corresponding accept states are identical. That says, when some sub-views are accessible for the same set of roles, they could combined. In Example 3, Views 1 and 2 are both accessible for AS and AM, but not UM, hence, we could combine those two sub-views.

Queries requiring multiple views. Not all queries could be answered by sub-views. Especially, some twig queries may require access to multiple views. In Example 3, a user from the AS role may submit this query:

/site/people/person[name='Alice']/address

This query will be accepted at State 7, however, the corresponding view (view 3) does not have "`<name>`" nodes to answer the twig query. Moreover, the XML engine may not be able to join views 2 and 3 – attribute "id" of "`<person>`" nodes is required for join, but it may not be preserved in the views. Therefore, for queries that access nodes outside of the destination views, they need to be answered by the original document, or by the views that correspond to the ancestor states of the NFA.

The portion of queries that require multiple views highly depends on the query pattern and design of access control rules. For instance, the design of R2 and R3 in Example 1 is highly likely to cause queries that cannot be answered by a sub-view. Such problems could be avoided by carefully designed access control rules, as well as forcing sub-views at ancestor states in the NFA. In particular, for *logically-related rules*, it is suggested to push the sub-view to their ancestor states in the NFA, so that twig queries could be answered by the sub-view. In the above example, a sub-view could be generated for NFA state 5 (Figure 2) to handle such twig queries. However, this move may slow down query processing by introducing larger views, which take more time to load, and decrease flexibility in view management. In real-world applications, we may often observe such logically-related rules, especially with complex ACR. An optimal solution is to observe the pattern of the queries, and merge views that are often requested in the same query. On the other hand, logically-unrelated rules, such as R3 and R4 in the example, would not cause such problem.

4. DYNAMIC VIEW MANAGEMENT

In Section 3, we have demonstrated the HyXAC framework with fine-grained views. In this section, we will look at the dynamic implementation of the HyXAC model. The main goal of HyXAC model is to improve the query performance under constrained situations where there are limited resources available. In particular, not all the views can be materialized and stored in system memory because of memory constraints. We select the views to be materialized to maximize the query evaluation performance. We first analyze the baseline without fine-grained views, so that queries are answered by the document. We then present the case where fine-grained views are materialized and stored on the hard drive. Finally, we introduce a cost-benefit model for dynamic view caching (i.e. loading to memory).

4.1 The Baseline

In the conventional pre-processing approach (e.g. [24]), safe queries are evaluated over the original XML document. In the first stage, all the queries are passed through the QFilter to get safe queries. Let the time taken for processing a query by QFilter be t_{QF,q_i}. Assuming that there are N safe queries that passed through the QFilter, then, the time taken for processing all the N queries by the QFilter will be $\sum_{i=1}^{N} t_{QF,q_i}$. The N queries are further evaluated against the original XML document on an XML engine. The total query processing time would be: $\sum_{i=1}^{N}(t_{L(D)} + t_{D,q_i})$, where $t_{L(D)}$ denotes the time to load the XML document (we assume that documents are loaded on-the-fly), and t_{D,q_i} denotes query processing time. Note that, the document load time linearly increases with the size of the document, and it is usually significantly larger than the query evaluation time. Assume that the document does not stay in memory – it is loaded for every query, the average end-to-end query processing time for all N queries would be:

$$\overline{T}_B = \frac{\sum_{i=1}^{N}(t_{QF,q_i} + t_{D,q_i})}{N} + t_{L(D)} \quad (1)$$

The first part (QFilter processing time and query evaluation time) is relatively moderate, but the second part is generally more expensive, because loading a document from hard drive is relatively time consuming.

4.2 HyXAC with fine grained views

Nowadays, cost for secondary storage, in particular, hard drives, are getting extremely low. On the other hand, the fine-grained view management in HyXAC minimizes the overlaps between sub-views. Hence, we could assume that all the sub-views are materialized but not pre-loaded in memory – each sub-view is stored in an XML file on hard drive (we will discuss dynamic view materialization later in the section). In HyXAC query processing, all queries from the NFA will be answered by the materialized sub-view that corresponds to the accept state. Hence, the time to load a sub-view to the memory could be denoted as $t_{L(V_k)}$, where $k = GetView(q_i)$ is a function that returns the ID of the view that answers q_i. In practise, the view ID is stored in the accept state. Let the time taken to answer query q_i over this sub-view be t_{V_k,q_i}. In this approach, we first assume that the memory is cleared of the view once the query is answered. Then the sub-view that answers the next query is loaded into memory

again. In HyXAC, the end-to-end query processing time for a single query q_i is given by:

$$T_{H,q_i} = t_{QF,q_i} + t_{L(V_{GetView(q_i)})} + t_{V_{GetView(q_i)},q_i}$$

For N queries, the average query processing time is:

$$\overline{T}_H = \frac{\sum_{i=1}^{N}(t_{QF,q_i} + t_{L(V_{GetView(q_i)})} + t_{V_{GetView(q_i)},q_i})}{N}$$

Assume that n_k queries are answered by view V_k, the above equation could be decomposed into:

$$\overline{T}_H = \frac{\sum_{i=1}^{N}(t_{QF,q_i} + t_{V_{GetView(q_i)},q_i})}{N} + \frac{\sum_{k=1}^{M}(t_{L(V_k)} \times n_k)}{N} \quad (2)$$

where M is the total number of views and $N = \sum_{k=1}^{M} n_k$.

The first part of $\overline{T}_H$ is slightly faster than the first part in $\overline{T}_B$ (Equation 1), since evaluating the query on a view is faster than evaluating the query on a document. The second part is significantly faster than $t_{L(D)}$ in Equation 1 – the time for loading the document is linear to the size of the document, and the view is much smaller compared with the document.

As we can see, HyXAC with fine grained views will perform better than traditional method. However, we still expect to improve it further. In the equation, the query processing by QFilter and the evaluation of the query over the views are optimized. Meanwhile, the second part (loading the view from secondary storage) can be enhanced. We came up with a new solution which can improve the average query processing time.

4.3 HyXAC with dynamic view caching

In database management systems, we always have a chunk of memory that could be used to cache data. Frequently queried tables or XML documents are temporarily kept in memory to expedite query processing. In this subsection, we introduce dynamic sub-view caching techniques to HyXAC, for better end-to-end query performance. In particular, we introduce a cost-benefit model for dynamic sub-view caching. First, we analyze the cost and benefit of caching a view V_k:

Cost. When the size of the view V_k is S_{V_k}, the cost of caching this view is a function of the size: $C_{V_k} = C(S_{V_k})$. In most cases, the cost increases linearly with the size: $C_{V_k} \propto S_{V_k}$. However, there are certain scenarios where the cost varies based on certain additional factors. For instance, in database-as-a-service scenarios, the price of renting the resources may vary. In this paper, we consider the size of the view as the cost: $C_{V_k} = S_{V_k}$.

On the other hand, the total affordable cost (e.g. total available memory) is limited to C_{max}. We assume that we cannot afford to cache all views: $\sum_{k=1}^{M} C_{V_k} > C_{max}$.

Benefit. Caching a view in memory saves the time required for loading the view every time a query needs to be answered by that view. This eliminates the loading time $t_{L(V_k)}$. So the query processing time reduces to:

$$T_{HD,q_i} = t_{QF,q_i} + t_{V_{GetView(q_i)},q_i}$$

while $b_{v_k} = \Delta t_{q_i} = t_{L(V_k)}$ is the benefit for q_i. Assuming that there are n_k queries being answered by view V_k, the total benefit of caching the view in memory is $b_{v_k} \times n_k$. Please note that, ultimately, benefit should be modeled as the "improvement of user satisfaction". Research from usability community has shown that the frustration of the user may not increase linearly with the waiting time. For instance, when wait time gets longer, user's frustration may increase exponentially. In this paper, we adopt the simple linear model, however, the b_{V_k} in our cost-benefit model could be easily altered to fit into more complicate usability models.

With the cost-benefit model, the problem becomes: to select a subset of views, so that the total cost is less than or equal to C_{max}, while maximize the total benefit. This is a classic *0/1 Knapsack Problem*, which could be described as: given a set of items, each has a weight and a value, fill the knapsack with a subset of items, so that the combined weight is under the capacity, while total value is maximized. In our scenario, we define a view loading vector $L = [l_1, l_2, ..., L_M]$, where $l_k \in \{0, 1\}$ indicating whether the view V_k is cached. The total cost is then denoted as:

$$C = \sum_{k=1}^{M} (C_{V_k} \times l_k) = \sum_{k=1}^{M} (S_{V_k} \times l_k) \quad (3)$$

And the total benefit is denoted as:

$$B = \sum_{k=1}^{M} (b_{V_k} \times n_k \times l_k) = \sum_{k=1}^{M} (t_{L(V_k)} \times n_k \times l_k) \quad (4)$$

Formally, our problem is to find a loading vector L, so that $C \leq C_{max}$, while B is maximized.

The knapsack problem is known to be NP-hard. Many polynomial time approximation approaches have been proposed in the literature [16, 25]. In this paper, we employ the classic *Greedy Approximation* [17], which has a $O(n)$ time complexity (assuming that the benefit-cost ratios (BCR) are already sorted), while provide good approximation when c_i is relatively small compared with C_{max}. Please note that any approximation approach of the knapsack problem could be employed in HyXAC. We choose greedy algorithm in this paper for its simplicity in presentation and relatively good performance; so that we do not deviate from the main contribution of HyXAC.

The benefit-cost ratio (BCR) is defined as the ratio of the benefit of caching a view, relative to the cost, i.e., benefit for unit cost. The BCR for caching view V_k is defined as:

$$BCR = \frac{b_{V_k} \times n_k}{C_{V_k}} = \frac{t_{L(V_k)} \times n_k}{S_{V_k}} \quad (5)$$

S_{V_k}, denoting the size of view V_k, could be easily measured. On the other hand, $t_{L(V_k)}$ is approximately linear to the size of V_k. It could be assessed with a simple experiment too. However, n_k, denoting the number of queries hitting view V_k, is not always available. We discuss three cases:

Case 1: known query pattern. Assume that we have observed the incoming query pattern (i.e., we know the fraction of queries that hit each view), and the future queries follow the same pattern as the observed queries. That is, n_k is known, and could be used to predict the number (or portion) of queries hitting view V_k in the future. In this case, we can employ the greedy approximation algorithm

illustrated in Algorithm 1 to get the view loading vector $L = [l_1, l_2, ...l_M]$, in which $l_i = 1$ indicates that view i would be cached in memory, and $l_i = 0$ indicates that view i would not be cached.

Algorithm 1 Greedy approximation for HyXAC view caching with know query pattern

---

Require: M: the total number of sub-views
Require: $Cmax$: the maximum cost
Require: $c[1, .., M]$: the cost of sub-views
Require: $n[1, .., M]$: number of queries hitting sub-views
Require: $b[1, .., M]$: the benefit of the sub-views
1: **return** $l[1, .., M]$: the view-loading vector
2: **for** $i = 1$ to M **do**
3: $\quad s[i] = b[i] \times n[i]/c[i]$;
4: **end for**
5: sort $s[i]$ in descending order, with index array $ind[1, ...M]$
6: $C = 0$;
7: **for** $i = 1$ to M **do**
8: $\quad l[ind[i]] = 0$
9: $\quad$ **if** $C + c[ind[i]] < Cmax$ **then**
10: $\quad\quad l[ind[i]] = 1$
11: $\quad\quad C = C + c[ind[i]]$
12: $\quad$ **end if**
13: **end for**

Note that, in line 2, the index array contains the original view ID of the sorted views, e.g. $ind[1]$ denotes the view ID of the view with highest benefit-cost ratio. The greedy algorithm starts from Line 4: we use a loop to go through the views, from the highest BCR to the lowest. In each iteration, we check whether there is capacity to load the current view. If yes, we load the view and move to the next.

Case 2: unknown query pattern. In the case that we do not know the distribution of the queries, we make the assumption that queries come in a unified pattern. That is, the number of queries answered by view V_k is proportional to the size of the view: $n_k \propto S_{V_k}$. Therefore, we can consider the total number of queries answered by a view V_k to be $n_k = \rho \times S_{V_k}$, where ρ is the number of queries answered by unit size. The benefit-cost ratio is now modified as:

$$BCR = \frac{b_{V_k} \times \rho \times S_{V_k}}{C_{V_k}} = \rho \times t_{L(V_k)} \quad (6)$$

Therefore, the greedy approximation will start from the largest view. In each iteration, the largest "affordable" view is set to be cached, until no more affordable views are available.

Case 3: dynamic decision. A more optimized solution will be to make view-caching decisions decanically. That is, at time t, use the view patterns observed during a time window $[t - t_0], t$, and apply Algorithm 1 to select views to be cached. Views may be unloaded from memory if they are not hit by queries during the time period, while frequently queried views are "promoted" to reside in memory. In the implementation, a counter (FIFO queue) is attached at every accept state, to store the number of queries in a unit time. Every period of t_0, the decision algorithm queries the accept states to get the query distribution to decide which views to be cached.

Algorithm 2 Greedy approximation for HyXAC view caching with unified query pattern

---

Require: M: the total number of sub-views
Require: $Smax$: the maximum cost (total available size)
Require: $s[1,..,M]$: the size of sub-views
1: **return** $l[1,..,M]$: the view-loading vector
2: sort $s[i]$ in descending order, with index array $ind[1,...M]$
3: $S = 0$;
4: **for** $i = 1$ to M **do**
5:    $l[ind[i]] = 0$
6:    **if** $S + s[ind[i]] < Smax$ **then**
7:       $l[ind[i]] = 1$
8:       $S = S + s[ind[i]]$
9:    **end if**
10: **end for**

4.4 Dynamic view materialization.

So far, we have assumed that the sub-views are all materialized and stored on hard drives. As we have introduced, with fine-grained view management, it is expected that overlaps between views are significantly reduced, when compared with conventional views. However, there still exist overlaps that cause redundancy in storage, such as Views 2, 3, 6 in Example 3 (Figure 3). As we introduced in previous section, contained views (e.g. Views 2, 3) do not need to be materialized, since the container view (View 6) could be employed to answer the queries. To further eliminate redundant storage in HyXAC, we only need to materialize the frequently queried views.

We can employ the cost-benefit analysis method, as introduced above, for dynamic view materialization. In view materialization, the benefit will be the difference between HyXAC query processing time ($\overline{T}_H$ in Equation 2) and baseline query processing time ($\overline{T}_B$ in Equation 1). The cost will be the storage for the corresponding view. Again, this becomes a knapsack problem, which could be approximated with polynomial-time solutions.

Moreover, if we combine both view materialization and view caching in one dynamic process, it becomes the classic *generalized assignment problem*. The generalized assignment problem could be described as: given N items and M bins, for each item x_i against each bin b_j, there is a weight $w_{i,j}$ and a value (also called profit) $v_{i,j}$. The goal is to assign items into bins so that (1) the total weights in each bin is under the capacity ω_j of the bin, and (2) the total value is maximized. The dynamic view materialization and caching problem in HyXAC is a generalized assignment problem with 2 bins ($M = 2$). The generalized assignment problem itself is known to be NP-hard and APX-hard. Various approximation methods have been proposed in the literature, e.g. [36, 32]; a survey is available at [9]. In HyXAC, as $M = 2$ and $w_{i,j}$ is much smaller than ω_j, a simple greedy approximation is expected to achieve relatively good result. In this paper, we do not go into further details of the 2-bin optimization problem, so that we do not deviate from the focus on access control.

5. EXPERIMENTAL RESULTS

Experiment settings. To demonstrate the effectiveness of our approach, we have performed intensive experiments to compare HyXAC and conventional approaches. First, we use an implementation of QFilter in [24]. We further implement HyXAC on top of QFilter in Java. We use Galax [13] for query evaluation, and use Galax's Java API to communicate between HyXAC and Galax.

We use the XMark benchmark [35] to generate XML documents of various sizes. We construct two sets of access control rules: each set contains approximately 10 rules, with RS1 grants access to a larger portion of the XML trees (portions of accessible nodes vary for different documents). Meanwhile, we construct 3 sets of XPath queries, with 250, 500, and 1000 queries (with different probabilities for wildcards in the XPath), respectively. Every query is submitted on behalf of both roles, and the average query processing time is recorded. Note that we do not include "access-denied" queries since they are rejected by the NFA and are not processed by the XML DB. Meanwhile, a very small portion of accepted twig queries require multiple sub-views in the evaluation, we eliminated such queries as well.

Baseline. The baseline is the conventional pre-processing approach. We use Multi-Role QFilter (MRQ) to process incoming queries. The output safe queries are then submitted to Galax, which loads the XML documents from hard drive, and evaluate the queries against the document. We used 5 documents: approximately 5 MB (MBytes), 11 MB, 25 MB, 43 MB and 52 MB, respectively. We assume that the available memory space is sufficient to load the queried document in its entirety, but cannot hold all of them in long-term. That is, documents are loaded on-the-fly during query processing. End-to-end query processing times are shown in Figure 5. The results confirm our assumption that query processing times are dominated by document loading and parsing times, and appear to be linear to the size of the documents.

HyXAC with fine grained views. In this experiment, we assume that fine-grained views are constructed and stored on hard drive, for every accept state in the MRQ constructed in the baseline approach. The queries are answered by the views, instead of the documents. Therefore, the document loading in the baseline approach is replaced by view loading. It is undoubtable that HyXAC significantly outperforms baseline when the document size increases. To demonstrate the advantage of HyXAC even with a smaller document (so that the constant overhead of MRQ and view management becomes relatively significant), we use the 5MB

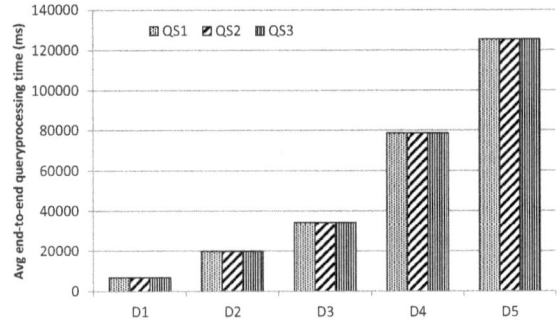

Figure 5: End-to-end query processing time for baseline approach.

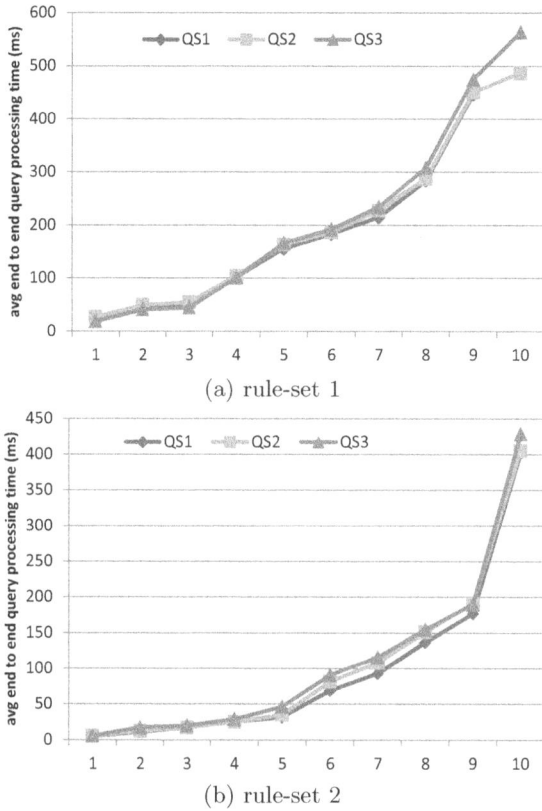

Figure 6: End-to-end query processing times for HyXAC with fine-grained views.

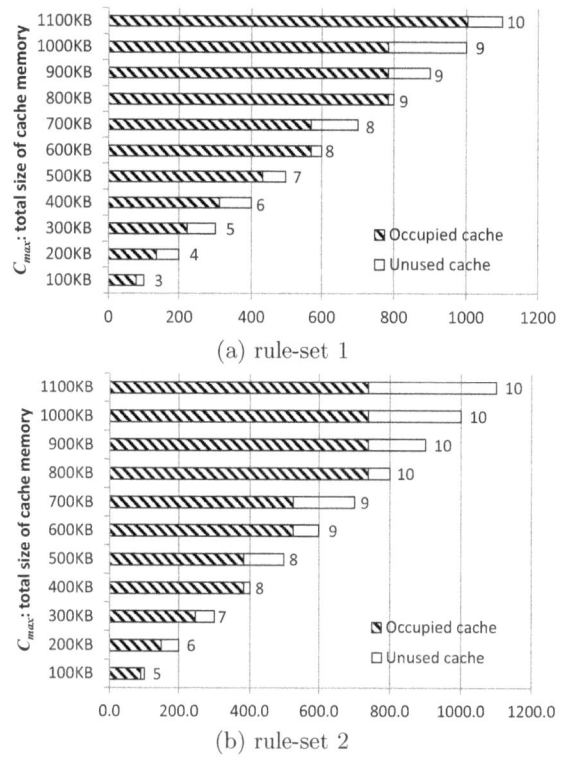

Figure 7: HyXAC with dynamic view management: cache memory utilization ratio. Numbers of cached sub-views are shown on the right of each bar.

XML document in the rest of the experiments. Role 1 has access to approximately 20% of the document (by size), while role 2 has access to approximately 15% of the document.

For each role, we sort the sub-views based on their costs (i.e. sizes), and record the average query processing times for queries hitting each sub-view. End-to-end query processing times for both roles are shown in Figure 6. Again, query processing time is mostly dominated by view loading and parsing times.

As we can see from the results, end-to-end query processing time is approximately linear to the size of the document. As the sizes of sub-views are significantly smaller than the original document, we have observed 12x to 600x improvement of query processing performance (compared with original QFilter approach). Meanwhile, if we utilize conventional view-based approaches, the view for each rule-set would be the combination of all sub-views for the RS. Compared with conventional views, the basic HyXAC approach could achieve approximately 3x-150x performance improvement.

HyXAC with dynamic views caching. In this experiment, we assume that a small chunk of memory (C_{max} KB) is available to cache the sub-views. We assume that the query pattern is known, and then employ the cost-benefit model to identify the views to be cached. We use the greedy approximation introduced in Algorithm 1. We conduct the experiments for two roles separately, to better illustrate incremental view caching. Figure 7 demonstrates the memory utilization ratio, when the available cache memory varies

from 100KB to 1100KB. Please note that 4 out of 10 views are shared between both roles, and 1400KB of cache is enough to host all views for two roles.

Next, we assess the query evaluation performance, with dynamic view caching. We submit queries from all query sets on behalf of each role, and record the average end-to-end query processing time. Again, the greedy approximation algorithm in Algorithm 1 was implemented to identify views to be cached, while the available memory for view caching varies from 100KB to 1100KB. The results are shown in Figure 8. Note that the white bars demonstrate the average query evaluation time when none of the views are cached, just for comparison. As expected, query evaluation performance improves when more views are cached in memory. In particular, when all the views are loaded in memory, the query processing time denotes the time for XML engine to evaluate the XPath queries and generate results, which cannot be further optimized outside the XML engine.

Discussions. In the experiments, we assumed that the XML engine does not have intelligent memory management – no built-in document caching capabilities. This is true for Galax and many other open source XML database engines, to the best of our knowledge. For instance, in Galax, `Galax.loadDocument()` needs to be explicitly invoked to load the document in memory. Meanwhile, for XML engines that could cache frequently queried XML documents, HyXAC still has significant advantages due to fine-grained view management. Smaller sub-views in HyXAC provides more flexibility for document caching: (1) memory utilization would be improved due to the smaller size of the views; (2) cache

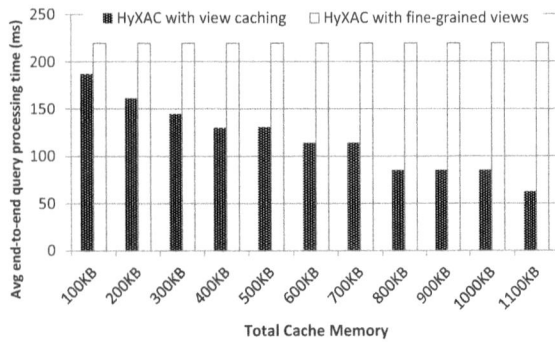

(a) rule-set 1

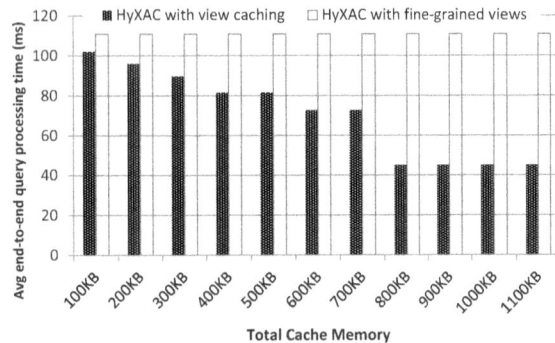

(b) rule-set 2

Figure 8: HyXAC with dynamic view management: average end-to-end query processing time with various cache memory size.

hit ratio is expected to be better again due to fine-grained views – it becomes possible to remove unused portion of the XML document from memory; and (3) cache update becomes more efficient since I/O is faster with smaller subviews.

6. CONCLUSION

In this paper, we present HyXAC, a hybrid XML access control enforcement mechanism. HyXAC first employs the pre-processing approach QFilter to process queries. With fine-grained view management, a sub-view is defined for each access control rule (i.e. an accept state in the NFA), and queries accepted by the access control rule are answered by the corresponding sub-view. In this way, views are not defined in a per-role basis, so that overlaps among views are minimized, and sub-views are shared among roles. Furthermore, the dynamic view management mechanism allocates the available resources (memory and secondary storage) to materialize and cache sub-views to improve query performance. Experimental results show that HyXAC optimizes the usage of system resource, and improves the performance of query processing.

7. ACKNOWLEDGEMENTS

Bo Luo is partially supported by NSF OIA-1028098, and University of Kansas General Research Fund (GRF-2301677). The authors would like to thank the anonymous reviewers for their valuable comments that helped improve the quality of the paper.

8. REFERENCES

[1] A. Balmin, F. Özcan, K. S. Beyer, R. J. Cochrane, and H. Pirahesh. A framework for using materialized xpath views in xml query processing. In *VLDB*, pages 60–71. VLDB Endowment, 2004.

[2] A. Berglund, S. Boag, D. Chamberlin, M. F. Fernández, M. Kay, J. Robie, and J. Simeon. "XML Path Language (XPath) 2.0". W3C Working Draft, Nov. 2003. http://www.w3.org/TR/xpath20.

[3] E. Bertino, S. Castano, and E. Ferrari. Securing xml documents with author-x. *IEEE Internet Computing*, 5(3):21–31, 2001.

[4] E. Bertino, S. Castano, E. Ferrari, and M. Mesiti. Specifying and enforcing access control policies for XML document sources. *World Wide Web*, 3(3):139–151, 2000.

[5] E. Bertino and E. Ferrari. Secure and selective dissemination of XML documents. *ACM Trans. Inf. Syst. Secur.*, 5(3):290–331, 2002.

[6] S. Boag, D. Chamberlin, M. F. Fernández, D. Florescu, J. Robie, and J. Simeon. "XQuery 1.0: An XML Query Language". W3C Working Draft, Nov. 2003. http://www.w3.org/TR/xquery.

[7] L. Bouganim, F. D. Ngoc, and P. Pucheral. "Client-Based Access Control Management for XML Documents". In *VLDB*, Toronto, Canada, 2004.

[8] T. Bray, J. Paoli, C. M. Sperberg-McQueen, E. Maler, F. Yergeau, and J. Cowan. XML 1.1 (Second Edition). W3C Recommendation, Aug. 2006. http://www.w3.org/TR/2006/REC-xml11-20060816/.

[9] D. Cattrysse and L. Van Wassenhove. A survey of algorithms for the generalized assignment problem. *European Journal of Operational Research*, 60(3):260–272, 1992.

[10] S. Cho, S. Amer-Yahia, L. V. Lakshmanan, and D. Srivastava. "Optimizing the Secure Evaluation of Twig Queries". In *VLDB*, Aug. 2002.

[11] E. Damiani, S. De Capitani di Vimercati, S. Paraboschi, and P. Samarati. "A Fine-Grained Access Control System for XML Documents". *ACM Trans. on Information and System Security (TISSEC)*, 5(2):169–202, May 2002.

[12] W. Fan, C.-Y. Chan, and M. Garofalakis. Secure xml querying with security views. In *SIGMOD*, pages 587–598, 2004.

[13] M. Fernandez and J. Simeon. Galax, 2009. http://galax.sourceforge.net/.

[14] J. Foster, B. Pierce, and S. Zdancewic. Updatable security views. In *Computer Security Foundations Symposium, 2009. CSF '09. 22nd IEEE*, pages 60 –74, july 2009.

[15] M. Jiang and A. W.-C. Fu. Integration and efficient lookup of compressed xml accessibility maps. *IEEE Transactions on Knowledge and Data Engineering*, 17(7):939–953, 2005.

[16] H. Kellerer and U. Pferschy. A new fully polynomial time approximation scheme for the knapsack problem. *Journal of Combinatorial Optimization*, 3:59–71, 1999.

[17] H. Kellerer, U. Pferschy, and D. Pisinger. *Knapsack problems*. Springer, 2004.

[18] M. Kudo and S. Hada. Xml document security based on provisional authorization. In *ACM CCS*, pages 87–96, 2000.

[19] G. Kuper, F. Massacci, and N. Rassadko. Generalized xml security views. In *SACMAT*, pages 77–84, 2005.

[20] F. Li, B. Luo, P. Liu, D. Lee, and C.-H. Chu. Automaton segmentation: a new approach to preserve privacy in xml information brokering. In *CCS '07: Proceedings of the 14th ACM conference on Computer and communications security*, pages 508–518, 2007.

[21] F. Li, B. Luo, P. Liu, D. Lee, P. Mitra, W.-C. Lee, and C.-H. Chu. In-broker access control: Towards efficient end-to-end performance of information brokerage systems. In *IEEE SUTC'06*, pages 252–259, 2006.

[22] B. Luo, D. Lee, W.-C. Lee, and P. Liu. "A Flexible Framework for Architecting XML Access Control Enforcement Mechanisms". In *VLDB Workshop on Secure Data Management in a Connected World (SDM)*, Toronto, Canada, Aug. 2004.

[23] B. Luo, D. Lee, W.-C. Lee, and P. Liu. "QFilter: Fine-Grained Run-Time XML Access Control via NFA-based Query Rewriting". In *ACM CIKM' 2004*, Washington D.C., USA, Nov. 2004.

[24] B. Luo, D. Lee, W.-C. Lee, and P. Liu. Qfilter: Rewriting insecure xml queries to secure ones using non-deterministic finite automata. *The VLDB Journal*, 20(3), 2011.

[25] M. Magazine and O. Oguz. A fully polynomial approximation algorithm for the 0Íc1 knapsack problem. *European Journal of Operational Research*, 8(3):270 – 273, 1981.

[26] S. Mohan, A. Sengupta, and Y. Wu. Access control for xml: a dynamic query rewriting approach. In *ACM CIKM*, pages 251–252, 2005.

[27] M. Murata, A. Tozawa, M. Kudo, and S. Hada. Xml access control using static analysis. In *ACM CCS*, pages 73–84, 2003.

[28] M. Murata, A. Tozawa, M. Kudo, and S. Hada. Xml access control using static analysis. *ACM Trans. Inf. Syst. Secur.*, 9(3):292–324, 2006.

[29] N. Qi and M. Kudo. Access-condition-table-driven access control for xml databases. In P. Samarati,

P. Y. A. Ryan, D. Gollmann, and R. Molva, editors, *ESORICS*, volume 3193 of *Lecture Notes in Computer Science*, pages 17–32. Springer, 2004.

[30] N. Qi and M. Kudo. Xml access control with policy matching tree. In *ESORICS 2005, 10th European Symposium on Research in Computer Security*, pages 3–23, 2005.

[31] N. Qi, M. Kudo, J. Myllymaki, and H. Pirahesh. A function-based access control model for xml databases. In *ACM CIKM*, pages 115–122, 2005.

[32] G. Ross and R. Soland. A branch and bound algorithm for the generalized assignment problem. *Mathematical programming*, 8(1):91–103, 1975.

[33] R. Sandhu and P. Samarati. Access control: principle and practice. *Communications Magazine, IEEE*, 32(9):40 –48, sept. 1994.

[34] R. S. Sandhu, E. J. Coyne, H. L. Feinstein, and C. E. Youman. Role-based access control models. *IEEE Computer*, 29(2):38–47, 1996.

[35] A. R. Schmidt, F. Waas, M. L. Kersten, D. Florescu, I. Manolescu, M. J. Carey, and R. Busse. "The XML Benchmark Project". Technical Report INS-R0103, CWI, April 2001.

[36] D. Shmoys and É. Tardos. An approximation algorithm for the generalized assignment problem. *Mathematical Programming*, 62(1):461–474, 1993.

[37] A. Stoica and C. Farkas. Secure xml views. In E. Gudes and S. Shenoi, editors, *DBSec*, volume 256 of *IFIP Conference Proceedings*, pages 133–146. Kluwer, 2002.

[38] X. Wu, D. Theodoratos, and W. H. Wang. Answering xml queries using materialized views revisited. In *Proceedings of the 18th ACM conference on Information and knowledge management*, CIKM '09, pages 475–484, 2009.

[39] T. Yu, D. Srivastava, L. V. S. Lakshmanan, and H. V. Jagadish. Compressed accessibility map: Efficient access control for XML. In *VLDB*, pages 478–489, China, 2002.

[40] H. Zhang, N. Zhang, K. Salem, and D. Zhuo. Compact access control labeling for efficient secure xml query evaluation. *Data Knowl. Eng.*, 60(2):326–344, 2007.

ERBAC: Event-Driven RBAC*

Piero Bonatti
Dip. di Ingegneria Elettrica e
Tecnologie dell'Informazione
Università di Napoli
"Federico II"
Compl. Univ. Monte S. Angelo
I-80126, Napoli, Italy
piero.bonatti@unina.it

Clemente Galdi
Dip. di Ingegneria Elettrica e
Tecnologie dell'Informazione
Università di Napoli
"Federico II"
Compl. Univ. Monte S. Angelo
I-80126, Napoli, Italy
clemente.galdi@unina.it

Davide Torres†
NTS Network S.p.A.
Corso Monforte, 2
20122 Milano, Italy
torres.davide@gmail.com

ABSTRACT

Context-aware access control systems should reactively adapt access control decisions to dynamic environmental conditions. In this paper we present an extension of the TRBAC model that allows the specification and enforcement of general reactive policies. Then we extend XACML to support the new model, and illustrate a prototype implementation of the PDP.

Categories and Subject Descriptors

D.4.6 [**OPERATING SYSTEMS**]: Security and Protection—*Access Controls*

General Terms

Security

Keywords

Event-driven access control, RBAC

1. INTRODUCTION

Role Based Access Control (RBAC) [25] models have received considerable attention in the last couple of decades. While early policy models associated permission directly to users, the RBAC paradigm interposes roles between users and permissions. In other words, permissions are assigned to roles and roles are assigned to users. This facilitates policy management, as every change to one of the user's roles is immediately reflected on the permissions available for that user. The success of RBAC models is also due to the fact that roles are a natural way of representing job functions within an organization [25, 12].

---

*Work partially supported by MIUR PRIN project Security Horizons.
†Work done while at the Università di Napoli "Federico II".

With the advent of pervasive/ubiquitous/mobile systems, the access control problem has become more complex. In such a systems, the decision of whether or not granting some permission might depend on a number of environmental conditions that might, by themselves, be dynamic in nature. First of all, such a decision might depend on *where* the user is, i.e., the current user position. Depending on the application scenario, the space might be divided into several logical areas. On one hand the access control system might be used to control the access of users to restricted areas, e.g., *accessing an operating room in a hospital should be allowed only to authorized personnel and patients.* On the other hand, the user location might be used as a condition for granting access to some resources, e.g., *an employee can read her work email marked "confidential" only whenever she is within specific offices in one of the company buildings.* A second important variable is *when* the access is required. An example is the case in which the policy needs to limit the access to some resource during specific time intervals, e.g., bank *the bank vault should be open every working day between 8:00 a.m. and 4:00 p.m.*

More generally, pervasive and ubiquitous systems are characterized by the possibility of *interacting* with an environment. Such systems are able to obtain information from the environment and possibly use them to influence it. Then naturally access control should *react* to a wide range of environmental conditions. Consider the following simple example: *Fire extinguishers should be, under normal circumstances, inaccessible; In case of fire, everybody who is close to the fire should be able to access fire extinguishers for 30 minutes after the alarm.* Such a scenario clearly describes the interplay between the environment and spatio-temporal conditions. If the environment does not sense any fire, nobody is able to access fire extinguishers. They should be unlocked only in case of fire, e.g., the rule enabling some user to access a resource is primarily driven by some environmental condition. Furthermore, the access permission is limited only to a category of resources (extinguishers) that are spatially and temporally limited (*close* to the fire and *for the first 30 minutes from the alarm*).

In this paper we extend the TRBAC model [7] (that dynamically (de)activates roles based on temporal conditions only) by supporting reactive policies based on a wider range of *events and environmental conditions.* For maximum flexibility, an environmental condition is seen as a triple consisting of a temporal, a spatial and an *event* condition. Spatio-temporal conditions can be expressed with powerful constructs based on hierarchies of calendars and logical/physical locations. The *event condition* will be used to model *every other measurable, dynamic context variable that can influence access decisions.* Such generic definition allows us to process event conditions ranging from *a user enters a new location* (that, in turn, is used to model user mobility) to events like *fire in room X* or *patient Y having a heart attack.* Then we describe and evaluate the prototype we have implemented by extending XACML and its Sun Microsystems' implementation [28].

2. PREVIOUS WORKS

In the classical RBAC model [25], permissions are *independent* from the actual object being manipulated. In other words, a user who has the permission to modify a patient record, can do it on *every patient record* in the system. In [14] the authors introduced the concept of *parametrized privilege* that is defined as a privilege that can be assigned only if some condition holds. A restricted privilege can be seen a triple $(op, o, exp(v_1, \ldots v_n))$, where op is an operation, o is a set of elements and $exp(v_1, \ldots v_n)$ is a logical expression over the cariables $v_1, \ldots v_n$. Whenever a parametric privilege is instantiated, i.e., a value is assigned to every variable $v_1, \ldots v_n$, the boolean expression identifies a subset of the objects in o on which the user has the permission to execute the operation op. Finally *role templates* are roles defined by using parametrized privileges.

Classical RBAC models have been shown to be unable to handle directly decision processes based on "static" user location or on "static" temporal conditions alone. A lot of attention has been devoted to manage policy driven by spatial [11, 21] or temporal conditions [6, 7, 15].

Context-aware systems should be able to adapt themselves to the surrounding environment. We observe that role templates might be a useful (but unfortunately not sufficient) tool in this direction, as conditions should be checked continuously as in usage control, as any change in the environment might (de)activate a role. Examples of context-aware RBAC models can be found in [4, 22, 23, 5, 10, 13, 15, 27, 24, 16, 17].

In [10], the authors introduce the concept of environmental role in the Generalized RBAC model, (GRBAC) as a mean for reducing the complexity of access control systems in ubiquitous computing. An environmental role is an abstract role that is activated whenever a number of environmental variables assume specific values, e.g. *temperature in room X in the morning below 32 °F.* In this model a permission, that can be associated with a set of environmental roles, become available to users whenever environmental conditions allow the activation of one of the roles in the set. In [9] the authors provide an implementation of GRBAC where access control is managed by means of environmental roles.

In [16, 17] the authors present Context Aware RBAC (CA-RBAC) and a framework that allows the specification of context aware policies. The system is centred around *applications*, each of which can define its own set of roles. Each role is defined by considering context-information like temporal and spatial conditions, pre-conditions that have to be met before the role can be activated and/or context events that describe specific environmental conditions. It is possible to associate to each event a *context guard*, i.e., a condition that has to be verified whenever the environmental condition changes. In this approach, the access policy for each role is not clearly separated from application definitions. This makes it hard to reason about access policies at a higher level, especially when a same policy spans over multiple applications.

In [4, 3, 22, 23] the authors present models in which both the spatial condition s and temporal condition t are managed as single spatio-temporal condition (s, t).

Our work is not subsumed by any of the above contributions. We cleanly separate policies from the application logic, while [13, 24, 16, 17] don't. In our reactive framework, the environment is monitored continuously (through an event-based mechanism) while [4, 22, 23, 13, 27, 24] check policy conditions only once before granting access. Joshi [15] deals only with time and [24] only with space. Neumann [27] does not provide a formal model. Finally, [4, 22, 23, 5, 10, 13, 15] do not illustrate any implementation, and [24] provides no experimental evaluation.

3. PRELIMINARIES

The RBAC model we are going to extend in this paper is the one introduced in [25] and consists, basically, of the following components: A set of users U, a set of roles R, a set of permission P and a set of sessions S. A user in U is actor, human or artificial, that can execute operations in the systems, each of which requiring a specific set of permissions. Finally sessions associates users to roles. After the authentication phase, the system creates a new session during which the user can require the activation of the roles she is allowed to play. Role activation is successful only if the required role is enabled and the user is entitled to require it. In such a case, the user is granted all the permissions contained in the activated role. The user assignment (UA) and the permission assignment (PA) functions are used to associate users and permissions to roles, respectively. As stated above, a user can be associated with many roles and every role can be played by many users. Similarly, a permission can be associated with many roles and a role can include many permissions. The *user* function maps each session to a single user, whereas the function *roles* establishes a mapping between a session and a set of roles. It is possible to define a hierarchy on the set of roles by means of the RH relation, where $(r_i, r_j) \in RH$ implies that r_i inherits the permissions of role r_j. In this paper we will extend one of RBAC successfull extensions, the TRBAC [7] whose components will be detailed in the next Section.

4. THE MODEL

In this section we present the formal model for ERBAC. We will first introduce the way in which we decided to represent the context and, then, we will use such a definition for extending the TRBAC model.

We consider the context in which an action takes place as identified by three major features. These are: *location* that describes where the action takes place, *time* identifying when the action takes place and *events*, that is the description of other relevant measurable features of the context that can influence the access control decision process.

Space Representation. A position in the space can be associated with three, orthogonal, representations. The first two are already been used in the context of time-space access control ([22, 23, 4]). The location of a device can be specified by its position within a Cartesian coordinate system. In this case, the *physical location* of the device is represented, say, by a triple of coordinates (x, y, z). We will denote by PL the set of physical locations. A second type of representation is strictly application dependent. The *logical location* of a device is an abstract notion like "Building A" or "Cardiology". The set of logical locations will be denoted by LL. We further define the logical locations "AnyPlace" and "NoPlace" that represent, respectively, the whole space (managed by an application) and the "empty" space. We assume the existence of a space hierarchy that characterizes containment relation among logical locations. We write $l_1 \subseteq_{LL} l_2$ whenever logical location l_1 is considered as a subspace of l_2. From the point of view of an application, the same (logical or physical) location is characterized by some extra information, its *type* that we will use to fine-tune context-dependent access control. Following [4], we will define *type* of a logical location an abstract notion characterizing its features or priority. We will denote by LT the set of location types.

Definition 1. In the space domain we define the following:
- $PtoL : PL \rightarrow 2^{LL} \cup \{\bot\}$. A partial function associating to each physical location the set of logical locations that contain it.
- $LtoT : LL \rightarrow 2^{LT}$. This function associates to each logical locations a set of type of locations that it represents.
- $LofT : LT \rightarrow 2^{LL} \cup \{\bot\}$. Partial function associating to each type of location the set of logical locations matching the given type.
- $UserPos : U \rightarrow PL$. This function returns the physical location of a given user.

We say that a location type T_1 is *more specific* than another type T_2 whenever the former type represents a finer granularity w.r.t. logical or physical representation or because T_1 has higher "priority" w.r.t. T_2. For example, location types "Operating room" and "patient room" are more specific than "room" or "floor" is more specific than "building". To formalize the hierarchy over the location types, we introduce a partial order ($\preceq_{LT}$) defined over the set LT. We further introduce a top element TOP_{LT} and a bottom element BOT_{LT}.

Definition 2. Location type ordering is defined as a partial order over the set of location types, $(LT, \preceq_{LT})$ such that:
- The relation $\preceq_{LT}$ is partial order over LT. If $lt_1, lt_2 \in LT$ and $lt_1 \preceq_{LT} lt_2$ then lt_1 is more specific than lt_2;
- LT contains the elements TOP_{LT} e BOT_{LT} such that:
  - $\forall lt \in LT : BOT_{LT} \preceq lt \preceq_{LT} TOP_{LT}$.
  - $LofT(TOP_{LT}) = \{AnyPlace\}$
  - $LofT(BOT_{LT}) = \{NoPlace\}$

Since each logical location can be associated with a number of location types, the relation $\preceq_{LT}$ might not be sufficient for identifying the "more specific" location between two arbitrary logical locations l_1 and l_2. The reason for this impossibility is, intuitively, that there might exist *some* location types for l_1 that are more specific than *some* location types for l_2 and, at the same time, the converse might also be true

Given the above discussion we define a *containment* relation between logical locations as follows:

Definition 3. Let $l_1, l_2 \in LL$. We say that l_1 is *more specific* in l_2, ($l_1 \subset_{LL} l_2$ in symbols) if the following hold:

- $l_1 \subseteq_{LL} l_2$.
- $\exists lt_i \in LtoT(l_1) \land \exists lt_j \in LtoT(l_2) : lt_i \prec_{LT} lt_j$;
- $\forall lt_i \in LtoT(l_1) \land \forall lt_j \in LtoT(l_2) : lt_j \not\prec_{LT} lt_i$.

We further define a notion of proximity based on the space representation just discussed. We notice that a possible definition of proximity for two physical locations p_1, p_2 might be the one based on the (Euclidean) distance between the two locations. Clearly such a definition does not consider constraints posed by the environment. For example, consider the case in which two "close" (w.r.t. the Euclidean distance) physical locations are separated by a wall. The existence of such an obstacle does not allow to move "directly" from one location to another.

Definition 4. Let $pl_1, pl_2 \in PL$. We say that pl_1 and pl_2 are *close* if the following holds: $\exists ll_1 \in PtoL(pl_1) \cap PtoL(pl_2)$ such that $\forall ll_2 \in PtoL(pl_1) \cup PtoL(pl_2)$ it holds that $ll_2 \not\subset_{LL} ll_1$

Intuitively, two physical locations are close if they both belong to the same logical location whose type is the most specific, i.e., the one that guarantees the maximum possible granularity for describing both the coordinates.

Time Representation. For the representation of temporal assertions we will use the classical formalism introduced by TRBAC [7], which we recall briefly for self-containment.

Informally a *temporal expression* is represented as a pair (I, P), where $I = [begin, end]$ identifies a time interval and P is a *periodic expression* that is used to specify repetitions of the interval I. Periodic expression P are specified by using the concept of *calendar*, that is a countable set of contiguous intervals, numbered by integers called *indexes* of the intervals. We say that C_1 is sub-calendar of C_2, $C_1 \sqsubseteq C_2$ in symbols, if each interval in C_2 is exactly covered by a finite number of intervals in C_1. In other words, for each interval I in C_2, there exist a set of intervals in C_1 whose union covers I. As in [7] we assume the existence of calendars, *hours, days, weeks, months* and *years* such that $hours \sqsubseteq days \sqsubseteq \ldots \sqsubseteq years$.

Let C be a calendar and $O \in 2^{\mathbb{N}} \cup \{all\}$ be its set of indices. We will denote by "$O \cdot C$" the set of intervals, defined in C whose indices correspond to the ones specified in O. If $O = all$, $all \cdot C$ denotes all the intervals in C. Formally we can define the following:

Definition 5. Given calendars $C_1, \ldots, C_n$ e C_d, a *periodic expression* P is defined as: $P = \sum_{i=1}^{n} O_i \cdot C_i \triangleright r \cdot C_d$ where $O_1 = all, O_i \in 2^{\mathbb{N}}, C_i \sqsubseteq C_{i-1}$ for $i \in [2, n], C_d \sqsubseteq C_n$ e $r \in \mathbb{N}$.

The symbol $\triangleright$ separates the set of starting points of the intervals from the specification of the duration of each interval. From TRBAC we further inherit the following functions. The $Sol(I, P)$ function is defined as follows: Given a temporal expression (I, P), outputs the (explicit) set of time intervals identified by the succinct representation. The $time()$ function returns the current time.

Event Representation. With the term *event* we describe all the aspects of the context that are different from time and space and that can be monitored and/or measured. An event can describe, for example "surgery in progress" or "open door". Events can be classified as *localized* or *global*. An event is localized if it is associated somehow with a specific location, e.g., a "surgery in progress" has an impact only in the "operating room" in which the surgery is performed. An event is *global* otherwise, e.g., a blackout is, in principle, a global event since it can affect the whole space.

We further classify the events based on their generation. In particular an event can be *system generated* or *user generated*. An example of the former is the automatic opening of a door while, for the second one, we can think to a medical emergency request by some patient.

Finally we can classify the events based on the set of users it affects. In particular, an event is *personalized* if it affects *some* users while it is *general* if it affects *all* the users.

We will denote by E the set of all possible events. We associate to each event a priority, that is a natural number in the set $Prios$. We will denote by Min_P and Max_P the minimum and maximum priority in $Prios$, respectively.

To formalize the above discussion, we will use the following:

Definition 6. Let U be the set of users. In the event domain we define the following functions:
- $generatedBy : E \rightarrow U \cup \{\bot\}$. Partial function associating to each event the user who generated it.
- $generatedFor : E \rightarrow 2^U \cup \{\bot\}$. Partial function associating to each event the set of users to whom it is addressed.
- $Eloc : E \rightarrow PL \cup \{\bot\}$. Partial function associating to each event the physical location where it has been generated.
- $EVisible : E \rightarrow LL \cup \{\bot\}$. Partial function associating to each event the set of logical locations where the event is visible.
- $Eprios : E \rightarrow Prios$. Partial function associating to each event its priority.

From the above discussion is clear that every event is, in principle, visible only to a subset of user. We will consider two types of visibility. In the first one, the generation of an event in a specific physical location needs to be "propagated" to some extent in the spatial hierarchy. Consider the case of a fire in a office. Although the event is localized, it is reasonable to assume that it will become visible to all the users to other levels in the hierarchy, say in the whole floor or in the whole building. Thus, on the one hand, we have a spatial hierarchy that maps a physical location p into a set of logical locations, $PtoL(p)$, containing p. On the other hand, every localized event ev, generated in a physical location p is associated with a set of logical locations in which it should be visible, i.e., $EVisible(ev)$. We assume a sort of consistency property that $EVisible(ev) \subseteq PtoL(Eloc(ev))$. Such a condition simply states that each event can only affect locations that contain the physical location in which the event has been generated.

A second type of visibility is related to the "presence" of a user in a specific place. Consider, for example, the case of a medical emergency. It is reasonable to assume that such an event is visible to doctors that are "close" to the event generation location. Similarly, it does not make much sense to alert a doctor that is miles away from the event location. We will discuss events of this type in Section 9.

Notice that a non-localized event is, by definition, visible everywhere. Finally, personalized events should be visible only to user to which it is addressed.

Given the above discussions and definitions we are now ready to formally define a state of the context in terms of time, space and events. Temporal conditions can be expressed either in the form of periodic intervals (I, P) or by means of the element "AnyTime". More formally:

Definition 7. The set of temporal condition TCond is such that: (a) Every periodic expression $(I, P) \in TCond$; (b) $AnyTime \in TCond$ and (c) $tcond \in TCond \Rightarrow \neg tcond \in TCond$.

A time instant t satisfies a temporal condition $tcond \in TCond$, denote by $t \models tcond$, if (a) $tcond = AnyTime$ or (b) $tcond = (I, P)$ and $t \in Sol(I, P)$ or (c) $tcond = \neg(I, P)$ and $t \notin Sol(I, P)$.

Similarly we can define spatial conditions as follows.

Definition 8. The set of spatial conditions SCond is such that (a) $\forall ll \in LL, ll \in SCond$; (b) $\forall tl \in LT, tl \in SCond$; (c) $AnyPlace \in SCond$ and (d) $scond \in SCond \Rightarrow \neg scond \in SCond$

Given a physical location pos, let $Locs = PtoL(pos) \cup \{LtoT(loc) \mid loc \in PtoL(pos)\}$. We say that pos satisfies $scond \in Scond$ (written, $pos \models scond$) if (a) $scond = AnyPlace$ or (b) $scond \in Locs$ if $scond \in LL \cup LT$ or (c) $scond = \neg A$ and, for all $l \in Locs, l \neq A$.

Using the same strategy we can define conditions on events as follows:

Definition 9. The set of event conditions ECond is such that: (a) $\forall ev \in E, ev \in ECond$; (b) $AnyEvent \in ECond$ and (c) $econd \in ECond \Rightarrow \neg econd \in ECond$.

A set of events evs satisfies an event condition $econd \in ECond$, in symbols $evs \models econd$, if one of the following holds: (a) econd=AnyEvent or (b) $econd \in evs$ if $econd \in E$ or (c) $econd \notin evs$ if $econd = \neg e$ for some $e \in E$.

A condition on the context can be expressed as the Cartesian product of $SCond$, $TCond$, and $ECond$, i.e., $STECond \subseteq SCond \times TCond \times ECond$. More formally:

Definition 10. Let $c = (s, t, e)$ be a triple identifying a physical location s, a time instant t and a set of events e. Let $cond = (sc, tc, ec) \in STECond$, where $sc \in SCond, tc \in TCond$ and $ec \in ECond$. We say that c satisfies $cond$ ($c \models cond$) if and only if $s \models sc$, $t \models tc$, and $e \models ec$.

5. SYNTAX

In this paper we will use role templates and parametrized privileges in order to make privileges context-dependent. For this reason, we need to redefine in the sets P of privileges and R of roles in the $RBAC$ model.

We will denote by OBJ the set of objects/resources managed by the access control system. A category is defined as a set of objects and the set of all categories will be denoted by OC.

Since objects and categories may be mapped arbitrarily, we define the following functions:

Definition 11. In the object domain we define:
- $ObjInCat : OC \rightarrow 2^{OBJ}$. Function mapping to each category the set of objects therein contained.
- $ObjCat : OBJ \rightarrow 2^{OC}$. Function mapping an object to the set of categories to which it belongs to.

Since we will use parametrized privileges, we need to define a privilege in terms of an operation, a category and an expression.

Definition 12. Let OPS be the set of operations. A *privilege* is represented by the triple $(op, oc, exp(v_1, \ldots, v_n))$, where $op \in OPS$, $oc \in OC$ and $exp(v_1, \ldots, v_n)$ is a logical expression over unbound variables $v_1, \ldots, v_n$. we will denote by P the set of privileges.

Similarly, we will use role templates as a mean for defining roles in our model. We will denote by R_T the set of role templates and by R_I the set of role instances. For example, we might define the following role template:
$Doctor\langle x \rangle = role((read, PatientRecord, record.dept = \text{``}x\text{''}))$

Given such a template, the role instance that will be instantiated for $Doctor\langle Cardiology \rangle$ will have the privilege:

$$(read, PatientRecord, record.dept = \text{``}Cardiology\text{''})$$

Classical RBAC model consider role activation always possible whenever a user requires to. According to [7, 4], role life-cycle is partitioned into two subsequent steps. Initially all roles are *disabled*. Role enabling modifies the role state from disabled to *enabled* making it ready the activation. Enabled roles are ready for the actual activation that is executed as an effect of the first granted access.

We thus need a way to formalize the role enabling/disabling rules. We will use the following

Definition 13. Let $(Prios, \leq_P)$ be a totally ordered set of priorities.
- (Simple) Event Expression: "*enable* r" or "*disable* r" are used to enable or disable a role $r \in R$; the syntax "*enable* r *for* u", "*disable* r *for* u" is used to enable or disable a role $r \in R$ for the specific user u. The set of simple event expressions will be denoted by $SEXP$.
- Prioritized Event Expression: These expressions have syntax $p : ev$, where $p \in Prios$, with $p \leq_P Max_P$, and ev is a simple event expression. The set of prioritized event expressions will be denoted by $PEXP$.
- Role Status Expression: In the form "*enabled* r" or "$\neg enabled$ r" denote, respectively, the enabled or disabled state for role r. The set of role status expressions will be denoted by $REXP$.

Given the above definition we can define the conflicts between expressions.

Definition 14. Let exp be an event expression in $SEXP$. The conflicting event $conf(exp)$ is defined as:
- $conf(enable\ r) = disable\ r$
- $conf(disable\ r) = enable\ r$
- $conf(enable\ r\ for\ u) = disable\ r\ for\ u$
- $conf(disable\ r\ for\ u) = enable\ r\ for\ u$

Finally we can encode the organization access control policy by coupling an event expression with a context-condition in what we call the *Conditional Event Expression*. From the TRBAC model we inherit the concept of *role trigger* in order to allow the possibility of enforcing the cascading enabling/disabling of roles as an effect of the enable/disable of other roles. For the sake of self-containment, we report the original definition.

Definition 15. A *Conditional Event Expression* is an expression $\langle cond, ev \rangle$, where $cond \in STECond$ and ev is a simple or prioritized event expression. A simple event expression is interpreted as prioritized event expression with

minimal priority. The set of conditional event expression is denoted by $CEXP$.

A *Role Trigger* is an element in the form:

$$E_1, \ldots, E_n, C_1, \ldots, C_k \rightarrow p : E \text{ after } \Delta t$$

where $E_1, \ldots, E_n \in SEXP$, $C_1, \ldots, C_k \in REXP$, $p : E \in PEXP$ ($p <_P Max_P$) and Δt denotes the offset after which it is possible to evaluate $p : E$. The set of role trigger is denoted by $TRIGGERS$.

A *Role Enabling Base* (REB) is a set of conditional event expressions and role triggers.

An example of conditional event expression is:
$\langle (Cardiology, WorkingHours, AnyEvent),$
$$\text{enable } Doctor\langle Cardiology \rangle \rangle$$
There are cases in which the access control system needs to enforce some specific behavior, e.g. enabling/disabling a specific role, independently from the current context. Such a possibility was provided in TRBAC by the *run-time request expression*.

Definition 16. A *Run-time Request Expression* is an expression $p : ev$ after Δt, where $p \in Prios$, $ev \in SEXP$ and Δt denoted the temporal offset after which the request $p : ev$ must be executed. A simple event expressions ev is intended to have maximum priority, i.e,. $Max_P : ev$.

Since run-time request expressions can assume maximum priority they can, in principle, override other context-dependent prioritized event expressions. As time passes, a number of run-time requests can presented to the system. The sequence of run-time requests (ordered by arrival time) is called *Request Stream* and is defined as follows:

Definition 17. A *Request Stream* (RQ) is an infinite sequence: $RQ = \langle RQ(1), \ldots, RQ(t), \ldots \rangle$ where $\forall t > 0$, $RQ(t)$ is the set of run-time request received at time t.

5.1 Usage of conditional event expressions

Conditional event expressions (Definition 15) allow the enabling/disabling of roles in response of environmental conditions. In particular, by using $STECond$ conditions, it is possible to refer to space, time and/or particular events that might happen in the system. Such conditions can thus be used to limit the release of privileges to users only in the case in which such privileges are actually needed for executing a specific task under some time-space constraints. Furthermore, the usage of events allow the possibility of specifying the behavior of the system under exceptional conditions.

Relaxing time constraints in response of events. As an example, it is possible to specify the policy that allows a doctor in a hospital to run his duties based on space-temporal conditions, e.g. a doctor has access to the medical records of his patients while he is in his office during the office hours. On the other hand, such type of specification cannot be flexibly used to specify critical "unconventional" conditions. As a simple example, consider the case in which in which a doctor needs to access the medical records of a person while he is off-duty, e.g., a person having a heart attack. In this case the event "heart attack" (assuming the patient is wearing a monitoring device that is able to recognize such a medical condition) might be used to loose the access policy to the patient medical record.

Let us assume that $Doctor\langle Department\rangle$ is the template that defines the privileges of doctors in a given department where $Department \in LT$. Furthermore, let $Cardiology \in LL$ and $Department \in LtoT(Cardiology)$. In this case $Doctor\langle Cardiology\rangle$ can be the specific role instance that limits the privileges of a doctor to the rooms that belong to the department of cardiology. If we assume that the system is able to recognize a patient in critical conditions within a given department by generating an event $CriticalPatient \in E$, we might specify the following policy:

$$\langle(Cardiology, WorkingHours, AnyEvent),$$
$$\text{enable } Doctor\langle Cardiology\rangle\rangle$$
$$\langle(Cardiology, AnyTime, CriticalPatient),$$
$$\text{enable } Doctor\langle Cardiology\rangle\rangle$$

The effects of the above rules is to enable, under normal conditions, permissions to doctors assigned to the cardiology department only during their $WorkingHours$ and within the logical locations belonging to the department of cardiology. At the same time, we can specify that, under specific medical conditions, a doctor might operate also while he is off-duty[1].

In this way we obtain a transparent management of permissions that, according to the minimum privilege principle, guarantees the granting of privileges only when they are actually needed.

Localized vs Global Events. We further notice that event localization allows the possibility to define special conditions in a flexible and compact way. Let $Loc = LofT(Department) \cap PtoL(Eloc(CriticalPatient))$. In the previous example, if we consider an access policy spanning over a number of departments, we might define the following:

$$\langle(Cardiology, WorkingHours, AnyEvent),$$
$$\text{enable } Doctor\langle Cardiology\rangle\rangle$$
$$\langle(Neurology, WorkingHours, AnyEvent),$$
$$\text{enable } Doctor\langle Neurology\rangle\rangle$$
$$\langle(Department, AnyTime, CriticalPatient),$$
$$\text{enable } Doctor\langle Loc\rangle\rangle.$$

If $Eloc(CriticalPatient) \neq \{\perp\}$, i.e., if the event *Critical-Patient* is localized, it is possible to obtain the department in which the event occurred and enable the roles of doctors in the specific department, independently from their office hours. Furthermore, the "level of visibility", i.e., the set of logical locations in which the event is visible, will be defined at the time of event definition and will be used to transparently enable the proper set of users. Let us now consider the following simple example of global event. Consider a web site that offers services to registered users only. The site policy might be to allow read-write access to users during normal operations but to restrict to read-only access during web the account check operations. We might model this policy using the event "ACheck" as a global-general event used to restrict the access to the users by defining the following roles:

$$FullMember\langle\rangle = role((\text{read-write}, Resource, true))$$
$$LimitedMember\langle\rangle = role((\text{read}, Resource, true))$$

Now, if $ACheck \in E$ is a global, general event, thus visible to all the users, it is possible to limit the implement the site policy using the following rules:

$$\langle(AnyPlace, AnyTime, ACheck), \text{disable } FullMember\langle\rangle\rangle$$
$$\langle(AnyPlace, AnyTime, ACheck), \text{enable } LimitedMember\langle\rangle\rangle$$

---

[1] We will show a more complex example that will relax also the requirement on the space conditions

Personalized vs General Events. By using the same role definitions, we can limit the access to a specific set of accounts, by turning the event into a personalized one. In other words, if we assume $user \in generatedFor(ACheck)$, the event $ACheck$ will be visible only to the users defined by $generatedFor(ACheck)$ and, thus, these users will be the only ones whose privileges will be restricted.

6. SEMANTICS

In complex Role Enabling Bases there might exist conflicting event expressions. Before defining the semantics of the ERBAC model, we need a way to cope with such conflicts. A we have seen, each event expression is associated with a priority and, thus, we can assume that in case two conflicting event expression have to be managed simultaneously, the one with higher priority takes precedence. However, there is still the possibility that the system will generate two (or more) conflicting event expressions with the same priority simultaneously. In this case, we adopt the strategy *denials take precedence*. This strategy can be restated as follows: a role is enabled only if there exists no disabling expression for the same role whose priority is greater than or equal to one of the enabling expression.

Definition 18. Let S be a set of event expressions, $r \in R$ and $u \in U$. An expression $p : ev \in S$ is said to be *blocked* by S if there exists $q \in Prios$ such that $q : conf(ev) \in S$ and one of the following holds:

1. $ev = \text{enable } r \text{ [for } u] \wedge (p \leq_P q)$
2. $ev = \text{disable } r \text{ [for } u] \wedge (p <_P q)$

The set of event expressions in S that are *not* blocked by S will be denoted by $NonBlocked(S)$.

Thus, given a set of event expressions S, the system actually processes at every time t, the set of $NonBlocked(S)$. Such set can depend on three distinct elements: the conditional event expressions, the role triggers in the role enabling base and the run-time requests received at time t. The only elements that depend on the context are the conditional event expression. Although we have just defined a priority based criterion for eliminating conflicting event expressions, there might still be cases in which such a criterion might not remove potentially dangerous ambiguities.

Before defining the sorting over conditional event expressions, we define a sorting criterion over spatial conditions.

Definition 19. Let $sc_1, sc_2 \in SCond$. Spatial condition sc_1 is said to be *more specific* than sc_2, denoted by $(sc_1 <_{SCond} s_2)$ is it holds that:
- $sc_1 \subset_{LL} s_2$, if $sc_1, sc_2 \in LL$
- $sc_1 \preceq_{LT} sc_2$, if $sc_1, sc_2 \in LT$
- if $sc_1 \in LL$ and $sc_2 \in LT$:
  - $\forall tl_1 \in LtoT(sc_1) : sc_2 \npreceq_{LT} tl_1$
  - $\exists tl_1 \in LtoT(sc_1) : tl_1 \preceq_{LT} sc_2$
- if $sc_1 \in LT$ and $sc_2 \in LL$:
  - $\forall tl_2 \in LtoT(sc_2) : tl_2 \npreceq_{LT} sc_1$
  - $\forall tl_2 \in LtoT(sc_2) : sc_1 \preceq_{LT} tl_2$

It is now possible to extend the concept of specificity to the conditional event expressions as follows:

Definition 20. Let $ce_1 = \langle(sc_1, tc_1, ec_1), p : ev_1\rangle$ and $ce_2 = \langle(sc_2, tc_2, ec_2), q : ev_2\rangle$ be conditional event expressions and

$ep1 = Eprios(ec_1)$, $ep2 = Eprios(ec_2)$. We say that ce_1 is more specific than ce_2, denote by $ce_1 < ce_2$, if one of the following holds:

- $p > q$. The priority of event expression ev_1 is greater than the priority of event expression ev_2;
- $p = q \wedge ep1 > ep2$. The priority of the event ec_1 is greater than the priority of event ec_1;
- $p = q \wedge ep1 = ep2 \wedge sc_1 <_{SCond} sc_2$. The events have the same priority but the spatial conditions sc_1 is more specific than sc_2.

This criterion defines a partial order over the conditional event expressions that might imply, depending on the context, the exclusions of some rules because their context is less specific than others. It is thus possible to define the set *MostSpecific* that, given a set S of rules, defines the subset of them that are most specific in S.

Definition 21. Let S be a set of conditional event expressions. We define the set $MostSpecific(S) \subseteq S$ as follows:

$$MostSpecific(S) = \{c \in S \mid \neg \exists c' \in S : c' < c\}$$

Notice that the definition of MostSpecific does not use time related constraints for classifying activation rules. This is due to the following observations. When we evaluate time conditions, their state depends on the moment in which a specific request enters the system. This means that the "same context" might (and should) lead to different behavior depending on the time in which the request is evaluated. Furthermore, if we try to specify the concept of "more specific" also in the case of temporal conditions, it is reasonable to assume that any time-interval is *less* specific than every its sub-interval. This implies a sort of absolute criterion that, on the one hand, might be in contrast with the policy the administrator needs to specify and, on the other hand, would reduce the specification flexibility.

Intuitively, the system should work as follows: in every instant a subset of the conditional event expressions are satisfied by the current context. The most specific rules in this set identify the set of roles and run-time requests that generate the role enabling/disabling requests that the system will process to determine the set of roles that are enabled at the next time instant. Such a behavior can be formalized by using the concept of *system trace* that can be used to describe the state of the system in every instant.

Definition 22. A *system trace* is a pair (EV, ST) of infinite sequences of sets defined as follows. For every $t \geq 0$:

- $EV(t)$ is the set of prioritized event expressions received at time t.
- $ST(t)$ is the set of roles that are globally enabled at time t and the set of pairs (r, u) that represent exceptions with with the specification of a given role $r \in R$ is disabled for the given user $u \in U$.

The sequence ST evolves as a function of event expressions evaluated at time t as follows:

$$
\begin{aligned}
ST(t+1) = \Big(& ST(t) \cup \\
& \{(r, u) \mid \text{disable } r \text{ for } u \in Nonblocked(EV(t))\} \cup \\
& \{r \mid \text{enable } r \in Nonblocked(EV(t))\} \Big) \setminus \\
& \Big(\{(r, u) \mid \text{enable } r \text{ for } u \in Nonblocked(EV(t))\} \cup \\
& \{r \mid \text{disable } r \in Nonblocked(EV(t))\} \Big)
\end{aligned}
$$

The sequence EV should instead include, in every time t, the event expressions generated by the role enabling base and the run-time request received at t. In particular, for the event expressions, it is necessary to consider the type of contextual condition. Indeed, some conditions express constraints that can be satisfied only by using the information carried by a specific user and, in this case, only such a user should be affected by such conditions. Other conditions, instead, might affect all the user in the system. For example, a contextual condition based on a spatial requirement restricts the effect of the role enabling/disabling only to users that posses a specific information, e.g., their physical position meets the spatial requirement. On the other hand, a contextual condition consisting only of a temporal requirement affects all the users in that specific time interval, independently from the specific information every user carries. In the following we will denote by $Q(t) = \{\langle(sc, tc, ec), p : ev\rangle \in \mathcal{R} \mid \exists e \in \text{ActiveEvents}(t) \wedge (t, EVisible(e), e) \models (sc, tc, ec)\}$. We can use the following formalization:

Definition 23. Let (EV, ST) be a system trace, $\mathcal{R}$ be a role enabling base and RQ be a request stream. We define $Caused(t, EV, ST, \mathcal{R}, RQ)$ to be the set of prioritized event expressions generated by the elements that satisfy the following conditions:

1. If $(p : ev \text{ after } \Delta t) \in RQ(t - \Delta t)$ and $\Delta t \leq t$, then $p : ev \in Caused(t, EV, ST, \mathcal{R}, RQ)$
2. If $[E_1, \ldots, E_n, C_1, \ldots, C_k \rightarrow p : ev \text{ after } \Delta t] \in c$ and the following hold:

   - $\Delta t \leq t$
   - for each state expression C_i in the form enabled R, $R \in ST(t - \Delta t)$
   - for each state expression C_i in the form $\neg$enabled R, $R \notin ST(t - \Delta t)$
   - for each event expression E_i there exists $\hat{E} p : E_i \in Caused(t - \Delta t, EV, ST, \mathcal{R}, RQ)$ not blocked by $EV(t - \Delta t)$

   then $p : ev \in Caused(t, EV, ST, \mathcal{R}, RQ)$
3. For each conditional event expression $ce = \langle(sc, tc, ec), p : ev\rangle \in MostSpecific(Q(t))$ we have $p : ev$ for $u \in Caused(t, EV, ST, \mathcal{R}, RQ)$ for each u in the following sets:

   1. Global, General Events:
      $\{v \in U \mid UserPos(v) \models sc\}$
   2. Global, Personalized Events:
      $\{v \in generatedFor(ec) \mid UserPos(v) \models sc\}$.
   3. Localized, General Events:
      $\{v \in U \mid UserPos(v) \models sc \wedge EVisible(ec) \cap PtoL(UserPos(v)) \cap \emptyset\}$.
   4. Localized, Personalized Events:
      $\{v \in generatedFor(ec) \mid UserPos(v) \models sc \wedge EVisible(ec) \cap PtoL(UserPos(v)) \neq \emptyset\}$.

The rational behind rules 1 to 4 is the following. The effect of a conditional event expression can either be bound by the features of the event ec or by the spatial constraints sc (or by both of them). The rule 1 is used to model the case in which the event in the conditional expression is neither a localized events nor a personalized one. In this case the prioritized event expression is global in the sense that it affects all the user that are satisfy the space condition sc. The rule 2 is used to model personalized global events. In this case the constraints posed by the personalized nature of the event, allows the prioritized event expression to affect only the users to which the event is addressed to. However, the spatial condition might further reduce such set of affected users by restricting it to contain only the ones that at time t, satisfy sc.

The rule 3 models localized and general events. In this case, the set of users that are affected by the prioritized event expression is the one that meets both the spatial conditions. Finally, the rule 4 manages personalized and localized events. In this case, the affected users are the ones for which the event has been generated for, whose position falls within the visibility range of the event and that satisfy the spatial condition.

At this point it is possible to define the behavior of the system introducing the concept of *execution model*.

Definition 24. A system trace (EV, ST) is said to be a *execution model* for a role enabling base $\mathcal{R}$ and a request stream RQ if, for each $t \geq 0$, it holds that:

$$EV(t) = Caused(t, EV, ST, \mathcal{R}, RQ)$$

7. AN EXAMPLE

Let us see an application of the rule ordering over the following set of rules:

1. $\langle (AnyPlace, WorkingHours, AnyEvent),$
   disable $Surgeon\langle OperatingRoom1 \rangle \rangle$
2. $\langle (SurgeryDepartment, WorkingHours, AnyEvent),$
   enable $Doctor\langle SurgeryDepartment \rangle \rangle$
3. $\langle (OperatingRoom1, WorkingHours, AnyEvent),$
   enable $Surgeon\langle OperatingRoom1 \rangle \rangle$
4. $\langle (OperatingRoom1, \neg WorkingHours, AnyEvent),$
   disable $Surgeon\langle OperatingRoom1 \rangle \rangle$
5. $\langle (OperatingRoom1, AnyTime, SurgeryInProgress),$
   enable $Surgeon\langle OperatingRoom1 \rangle \rangle$

where $OperatingRoom1$ and $SurgeryDepartment$ are logical locations of types $OperatingRooms$ and $Department$, respectively. We assume $OperatingRooms$ to be more specific of $Department$, i.e., $OperatingRooms \preceq_{LT} Department$. Finally, the event $SurgeryInProgress$ is a localized event with priority greater than Min_P.

Let us consider the triple $\sigma = (s, t, e)$ where t is in WorkingHours and the user is physically inside the operating room 1 (that is part of the surgery department), that is, $PtoL(s) = \{OperatingRoom1, SurgeryDepartment\}$. In state σ there are no visible events, i.e, $evs = \emptyset$. The set S of rules satisfied by the triple (s, t, evs) is $A = \{1, 2, 3\}$, two of which, rules 1 and 3, are conflicting. However, since $OperatingRooms \preceq_{LT} Department \preceq_{LT} AnyPlace$, it is possible to derive that $OperatingRoom1$ is more specific than $SurgeryDepartment$ and thus MostSpecific(S)=\{3\}.

Let us now consider the case in which $\sigma' = (s, t', e)$, where $t' \notin WorkingHours$. In this case it is immediate that $MostSpecific(S) = \{4\}$. Such a rule models the policy that does not allow a surgeon to enable the $Surgeon$ role in the OperatingRoom1 outside her working hours. On the other hand, let us assume that, under the same space and time conditions, the event $SurgeryInProgress$ becomes visible, i.e., $\sigma'' = (s, t', e')$ and $SurgeryInProgress \in e'$.

This case models the typical medical emergency in which the surgeon, independently from the working hours, should be able to run the surgery. In this case the conflicting rules 4 and 5 in S meet the triple σ''. However, since $Eprios(SurgeryInProgress) >_P Eprios(AnyEvent) = Min_P$, it follows that MostSpecific(S)=\{5\}.

8. EXTENDING THE RBAC MODEL

Although most of the logic that binds the context to the system state has been limited to the concept of role enabling and disabling, the presence of role templates, role instances and parametrized privileges requires that in order to obtain the desired behavior we need to redefine the $RBAC$ model as defined in Section 3. In particular we need (a) to modify the assignment relation as function of the new elements that have been introduced or restated in Section 5 and (b) to redefine the relation within a session in a way to keep the "transparency" goal we had. Indeed, if we want that the system automatically guarantees the "required" privileges as a function of the context, we need to redefine the concept of role activation (represented in RBAC by the function $roles$) in a way that active roles are defined as all the roles assigned to a specific user that the system considers to be enabled.

Definition 25. The $ERBAC$ model consists of the following components:
- U, S: sets of users and sessions;
- P: set of parametrized privileges as defined in Definition 12;
- $R = R_T \cup R_I$: set of roles composed by the union of the role templates (R_T) and role instances (R_I);
- $PA \subseteq P \times R_T$: relation associating permissions to role templates;
- $UA \subseteq U \times R_I$: relation associating role instances to users;
- $RH \subseteq R \times R$, a partially ordered role hierarchy;
- $user : S \to U$. Function associating every session to the user that generated it;
- $eSR(s, t)$: function associating to each session s the enabled roles at time t such that:

$$eSR(s, t) = \{r \in R_I \mid (user(s), r) \in UA \wedge \\ \wedge (r \in ST(t) \wedge (r, user(s)) \notin ST(t)\}$$

where (EV, ST) is the execution model (Definition 24) that describes the system.
- $roles : S \to 2^R$. Function associating to each session the active roles. Given a session $s \in S$, it holds that:

$$\forall t \geq 0, \ r \in roles(s) \Leftrightarrow r \in eSR(s, t)$$

Given the model just defined, an access request should, intuitively, be allowed only if there exists a parametrized privilege (a) whose conditional expression is satisfied and (b) that is associated with a currently enabled role for the user who made the request. More formally, let $ar = \langle s, op, o \rangle$ be an access request generated at time t, where s is a session, op is an operation and o is an object; furthermore, let $perm(y)$ be the permissions associated with the role instance y. The model allows the right to execute the operation op over the object o if and only if the following holds:

$$(op, o) \in \bigcup_{y \in eSR(s,t)} \{(op, o) \mid \exists (op, oc, exp) \in Perm(y) \land$$

$$\land\, oc \in ObjCat(o) \land exp\}$$

9. PROXIMITY-BASED VISIBILITY

In the previous sections we have considered the case in which the event visibility was only related to the space hierarchy. In other words, whenever an event is defined, the administrator also defines the set of locations in which such an event is visible. There are cases, however, in which the event should reach a subset of users that are somehow "close" to the location in which the event has been generated. In this paper we will only present a case in which, informally, the notion of "closeness" corresponds to the one in which two users are close if they are in the same logical location. We stress, however, that other notions of "closeness" might be defined as well.

We present a concrete application scenario. We consider the case in which patients carry mobile monitoring devices that are able to (a) store the medical records of the patient and (b) generate alerts in case some medical emergencies, e.g., heart attack. Clearly the protection of the patient's medical record is a sensitive task that should be specified by a proper access policy. However, it is reasonable to assume that every patient would be willing to disclose her medical records *to every doctor in case of real medical emergency*.

In order to allow *whoever qualifies as a doctor* to access such information, we need to provide each such user with a minimal set of privileges that are usable even outside the logical location in which they are *usually* assumed to be used. This means that a user that belongs to the medical staff in some hospital, even if she is provided with "special" permissions within her institution, will also be provided with a set of minimal privileges that can be user *outside* her home institution. From the technological point of view, such type of definition assume the existence of a federation of institutions including all the hospitals and medical institutions in a given area[2]. We might, thus, imagine the existence of a generic role "Doctor", shared by all the institutions in the federation, with a set of minimal privileges.

Among the permissions associated with the role $Doctor\langle\rangle$ we might add the one of accessing the medical records of a patient in case of medical emergency. Notice, however, that such a simple solution relaxes too much the privacy constraints related to the medical records. Indeed, we need a way to specify that, in case of emergency, the patient's medical records should be released only to a doctor that is *close-by*. In other words, we need a way to *relax* the access policy while *binding* its applicability to some concept of physical closeness. In this way we do not release sensitive information to personnel that could not use it while, at the same time, we guarantee the maximum possible disclosure of the patient records to all the users that can save her life.

Let us assume $MedicalDevices \in OC$ be the category of objects containing the patients monitoring devices. Furthermore, let $MedicalEmergency \in E$ be the localized event generated a medical emergency. Let $p, q \in PL$. We define

---

[2]Clearly the need of a federation is due to the fact that it is impossible to think to a *unique* institution that employs all the doctors in a wide area.

the predicate $AreClose(p, q)$ to be true whenever p and q are close according to Definition 4. We might define the template $Doctor\langle\rangle$ as follows:

$$Doctor\langle ev \rangle = role($$
$$(read, MedicalDevice, ev = "MedicalEmergency" \land$$
$$MedicalDevice.Owner = generatedBy(ev) \land$$
$$AreClose(Eloc(ev), CurrentPosition)\})$$
$$)$$

The policy that every institution should implement, must ensure the preservation of such minimal role within the federation.

$$\langle (AnyPlace, AnyTime, MedicalEmergency),$$
$$\text{enable } Doctor\langle MedicalEmergency \rangle \rangle$$

10. PROTOTYPE IMPLEMENTATION

We implemented a prototype system for the specification and enforcement of ERBAC policies. Our prototype implementation is based on the XACML standard [19] for policy specification. We extended such standard to support event-based policies. We have evaluated three different implementation of XACML, Sun's XACML [19], XACML Enterprise [1] and XACML Light [2]. Among the available implementations, we have extended the open source java SUN's implementation XACML [19] since it has a modular and easily extendible architecture. Furthermore, as noted in [29], Sun's implementation, has a good trade-off between time needed to load policies and time needed to compute access decisions.

10.1 XACML Standard and extension

OASIS Standard [19] introduces both a standard for policy specification and the description of an architecture that could be implemented to enforce such policies. The core element in the architecture is the Policy Decision Point (PDP), that is responsible for access control decisions. This module communicates with other modules in the architecture for obtaining policy descriptions, context information and values of attributes. The PDP receives access requests and sends replies to the Policy Enforcement Point. The communication between the PDP and the PEP must be encoded using a *canonical form*, called the *XACML Context*

Every access policy can be seen, informally, as a set of *Rules*. A *Rule* is the basic element in the language and it is defined by the triple (*Target, Effect, Condition*), where the Target identifies the circumstances to which the rule applies, the Effect specifies the outcome of the decision process Permit, Deny, Indeterminate, NotApplicable) and the Condition is a boolean expression over the set of attributes that can be used to further restrict the applicability of the rule.

XACML defines *Policies* as the set of rules that can be applied to the same Target, along with a specification of the algorithm for composing the effect of different rules in case more than one is applicable, e.g., permit overrides deny. Furthermore, a policy might include a set of obligations, i.e., operations that should be enforce by the PEP in conjunction with the authorisation decision. A Policy set is, informally, a set of policies. In [18] the OASIS consortium provides a profile for specifying RBAC policies using XACML. Roles and permissions specifications are obtained by two distinct Policy Sets. The Permission Policy Set (or PPS) is used to define a set of permission. A Role Policy Set (RPS) is a policy set associating the holder of a given role to the

PPS containing the associated permissions. The Target of an RPS limits the set of subjects to which the role can be assigned. Finally a RPS can reference only a single PPS. A Role Assignment policy or policy set defines the association of users to roles. Notice that each PPS or RPS is astatic object uniquely identified by a Uniform Resource Identifier (URI).

In order to allow the write-up of policies based on STE-Conditions we needed to extend XACML standard [19] by defining new data types and functions that are needed to process the new types.

For spatial conditions we need to be able to represent physical locations, logical locations and location types. Logical locations and location types can be represented as strings. A more complex representation is required tfor physical locations. In this case we need a way of representing coordinates and, more generally, geometrical shapes in two-three dimensional spaces. For these reasons we decided to adopt GeoXACML [20], an extension of the XACML standard by the OpenGIS Consortium. GeoXACML provides the possibility of describing arbitrary geometric shapes starting from the following base types:Point, LineString, Polygon, MultiPoint (a set of points), MultiLine(a set of LineString) and Multi-Polygon (a collection of Polygon). The XACML schema is extended to allow the possibility of describing such new type of geometries by means of an extension of XML, known as Geography Markup Language (GML).

As for temporal conditions we needed to introduce a new data type in order to represent periodic expressions. The pair (I, P) is represented as follows: The interval I is defined as the pair of its endpoints. Furthermore, we have defined the basic calendars Hours, Days, Weeks, Months and Years used to specify periodic expressions. Finally event are represented by means of strings. For each data type we defined the function needed to operate on it.

The representation of role templates in XACML using RPS and PPS is not immediate. The basic reason is that a role template is essentially a parametric role and, thus, it is not sufficient to define a new static object to represent it. Furthermore, a role instance is defined by assigning specific values to each role parameter. for this reason it is, in principle, impossible to define all possible role instance *a priori*. A second problem arises from the fact that the variables that are used to define parametrized privileges must be a subset of the variables of the role template that contains it. For this reason we extended the XACML grammar in order to identify the variables in the role instance definition in order to use them in the instantiation process.

10.2 XACML Syntax Extension

In this section we briefly describe the XACML extension we have implemented in our prototype. A role template is defined as follows:

```
<Attribute>
  <AttributeValue DataType="urn:my:dataType:role">
    <RoleName>string</RoleName>
    <RoleParams [number=int]>
      {<Param Name=String DataType=type>value</Param>}
    </RoleParams>
  </AttributeValue>
</Attribute>
```

The *number* parameter indicates the number of free variables in the template. Furthermore, the *value* parameter,

one for each free variable, is required for role instances but is omitted for role tempates.

The data type used for periodic expressions is as follows:

```
<AttributeValue DataType="urn:my:periodic-expression"
              [TimeZone=String]>
  [<Interval [DateFormat=String]>
    <Start></Start>
    <End></End>
  </Interval>]
  [{<PeriodicExp>
    <CalendarStart Type=String>s1-e1,s2-e2,...
                                  </CalendarStart>
    {<CalendarStart Type=String>...</CalendarStart>}
    <CalendarLength Type=String>int</CalendarLength>
  </PeriodicExp>]
</AttributeValue>
```

In the above definition, the available calendar types are Years, Months, Weeks, Days, Hours and we denote an interval of indices by `si-ei`.

We have defined a number of functions for managing the new conditions. More specifically, we have defined the following functions:

- urn:my:function:spatial:point-within-location-logical takes as inputs a logical location and a point and checks if the point belongs to the logical location.
- urn:my:function:spatial:point-within-location-type takes as inputs a location type and a point and checks if the point belongs to some logical location of the specified type;
- urn:my:function:role:is-instance takes as inputs a template T and an instance I and checks whether I is a proper instance of T;
- urn:my:function:role:is-instance takes as inputs two instances I_1 and I_2 and checks if they are instances of the same template.
- urn:my:function:time:inside takes as inputs a date D and a periodic expression P and checks if $D \in Sol(P)$.
- urn:my:function:event:visible-at takes as inputs an event name, a point and a username and checks if the event is visible by the user at the specified point;
- urn:my:function:event:visible-in takes as inputs an event name, a logical location and a username and checks if the event is visible by the user at the specified logical location;
- urn:my:function:event:generated-by-and-visible-at takes as inputs a username U, an event name E, a logical location L and a username T and checks if E has been generated by U in location L and is visible by T.
- my:rule-combining-algorithm:deny-overrides, a rule combining algorithm evaluating the MostSpecific rule.

10.3 SUN XACML Extension

Our prototype implementation extends SUN's XACML [28]. In this paragraph we will discuss some implementation issues. Our work essentially consists in the extension of the PDP, i.e., the module that is responsible for policy decision. We have focussed our work on the issues related to context-dependent decisions, leaving out context-indepedent matters, e.g., triggers.

In our implementation we used the JTS [26] library. The implemented prototype supports *point* and *polygon* types, that are necessary to define the physical location of an object and logical locations. Location types are represented by means of directed graph in which an edge between types A

and B indicates that B is more specific than A. A *Location Handler* has been implemented in order to support the PDP in all decisions related to spatial conditions.

In order to make event management more flexible, we have defined an interface that every event must implement. In other words, every event must be associated by the administrator to a name and a priority and, optionally, to the user who generated it, the user to whom the event is addressed to and the location in which the event occurred. Given such information the *Event Handler* will be able to support the PDP in the decision process.

10.3.1 *Complexity considerations*

Since we have extended the Sun XACML implementation, all the considerations in [29] still hold. In particular, the time needed for policy parsing is still proportional to the size of the policies. What we are most interested in is evaluating the impact on running time of the new elements introduced in this paper. In particular, whenever more than one rule applies to the received access request, the PDP should compute the *most specific* context and apply the corresponding rule. On the other hand, finding the most specific rule the PDP needs to sort them using (a) the event expression priority, (b) the event priority and finally (c) spatial specificity, in this order. While the first two are immediate, the third test required a DFS over the graph representing location types. However, the probability with which an access request requires the discrimination of a high number of rules based on the spatial condition is low. Indeed, the Target in the XACML rule will be used to filter the rules in the policy. It is reasonable to assume that, for well designed policies, the number rules matching a given access request should be low.

Another operation that could heavily affect the running time is the need to retrieve all logical locations to which a given physical location belongs to (e.g., the user location). Such an operation clearly depends on the number of logical locations and, thus, on the complexity of the spatial hierarchy the system has to manage. Furthermore, the higher is the complexity of the polygon (i.e., the shape) that describes a logical location, the higher is the actual time needed to check containment. A naive way of performing such operation is to check if a given point belongs to each logical location in the hierarchy. Such strategy takes time that is linear in the (total) number of logical locations. In order to reduce the computational burden for this operation, we have implemented the following strategy. Each logical location is identified by a set of polygons. For each logical location we consider the smallest rectangle (aligned to two given axis) that includes all its polygons and we identify the two intervals on the x and y axis corresponding to the rectangle sides. We construct two interval trees, an X-tree and a Y-tree, each including the coordinates of all the identified intervals on the corresponding axis. Whenever we need to recover the logical locations including given physical location (x, y), we extract from the X-tree all rectangles having a side intersecting x and from the Y-tree all rectangles having a side intersecting y. At this point we compute the intersection of the two list of rectangles obtained so far, since every logical location containing (x, y) must belong to both list. We finally check all the polygons contained in the identified rectangles. In this way, by using the proper data structures [8], if the number of intervals containing x in the X-tree and y in the Y-tree are both $O(k)$, our strategy takes $O(k + \log n)$ time

instead of $O(n)$. Clearly, we need a $O(n \log n)$ time to build up the trees. However such time is required only during the start-up time.

10.3.2 *Performance Evaluation*

In real-life scenarios the system's response time clearly depends on a number of factors ranging from size of the access policy to the efficiency with which the devices provide the data they are required to deliver to the PDP. In this section we report the results of a set of preliminary tests aimed at evaluating the response time of the prototype. Our tests are meant to verify the usability of the provided prototype having in mind the need of scalability w.r.t. a number of variables. As stated before, our prototype at start-up loads and parses the files describing the access policy and the spatial hierarchy, building up in memory their internal representation that will be used during the evaluation of an access request. Although expensive, this first phase takes place only once.

Then we evaluated response time as a function of the number of different policies the system needs to manage. Specifically, following what has been done in [29], we have run tests wth $10, 100, 1000$ and 10000 different policies. All the policies have the same target and a single rule. In Figure 1 (left) we report the response time in our experiments. We have then evaluated a slightly different scenario. We evaluate the response time as function of the number of roles in the system with each role having 9 rules. In this scenario, the rules for each role are designed in a way to force the system to evaluate all of them for computing the "most specific" one. Figure 1 (right) reports the obtained results. As it can be seen by the figures, in all cases the (average) response time is well below half-second.

11. CONCLUSIONS AND FUTURE WORK

We introduced an extension of the TRBAC model supporting reactive policies that can be triggered by a wide range of environment-generated events. Spatio-temporal conditions are supported at different levels of abstractions by powerful constructs based on calendars and logical locations.

We extended XACML for specifying this kind of policies, then we implemented and tested a prototype that enriches the SUN-XACML implementation.

We are currently working on extending ERBAC in order to support role/permission delegation under event constraints.

As an interesting subject for further research we mention the definition of methods and algorithms for checking whether policies are safe.

12. REFERENCES

[1] XACML enterprise. http://code.google.com/p/enterprise-java-xacml/.
[2] XACML light. http://sourceforge.net/projects/xacmllight/.
[3] S. Aich, S. Mondal, S. Sural, and A. Majumdar. Role based access control with spatiotemporal context for mobile applications. In *Transactions on Computational Science IV*, volume 5430 of *LNCS*, pages 177–199. Springer, 2009.
[4] S. Aich, S. Sural, and A. Majumdar. STARBAC: Spatiotemporal role based access control. In

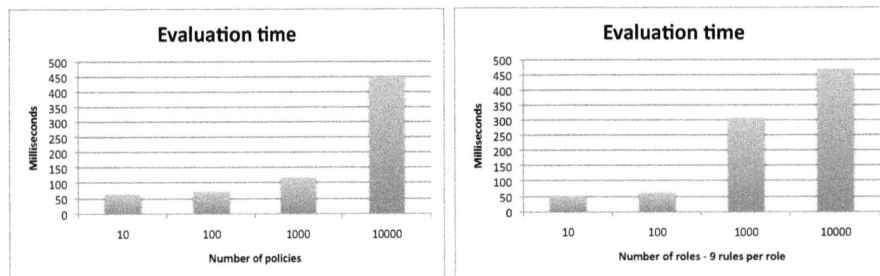

Figure 1: Evaluation time as function of (left) number of policies and (right) number of roles.

Proceedings of the 2007 OTM confederated international conference: CoopIS, DOA, ODBASE, GADA, and IS-Volume Part II, pages 1567–1582. Springer-Verlag, 2007.

[5] J. Bacon, K. Moody, and W. Yao. A model of OASIS role-based access control and its support for active security. *ACM Trans. Inf. Syst. Secur.*, 5(4):492–540, 2002.

[6] E. Bertino, C. Bettini, E. Ferrari, and P. Samarati. An access control model supporting periodicity constraints and temporal reasoning. *ACM Trans. Database Syst.*, 23(3):231–285, 1998.

[7] E. Bertino, P. A. Bonatti, and E. Ferrari. TRBAC: A temporal role-based access control model. *ACM Trans. Inf. Syst. Secur.*, 4:191–233, August 2001.

[8] T. H. Cormen, C. E. Leiserson, R. L. Rivest, and C. Stein. *Introduction to Algorithms (3. ed.)*. MIT Press, 2009.

[9] M. J. Covington, P. Fogla, Z. Zhan, and M. Ahamad. A context-aware security architecture for emerging applications. In *Proceedings of the 18th Annual Computer Security Applications Conference*, ACSAC '02, pages 249–, Washington, DC, USA, 2002. IEEE Computer Society.

[10] M. J. Covington, W. Long, S. Srinivasan, A. K. Dev, M. Ahamad, and G. D. Abowd. Securing context-aware applications using environment roles. In *Proceedings of the sixth ACM symposium on Access control models and technologies*, SACMAT '01, pages 10–20. ACM, 2001.

[11] M. L. Damiani, E. Bertino, B. Catania, and P. Perlasca. GEO-RBAC: A spatially aware RBAC. *ACM Trans. Inf. Syst. Secur.*, 10(1), 2007.

[12] D. F. Ferraiolo, R. S. Sandhu, S. I. Gavrila, D. R. Kuhn, and R. Chandramouli. Proposed NIST standard for role-based access control. *ACM Trans. Inf. Syst. Secur.*, 4(3):224–274, 2001.

[13] C. K. Georgiadis, I. Mavridis, G. Pangalos, and R. K. Thomas. Flexible team-based access control using contexts. In *SACMAT*, pages 21–27, 2001.

[14] L. Giuri and P. Iglio. Role templates for content-based access control. In *Second ACM Workshop on Role-Based Access Control*, pages 153–159, 1997.

[15] J. Joshi, E. Bertino, U. Latif, and A. Ghafoor. A generalized temporal role-based access control model. *IEEE Trans. Knowl. Data Eng.*, 17(1):4–23, 2005.

[16] D. Kulkarni and A. Tripathi. Context-aware role-based access control in pervasive computing systems. In *13th*

ACM Symposium on Access Control Models and Technologies (SACMAT 2008), pages 113–122, 2008.

[17] D. Kulkarni and A. R. Tripathi. A framework for programming robust context-aware applications. *IEEE Trans. Software Eng.*, 36(2):184–197, 2010.

[18] OASIS Consortium. Core and hierarchical role based access control (rbac) profile of xacml v2.0. http://docs.oasis-open.org/xacml/2.0/access_control-xacml-2.0-rbac-profile1-spec-os.pdf.

[19] OASIS Consortium. extensible access control markup language (XACML), v. 2.0.

[20] OpenGIS Consortium. Geospatial eXtensible Access Control Markup Language (GeoXACML) v 1.0. http://www.opengeospatial.org/standards/geoxacml.

[21] I. Ray, M. Kumar, and L. Yu. Lrbac: A location-aware role-based access control model. In A. Bagchi and V. Atluri, editors, *ICISS*, volume 4332 of *Lecture Notes in Computer Science*, pages 147–161. Springer, 2006.

[22] I. Ray and M. Toahchoodee. A spatio-temporal role-based access control model. In S. Barker and G.-J. Ahn, editors, *Data and Applications Security XXI*, volume 4602 of *Lecture Notes in Computer Science*, pages 211–226. Springer Berlin / Heidelberg, 2007.

[23] I. Ray and M. Toahchoodee. A spatio-temporal access control model supporting delegation for pervasive computing applications. *Trust, Privacy and Security in Digital Business*, pages 48–58, 2008.

[24] G. Sampemane, P. Naldurg, and R. H. Campbell. Access control for active spaces. In *Proceedings of the 18th Annual Computer Security Applications Conference*, ACSAC '02, pages 343–, Washington, DC, USA, 2002. IEEE Computer Society.

[25] R. S. Sandhu, E. J. Coyne, H. L. Feinstein, and C. E. Youman. Role-based access control models. *IEEE Computer*, 29(2):38–47, 1996.

[26] V. Solutions. JTS topology suite. http://www.vividsolutions.com/jts/jtshome.htm.

[27] M. Strembeck and G. Neumann. An integrated approach to engineer and enforce context constraints in rbac environments. *ACM Trans. Inf. Syst. Secur.*, 7(3):392–427, Aug. 2004.

[28] Sun Microsystems. Sun's xacml implementation. http://sunxacml.sourceforge.net.

[29] F. Turkmen and B. Crispo. Performance evaluation of XACML PDP implementations. In *Proceedings of the 2008 ACM workshop on Secure web services*, SWS '08, pages 37–44, New York, NY, USA, 2008. ACM.

Heuristic Safety Analysis of Access Control Models

Peter Amthor
Ilmenau University of
Technology
Germany
peter.amthor@tu-
ilmenau.de

Winfried E. Kühnhauser
Ilmenau University of
Technology
Germany
winfried.kuehnhauser@tu-
ilmenau.de

Anja Pölck
Ilmenau University of
Technology
Germany
anja.poelck@tu-
ilmenau.de

ABSTRACT

Model-based security engineering uses formal security models for specifying and analyzing access control systems. Tool-based model analysis encounters a fundamental difficulty here: on the one hand, real-world access control systems generally are quite large and complex and require models that have high expressive power. On the other hand, analysis of such models is often pestered by computational complexity or even non-decidability, making it difficult to devise algorithms for automated analysis tools.

One approach to this problem is to limiting the expressive power of the modeling calculus, resulting in restrictions to the spectrum of application scenarios that can be modeled. In this paper we propose a different approach: a heuristic-based method for analyzing the safety properties of access control models with full expressive power. Aiming at generality, the paper focuses on the lineage of HRU-style, automaton-based access control models that are fundamental for modeling the dynamic behavior of contemporary role-based or attribute-based access control systems.

The paper motivates a heuristics-based approach to model analysis, describes in detail a heuristic model safety analysis algorithm, and discusses its computational complexity. The algorithm is the core of a security model analysis tool within the context of a security policy engineering workbench; a formal description of major components of its heuristic-based symbolic model execution engine is given, and its capacity to analyze complex real-world access control systems is evaluated.

Categories and Subject Descriptors

D.4.6 [**Operating Systems**]: Security and Protection—*Access controls*; D.2.4 [**Software Engineering**]: Software/Program Verification—*Formal methods, Model checking*

Keywords

Security engineering, access control systems, access control models, model safety, symbolic model execution

1. INTRODUCTION

In the last decade, advances in systems security have evolved into new system paradigms that support the design, specification, and implementation of sophisticated security concepts. Systems with advanced security requirements increasingly apply problem-specific security policies for describing, analyzing, and implementing strategic security concepts, and policy-controlled operating systems emerge that are capable of directly supporting and enforcing security policies [LS01, WV03].

Due to their key role in defining, implementing, and enforcing strategic security concepts, security polices are extremely critical, and quality assets such as correctness or consistency are essential objectives in policy engineering. On the other hand, given the large amount of their responsibilities, experiences with policy-controlled systems point out that security policies usually are large and complex, rendering analyses and quality guarantees difficult.

In order to improve policy quality, model-based security engineering uses formal security models such as [BL73, HRU76, BN89, SCFY96, CS96, EK08] for analyzing and proving critical policy properties. In the domain of access control policies, a core objective is to study the proliferation of access rights. This problem was first formalized in HRU access control models in order to find proliferation boundaries and to prove that, for a given security model, these boundaries will never be crossed – a security property known as HRU safety. Unfortunately, safety analysis of automaton-based security models has always been constricted by its general non-decidability for a large class of powerful HRU-style access control models, rendering it difficult to devise algorithms for automated safety analysis tools. As a consequence, several safety-decidable fragments of the HRU calculus emerged [HR78, LS78, San92] that bought safety decidability by limiting the expressive power of the calculus. Unfortunately, these fragments generally have severe limitations in their ability to model the complex policies of contemporary real-world systems.

Our approach to model safety analysis fundamentally differs from these approaches. Instead of restricting model expressiveness, our safety analysis technique works on unrestricted access control models and aims at a practical method for dealing with the complexity of large real-world security models. We tackle the problem by a family of heuristic model analysis algorithms that exploit the fact that the safety problem is semi-decidable: once given two states of a model we may efficiently decide whether one state renders the other unsafe with respect to a given right. The core of the algorithm is to explore a model's state space by symbolic model execution, cutting through complexity using heuristic algorithms that exploit structural properties of a model's authorization scheme.

The paper motivates heuristic algorithms for safety analyses, describes the most efficient member of the family of heuristic algorithms we developed, provides formal descriptions of major components of a heuristic-based symbolic execution engine, and discusses its computational complexity. Aiming at generality, the paper focuses on the lineage of HRU-style, automaton-based access control models that are fundamental for modeling the dynamic behavior of contemporary role-based or attribute-based access control systems. An evaluation of the algorithm's performance as the core of a safety analysis tool within the framework of a security engineering workbench concludes the work.

2. MODEL SAFETY ANALYSIS

This section briefly recapitulates HRU security models and the HRU safety problem, discusses their role within this work, and motivates the use of heuristic algorithms for safety analysis.

2.1 HRU Security Models

HRU security models [HRU76] are among the most powerful and general access control security models to date. In order to model dynamic behavior of access control systems, HRU security models combine access control matrices [Lam74] with deterministic state machines. Each state of an HRU model reflects a single protection state of an access control system; state transitions are triggered by system-specific operations that modify this state. Security properties such as right proliferation now can be analyzed by observing state transitions caused by input sequences; in particular, the boundaries of right proliferation can be explored by state reachability analyses.

Right proliferation analysis focuses on a fundamental family of questions: Given some model state, is it possible that a specific subject ever may obtain a specific right with respect to a specific object? Or, in terms of model abstractions, given an access control matrix (ACM), is it ever possible that a specific right is written into a specific matrix cell? If this may happen, such a state is not considered *safe* with respect to that right. Precisely, a model state q is called *HRU-safe* with respect to a right r if there is no sequence of inputs that writes r into an ACM cell that in q did not contain r. A general answer to this family of questions provides fundamental insights on right proliferation in access control systems.

Formally, any HRU security model is a state machine (Q, Σ, δ, q_0) with a state set Q, an input alphabet Σ, a state transition function δ, and an initial state q_0. Each state $q \in Q$ is a triple (S_q, O_q, m_q) where S_q and O_q are the subject and object set of that state, and $m_q : S_q \times O_q \to 2^R$ is the state's ACM with a finite right set R. Model dynamics are defined by the transition function $\delta : Q \times \Sigma \to Q$ (called the model's *authorization scheme*) modeling the impact of application-specific operations on the model's state. As an example, a state transition effected by an operation *delegateReadRight* that allows the delegation of a right by a subject s_1 to a subject s_2 only the delegating subject already has this right is modeled by

$\delta(q, (delegateReadRight, s_1, s_2, o)) ::=$
   if $read\_right \in m_q(s_1, o)$ **then**
      enter $read\_right$ into $m_q(s_2, o)$
   fi.

In the original HRU papers [HRU75, HRU76], operations that affect the model state are called *commands* from a finite command set C. Commands may have parameters (e.g. s_1, s_2, and o) from the sets S and O. Thus the input set Σ is a tuple set $\Sigma = C \times (S \cup O)^k$, k denoting the maximum number of parameters in a model's command set.

Precisely, the state transition function δ of an HRU model is defined by a finite set of partial definitions where each definition specifies the parameters, conditions, and effect of a single command in C. In the example above, the condition $read\_right \in m_q(s_1, o)$ controls the execution of the command. If satisfied, $read\_right$ is entered into a matrix cell, effected by an operation *enter*, which is one of six HRU-specific primitive operations for modifying a model's state. Formally, any command $c \in C$ is defined by a tuple $(X, Cond, Body)$ consisting of

(1) the formal parameter vector $X \in (S \cup O)^k$

(2) the set of conditions *Cond* where each condition has the form $r \in m(s_i, o_j)$ where $s_i \in S, o_j \in O$ are elements in X and $r \in R$

(3) a sequence of HRU primitives *Body* where each primitive is from the set {enter r into $m(s_i, o_j)$, remove r from $m(s_i, o_j)$, create subject s_i, create object o_i, destroy subject s_i, destroy object o_i}, each primitive having the obvious effect.

2.2 The Role of HRU Models

HRU security models have been first to study the dynamic behavior of access control systems. They focus on the right proliferation problem and especially on the feasibility and computational complexity of the analysis itself. The model's basic abstractions (subjects, objects, ACMs) are aligned to the intended application area of HRU models (access control systems of operating systems) and match the needs at the time the model was devised (1975). From today's point of view, these abstractions are rather low-level, making it difficult to actually use the model for designing and managing contemporary real-world access control systems.

Contemporary access control models provide application-friendly abstractions such as roles (RBAC) or attributes (ABAC) and define access control rules based on classes of subjects and objects. The earlier of these models only provide a rather static view on an access control system (e.g. [SCFY96]), while more recent models continue the lineage of HRU models and use deterministic automata to model dynamic behavior [ZLN05, MSA09, SYGR11].

From a fundamental point of view, while high-level abstractions introduced e.g. by RBAC or ABAC models improve model usability and manageability, any such model can still be represented in the basic abstractions of a (larger and more complex) HRU model [KP11], in the same way that programs in high-level languages still can be (and are) represented in low-level machine language. Especially, high-level abstractions have no impact on the basic computational complexity of model analysis.

As a consequence and aiming at generality, the approach taken in this paper is to build the foundations of our work on HRU-style access control models the dynamic behavior of which is modeled by deterministic automatons and then proceed to apply the results to the more application-friendly abstractions of contemporary access control models.

2.3 The Role of Heuristics

Safety properties of HRU security models in general are undecidable. In other words, there is no algorithm that, given some arbitrary HRU model, will always terminate and tell us whether a given state is safe, rendering it difficult to devise algorithms for automated safety analysis tools. Because safety-decidable fragments of the HRU calculus generally have considerable limitations in their ability to model complex real-world policies, safety analysis tools based on restricted calculi have only a limited applicability.

A fundamentally different approach to safety analysis are heuristic search algorithms. Heuristic search algorithms exploit the fact that HRU safety is semi-decidable and try to prove that some given state q is *not* safe with respect to a right r by finding an input sequence that, starting in q leaks r into a matrix cell of some follow-up state q_{target}. To this end, each state reachable from q by a finite input sequence is checked whether r has leaked into a cell of its ACM. If such a target state is found, q is proven to be unsafe with respect to r, and the state sequence from q to q_{target} reflects an input sequence violating the safety property. As long as no such target state is found, the search continues.

Heuristic-based approaches trade accuracy for tractability. Especially, for models with infinite state spaces where all states actually are safe with respect to all rights, the problem's undecidability will render a heuristic search unsuccessful without the algorithm actually terminating with that result. On the other hand, valuable hints on model correctness are obtained if model analysts are pointed to unsafe states and input sequences that lead to in these states.

Starting with a state q the safety of which is to be analyzed heuristic-based search algorithms symbolically execute a model and assemble all encountered states into a state transition tree – a digraph (V, E), $V \subseteq Q$, $E \subseteq Q \times Q$, where each vertex q_i represents a state from the model's state space that is reachable from q by $\delta^*(q, a)$ (where δ^* is the successive application of δ to an input sequence $a \in \Sigma^*$), and any direct successor of q_i is a state $\delta(q_i, \alpha)$ where α is a single input from Σ (Fig. 1).

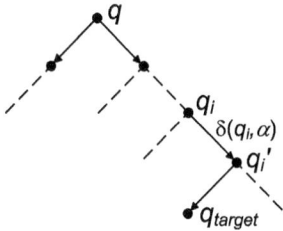

Figure 1: State Transition Tree

The challenge now is to restrict the rapidly growing state transition tree by a proper heuristic that channels its growth. Adding a new vertex q_i' to the tree corresponds to a state transition from q_i to $q_i' = \delta(q_i, \alpha)$; a heuristic thus has to decide which vertex q_i and which input α will be chosen for generating a follow-up vertex. An optimal choice of course will select q_i and α such that (q_i, q_i') is an edge on the path from q to the target state q_{target}. Because q_{target} is yet unknown, q_i and α are heuristically chosen.

3. HEURISTIC

For heuristic approaches to be successful the heuristic should be well-tailored to the specific problem to be solved. When building the state transition tree step-by-step, the challenge is to find model properties that have an impact on the probability of a state or an input to contribute to a path from q to q_{target}. As an example, for a right to be leaked into some matrix cell the conditions of a command entering this right must be satisfied. Because HRU authorization schemes do not check for the absence of rights, states with well-populated ACMs satisfy this condition with a higher probability and thus might be preferred.

In general, several model properties exist that provide such hints, and consequently, several heuristic metrics exist that combine into functions for selecting promising candidates for q_i and α, and many of them have been integrated in our security model engineering workbench WORSE. This section focuses on our most efficient heuristic that has become the core of the DEPSEARCH safety analysis algorithm; the section motivates the heuristic, infers appropri-

ate metrics, sketches their composition into a selection function for q_i and α, provides the formal definition of the DEPSEARCH algorithm, and discusses its computational complexity.

3.1 Heuristic Search Algorithms

Basically, the goal of each heuristic safety analysis algorithm is to find a command sequence that transits the model from a state q to a state q_{target}. The idea behind the DEPSEARCH heuristic is that hints for a successful command sequence can be mined from a model's authorization scheme. Because authorization schemes consist of a finite and usually manageable number of commands, this approach is fast and efficient.

The core of the DEPSEARCH heuristic is a recursive algorithm that gradually establishes necessary conditions for leaking some target right r_{target}. In the first step, the heuristic looks for commands in the authorization scheme that directly enter r_{target} into a matrix cell: if q is not safe with respect to r_{target}, at least one such command must exist, and the execution of at least one such command is a necessary condition for a leakage of r_{target}. Because a command in general is guarded by conditions, the presence of the rights of its condition in the ACM is necessary condition for its execution, and the process starts all over again with these rights added to the set of target rights, until we finally either encounter only commands that have no conditions at all, or we only have conditions that already are satisfied by the initial state q.

This recursive process assembles a command dependency graph (CDG, see Fig. 2) whose vertices are commands, and an edge from vertex c_1 to c_2 denotes that c_1 establishes at least one condition necessary for executing c_2. Each path to q_{target} reflects a command sequence where each command has a role in establishing necessary conditions for reaching q_{target}. Fig. 2 shows an example CDG generated from a small authorization scheme consisting of 5 commands $c_1...c_5$. c_5 is a command that enters the target right into a matrix cell, and c_1's conditions are already satisfied, either by q or by the fact that c_1 simply has no conditions; command c_2 for example has conditions that can be satisfied by the execution of either c_1 or c_4 or both.[1]

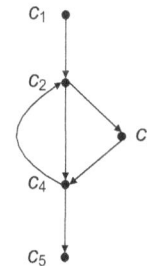

Figure 2: A Command Dependency Graph

Formally, a command dependency graph of an HRU access control model is a connected digraph $CDG = (V, E)$ where

$V = C \cup \{c_q, c_{target}\}$ where
  C is the set of commands in the model's authorization scheme
  c_q is a virtual command without any conditions that enters each right present in m_q

---

[1] Note that a CDG is the result of a *static* analysis and thus only can provide *necessary* conditions; whether a command also establishes sufficient conditions depends on the actual state of the ACM as well as on the commands parameters when a model is symbolically executed.

c_{target} is a virtual command without any primitives that requires the target right as a condition

$E \subseteq V \times V$ where $(c_i, c_j) \in E \Leftrightarrow$
$c_i.Prim.Enter.Rights \cap c_j.Cond.Rights \neq \emptyset$ where $c_i.Prim.Enter.Rights$ denotes the set of rights entered by the primitives of c_i, and $c_j.Cond.Rights$ denotes the rights needed to satisfy the conditions of c_j.

c_q and c_{target} are virtual commands that are added to a CDG for convenience of the command sequence generation algorithm (Alg. 2) discussed below.

Alg. 1 builds a CDG from the authorization scheme of a model. Starting with c_{target}, it recursively computes the predecessors of all vertices. The algorithm terminates when all those commands without conditions (vertices without incoming edges) are included in V for which a path to c_{target} exists.

Algorithm 1: Dependency Graph Assembly

Input: a model's authorization scheme C, a model state q (so that we can assemble c_q), a target right r_{target}
Output: a command dependency graph $CDG = (V, E)$

procedure predecessors(**in** $v \in V$)
$\quad | \quad P \leftarrow \{c | c \in C, c.Prim.Enter.Rights \cap v.Cond.Rights \neq \emptyset\}$;
$\quad | \quad$ **for** $c_i \in P$ **do**
$\quad | \quad | \quad$ **if** $c_i \notin V$ **then**
$\quad | \quad | \quad | \quad V \leftarrow V \cup \{c_i\}$;
$\quad | \quad | \quad | \quad$ predecessors(c_i);
$\quad | \quad | \quad E \leftarrow E \cup \{(c_i, v)\}$;

assemble virtual vertices c_q and c_{target};
$C \leftarrow C \cup \{c_q\}$;
$V \leftarrow \{c_{target}\}$;
$E \leftarrow \emptyset$;
predecessors(c_{target});

Before addressing the CDG's role in channeling the growth of the state transition tree let us first look at some of its properties.

- The existence of a path from a vertex with no incoming edges (e.g. c_1 in Fig. 2) to c_{target} is a necessary condition for q to not be safe. It is by no means sufficient, because the CDG is the result of a static analysis, and only the parameters of a command at runtime determine its actual effect. A path $c_q, c_1, c_2, ..., c_{target}$ only tells us that a command sequence $c_q, c_1^+, c_2^+, ..., c_{target}$ (where c_i^+ denotes the at-least-once execution of c_i) has the *potential* to leak r_{target}.

- Paths may contain cycles; these must not be ignored, because multiple runs of the same cycle may result in different rights being entered into different matrix cells; e.g. in Fig. 2 with cycles c_2, c_4, c_2 and c_2, c_3, c_4, c_2 we only know that a successful command sequence has the pattern $c_1^+, [c_2^+, [c_4^+ | c_3^+, c_4^+],]^+ c_5^+$.

- If a command sequence is found that actually leaks r_{target} and this sequence matches the shortest path in the CDG from c_q to c_{target}, then this is the shortest existing sequence.

Based on these properties, the DEPSEARCH heuristic makes three fundamental assumptions.

1st Assumption. Command sequences that have the property of establishing necessary conditions for a right leakage are more promising in comparison to arbitrary sequences without this property. Consequently, the DEPSEARCH heuristic chooses command sequences that are paths in the CDG, beginning at a node without incoming edges (meaning that all conditions of this command are already met) and ending at a node that has an edge to c_{target}. Such a path $c_1...c_n$ is then fed into the symbolic execution engine that updates the state transition tree by executing model transitions $\delta(q, c_1, x_1) = q_1, \delta(q_1, c_2, x_2) = q_2, ..., \delta(q_{n-1}, c_n, x_n) = q_n$, registering all states q_i as a single branch in the state transition tree (we will discuss the command parameters x_i below).
If q_{target} (any state where r_{target} has leaked into a matrix cell) is found, a command sequence was found that leaked r_{target}, and q is proved to not be safe with respect to r_{target}. Otherwise, we proceed with a new command sequence by generating a new path from the CDG.

2nd Assumption. If a command sequence was used once, the probability that a second execution of the same sequence will establish additional necessary condition decreases. Consequently, each path generation in the CDG decreases the probability that the same path will be generated again. Especially, each run of a cycle decreases the probability of a second run.
Generating different paths follows the idea of ant algorithms, although in a variation where the scent of an edge acts repelling. Scent is implemented by an edge attribute (*flavor* in Alg. 2) where the flavor of an edge is incremented whenever it is used in a path. Thus paths are always minimal with respect to the accumulated scent of its edges. Scent minimality enforces path diversity, dealing with the situation that commands can have conditions that can only be satisfied by prior execution of two or more different commands (advertised by more than one incoming edges in the CDG).

3rd Assumption. If the same path is used more than once, then a modification of the command's parameters improves the probability that the same path will establish new necessary conditions. Consequently, the DEPSEARCH algorithm outlined in Alg. 3 modifies the command parameters in each run.

These three assumptions have been combined into a path generation algorithm outlined in Alg. 2.

Algorithm 2: CDG Path Generation

Input: a CDG as generated by Alg. 1, c_{target}
Output: a path in the CDG, represented as a sequence of vertices; a modified CDG where all edges of this path have a stronger flavor

$currentVertex \leftarrow c_{target}$;
$path \leftarrow currentVertex$;
repeat
$\quad | \quad edge \leftarrow$ lowestFlavor($currentVertex.incomingEdges$);
$\quad | \quad currentVertex \leftarrow edge.origin$;
$\quad | \quad path \leftarrow path + currentVertex$;
$\quad | \quad edge.flavor \leftarrow edge.flavor + 1$;
until $currentVertex.incomingEdges = \emptyset$;

3.2 The DEPSEARCH Algorithm

Starting at q, the DEPSEARCH safety analysis algorithm explores the state space of a model in order to find a state where r_{target} has leaked into some matrix cell. The growth of the state transition tree is channeled by generating command sequences that gradually establish necessary conditions for the model to reach q_{target}. Command sequences repeatedly are generated according to the heuristic discussed in section 3.1 by Alg. 2.

Algorithm 3: DEPSEARCH Algorithm

Input: a model's authorization scheme C, a model state q, a
   target right r_{target}
Output: a state transition sequence STS that leaks r_{target}

$CDG \leftarrow$ DependencyGraphAssembly(C, q, r_{target});
$STS \leftarrow q$;

repeat
 | $path \leftarrow$ CDGPathGeneration(CDG, r_{target});
 | **while** $c \leftarrow path.next$ **do**
 | | $q \leftarrow \delta(q, c, s_{param}(q, c))$;
 | | $STS \leftarrow STS + q$;
until q contains right leakage;

Two problems remain to be addressed: termination conditions and the selection of a parameter vector for each state transition.

With respect to termination, the algorithm of course does not terminate if q is safe with respect to r_{target}. This problem will be addressed in the evaluation section 4.1. Selection of a parameter vector is discussed in the next section.

3.3 Command Parameter Selection

The problem of selecting a command's parameter vector is basically a constraint satisfaction problem [Lau78, JM94]. A constraint satisfaction problem (CSP) is a tuple (V, D, P) with a set of variables $V = (v_1, ..., v_k)$ each of which is instantiated in a particular domain $\in D = (D_1, ..., D_k)$ where D_i defines the range of value of v_i. P is a set of predicates defining constraints that the values of the variables must simultaneously satisfy. A solution of a CSP is an assignment of values to the variables which satisfies all constraints.

The problem of finding "good" parameters for a command can be modeled as a CSP by perceiving the set of formal parameters as the set V, the domains being either S_q or O_q (depending on the formal parameter being a subject or object), and the constraints defining restrictions on the variables such that only "good" values solve the CSP. Then, any one of the several well known CSP solving algorithms (e.g. AC-3 [Mac77]) can be applied.

Whether parameters are "good" or "bad" is decided by a heuristic metric that reflects the probability of a parameter vector to promote right leakages. As already argued in the introduction of this section, states with large numbers of rights generally provide better chances for right leakages. Given a state q, a command c, and a parameter vector x, this can easily be captured by a simple heuristic metric h_{param} comparing the number of rights in the matrices of q and q' where q' is the follow-up state of q obtained by $\delta(q, c, x)$. Thus $h_{param} : Q \times C \times (S \cup O)^k \to \mathbb{Z}$ is computed by

$$h_{param}(q, c, x) \mapsto$$
$$\sum_{(s,o) \in S_q' \times O_q'} |m_q'(s, o)| - \sum_{(s,o) \in S_q \times O_q} |m_q(s, o)| .$$

Parameter selection then is captured by a function $s_{param} : Q \times C \to (S \cup O)^k$ that is computed by a CSP solving algorithm where

$$s_{param}(q, c) \mapsto x \in (S_q \cup O_q)^k \quad \text{such that}$$

$$h_{param}(q, c, x) = \max_{z \in (S_q \cup O_q)^k} h_{param}(q, c, z) .$$

3.4 DEPSEARCH Summary

Concluding, we have presented a heuristic safety analysis algorithm for security models of the HRU automaton-based lineage.

The heuristic is based on static analysis of a model's authorization scheme, similar to the idea that led to the Bell/LaPadula basic security theorem for proving BLP model security [BL76].

Computational complexity of assembling the CDG is $O(n^2)$, where n is the number of commands in a model's authorization scheme. Generating a path in the CDG runs in $O(n)$, because due to the minimum scent of each path, eventual cycles occur at most once in a path. For selecting the parameters for a command execution we currently use a brute force approach running in $O(max(|S_q|, |O_q|)^p)$, where S_q and O_q are the subject and object sets in q, and p denotes the maximum number of parameters in a model's authorization scheme.

The DEPSEARCH heuristic originally was developed as a consequence of failures of earlier heuristics in analyzing atypical models where right leakages were well hidden and appeared only after long command sequences where each command depended exactly on the execution of its predecessor. For such models, DEPSEARCH has turned out to be quite successful, and its application to more regular models also demonstrated its superiority to earlier approaches.

4. EVALUATION

This section is an evaluation of the heuristic analysis approach and addresses to two major points: (i) practical feasibility in terms of runtime performance for analyzing real-world access control models and (ii) relative quality of the heuristic. Subject of the evaluation is the DEPSEARCH heuristic algorithm.

4.1 Evaluation Method

Practical feasibility is evaluated using two different model types: Role-based Access Control (RBAC) models demonstrate the analysis of a real-world scenario, and synthetic High-Dependency Models that maliciously are designed to stress-test the analysis with well-hidden right leaks. The RBAC models are based on a health care security policy and used to demonstrate the performance of the DEPSEARCH algorithm on a realistic authorization scheme. High-Dependency Models on the other hand will serve as a benchmark-test that imposes maximal calculation effort.

The relative quality of the DEPSEARCH algorithm is evaluated by comparing it with a randomized heuristic, a simple heuristic that does not exploit any specific model knowledge and that serves as a baseline. The same real-world and synthetic model types as mentioned above are used as test cases.

The basic test procedure is executing our DEPSEARCH implementation to find a specific right leakage. Therefore, randomly initialized ACMs have been generated for each model, featuring a increasing number of matrix cells. This way, we have covered the two main indicators of analysis performance in practice: general matrix size and authorization scheme complexity in terms of command dependencies.

The remainder of this section addresses the evaluation method: it describes the two model types and the RANDOM heuristic (4.1.1), the execution environment "WorSE" (4.1.2), and finally test conditions such as execution parameters and evaluation metrics (4.1.3).

4.1.1 Test Cases

RBAC Models.

The RBAC models used in this paper are generally based on a security policy of a real-world Health Information System (HIS) for an aged-care facility introduced by [EB04]. This policy was extended and rendered more precisely by [GRSY09, SYGR09, SYRG07] to develop a formal security model. We have enhanced this model by a state automaton along with an authorization scheme for modeling dynamic behavior of the policy. The result is an RBAC model based on [SFK00] with 20 roles, 15 commands in the authorization scheme, a role hierarchy, and separation-of-duty focusing on role exclusion.

When analyzing the dynamic behavior of RBAC models, two main questions are significant. (i) Given some model state, is it possible that a specific user is ever assigned a specific role? In terms of model abstractions, we have to analyze the behavior of the user-to-role assignment (UA) relation, which is a many-to-many relation between users and roles. More precisely, given a user-to-role assignment relation, we have to monitor whether a tuple (u, r) with a specific user u and a specific role r can under a given authorization scheme become an element in this relation. If this may happen, such a state is not considered *safe* with respect to that role. Analogously, the second question deals with the permission-to-role assignment (PA) relation, which is a many-to-many relation between roles and permissions: (ii) Given some model state, is it possible that a specific role is assigned a specific permission, i.e. a specific operation on a specific object? In this case, we call such a state not *safe* with respect to that operation. Both of these safety flavors are quite relevant in practice.

Since the DEPSEARCH algorithm focuses on HRU-style model abstractions, we rewrote the RBAC model in HRU style. In analogy to [SYRG07, SYSR06], we omit sessions because the above addressed safety properties are independent of sessions. Additionally, due to demonstration purposes, we adopt a simplified model where object attributes for mapping users to their objects, e.g. the electronic health record of a specific patient, are also omitted. This is reasonable because on the one hand it promotes unfogged evaluation results, and on the other it is no restriction to generality because object attributes may be reproduced by simply using the product set of objects and attributes. Result of this model rewriting are two HRU-type models *HIS I* and *HIS II*, each of which focusing on certain parts of the original RBAC model.

The HIS I model focuses on the user-to-role assignment and separation-of-duty based on role exclusion. Its state $q = (S_q, O_q, m_q)$ is described by the user set of the original RBAC model as the subject set S_q, the RBAC object set as O_q, and an ACM $m_q : S_q \times O_q \to 2^{roles}$ which maps a user-object-pair to a set of roles. Any command of the authorization scheme is then guarded by at least one condition of the following type: a user has to own a specific role for a specific object (cf. authorization scheme specification, section 2.1). The HIS I model implements role exclusion by negative roles: since conditions in HRU-like models cannot test the absence of rights in the ACM, we add one negative role for each role, that simulates its absence. Finally, for modeling the health care policy, our authorization scheme contains 7 commands that modify the user-to-role assignment of the original RBAC model under consideration of its role exclusion relation. Analyzing the HIS I with respect to HRU safety is then equivalent to analyzing the original model regarding RBAC safety flavor (i).

The HIS II model implements the permission-to-role assignment and the role hierarchy of the original model. As in HIS I, its state $q = (S_q, O_q, m_q)$ includes the object set of the original RBAC model O_q. S_q is now defined as the role set of the original RBAC model and the ACM $m_q : S_q \times O_q \to 2^{operations}$ maps a role-object-pair to a set of operations. The ACM hence exactly represents the PA relation of the original model, omitting the indirection level of permissions. The authorization scheme incorporates the role hierarchy relation by solving the level of indirections of PA, resulting in a HRU-like RBAC model with 7 commands. HRU safety analyses of the HIS II model equals the analysis of the original RBAC model regarding safety flavor (ii).

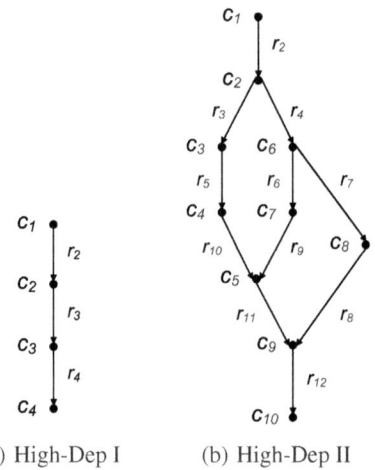

(a) High-Dep I   (b) High-Dep II

Figure 3: CDG of High-Dependency Models

High-Dependency Models.

As mentioned earlier, the motivation for the DEPSEARCH approach was to analyze a special case of access control models, featuring sequences of causally dependent commands that require each predecessor's execution to satisfy their conditions. Such models have proven to be a worst-case scenario for previous heuristic analysis approaches; they highlight a type of complexity that is effectively part of almost any real-world security policy. For this reason, two of these models will serve as an artificial benchmark-test to scale up this dimension of authorization scheme complexity. They are used to judge both feasibility in terms of absolute runtime as well as relative quality of DEPSEARCH compared to RANDOM.

The high-dependency models, referred to as High-Dep I and High-Dep II, are traditional HRU models, solely designed to incorporate many different command dependencies. Their initial state and authorization scheme implement the dependencies shown in Fig. 3: In High-Dep I, the target right r_5 is entered by command c_4. Each label of an edge (c_i, c_j) denotes a right that is entered by c_i and required by c_j; the initial state q_0 is chosen so that $\forall (s, o) \in S_0 \times O_0 : \{r_2, \dots, r_5\} \notin m_0(s, o)$ (apart from this, all matrix cells are initialized randomly based on a generic right set $R = \{r_1, \dots, r_{20}\}$). No command requires or enters more than one right out of $\{r_2, \dots, r_5\}$. High-Dep II is analogously constructed (target right r_{13}, leaked by c_{10}), just with the more complex dependencies shown by Fig. 3(b). Note that in case of our test models, each node of the CDG has to be visited at least once because none of the rights that impose the dependencies are present in the initial matrix. Therefore, a minimum number of state transitions is required to discover a right leakage.

Random Heuristic.

The RANDOM heuristic serves as a baseline to judge the performance of DEPSEARCH, since it uses a poor algorithm that requires zero knowledge about any part of the model. Its basic mode of operation is simple: it selects (i) a random state q from the state transition tree, (ii) a random command from the authorization scheme, and (iii) a random parameter vector $x \in (S_q \cup O_q)^k$. Each of these selections runs in $O(1)$, so each input set generation by RANDOM takes constant time.

Yet the runtime behavior of RANDOM is not uniformly distributed. While for a small initial matrix the brute force approach tends to be quite fast, for larger matrices it becomes increasingly unlikely to find a viable parameter vector that actually results in a state transition. However, since no heuristic knowledge about the model is used, there is of course no guarantee that even frequent state transitions gain progress towards finding the desired right leakage, so the overall success of this heuristic is largely random.

4.1.2 Execution Environment

The experimental evaluation of the DEPSEARCH heuristic is performed in the security policy engineering framework "WorSE". WorSE enables automated symbolic execution of access control models employing variable heuristic algorithms. This section outlines the WorSE implementation of the DEPSEARCH algorithm and its data structures.

The overall architecture of WorSE is module-based, featuring tools for different security engineering and analysis problems. The DEPSEARCH algorithm has been implemented as a module of the model safety analysis tool. At present, WorSE focuses on symbolic execution of HRU-type access control models. However, since our goal is to provide method and tool support for analyzing more up-to-date security models like role-based or attribute-based access control models, a symbolic model execution engine class (SMEE class) based on a generic deterministic state machine is implemented here. For evaluating the DEPSEARCH heuristic, we used a HRU automaton class derived from the SMEE class. The implementation of the algorithm itself is likewise derived from a heuristic base class[2] that allows for using and comparing different heuristics independent of the actual model. The model itself is a shared data structure accessible from both the SMEE and the heuristic, which basically contains the state transition tree and the authorization scheme.

Both the SMEE and the heuristic interact via a a tuple space, a flexible, anonymous communication architecture which allows for an easy integration of new SMEEs (such as for role-based models) and heuristics into WorSE. The interaction basically follows a simple pattern: Whenever the current heuristic is executed, it selects a particular state from the state transition tree, a command from the authorization scheme, and a parameter vector. This information is sent to the SMEE, eventually triggering a state transition, depending on the given combination of state, command, and parameters. Possible reasons for a failing state transition may be that conditions of the given command cannot be satisfied using the given state and parameter vector, or that primitives of the given command do not affect the given state at all (if it only enters rights that are already present in the matrix and/or only deletes rights that are not). If, on the other hand, a successful state transition has occurred, the follow-up state is inserted into the state transition tree (see section 2.3).

The result of the transition attempt is sent back to the heuristic that is then re-executed on the (possibly enhanced) state tree. Each of these iterations is called a *step*. Since a heuristic step does not necessarily trigger a transition to a new state, we distinguish those steps that actually do by calling them *effective* in the following.

WorSE is under ongoing development. Current work focuses on enhancing its analysis tool to support automaton-based access control models beyond HRU, such as dynamic RBAC models.

4.1.3 Test Conditions

All test models used for evaluation are not safe by construction, i.e. we will only analyze known-positive cases of the safety problem. However, due to its semi-decidable nature, our algorithm im-

plementation has to decide when to terminate without result based on a certain criterion. For this purpose, the overall number of heuristic steps is limited to a certain upper bound, called *step limit*, which is left to the user for the following reason: The concrete number of necessary steps heavily depends on the operation principle of a certain heuristic. With respect to a particular access control model, only a "model administrator" (who knows about the context and impact of the safety property of this model) can decide, how many steps are feasible to make a justified statement about safety using the given heuristic. For the purpose of this evaluation, we will define the step limit as part of an input configuration (see below). Due to the generally large number of heuristic steps performed by the RANDOM algorithm, all runs using this heuristic are assigned a step limit one order of magnitude greater than the corresponding run using DEPSEARCH.

Test Parameters.

The following parameters determine an input configuration of our test runs: Initial subject and object count ($|S_0|$ and $|O_0|$), ACM initialization (m_0), target right, and step limit. Here, the object count of the initial state and its respective matrix contents are varied, whereas the initial subject count is kept constant (since only the number of cells in the matrix impacts the behavior of both heuristics, not their layout). We used matrix dimensions starting from 20x20 and ending with 20x500, increasing in steps of 20 objects (i.e. 400 cells); the initial matrix contents are randomized using a fixed, model-specific right set R. Moreover, the target right (that *safety* is analyzed for) and the step limit are fixed, but also model-specific. In case of the step limit, values of 1,000,000 and 10,000,000 are used.

For each of these configurations, at least 10 successful runs per model have been performed (plus those aborted without result), with one exception: For the High-Dep II model, the RANDOM algorithm did not terminate within the steps limit for any input (including those featuring the smallest, 20x20 matrix). To this end, we did not include this model in our comparison of heuristics quality.

The WorSE framework is implemented in C++ under Ubuntu Linux 12.04. All runs were performed on contemporary desktop hardware (Intel Core i7-2600 3.4 GHz CPU, 16 GB RAM).

Metrics.

Three different measures are used in the following: Effective step count (ESC), effective step time (EST), and total runtime of a heuristic. The ESC measure is the total count of effective steps required to leak a target right, while EST is the average time required by a heuristic to make an effective step (including any ineffective steps within that time). For the feasibility criteria, we performed a straight-forward runtime comparison of the DEPSEARCH algorithm for both model types, that allows for educated performance estimations in a real-world analysis session regarding both average and worst-case runtime. The quality comparison with the RANDOM algorithm turns out to be slightly more difficult due to the fundamentally different operation of both heuristics. In addition to total runtime, we use the measures of ESC and EST here.

4.2 Evaluation Results

We will now discuss the results of the experimental evaluation with respect to feasible runtime performance and heuristic quality.

4.2.1 Feasible Runtime Performance

We compared the total runtime of the DEPSEARCH algorithm for all four access control models with matrix sizes from 20x20 to 20x500 cells. The results are shown in Fig. 4.

---

[2]Where a subclass for a concrete heuristic algorithm may hold its individual state, such as the CDG described in section 3.1.

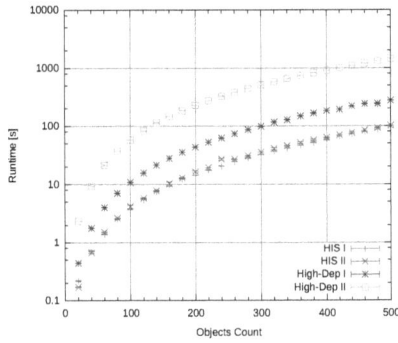

Figure 4: Runtime performance of the DEPSEARCH heuristic (error bars show standard deviation)

While still bound by the $O(n^4)$ complexity of parameter selection (cf. section 3.4), we argue that the absolute runtime behavior on the used, common hardware suggests reasonable feasibility in practice: Even for a worst-case in model complexity, illustrated by the High-Dep II model, the absolute runtime (up to several thousands of seconds) does not exceed the scale of a real-world analysis session. Also, it is observable that on both real-world models (HIS I and HIS II), DEPSEARCH does not show a significant difference in runtime behavior due to the common number of command dependencies (cf. "Minimal ESC" in Tab. 1).

However, one should bear in mind that we base the assessment of these numbers on two assumptions: (1) ACMs of several thousand cells are a realistic quantitative bound for most contemporary access control systems; (2) the complexity of real-world access control policies does not excess the degree of dependencies imposed by our High-Dep models (independent from application domain). Assumption 1 may be too strong in a traditional IBAC context, e.g. when analyzing a file system on Unix-permission level. However, according to our belief, it should be suitable in context of contemporary access control policies that are usually written on a much higher level of abstraction and thus also analyzed on that level. An example are policies based on an RBAC model, such as modeled by HIS I and HIS II. Assumption 2 appears legitimate, since the design of our High-Dep models (strict single-permission dependencies over several state-modifying operations in succession) is largely removed from realistic policy design goals and thus provides a reasonable upper bound for the degree of dependency imposed by current real-world access control policies.

Finally, it should be noted that our present implementation still leaves room for improvement in runtime performance. Besides this, current work focuses on an advanced heuristic parameter selection algorithm that may break this major drawback in runtime: One approach here is to weight the rights that are entered, exploiting already gathered information such as search path length or previously used matrix cells.

4.2.2 Heuristic Quality

For quality evaluation, we compared the DEPSEARCH performance with the RANDOM algorithm as a baseline.

Effective Step Quality.
Table 1 shows the mean ESC of both algorithms for each model, along with its standard deviation and the percentage of aborted runs. These values apply to all successful runs, since matrix size is not relevant here: The ESC value of both algorithms only depends on the model's authorization scheme.[3] To judge heuristic quality based on ESC, the ratio of minimal to mean ESC is given, called *effective step quality* (Q_{ESC}).

	HIS I	**HIS II**	**High-Dep I**	**High-Dep II**
Minimal ESC	2	2	4	10
RANDOM heuristic				
Mean ESC	136.3	143.6	10,758.9	–
Std. Dev.	134.4	138.8	9,570.3	–
Q_{ESC}	0.015	0.014	$\ll 0.01$	
Abort rate	0%	0%	21%	100%
DEPSEARCH heuristic				
Mean ESC	2.0	2.0	4.1	15.2
Std. Dev.	< 0.1	< 0.1	0.2	0.4
Q_{ESC}	0.984	0.981	0.973	0.658
Abort rate	0%	0%	0%	0%

Table 1: Mean ESC and effective step quality

As expected, the target-oriented DEPSEARCH approach only requires a fraction of the state transitions needed by RANDOM. More important, Q_{ESC} is nearly optimal for DEPSEARCH on all models but the most complex High-Dep II. This means that, judged by pure path length in the state transition tree, DEPSEARCH outperforms the brute-force approach even in the low-dependency models HIS I and HIS II by about two orders of magnitude.

With respect to the high-dependency models, it becomes clear that a zero-knowledge approach as employed by RANDOM is futile: As soon as authorization scheme complexity rises only slightly in terms of dependency, the ESC of this heuristic increases exponentially and, consequentially, so do total step count and runtime. This led to a 100% abort rate in case of the High-Dep II model, even under a step limit of 10,000,000.

Runtime Quality.
To evaluate the heuristic quality based on runtime performance, both EST and total runtime of DEPSEARCH and RANDOM were compared for each model. As mentioned above, the High-Dep II model could not be analyzed with the RANDOM heuristic under the given step limit and is thus excluded here.

Fig. 5 depicts a per-model comparison of DEPSEARCH and RANDOM heuristics regarding average EST. It can be noticed that the huge impact of DEPSEARCH on effective step quality does not equally reflect in per-step runtime: In case of both HIS models, DEPSEARCH EST largely exceeds that of RANDOM, which raises by magnitudes slower. Even in case of High-Dep I, where RANDOM features a Q_{ESC} several orders of magnitudes worse, the EST is on a comparable level here. This striking discrepancy is explainable with the parameter selection performance, that features $O(n^4)$ runtime (for a matrix size n) for DEPSEARCH, while the RANDOM approach requires constant time. This result emphasizes the importance to eliminate this algorithmic bottleneck in order to take full advantage of the efficient dependency-based path generation algorithm of the DEPSEARCH heuristic.

The average total runtime of both algorithms is compared in Fig. 6. Here, DEPSEARCH generally outperforms RANDOM. This

---

[3]Remember that, however, matrix size may influence the number of *total* steps of the RANDOM heuristic: With a rising number of subjects and objects, parameter vectors that do not satisfy all conditions of the selected command and thus produce ineffective steps become increasingly common.

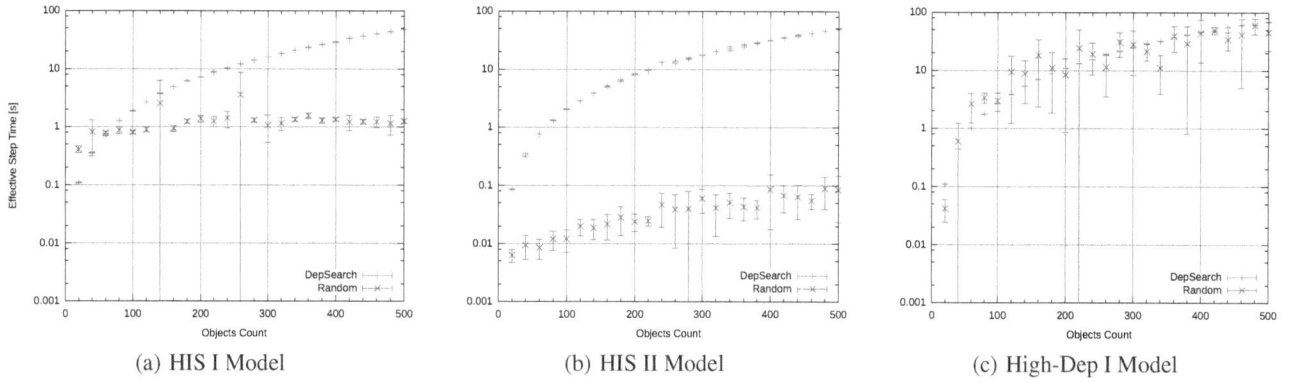

(a) HIS I Model   (b) HIS II Model   (c) High-Dep I Model

Figure 5: EST comparison of DEPSEARCH and RANDOM heuristics (error bars show standard deviation)

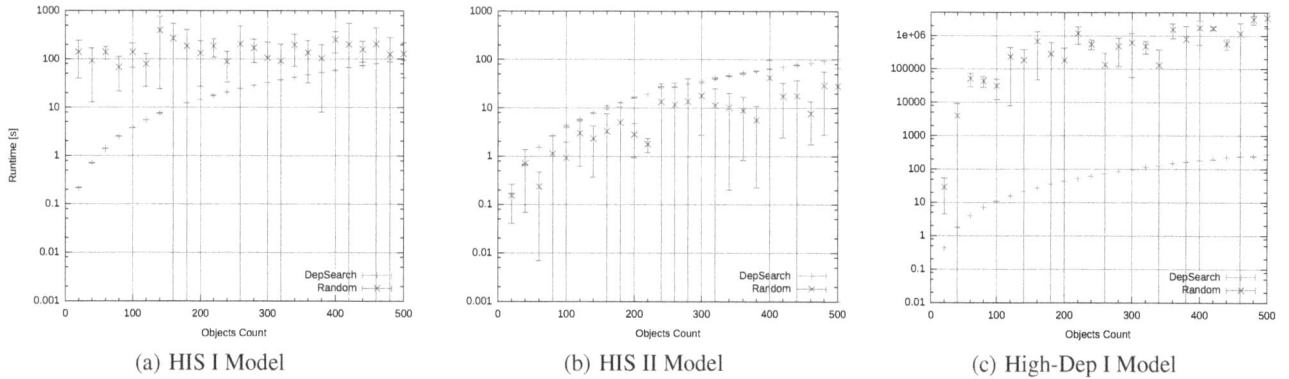

(a) HIS I Model   (b) HIS II Model   (c) High-Dep I Model

Figure 6: Runtime comparison of DEPSEARCH and RANDOM heuristics (error bars show standard deviation)

becomes especially clear in case of HIS I and High-Dep I, were the idea of a dependency-based path to approach a leaking state pays off. The brute force approach, in contrast, does not use any additional information to narrow down the state space; consequently, a heavily varying runtime with large standard deviations is observable. In accordance to the ESC evaluation, the High-Dep model shows again that a slight rise in authorization scheme complexity yields dramatic performance drops for the RANDOM approach.

As a side note, Fig. 6(b) illustrates a difference in model complexity between HIS I and HIS II that is not directly related to command dependencies: since HIS II commands include maximal 2 conditions (as opposed to 6 in HIS I), a notable improvement of EST is possible here for the probabilistic parameter selection of the RANDOM heuristic (cf. Fig. 5(b)). The DEPSEARCH heuristic on the other hand tries to minimize the number of steps by always selecting parameters that satisfy *all* conditions of the current command; consequently, average EST does not improve in the same extent.

A comparison of Figs. 5 and 6 emphasizes that pure throughput in triggering state transitions is not a crucial parameter for overall performance of the safety-analysis, while exploiting model-specific knowledge about structural properties of the authorization scheme and state components can lead to a significant increase in analysis quality.

5. RELATED WORK

Extensive research work has been done to develop methods that analyze specific properties of security policies. This work can be classified in several ways; in terms of analysis goals we distinguish between static and dynamic policy analyses.

Much work has focused on static analysis, which analyses a specific policy state with respect to some security requirements. For example, [NRN07] develops a deterministic heuristic using a flow logic approach. The authors have demonstrated their work by means of the Bell-LaPadula model, where the heuristic analyzes entity classifications against a policy's mandatory part. In case of policy violation, the heuristic suggests actions to reclassify specific entities such that the classifications become legitimate. On the other hand, [JZE03] has developed and implemented an analysis algorithm for access control models, which system administrators can apply for analyzing real-world policies, e.g. an SELinux policy, regarding incomplete or conflicting right assignments.

The appraoch in this paper focuses on dynamic policy analysis like [ZLN05, KN07, LT06, SYGR11, JGT+11, MSA09, AAR11]. The latter have in common that their analysis methods are developed for specific security models. For example, while [ZLN05] develops an HRU-style ABAC model and analyses the decidability of its safety problem, [LT06] deals with safety analysis for RBAC models. Following, others such as [SYGR11, JGT+11, MSA09, AAR11] have researched analysis methods for specialized variants of RBAC models. In [JGT+11], an iterative abstraction-refinement approach is used to perform symbolic execution and leakage search in administrative RBAC policies. As with our method, the algorithm cannot terminate with a "no leakage" result due to the semi-decidability of the reachability problem.

Most closely related to our DEPSEARCH heuristic is [SYGR11]. Here, the authors have developed an algorithm for analyzing user-role-reachability for parameterized administrative RBAC models. Just like DEPSEARCH, their algorithm contains two stages: The first stage performs a backward search from the goal to the initial state; the second stage runs a forward search from the initial state by limiting the search based on the results of the first stage [SYGR11]. Analogously, DEPSEARCH first generates the CDG, which is then used to limit the search by command sequences. The significant difference is that our heuristics have not been developed for a specific security model, but to analyze any automaton-based model and their respective safety problems.[4] This is also the reason why DEPSEARCH in general cannot prove the absence of a right leakage (policy *safety*). It should be noted that the algorithm in [SYGR11] achieves decidability under some conditions by exploiting specific properties of a model calculus more restrictive than general HRU. Thus, the termination issue with DEPSEARCH is part of the trade-off between accuracy and generality. However, our approach still leaves room for model-dependent tuning of the heuristic based on a more constrained authorization scheme, e.g. involving role hierarchies or separation-of-duty constraints.

6. CONCLUSIONS

This paper addresses the computational complexity problem of access control model safety analysis. The idea is to use heuristic analysis algorithms that exploit model-specific properties gained from a static analysis of a model's authorization scheme, resulting in necessary conditions for safety violations. These conditions then are used for restricting model input sequences that are fed into a symbolic model execution engine and guide the model to an unsafe state.

The paper focuses on the lineage of HRU-style, automaton-based access control models with sufficient power to model the dynamic behavior of real-world access control systems. The results provide the foundations for heuristic-based safety analysis of contemporary role-based or attribute-based access control models that integrate automatons to model their dynamic behavior.

There is a huge potential in static model-specific properties that still remains to be exploited. The effectiveness of the necessary conditions restricting the search paths will be fueled by models with constraints in the authorization scheme such as $RBAC_2$. For boosting the success of a search path, the command parameter selection algorithm can be furnished with a scheme that exploits hot spots in the ACM similar to the concept of working sets in virtual memory management algorithms. Then, in role-based or attribute-based models the focus of analysis goals can be narrowed down, distinguishing e.g. in RBAC models between role-safety, permission-safety, or session-safety, or in ABAC models between the safety of different attributes.

An implementation of the analysis heuristic was integrated into the security policy engineering framework "WorSE". Its evaluation points out that the approach allows for safety analysis in many practical cases.

7. REFERENCES

[AAR11]   Francesco Alberti, Alessandro Armando, and Silvio Ranise. Efficient Symbolic Automated Analysis of Administrative Attribute-based RBAC-Policies. In *Proc. 6th ACM Symposium on Information, Computer and Communications Security*, ASIACCS '11, pages 165–175, New York, NY, USA, 2011. ACM.

[BL73]   D. Elliott Bell and Leonard J. LaPadula. Secure Computer Systems: Mathematical Foundations (Vol.I). Technical Report AD 770 768, MITRE, Bedford, Massachusetts, November 1973.

[BL76]   D.E. Bell and L.J. LaPadula. Secure Computer System: Unified Exposition and Multics Interpretation. Technical Report AD-A023 588, MITRE, March 1976.

[BN89]   David F.C. Brewer and Michael J. Nash. The Chinese Wall Security Policy. In *Proc. IEEE Symposium on Security and Privacy*, pages 206–214. IEEE Press, May 1989.

[CS96]   Frédéric Cuppens and Claire Saurel. Specifying a Security Policy: A Case Study. In *Proc. Computer Security Foundations Workshop*, Kenmare, Ireland, 1996. IEEE Press.

[EB04]   Mark Evered and Serge Bögeholz. A Case Study in Access Control Requirements for a Health Information System. In *Proc. 2nd Workshop on Australasian Information Security, Conferences in Research and Practice in Information Technology, Vol. 32*, ACSW Frontiers '04, pages 53–61, Darlinghurst, Australia, Australia, 2004. Australian Computer Society, Inc.

[EK08]   Petros Efstathopoulos and Eddie Kohler. Manageable Fine-Grained Information Flow. In *Proc. 2008 EuroSys Conference*, pages 301–313. ACM SIGOPS, April 2008.

[GRSY09] Mikhail I. Gofman, C.R. Ramakrishnan, Scott D. Stoller, and Ping Yang. Parameterized RBAC and ARBAC Policies for a Small Health Care Facility. http://www.cs.stonybrook.edu/~stoller/parbac/healthcare.txt, 2009. [Online; accessed 24-August-2011].

[HR78]   Michael A. Harrison and Walter L. Ruzzo. Monotonic Protection Systems. In R. DeMillo, D. Dobkin, A. Jones, and R. Lipton, editors, *Foundations of Secure Computation*, pages 337–365. Academic Press, 1978.

[HRU75]   Michael A. Harrison, Walter L. Ruzzo, and Jeffrey D. Ullman. On Protection in Operating Systems. *Operating Systems Review, special issue for the 5th Symposium on Operating Systems Principles*, 9(5):14–24, November 1975.

[HRU76]   Michael A. Harrison, Walter L. Ruzzo, and Jeffrey D. Ullman. Protection in Operating Systems. *Communications of the ACM*, 19(8):461–471, August 1976.

[JGT+11] Karthick Jayaraman, Vijay Ganesh, Mahesh Tripunitara, Martin Rinard, and Steve Chapin. Automatic Error Finding in Access-Control Policies. In *Proceedings of the 18th ACM conference on Computer and communications security*, CCS '11, pages 163–174, New York, NY, USA, 2011. ACM.

[JM94]   Joxan Jaffar and Michael J. Maher. Constraint Logic Programming: a Survey. *Journal of Logic Programming*, 19/20:503–581, 1994.

[JZE03]   Trent Jaeger, Xiaolan Zhang, and Antony Edwards. Policy Management using Access Control Spaces. *ACM Transactions on Information and System Security*, 6:327–364, August 2003.

[KN07]   Eldgar Kleiner and Tom Newcomb. On the

---

[4] Note that the WorSE implementation focuses on HRU models basically to study the performance properties of a prototype.

Decidability of the Safety Problem for Access Control Policies. *Electronic Notes in Theoretical Computer Science (ENTCS)*, 185:107–120, July 2007.

[KP11]   Winfried E. Kühnhauser and Anja Pölck. Towards access control model engineering. In *Proc. 7th Int. Conf. on Information Systems Security*, ICISS'11, pages 379–382, Berlin, Heidelberg, 2011. Springer-Verlag.

[Lam74]   Butler W. Lampson. Protection. *Operating Systems Review*, 8(1):18–24, January 1974.

[Lau78]   Jean-Louis Lauriere. A Language and a Program for Stating and Solving Combinatorial Problems. *Artificial Intelligence*, 10(1):29–127, 1978.

[LS78]   R. Lipton and L. Snyder. On Synchronization and Security. In R. DeMillo, D. Dobkin, A. Jones, and R. Lipton, editors, *Foundations of Secure Computation*, pages 367–385. Academic Press, 1978.

[LS01]   Peter A. Loscocco and Stephen D. Smalley. Integrating Flexible Support for Security Policies into the Linux Operating System. In Clem Cole, editor, *2001 USENIX Annual Technical Conference*, pages 29–42, 2001.

[LT06]   Ninghui Li and Mahesh V. Tripunitara. Security Analysis in Role-Based Access Control. *ACM Transactions on Information and System Security (TISSEC)*, 9(4):391–420, November 2006.

[Mac77]   Alan K. Mackworth. Consistency in Networks of Relations. *Artificial Intelligence*, 8(1):99–118, 1977.

[MSA09]   Samrat Mondal, Shamik Sural, and Vijayalakshmi Atluri. Towards Formal Security Analysis of GTRBAC using Timed Automata. In *Proc. 14th ACM Symp. on Access Control Models and Technologies*, SACMAT '09, pages 33–42, New York, NY, USA, 2009. ACM.

[NRN07]   Flemming Nielson and Hanne Riis Nielson. Heuristics for Safety and Security Constraints. *Electron. Notes Theor. Comput. Sci.*, 172:523–543, 2007.

[San92]   Ravi S. Sandhu. The Typed Access Matrix Model. In *Proc. IEEE Symposium on Security and Privacy*, pages 122–136. IEEE, May 1992.

[SCFY96]   Ravi S. Sandhu, Edward J. Coyne, Hal L. Feinstein, and Charles E. Youman. Role-Based Access Control Models. *IEEE Computer*, 29(2):38–47, 1996.

[SFK00]   Ravi Sandhu, David Ferraiolo, and Richard Kuhn. The NIST Model for Role-Based Access Control: Towards a Unified Standard. In *Proc. 5th ACM Workshop on Role-Based Access Control*, pages 47–63, New York, NY, USA, 2000. ACM. ISBN 1-58113-259-X.

[SYGR09]   Scott D. Stoller, Ping Yang, Mikhail Gofman, and C. R. Ramakrishnan. Symbolic Reachability Analysis for Parameterized Administrative Role Based Access Control. In *Proc. 14th ACM Symposium on Access Control Models and Technologies*, SACMAT '09, pages 165–174, New York, NY, USA, 2009. ACM.

[SYGR11]   Scott D. Stoller, Ping Yang, Mikhail Gofman, and C. R. Ramakrishnan. Symbolic Reachability Analysis for Parameterized Administrative Role Based Access Control. *Computers & Security*, 30(2-3):148–164, 2011.

[SYRG07]   Scott D. Stoller, Ping Yang, C R. Ramakrishnan, and Mikhail I. Gofman. Efficient Policy Analysis for Administrative Role Based Access Control. In *Proc. 14th ACM Conference on Computer and Communications Security*, CCS '07, pages 445–455, New York, NY, USA, 2007. ACM.

[SYSR06]   Amit Sasturkar, Ping Yang, Scott D. Stoller, and C. R. Ramakrishnan. Policy Analysis for Administrative Role Based Access Control. In *Proc. 19th IEEE Workshop on Computer Security Foundations*, CSFW '06, pages 124–138, Washington, DC, USA, 2006. IEEE Computer Society.

[WV03]   Robert Watson and Chris Vance. The TrustedBSD MAC Framework: Extensible Kernel Access Control for FreeBSD 5.0. In *In USENIX Annual Technical Conference*, pages 285–296, 2003.

[ZLN05]   Xinwen Zhang, Yingjiu Li, and Divya Nalla. An Attribute-based Access Matrix Model. In *Proc. 2005 ACM Symposium on Applied Computing*, pages 359–363. ACM, 2005.

A White-Box Policy Analysis and its Efficient Implementation

Jayalakshmi Balasubramaniam   Philip W. L. Fong
Department of Computer Science
University of Calgary
Calgary, Alberta, Canada
{ jbalasub, pwlfong }@ucalgary.ca

ABSTRACT

In policy composition frameworks, such as XACML, composite policies can be formed by the application of policy composition algorithms (PCAs), which combine authorization decisions of component policies. Understanding the behaviour of composite policies is a non-trivial endeavour, but instrumental in the engineering of correct access control policies. Existing policy analyses take a black-box approach, in which the global behaviour of the composite policy is assessed. A black-box approach is useful for detecting the presence of erroneous behaviour, but not particularly useful for locating the source of the error.

In this work, we propose a white-box policy analysis, known as Decision in Context (DIC), that assesses the behaviour of component policies situated in a composite policy. We show that the DIC query can be applied to facilitate policy change impact analysis, break-glass reduction analysis, dead policy identification, as well as the pruning of redundant subpolicies. For generality, the DIC query is defined in an XACML-style policy composition framework that is agnostic of the underlying access control model. The DIC query is implemented via a reduction to either propositional satisfiability (SAT) or pseudo boolean satisfiability (PBS) instances, after which standard solvers can be invoked to complete the evaluation. Empirical analyses have been conducted to compare the relative efficiency of the SAT and PBS encodings. The latter is found to be a more effective encoding, especially for composite policies containing majority-voting PCAs.

Categories and Subject Descriptors

D.4.6 [**Security and Protection**]: Access Controls

General Terms

Security, Theory

Keywords

Policy analysis, white-box testing, change impact analysis, break-glass reduction, dead policy, policy pruning, policy composition, XACML, propositional satisfiability, pseudo boolean satisfiability

1. INTRODUCTION

A typical organization is divided into a number of work units. For example, a hospital has different departments, such as cardiology, neurology, anaesthetics, critical care, etc; a bank is composed of units such as legal, financial management, marketing, etc. Each work unit may have a different set of policies governing the disclosure and usage of data. In such an organizational setting, an access control system must (i) consult the policies of the many work units, and (ii) combine, weigh and prioritize their individual authorization decisions in order to reach a final authorization decision. This creates the need for a policy composition framework [25, 10, 26, 21, 8, 11]. A typical policy composition framework, such as XACML [25], offers policy combinators called Policy Combining Algorithms (PCAs) for constructing composite policies out of component policies. These PCAs specify procedures for harmonizing the potentially conflicting decisions of their component policies.

Being able to comprehend and assess the behaviour of a composite policy specified in a policy composition framework is both important and challenging. Important because the formulation of correct policy depends on it. Challenging because of the sheer size of organizational policies, as well as the fact that, in an organizational setting, components policies may undergo constant revisions motivated by changing organizational needs. Various policy analyses have been proposed to alleviate this need [14, 20, 29, 23, 24, 17, 19, 7, 22, 18, 10, 31].

Many of the previously proposed policy analyses [14, 17, 22, 10] are *black-box analyses*. They assess the global behaviour of a composite policy: e.g., under such and such a condition, would the composite policy return such and such authorization decisions? That is, the composite policy is seen as a black box, in the sense that the concern is on the global behaviour of the entire policy rather than the local behaviour of subpolicies.

Black-box analyses is important, as they help us identify any problematic behaviour of the composite policy. Yet they are not designed for locating the source of error: i.e., determining which subpolicy of the composite policy produces the error. To facilitate the location of error sources, we need analysis techniques that would assess the behaviour of subpolicies in the execution context of the composite policy. In other words, the composite policy is now seen as a white box. ***White-box analyses*** are analogous to debugging tools. It is the position of this work that we need to develop white-box policy analysis techniques.

Yet the behaviour of subpolicies are difficult to understand due to at least two reasons. First, realistic policy analysis frameworks offer PCAs that have procedural semantics. For example, the First-Applicable PCA of XACML may opportunistically terminate the evaluation of subpolicies when an applicable subpolicy is found. Reasoning about such behaviour is challenging. Second, a breed of PCAs known as majority-voting algorithms have not been given proper treatment in previous work on policy analyses [14, 17, 22, 10]. Inefficient implementation, by way of brute-force encoding, is usually adopted.

To bridge the above gaps, this work proposes a novel white-box policy analysis, as well as corresponding implementation techniques that can gracefully cope with the presence of majority-voting PCAs. Specifically, the contributions of this work are the following.

1. A new policy analysis, Decision in Context (DIC), has been proposed. The DIC analysis can be used for understanding the behaviour of a subpolicy that is situated within a composite policy, when the latter is being evaluated. Specifically, given a subpolicy contained within a composite policy, a DIC query determines (a) whether the subpolicy will be evaluated when the composite policy is evaluated, and (b) the potential authorization decisions that the subpolicy may return. The DIC analysis has a wide range of applications, including that of change impact analysis, reduction of breakglass accesses, dead policy identification, and complex policy pruning. The definition and applications of DIC analysis are discussed in §4.

2. The DIC analysis is defined in terms of a policy composition language called μ-XACML, which is a lightweight, idealized version of XACML 2.0 [25]. Defining DIC in terms of μ-XACML demonstrates that the analysis can be conducted against policy composition frameworks with complex policy combinators, including those that exhibit procedural characteristics as well as those that employ majority-voting schemes. This language is also independent of the choice of access control models, thereby rendering the DIC analysis widely applicable. Details of μ-XACML can be found in §3.

3. We demonstrate how the DIC query can be answered by a reduction to either propositional satisfiability (SAT) or pseudo boolean satisfiability (PBS) instances. While the SAT compilation is now a standard technique for implementing policy analyses, the application of PBS as an encoding technique is a novel contribution of this work. The motivation is to cope with the complexity introduced by majority-voting PCAs. A standard SAT-based compilation would lead to an exponential growth in encoding size, whereas a PBS encoding is much more compact. Details of these compilation can be found in §5 and §6. An empirical study for demonstrating the efficiency of the PBS encoding over the SAT encoding, especially in the presence of majority-voting PCAs, is reported in §7.

2. RELATED WORK

We compare our work to related research in three aspects: (i) policy composition frameworks, (ii) policy analysis and testing, and (iii) policy analysis implementation approaches.

2.1 Policy Composition Frameworks

D-Algebra [26] is an algebraic framework for policy composition. Algebraic operations have been designed for policy composition. A technique has been developed to convert tabular specification of policy combinators into D-Algebra functions. The framework is expressive enough for capturing standard PCAs of XACML. The algebra can also be interpreted in such a way to support majority voting.

The Policy Combining Language (PCL) [21] is another policy composition framework. The language has two variants: one for representing majority-voting PCAs, and the other for standard PCAs. Majority voting PCAs are specified using linear constraints on variables representing the number of policies returning a specific decision. Standard PCAs are represented as finite-state automata. PCL also handles obligations.

Bruns and Huth [10] base their policy composition language on Belnap Logic (a four-valued logic). The ***meet*** and ***join*** operators of the Belnap bilattice are taken as policy combinators. The language is capable of representing every possible four-valued functions (and thus all PCAs). The language is parameterized on abstract access control systems, which abstract away the idiosyncrasies of individual access control model.

The goal of this present work is not to innovate in the design of policy composition languages. Our policy composition language, μ-XACML, is designed only for capturing the essential complexity of XACML 2.0 [25]. It forms the basis for demonstrating the feasibility of defining the DIC analysis for realistic policy composition languages. We also borrowed the idea of abstract access control systems from [10], to render our work applicable to a wide range of access control models.

2.2 Policy Analysis and Testing

Various policy analyses have been proposed previously [20, 29, 24, 19, 7, 18, 31]. The following discusses the ones that are particularly related to the DIC analysis.

A number of types of policy analyses have been presented in [22]: analysis of information about the policy, analysis of information about the structure of the policy, analysis of the decisions returned by a policy, and analysis of the type of access requests to which the policy is applicable. They provide a method to determine, given requests satisfying a request predicate, whether a policy applicable to such requests can return a specific decision. They also provide techniques for analyzing the similarity between two policies.

Two kinds of policy analyses are considered in [10]. First, they provide a technique to determine if a policy returns a specific decision on at least one access request. Second, they provide techniques to compare two policies: (a) they provide a technique to determine whether a policy is more permissive than another policy, and (b) they determine policy similarity by determining whether two policies return the same access decision for all access requests, or, for all access requests that satisfy a request predicate.

Hughes and Bultan [17] compare the extent of similarity between two access control policies, by determining the number of access requests to which these policies are applicable.

Two kinds of policy analyses are proposed in [14] The first one determines whether an access control policy satisfies a safety property. The second is change impact analysis on two versions of a policy. Multi Terminal Binary Decision Diagrams (MTBDDs) [5, pages 392–422] are adopted for representing policies. The MTBDDs of the policy before and after change are combined to represent the change in behaviour. From this combined diagram, one can effectively determine the access requests for which the policy returns a different authorization decision before and after the change.

In [23], a mechanism has been devised to generate test cases for XACML policies. Each test case is a pair composed of an access request and an authorization decision. Each rule in a policy is examined in turn, to determine an access request for which the corresponding authorization decision is affected by that rule. Then, a new request-decision pair is introduced into the set of test cases.

All the above analyses (with the exception of [23]) are black-box analyses. A policy is analyzed based on either the type of access requests to which it is applicable, or the authorization decision that is returned for a specific access request. The position of this work is that assessing the behaviour of individual subpolicies is important during policy debugging. This work differs from all of the above in that it is possible for the policy analyst to examine the behaviour of a subpolicy situated within a composite policy.

2.3 Approach to Implement Policy Analyses

The policy analyses of [10] and [17] are realized by translating analysis instances to SAT instances. This approach produces SAT instances of exponential size in cases involving majority voting. In [14] and [22], change impact analysis is conducted by generating Multi-Terminal Binary Decision Diagrams (MTBDDs) to represent the difference between two policies. In our work, the DIC query is translated into either SAT or PBS instances. PBS is employed to produce a compact encoding for policies involving majority-voting PCAs, and we rely on state-of-the-art PBS solvers to solve PBS instance efficiently, or to convert an PBS instance to an optimized SAT instance [13]. To the best of our knowledge, our work is the first to implement policy analysis queries via a PBS encoding.

3. μ-XACML

Our proposed policy analysis will be specified in terms of a policy composition language called μ-XACML, which is a lightweight, idealized version of XACML 2.0 [25]. The goal here is not to capture the entirety of XACML. Instead, we want to demonstrate that, even in the presence of complex policy combinators such as XACML PCAs, which feature imperative characteristics as well as majority-voting schemes, our policy analysis can still be properly defined.

Following the approach of Bruns and Huth [10], the definition of μ-XACML is parameterized by abstract access control systems. The interface between an abstract access control system and the policy composition language takes the form of request predicates. By following this design, it allows the μ-XACML and the proposed policy analysis to be independent of the choice of the underlying access control models, thereby widening the applicability of the policy analysis.

3.1 Abstract Access Control System

An access control system S is a 4-tuple $\langle PS, R, RP, \Vdash \rangle$. PS is a set of **protection states**. R is a set of **requests**. RP is a set of **request predicates**. Typical members of PS, R and RP are denoted respectively by ps, r and rp. A request predicate rp describes a property of a request that is issued in a given protection state. Specifically, each pair (ps, r) either satisfies a request predicate rp, or not. The ternary relation $\Vdash \subseteq PS \times R \times RP$ specifies the semantics of a request predicate. We write $ps, r \Vdash rp$ whenever $(ps, r, rp) \in \Vdash$. Every state-request pair (ps, r) induces a variable assignment $\sigma_{ps,r} : RP \to \{0, 1\}$ such that $\sigma_{ps,r}(rp) = 1$ iff $ps, r \Vdash rp$. An access control system S is **uniform** iff, for every variable assignment $\sigma : RP \to \{0, 1\}$, there exists a state-request pair (ps, r) such that $\sigma_{ps,r} = \sigma$.

As one can easily see, the above notion of access control systems abstracts away the idiosyncrasy of individual access control model. So long as an access control model can be abstracted into a system of the above form, then our policy composition framework and policy analysis techniques will be applicable.

3.2 Policy Evaluation

The policy language μ-XACML offers syntax for specifying policy *expressions*. Each expression is evaluated against a state-request pair (ps, r). The result of evaluation is one of four **authorization decisions**. The decisions "**permit**" and "**deny**" have obvious meaning. The decision "**indeterminate**" is returned when a PCA fails to harmonize the conflicting decisions returned by its component policies. The decision "**not applicable**" is returned when a policy is not applicable for the given state-request pair. Let $DS = \{\mathbf{p}, \mathbf{d}, \mathbf{i}, \mathbf{n}\}$ be the set of authorization decision values.

3.3 Syntax

The abstract syntax of μ-XACML is given in the following context free grammar:

$$pol ::= \mathsf{permit} \mid \mathsf{deny} \mid con \to pol \mid pca(pol^+)$$
$$pca ::= \mathsf{po} \mid \mathsf{do} \mid \mathsf{fa} \mid \mathsf{oa} \mid \mathsf{smv} \mid \mathsf{amv} \mid \mathsf{spmv}$$
$$con ::= rp \mid \top \mid \bot$$

where $rp \in RP$ is a request predicate. The atomic policies permit and deny return fixed decision values. The conditional policy $con \to pol$ restricts the applicability of pol based on the satisfiability of the request predicate con. The PCA policy $pca(pol_1, \ldots, pol_k)$ combines the decisions of the subpolicies $pol_1, \ldots, pol_k$ using the PCA pca. Seven PCAs are supported in μ-XACML: (a) four standard XACML policy combining algorithms — permit-overrides (po), deny-overrides (do), first-applicable (fa), and only-applicable (oa); (b) three majority voting algorithms — simple majority voting (smv), absolute majority voting (amv), and super permit majority voting (spmv).

We write $vars(pol)$ to denote the set of request predicates appearing in policy pol.

3.4 Semantics and Derived Forms

The evaluation function $eval(\sigma, pol)$ returns the decision of policy pol when it is evaluated against the variable assignment σ. Its definition is given below.

- $eval(\sigma, \mathsf{permit}) = \mathbf{p}$.

- $eval(\sigma, \mathsf{deny}) = \mathbf{d}$.

- $eval(\sigma, con \to pol) = eval(\sigma, pol)$ if either $con = \top$, or $con = rp$ and $\sigma(rp) = 1$; otherwise, $eval(\sigma, con \to pol) = \mathbf{n}$.

The decision value returned by $eval(\sigma, pca(pol_1, \dots, pol_k))$ depends on pca.

- Case $pca = \mathsf{po}$: If $eval(\sigma, pol_i) = \mathbf{p}$ for some $1 \le i \le k$, then return $\mathbf{p}$. Otherwise, if $eval(\sigma, pol_i) = \mathbf{d}$ for some $1 \le i \le k$, then return $\mathbf{d}$. Otherwise, if $eval(\sigma, pol_i) = \mathbf{i}$ for some $1 \le i \le k$, then return $\mathbf{i}$. Otherwise, return $\mathbf{n}$. Operationally, the subpolicies pol_i are evaluated from left to right, and evaluation stops as soon as one of the subpolicies evaluates to a $\mathbf{p}$.

- Case $pca = \mathsf{do}$: Similar to the case of po, except that the order of precedence is: $\mathbf{d}, \mathbf{i}, \mathbf{p}, \mathbf{n}$.

- Case $pca = \mathsf{fa}$: If $eval(\sigma, pol_i) = \mathbf{n}$ for all $1 \le i \le k$, then return $\mathbf{n}$. Otherwise, let i be the smallest index for which (a) $eval(\sigma, pol_j) = \mathbf{n}$ for $1 \le j < i$, and (b) $eval(\sigma, pol_i) = v$, where $v \ne \mathbf{n}$. Return v. Operationally, the subpolicies pol_i are evaluated from left to right, and evaluation stops as soon as one of the subpolicies evaluates to a decision that is not $\mathbf{n}$.

- Case $pca = \mathsf{oa}$: If $eval(\sigma, pol_i) = v$ for some $1 \le i \le k$, where $v \in \{\mathbf{p}, \mathbf{d}\}$, but $eval(\sigma, pol_j) = \mathbf{n}$ for $j \ne i$, then return v. Otherwise, if $eval(\sigma, pol_i) = \mathbf{n}$ for all $1 \le i \le k$, then return $\mathbf{n}$. Otherwise, return $\mathbf{i}$. Operationally, all subpolicies pol_i are evaluated before the final decision is computed.

To articulate the decision value returned by the majority voting algorithms smv, amv and spmv, we define additional notation. We associate with each subpolicy pol_i and each decision value v a variable x_i^v, such that variable can take on a value of either 0 or 1, and $x_i^v = 1$ iff $eval(\sigma, pol_i) = v$.

- Case $pca = \mathsf{smv}$: If $\Sigma_{i=1}^k x_i^{\mathbf{p}} > \Sigma_{i=1}^k x_i^{\mathbf{d}}$, then return $\mathbf{p}$. If $\Sigma_{i=1}^k x_i^{\mathbf{d}} > \Sigma_{i=1}^k x_i^{\mathbf{p}}$, then return $\mathbf{d}$. If $\Sigma_{i=1}^k x_i^{\mathbf{n}} = k$, then return $\mathbf{n}$. Otherwise, return $\mathbf{i}$.

- Case $pca = \mathsf{amv}$: If $\Sigma_{i=1}^k x_i^{\mathbf{p}} \ge \lfloor k/2 \rfloor + 1$, then return $\mathbf{p}$. If $\Sigma_{i=1}^k x_i^{\mathbf{d}} \ge \lfloor k/2 \rfloor + 1$, then return $\mathbf{d}$. If $\Sigma_{i=1}^k x_i^{\mathbf{n}} = k$, then return $\mathbf{n}$. Otherwise, return $\mathbf{i}$.

- Case $pca = \mathsf{spmv}$: Similar to the case of amv, except that the threshold is $\lfloor 2k/3 \rfloor + 1$ rather than $\lfloor k/2 \rfloor + 1$.

Operationally, majority voting algorithms evaluate all their subpolicies pol_i before a final decision is computed.

We write $eval(ps, r, pol)$ to denote $eval(\sigma_{ps,r}, pol)$, that is, the evaluation of pol against the state-request pair (ps, r). We also define the following derived forms.

$$\mathsf{in} \overset{def}{=} \mathsf{oa}(\mathsf{permit}, \mathsf{deny}) \qquad \mathsf{na} \overset{def}{=} \bot \to \mathsf{permit}$$

The above derived forms essentially evaluate to the decision values $\mathbf{i}$ and $\mathbf{n}$ respectively.

3.5 Comparing with XACML

As disclaimed before, μ-XACML is never intended to capture the entirety of XACML. Instead, μ-XACML is designed to capture only the essential complexities of XACML so as to demonstrate that our policy analysis can be applied to realistic policy languages. We outline below the major ways in which μ-XACML deviates from XACML.

1. XACML feature rules, policies and policy sets. We flatten the hierarchy in μ-XACML, and consider only one syntactic category — policies. Therefore, we do not differentiate between rule combining algorithms and policy combining algorithms.

2. In XACML, applicability testing and decision combination are merged in a single construct (e.g., policy). In μ-XACML, we separate them into two constructs — conditional and PCA policies. This produces a more composeable and uniform language design.

3. In XACML, an indeterminate decision may be returned for two reasons: (a) a PCA fails to harmonize contradicting decisions of the component policies, or (b) an error occurs during the evaluation of a policy. In μ-XACML, we ignore possibility (b).

4. XACML supports dynamic retrieval of policies at the time of their evaluation, as well as the specification of obligations; μ-XACML supports neither.

4. DECISION IN CONTEXT

We define in this section a white-box policy analysis, Decision in Context (DIC), and showcase some useful applications of the analysis.

4.1 Preliminaries

We assume that policies are represented as abstract syntax trees (ASTs) [3] according to the grammar of §3.3. Subpolicies correspond to subtrees.

We further assume that every tree node is uniquely labelled within the AST. Thus, we identify a subpolicy by the label of the root of the corresponding subtree. We write $\mathsf{root}(pol)$ for the label of the root node of pol. Let l_1 and l_2 be the labels of two AST nodes. We write $l_1 \sqsubseteq l_2$ if l_1 is either l_2 or one of its descendants, and say that l_1 is a subpolicy of l_2. We write $l_1 \sqsubset l_2$ if $l_1 \sqsubseteq l_2$ and $l_1 \ne l_2$, and we say that l_1 is a **proper** subpolicy of l_2.

4.2 The DIC Query

An **atomic DIC query** has the form:

$$DIC(pol, l, ds)$$

where pol is a policy to be analyzed, l is the label of a subpolicy of pol, and ds is a *non-empty* subset of DS.

The above query is said to be **satisfied** by a variable assignment σ iff, during the evaluation of $eval(\sigma, pol)$, (a) the subpolicy referenced by l is recursively evaluated, and (b) the evaluation of this subpolicy returns one of the authorization decisions in ds. The query is said to be **satisfied** by a state-request pair (ps, r) iff it is satisfied by the variable assignment $\sigma_{ps,r}$. The query is **satisfiable** iff it is satisfied by some state-request pair. The query is **valid** iff it is satisfied by every state-request pair.

Note that, in order for a DIC query to be satisfied by a variable assignment, both conditions (a) and (b) must hold. That is, if a variable assignment fails to satisfy the DIC query, then either the subpolicy is not evaluated, or else its evaluation yields a decision value that is not in ds.

Condition (a) is significant because of the operational semantics of μ-XACML. Specifically, the conditional as well as the PCAs fa, po and do may not evaluate all its subpolicies due to its opportunistic semantics.

Note also that, in order for the DIC query to be well-formed, l must reference a subpolicy of pol. That is, if pol is itself a subpolicy of some bigger policy pol', and l references some subpolicy of pol' that is not a subpolicy of pol, then the DIC query is not well defined.

A **composite DIC query** is a boolean combination of atomic DIC queries:

$$q ::= DIC(pol, l, ds) \mid \neg q \mid q \vee q$$

The composite query $q_1 \vee q_2$ is satisfied by variable assignment σ iff σ satisfies either q_1 or q_2. The query $\neg q$ is satisfied by σ iff q is not satisfied by σ. The satisfaction of composite DIC queries by state-request pairs and the satisfiability and validity of composite DIC queries can be defined in a straightforward manner. Also, we define the derived form $q_1 \wedge q_2 \stackrel{def}{=} \neg(\neg q_1 \vee \neg q_2)$.

4.3 Applications

As a white-box policy analysis is like a debugger: it checks whether a subpolicy will be evaluated, and if so what decision values it will return. As such, the DIC query has a wide range of applications. The following are four examples.

4.3.1 Change Impact Analysis

Complex policies are prone to frequent changes. When the administrator adds new policy components, or remove or modify existing policy components, there is bound to be unanticipated changes to the behaviour of other policy components. DIC queries can be formulated to facilitate the effective identification of such unanticipated changes.

Suppose a policy pol_1 has been revised to pol_2. More specifically, the subpolicy l_1 in pol_1 has been revised into subpolicy l_2 in pol_2. We further suppose that the labels of the two ASTs are disjoint.

An policy analyst wishing to perform change impact analysis proceeds in two steps.

Step 1: Expansion or contraction of applicability.

Given a state-request pair (ps, r), a subpolicy l of policy pol is said to be **applicable** if the evaluation of $eval(ps, r, pol)$ results in the recursive evaluation of subpolicy l. The analyst begins by determining if the policy revision results in a change of applicability of l_1. If there has been an increase (resp. decrease) in the number of state-request pairs in which l_1 is applicable, then it is called an **expansion (resp. contraction) of applicability**. The analyst usually has a prior expectation of whether the revision should result in expansion or contraction of applicability for the target subpolicy. A DIC query can be formulated to confirm this expectation.

Consider the following atomic DIC queries:

$$q_1^{app} = DIC(pol_1, l_1, \{\mathbf{p}, \mathbf{d}, \mathbf{i}, \mathbf{n}\})$$
$$q_2^{app} = DIC(pol_2, l_2, \{\mathbf{p}, \mathbf{d}, \mathbf{i}, \mathbf{n}\})$$

There is no contraction of applicability iff $\neg q_1^{app} \vee q_2^{app}$ is valid. Actual expansion of applicability can then be confirmed by further checking that $q_2^{app} \wedge \neg q_1^{app}$ is satisfiable.

Similarly, there is no expansion of applicability iff $\neg q_2^{app} \vee q_1^{app}$ is valid. Actual contraction of applicability can then be confirmed by further verifying that $q_1^{app} \wedge \neg q_2^{app}$ is satisfiable.

Step 2: Change of authorization decision.

Once the policy analyst has determined whether the applicability of the target subpolicy has changed, he may wish to determine whether the decision returned by that subpolicy has changed between the old and new versions. The policy analyst usually has prior expectation on whether there is a change in authorization, or what the change should be like.

Suppose $q = DIC(pol, l, ds)$, where $\emptyset \subset ds \subseteq DS$. The **complement query** q^c is defined to be $DIC(pol, l, DS \setminus ds)$. Note that q^c is not equivalent to $\neg q$. The query q^c checks if there can ever be a case when subpolicy l is evaluated, but the evaluation returns a decision outside of ds.

Consider the following atomic DIC queries:

$$q_1^v = DIC(pol_1, l_1, \{v\}) \qquad q_2^v = DIC(pol_2, l_2, \{v\})$$

The DIC query $q_1^v \wedge (q_2^v)^c$ is satisfiable iff there is a case when both the old and new version of the target subpolicy are applicable, but the old version returns the decision v while the new version returns a different decision.

4.3.2 Break-Glass Reduction Analysis

In [4], Ardagna *et al.* introduced the concept of **policy spaces** for reducing the number of emergency accesses (aka break-glass accesses) made to healthcare information systems to access patient health records.

Policy spaces are partitions (i.e., disjoint subsets) of policies in an access control system. Four such policy spaces are described in [4]:

- The **positive authorization policy space**, denoted by ρ^+, is the set of policies that grant access under normal circumstances.

- The **negative authorization policy space**, denoted by ρ^-, consists of those policies denying access under normal circumstances.

- The **planned exception policy space**, denoted by ε^P, contains policies that grant access under known exceptional circumstances, which under normal circumstances will not be granted.

- The **unplanned exception policy space**, denoted by ε^U, contains a single policy that grants access to all access requests. This covers circumstances that do not satisfy the conditions stipulated in the other three policy spaces. This policy grants access with certain obligations such as logging and manual auditing.

Such a scheme can be modelled in our policy composition framework using the following policy:

$$\mathsf{fa}(\rho^+, \rho^-, \varepsilon^P, \varepsilon^U) \tag{1}$$

The atomic policy deny (resp. permit) is not allowed to appear in ρ^+ and ε^P (resp. ρ^-). The policy space ε^U is simply the atomic policy permit.

Ardagna *et al.* propose to reduce the occurrence of exceptions (requests to which access is granted by ε^P and ε^U) in the following ways: (1) by moving frequent applicable policies from ε^P to the policy spaces ρ^+ and ρ^-, and (2) adding new policies in ρ^+ and ρ^- that will capture the frequently applicable conditions under which requests are granted from ε^U (by reviewing access logs).

A policy analyst may want to verify that the two kinds of periodic policy updates advocated by Ardagna *et al.* actually achieve the intended effects. This can be summarized by the following.

before\after	ρ_{new}^+	ρ_{new}^-	ε_{new}^P	ε_{new}^U
ρ_{old}^+			$\times$	$\times$
ρ_{old}^-			$\times$	$\times$
ε_{old}^P	$\checkmark$	$\checkmark$		
ε_{old}^U	$\checkmark$	$\checkmark$		

A checkmark ($\checkmark$) indicates that we would like to see if there exists state-request pair in which the old version of either ε^P or ε^U is applicable, and the new version of either ρ^+ or ρ^- is applicable. This check gauges if the update produces actual benefits.

A cross ($\times$) indicates that we would like to ensure that there is no state-request pair in which the old version of either ρ^+ or ρ^- is applicable, but the new version of either ε^P or ε^U is applicable. This check ensures that the update produces no error.

Let pol_1 and pol_2 be the old and new version of the policy in (1). Let l_1^+, l_1^-, l_1^P, l_1^U, l_2^+, l_2^-, l_2^P and l_2^U be the labels of the four policy spaces in the two policy versions. Define the following DIC query:

$$q_i^j = DIC(pol_i, l_i^j, \{\mathbf{p}, \mathbf{d}, \mathbf{i}, \mathbf{n}\})$$

where $i \in \{1, 2\}$ and $j \in \{+, -, P, U\}$.

To gauge if there is any real benefit for the update, the policy analyst can test if the following is satisfiable: $q_1^i \wedge q_2^j$, where $i \in \{P, U\}$ and $j \in \{+, -\}$. To verify if there is no error produced by the update, the policy analyst can test if the following is valid: $\neg(q_1^i \wedge q_2^j)$, where $i \in \{+, -\}$ and $j \in \{P, U\}$.

4.3.3 Dead Policy Identification

Another application of the DIC query is in the identification of dead policies. By dead policies (analogous to dead code [3]) we refer to those subpolicies of a composite policy that are never evaluated. For example, in the policy $\mathsf{po}(pol_1, pol_2, pol_3)$, if, for every state-request pair, at least one of pol_1 and pol_2 evaluates to $\mathbf{p}$, then pol_3 is a dead policy. A dead policy may be accidentally produced as a by-product of policy revision, or it may reflect a design flaw. Once a dead policy has been identified, the composite policy can usually be simplified.

Formally, a subpolicy referenced by l is a dead policy iff the following DIC query is *not* satisfiable (i.e., its negation is valid):

$$DIC(pol, l, \{\mathbf{p}, \mathbf{d}, \mathbf{i}, \mathbf{n}\})$$

In a sizeable composite policy, the search for dead policies can be performed in a top-down manner. More specifically, the AST of the composite policy can be traversed in a pre-order fashion, and each node is checked to see if it is a dead policy.

4.3.4 Complex Policy Pruning

Another useful application of the DIC query is in determining the parts of the composite policy that can be pruned (to be replaced by simpler policies). Specifically, a subpolicy that always returns the same decision can be replaced by a constant policy (i.e., permit, deny, in, na). This is comparable to constant folding in compilers [3] as well as the policy tree pruning method in [11]. Again, the presence of such a subpolicy may be the result of policy revision or design flaw.

Suppose we are to check if the subpolicy l of policy pol always return the same decision v. This can be achieved by checking if the *complement* (§4.3.1) of $DIC(pol, l, \{v\})$ is *not* satisfiable (i.e., the negation of the complement is valid). When this is the case, we know that either l is not evaluated, or else its evaluation never yields any decision other than v.

Again, the search for subpolicies to prune can be performed in a top-down manner: i.e., the AST of the composite policy is traversed in a pre-order fashion.

4.4 Complexity

The satisfiability of DIC queries naturally induces a decision problem.

The DIC-SAT Problem Given a well-formed, atomic DIC query $DIC(pol, l, ds)$ of a uniform access control system, is the DIC query satisfiable?

THEOREM 1. *The DIC-SAT problem is NP complete.*

That DIC-SAT is in NP is elementary. The NP-hardness of DIC-SAT is demonstrated in Appendix A through a reduction from monotone one-in-three 3SAT [28].

5. REDUCTION TO SAT

To test the satisfiability of a DIC query, a standard implementation is to compile the DIC query into an equivalent propositional satisfiability (SAT) problem instance, and then employ a standard SAT solver to solve the SAT instance. We derived such a compilation algorithm, DIC2SAT, the design of which is the topic of this section. Our goal here is to outline the baseline implementation technique, and then point out its weakness in handling majority-voting PCAs, so as to prepare for the presentation of the alternative reduction in the next section.

5.1 The DIC2SAT Algorithm

We assume that the underlying access control system is uniform (that is, every variable assignment is realized by some state-request pair). §5.2 explains how this assumption can be relaxed.

The input and output of DIC2SAT is given below.

Input A policy pol, a label l, and a set ds of decision values, such that $DIC(pol, l, ds)$ is a well-formed DIC query.

Output A propositional formula ϕ such that $DIC(pol, l, ds)$ is satisfiable iff ϕ is satisfiable.

Specifically, the request predicates that appear in pol are taken as propositional variables in ϕ. Since the access control system is assumed to be uniform, the existence of a variable assignment that satisfies the DIC query implies that the DIC query is satisfiable.

5.2 Alternative Usages

The DIC2SAT algorithm can be used for testing the satisfiability of a composite DIC query. Suppose $q_1, \ldots, q_k$ are atomic DIC queries, and $f(q_1, \ldots, q_k)$ is a boolean combination of the atomic queries. Suppose further that ϕ_i is the SAT encoding of q_i (as returned by DIC2SAT). Then the satisfiability of $f(q_1, \ldots, q_k)$ (as a composite query) can be determined by testing the satisfiability of $f(\phi_1, \ldots, \phi_k)$ (as a propositional formula).

While the DIC2SAT algorithm can be applied directly to uniform systems, it can be easily adapted to handle non-uniform systems. Given a DIC query q, there may be dependencies among the truth values of the request predicates appearing in q, because not every variable assignment is realized by some state-request pair. In such cases, it is usually possible to capture these dependencies in a propositional formula ψ (because there can only be finitely many request predicates appearing in q). If DIC2SAT returns a formula ϕ, then we test the satisfiability of $\phi \wedge \psi$ to find out if q is satisfiable.

As an example, suppose resource predicates rp_1 and rp_2 respectively indicate if the resource being accessed is a departmental or university resource. Suppose further that every departmental resource is considered a university resource. Then we can capture this dependency by the propositional formula $\neg rp_1 \vee rp_2$. If DIC2SAT returns ϕ, then we test the satisfiability of $\phi \wedge (\neg rp_1 \vee rp_2)$.

Generalizing the above technique, one can actually perform what-if analysis using DIC2SAT. By what-if analysis, we mean to ask if a DIC query is satisfiable by specific kinds of state-request pairs for which certain conditions (expressed in terms of a boolean combination of some request predicates) hold. For example, "is this DIC query satisfiable if the requested resource is a university equipment but the user is not an academic staff?" Suppose the condition can be captured by a propositional formula ψ, and DIC2SAT converts the DIC query to ϕ, then we test the satisfiability of $\psi \wedge \phi$.

5.3 The Overall Structure of DIC2SAT

DIC2SAT is syntax directed. That is, given a policy pol, DIC2SAT performs case analysis to see which variant of policy pol is, based on the grammar of §3.3. If pol is atomic, DIC2SAT returns a simple propositional formula as the encoding of pol. If pol is composite, DIC2SAT recursively invokes itself to process the subpolicies, and then combines the returned formulas to build an encoding for pol.

The full pseudocode of the DIC2SAT algorithm is given in the companion technical report [6]. Here we illustrate how the algorithm behaves by listing the pseudocode for the case of conditional policy.

case $pol = rp \rightarrow pol'$:
  if $l = \mathsf{root}(pol)$ **then**
    if $\mathbf{n} \in ds$ **then**
      return $\neg rp \vee \mathrm{DIC2SAT}(pol', \mathsf{root}(pol'), ds)$;
    else
      return $rp \wedge \mathrm{DIC2SAT}(pol', \mathsf{root}(pol'), ds)$;
  else /* $l \sqsubset \mathsf{root}(pol)$ */
    return $rp \wedge \mathrm{DIC2SAT}(pol', l, ds)$;

We explain the intuition behind the pseudocode. The outer **if-then-else** indicates that there are two main cases: (1) the subpolicy l is pol itself, or (2) l is a proper subpolicy of pol. In case (1), subpolicy l is obviously evaluated when pol is evaluated. So the question is whether pol returns a member of ds. Now there are two subcases: (a) the decision $\mathbf{n}$ is one of the decisions in ds, or (b) otherwise. In subcase (a), there are two ways in which a member of ds is returned: either rp does not hold, and thus the conditional policy returns $\mathbf{n}$, or else the evaluation of the subpolicy pol'

yields a member of ds. In subcase (b), $\mathbf{n} \notin ds$, and thus the only way for a member of ds to be returned is when the condition rp holds, and also when the subpolicy pol' returns such a member.

In main case (2), l is a proper subpolicy of pol. We need rp to hold in order for pol' to be evaluated, and recursively we need subpolicy l to be evaluated to a member of ds when pol' is evaluated.

5.4 Compiling Standard PCAs

The compilation of the four standard PCAs is more involved. We illustrate this by considering the compilation of the first-applicable (fa) PCA.

We begin by defining some shorthands. Suppose $\langle pol_1, \ldots, pol_k \rangle$ is a sequence of policies, l is a label for which $l \sqsubseteq \mathsf{root}(pol_k)$, and ds is a non-empty set of decisions.

$$AllN(\langle pol_1, \ldots, pol_k \rangle) \stackrel{def}{=} \bigwedge_{i=1}^{k} \mathrm{DIC2SAT}(pol_i, \mathsf{root}(pol_i), \{\mathbf{n}\})$$

Intuitively, the formula $AllN(\langle pol_1, \ldots, pol_k \rangle)$ is satisfiable iff every pol_i evaluates to $\mathbf{n}$.

$$FA(\langle pol_1, \ldots, pol_k \rangle, l, ds) \stackrel{def}{=} AllN(\langle pol_1, \ldots, pol_{k-1} \rangle) \wedge \mathrm{DIC2SAT}(pol_k, l, ds)$$

Intuitively, the formula $FA(\langle pol_1, \ldots, pol_k \rangle, l, ds)$ is satisfiable iff (a) each of $pol_1, \ldots, pol_{k-1}$ evaluates to $\mathbf{n}$, and (b) subpolicy l of pol_k is evaluated to a decision in ds.

The compilation of fa is shown below:

case $pol = \mathsf{fa}(pol_1, \ldots, pol_k)$:
  if $l = \mathsf{root}(pol)$ **then**
    $\phi := \bot$;
    if $ds \cap \{\mathbf{p}, \mathbf{d}, \mathbf{i}\} \neq \emptyset$ **then**
      $\phi := \phi \vee \bigvee_{j=1}^{k} FA(\langle pol_1, \ldots, pol_j \rangle,$
                $\mathsf{root}(pol_j), ds \cap \{\mathbf{p}, \mathbf{d}, \mathbf{i}\})$;
    if $\mathbf{n} \in ds$ **then**
      $\phi := \phi \vee AllN(pol_1, \ldots, pol_k)$;
    return ϕ;
  else /* $l \sqsubset \mathsf{root}(pol)$ */
    let j be the index for which $l \sqsubseteq \mathsf{root}(pol_j)$;
    return $FA(\langle pol_1, \ldots, pol_j \rangle, l, ds)$;

The case handled by the **else** is easier to explain, so we start with that. In this case, l refers to a proper subpolicy of pol. So, l must be pointing to a subpolicy of one of $pol_1, \ldots, pol_k$. Let's say it is pointing to a subpolicy of pol_j. Then a simple invocation of $FA(\langle pol_1, \ldots, pol_j \rangle, l, ds)$ gives us exactly what we need.

In case l is referring to pol, the evaluation of l is guaranteed. We just need to ensure that the evaluation of pol returns a member of ds. The pseudocode initializes a formula ϕ to $\bot$ (the boolean constant false). The intention is that this formula will be a disjunction of further subformulas. As the construction progresses, more disjuncts will be put into the disjunction, and ϕ will be returned when the construction is complete. The first nested **if** builds disjuncts that account for pol returning a non-$\mathbf{n}$ member of ds. The second nested **if** builds disjuncts that account for pol returning $\mathbf{n}$ (in case the latter is a member of ds).

5.5 Compiling Majority Voting Algorithms

In [10], Bruns and Huth give a brute force SAT encoding of policies involving majority voting. The compilation techniques presented in the previous subsections can be applied to produce a brute-force compilation for the three majority-voting PCAs smv, amv and spmv. Rather than detailing the compilation here, we discuss below the problem of such an encoding.

Majority-voting PCAs consider the *number* of subpolicies returning a decision when a final decision is computed. Consider as an example the PCA policy $\mathsf{amv}(pol_1, \ldots, pol_n)$. A final decision of $\mathbf{p}$ is returned if at least $k = \lfloor \frac{n}{2} \rfloor + 1$ subpolicies return $\mathbf{p}$. A brute-force encoding will have to formulate a disjunction of k sub-formulas, with each sub-formula representing the condition under which one of the $\binom{n}{k}$ combinations of subpolicies return $\mathbf{p}$. So the size of the output formula produced by such an encoding will be at least $\binom{n}{k} = \Omega(2^{\frac{n}{2}})$.

The number of combinations that need to be generated by smv, amv and spmv are respectively $\Omega(2^n)$, $\Omega(2^{\frac{n}{2}})$ and $\Omega((\frac{3}{2})^{\frac{2 \times n}{3}})$. This exponential growth in the size of the output formula underlines the need for a more compact encoding of DIC satisfiability, a topic to which we now turn.

6. REDUCTION TO PBS

A more compact encoding of DIC satisfiability can by obtained by PBS. This section begins with an introduction of PBS, and then proceeds to present the compilation techniques behind our DIC2PBS compiler.

6.1 Pseudo Boolean Satisfiability

A *pseudo boolean variable* is an integer variable that can be assigned a value of 0 or 1. A (linear) *pseudo boolean constraint* has one of the following general forms.

$$a_1 y_1 + a_2 y_2 + \ldots + a_n y_n \leq b$$
$$a_1 y_1 + a_2 y_2 + \ldots + a_n y_n = b$$
$$a_1 y_1 + a_2 y_2 + \ldots + a_n y_n \geq b$$

where a_i's and b are integer constants, and y_i's are pseudo boolean variables. A *pseudo boolean constraint set* is a finite set of pseudo boolean constraints. An assignment of 0 or 1 to each variable appearing in the constraint set is called a *variable assignment*. If the variable assignment satisfies all the constraints in the constraint set, then it is a *solution* to the constraint set. A constraint set is *satisfiable* iff it has a solution. Pseudo boolean satisfiability (PBS), that is, deciding if a given pseudo boolean constraint set is satisfiable, is known to be NP complete.

6.2 The DIC2PBS Algorithm

We again assume that the underlying access control system is uniform. (Non-uniform systems can be handled in exactly the same way as discussed in §5.2.) We devised a compilation algorithm, DIC2PBS, that reduces a DIC satisfiability instance to a PBS instance. The request predicates in the DIC query appear as pseudo boolean variables in the PBS instance.

We define further notions before presenting DIC2PBS. Suppose CS is a *satisfiable* pseudo boolean constraint set, and x is a pseudo boolean variable that appears in CS. Then the pair (CS, x) is called an *instrumented constraint set*. That CS is satisfiable is already given; the question is whether there exists a solution to CS that assigns 1 to x. An instrumented constraint set is used for representing a boolean condition: the condition holds iff there exists a solution to CS such that x is set to 1.

The input and output of DIC2PBS is given below.

Input A policy pol, a label l, and a set ds of decision values, such that $DIC(pol, l, ds)$ is a well-formed DIC query.

Output An instrumented constraint set (CS, x) such that:

- The request predicates appearing in pol will appear in CS as pseudo boolean variables. Let RV be the set of variables in CS that correspond to request predicates. Let AV be the rest of variables in CS.

- $x \in AV$.

- Every variable assignment for the variables in RV can be extended to a solution of CS.

- Suppose σ is a variable assignment for the request predicates in pol. If σ satisfies the input DIC query, then every extension of σ to a solution of CS will assign 1 to x. If σ does not satisfy the input DIC query, then every extension of σ to a solution of CS will assign 0 to x. Consequently, the input DIC query is satisfiable iff there is a solution for CS for which x is set to 1.

Suppose the instrumented constraint set (CS, x) is returned by DIC2PBS. Consider the pseudo boolean constraint set $CS' = CS \cup \{x = 1\}$. The constraint set CS' is satisfiable iff the input DIC query is satisfiable.

6.3 Compiling Majority-Voting PCAs

To demonstrate the compactness of the PBS encoding, we here outline the compilation for the query $DIC(pol, l, ds)$, where:

- $pol = \mathsf{smv}(pol_1, \ldots, pol_n)$,

- $l = \mathsf{root}(pol)$, and

- $ds = \{\mathbf{p}\}$.

Recall that the simple majority voting PCA (smv) returns $\mathbf{p}$ iff the number of subpolicies returning $\mathbf{p}$ is strictly larger than the number of subpolicies returning $\mathbf{d}$. The compilation proceeds in three steps.

1. For $1 \leq i \leq n$, let $(CS_i^{\mathbf{p}}, x_i^{\mathbf{p}})$ be the return value of $DIC2PBS(pol_i, \mathsf{root}(pol_i), \{\mathbf{p}\})$. (That is, $(CS_i^{\mathbf{p}}, x_i^{\mathbf{p}})$ captures the condition that pol_i evaluates to $\mathbf{p}$.)

2. For $1 \leq i \leq n$, let $(CS_i^{\mathbf{d}}, x_i^{\mathbf{d}})$ be the return value of $DIC2PBS(pol_i, \mathsf{root}(pol_i), \{\mathbf{d}\})$. (That is, similar to Step 1, the variable $x_i^{\mathbf{d}}$ will assume the value 1 iff pol_i evaluates to $\mathbf{d}$.)

3. Return (CS, y), where y is a fresh variable, and CS is the union of the following three sets.

   (a) $CS_1^{\mathbf{p}} \cup \ldots \cup CS_n^{\mathbf{p}}$,

   (b) $CS_1^{\mathbf{d}} \cup \ldots \cup CS_n^{\mathbf{d}}$, and

(c) the set containing the following two constraints:

$$\sum_{i=1}^{n} x_i^{\mathsf{p}} - \sum_{i=1}^{n} x_i^{\mathsf{d}} \geq y + (1 - y) \times (-n) \quad (2)$$

$$\sum_{i=1}^{n} x_i^{\mathsf{p}} - \sum_{i=1}^{n} x_i^{\mathsf{d}} \leq y \times n \quad (3)$$

To understand Step 3, note that $\sum_{i=1}^{n} x_i^{\mathsf{p}}$ is the number of subpolicies returning $\mathbf{p}$, $\sum_{i=1}^{n} x_i^{\mathsf{d}}$ is the number of subpolicies returning $\mathbf{d}$, constraint (3) forces y to 1 when $\sum_{i=1}^{n} x_i^{\mathsf{p}} > \sum_{i=1}^{n} x_i^{\mathsf{d}}$, and constraint (2) forces y to 0 when $\sum_{i=1}^{n} x_i^{\mathsf{p}} \leq \sum_{i=1}^{n} x_i^{\mathsf{d}}$.

Note that the growth in size of the output is polynomial rather than exponential.

The compilation of other cases of majority-voting PCAs are similar. For details please consult the companion technical report [6].

6.4   Compiling the Rest of the Policy Language

While PBS provides a more compact encoding for majority-voting PCAs, the compilation strategy of DIC2SAT for conditional policies and standard PCA policies can be reused as is in DIC2PBS. The role of a propositional formula in DIC2SAT is now assumed by an instrumented constraint set in DIC2PBS. DIC2SAT constructs boolean combinations of formulas returned by recursive calls. Therefore, for DIC2PBS, we need a way to formulate instrumented constraint sets that express the conjunction, disjunction and negation of boolean conditions encoded as instrumented constraint sets.

In the following, we present two algorithms, *AtLeast* and *AtMost*, that can be used for encoding boolean combinations.

Suppose $\langle (CS_1, x_1), \ldots, (CS_n, x_n) \rangle$ is a *non-empty* sequence of instrumented constraint sets (with distinct variables $x_1, \ldots, x_n$). Suppose further than m is a *non-negative* integer. The function $AtLeast(\langle (CS_1, x_1), \ldots, (CS_n, x_n) \rangle, m)$ returns an instrumented constraint set (CS, y). The variable y is a fresh variable. The constraint set CS contains all the constraints in $CS_1 \cup CS_2 \cup \ldots CS_k$, plus the following two constraints.

$$\sum_{i=1}^{n} x_i \geq y \times m \quad (4)$$

$$\sum_{i=1}^{n} x_i \leq y \times n + (1 - y) \times (m - 1) \quad (5)$$

If $\sum_{i=1}^{n} x_i$ is at least m, then constraint (5) forces y to 1. If $\sum_{i=1}^{n} x_i$ is smaller than m, then constraint (4) forces y to 0.

The intention is that, if each instrumented constraint set (CS_i, x_i) represents a boolean condition, then the output (CS, y) expresses the boolean condition that at least m of the input variables (x_i) are set to 1. The *AtLeast* function can be used for encoding disjunction (with m set to 1) and conjunction (with m set to n).

We also devised a function *AtMost* for ensuring that no more than a certain number of conditions hold. This function can be used for encoding negation (with a single instrumented constraint set as input and with the threshold set to zero).

In summary, with the use of instrumented constraint sets, one can encode boolean combinations, and thus the rest of

the policy language can be compiled using exactly the same compilation strategy previously used in DIC2SAT.

7.   EMPIRICAL STUDY

This section reports an empirical study that was conducted to compare the relative efficiency of testing DIC satisfiability via the PBS encoding versus the SAT encoding.

7.1   Prototype Implementation

The DIC2SAT and DIC2PBS algorithms were implemented in respectively 2210 and 1949 lines of Java code, among which 1176 lines are shared between the two implementations.

The DIC2SAT implementation returns the abstract syntax tree of a propositional formula. It further performs a post-processing step to convert the generated formula into CNF form. This transformation is based on the Tseitin transformation [30]. The CNF formula is then fed to the MINISAT Solver [12, 2]. The MINISAT Solver is an open-source SAT solver implemented in C++. The conversion to CNF is necessary because MINISAT expects its input in CNF. The solver reports the satisfiability of its input, and the time in seconds taken to determine satisfiability.

The DIC2PBS implementation constructs an instrumented constraint set (CS, x) as specified in §6. It then passes the constraint set $CS \cup \{x = 1\}$ to the MINISAT+ Solver [13, 1], which is an open-source PBS solver implemented in C++. Again, the solver reports satisfiability and timing in seconds.

7.2   Experiment Setup

Overall Design.

Random instances of DIC queries were generated for various ranges of policy size. For each randomly generated DIC query, the aforementioned DIC2SAT and DIC2PBS implementations were invoked to compile the DIC query into a corresponding SAT and PBS instance. MINISAT and MINISAT+ were invoked to solve that instance. The average compile time and the average solver time for each size range is computed. Details are given in the following.

Hardware.

The experiment was conducted on a High Performance Computing Unix server, named BigBox, at the University of Calgary. The server features a 16-core processor and 128 GB RAM. A total of 10 GB RAM has been allocated to the Java Virtual Machine (JVM) for this experiment.

DIC Instances.

Random instances of the atomic DIC query were generated according to the scheme sketched below. DIC instances are generated for different policy sizes, ranging from 3 to 300. We divide the size range into intervals. The first interval is 3–20. Thereafter, each interval covers 20 policy sizes, such that the last interval is 281–300. A total of 50 random DIC instances were generated for each interval.

Generation of DIC Instances.

Each randomly generated DIC instance has the form (pol, root(pol), ds), where pol is a policy, and ds is a non-empty subset of $\{\mathbf{p}, \mathbf{d}, \mathbf{i}, \mathbf{n}\}$. Each of the 15 possible non-empty subsets is selected with equal probability.

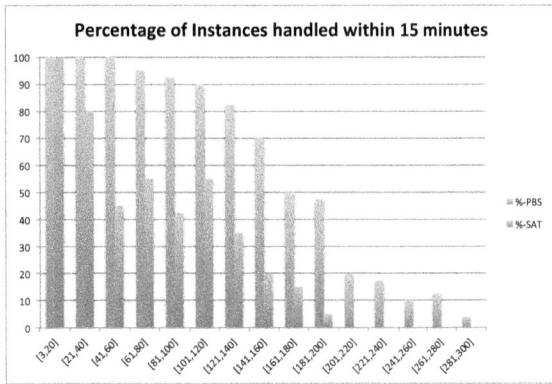

Figure 1: Comparison of Percentage of Handled Instances by DIC2SAT and DIC2PBS.

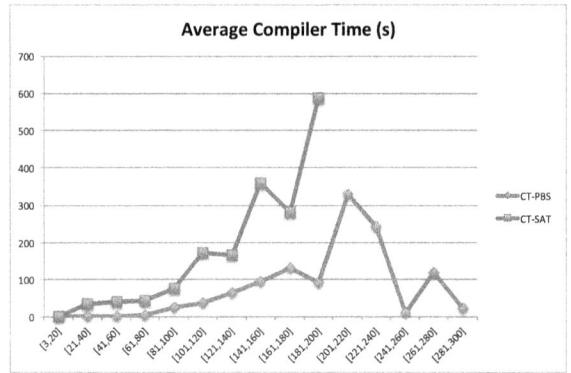

Figure 2: Comparison of Average Compile Times of DIC2SAT and DIC2PBS.

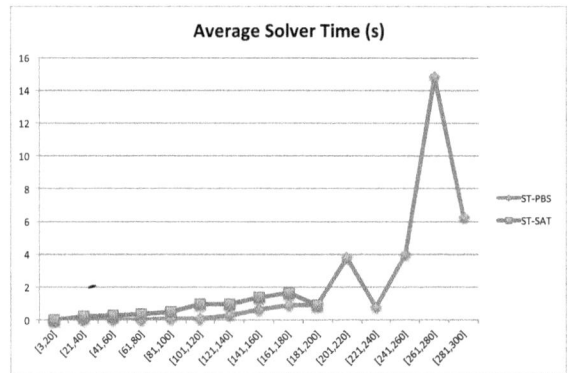

Figure 3: Comparison of Average Solver Times of SAT and PBS Instances.

Given a size parameter n, a random policy of size n is generated using the algorithm *PolGen* in Appendix B, with minor variations to be discussed below. The policies generated by *PolGen* contains both standard as well as majority-voting PCAs. We adapt *PolGen* so that the top-level AST node of the generated policy must of the form $pca(pol_1, \ldots, pol_k)$ (i.e., it can be neither an atomic nor conditional policy). In addition, pca must be one of the three majority-voting algorithms (each chosen with probability 1/3). Note that these restrictions apply only to the top-level AST node. The other subpolicies are generated with the probability distribution specified in Appendix B, and thus they contain either standard or majority-voting PCAs.

We introduced the above bias to the top-level AST node because we want to compare the relative performance of the two encodings in the case of majority-voting PCAs.

Time Out.

During pilot runs of the experiment (with a less capable hardware environment), we noticed that DIC2SAT would completely exhaust its heap space when dealing with DIC queries with large SAT encodings, resulting either in an out-of-memory error (usually accompanied by numerous invocations of the garbage collector), or in thrashing of memory pages. In either cases, the compile time is either unavailable or prohibitively large. To prevent this from happening in the real experiment, we set a time-out bound of 15 minutes for the compile time. If a DIC query can be compiled within the time-out bound, then that query is said to be "**handled**" by the compiler. We recorded the percentage of randomly generated DIC queries that were successfully handled by each of DIC2SAT and DIC2PBS.

Measurements.

The following four measurements were made for each randomly generated DIC instance that could be properly handled by a compiler within the time-out bound.

- **CT-SAT** (resp. **CT-PBS**) is the time in seconds to compile a DIC query to a SAT (resp. PBS) instance, using the DIC2SAT (resp. DIC2PBS) implementation.

- **ST-SAT** (resp. **ST-PBS**) is the time in seconds taken by the MiniSat SAT solver (resp. MiniSat+ PBS

solver) to determine the satisfiability of the compiled SAT (resp. PBS) instance.

CT-SAT and **CT-PBS** were measured using JETM, the Java Execution Time Monitor. **ST-SAT** and **ST-PBS** were reported by MiniSat and MiniSat+.

7.3 Experiment Results

Figure 1 depicts, for each policy size interval, the percentage of DIC instances that were successfully handled by each of DIC2SAT and DIC2PBS without triggering time out. The vertical axis corresponds to percentages of handled DIC instances, and the horizontal axis corresponds to policy size intervals. In all input intervals, DIC2PBS handled more DIC instances than DIC2SAT. For instance, DIC2SAT began not to be able to handle all instances when policy size reaches 21. After than point, percentage of handled instances dropped to around 50% or below in the next few intervals. DIC2SAT failed to handle any instances of size 201 or more. In contrast, DIC2PBS demonstrated a more graceful degradation. The percentage of handled instances remains roughly 50% even for input sizes of 181–200, and remains non-zero even up to input sizes of 281–300. This is explained by noticing that the SAT instances produced by DIC2SAT are much bigger than those generated by DIC2PBS.

Figure 2 depicts the average compile time (i.e., **CT-SAT** and **CT-PBS**), in seconds, for each policy size interval. Note that as DIC2SAT failed to handle any DIC instances of policy size 200 or above, the line for **CT-SAT** broke off after that point. Except for very small DIC instances, **CT-SAT** consistently exceeded **CT-PBS**. This, again, is explained by difference in encoding size produced by the two compilers. Note that the line for CT-PBS actually decreased for large DIC instances. The reason is that, for bigger input size, many of the difficult instances are not handled by DIC2PBS, and it is likely that the remaining instances are not particularly challenging.

Figure 3 depicts the average solver time (i.e., **ST-SAT** and **CT-PBS**), in seconds, for each policy size interval. Note that, if the DIC instance can be handled by the compiler, the solver time is actually insignificant.

8. CONCLUSION AND FUTURE WORK

The DIC analysis has been proposed as a white-box policy analysis. We demonstrated both the wide range of applications of the analysis, as well as the feasibility of the analysis via SAT and PBS encodings. Of particular interest is our novel application of PBS to achieve a compact encoding for policies containing majority-voting PCAs.

We are currently extending our work to adapt DIC analysis to Relationship-Based Access Control [15, 16, 9]. Research challenges include the choice of request predicates as well as formalizing their dependencies.

Acknowledgments

This work is supported in part by an NSERC Discovery Grant and a Canada Research Chair.

9. REFERENCES

[1] MINISAT+ PBS Solver. http://minisat.se/MiniSat+.html.

[2] MINISAT SAT Solver. http://minisat.se/MiniSat.html.

[3] Alfred V. Aho, Monica S. Lam, Ravi Sethi, and Jeffrey D. Ullman. *Compilers: Principles, Techniques, and Tools*. Prentice Hall, 2nd edition, 2006.

[4] Claudio Agostino Ardagna, Sabrina Capitani di Vimercati, Tyrone Grandison, Sushil Jajodia, and Pierangela Samarati. Regulating Exceptions in Healthcare Using Policy Spaces. In *Data and Applications Security XXII*, volume 5094 of *LNCS*, pages 254–267, London, UK, 2008. Springer.

[5] Christel Baier and Joost-Pieter Katoen. *Principles of Model Checking*. MIT Press, 2008.

[6] Jayalakshmi Balasubramaniam and Philip W. L. Fong. A white-box policy analysis and its efficient implementation. Technical Report 2013-1042-09, Department of Computer Science, University of Calgary, Alberta, Canada, 2013.

[7] Moritz Y. Becker. Specification and analysis of dynamic authorization policies. In *Proceedings of the 22nd IEEE Computer Security Foundations Symposium (CSF'09)*, pages 203–217, Port Jefferson, New York, USA, 2009.

[8] Piero Bonatti, Sabrina De Capitani di Vimercati, and Pierangela Samarati. An Algebra for Composing Access Control Policies. *ACM Transactions on Information and System Security*, 5(1):1–35, February 2002.

[9] Glenn Bruns, Philip W. L. Fong, Ida Siahaan, and Michael Huth. Relationship-based access control: Its expression and enforcement through hybrid logic. In *Proceedings of the 2nd ACM Conference on Data and Application Security (CODASPY'2012)*, San Antonio, TX, USA, February 2012.

[10] Glenn Bruns and Michael Huth. Access Control via Belnap logic: Intuitive, Expressive, and Analyzable Policy Composition. *ACM Transactions on Information and System Security*, 14(1):9:1–9:27, June 2011.

[11] Jason Crampton and Michael Huth. An Authorization Framework Resilient to Policy Evaluation Failures. In *Proceedings of the 15th European Symposium on Research in Computer Security (ESORICS'10)*, pages 472–487, Athens, Greece, 2010. Springer.

[12] Niklas Eén and Niklas Sörensson. An Extensible SAT-solver. In *6th International Conference on Theory and Applications of Satisfiability Testing*, volume 2919 of *LNCS*, pages 502–518, Santa Margherita Ligure, Italy, 2004. Springer.

[13] Niklas Eén and Niklas Sörensson. Translating Pseudo-Boolean Constraints into SAT. *Journal on Satisfiability, Boolean Modeling and Computation*, 2(1–4):1–26, March 2006.

[14] Kathi Fisler, Shriram Krishnamurthi, Leo A. Meyerovich, and Michael Carl Tschantz. Verification and change-impact analysis of access-control policies. In *Proceedings of the 27th International Conference on Software Engineering (ICSE'05)*, pages 196–205, St. Louis, Missouri, USA, 2005.

[15] Philip W. L. Fong. Relationship-based access control: Protection model and policy language. In *Proceedings of the First ACM Conference on Data and Application Security and Privacy (CODASPY'11)*, pages 191–202, San Antonio, Texas, USA, February 2011.

[16] Philip W. L. Fong and Ida Siahaan. Relationship-based access control policies and their policy languages. In *Proceedings of the 16th ACM Symposium on Access Control Models and Technologies (SACMAT'11)*, pages 51–60, Innsbruck, Austria, June 2011.

[17] Graham Hughes and Tevfik Bultan. Automated Verification of Access Control Policies Using a SAT Solver. *International Journal of Software Tools for Technology Transfer*, 10(6):503–520, December 2008.

[18] Karthick Jayaraman, Vijay Ganesh, Mahesh Tripunitara, Martin Rinard, and Steve Chapin. Automatic Error Finding in Access-Control Policies. In *Proceedings of the 18th ACM Conference on Computer and Communications Security (CCS'11)*, pages 163–174, Chicago, IL, USA, 2011. ACM.

[19] Vahid R. Karimi. Formal analysis of access control policies for pattern-based business processes. In *Proceedings of the 2009 World Congress on Privacy, Security, Trust and the Management of e-Business*, pages 239–242, Saint John, New Brunswick, Canada, 2009. IEEE Computer Society.

[20] Vladimir Kolovski, James Hendler, and Bijan Parsia. Analyzing web access control policies. In *Proceedings of the 16th International Conference on World Wide*

Web (WWW'07), pages 677–686, Banff, Alberta, Canada, 2007. ACM.

[21] Ninghui Li, Qihua Wang, Wahbeh Qardaji, Elisa Bertino, Prathima Rao, Jorge Lobo, and Dan Lin. Access control policy combinination: Theory meets practice. In *Proceedings of the 14th ACM symposium on Access Control Models and Technologies (SACMAT'09)*, Stresa, Italy, 2009. ACM.

[22] Dan Lin, Prathima Rao, Elisa Bertino, Ninghui Li, and Jorge Lobo. EXAM: a comprehensive environment for the analysis of access control policies. *International Journal of Information Security*, 9(4):253–273, August 2010.

[23] Evan Martin and Tao Xie. Automated test generation for access control policies via change-impact analysis. In *Proceedings of the 3rd International Workshop on Software Engineering for Secure Systems (SESS'07)*, page 5, Minneapolis, MN, USA, 2007. IEEE Computer Society.

[24] Fabio Massacci and Nicola Zannone. A model-driven approach for the specification and analysis of access control policies. In *Proceedings of On the Move to Meaningful Internet Systems: OTM 2008, OTM 2008 Confederated International Conferences, CoopIS, DOA, GADA, IS, and ODBASE 2008 — Part II*, pages 1087–1103, Monterrey, Mexico, 2008. Springer.

[25] Tim Moses. eXtensible Access Control Markup Language (XACML) Version 2.0. Technical report, OASIS Access Control TC, 2005.

[26] Qun Ni, Elisa Bertino, and Jorge Lobo. D-algebra for composing access control policy decisions. In *Proceedings of the 2009 ACM Symposium on Information, Computer, and Communications Security (ASIACCS'09)*, Sydney, Australia, 2009. ACM.

[27] Edward M. Reingold, Jurg Nievergelt, and Narsingh Deo. *Combinatorial Algorithms*. Prentice Hall, 1977.

[28] Thomas J. Schaefer. The complexity of satisfiability problems. In *Proceedings of the 10th Annual ACM Symposium on Theory of Computing (STOC'78)*, pages 216–226, San Diego, CA, USA, May 1978.

[29] Scott D. Stoller, Ping Yang, C R. Ramakrishnan, and Mikhail I. Gofman. Efficient policy analysis for administrative role based access control. In *Proceedings of the 14th ACM Conference on Computer and Communications Security (CCS'07)*, pages 445–455, Alexandria, Virginia, USA, 2007. ACM.

[30] G. S. Tseitin. On the Complexity of Derivations in the Propositional Calculus. *Studies in Mathematics and Mathematical Logic*, Part II:115–125, 1968.

[31] Dianxiang Xu, Lijo Thomas, Michael Kent, Tejeddine Mouelhi, and Yves Le Traon. A model-based approach to automated testing of access control policies. In *Proceedings of the 17th ACM symposium on Access Control Models and Technologies (SACMAT'12)*, pages 209–218, Newark, New Jersey, USA, 2012.

APPENDIX

A. NP-HARDNESS OF DIC-SAT

To demonstrate the NP-hardness of DIC-SAT, we outline below a reduction from monotone one-in-three 3SAT [28].

An instance of monotone one-in-three 3SAT problem is similar to an instance of 3SAT, except that all literals are positive. That is, every clause is a disjunction of three variables. Monotone one-in-three 3SAT decides whether there exists a truth assignment that satisfies exactly one variable in each of the clauses. The problem is known to be NP-complete [28].

Given an instance of montone one-in-three 3SAT, $\phi = C_1 \wedge C_2 \wedge \ldots \wedge C_k$, where each C_i is of the form $x_1^i \vee x_2^i \vee x_3^i$, we construct a corresponding DIC-SAT instance $q_\phi = DIC(pol, \mathsf{root}(pol), \{\mathbf{p}\})$, where pol is defined as follows

$$\mathsf{amv}(pol_1, \ldots, pol_k, \overbrace{\mathsf{deny}, \ldots, \mathsf{deny}}^{k-1 \text{ times}})$$

and each pol_i is defined as follows

$$\mathsf{oa}(x_1^i \to \mathsf{permit}, x_2^i \to \mathsf{permit}, x_3^i \to \mathsf{permit})$$

It is easy to see that q_ϕ is satisfiable iff there is a truth assignment that satisfies exactly one variable in each clause of ϕ.

B. GENERATION OF RANDOM POLICIES

The following specifies an algorithm *PolGen* for generating a random policy of size n, with RP as the set of request predicates. We write m as a shorthand for the size of RP. Note that the policy returned *PolGen* does not contain $\top$ and $\bot$.

Algorithm *PolGen(n, RP)*:

Case $n = 1$. Each of deny and permit is generated with probability $1/2$.

Case $n = 2$. A conditional policy $rp \to pol$ will be generated. One of the m request predicates from RP is selected to be rp, each with probability $1/m$. Either deny or permit is selected to be pol, each with probability $1/2$.

Case $n \geq 3$. Either a conditional policy $rp \to pol$ or a PCA policy $pca(pol_1, \ldots, pol_k)$ is generated, each with probability $1/2$. The following specifies the procedure for each of the two subcases.

  Subcase $rp \to pol$. One of the m members of RP is selected to be rp, with probability $1/m$. The subpolicy pol is generated by a recursive call to $PolGen(n-1, RP)$.

  Subcase $pca(pol_1, \ldots, pol_k)$. Firstly, *pca* will be selected from one of the seven combining algorithms (i.e., po, do, fa, oa, smv, amv, and spmv), each with probability $1/7$. Secondly, we generate k and $pol_1, \ldots, pol_k$. To understand how this is done, we digress to introduce the idea of **compositions**.
  A composition of a positive integer n is a sequence of positive integers $n_1, \ldots, n_k$ such that $k \leq n$ and $n = n_1 + \cdots + n_k$. There is a total of 2^{n-1} compositions. The composition with $k = 1$ is said to be **degenerate**. So there is a total of $2^{n-1} - 1$ nondegenerate compositions. See [27, §5.3.1] for an algorithm for generating random compositions.
  We randomly generate a nondegenerate composition of $n - 1$, so that each nondegenerate composition is generated with equal probability. Suppose the selected composition is $n_1, \ldots, n_k$. Then we recursively invoke $PolGen(n_i, m)$ to generate pol_i.

On the Notion of Redundancy in Access Control Policies*

Marco Guarnieri [†]
Institute of Information
Security, ETH Zürich,
Switzerland
marco.guarnieri@inf.ethz.ch

Mario Arrigoni Neri
Università degli Studi di
Bergamo, Italy
mario.arrigonineri@unibg.it

Eros Magri [†]
Comelit R & D,
Comelit Group S.p.A, Italy
eros.magri@comelit.it

Simone Mutti
Università degli Studi di
Bergamo, Italy
simone.mutti@unibg.it

ABSTRACT

The evolution of information systems sees an increasing need of flexible and sophisticated approaches for the automated detection of anomalies in security policies. One of these anomalies is redundancy, which may increase the total cost of management of the policies and may reduce the performance of access control mechanisms and of other anomaly detection techniques.

We consider three approaches that can remove redundancy from access control policies, progressively reducing the number of authorizations in the policy itself. We show that several problems associated with redundancy are NP-hard. We propose exact solutions to two of these problems, namely the Minimum Policy Problem, which consists in computing the minimum policy that represents the behaviour of the system, and the Minimum Irreducible Policy Problem, consisting in computing the redundancy-free version of a policy with the smallest number of authorizations. Furthermore we propose heuristic solutions to those problems. We also present a comparison between the exact and heuristics solutions based on experiments that use policies derived from bibliographical databases.

Categories and Subject Descriptors

D.4.6 [**Operating Systems**]: Security and Protection

General Terms

Algorithms, Security, Theory

*This work was partially supported by the EC within the 7FP, under grant agreement 257129 "PoSecCo" and 256980 "NESSoS", by the Italian Ministry of Research within the PRIN projects "PEPPER", "GATECOM" and "GenData 2020".

[†]This work was partially done while the author was with Dipartimento di Ingegneria, Università degli Studi di Bergamo, Italy.

Keywords

Redundancy, Access Control, Minimization

1 Introduction

Access control policies used in real systems are often unnecessarily large due to redundancy. Since the size of the policy is one of the main factors that determine the cost of managing the security configuration of a system, minimizing the size of a policy can ease the management of the policy itself and can reduce the cost of the management process. Furthermore the size of a policy influences the performance of the access control system, and thus minimizing the size of the policy can improve the access control system performance [11, 16].

Although *redundancy* seems a natural and quite simple concept, providing a formal definition of it in case of access control policies is not trivial for several reasons. One of the reasons is that we may have to deal with conflicts between authorizations that may influence the result of our redundancy detection process. Another reason is that at a certain point during our redundancy detection process we may consider as redundant a subset of the authorizations in the policy, and the choice of the authorizations to effectively tag as redundant may influence the redundancy of the others. In the following, we are going to survey several definitions of redundancy that were presented in the literature. Al-Shaer et al. in [1–3] define a rule r as *redundant* iff there are other rules that produce the same actions as r, such that the removal of r does not affect the security policy. A similar definition can be found in the work of Kolovski et al. [10], which defines a policy element as *redundant* if its removal does not change the final behavior of the policy. Also Liu et al. [11] and Yuan et al. [16] agree with the definition of redundancy given above by saying that a rule is redundant iff its removal does not influence at all the behavior of the firewall. All these authors give a very similar definition of *redundancy* (which we call *basic definition* in the following) and we can consider all the definitions as equivalent to saying that an authorization (or a rule) is *redundant* iff it does not affect the behavior of the access control mechanisms (i.e., its presence or absence in a policy passes unnoticed). The main problem of this definition is that, although it is very simple and intuitive, it often lacks in precision and flexibility: the definition of behavior of a policy is usually not specified in a formal way and it is only defined in terms of a specific and concrete access control system. Hu et al. [9] try to overcome this problem by providing a more formal definition, saying that a rule r is redundant in case the *authorization space* (which is a collection of access requests to which a policy element is applicable) derived from the policy that contains r is the same as the one derived from the policy without r.

Although the definition given above seems clear, it presents subtle side-effects that we show with a simple example. Let P be a policy composed by the authorizations a_1, a_2, a_3 where a_1 produces exactly the same effect as the combination of authorizations a_2 and a_3.

A first problem is that the *basic definition* of *redundancy* is not invariant w.r.t. the decisions of our redundancy-removal process. This fact means that a rule may be considered redundant at a certain point in time during the redundancy-removal process, and lose this property at a later time. For instance, if we consider the policy P, the redundant authorizations are a_1, a_2, a_3 (i.e., the complete policy), but if we remove authorization a_3, then a_1 is not redundant anymore. This means that we cannot safely remove sets of redundant authorizations and the definition cannot be applied looking only at the starting policy state. The definition of *redundancy* should take into account all the decisions taken during the redundancy-removal process.

Furthermore, by iteratively removing authorizations that satisfy the *basic definition*, we usually do not obtain a unique solution. Rather, we can obtain several equivalent policies with different number of authorizations. For instance, in our example both policies $\{a_1\}$ and $\{a_2, a_3\}$ are equivalent and redundancy-free, but they have different size. The fact that the *basic definition* of *redundancy* does not take into account the number of authorizations in the final policy can be surprising, since the main motivation behind the development of redundancy detection techniques is the improvement of access control mechanisms' performance, which primarily depends on the size of the access control policies. This aspect of the redundancy problem is important, because an effective redundancy-removal process should always aim at computing the minimum redundancy-free version of the given policy, not limiting the goal to the identification of one of the redundancy-free versions.

An underlying assumption in all the previous definitions is that the only way on which we can act on a policy is by removing redundant authorizations. This assumption introduces some limitations in the search for performance improvements. For instance, if P is a policy with 6 authorizations, there may exist another policy P' that is equivalent to P but it contains only 4 authorizations that were not in P. In this case, we should prefer P' over P because it can lead to an improvement in system performance. We consider as another aspect of the *redundancy* problem the computation of the policy that models the behavior of the system with the minimum number of authorizations.

It is then obvious that the *basic definition* of *redundancy* is not enough for handling this issue effectively. There is the need of one or more definitions for several aspects of the redundancy problem that take into account the size of the resulting policy, and the dependency between actions performed at different steps of the redundancy-removal process.

In this work we present a formalization of the redundancy problem in access control policies that considers three different ways in which a security administrator can act on a policy containing redundancy. In the first approach, the administrator can compute an equivalent policy that does not contain redundancy anymore, i.e., she computes an *irreducible policy*. However, given a certain policy there usually are several irreducible versions of the same policy. Given the fact that the number of authorizations of the policy is one of the major factors that influence the management cost of the policy itself, in the second approach the security administrator identifies among the *irreducible policies* obtained by the original policy one with the minimum number of authorizations, which is the *minimum irreducible policy*. With the third approach, the security administrator may be interested in computing the representation of the access control system with the minimum number of authorizations, i.e., the *minimum policy*.

Main contributions: The main contributions of our work are: (a) we propose a definition of the redundancy removal problem in access control policies; (b) we study in detail two new problems related with redundancy; (c) we provide two exact solutions and two heuristic solutions for these problems; (d) we provide an evaluation of the various approaches based on data extracted from bibliographical databases.

Structure of the paper: Section 2 describes the underlying model used in our approach. In Section 3 we study in detail the problem of removing redundancy from security policies. Section 4 presents exact solutions and heuristic algorithms for solving two different redundancy-removal problems; we present also a detailed performance analysis. In Section 5 we illustrate an analysis of the state of the art with respect to redundancy detection. Finally, Section 6 draws our conclusions.

2 Model

In enterprise scenarios, policy definition and management systems are needed that provide a high level of flexibility, to correctly represent the large number and variety of security requirements. In order to achieve this goal, we have defined an access control model containing the following entities:

- **Principals**: represent users and groups of principals. Each *Principal* may contain one or more other *Principals* and this fact is represented by the function $contains:Principal \rightarrow 2^{Principal}$. The function $contains+:Principal \rightarrow 2^{Principal}$ is the transitive closure of $contains$.

- **Actions**: represent the actions that users can execute. Each *Action* may be composed by one or more *Actions* and this fact is represented by the function $composed:Action \rightarrow 2^{Action}$. The function $composed+:Action \rightarrow 2^{Action}$ is the transitive closure of $composed$.

- **Resources**: represent the resources on which users can act. Each *Resource* may contain one or more *Resources* and this fact is represented by the function $containsResources:Resource \rightarrow 2^{Resource}$. The function $containsResources+:Resource \rightarrow 2^{Resource}$ is the transitive closure of $containsResources$.

An instance $\mathcal{M}$ of our model is a list of *Principals*, *Actions* and *Resources* with the associated functions[1]. $\preceq_P$, $\preceq_A$ and $\preceq_R$ are partial orders defined over *Principals*, *Actions* and *Resources* respectively. For instance, given two principals p_1 and p_2 we say that $p_1 \preceq_P p_2$ iff $p_1 \in contains+(p_2) \cup \{p_2\}$. The definition of $\preceq_A$ and $\preceq_R$ can be obtained in a similar way (the fact that $\preceq_P$, $\preceq_A$ and $\preceq_R$ are partial orders is

---

[1]The hierarchies defined in $\mathcal{M}$ must be acyclic.

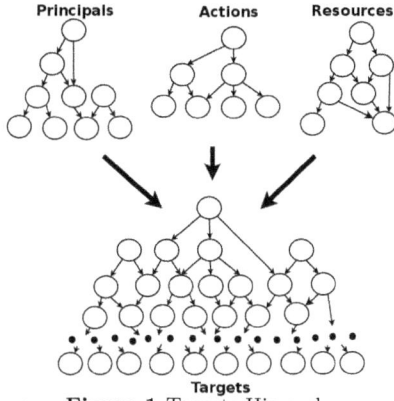

Figure 1 Targets Hierarchy

enforced by the fact that the hierarchies over *Principals*, *Actions* and *Resources* are acyclic). We say that an element of one of the hierarchies in $\mathcal{M}$ is *primitive* iff it is a leaf of the hierarchy (e.g., a principal p is a primitive element iff $contains(p) = \emptyset$).

We assume that the assignment of permissions to users can be derived from the system, e.g. in Role-Based Access Control (RBAC) [14] the user-permission assignment matrix can be directly computed from the user-role assignment and the role-permission assignment matrices.

The basic element about which we can express access control decisions is called a *Target*, and it is defined in the following way:

Definition 1. **Target:** a target consists of a *Principal* p, an *Action* a and a *Resource* r. We represent a target as a triple $< p, a, r >$. We say that a target $< p, a, r >$ is *primitive* iff p, a and r are primitive elements.

Given two targets $t_1 = < p_1, a_1, r_1 >$ and $t_2 = < p_2, a_2, r_2 >$, we say that t_1 implies t_2, denoted by $t_1 \preceq_T t_2$, iff $p_1 \preceq_P p_2 \wedge a_1 \preceq_A a_2 \wedge r_1 \preceq_R r_2$. The partial order $\preceq_T$ defines the *Target Hierarchy* $TH_\mathcal{M}$, shown in Figure 1. Primitive targets are the leafs of the hierarchy.

Security administrators can define access rights on the targets by means of authorizations, which are defined in the following way:

Definition 2. **Authorization**: An authorization consists of a triple composed by a set of *Principals* P, a set of *Actions* A and a set of *Resources* R. Each authorization has a sign s that can be $+$ or $-$. It is used in order to state, respectively, whether an authorization is *positive* (i.e., it grants the permission to do something) or *negative* (i.e., it denies the permission to do something). We graphically represent an authorization in the following way: $< s, P, A, R >$.

An authorization $auth = < s, P, A, R >$ defined over the model $\mathcal{M}$ is associated in an unique way to a set of *Targets* $T_{auth} = P \times A \times R$ on which the authorization acts. Without loss of generality, we can express access control decisions only in terms of primitive targets (and thus we consider only primitive targets when we compute the set T_{auth}). Given an authorization, the following functions can be used in order to obtain the elements contained in it:

- $principals$:$Authorization \rightarrow 2^{Principal}$ retrieves the set of *Principals* involved in the authorization,

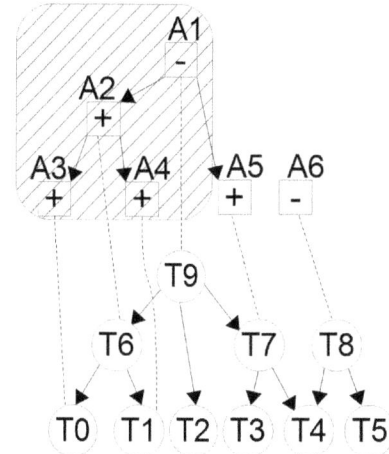

Figure 2 Graphical representation of authorizations

- $actions$:$Authorization \rightarrow 2^{Action}$ retrieves the set of *Actions* involved in the authorization,
- $resources$:$Authorization \rightarrow 2^{Resource}$ retrieves the set of *Resources* involved in the authorization,
- $sign$:$Authorization \rightarrow \{+, -\}$ retrieves the *sign* of the authorization.

Given a set of authorizations Δ and an authorization $a \in \Delta$, the *region* defined by a over Δ is $R_a^\Delta = \{a' \in \Delta | T_a \cap T_{a'} = \emptyset\}$. The region of an authorization a contains all the authorizations that may interact with a. We can define a hierarchy over authorizations in the following way: given two authorizations $auth_1$ and $auth_2$, we say that $auth_1$ is dominated by $auth_2$, i.e., $auth_1 \preceq auth_2$, iff $T_{auth_1} \subseteq T_{auth_2}$.

Example 1. Figure 2 shows a graphical representation of a set of authorizations applied over a set of targets. This example will be used in the next sections as running example. The graph is composed by two different components (a) the authorizations, represented by squares labeled with a sign, and (b) the targets, represented by circles (this set of targets represent a part of the target hierarchy shown in Figure 1). Edges between authorizations represent the $\preceq$ ordering relation, whereas edges between targets represent the $\preceq_T$ ordering relation. In this representation, given an authorization $auth$ the set T_{auth} is defined by all the nodes in the target hierarchy reachable from the node representing $auth$. For instance, if we consider the authorization $A2$ then T_{A2} is the set $\{T0, T1, T6\}$. The region defined by the authorization $A2$ is $\{A1, A2, A3, A4\}$.

Let $auth$ be an authorization. $auth$ specifies an access control decision on the targets on which it can act (represented by the sign $sign(auth)$), and we represent this fact by saying that $auth$ assigns a label $sign(auth)$ to the targets in T_{auth}. We represent the basic access control decision by means of the concept of *Privilege*, which represents a *Target* labeled with a sign s, defined in the following way:

Definition 3. **Privilege**: A privilege consists of a target $t = < p, a, r >$ and a sign $s \in \{+, -\}$ (inherited from an authorization). We graphically represent a privilege in the following way: $< s, p, a, r >$. If the sign s is $+$ then the privilege represents the fact that the *Principal* p is allowed to do the *Action* a on the *Resource* r. On the contrary, if the sign s is $-$ then the privilege represents the fact that the

Principal p is not allowed to do the *Action* a on the *Resource* r. We say that a privilege $< s, p, a, r >$ is *primitive*, i.e., it does not imply other privileges, iff the target $< p, a, r >$ is primitive.

Given a privilege the following functions can be used in order to obtain the elements of the model contained in it:

- *principal*:*Privilege*→*Principal* retrieves the *Principal* involved in the privilege,
- *action*:*Privilege*→*Action* retrieves the *Action* involved in the privilege,
- *resource*:*Privilege*→*Resource* retrieves the *Resource* involved in the privilege,
- *sign*:*Privilege*→ $\{+, -\}$ retrieves the *sign* of the privilege.

Each authorization *auth*, thus, grants a set of privileges (i.e., a set of labeled targets). More formally, we say that each authorization *auth* associates a sign s to the targets in the set T_{auth}. The procedure shown in Algorithm 1 can be used to compute the set of privileges associated with an authorization. We denote the set of privileges associated with the authorization *auth* as *privileges(auth)*.

Algorithm 1: *privileges* procedure for authorizations

Input : Authorization *auth*
Output: *Privileges*
begin
    $Privileges = \emptyset$;
    for $p \in principals(auth)$, $a \in actions(auth)$, $r \in resources(auth)$ **do**
        for $p' \in contains + (p) \bigcup \{p\}$,
        $a' \in composed + (a) \bigcup \{a\}$,
        $r' \in containsResources(r) \bigcup \{r\}$ **do**
            if $contains(p') = \emptyset \wedge composed(a') = \emptyset \wedge containsResources(r') = \emptyset$ **then**
                $Privileges = Privileges \bigcup \{< sign(auth), p', a', r' >\}$;

Due to the fact that authorizations and privileges have a sign, we may have conflicts between different authorizations and privileges in the same policy P. Several approaches have been proposed in the literature for the solution of conflicts between authorizations [6, 12, 15]. Our approach is not tied to any particular conflict resolution strategy, indeed it can be used with any conflict resolution strategy that satisfies certain requirements, explained in detail in Section 2.1. Let $\mathcal{M}$ be a model, let $P_{\mathcal{M}}$, $A_{\mathcal{M}}$ and $R_{\mathcal{M}}$ be the set of principals, actions and resources associated with the model, and let Δ be the set of all possible authorizations that can be defined over $\mathcal{M}$. We represent a conflict resolution strategy as a function $\psi : P_{\mathcal{M}} \times A_{\mathcal{M}} \times R_{\mathcal{M}} \times \mathbb{P}(\Delta) \to \Delta \cup \{\bot\}$ that takes as input a target $< p, a, r >$ and a set of authorizations A and returns the authorization in A that determines the privilege granted by the set A w.r.t. the $< p, a, r >$ (if no authorization in Δ can be applied to $< p, a, r >$ then ψ returns $\bot$).

Let Δ be a set of authorizations, we denote with *privileges*(Δ, ψ) the set of privileges granted by Δ w.r.t. the conflict resolution strategy ψ. In this case *privileges*(Δ, ψ) can be computed by using the procedure shown in Algorithm 2 that returns the set of labeled targets associated with Δ w.r.t. the strategy ψ. Given a set of authorizations Δ, a conflict resolution strategy ψ and an authorization *auth*, we

say that Δ dominates *auth* w.r.t. ψ, denoted by *auth* $\preceq \Delta$, iff *privileges(auth)* $\subseteq$ *privileges*(Δ, ψ).

Algorithm 2: *privileges* procedure for sets of authorizations

---

Input : Set of authorizations Δ, Conflict resolution strategy ψ
Output: *Privileges*
begin
    $Privileges = \emptyset$;
    for $auth \in \Delta$ **do**
        for $p \in principals(auth)$, $a \in actions(auth)$, $r \in resources(auth)$ **do**
            for $p' \in contains + (p) \bigcup \{p\}$,
            $a' \in composed + (a) \bigcup \{a\}$,
            $r' \in containsResources(r) \bigcup \{r\}$ **do**
                if $contains(p') = \emptyset \wedge composed(a') = \emptyset \wedge containsResources(r') = \emptyset$ **then**
                    $a = \psi(p', a', r', \Delta)$;
                    $Privileges = Privileges \bigcup \{< sign(a), p', a', r' >\}$;

Definition 4. **Policy**: A policy consists of a set of authorizations Δ and a conflict resolution strategy ψ. We represent a policy as a pair $< \Delta, \psi >$.

Let $P = < \Delta, \psi >$ be a policy, we denote with $P' \subset P$ a policy $P' = < \Delta', \psi' >$ such that $\Delta' \subset \Delta$ and $\psi' = \psi$.

Each policy is identified by its behaviour, which is defined in the following way:

Definition 5. **Behaviour of a Policy**: the behaviour of a policy P is the set of privileges granted, directly or indirectly, by the policy.

The behaviour of a policy P can be computed using the function *privileges* presented in Algorithm 2, thus we can check whether two different policies are equivalent by checking whether they enable the same set of privileges. The behaviour of the policy models how the real access control system behaves. Given the fact that the same behaviour can be modeled by means of several different policies, the equivalence relation between policies is defined in the following way:

Definition 6. **Equivalence of Policies**: Two policies $P = < \Delta, \psi >$ and $P' = < \Delta', \psi' >$ are equivalent, $P \equiv P'$, iff they have the same behaviour, i.e., iff *privileges*$(\Delta, \psi) =$ *privileges*(Δ', ψ').

Let P be a policy defined over the model $\mathcal{M}$. There exists always a policy P' expressed only in terms of primitive elements of $\mathcal{M}$ which is equivalent to P and such that $|P| = |P'|$. In order to obtain P' we can proceed in the following way: we define an authorization $< s, Pr', A', R' > \in P'$ for each authorization $< s, Pr, A, R > \in P$ where Pr', A' and R' contains only the primitive elements that can be derived from the elements in Pr, A, and R respectively. The fact that $P \equiv P'$ follows trivially from the definition of equivalence and from the *privilege* procedure. In the following we can thus consider, without loss of generality, policies expressed only in terms of primitive elements.

2.1 Conflict resolution strategies

Let $\mathcal{M}$ be a model, let $P_\mathcal{M}$, $A_\mathcal{M}$ and $R_\mathcal{M}$ be the set of principals, actions and resources associated with the model and let Δ be the set of all possible authorizations that can be defined over $\mathcal{M}$.

A conflict resolution strategy is a function $\psi : P_\mathcal{M} \times A_\mathcal{M} \times R_\mathcal{M} \times \mathbb{P}(\Delta) \to \Delta \cup \{\bot\}$. ψ takes as input a set of authorizations Δ and a target $< p, a, r >$, and it returns as output the authorization $auth \in \Delta$ that is applied over $< p, a, r >$ according to the strategy (if no authorization in Δ can be applied to $< p, a, r >$ then ψ returns $\bot$).

A conflict resolution strategy ψ may satisfy one or more of the following properties:

- **Polynomiality:** we say that ψ is polynomial (in the size of Δ and of the target hierarchy) iff there is an algorithm that implements ψ which is in **P**,
- **Completeness:** we say that ψ is complete iff for any possible set of authorizations Δ and for any target $t = < p, a, r >$ if $\exists auth \in \Delta : < p, a, r > \in T_{auth}$ then $\psi(p, a, r, \Delta) \neq \bot$,
- **Monotonicity:** we say that ψ is *monotone* iff for any possible set of authorizations Δ and for any target $t = < p, a, r >$ then $\psi(p, a, r, \Delta) = \psi(p, a, r, \Delta \cup \{auth\})$ holds for any authorization $auth$ such that $< p, a, r > \notin T_{auth}$. A monotone conflict resolution strategy is one that produces a result that depends only on the authorizations in Δ that are related with $< p, a, r >$ (i.e., adding unrelevant authorizations do not change the outcome of the strategy).

We say that ψ is a *valid* conflict resolution strategy for our framework, iff ψ satisfies the three properties above.

For instance, we can represent the *Denial takes precedence* strategy in the following way:

$$\psi_{DTP}(p, a, r, \Delta) = \begin{cases} a_i & if \ < +, p, a, r > \in privileges(a_i) \land \\ & \not\exists a_j \in \Delta \setminus \{a_i\} : \\ & < -, p, a, r > \in privileges(a_j) \\ a_i & if \ < -, p, a, r > \in privileges(a_i) \\ \bot & otherwise \end{cases}$$

It is easy to see that the *Denial takes precedence* strategy satisfies all the requirements stated above.

Example 2. If we consider only the authorizations $A5$ and $A6$ of Figure 2, we can define the sets (a) $T_{A5} = \{T3, T4, T7\}$, and (b) $T_{A6} = \{T4, T5, T8\}$. We can notice that there is an intersection between T_{A5} and T_{A6}, and the two authorizations have a different sign. The application of the strategy *Denial takes precedence* means that for the target $T4$ (i.e., the intersection) will be applied the authorization $A6$, the negative one.

The *Most Specific Wins* strategy can be represented by the following function ψ_{MSW}:

$$\psi_{MSW}(p, a, r, \Delta) = \begin{cases} a_i & if \ < p, a, r > \in T_{a_i} \land \\ & \not\exists a_j \in \Delta \setminus \{a_i\} : \\ & (< p, a, r > \in T_{a_j} \land a_j \preceq a_i) \\ \bot & if \ \exists a_i, a_j \in \Delta : < p, a, r > \in T_{a_i} \\ & \land < p, a, r > \in T_{a_j} \land \\ & a_i \not\preceq a_j \land a_j \not\preceq a_i \\ \bot & otherwise \end{cases}$$

It is easy to see that ψ_{MSW} is not complete because it may return $\bot$ also in case there are authorizations in Δ that can be applied to the target $< p, a, r >$ but these authorizations are not comparable.

Example 3. If we consider only the authorizations $A2$ and $A3$ of Figure 2, we can define the sets (a) $T_{A2} = \{T0, T1, T6\}$, and (b) $T_{A3} = \{T0\}$. We can notice that $A3 \preceq A2$ because $T_{A3} \subseteq T_{A2}$. For instance, for the target $T0$ we can apply two authorizations $A2$ and $A3$. The *Most Specific Wins* strategy chooses to apply the authorization $A3$ because it is more specific than $A2$.

Although our framework is independent from a specific conflict resolution strategy, for concreteness in the the running example and in Section 4 we consider the conflict resolution strategy ψ that applies the *Most Specific Wins* and *Denial takes precedence* criteria. This strategy can be modeled in the following way:

$$\psi(p, a, r, \Delta) = \begin{cases} \psi_{MSW}(p, a, r, \Delta) & if \ \psi_{MSW}(p, a, r, \Delta) \neq \bot \\ \psi_{DTP}(p, a, r, \Delta) & otherwise \end{cases}$$

ψ satisfies all the requirements stated above.

3 Redundancy

Sometimes real policies contain redundancy [13], for several reasons caused by the evolution of security policies during time. Although the concept of *redundancy* is easy to understand, defining it formally is not trivial, especially, as in our case, when we consider conflicts.

A simple definition of *redundancy* may be the following: "Given a policy P, we can define an authorization $auth$ as *redundant* when it does not add anything to the behaviour of P.". The process of removing redundancy is called *redundancy-removal* process. The problem of this definition is that redundancy is not invariant, i.e., it depends on the sequences of decisions taken during the redundancy-removal process. Indeed, by solving a conflict between authorizations or by removing an authorization from the policy, we may change the set of authorizations that are redundant. As a consequence, the sequence of decisions taken during the redundancy-removal process in order to achieve a redundancy-free equivalent policy, may lead to significantly different results in terms of size of the final policy.

In the following we try to formalize the *redundancy* problem. The proof of all the theorems are given in the appendix.

We start by defining the concept of *redundancy condition*, which refines the definition given above.

Definition 7. **Redundancy Condition:** An authorization $auth \in P$ satisfies the *redundancy condition* w.r.t. the policy $P = < \Delta, \psi >$ iff $\forall < p, a, r > \in T_{auth} :$
$sign(\psi(p, a, r, R_{auth}^\Delta \setminus \{auth\})) = sign(\psi(p, a, r, R_{auth}^\Delta)) \land$
$\psi(p, a, r, R_{auth}^\Delta \setminus \{auth\}) \neq \bot$.

In other words, $auth$ satisfies the redundancy condition w.r.t. P iff its presence or absence does not influence the access control decision for any possible target $< p, a, r >$ on which it can act.

Example 4. For instance, authorization $A2$ in Figure 2 satisfies the redundancy condition. The set T_{A2} contains the targets $T0$, $T1$ and $T6$ and for each of these targets the presence of $A2$ does not influence the behaviour of the policy. Hence, we can safely remove $A2$.

Given a policy P, we can remove one by one all the authorizations that satisfy the redundancy condition without changing the behaviour of the policy. However, by removing authorizations from P we may change the redundancy condition for other authorizations. We model this phenomenon with the concept of *sequence of reductions*.

Definition 8. **Sequence of Reductions (SoR):** let P_0 be a policy, and let $P_1, \ldots, P_n$ be a sequence of policies. The sequence $P_0, P_1, \ldots, P_n$ is a *sequence of reductions* iff it satisfies the following requirements:

- $P_n \subset P_{n-1} \subset \ldots \subset P_1 \subset P_0$,
- for each $i \in \{1, \ldots, n\}$, $P_{i+1} = P_i \setminus \{\gamma_i\}$ and γ_i is an authorization that satisfies the *redundancy condition* w.r.t. P_i,
- there are no authorizations in P_n that satisfy the redundancy condition w.r.t. P_n.

We say that P_0 is the *begin* of the sequence, and that P_n is the end of the sequence. We say that the reduction from P_i to P_{i+1} is a *step* in the sequence.

Due to the fact that the authorization removed at each step satisfies the redundancy condition, the behaviour of the policy does not change along the sequence of reduction, as stated in Theorem 1.

Theorem 1. Let $P_0, \ldots, P_n$ be a sequence of reductions. All the policies in the sequence have the same behaviour, i.e., they are equivalent.

An interesting property of *SoRs* is that once we reach a point P_i in a sequence $P_0, \ldots, P_n$ then all the authorizations that satisfy the redundancy condition at P_i satisfy the redundancy condition also at the following steps of the sequence, as stated in Theorem 2. This means that, although the choice of the authorization to remove may influence the final outcome, the order in which we remove these authorizations does not influence the result (i.e., what influences the size of the final policy is only $\Gamma = \{\gamma_0, \ldots, \gamma_{n-1}\}$ and not the order in the SoR in which we remove authorizations that satisfy the redundancy condition).

Theorem 2. Let $P_0, P_1, \ldots, P_n$ be a sequence of reductions. Let $auth \in P_0$ be an authorization such that there exists a value $j \in \{1, \ldots, n\}$ for which $\forall j' < j : auth \in P_{j'}$ and $auth$ satisfies the redundancy condition w.r.t. P_j. In this case $auth$ satisfies the redundancy condition w.r.t. all $P_i \cup \{auth\}$ where $j < i \leq n$.

Another important property of *SoRs* is stated in Theorem 3. The theorem says that whenever there are two equivalent policies P and P' such that P' is a subset of P, then there is always at least a sequence of reductions that starts from P and passes through P'. This means that we can reduce the problem of finding a redundancy-free version of a policy P to the one of finding an adequate *SoR* starting from P.

Theorem 3. Let P be a security policy and let $P' \subset P$ be another policy such that P and P' are equivalent. There is always at least one sequence of reductions of the form $P, \ldots, P', \ldots, P_n$.

We can now define the concept of redundancy-free policy, called *irreducible policy*, in the following way:

Definition 9. **Irreducible Policy (IP):** A policy P is an irreducible version of the policy P' iff it does not contain any authorization that satisfies the redundancy condition w.r.t. P and $P \subseteq P'$. This is equivalent to say that there is a sequence of reductions from P' to P, i.e., $P', \ldots, P$.

From Theorem 3 follows that in case we reach a policy P in a SoR such that there are no authorizations satisfying the redundancy condition w.r.t. P, then we can soundly say that an equivalent policy $P' \subset P$ does not exist. Hence given a policy P, we can compute an equivalent irreducible version P' in a simple, although sometimes inefficient, way. Initially let $P' = P$, then we iterate over all the authorizations in P', and we check for each authorization $a \in P'$ whether it satisfies the redundancy condition w.r.t. P' or not, if this is the case then we remove the authorization (i.e., $P' = P' \setminus \{a\}$). We iterate the above procedure until no more authorizations satisfy the redundancy condition. It is easy to see that this algorithm is polynomial w.r.t. the number of authorizations in P.

Checking whether a certain policy P is irreducible or not is the Irreducible Policy Problem (IPP) and it can be solved in **P-TIME**, as demonstrated by Theorem 4.

Definition 10. **Irreducible Policy Problem:** Given a policy P, checking whether P is irreducible is called Irreducible Policy Problem (IPP).

Theorem 4. The *IPP* is in **P**.

Example 5. Figure 3(a) shows an irreducible version of the policy in Figure 2. The new policy was obtained by removing the authorization $A2$ which satisfies the redundancy condition, as shown in Example 4.

Given a policy P, several different irreducible versions of it may exist. In order to improve the performance of access control mechanisms, a possible solution is to compute the irreducible version of P with the minimum number of authorizations. We call this policy a *Minimum Irreducible Policy*.

Definition 11. **Minimum Irreducible Policy (MIP):** A policy P is a minimum irreducible version of the policy P' iff a policy P'' does not exist such that P'' is irreducible, P'' is equivalent to P', $|P''| < |P|$, $P \subseteq P'$ and $P'' \subseteq P'$. In an equivalent way, we can say that P is a minimum irreducible version of the policy P' iff P is the end of the longest SoR that can be computed starting from P'.

The problem of checking whether a certain policy P is a minimum irreducible policy with respect to the original policy P' is called Minimum Irreducible Policy Problem.

Definition 12. **Minimum Irreducible Policy Problem:** Given two policies P and P', checking whether P is a minimum irreducible policy with respect to P' is called Minimum Irreducible Policy Problem (MIPP).

We are more interested in the the problem of finding a minimum irreducible version of a given policy P (which is the search problem associated with the MIPP). Since the associated decision problem is **coNP-complete**, the search problem is **NP-hard**.

Theorem 5. The *MIPP* is **coNP-complete**.

166

Example 6. Although in Example 4, we have shown a redundancy-free version of the policy in Figure 2, the resulting policy (obtained by removing $A2$) was not the minimum irreducible one. Indeed a smaller irreducible policy can be computed by removing $A3$ and $A4$ instead of $A2$. This policy, shown in Figure 3(b), is the minimum irreducible one, since no smaller irreducible policies exist.

Given the fact that the behaviour of an access control system may be modeled by means of different equivalent policies, security administrators may be interested in computing the policy with the minimum number of authorizations that models the system, i.e., the *minimum policy*.

Definition 13. **Minimum Policy (MP)**: A policy P is said to be minimum iff an equivalent policy P' does not exist such that $|P'| < |P|$.

Given a policy P we can compute an irreducible policy P' equivalent to P by removing authorizations that satisfy the redundancy condition. However, in order to compute the minimum policy P'' we may have to define new authorizations that do not exist in P or remove authorizations in P with the only constraint that the resulting policy P'' must have the same behaviour as the original one. The problem of checking whether a policy is minimum or not can be defined in the following way:

Definition 14. **Minimum Policy Problem**: Given a policy P, checking whether P is minimum is called Minimum Policy Problem (MPP).

Theorem 6. The *MPP* is **coNP-complete**.

We are more interested in the the problem of computing a minimum version P' of a given policy P (which is the search problem associated with the MPP). Since the associated decision problem is **coNP-complete**, the search problem is **NP-hard**. It is worth pointing out that depending on the given policy P, the search problems associated with *MIPP* and *MPP* may do not have a unique solution, i.e., there may be several different *minimum irreducible* and *minimum* versions of the same policy P (all with the same size).

Example 7. Although the policy computed in Example 6, is the minimum irreducible policy, a smaller policy exists and it is shown in Figure 3(c)[2]. This policy is the minimum policy.

4 Implementation

In this section, we present techniques for solving the *MIPP* and *MPP* problems. We ignore the *IPP* because several algorithms were proposed in the literature to solve this problem [5,9–11,16] (and also because any solution for *MIPP* is a solution for *IPP*). In the following we show how *MIPP* and *MPP* can be mapped on the *Weighted SAT* problem. The *Weighted SAT* problem is an extension of the SAT problem, and it is defined as follows:

Definition 15. **Weighted SAT**: Given a set of variables U and a collection C of clauses over U, computing, in case it exists, the truth assignment $t : U \rightarrow \{0, 1\}$ which satisfies C and minimizes a certain cost function $\sum_{u_i \in U'} k_i * u_i$, where $U' \subseteq U$ and $k_i \in \Re$, is called the **Weighted Satisfiability Problem**.

---

[2]We assume that the parent node is equal to the union of its children.

Section 4.1 presents how the *MIPP* can be mapped to the *Weighted SAT* problem, whereas in Section 4.2 we present a heuristic technique for solving *MIPP*. In Section 4.3 we present how the *MPP* can be mapped to the *Weighted SAT* problem. In Section 4.4 we present an algorithm that uses a heuristic approach to solve *MPP*. Section 4.5 presents some experimental results.

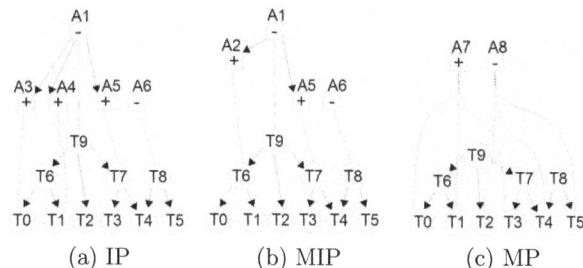

(a) IP   (b) MIP   (c) MP

Figure 3 Redundancy-free policies

4.1 MIPP to Weighted SAT

We can map the *MIPP* to the *Weighted SAT* problem, and we can use efficient *SAT*-solvers in order to identify the minimum irreducible version of the input policy. Let $P = < \Delta, \psi >$ be the input policy, we want to produce a policy $P' = < \Delta', \psi >$ such that $\Delta' \subseteq \Delta$ and P' is a minimum irreducible version of P. We denote with G the set *privileges*(Δ, ψ).

We define a variable a_i for each authorization $a_i \in \Delta$. Due to the fact that the correspondence between variables and authorizations is clear, in the following we switch freely between the two notations (e.g., sometimes a_i may refer to an authorization and sometimes it may refer to the variable associated with that authorization). For simplicity's sake, we do not present formulae in CNF (this is not a problem because it is always possible to translate a formula to an equivalent one in CNF).

The cost function $min \sum_{a_i \in \Delta} a_i$ aims at minimizing the number of authorizations in the resulting policy (and thus it guarantees that the resulting policy is the minimal irreducible one).

We still have to handle conflicts and the conflict resolution strategy in our *Weighted SAT* instance. Our approach considers a general conflict resolution strategy ψ. Let $t = < p, a, r >$ be a target defined in our model, we denote with K_t the set containing all the authorizations that act on the target t (i.e., $K_t = \{a_i \in \Delta | t \in T_{a_i}\}$). Given a target $t = < p, a, r >$ and a privilege $p = < s, p, a, r >$ we define $C(p)$ in following way:

$$C(p) = \bigvee_{X \in \mathbb{P}(K_t) \wedge sign(\psi(p,a,r,X)) = sign(p)} (\bigwedge_{a_i \in X} a_i \wedge \bigwedge_{a_i \in K_j \setminus X} \neg a_i)$$

For each privilege $p_j \in G$ we add a constraint in the form $C(p_j)$, this constraint enumerates all the possible combinations of authorizations that effectively grant the privilege p_j. By enforcing these constraints we ensure that the behaviour of the resulting policy is equivalent to the behaviour of P. An authorization $a_i \in \Delta$ is in Δ' iff the variable associated with a_i is set to one in the result of the *Weighted SAT* problem. It is easy to see that the result of the *Weighted SAT* problem produces a *Minimum Irreducible Policy*.

4.2 Heuristic Algorithm for MIPP

As described above the MIPP is a **coNP-complete** problem. Hence, in this Section we propose a heuristic algorithm that allows to find, in an efficient way, an irreducible policy close to one of the exact solutions.

Algorithm 3: Heuristic Algorithm for MIPP

Input : Policy P, Conflict Resolution Strategy CRS
Output: MIP P
begin

    bool removed;
    repeat
        removed = false;
        for $a \in P$ **do**
            List region = computeRegion(a, P);
            if *isRemovable(a, region, CRS)* **then**
                P.removeAuthorization(a);
                removed = true;
    until *removed;*

Our approach, shown in Algorithm 3, is based on an iterative process. Let $P =< \Delta, \psi >$ be the initial policy. At each iteration, the algorithm iterates over the authorizations and for each authorization a computes its region R_a^Δ by means of the *computeRegion* procedure. Then the algorithm checks whether the authorization satisfies the redundancy condition w.r.t. P by means of the *isRemovable* procedure, which takes as input (a) the selected authorization, (b) the region, and (c) the resolution strategy. If the authorization a satisfies the redundancy condition, then the algorithm removes it from the policy. The algorithm ends when no more authorizations satisfy the redundancy condition w.r.t. P; this means that the algorithm has reached a fixed point, and from Theorem 3 further reductions are not possible.

In order to improve the performance of the algorithm, we can optimize the *computeRegion* and the *isRemovable* procedures, by taking into account a specific conflict resolution strategy. For instance, if we consider the conflict resolution strategy presented in Section 2.1 we can tune both procedures in the following way. Let a be an authorization and P be the policy, the *computeRegion* procedure can produce a restricted region $R_a' = A_a \cup D_a \cup I_a$ where A_a is the set of direct ancestors of a (i.e., $A_a = \{a' \in \Delta | a \preceq a' \wedge \nexists a'' \in \Delta \setminus \{a, a'\} : (a \preceq a'' \wedge a'' \preceq a')\}$), D_a is the set of direct descendants of a (i.e., $D_a = \{a' \in \Delta | a' \preceq a \wedge \nexists a'' \in \Delta \setminus \{a, a'\} : (a'' \preceq a \wedge a' \preceq a'')\}$) and I_a is the set of most specific authorizations that have an intersection (at the target level) with a (i.e., $I_a = \{a' \in \Delta | a' \npreceq a \wedge a \npreceq a' \wedge T_a \cap T_{a'} \neq \emptyset \wedge \nexists a'' \in P \setminus \{a, a'\} : (a'' \preceq a' \wedge T_a \cap T_{a''} \neq \emptyset)\}$). The region R_a' is a subset of the region R_a and usually R_a' is quite smaller than R_a. In the same way we can improve the performance of the *isRemovable* procedure by leveraging the characteristics of the conflict resolution strategy, e.g, first we may check whether the *Most Specific Wins* criterion can be applied; if this is the case, then we need only to find the most specific authorization, otherwise we know that if at least one negative authorization is in the region, then the sign of the resulting authorization will be $-$ otherwise $+$.

4.3 MPP to Weighted SAT

In order to obtain an exact solution to the *MPP* problem, we can map it to the *Weighted SAT* problem, and we can use efficient *SAT*-solvers in order to identify the minimum version of the input policy. Let $P =< \Delta, \psi >$ be the input

---

Algorithm 4: Heuristic Algorithm for MPP

Input : Policy $P =< \Delta, \psi >$
Output: Policy $P' =< \Delta', \psi >$
begin

    $\Delta' = \emptyset;$
    $Pr = privileges(\Delta, \psi);$
    List pList = new List(Pr);
    while $pList \neq \emptyset$ **do**
        $p = pList[0];$
        $pList = pList.remove(p);$
        $added = false;$
        for $a \in P'$ **do**
            if *isCompatible(p, a, Pr)* **then**
                $added = true;$
                $T = privileges(a);$
                if $p \notin T$ **then**
                    $principals(a) = principals(a) \cup principal(p);$
                    $actions(a) = actions(a) \cup action(p);$
                    $resources(a) = resources(a) \cup resource(p);$
                    break;
        if *!added* **then**
            $a =< \{principal(p)\}, \{action(p)\}, \{resource(p)\} >;$
            $\Delta' = \Delta' \cup \{a\};$

---

policy, we want to produce a policy $P' =< \Delta', \psi >$ where P' is a minimum version of P. We denote with G the set $privileges(\Delta, \psi)$. Let k be $|G|$ and n be $|\Delta|$.

We define the following variables:

- $auth_1, \ldots, auth_n$ where each $auth_i$ represents an authorization,
- $p_{i,j}$ for each $i \in [1, n]$, $j \in [1, k]$. Each variable $p_{i,j}$ represents the fact that the privilege $p_j \in G$ is assigned to the authorization a_i,

The cost function $min \sum_{j \in [1,n]} auth_j$ aims at minimizing the number of authorizations in the resulting policy. We define the following clauses that aim at ensuring that the resulting policy is equivalent to the initial policy:

- For each privilege p_j we define a clause in the form $\bigvee_{i \in [1,n]} p_{i,j}$. The clause aims at enforcing the fact that the privilege has to be assigned to at least one authorization.
- For each authorization $auth_i$ we define the clauses in the form $\neg p_{i,j} \vee auth_i$ for each $j \in [1, k]$, which enforce the fact that if one of the privileges is assigned to an authorization, then the variable associated with the authorization is enabled.
- For each pair of privileges p_l and p_m such that $p_l \neq p_m$ and $sign(p_l) \neq sign(p_m)$ and $privileges(\{<\{principal(p_l), principal(p_m)\}, \{action(p_l), action(p_m)\}, \{resource(p_l), resource(p_m)\} >\}) \nsubseteq Z$ we define the clauses in the form $\overline{p_{i,l}} \vee \overline{p_{i,m}}$ for each $i \in [1, n]$ that enforce the fact that two incompatible privileges cannot be assigned to the same authorization.

The resulting policy P' is obtained by creating the authorizations $auth_i$ where $i \in [1, n]$ to which at least one privilege has been assigned to.

4.4 Heuristic Algorithm for MPP

We defined a heuristic algorithm, shown in Algorithm 4, which iteratively tries to build the minimum policy by adding a privilege at a time. First the algorithm computes the set of privileges granted by the policy P given as input. The algorithm tries to group together compatible privileges. In order to do this it iterates over the privileges, and at each iteration it tries to add the current privilege to the already existing authorizations. If no compatible authorization exists, it creates a new authorization. The *isCompatible* procedure takes as input a privilege p, an authorization a and the set of privileges Pr granted by the original policy and checks whether a and p can be merged or not, i.e., *isCompatible(p,a,Pr)* = $privileges(\{<principal(p)\cup principals(a), action(p)\cup actions(a), resource(p)\cup resources(a) >\}) \subseteq Pr \wedge sign(p) = sign(a)$.

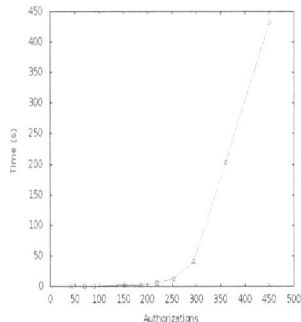

Figure 4 SAT MIPP   **Figure 5** Heuristic MIPP

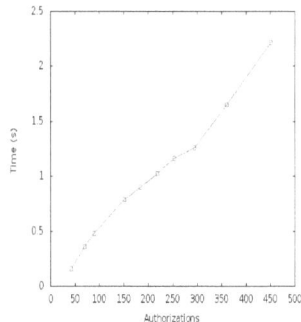

Original Size	Final Size	Delta Time %
43	22	25.58%
70	29	10.19%
88	25	3.78%
151	47	60.74%
184	58	58.86%
219	76	83.08%
253	92	90.64%
295	98	96.88%
360	112	99.19%
451	149	99.49%

Table 1 Comparison between the two MIPP methods

4.5 Experimental Results

We implemented a prototype for the evaluation of the performance of the techniques presented in this paper. The prototype consists of a Java module that invokes the implementation of the four approaches presented above. The exact solutions use the SAT4J[3] SAT solver. Since there are no freely available large datasets of real security policies, we chose to test our prototype against policies built according to an interpretation of the data in bibliographic databases. We used randomly selected subsets of *PubMed Central*[4] (PMC) which provides a rich set of attributes and relationships that represent a real and extensive social network. It has rich information about journals, with a description of editorships and the funding of papers.

Given a random sample of the *PMC* database, we built an instance of our model in the following way: (a) for each author or editor, we create a *principal*, (b) for each group of authors that have written a paper together, we create a *principal* containing the *principals* associated with the authors, (c) for each group of editors of a conference or a journal, we create a *principal* containing the *principals* associated with the groups (d) we defined three different actions *read*, *write* and *review*. We then created the following authorizations: (a) for each paper author we create the authorizations to

http://www.sat4j.org - Sat4j library for Java
[4]http://www.ncbi.nlm.nih.gov/pmc/

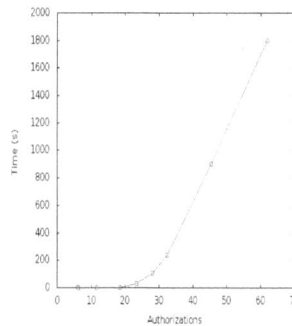

Figure 6 SAT MPP   **Figure 7** Heuristic MPP

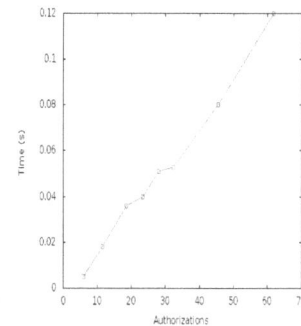

Original Size	Final Size	Delta Time %
6	4	93.67%
12	4	83.94%
19	4	76.70%
23	8	99.86%
28	9	99.95%
32	10	99.98%
45	11	99.99%
62	13	99.99%

Table 2 Comparison between the two MPP methods

read and *write* the paper and the negative authorization to *review* the paper, (b) for each editor of the issue of the journal containing the paper we add the authorizations to *read* and *review* the paper and the negative authorization to *write* the paper, (c) for each author that receives funding from the same grant that funded the paper, we add a negative authorization to *review* the paper and an authorization to *read* the paper, (d) for each group representing the institution to which the author is affiliated, we add the authorization to *read* the paper, (e) for each group representing the editorial board of the journal that published the paper we add the authorizations to *read* and *review* the paper and the negative authorization to *write* the paper. Experiments have been run on a PC with two Intel Xeon 2.0GHz/L3-4MB processors, 12GB RAM, four 1-Tbyte disks and Linux operating system. Each observation is the average of the execution of ten runs.

The results of the exact approach for the MIPP problem are shown in Figure 4, whereas the performance of the heuristic algorithm are shown in Figure 5. Table 1 shows a detailed comparison between the results of the two approaches. The heuristic approach is always able to identify the exact solution and the savings in execution time range from 3.78% to 99.49%.

The results of the exact approach for the MPP problem are shown in Figure 6, whereas the performance of the heuristic algorithm are shown in Figure 6. Table 2 shows a detailed comparison between the results of the two approaches. Also in this case the heuristic approach is always able to identify the exact solution and the savings in execution time range from 76.70% to 99.99%. However the MIPP exact solution scales better than the MPP one.

Empirical results show that both heuristic algorithms could be a good approximation of the exact ones. They allow the analysis of real policies with a good precision and with good response time. Figure 8 and Figure 9 compare the performance of the two heuristic algorithms, both in terms of execution time and reduction. The execution time of the two algorithms is very similar with policy with a size lower

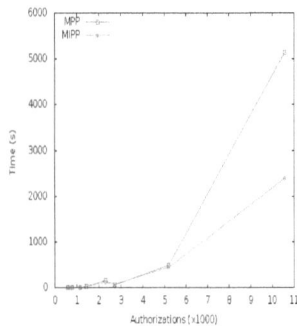

Figure 8 Time Comparison   **Figure 9** Size Comparison

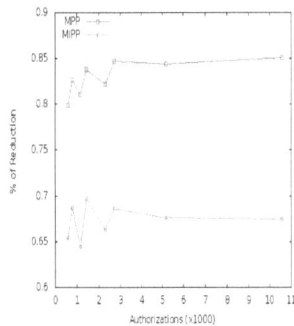

than 5000 authorizations. After that threshold the MIPP algorithm performs better. On the other hand, the MPP algorithm allows to compute smaller policies than the MIPP. The MPP allows to obtain a policy which is usually 20% smaller than the policies resulting from the MIPP, but its execution may take more time.

5   Related Work

Several works recognize that real security policies may contain redundancy [13, 16], and that this fact may lead to an increase in the total management costs of the policies. Redundancy may also reduce the efficiency of the global access control system.

The firewall community has shown a great interest in detection and removal of redundancy from firewall policies [1–3, 5, 11, 16].

Basile et al. [5] present an approach to anomaly detection which is based on the representation of policies by means of hyper-rectangles. Their approach can be used to identify redundant rules in firewall policies. Fireman [16] is a tool that can be used also to detect redundant rules in firewall policies by using Binary Decision Diagrams. Al-Shaer and Hamed proposed *Firewall Policy Advisor* [1–3], a tool that is able to detect several anomalies in firewall policies and also redundancies. In [11] Liu and Gouda model policies by means of *Firewall Decision Trees*, and present an algorithm that can be used to detect redundant rules.

In our opinion the models used in these works are quite simple, because they usually have only two actions, i.e. *accept* and *deny*, and they consider only the hierarchy of IP addresses, and thus comparison with approaches that consider more complex models may be difficult.

An interest in anomaly detection for access control policies has grown also in the computer security community [4, 8–10].

Kolovski et al. [10] tackle the fact that complex XACML policies are hard to understand and evaluate manually, and, thus, automated tools are needed. They propose to map XACML to Description Logics (DL), to benefit from off-the-shelf DL reasoners. They implement in DL a reasoning service that can be used to identify redundant authorizations. Also Hu et al. [9] provide a way to detect redundant authorizations in XACML policies. They model access control policies by means of boolean expressions, and then they represent these expressions using BDDs.

Although our work does not consider explicitly a particular scenario, our model is general enough to be adapted to represent both firewall policies (there is only one *Principal* which represents any incoming packet, *Actions* are only

deny and *accept*, and *Resources* represent IP addresses) and XACML policies (the mapping from XACML to our model is trivial in case of stateless XACML policies).

All the works presented above propose only solutions that compute an *irreducible version* of the original policy given as input, they do not try to compute the *minimum irreducible version* nor the *minimum version* of the original policy. To the best of our knowledge no algorithms for the *Minimum Irreducible Policy Problem* and *Minimum Policy Problem* exist.

Despite the fact that the *Minimum Policy Problem* may have some aspects in common with Role Mining [7], i.e., it tries to compute a minimum representation of the behaviour of the access control mechanism, there are also several differences, i.e. (a) *MPP* can be applied also to situations in which no roles exist (e.g. in firewalls), (b) *MPP* does not try to extract any meaningful information from the user-permission assignments, (c) *MPP* can be applied also as an optimization step just before the actual deployment of the policy; in this way by obtaining a smaller equivalent policy security administrators can implement a policy that achieves better performance [11, 16].

6   Conclusions

We analyzed the presence of redundancies in access control policies and we have shown that the interesting problems related with redundancy are NP-hard. Although exact solutions can be found by means of *SAT solvers*, the empirical evidence we reported confirms that the approaches do not scale well. Thus, we proposed two *heuristic algorithms*. For the *Minimum Irreducible Policy Problem* we defined a heuristic approach that iteratively computes which authorizations satisfy the redundancy condition by computing their regions. For the *Minimum Policy Problem* we defined a heuristic approach that iteratively tries to identify compatible privileges. We conducted a detailed performance analysis, which shows that our heuristic solutions can compute solutions very close to the optimal one, with a performance that, as expected, significantly outperforms exact solutions in terms of execution time and remains applicable even with large policies.

7   References

[1] AL-SHAER, E., AND HAMED, H. Firewall policy advisor for anomaly detection and rule editing. In *Proc. of IEEE/IFIP Integrated Management* (2003).

[2] AL-SHAER, E., AND HAMED, H. Discovery of policy anomalies in distributed firewalls. In *Proc. of IEEE Infocom* (2004).

[3] AL-SHAER, E., AND HAMED, H. Modeling and management of firewall policies. *IEEE Transactions on Network and Service Management 1*, 1 (2004).

[4] ARRIGONI NERI, M., GUARNIERI, M., MAGRI, E., MUTTI, S., AND PARABOSCHI, S. Conflict detection in security policies using semantic web technology. In *Proc. of the ESTEL 2012 - Security Track*.

[5] BASILE, C., CAPPADONIA, A., AND LIOY, A. Network-level access control policy analysis and transformation. *Networking, IEEE/ACM Transactions on, 99* (2011).

[6] BONATTI, P., DE CAPITANI DI VIMERCATI, S., AND SAMARATI, P. An algebra for composing access control policies. *ACM TISSEC 5*, 1 (2002).

[7] FRANK, M., BUHMANN, J. M., AND BASIN, D. On the definition of role mining. In *Proc. of SACMAT 2010*, ACM.

[8] GUARNIERI, M., MAGRI, E., AND MUTTI, S. Automated management and analysis of security policies using eclipse. In *Proc. of the Eclipse-IT 2012*.

[9] HU, H., AHN, G., AND KULKARNI, K. Anomaly discovery and resolution in web access control policies. In *Proc. of SACMAT '11*, ACM.

[10] KOLOVSKI, V., HENDLER, J., AND PARSIA, B. Analyzing web access control policies. In *Proc. of WWW 2007*, ACM.

[11] LIU, A., AND GOUDA, M. Complete redundancy detection in firewalls. In *Data and Applications Security XIX*, vol. 3654. 2005.

[12] LUPU, E., AND SLOMAN, M. Conflicts in policy-based distributed systems management. *IEEE TSE 25*, 6 (1999).

[13] MOLLOY, I., CHEN, H., LI, T., WANG, Q., LI, N., BERTINO, E., CALO, S., AND LOBO, J. Mining roles with multiple objectives. *ACM TISSEC 2010*.

[14] SANDHU, R. Role-based access control. *Advances in computers 46* (1998).

[15] SHEN, H., AND DEWAN, P. Access control for collaborative environments. In *Proc. of the CSCW'92*, ACM.

[16] YUAN, L., CHEN, H., MAI, J., CHUAH, C., SU, Z., AND MOHAPATRA, P. FIREMAN: a toolkit for firewall modeling and analysis. In *Proc. of IEEE S&P* (2006).

APPENDIX

Lemma 1. Let $P = < \Delta, \psi >$ be a policy and let $auth$ an authorization in Δ. If $auth$ satisfies the *redundancy condition* w.r.t. P then $privileges(\Delta, \psi) = privileges(\Delta \setminus \{auth\}, \psi)$.

Proof of Lemma 1 We prove the lemma by contradiction. We assume that $auth$ satisfies the *redundancy condition* w.r.t. P, and that $privileges(\Delta, \psi) \neq privileges(\Delta \setminus \{auth\}, \psi)$. This means that there is at least a target $< p, a, r >$ that behaves in a different way under P and under $P \setminus \{auth\}$. This fact implies that $\exists s \in \{+, -\}$: $< s, p, a, r > \in privileges(auth)$ such that one of the two following cases holds:

1. $< s, p, a, r > \in privileges(\Delta, \psi)$ and does not exist any sign $s' \in \{+, -\}$ such that $< s', p, a, r > \in privileges(\Delta \setminus \{auth\}, \psi)$. This means that $\psi(p, a, r, \Delta \setminus \{auth\}) = \perp$, but this generates a contradiction due to the *completeness* property of ψ and the definition of the *redundancy condition*.

2. $< s, p, a, r > \in privileges(\Delta, \psi) \land$ $< s', p, a, r > \in privileges(\Delta \setminus \{auth\}, \psi)$ where s' is the opposite sign of s (i.e., if $s = +$ then $s' = -$ and viceversa), but this fact contradicts the definition of the *redundancy condition*. $\square$

Proof of Theorem 1 It follows trivially from Lemma 1. $\square$

Proof of Theorem 2 We prove the theorem by contradiction. We assume that there is an $auth$ that satisfies the redundancy condition w.r.t. P_j but does not satisfies the redundancy condition w.r.t. a $P_i \cup \{auth\}$ where $j < i \leq n$. Due to the fact that $R_{auth}^{P_i \cup \{auth\}} \subseteq R_{auth}^{P_j}$, it follows that there is at least a privilege $< s, p, a, r > \in privileges(auth)$ for which one of the following holds:

1. $\psi(p, a, r, R_{auth}^{P_i \cup \{auth\}}) = \perp$, but this is impossible because $R_{auth}^{P_i \cup \{auth\}}$ contains $auth$ and ψ is complete.

2. $sign(\psi(p, a, r, R_{auth}^{P_i \cup \{auth\}} \setminus \{auth\})) \neq$ $sign(\psi(p, a, r, R_{auth}^{P_i \cup \{auth\}}))$ (we refer in the following to this property as $\circ$). From the fact that all the authorizations that are in P_j but not in $P_i \cup \{auth\}$ satisfies the redundancy condition, it follows that also if we add them to $P_i \cup \{auth\}$ they preserve the $\circ$ property. This means that also $P_i \cup \{auth\} \cup (P_j \setminus (P_i \cup \{auth\})) = P_j$ satisfies the $\circ$ property, but this is a contradiction.

In both cases we have a contradiction, so we have proved the theorem. $\square$

Lemma 2. Let P be a security policy. There is a $P' \subset P$ equivalent to P iff there is at least an authorization $auth \in P$ that satisfies the redundancy condition w.r.t. P.

Proof of Lemma 2 $\Leftarrow$) Suppose there is an authorization $auth \in P$ that satisfies the redundancy condition w.r.t. P. This means that there is a sequence of reductions in which P and $P' = P \setminus \{auth\}$ appear, and thus from Theorem 1 we know that P and P' are equivalent (and $P' \subset P$ holds). $\Rightarrow$) We prove this part by contradiction. Let $P' \subset P$ be equivalent to P and let $S \subseteq P$ be the set of authorizations that satisfies the redundancy condition w.r.t. P. We assume that $S = \emptyset$. From the fact that $P' \subset P$ and P' is equivalent to P, follows that all the authorizations in $K = P \setminus P'$ do not influence the behaviour of P. Without loss of generality, we consider only the case in which $|K| = 1$ (i.e., $K = \{auth'\}$). The fact that $auth'$ does not influence the behaviour of P means that for each privilege $< s, p, a, r > \in privileges(auth')$ the following statements hold:

- $sign(\psi(p, a, r, P \setminus \{auth'\})) = sign(\psi(p, a, r, P))$ and from the fact that ψ satisfies the monotonicity property this is equivalent to $sign(\psi(p, a, r, R_{auth'}^P \setminus \{auth'\})) = sign(\psi(p, a, r, R_{auth'}^P))$,
- $\psi(p, a, r, P \setminus \{auth'\}) \neq \perp$, but since ψ satisfies the completeness property this implies the fact that $\psi(p, a, r, R_{auth'}^P \setminus \{auth\}) \neq \perp$.

This means that $auth'$ is redundant w.r.t. P, and thus $S \neq \emptyset$ which lead to a contradiction. $\square$

Proof of Theorem 3 It follows trivially from Lemma 2. $\square$

Algorithm 5: *irreduciblePolicy* procedure

Input : Policy $P = < \Delta, \psi >$
Output: Policy $P' = < \Delta', \psi >$ where $P' \subseteq P$
begin
    $\Delta' = \Delta$;
    bool continue =**true**;
    while *continue* **do**
        $\Gamma = \emptyset$;
        continue =**false**;
        for $auth \in \Delta'$ **do**
            if *satisfies*$(auth, \Delta')$ **then**
                $\Gamma = \Gamma \cup \{auth\}$;
                continue =**true**;
                Break;
        $\Delta' = \Delta' \setminus \Gamma$;

Proof of Theorem 4 Algorithm 5 computes an irreducible version of the policy P given as input, and it can be executed in polynomial time (the procedure $satisfies(auth, \Delta')$ checks whether the authorization $auth$ satisfy the redundancy condition w.r.t. Δ' and it can be executed in time polynomial in the size of the set Δ and in the size of the Target Hierarchy). Given a policy P we can check if P is irreducible by checking whether $P = irreduciblePolicy(P)$. $\square$

Proof of Theorem 5 A nondeterministic algorithm need only to guess a sequence of reduction R starting from P. If $|end(S)| < |P|$ we have found an irreducible version of the policy P' with less authorizations than P, and thus P is not a Minimum Irreducible Policy and we have found a solution to the $\overline{MIPP}$. We have already shown that the $\overline{MIPP}$ is in **NP**. Now we have to show that a **NP-complete** problem can be reduced in polynomial time to $\overline{MIPP}$. We consider the *Set Covering Problem* (SCP). The SCP is defined in the following way: given a set X, a collection of subsets of X called C, such that $X = \bigcup_{C_i \in C} C_i$, and an integer value $k < |C|$, does exist a $C' \subset C$ such that $X = \bigcup_{C'_i \in C'} C'_i$ and $|C'| \leq k$?

We can map SCP to $\overline{MIPP}$ in the following way:

- we define an action a and a resource r,
- for each element $x_i \in X$ we define a principal p_i and a privilege $< +, p_i, a, r >$,
- for each element $C_i \in C$ we define an authorization $< +, P_i, a, r >$ where P_i is the set containing all the principals associated with the elements $x_j \in C_i$,
- we define the original policy P' composed by all the authorizations associated with each $C_i \in C$. The policy P' has $|C|$ authorizations,
- we define the policy P composed by $k+1$ authorizations in the following way: it contains the k authorizations associated with $C_1, \ldots, C_k$, it contains an authorization $< +, P_{all}, a, r >$ where P_{all} contains all the principals associated with the elements in $C_{k+1}, \ldots, C_{|C|}$.

The algorithm presented above is obviously polynomial, and it produces a pair of policies. The original policy P' is composed by $|C|$ authorizations, each one with the form $auth_i = < +, \{p_1, \ldots, p_j\}, a, r >$ where $p_1, \ldots, p_j$ are the principals associated with the elements of X which belong to C_i. The policy P which has to be checked for minimum irreducibility is composed by $k+1$ authorizations.

We have only to show that $SCP \Longleftrightarrow \overline{MIPP}$. On the one hand we assume that there exists a $C' \subset C$ such that $X = \bigcup_{C'_i \in C'} C'_i$ and $|C'| \leq k < |C|$. This means that we can create a policy P'' composed by $|C'|$ authorizations (we generate an authorization $auth_i$ that contains all the privileges associated with the elements of C'_i for each element $C'_i \in C$) that is equivalent to P', because the privileges in P'' and P' are the same given the fact that C' is a cover for X. In addition, P'' is smaller than P ($|P''| \leq k \leq |P|$) and $P'' \subset P'$, and thus we have found an equivalent policy smaller than P. Also the $\overline{MIPP}$ evaluates to *yes* because P is not a minimum irreducible policy. Conversely, we assume that $\overline{MIPP}$ evaluates to *yes* and thus the policy P is not a minimum irreducible version of P'. This means that there exists a policy P'', equivalent to P', such that $|P''| < |P| = k + 1$ and $P'' \subseteq P'$ and this means that there exists a cover $C' \subset C$ with the same cardinality of P'' and thus $|C'| \leq k$. $\square$

Given a set of authorizations A and an authorization $auth$, we can compute whether $auth$ implies all the authorizations in the set A by means of the function *implies(auth, A)* shown in Algorithm 6 (the functions *principals+*, *actions+* and *resources+* are the transitive closures of *principals*, *actions* and *resources* over the respective hierarchies).

Proof of Theorem 6 A nondeterministic algorithm need only to guess a set of authorizations A, and an authorization $auth$ such that $|A| \geq 2$, $A \subseteq P$ and $auth \notin A$, and then we can check in polynomial time, using the Algorithm 6,

---

Algorithm 6: *implies* procedure

Input : *auth, A*
Output: *True* or *False*
begin
  for $auth' \in A$ **do**
    if $sign(auth) = sign(auth')$ **then**
      if $principals+(auth') \not\subseteq$
      $principals+(auth) \vee actions+(auth') \not\subseteq$
      $actions+(auth) \vee resources+(auth') \not\subseteq$
      $resources+(auth)$ **then**
        return *False*;
    else
      return *False*;
  return *True*;

---

whether the policy is not minimum. If the *implies* procedure returns *True*, this means that an equivalent policy P' with a size of $|P| - |A| + 1$ exists (this policy is the one that we can obtain by removing from P all the authorizations in A and adding *auth*) and thus we have found a solution to the $\overline{MPP}$ (i.e., given a policy P checking whether P is not minimum). We have already shown that the $\overline{MPP}$ is in **NP**. Now we have to show that an **NP-complete** problem can be reduced in polynomial time to $\overline{MPP}$. We consider the *Set Covering Problem* (SCP). The SCP is defined in the following way: given a set X, a collection of subsets of X called C, such that $X = \bigcup_{C_i \in C} C_i$, and an integer value $k < |C|$, does exist a $C' \subset C$ such that $X = \bigcup_{C'_i \in C'} C'_i$ and $|C'| \leq k$?

We can map SCP to $\overline{MPP}$ in the following way:

- we define an action a and a resource r,
- for each element $x_i \in X$ we define a principal p_i and a privilege $< +, p_i, a, r >$,
- we define a policy composed by $k + 1$ authorizations $auth_0, \ldots, auth_k$,
- for each element $C_i \in C$ we add the privileges associated with all the elements in C_i to the authorization $auth_{i \bmod(k+1)}$.

The algorithm presented above is obviously polynomial, and it produces a policy composed by $k+1$ authorizations, each one with the form $auth_i = < +, \{p_1, \ldots, p_{l_i}\}, a, r >$ where l_i is the number of principals in the authorization $auth_i$.

We have only to show that $SCP \Longleftrightarrow \overline{MPP}$. On the one hand we assume that there exists a $C' \subset C$ such that $X = \bigcup_{C'_i \in C'} C'_i$ and $|C'| \leq k$. This means that we can create a policy P' composed by $|C'|$ authorizations (we generate an authorization $auth_i$ for each element $C'_i \in C$ that contains all the privileges associated with the elements of C'_i) that is equivalent to P, because the privileges in P and P' are the same given the fact that C' is a cover for X. In addition, the size of P is at most k that is smaller than P, and thus also the $\overline{MPP}$ evaluates to *yes*. Conversely, we assume that $\overline{MPP}$ evaluates to *yes* and thus the policy P is not minimum. This means that there exists a policy P', equivalent to P, such that $|P'| < |P| = k + 1$ and thus this means that there exists a cover $C' \subset C$ with the same cardinality of P' and thus $|C'| \leq k$. $\square$

Specification and Analysis of Access Control Policies for Mobile Applications

Ramadan Abdunabi
Computer Science Dept.
Colorado State University
Fort Collins, CO 80523
rabdunab@cs.colostate.edu

Indrakshi Ray
Computer Science Dept.
Colorado State University
Fort Collins, CO 80523
iray@cs.colostate.edu

Robert France
Computer Science Dept.
Colorado State University
Fort Collins, CO 80523
france@cs.colostate.edu

ABSTRACT

Mobile applications allow individuals on-the-move access to resources "anytime, anywhere" using hand-held mobile devices. We argue that for critical and sensitive resources this is often times not desirable – a lost or stolen mobile device can be tampered with to view or alter sensitive information. We need authorization policies that take into account time of access and location of the user in addition to the credentials of the user. Towards this end, we propose a new spatio-temporal role-based access control model. It improves upon existing models by providing features that are useful for mobile applications. Thus, an application using our model can specify different types of spatio-temporal constraints. We discuss how such an application using our spatio-temporal access control model can be verified using the UPPAAL model checker. We also demonstrate how to reduce the state-space explosion problem that is inherent in model checkers.

Categories and Subject Descriptors

D.2.1 [**Requirements/Specifications**]: [Languages, Methodologies]; K.6.5 [**Management of Computing and Information Systems**]: [Security and Protection]

Keywords

spatio-temporal access control; policy analysis

1. INTRODUCTION

The growth of mobile device technology has benefited numerous applications domains including e-commerce, electronic government, health care, and power-control systems. For example, mobile health care applications can detect and alert medical professionals of a patient's fall anytime and anywhere[30]. These enhanced features come with a cost – mobile devices may get lost or stolen and they can be used to launch an attack. Consequently, access to critical resources and services should not only depend on the credentials of

the user, but also on the time and place of access. Towards this end, we propose a spatio-temporal access control model for mobile applications and discuss how the authorization policies can be automatically verified to provide assurance about secure executions.

The need for spatio-temporal access control arises in many applications. The iMedik [23] is a mobile telemedicine application accessible by handheld devices that are integrated with Global Positioning System (GPS). With the help of mobile devices, doctors can access their patient information on the move. The security policy allows doctors to use handheld devices to view complete Patient Medical Record (PMR) information in the clinic during day-time, but for reasons of privacy allows them to view only partial PMR information outside the clinic during night-time. Incorrect specification and enforcement of such policies may cause the system to malfunction and in the worst case scenario may cause a patient to lose his life. Spatio-temporal access control can also be used to enforce that only on-campus students have access to digital libraries, campus licenses, and Internet movies during the semester. Proper spatio-temporal access control can prevent a malicious user in a public location from activating a missile launcher system in order to fire a missile.

There is a lot of research in spatio-temporal access control. Researchers have advocated extending Role-Based Access Control (RBAC) with spatial and temporal constraints, such that authorization is contingent upon time and place of access. To the best of our knowledge, the most known and detailed spatio-temporal RBAC extensions are in [3, 4, 12, 29, 36]. Most of the work on spatio-temporal RBAC associate two entities, namely, location and time with users, roles, and permissions. The location and time associated with a user gives the current time and his present location. The location and time associated with a role designate when and where the role can be activated. The location and time associated with a permission signify when and where a permission can be invoked. In addition, researchers have also suggested how spatio-temporal constraints can be associated with role hierarchy (RH) and separation of duties (SoD) relations.

Existing works on extending RBAC with spatio-temporal constraints authorize access based on the *present* environmental conditions related to a user, but do not provide mechanisms for *persistent* spatio-temporal control enforcement after resources have been accessed. Most of the existing work also do not allow for the specification of the spatio-temporal prerequisite or triggers constraints. In existing models, the resource is also not explicitly modeled; however, mobile applications may access moving objects and the access to such objects may be contingent on its location. In existing models, the location and time information are represented as an external data structure for determining access apart from the model structure. The relationship between such information and RBAC components in the model structure is often unclear. In other words, these models define user, role, permission entities and entity relationships as their core components; but they lack the definition of an entity that contains spatio-temporal information in the model and also its association with the model entities.

Treating location and time separately makes policy specifications harder and non-intuitive. Moreover, the number of entities increases significantly making the comprehension and analysis of the policies more challenging. Automated verification becomes harder because of the increase in search space. Policy evolution is also non-trivial. Let us explain this with an example. Suppose a *doctor* role can be activated at locations {*hospital, clinic*} in the interval *[8:00 a.m. - 5:00 p.m.]*. This means that the *doctor* can activate his/her role either in the *hospital* or *clinic* anytime from 8:00 a.m. to 5:00 p.m. Suppose the medical board decides to change the spatio-temporal constraints such that the *doctor* can only activate his/her role in the *hospital* in the interval *[8:00 a.m. - 1:00 p.m.]* and can only activate his/her role in the *clinic* during *[12:00 p.m. - 5:00 p.m.]*. In order to specify such a constraint, we would have to split the doctor role into two roles, namely, *hospital doctor* and *clinic doctor* and associate the respective location and temporal constraints with each of them. Such a change is non-trivial. Consequently, we propose to introduce a new concept, *spatio-temporal zone*, that abstracts location and time into a single entity and avoids the problems mentioned earlier.

We introduce the concept of spatio-temporal zone that makes it possible to abstract location and time into one single entity. This, in turn, reduces the number of entities that must be managed and also prevents creation of new roles or permissions when spatio-temporal constraints associated with them change. The spatio-temporal zone is a new logical RBAC entity that encapsulates location and time information. The spatio-temporal zone is referred to as *STZone* and is denoted by a pair of location and time values that is of interest to some RBAC entity. In the previous example, the *doctor* role is initially associated with the following set of STZones: { <*hospital, [8:00 a.m. − 5:00 p.m.]*>, <*clinic, [8:00 a.m. − 5 p.m.]*> }. When the medical board decides to change the policy, this can be achieved by simply changing the *STZones* associated with the *doctor* role as follows: { <*hospital, [8:00 a.m. − 1:00 p.m.]* >, <*clinic, [12:00 p.m. − 5 p.m.]*> }. Abstracting location and time into a single STZone also reduces the number of entities in the model, making it easier to understand, manage, and verify.

Our model has many features that may interact in subtle ways to produce inconsistencies and conflicts. Incorrect policies may cause security breaches. Consequently, the security policies of an application must be analyzed. Researchers have proposed automated analysis approaches for verifying spatio-temporal RBAC policies using existing formal method notations and tools. Examples include UML/OCL [28, 33], Alloy [31, 35], and Colored Petri Nets [32, 27]. Most of these approaches perform rigorous analysis of temporal behaviors, but hard real-time properties cannot be verified using these approaches. Most approaches express the be-

havior of real-time systems as discrete time behaviors using many integer valued variables. In such techniques, continuous time is approximated to some fixed quantum. However, events do not always happen at integer-valued times. This, in turn, limits the accuracy of the real-time verification.

The notion of complex real-time in spatio-temporal policies necessitates the use of a formalization that supports quantitative analysis of temporal properties and makes it easy to specify temporal properties. We need to consider temporal properties that not only refer to the order in which certain events take place (before and after), but also the properties that take place or change over time at exact real-time units.

Timed-automata [5] provide a framework to model the behavior of real-time systems in annotated state transition graphs that have timed transitions labeled with piece-wise real-valued clocks. Timed-automata has been successfully applied in many case studies [7, 16, 10, 17] to verify complex real-time systems that rely on strict timing constraints, including timing delays, periodicity, bounded response time, and execution time. A number of automated tools, such as COSPAN [6], KRONOS [13], and UPPAAL [8] are available for modeling, specifying, and verifying the correctness of timed-automaton models. Spatio-temporal access control policies can be viewed as a timed state transition system. Temporal constraints are expressed by real-timed clocks that precisely capture the elapsed time between events since the last reset of the clocks. Spatial constraints are specified by using shared integer variables and control states. We use the model checker UPPAAL for our work.

In order to verify real-world problems, we often encounter the state explosion problem in model checkers. Towards this end, we explore some optimization techniques supported by UPPAAL for improving the performance analysis and carefully reduce the temporal conditions that need to be verified. We also provide techniques for abstracting away the unnecessary details to reduce the state-space being verified. This technique excludes the non-dependent timed-automata processes during the verification of certain properties, and as such, improves the analysis accuracy and performance.

The remainder of this paper is organized as follows. Section 2 formalizes the features of our proposed model. Section 3 demonstrates how a real world application policy, the Dengue Decision Support System (DDSS), can be specified using our model. Section 4 elaborates on our analysis approach. Specifically, it describes how the spatio-temporal RBAC components can be expressed by timed-automata, provides the algorithms for constructing a timed-automata model for a spatio-temporal policy, and also discusses the state-space reduction technique that is important for automated verification. Section 5 describes the analysis of the DDSS policy using UPPAAL and also presents the analysis results. Section 6 lists a few works that are related to this work. Section 7 concludes the paper with pointers to future work directions.

2. SPATIO-TEMPORAL ACCESS CONTROL MODEL

Figure 1 shows our spatio-temporal RBAC. The models' entities are represented by oval shapes, and the single directional and bi-directional arrows respectively represent one-to-one and many-to-many relations between those entities.

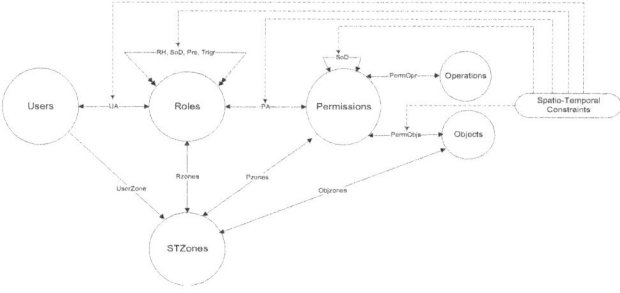

Figure 1: A Conceptual Model of the Proposed Spatio-Temporal RBAC

The bi-directional arrow with double heads represents multiple relations between the same entities. Most entities in the graph are connected to the STZone entity in order to express the spatio-temporal constraints. The cylinder shape depicts the spatio-temporal constraints on model relationships.

2.1 Spatio-Temporal Zone Representation

In our model, each entity and relation is associated with a spatio-temporal zone. Before describing these associations in details, we show how spatio-temporal information is represented in our models.

A spatio-temporal zone $STZone$ is an abstract logical unit that encapsulates both spatial and temporal information. A spatio-temporal zone z_i is represented as a pair: $< l_i, d_i >$ where l_i, d_i denote the spatial and the temporal component, respectively.

DEFINITION 1. **[Spatio-Temporal Zone]** *A spatio-temporal zone STZone is a pair of the form $< l, d >$ where l and d represent the logical location and time interval, respectively.*

The logical locations pertaining to an application are organized using a *containment* relationship, which is reflexive, transitive, and anti-symmetric. For example, *Colorado* is contained in U.S.A. A *containment* relationship can also be defined over time intervals, which consists of sets of time instants.

DEFINITION 2. **[Operators on Spatio-Temporal Zone]** *We define the following operators on spatio-temporal zones.*

- *Spatio-temporal Zone Containment $z_j \subseteq z_i$: Spatio-temporal zone $z_j =< l_j, d_j >$ is said to be contained in zone $z_i =< l_i, d_i >$, denoted by, $z_j \subseteq z_i$, if $d_i \subseteq d_j$ and $l_i \subseteq l_j$.*

- *Spatio-temporal Zone Equality $z_i = z_j$: Two spatio-temporal zones $z_i =< l_i, d_i >$ and $z_j =< l_j, d_j >$ are equal, denoted by $z_i = z_j$, if $d_i = d_j$ and $l_i = l_j$.*

- *Spatio-temporal Zone Overlap $z_j \subseteq z_i$: Two spatio-temporal zones $z_i =< l_i, d_i >$ and $z_j =< l_j, d_j >$ overlap, denoted by $z_i \cap z_j$, if $d_i \cap d_j \neq \{\}$ and $l_i \cap l_j \neq \{\}$.*

Consider the following example of STZones containment. $< FortCollinsOffice, May2013 > \subseteq < Colorado, Year2013 >$ since $FortCollins \subseteq Colorado$ and $May2013 \subseteq Year2013$. However, $< FortCollins, May2013 > \not\subseteq < Colorado, Year2010 >$ since $May2013 \not\subseteq Year2010$. Similarly, $< FortCollins, May2013 > \not\subseteq < Nevada, Year2013 >$ because $FortCollins \not\subseteq Nevada$.

2.2 Entities and Relationships

Model entities and relationships are associated with spatio-temporal zones to constrain access.
Users:

Users are mobile and may issue access requests from anywhere and at any place. The model assumes that tamper-proof location and time devices are attached to the user that reports her spatio-temporal zone. *Users* is the set of all authorized users in the system. A *UserZone* function that gives the current spatio-temporal zone associated with the user is defined in the model. The model also requires that the user zone be reported at the minimum granularity permitted by the application.

- $UserZone : Users \rightarrow STZones$

Roles:

A role is available for activation or assignment in some predefined spatio-temporal zones referred to as *role zones*. The set of all role identifiers in a system is denoted as *Roles*. The function *Rzones* gives the set of spatio-temporal zones associated with a role.

- $Rzones : Roles \rightarrow 2^{STZones}$

User Role Assignment:

The $can\_AssignRole(u, r, z)$ predicate holds when the current user zone z is contained in the set of role zones for r. If this predicate is true, $AssignRole(u, r, z)$ action can take place either automatically or initiated by the security administrator. Execution of the action will change the function $assigned\_roles(u, z)$. The $assigned\_roles(u, z)$ function returns the roles assigned to the user in a particular zone. The user-role assignment is defined in the UA relation.

- $can\_AssignRole(u, r, z) \Rightarrow UserZone(u) = z \wedge$
  $(\exists z' \in Rzones(r) \bullet z \subseteq z')$
- $assigned\_roles : (Users \times STZones) \rightarrow 2^{Roles}$

Role Enabling:

Once a role is enabled in a spatio-temporal zone, the role can be activated. The predicate $can\_EnableRole(r, z)$ specifies where and when the role can be enabled. If the predicate $can\_Enable(r, z)$ returns true, then action $EnableRole(r, z)$ can take place. This action takes place automatically and is enforced through triggers. $can\_Enable(r, z)$ is true implies that z is contained in the zones associated with role r. The function $enabled\_roles(z)$ returns the current enabled roles in zone z.

- $can\_EnableRole(r, z) \Rightarrow \exists z' \in Rzones(r) \bullet z \subseteq z'$
- $enabled\_roles : STZones \rightarrow 2^{Roles}$

User Role Activation:

For a user to activate a role, the $can\_ActivateRole(u, r, z)$ predicate must be satisfied. Only when this predicate is satisfied, the action $ActivateRole(u, r, z)$ can take place. Execution of this action causes the set $active\_roles(u, z)$ to be modified. $can\_ActivateRole(u, r, z)$ holds if the role r can be enabled in zone z, the current user zone is z, and role r can be assigned to user u in zone z. Function $active\_roles(u, z)$ maps a user u in zone z to the set of roles that he has activated.

175

- $can\_ActivateRole(u, r, z) \Rightarrow r \in enabled\_roles(z) \land r \in$ $assigned\_roles(u, z) \land UserZone(u) = z$
- $active\_roles : (Users \times STZones) \rightarrow 2^{Roles}$

Objects:

The *Objects* set defines the objects in a system. The function *Objzones(obj)* associates object *obj* with its set of spatio-temporal zones.

- $Objzones : Objects \rightarrow 2^{STZones}$

Operations:

Operations is the set of all operations performed in a system.

Permissions:

Permissions is the set of all permissions in the system. Spatio-temporal zones are also associated with permissions that determine where and when a permission can be used. The function *Pzones* gives the set of zones where the corresponding permission can be invoked.

- $Pzones : Permissions \rightarrow 2^{STZones}$

The following functions define the operations and objects respectively associated with a given permission in some spatio-temporal zone.

- $permObjs : (Permissions \times STZones) \rightarrow 2^{Objects}$
- $permOpr : (Permissions \times STZones) \rightarrow 2^{Operations}$

Permission Role Assignment:

The predicate *can_AssignPerm(r, p, z)* evaluates to true if permission p can be assigned to role r in zone z. When this predicate is true, the action *AssignPerm(r, p, z)* can take place. The function *assigned_perms(r, z)* determines all the explicitly assigned permissions to role r in zone z. The permission-role assignment is defined by relation PA.

- $can\_AssignPerm(r, p, z) \Rightarrow \exists z' \in Rzones(r) \land \exists z'' \in$ $Pzones(p) \land z \subseteq (z' \cap z'')$
- $assigned\_perms : (Roles \times STZones) \rightarrow 2^{Permissions}$

User Permission Authorization:

The predicate *can_InvokePerm(u, p, z)* evaluates whether user u is authorized to invoke permission p in zone z. The predicate returns true if there is a role r assigned to user in zone z, p is assigned to role r in z, and zone of u is z.

- $can\_InvokePerm(u, p, z) \Rightarrow \exists r \in assigned\_roles(u, z) \bullet$ $p \in assigned\_perms(r, z) \land UserZone(u) = z$

2.3 Role Hierarchy

In a role hierarchy (RH), senior roles inherit the permissions of the junior role or can activate a junior role depending on whether the roles are related by permission inheritance hierarchy (RH_I) or role activation hierarchy (RH_A) [21, 14]. Both hierarchies are supported by our model and the hierarchies are related by spatio-temporal constraints. The spatio-temporal role hierarchies are formally defined as follows:

- $RH \subseteq Roles \times Roles \times STZones$

- $RH_I \subseteq RH$, $RH_A \subseteq RH$, $RH_I \cap RH_A = \phi$, $RH_I \cup$ $RH_A = RH$

Permission-Inheritance Hierarchy (RH_I):

When role r inherits role r' in zone z, denoted by $r \succeq_{I,z} r'$, all permissions of role r' are permissions of role r in zone z. The function $junior_I(r, z)$ returns the set of junior roles whose permission is inherited by the senior role in zone z. The function *authorized_perms(r, z)* returns a subset of permissions that are either assigned to role r or inherited by role r in zone z.

- $authorized\_perms(r, z) = \{(p \in assigned\_perms(r, z))$ $\lor (p \in authorized\_perms(r', z) | r' \in junior_I(r, z))\}$.

All permissions authorized to a role, either assigned or inherited, are authorized to all the role's members. The permissions a user can invoke are determined as follows.

- $can\_InvokePerm(u, p, z) \Rightarrow \exists r \in assigned\_roles(u, z) \bullet$ $p \in authorized\_perms(r, z) \land UserZone(u) = z$

Role Activation Hierarchy (RH_A):

When roles r and r' are related by RH_A, denoted by $r \succeq_{A,z} r'$, the senior role r can activate junior role r' in zone z. The function $junior_A(r, z)$ returns the set of junior roles which can be activated once the senior role r is activated in zone z. Based on the RH_A relation, the user activation predicate is revised:

- $can\_ActivateRole(u, r, z) \Rightarrow r \in enabled\_roles(z) \land$ $r \in (assigned\_roles(u, z) \lor junior_A(r', z))$ $\land UserZone(u) = z$

2.4 Separation of Duty (SoD) Constraints

Static SoD (SSoD) and Dynamic SoD (DSoD) constraints are two types of SoD in RBAC [2]. In our model, spatial and temporal factors are applied to the SoD constraints. Role SSoD relation ($SSoD_r$) determines the set of conflicting roles that should not be assigned to the same individual in some spatio-temporal zones. The permission SSoD relation $SSoD_p$ defines the conflicting permissions that are not allowed to be invoked by the same role in some spatio-temporal zones. The conflicting activation roles in undesirable spatio-temporal zones are defined by the $DSoD_r$ relation. The functions $ssod\_Roles(r, z)$ and $dsod\_Roles(r', z)$ determine the conflicting roles in zone z for role r and r', respectively. The spatio-temporal $SSoD_r$, $SSoD_p$, $DSoD_r$ relations are formally defined as follows:

- $SSoD_r \subseteq Roles \times Roles \times STZones$
- $DSoD_r \subseteq Roles \times Roles \times STZones$, and $SSoD_r \cap$ $DSoD_r = \phi$
- $SSoD_p \subseteq Permissions \times Permissions \times STZones$
- $ssod\_Roles : (r : Roles, z : Stzone) \rightarrow 2^{Roles}$
- $dsod\_Roles : (r : Roles, z : Stzone) \rightarrow 2^{Roles}$

In the following, we discuss how SoD constraints are specified in our model.

Role SSoD:

The same individual cannot be assigned two conflicting roles defined by $SSoD_r$ in the context of zones.

- $\forall u \in Users \bullet (r,r',z) \in SSoD_r \Rightarrow$
  $\neg(r \in assigned\_roles(u,z) \wedge r' \in assigned\_roles(u,z))$

Permission SSoD:

Mutual exclusive permissions defined by $SSoD_p$ cannot be assigned to the same role in some zones.

- $\forall r \in Roles \bullet (p,p',z) \in SSoD_p \Rightarrow$
  $\neg(p \in authorized\_perms(r,z) \wedge$
  $p \in authorized\_perms(r,z))$

Role DSoD:

A pair of mutual exclusive roles related by $DSoD_r$ are not allowed to be activated by the same individual in some zones.

- $\forall u \in Users \bullet (r,r',z) \in DSoD_r \Rightarrow$
  $\neg(r \in active\_roles(u,z)$
  $\wedge r' \in active\_roles(u,z))$

2.5 Prerequisite Constraints

The prerequisite constraints impose some actions to be performed before executing operations on critical entities. For example, the role of nurse-on-night-duty at a hospital can be enabled in the urgent care unit only if the role of doctor-on-night-duty is already enabled in the same urgent care unit during night-time. Similarly, a nurse role can be disabled only after nurse-in-training role has been disabled in the emergency unit.

Prerequisite on Role-Enabling:

An access control policy might require that a role can be enabled if some other roles are already enabled in a certain location and time. To capture this requirement in our model, we define the function $pre\_EnableRoles(r,z)$ which retrieves the set of roles together with the zones where they should be enabled in order to enable role r in zone z. The role enabling prerequisite is formalized as follows.

- $\forall(r',z') \in pre\_EnableRoles(r,z) \bullet can\_EnableRole(r,z)$
  $\Rightarrow r' \in enabled\_roles(z')$

Prerequisite on Role-Disabling:

Sometimes before a role can be disabled, other critical roles must be disabled. $pre\_DisableRoles(r,z)$ defines the set of roles that must be disabled in certain zones prior to disabling role r in z. $can\_Disable(r,z)$ predicate defines when role r can be disabled in zone z.

- $\forall(r',z') \in pre\_DisableRoles(r,z) \bullet can\_Disable(r,z)$
  $\Rightarrow r' \notin enabled\_roles(z')$

Prerequisite on Role Assignment:

This constraint imposes that a user must be assigned to some less critical roles before being assigned more critical roles in specific zones. We define the function $pre\_AssignRoles(r,z)$ in order to obtain the prerequisite roles that should be already assigned to a user in order to assign role r in zone z to a user.

- $\forall(r',z') \in pre\_AssignRoles(r,z) \bullet can\_AssignRole(u,r,z)$
  $\Rightarrow r' \in assigned\_roles(u,z')$

Prerequisite on Role Deassignment:

Some critical roles must be deassigned from a user before deassigning other roles. The function $pre\_DeassignRoles$ (r,z) gives the set of roles that must be deassigned before deassigning role in zone z. The predicate $can\_DeassignRoles$ (u,r,z) says whether or not role r can be deassigned for the user u in zone z.

- $\forall(r',z') \in pre\_DeassignRoles(r,z) \bullet$
  $can\_DeassignRole(u,r,z) \Rightarrow r' \notin assigned\_roles(u,z')$

Prerequisite on Role Activation:

This condition states that a user can activate a particular role only if some roles are already activated by the user in certain critical zones. Function $pre\_ActivateRoles(r,z)$ determines the set of roles that have to be previously activated by a user in zone z in order to activate r.

- $\forall(r',z') \in pre\_ActivateRoles(r,z) \bullet$
  $can\_ActivateRole(u,r,z) \Rightarrow r' \in active\_roles(u,z')$

Prerequisite on on Role Deactivation:

Some critical roles must be deactivated before deactivating other less important roles. The function $pre\_DeactivateRoles$ (r,z) gives the set of roles that must be deactivated before deactivating role r in zone z. The predicate $can\_DeactivateRole$ (u,r,z) states whether role r can be deactivated from user u in zone z. The following constraint captures this.

- $\forall(r',z') \in pre\_DeactivateRoles(r,z) \bullet$
  $can\_DeactivateRoles(u,r,z) \Rightarrow r' \notin active\_roles(u,z')$

2.6 Trigger Constraints

We may need some actions to take place instantly when some events of interest happens. We can formalize trigger constraints for this purpose. Explicitly identifying such constraints allows us to analyze them together with the other constraints. For example, if a user moves out of a spatio-temporal zone, his role must be automatically deactivated. The triggers are described using the notation $event\{cond\} \rightarrow action$, where $event$ triggers $action$ if the predicate $cond$ is true. $event$ can be a spatio-temporal zone change or some operation in the access control model.

2.6.1 Spatio-Temporal Zone Change of User

Let $ZoneChange(u,z,z')$ represent the event where the spatio-temporal zone associated with the user u changes from z to z'. Note that, for the action $DeactivateRole$ to take place, the conditions that r must be active in zone z and r cannot be activated in z' must also be true.

Role Deactivation: $ZoneChange(u,z,z')$
$\{r \in active\_roles(u,z) \wedge \neg can\_ActivateRole(u,r,z')\}$
$\rightarrow DeactivateRole(u,r,z')$

Role Deassign: $ZoneChange(u,z,z')$
$\{r \in assigned\_roles(u,z) \wedge \neg can\_AssignRole(u,r,z')\}$
$\rightarrow DeassignRole(u,r,z')$

2.6.2 Enforcing Prerequisite Constraints

Role Enabling: $EnableRoles(r',z)\{true\} \rightarrow$
$EnableRole(r,z)$ where $r' \in pre\_EnableRole(r,z)$

Role Disabling: $DisableRole(r', z)\{true\} \rightarrow DisableRole(r, z)$ where $r' \in pre\_DisableRole(r, z)$

Role Activation: $ActivateRole(u, r', z)\{true\} \rightarrow ActivateRole(u, r, z)$ where $r' \in pre\_ActiveRoles(r, z)$

Role Deactivation: $DeactivateRole(u, r', z)\{true\} \rightarrow DeactivateRole(u, r, z)$ where $r' \in pre\_DeactivateRole(r, z)$

Assign Role: $AssignRole(u, r', z)\{true\} \rightarrow AssignRole(u, r, z)$ where $r' \in pre\_AssignRole(r, z)$

Deassign Role: $DeassignRole(r', z)\{true\} \rightarrow DeassignRole(r, z)$ where $r' \in pre\_DeassignRoles(r, z)$

3. REAL-WORLD MOBILE APPLICATION

We use a few example policies from a real-world Dengue Decision Support System (DDSS) deployed in Mexico. DDSS aims to improve prevention, surveillance, and control of the dengue vector-borne disease. The DDSS helps state-level public health officials respond to local outbreaks of dengue. Response consists of vector control and vector surveillance, namely spraying for mosquitoes (control) and investigating locations where they might be breeding and living (surveillance) in areas where the level of confirmed dengue cases has increased above a prescribed threshold. Public health officials are organized in jurisdictions, based on population, and multiple jurisdictions are included in a single state. When the threshold is reached, officials at both levels respond. The jurisdiction officer activates vector control and surveillance teams that are local to the jurisdiction, with instructions regarding the specific control and surveillance protocols to follow and the locations where they are to be performed. The state officer releases materials for control to the team, and the local team then performs the controls and surveillance ordered. The jurisdiction and state vector control officials are often located in different buildings, although the vector control team is co-located with the jurisdiction officer. All control materials are located in warehouses elsewhere, and for coordination reasons are controlled by the state officer. Information about specific cases of dengue is retained in what is called an epidemiological study. This data includes information about the patient, the location where the patient lives (the premise), the case, and control and surveillance actions performed at the premise. The patient and case data are considered private information, and are only available to epidemiologists at the jurisdiction and state levels.

DDSS has the following job functions: Personal managers are responsible for assigning roles, tasks, and privileges to users. Clinicians review patient personal information (e.g., names, gender, date of birth), premises of the patient (e.g., residence, and optionally work or school), past hospitalization and treatment information (e.g., clinic, physicians, disease), and clinical findings (e.g., presence/absence of fever, nausea, or headache). Laboratory technicians collect laboratory test data including type of samples, method(s) used to test the samples, framework for interpreting test results, and interpreted results. Epidemiologists access patient and laboratory test information with regard to evaluating and changing health safety standards and programs. Vector control team members spray houses in infected areas. Vector surveillance team members perform mosquito collection and testing tasks intended for developing insecticide resistance

methods. Vector control and surveillance members are provided with needed materials to use for their tasks. Such material allocation is done by material managers at the state or city level. Material managers are also responsible for updating the local materials inventories. Vector manager designates the tasks that must be performed by vector control and surveillance teams.

Healthcare professionals are only allowed to access their patients' records in the areas where the dengue case occurred and during the course of dengue. Moreover, to prevent fraudulent entries, the vector control and surveillance teams must perform their tasks in the designated places and at specified times. Location hierarchy in DDSS imposes restrictions on both permission-inheritance, role-activation hierarchies, role assignments, and activation relationships. For example, a clinician working at the state level can inherit permissions from the clinician at the city level. Therefore, a spatio-temporal policy should be in place to define these requirements in DDSS. Below we give some of the policies used in DDSS.

-Users:

$Users = \{ Dan, Alice, Tom, Sam, Yue, Lura \}$

-Roles:

$Roles = \{ Personal\ Manager\ (PM),\ State\ Hospital\ Clinician\ (SHC),\ City\ Hospital\ Clinician\ (CHC),\ City\ Material\ Manager\ (CMM),\ City\ Vector\ Manager\ (CVM),\ Vector\ Control\ Team\ Member\ (VCT),\ Vector\ Surveillance\ Team\ Member\ (VST) \}$

-Permissions:

$Permissions = \{ UpdateUsersData(p_1),\ UpdatePatientRecord(p_2),\ UpdateControlMaterial(p_3),\ UpdateVectorInfo(p_4),\ ReadScheduledTasks(p_5),\ CollectVectorInfo(p_6),\ SprayHouses(p_7) \}$

-Objects:

$Objects = \{ Personal\ User\ Data\ (o_1),\ Patient\ Clinical\ Data\ (o_2),\ Materials\ Inventory\ Data\ (o_3),\ Vector\ Data(o_4) \}$

-Spatio-temporal zones:

$STZones = \{z_0:<State, DayTime>,\ z_1:<MainOffice, DayTime>,\ z_2:<StateClinic, DayTime>,\ z_3:<CityClinic, DayTime>,\ z_4:<CityWarehouse, DayTime>,\ z_5:<VectorCityOffice, DayTime>,\ z_6:<City, Dayime> \},$ $DayTime = [8 - 17]$ and zone z_0 is the zone that contains all other zones.

-Role zones:

$Rzones = \{(PM, z_1),\ (SHC, z_2), (SHC, z_3),\ (CHC, z_3), (CMM, z_4), (CMM, z_6),\ (CVM, z_5),\ (CVM, z_6),\ (VCT, z_6), (VST, z_6) \}.$

-Permissions zones:

$Pzones = \{ (p_1, z_1),\ (p_2, z_3),\ (p_3, z_4),$

(p_4, z_5), (p_5, z_6), (p_6, z_6), (p_7, z_6)}

- Object zones:

$Objzones = \{(o_1, z_1), (o_2, z_3), (o_3, z_4),$
$(o_4, z_5), (o_4, z_6) \}$

- User Role Assignments:

$UA_z = \{(Dan, PM, z_1),$
$(Alice, SHC, z_2), (Alice, SHC, z_3), (Tom, CMM, z_4),$
$(Tom, CMM, z_6), (Tom, CVM, z_6), (Sam, CVM, z_5),$
$(Sam, CVM, z_6), (Yue, VCT, z_6), (Lura, VST, z_6)\}$

-Permission Role Assignments:

$PA_z = \{(PM, p_1, z_1),$
$(CHC, p_2, z_3), (CMM, p_3, z_4), (CVM, p_4, z_5), (VCT, p_5, z_6),$
$(VCT, p_6, z_6), (VST, p_5, z_6), (VST, p_7, z_6)\}$

-Permission Object Access:

Table 1 shows the zones where the permissions access objects.

Permission	Object	Zone	Permission	Object	Zone
p_1	o_1	z_1	p_2	o_2	z_3
p_3	o_3	z_4	p_4	o_4	z_5
p_5	o_4	z_6	p_6	o_4	z_6
p_7	o_4	z_6			

Table 1: Permission Object Access Zones

-Role Activation Hierarchy:

A user assigned the *State Hospital Clinician* role can activate the *City Hospital Clinician* role in the *CityClinic* at *DayTime*. This is expressed as follows.

$RH_A = \{(SHC, CHC, z_3)\}$

-Trigger Constraints:

When the *Vector Control Team Member* or *Vector Surveillance Team Member* Role is enabled, the *City Material Manager* role gets enabled as well. Formally, these are expressed as follows.

$enable(VCT, z_6)\{true\} \rightarrow enable(CMM, z_4)$
$enable(VST, z_6)\{true\} \rightarrow enable(CMM, z_4)$

- SoD Constraints:

We have two dynamic separation of duty constraints. The *City Material Manager* and the *City Vector Manager* roles cannot both be activated in the *City* at *DayTime*. We also have one static separation of duty constraint: *ReadScheduledTasks* and *CollectVectorInfo* cannot both be invoked in the *City* at *DayTime*.

$DSoD_r = \{(CMM, CVM, z_6), (VCT, VST, z_6)\}$
$SSoD_p = \{(p_5, p_6, z_6) \}$

The DDSS policy is graphically visualized in Figure 2.

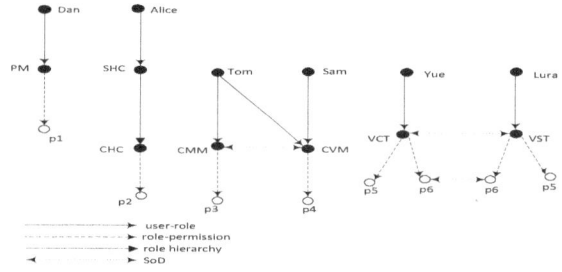

Figure 2: Access Control Graph for Mobile DDSS Policy

4. ANALYSIS APPROACH

The proposed model supports many spatio-temporal properties that might incorrectly interact and result in conflicts and inconsistencies. An error in spatio-temporal authorization constraints might deny authorized users' requests for invoking allowed roles from valid zones. Other constraint inconsistencies might allow unauthorized users to access critical objects and hence perform malicious operations from incorrect zones.

We propose a timed-automata based analysis approach to check spatio-temporal policies. With the timed-automata approach, we build a formal model 'M' describing the behavior of a mobile policy under verification, the correctness of temporal property 'P' is expressed with Timed Computational Tree Logic (TCTL) [18], and then a model-checker UPPAAL is used to automatically decide whether 'M' satisfies 'P' or not. If successful, UPPAAL reports *"a property is satisfied"*. If unsuccessful, it reports *"a property is not satisfied"* and a counterexample trace helps the user to identify the source of the errors. Figure 3 illustrates the flow of the timed-automata approach.

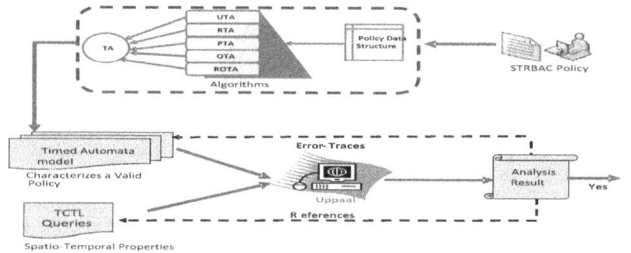

Figure 3: Timed-Automata Verification Approach

4.1 Timed-Automata Model

A spatio-temporal policy of an application is first converted into a network of timed-automata model. Each timed automaton represents the behavior of an entity at a particular spatio-temporal zone. Thus, a number of timed-automata are instantiated for each user, role, object, and permission zone in a system.

Syntactically, timed-automaton TA is a 6-tuple $< L, l_0, C, A, E, I >$ where: L is a set of nodes, l_0 is the initial node, C is a set of clock variables, A is a set of synchronized actions, E is a finite set of directed edges depicting transitions between nodes. I is a function that assigns invariants to nodes, i.e., $I : L \rightarrow B(C)$, and $B(C)$ represents the clock constraints over the set C. Nodes in a timed-automaton can be labeled as *committed* to disallow the passing of time (that is, nodes must be left without delay). *Committed* nodes are commonly used to express atomic transactions. Furthermore, actions defined as *urgent* are taken without any delay when they are enabled.

Timed-automata interact with each other through synchronization channels. For example, two timed-automata T_1 and T_2 can synchronize over two edges e_1 and e_2 labelled with $a_1!$ and $a_2?$, respectively. The former automaton T_1 is referred to as "sending" automaton, and the later automaton T_2 is referred to as "receiving" automaton (i.e., there might be more than one receiving automata). In the following, we will discuss how timed-automata are constructed for entities in the DDSS policy.

Role Observer Timed-Automata ROTA:

Global clock t is used by all timed-automata to express temporal constraints. For each role zone, we develop a timed-automata that describes the behavior of the role for the corresponding zone. We also develop a Role Observer Timed-Automaton ($ROTA$) that is responsible for clock reset, enabling and disabling of all roles. $ROTA$ explores the set $Rzones$ to determine the zones where a role can be enabled. Nodes in the $ROTA$ represent the states signifying the enabling and disabling of roles in zones.

Figure 4 shows a partial $ROTA$ for roles SHC, CHC, and PM. Recall that PM is enabled in zone $z_1:<MainOffice,[8-17]>$ and SHC and CHC are enabled in $z_3:<CityClinic,[8-17]>$. *Init* node signifies the state where all the roles are disabled. The transition from node $Init$ to node ER_{SHC} with action $enable\_SHC[CityClinic]!$ enables role SHC at time instant $t_1 = 8$. Firing this transition changes the state of the receiving role SHC timed-automaton at zone z_3. Node ER_{SHC} represents the state where role SHC is enabled. Since roles CHC and PM are enabled at the same time instant, the intermediate nodes ER_{SHC} and ER_{CHC} are labeled as *committed*. These nodes allow more than a single action to be taken at the same time. The transitions enabling roles CHC and PM are labeled with sending actions $enable\_CHC[CityClinic]!$ and $enable\_PM[MainOffice]!$ respectively. Thus, these action will change the states of roles PM and CHC timed-automata at zone z_3. Node ER_{CHC} and ER_{PM} represent the state where role CHC and PM are respectively enabled.

$ROTA$ remains in node ER_{PM} as long as the clock invariant $t < t_1'$, (note that, $t_1' = 17$). At time $t = 17$, roles SHC, CHC, and PM are simultaneously disabled by transitions labeled with synchronous actions $disable\_SHC[CityClinic]!$, $disable\_CHC[CityClinic]!$, and $disable\_PM[MainOffice]!$, respectively. The states, DR_{SHC}, DR_{CHC}, and ER_{PM}, express that roles SHC, CHC, PM are disabled, respectively.

On the event of firing the input transition to node $Init$ coming from node DR_{PM}, at $t = t_3$ (note that, $t_3 = 24$), the function $reset\_clock()$ resets clock variable t. The nodes that are not *committed* are labeled with invariants that strictly express the start and end of time intervals at which roles are enabled or disabled.

Role Timed-Automata RTA:

For each role in set $Roles$, a parametrized automaton is constructed for each role zone in set $Rzones$ to capture the states at which the role is enabled, disabled, activated, or deactivated at that zone. In the DDSS policy, we have *10* timed-automata corresponding to the roles. The timed-

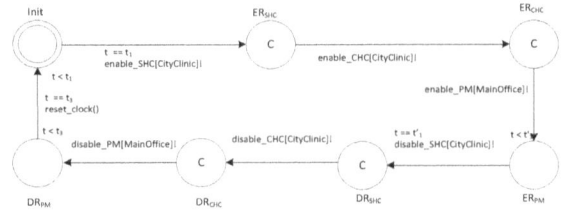

Figure 4: Role Observer Timed-Automata

automaton in Figure 5 represents the enable, disable, active, inactive states of role CHC at role zone $z_3 = <CityClinic, [8-17]>$.

$DisabledInCityClinic$ is the initial state of role CHC where it is disabled, and $EnabledInCityClinic$ is the target state of the $DisabledInCityClinic$ state that represents the enable state of role CHC. Edges between these two control states synchronize with sending edges in $ROTA$ (see Fig. 4) through receiving action $enable\_CHC[CityClinic]?$. Firing this action changes the state of role CHC at zone z_3 to the enable state.

The receiving action $activate\_CHC[CityClinic]?$ activates role CHC. This action synchronizes with a sending activation action at user $Alice$ timed-automaton. Firing this action changes the state of role CHC from an enabled to an active state. Note that, a role may be assigned to multiple users in zone z_3. Thus, any subsequent activation of role CHC in $ActivatedInCityClinic$ does not change the state of role CHC. The self-loop transitions at $ActivatedInCityClinic$ indicate that role CHC remains in an active state as long as there is at least one user activating role CHC. The variable $Cont\_CHC[CityClinic]$ records the number of users who activate role CHC. When no user is using role CHC, it goes back to the $EnabledInCityClinic$ state. Role CHC goes from $EnabledInCityClinic$ state to $DisabledInCityClinic$ state at the end of the enabling duration through *urgent* synchronization action $disable\_CHC[CityClinic]?$. Since CHC is only accessed by $Alice$ via RH_A, these self-loop edges are not needed, but we present them for the clarity of discussion.

The *committed* $Aperm_2$ node is added between the states $EnabledInCityClinic$ and $ActivatedInCityClinic$ to capture the permissions p_2 access at the time role CHC is activated. The sending $access\_p_2[CityClinic]!$ action synchronize with a receiving action at the corresponding permission timed-automaton of p_2 in zone z_3. The *committed* $Eperm_2$ node is also added between $ActivatedInCityClinic$ and $EnabledInCityClinic$ to remove permission p_2 when role CHC is deactivated by the user. The sending channel $exit\_p_2[CityClinic]!$ has a corresponding receiving action at permission p_2 timed-automaton.

The deactivation of role CHC is represented by *urgent* synchronization channel $deactivate\_CHC[CityClinic]?$. Thus, if a user suddenly moves to an invalid location while a role is in an active state by that user, that role must be deactivated. Similarly, when a role activation time has expired, role CHC must be instantly revoked from the user. Such requirements are expressed by the deactivation triggers at user timed-automata (e.g., *urgent* actions and node invariants). Timed-automata for other roles are formulated in a similar manner.

Permission Timed-Automata (PTA) and Object Timed-

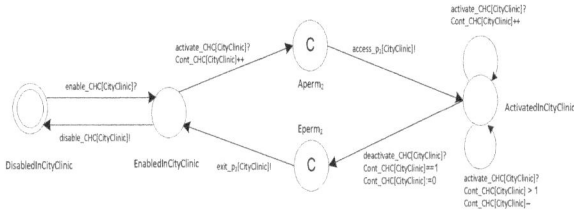

Figure 5: Timed-Automata of Role CHC at zone z_3

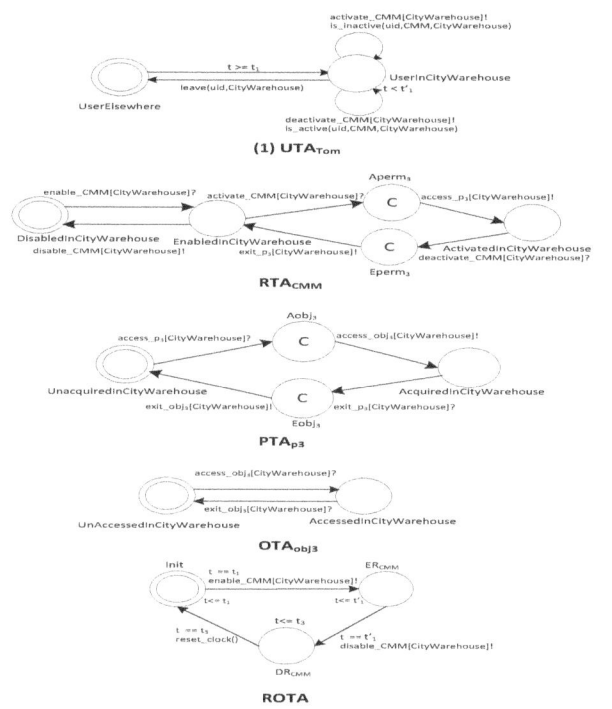

Figure 6: Timed-Automata Model M

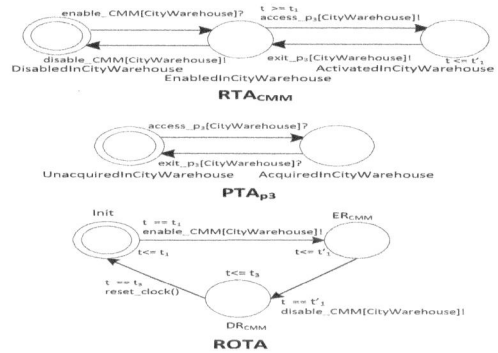

Figure 7: sub-Timed-Automata Model M_i

Automata (OTA) are created in a similar manner. For the lack of space, we eliminated the discussions of User Timed-Automata (UTA). Please refer to [1] for algorithms generating the timed-automata ROTA, RTA, and UTA.

4.2 Improving Efficiency of Analysis

We use the optimizations available in UPPAAL to reduce the size of the state space. In addition, we design the timed-automata in a manner such that the temporal guards, responsible for increasing the state space, are minimized. For our example application, only the *ROTA* and *UTA* have temporal guards.

Analyzing the entire network of timed-automata model for a particular property is time consuming. We propose a technique which minimizes the size of the network that must be analyzed for checking the existence of some property. The smaller network has only the entities and relationships that are relevant to the property of interest. For lack of space, we do not give the algorithm for doing the state space reduction. Note that, the detailed algorithm appears in [1]. Here we illustrate our ideas with an example.

Consider a partial simple timed-automata model **M** for the DDSS policy in the left rounded rectangle of Figure 6, $M = UTA_{Tom} \parallel RTA_{CMM} \parallel PTA_{p3} \parallel OTA_{obj3} \parallel ROTA$. Timed-automata **M** has 5 automata. In this model, role CMM can only be activated by user Tom in zone $z_4 = <$ $CityWarehouse, [t_1 - t'_1] >$, where $[t_1 - t'_1] = [8 - 17]$. At the moment role *CMM* is activated by *Tom*, permission p_3 is acquired and object obj_3 is accessed.

Suppose now a policy verifier tends to check property pr_1 that verifies whether *CMM* can invoke permission p_3 in the **M** model. Using the reduction algoithm, we create **M₁** shown in the rounded rectangle of Figure 7. The reduction algorithm eliminates the timed-automata UTA_{Tom} and OTA_{obj3}. Furthermore, the edges and guards are also reconstructed for RTA_{CMM} and PTA_{p3} as a consequence of removing the user and object timed-automata. Note that, the observer timed-automaton remains intact because it is not directly related to the required changes for checking property pr_1. In the subsequent section, we evaluate the effectiveness of our approach on sample queries w.r.t. state space and searching time reduction.

5. DDSS POLICY ANALYSIS

In the analysis of the DDSS policy, we construct timed-automata model **M**. **M** is composite from a number of timed-automata operating in parallel, i.e., $\mathbf{M} = \mathbf{M_0} \parallel \mathbf{M_1} \parallel \mathbf{M_2} \parallel \cdots \parallel \mathbf{M_n}$, where n is the number of timed-automata. The total number of timed-automata in **M** is computed by $N_{TA} = N_{RTA} + N_{PTA} + N_{OTA} + N_{UTA} + 1$., where, $N_{UTA} = 6$

for users automata, $N_{RTA} = 10$ for roles, $N_{PTA} = 7$ for permissions, $N_{OTA} = 5$ for objects, and 1 for $ROTA$, in total, $N_{TA} = 29$ automata in **M**. The verification is carried out on the Windows platform using 4GB RAM with Intel(R) Core(TM) 2Due CPU. Furthermore, our optimization techniques in Section 4.2 are applied for improving the analysis performance.

We first simulate model **M** using UPPAAL to see if all the states are reachable and there are no deadlocks. We then check to see if the DDSS policy satisfies some properties.

```
(Q1): CMM(CityWarehouse).Enlabled && x>=8 -->
      CMM(CityWarehouse).Disabled && x>17
```

Q1 checks if the role *CMM* is enabled, it will be eventually disabled in location *CityWarehouse* before time instant 17.

```
(Q2): E<> p2(CityClinic).Acquired and (x>=8 and x<=17)
```

Q2 checks if permission p_2 can be acquired by some role in

181

zone z_3. The query result shows that there are some states where permission p_2 is accessed.

```
(Q3): E<> obj2(CityClinic).Accessed and (p2(CityClinic).
      Acquired and (x> 8 && x<17))
```

Q3 checks whether object obj_2 can be accessed by permission p_2 in zone z_3. This property is satisfied and the object is correctly accessed.

```
(Q4): A[] forall(i:uid)(CMM(City).Activated and
      CMM_u[i] == 1) and forall(j:uid)(CVM(City).Activated
      and CVM_u[j] == 1) and (x >= 8 && x < 17)
      imply  i != j
```

Q4 checks for the violations of $DSoD_r$ constraint involving roles CMM and CVM in zone z_6. The results shows that this $DSoD_r$ constraint is satisfied.

```
(Q5): E<> SHC(CityClinic).Activated and
      SHC_u[Alice.uid] == 1 and CHC(CityClinic).Activated
      and (CHC_u[Alice.uid]==1 and (x>=8 and x<=17))
```

Q5 checks the activation of junior role CHC of senior role SHC in zone z_3 for user $Alice$. This property is satisfied.

```
(Q6): VCT(City).Enabled --> (CMM(CityWarehouse).Enabled
      and (x>=8 && x<=17))
```

This query checks whether enabling role VCT causes the $CityWarehouse$ role to be enabled in zone z_6. This property is satisfied.

Table 2 compares the average number of the explored states and the consumed time for checking quires: Q_1, Q_2, Q_3, Q_4, Q_5, and Q_6, for the entire policy model $\mathbf{M}$ versus the sub-automata models that are generated by the reduction algorithm.

In our analysis scenario, we have four models, timed-automata model $\mathbf{M}$ and three smaller automata models: $\mathbf{M}_1$ for checking the interaction between users and roles, $\mathbf{M}_2$ for verifying the roles and permissions relationships, and $\mathbf{M}_3$ concerning about the access to objects via permissions.

Queries	Model		Sub-Models		Reduction %	
	States	Time	States	textbfTime	States%	Time%
$Q_1 : \mathbf{M}_1$	26	628ms	4	102ms	85%	84%
$Q_2 : \mathbf{M}_2$	1019	230ms	1	12ms	99%	94%
$Q_3 : \mathbf{M}_3$	1028	175ms	1	11ms	99%	93%
$Q_4 : \mathbf{M}_1$	95616	7.018ms	5184	644ms	94%	90%
$Q_5 : \mathbf{M}_1$	622	193ms	30	79ms	95%	59%
$Q_6 : \mathbf{M}_1$	95616	6,968ms	5184	866ms	94%	87%
Reduction Average					94%	85%

Table 2: Evaluation of the State-Space Reduction Technique

$\mathbf{M}_1$ has timed-automata for users (6 timed-automata) and roles (10 timed-automata), in total is 17 automata including the observer automata. Thus, the number of automata in $\mathbf{M}_1$ is reduced to 41% from the number of automata in $\mathbf{M}$. $\mathbf{M}_2$ includes on 18 timed-automata: 10 automata for roles, 7 automata for permissions, and the observer automata. The number of automata in $\mathbf{M}_2$ is 37% smaller than the number of automata in $\mathbf{M}$. $\mathbf{M}_3$ has 7 permissions automata, 5 objects automata, and the observer automata, thereby in total 13 automata. The number of automata in $\mathbf{M}_3$ is reduced to 55% in comparison to the number of automata in $\mathbf{M}$. Table 2

shows that the average number of explored states is reduced by 94% and the average elapsed time is decreased by value of 85% in the sub-models in a comparison to check those queries against the entire policy model $\mathbf{M}$. Consequently, these values demonstrate the effectiveness of the proposed reduction technique in verifying spatio-temporal properties in our model.

6. RELATED WORK

Researchers have proposed numerous spatio-temporal models in the past decade [4, 21, 11, 31, 3, 29, 12, 36]. The models differ with respect to which entities and relationships can support spatio-temporal constraints. Our current work is able to represent all these different types of spatio-temporal constraints. In addition, we introduce the concept of trigger constraints – constraints that must be automatically enforced by the underlying implementation mechanisms. We also introduce the concept of spatio-temporal zone that abstracts location and time into a single entity which makes it easier to understand, analyze, and evolve policy specifications.

Some of the works [31] focus on using Alloy [19] for verifying spatio-temporal access control model and policies [31, 34, 35, 37]. Alloy specification is automatically translated into a Boolean expression, which is analyzed by the SAT solver. A user specified scope on the model elements bounds the domain, making it possible to create finite Boolean formulas that can be evaluated by the SAT-solver. Often times, the scope must be kept small for the analysis to terminate in a timely manner. Consequently, real-world applications often must be abstracted for automated verification. Abstraction may alter the properties of interest that are being verified, resulting in incorrect results. Alloy also does not support temporal logic, so some spatio-temporal properties cannot be directly verified.

Researchers [22, 27, 32, 36] have also proposed the use of Colored Petri Nets (CPN) [20] for verifying RBAC and its extensions. CPN treats time as any variable and cannot check real-time constraints. Consequently, temporal properties were not verified in these works. Timed Petri Nets overcome these shortcomings, but as per Godray et al. [15] they are not as intuitive and usable as Timed Automata [5] although both have similar expressive power.

Researchers have also proposed a Timed Automata (TA) for checking temporal properties in RBAC. Mondal et al. [25, 24, 26] have used timed-automata for specifying properties in TRBAC [9] and GTRBAC [21] models and using UP-PAAL [8] for automated verification. However, the authors have verified very simple temporal properties and made assumptions that often do not hold in the real-world. Examples of such assumptions include activating a single role at any time or the absence of multilevel role hierarchies. Moreover, the authors also do not consider spatio-temporal constraints which makes verification in timed automata significantly harder because of the increase in the number of constraints and entities and the change of location of users and objects. The authors also do not provide any state space reduction technique. Our work fills this gap.

Verification of Temporal-RBAC using approaches based on a discrete time model has been proposed by Uzun et al. [38]. Our analysis approach assumes the continuous time model. Continuous time analysis is expensive and we propose a number of techniques to reduce this cost. We also checked some critical temporal properties, such as trigger constraints, that have not been considered in their work.

7. CONCLUSION AND FUTURE WORK

We proposed a spatio-temporal access control model based on RBAC for mobile applications. We describe how to specify spatio-temporal access control constraints on the various entities and relationships in RBAC. We demonstrated how such a model can be verified using timed-automata and how to make the analysis more efficient. Our future work includes implementing our model for real-world applications, extending this model for workflows and understanding the interplay of workflow constraints with the spatio-temporal requirements.

8. ACKNOWLEDGEMENT

The work described in this report was partially supported by the National Science Foundation grant CCF-1018711.

9. REFERENCES

[1] R. Abdunabi. *An Access Control Framework for Mobile Applications*. PhD thesis, Colorado State University, January 2013.

[2] G.-J. Ahn and R. Sandhu. Role-based Authorization Constraints Specification. *ACM Transactions on Information Systems Security*, 3(4):207–226, 2000.

[3] S. Aich, S. Mondal, S. Sural, and A. K. Majumdar. Role Based Access Control with Spatiotemporal Context for Mobile Applications. *Transactions on Computational Science*, 4:177–199, 2009.

[4] S. Aich, S. Sural, and A. K. Majumdar. STARBAC: Spatio temporal Role Based Access Control. In *OTM Conferences (2)*, pages 1567–1582, 2007.

[5] R. Alur and D. Dill. A Theory of Timed Automata. *Theoretical Computer Science*, 126(2):183–235, 1994.

[6] R. Alur and R. Kurshan. Timing Analysis in COSPAN. In *Hybrid Systems*, pages 220–231, 1995.

[7] P. Argenio, J. Katoen, T. Ruys, and J. Tretmans. The Bounded Retransmission Protocol must be on time! In *TACAS*, pages 416–431. Springer, 1997.

[8] G. Behrmann, A. David, and K. G. Larsen. A Tutorial on UPPAAL. In *SFM*, pages 200–236, 2004.

[9] E. Bertino, P. Bonatti, and E. Ferrari. TRBAC: A Temporal Role-Based Access Control Model. *ACM Transactions on Information Systems Security*, 4(3):191–233, 2001.

[10] M. Bozga, J. Hou, O. Maler, and S. Yovine. Verification of Asynchronous Circuits using Timed Automata. *Electr. Notes Theor. Comput. Sci.*, 65(6):47–59, 2002.

[11] S. Chandran and J. Joshi. *LoT-RBAC*: A Location and Time-Based RBAC Model. In *WISE*, pages 361–375, 2005.

[12] L. Chen and J. Crampton. On Spatio-Temporal Constraints and Inheritance in Role-Based Access Control. In *ASIACCS*, pages 205–216, 2008.

[13] C. Daws, A. Olivero, S. Tripakis, and S. Yovine. The Tool KRONOS. In *Hybrid Systems*, pages 208–219, 1995.

[14] D. Ferraiolo, R. Sandhu, S. Gavrila, D. Kuhn, and R. Chandramouli. Proposed NIST Standard for Role-Based Access Control. *ACM Transactions on Information Systems Security*, 4(3):224–274, 2001.

[15] K. Godary, I. Augé-Blum, and A. Mignotte. SDL and Timed Petri Nets versus UPPAAL for the Validation of Embedded Architecture in Automotive. In *FDL*, pages 672–684, 2004.

[16] K. Havelund, K. Larsen, and A. Skou. Formal Verification of a Power Controller Using the Real-Time Model Checker UPPAAL. In *ARTS*, pages 277–298, 1999.

[17] K. Havelund, A. Skou, K. Larsen, and K. Lund. Formal Modeling and Analysis of an Audio/Video Protocol: an Industrial Case Study using UPPAAL. In *RTSS*, pages 2–13, 1997.

[18] T. A. Henzinger, X. Nicollin, J. Sifakis, and S. Yovine. Symbolic Model Checking for Real-Time Systems. *Information and Computation*, 111(2):193–244, 1994.

[19] D. Jackson. Alloy: A Lightweight Object Modelling Notation. *ACM Transactions on Software Engneering Methodology*, 11(2):256–290, 2002.

[20] K. Jensen, L. Kristensen, and L. Wells. Coloured Petri Nets and CPN Tools for Modelling and Validation of Concurrent Systems. *International Journal on Software Tools for Technology Transfer*, 9(3-4):213–254, 2007.

[21] J. Joshi, E. Bertino, U. Latif, and A. Ghafoor. A Generalized Temporal Role-Based Access Control Model. *IEEE Transactions on Knowledge and Data Engineering*, 17(1):4–23, 2005.

[22] R. Laborde, B. Nasser, F. Grasset, F. Barrère, and A. Benzekri. A Formal Approach for the Evaluation of Network Security Mechanisms Based on RBAC Policies. *Electronic Notes in Theoretical Computer Science*, 121:117–142, 2005.

[23] A. Maji, A. Mukhoty, A. Majumdar, J. Mukhopadhyay, S. Sural, S. Paul, and B. Majumdar. Security Analysis and Implementation of Web-Based Telemedicine Services with a Four-Tier Architecture. In *PCTHEALTH*, pages 46–54, 2008.

[24] S. Mondal and S. Sural. A Verification Framework for Temporal RBAC with Role Hierarchy (Short Paper). In *ICISS*, pages 140–147, 2008.

[25] S. Mondal and S. Sural. Security Analysis of Temporal-RBAC Using Timed Automata. In *IAS*, pages 37–40, 2008.

[26] S. Mondal, S. Sural, and V. Atluri. Towards Formal Security Analysis of GTRBAC Using Timed Automata. In *SACMAT*, pages 33–42, 2009.

[27] H. Rakkay and H. Boucheneb. Security Analysis of Role Based Access Control Models Using Colored Petri Nets and CPNtools. *Transactions on Computational Science*, 4:149–176, 2009.

[28] I. Ray, N. Li, R. France, and D.-K. Kim. Using UML to Visualize Role-Based Access Control Constraints. In *SACMAT*, pages 115–124, 2004.

[29] I. Ray and M. Toahchoodee. A Spatio-temporal Role-Based Access Control Model. In *DBSec*, pages 211–226, 2007.

[30] R. Salomon, M. Lüder, and G. Bieber. iFall - A New Embedded System for The Detection of Unexpected Falls. In *PerCom Workshops*, pages 286–291, 2010.

[31] A. Samuel, A. Ghafoor, and E. Bertino. A Framework for Specification and Verification of Generalized Spatio-Temporal Role Based Access Control Model. Technical Report CERIAS TR 2007-08, Purdue University, February 2007.

[32] B. Shafiq, A. Masood, J. Joshi, and A. Ghafoor. A Role-Based Access Control Policy Verification Framework for Real-Time Systems. In *WORDS*, pages 13–20, 2005.

[33] K. Sohr, G.-J. Ahn, M. Gogolla, and L. Migge. Specification and Validation of Authorisation Constraints Using UML and OCL. In *ESORICS*, pages 64–79, 2005.

[34] M. Toahchoodee and I. Ray. On the Formal Analysis of a Spatio-temporal Role-Based Access Control Model. In *DBSec*, pages 17–32, 2008.

[35] M. Toahchoodee and I. Ray. Using Alloy to Analyse a Spatio-Temporal Access Control Model Supporting Delegation. *IET Information Security*, 3(3):75–113, 2009.

[36] M. Toahchoodee and I. Ray. On the Formalization and Analysis of a Spatio-Temporal Role-Based Access Control Model. *Journal of Computer Security*, 19(3):399–452, 2011.

[37] M. Toahchoodee, I. Ray, K. Anastasakis, G. Georg, and B. Bordbar. Ensuring spatio-temporal access control for real-world applications. In *SACMAT*, pages 13–22, 2009.

[38] E. Uzun, V. Atluri, S. Sural, J. Vaidya, G. Parlato, A. L. Ferrara, and P. Madhusudan. Analyzing Temporal Role Based Access Control models. In *SACMAT*, pages 177–186, 2012.

A BigData Platform for Analytics on Access Control Policies and Logs

Suresh Chari, Ted Habeck, Ian Molloy, Youngja Park, Wilfried Teiken
IBM Research T.J. Watson
Yorktown Heights, NY
{schari,habeck,molloyim,young_park,wteiken}@us.ibm.com

ABSTRACT

Relying on an access control security policy alone to protect valuable resources is a dangerous practice. Prudent security must engage in other risk management and mitigation techniques to rapidly detect and recover from breaches. In reality, many security policies are either wrong, containing errors, or are misused and abused by malicious employees or compromised accounts; not all granted access is desirable. A popular approach to mitigate against these and other residual threats is to monitor applications to detect misuse and abuse of credentials in near real-time.

We will show a platform for monitoring applications and the use of analytic models on diverse datasets for detecting suspicious user activity. Our platform combines traditional data management systems with BigData platforms to efficiently apply analytics across security relevant data (policies, logs, metadata) and provide administrators a dashboard of the current security status of the organization, and the ability to investigate prioritized alerts. One key analytic in the demo is a novel generalization of the role mining problem as applied to access logs and modeling user behavior for anomalies. Other analytics include conventional statistical measures, Gaussian mixture models and clustering, Markov models, and entropic analysis of requests. This demonstration will walk through a prototype system and describe the analytics and underlying architecture.

Categories and Subject Descriptors

H.2.8 [**Information Systems**]: Database Applications— *Data mining*; D.4.7 [**Operating Security**]: Organization and Design—*Batch processing systems*

General Terms

Management, Security, Human Factors

Keywords

insider threat, log analysis, demonstration

1. INTRODUCTION

Organizations are increasing subjected to sophisticated attacks from nation states, vigilante groups, and 0-day exploits, targeted at information pilfering and theft. These breaches are not the result of improper policy specifications. Rather, user credentials are misused and abused within the valid confines of the possibly provably secure policy.

There are many security monitoring tools organization can leverage to help mitigate these threats. For example, Splunk[1] and Bro[2] [3] for networks, and ArcSight[3] and QRadar[4] allow administrators to monitor user activity. These systems are mostly rule based, and are most useful for detecting known pattens of bad behavior and enforcing compliance conditions. We demonstrate a system which is a hybrid of traditional data management (RDBMS) and big data platform for detecting malicious user activity, either willful or under the control of malware. This allows us to sore vast historical logs while being able to quickly extract information for efficient processing and visualization.

Our system experiments with handling an abundance of data, diverse systems, and unknown attacks, using machine learning based approaches and profiling. One drawback of using machine learning and data mining techniques is the high false positive rate. We have taken care to integrate methods to reduce false positives and alerts and integrate administrative feedback when evaluating future alerts.

Our demonstration will include the system architecture and components, data sources, their rates and characteristics, analytic models employed, and sample alerts and results. This is presented using our novel visualizations that provides an analyst sophisticated drill down capabilities.

In this work we demonstrate a prototype system that presents a unified framework balancing the strengths of relational databases and big data platforms. We marry this platform with an extensible suite of analytics against both security policies and application logs to learn the dynamic and unique normal behaviors of the user (or subject) populations and produce tickets or alerts when we observe a deviation. Our analytics can correlate user behavior across multiple applications and attributes obtained from other sources, such as a human resources LDAP server, that can be used to elevate an alert when it is both anomalous for the user, and "out of character" given the user's attributes.

---

[1] http://www.splunk.com

[2] http://www.bro-ids.org

[3] http://www8.hp.com/us/en/software-solutions/software.html?compURI=1214365

[4] http://q11abs.com

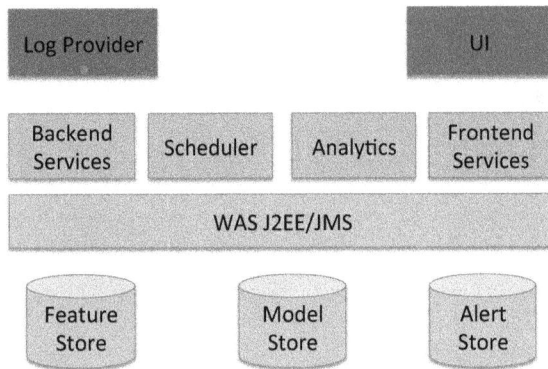

Figure 1: High-Level Architecture Overview

2. PLATFORM ARCHITECTURE

The analytics platform provides a framework to run the various analytics on the log and policy data. The framework abstracts storage of data and distribution of analytics jobs across a research cluster. The current implementation uses DB2 for data storage and the WebSphere Application Server for process control job distribution, but we are experimenting with alternate storage mechanisms and job scheduling mechanisms (e.g., HDFS and HBase) to optimize the platform for the various load profiles of different analytics. Logs are provided to the system using a set of backend REST services that feed the data into the platform. The scheduler determines which analytics need to be run on the data and schedules appropriate jobs across the cluster. The UI uses frontend REST services to access the analytics results and visualize them for the users.

Figure 2 shows the framework separates the analytics into a pipeline handling various different tasks: The first step after receiving new log data is to run the feature extraction for the various analytics. The feature store is used to aggregate the data for time periods specific to the analytics. Once all data for a time period is aggregated the platform will call the various analytic modules to generate appropriate alerts for the log data. They are passed on to an alert aggregation that applies filters to re-prioritize and de-duplicate alerts to reduce the number of false positives.

Extracted features are passed to model generation components that create generative models used by analytics. The platform allows various rule mechanisms to determine how models are built based on the extracted features.

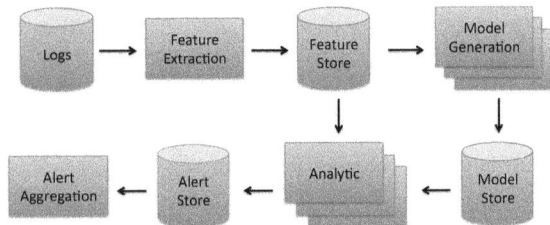

Figure 2: Schematic Overview of the Data Flow

3. MODELS

We have implemented a number of analytical models that can be applied to a wide variety of applications. These models make no assumptions regarding domain knowledge and are not application specific. For succinctness, we will present some of the existing analytics, some example applications, and possible visualizations.

Generative Models

The concept of a role used in role-based access control is a powerful primitive that can be abstracted beyond binary relations frequently to define common tasks performed by users. Recently, Molloy et al. [2] presented a way to extract a set of tasks from usage logs. These generative models naturally produce probability distributions over latent tasks[5]. Instead, we produce baseline distributions for each user over the set of tasks and measure deviations from this baseline. When the deviation, e.g., using KL divergence, becomes statistically significant or exceeds a threshold, we raise an alert. An example deviation in shown in Figure 3 plotting the user's past five years of task-based activity. We see two sudden changes: when the user stops acting in the purple role for 18 months, and when they resume.

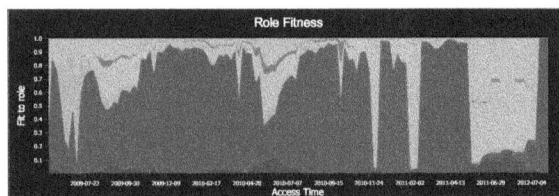

Figure 3: Example role fitness deviation. Note that user stops acting in the purple role for 18 months.

Clustering and Mixture Models

General clustering techniques, such as Gaussian mixture models, are a powerful mechanism to group users into subsets for easy comparison, and determine if a behavioral change is *significant*. User activity can be clusters using many different criteria. For example, frequency of the action, bytes read from a server, time of day, or even user attributes. These clusters are useful for subsequent analysis. For example, within a cluster—a peer group—is there a user that is an outlier. We have used this technique to identify users who are anomalies based on their attributes ("why is the VP checking out source code"), and detect transitions from one peer group to another.

We visualize clusters in using a radar plot. Here, we plot the top n dimensions that contributed to the deviation score, as shown in Figure 4. When higher dimensions are desirable, box plots are a powerful way to visualize dimensions of significant deviation from insignificant deviation.

Markov Models

Many common tasks performed by users are based around workflows that employees adhere to. Such activities often have a Markov property that can be easily learned and scored against. For example, in a source code management application, a user will often update their local brach, view outstanding tasks and defects assigned to them, make code changes and check them in, and close completed tasks and defects. We extract Markov models of various orders and score future behavior for significant deviations. These models can be conveniently visualized as weighted paths through

---

[5] [2] discretizes to produce a set of roles

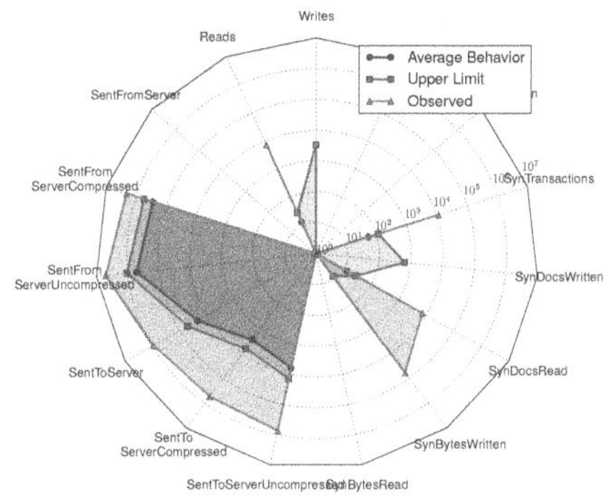

Figure 4: Comparing a user's actions to prior behavior and their peer group found via clustering

a graph, as shown in Figure 5, where the anomalous, low probability transitions are shown in red.

Statistical Measures

A classical model proposed by Denning [1] is statistical deviations. For example, for a given time period calculate a historical distribution and measure the probability a sample was drawn from the distribution. These types of analytics are common in most commodity systems, and we have implemented them as well, but note they yield high false positive rates.

Entropy Based Methods

There are many entropy based analytic methods that can be deployed, that we can use to differentiate human from malware derived behavior. One example assumes the distribution of high entropy time bits, the seconds of the minute and minute of the hour, are uniform distributed [4]. On our mainframe dataset, this analytic differentiates human users from batch processes with high accuracy.

Location Awareness

Users sign onto servers, we use IP geolocation to determine the location they are logging in from. Correlate their location, the location of the resources they are accessing, and their locations as provided by LDAP to produce actionable aggregate results.

Concurrent Access to Resources

Logs across multiple systems indicate when an account has been used to access multiple resources concurrently, or access the same resource from multiple locations. This may be an indication of credential sharing, a violation of many

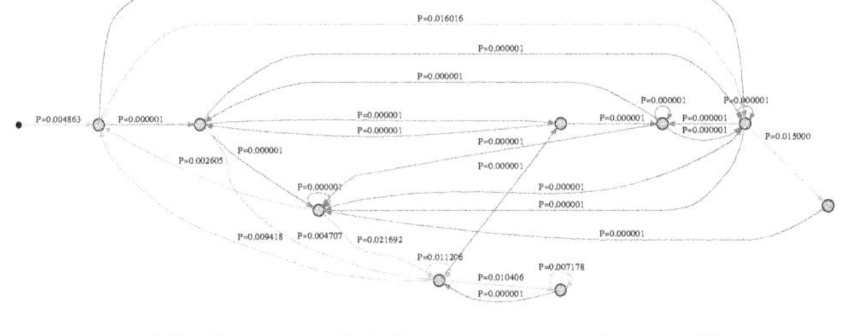

Figure 5: Markov model for an example application with low probability transitions.

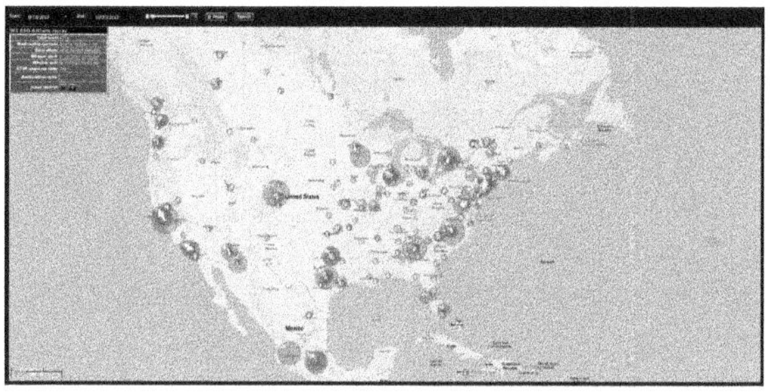

Figure 6: World map displaying the location of users accessing web applications

security policies. Such behavior can be integrated into a risk profile for a user for later prioritization of aggregate alerts.

4. DATA, APPLICATIONS, AND RESULTS

In our initial exploration, we have been able to ingest and process a wide variety of applications. In this section we describe some of the application logs we currently process, and some results, indicating strengths of the platform.

4.1 Data Sources

Web Applications

There is a recent trend in replacing platform specific applications, e.g., Windows or Java, with web applications. A common platform is LAMP: Linux, Apache, MySQL, and PHP. This architecture provide diverse application logs along the entire application stack that can be monitored and analyzed, each with its own policy and security model. Web-facing web applications are typically under constant attack by script kiddies and people "jiggling the doors" to see if systems have been left open. These requests typically attack old, known vulnerabilities and pollute application logs and should be suppressed for alerting to reduce false positive. We have begun to process a wide variety of such applications, ranging from custom content pages for researchers at IBM, customer serving help forums, and business critical applications.

Source Code Monitoring

Many of our tools were originally developed as a means to monitor for suspicious access to source code for commercial applications. We currently monitor around 70 CMVC applications, and a dozen or more applications using the Rational Team Concert source code management system. These source code management tools provide workflow management, bug and task tracking, automatic build systems, and a separation of components and job functions, such as developers and debuggers.

Custom Applications

We monitor a custom application managing a database of patent disclosures. The application is used to store, manage, and coordinate patent drafts between inventors, evaluators, and lawyers. This is an extremely valuable datasource containing unreleased, high value data that directly impacts a businesses ability to protect it's investments in research and development. We mine the logs for suspicious behavior, looking for users accessing patents they have no need for

Application	Avg. Rate	Max Rate	Avg. Time
z/OS (Daily)	16.4 GB	174.6 GB	1732s
Patent DB (Daily)	9.66 MB	93.9 MB	12s
W3 (Daily)	522 MB	2.27 GB	10250s
SSO (Daily)	146 MB	472 MB	3106s
CMVC-1 (Weekly)	945 MB	3.8 GB	921s
CMVC-2 (Weekly)	692 MB	4.3 GB	1272s

Table 1: Example data sizes for the datasets

(a security researcher won't typically evaluate a patent application for a semiconductor group), and correlation with the attributes of the employee. This allows us to treat researchers differently than evaluators, managers, and lawyers.

Syslog and z/OS RACF

Servers and mainframes can be configured to log security sensitive applications. We process syslogs for our web servers (in addition to any PHP, MySQL, and Apache logs), and for z/OS mainframes we process unloaded SMF records. On systems such as z/OS, we can process log files against the original RACF policy. RACF provides an expressive security policy containing a group-like structure with administrative hierarchies, multi-level security and mandatory access control, digital certificates, and grants access to resources using rules based on regular expressions over a resource path in the system (known as profiles). Here, small errors can vastly alter a user's access rights. We process the RACF policy for possible misconfigurations, such as overly expressive groups or profiles. This allows us to alert when users perform mildly suspicious behavior on resources they have a low probability right to access. (We can also suppress access to resources we believe a user has a high probability right to access).

4.2 Data Rates and Throughput

We are currently processing incremental data from the various sources in our platform. Table 1 show the amount of data imported from the various sources and their average processing time. The average time needed to process the data is depending on the type of analytics run. The W3 and SSO data sets are running the Markov Model analytics that requires a significantly longer time as the size of the extracted features is significantly larger causing a different IO behavior. We expect significant improvement in the processing speed by using a distributed data store and a data-location-aware scheduler.

4.3 Unified Models for Users

In all instances, when possible, we associate any application user id back to an owning company employee. This allows us to associate user attributes obtained from an LDAP database and social connections based on collaborations obtained from project wikis and other internal project management tools, with the application subject. After performing this correlation, we can provide a unified view of a user's activities. For example, if a user is behaving suspiciously with their access patterns to a source code repository, have they been performing anomalous actions against a web application or other database? Are similar users or colleagues behaving in a similar fashion? This could be an indication of collusion or more benign project constraints, such as an impending deadline or demonstration.

4.4 False Positive Reduction

We perform false positive reduction by grouping multiple alerts from similar analytics into a representative meta alert, suppress alerts we have already seen from being re-thrown, and processing alerts similar to those an administrator has already commented on (e.g., when closed or marked as duplicate).

We use a number of different techniques:

- *Alert grouping* Alerts for related analytics are grouped into a representative alert
- *Alert prioritization* suppresses a low priority alert for a higher analytic.
- *Duplicate and redundant alert elimination* We compare alerts to past alerts and eliminate alerts that have already been raised. This requires custom distance functions over alerts.
- *Administrative feedback* When an administrator has provided feedback for an alert, e.g., benign alert, we apply this label to similar, future alerts with a few caveats (increases in score or significance, time since last alert, etc.).
- *Asset prioritization* Some applications or datasets are more valuable than others, such as jewel code versus code contributed to an open source project. Alerts can be prioritized by asset value.

4.5 Results

The analytics provided by our platform have identified several interesting security incidents and misconfigurations. For some analytics and applications, such as those based on generative models, we observe low false positive rates from short durations of input data. We note that geolocation data is error produce due to the tendency of users to login remotely on multiple systems.

Finally, we present some interesting cases we uncovered:

- *Excessive File Replication* Employees in some demographics replicate document repositories on their local machines, beyond their need-to-know and increasing damage if laptops are lost of stolen.
- *Generative models track role transitions* For our source code monitoring application, we are able to detect employees changing their roles, such debuggers and testers checking out non-test source code, or checking out code for components they no longer work on.
- *Web vulnerabilities* Using our markov models, we identified several web server misconfigurations resulting in an administrative application listening on the external, and not internal IP, and mod rewrite not forwarding some port HTTP traffic to HTTPS.

5. REFERENCES

[1] D. E. Denning. An Intrusion-Detection Model. *IEEE TSE*, SE-13(2), 1987.

[2] I. Molloy, Y. Park, and S. Chari. Generative Models for Access Control Policies: Applications to Role Mining Over Logs with Attribution. In *SACMAT*, 2012.

[3] V. Paxson. Bro: A System for Detecting Network Intruders in Real-Time. *Computer Networks*, 31(23–24), 1999.

[4] C. M. Zhang and V. Paxson. Detecting and Analyzing Automated Activity on Twitter. *Proc. Passive & Active Measurement: PAM*, 2011.

Enabling Intensional Access Control via Preference-aware Query Optimization

Nicholas L. Farnan, Adam J. Lee, Panos K. Chrysanthis[1]
{nlf4, adamlee, panos}@cs.pitt.edu

Ting Yu[2]
yu@csc.ncsu.edu

[1]Department of Computer Science, University of Pittsburgh, Pittsburgh, PA, USA
[2]Department of Computer Science, North Carolina State University, Raleigh, NC, USA

ABSTRACT

Although the declarative nature of SQL provides great utility to database users, its use in *distributed* database management systems can result in unintended consequences to user privacy over the course of query evaluation. By allowing users to merely say *what* data they are interested in accessing without providing guidance regarding *how* to retrieve it, query optimizers can generate plans that leak sensitive query intension. To address these types of issues, we have created a framework that empowers users with the ability to specify access controls on the intension of their queries through extensions to the SQL SELECT statement. In this demonstration, we present a version of PostgreSQL's query optimizer that we have modified to produce plans that respect these constraints while optimizing user-specified SQL queries in terms of performance.

Categories and Subject Descriptors

K.4.1 [**Computers and Society**]: Public Policy Issues—*Privacy*; H.2.4 [**Database Management**]: Systems—*Distributed databases, Query processing*

Keywords

query optimization, privacy, distributed databases, preference SQL

1. INTRODUCTION

The declarative nature of SQL has been a major strength of relational database systems: users can simply specify *what* data they are interested in accessing and the database management system will determine the *best* plan for accessing that data. Plans for query evaluation detail what operations need to be performed to produce the result of an SQL query, what order these operations should be completed in, and what server should actually execute each operation. Traditionally, the *best* plan has been simply the plan that returns results to the user in the shortest amount of time. When

user queries are issued to distributed database management systems, however, two plans generating the same results for the same query can vary greatly in how they disseminate portions of that query during its evaluation.

In issuing a query to a database management system, the user is specifying exactly what information she wishes to retrieve from the system. This description is called the *intension* of a user's query. Users may consider some of the intension of their queries to be sensitive and wish to keep such sensitive intension hidden from remote servers. Hence, in order to protect their privacy, users must be empowered with the ability to control who is granted access to the intension of their queries.

In centralized database systems, the whole of the intension of a user's query is disclosed to a single system that optimizes and evaluates the query itself. As such, *how* the system optimizes and evaluates the query has no effect on the intensional privacy afforded to the user. With distributed database systems, however, though the whole intension of a user query is still disclosed to the optimizer, the optimizer may construct an evaluation plan for the query that distributes portions of query intension to a large number of remote servers needed to evaluate some part of that plan. Further, the user is left completely unaware of how the intension of her query is disseminated during its evaluation. Though these servers are trusted to store data and correctly process queries, the user may not trust them to learn sensitive portions of the intension of her query. Hence, access controls over the intension of SQL queries are needed to uphold user privacy.

Towards this goal, we have developed a framework for users to author declarative constraints on the query evaluation plans generated by a query optimizer for resolving SQL queries. The goal of our demonstration is to show how our framework can be used to establish access controls and protect the intension of SQL queries in distributed database systems, such as by keeping sensitive join conditions from being revealed to untrusted servers.

The remainder of this demonstration paper is structured as follows: Section 2 will describe the system model that we assume for this work and present a motivating example that will be used as the core of our demonstration. Section 3 will describe our framework, the extensions to SQL that we have developed as an interface to it, and further our implementation of this framework within PostgreSQL's optimizer. Finally, Section 4 will describe the details of the demonstration.

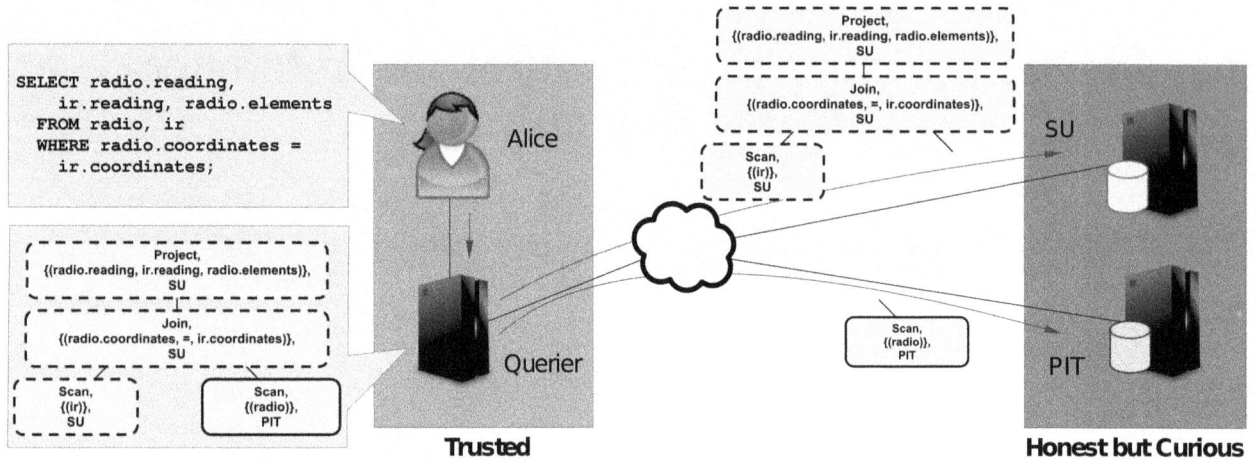

Figure 1: An illustration of the workflow of distributed query processing. Here, Alice's issuance of Query 1 and the dissemination of the query plan presented in Figure 2 is shown.

2. SYSTEM MODEL AND USE CASE

In our work, we consider the system model illustrated in Figure 1. The distributed query evaluation process begins when a user constructs the query she wishes to issue and passes it to a query optimizer. The optimizer then determines the best plan for evaluating the user's query, and distributes a portion of this plan to each server needed to evaluate the query. These database servers will evaluate their assigned portions of the query, combine their intermediate results as needed, and return the final query result to the user.

As can be seen here, the user has no part in deciding to or actually disseminating partial query plans to database servers. This provides the opportunity for violations of the user's privacy to occur. To highlight this issue, consider the following example:

Example 1. Alice is an astronomy researcher working at the Polytechnic Institute of Technology (PIT). Alice has recently decided to investigate whether combined readings from radio and infrared telescopes viewing the same stellar object can be used to efficiently predict the elements that make up that object in a novel way. Towards investigating this theory, she will query a small database of radio telescope readings and the elements known to be found in those objects that is maintained by PIT (in a table called simply "radio"). To get infrared readings to work with as well, however, Alice will have to query a much larger database maintained by State University (SU), specifically their "ir" table. For the greater good, the PIT and SU astronomy departments allow each other access to their respective databases. In spite of this, though, Alice would like to keep her new theory secret from researchers at SU to ensure she is the first to publish it in the case that she is, indeed, on to something.

Alice is interested in the result of the following SQL query:

```
SELECT radio.reading, ir.reading, radio.elements
   FROM radio, ir                                      (1)
   WHERE radio.coordinates = ir.coordinates;
```

Without the aid of our framework, an optimizer could produce a plan like the one shown in Figure 2. Here (and

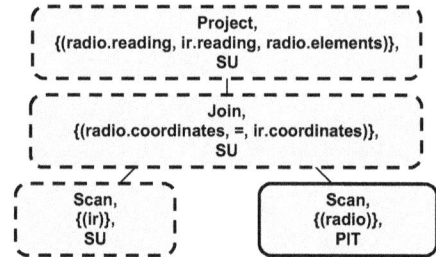

Figure 2: A potential plan for evaluating Alice's query that reveals sensitive intension to the adversarial server SU. The execution location of each node is represented by its border. Nodes with a dashed border are to be executed by SU, while those with a solid border are assigned to PIT.

throughout this demonstration paper) we represent a query plans as trees of relational algebra operations where the leaves of this tree scan the base tables containing needed data, the root produces the result of the query, and intermediate nodes process data from the relations scanned at the leaves. The relational algebra operations that make up the nodes of this tree can be represented as ternaries of the following form:

$$\langle op, params, p \rangle$$

Here, op represents the operation to be performed. We consider valid operators to be either one of the core relational algebra operators (selection, projection, rename, set union, set difference, and cross product), a scan, or a join. $params$ is a set of sets that represents the parameters to that operation (e.g., the table to be scanned, the condition on a join of two relations, the attributes that tuples should be projected down to, etc.); and p represents the site annotated to evaluate this operation.

It can be seen in Figure 2 that this example plan reveals to SU sensitive aspects of the intension of Alice's query: by having SU evaluate the join of data from the radio and ir tables, SU learns that Alice is interested in both radio and ir telescope readings, the very information that she wished to keep private. To solve this problem for Alice and users like her, we provide a way for users to specify what portions of the intension of their queries they consider to be sensitive, and whom that sensitive intension should be kept from.

3. OUR APPROACH

To give users control over what parties are granted access to sensitive portions of the intension of their queries, we modify the query optimizer from our system model to accept not only user queries, but also constraints on the plans that can be generated to evaluate those queries. The optimizer will then utilize these constraints during the optimization process and produce plans that uphold them. Through this approach, we can effectively include privacy as an optimization metric.

3.1 SQL Extensions

Constraints can be specified as either *requirements* (constraints that *must* be upheld by any plan to evaluate the query) or *preferences* (constraints that may not be upheld if they conflict with other constraints or render the optimizer unable to generate a feasible query plan). To express each of these to the optimizer, in [1] we developed two extensions to the SQL `SELECT` statement: the `REQUIRING` and `PREFERRING` clauses.

Required constraints are fairly straightforward: Alice (from Example 1) could require that any plan produced by the optimizer for her query presented in Section 2 keeps her interest in radio and infrared telescope readings from SU. The `REQUIRING` clause takes the following general form:

> `REQUIRING` *condition* `HOLDS OVER` *node descriptors*
>
> `AND` *another condition* `HOLDS OVER` *node descriptors*

Node descriptors are used to identify the intensional region that the user wishes to constrain. Node descriptors are defined as a mirror to our representation of query tree nodes, ternaries consisting of *op*, *params*, and *p*. They are used to "match" query tree nodes that contain sensitive pieces of query intension. A node descriptor designed to specify the mention of radio and infrared telescope readings as sensitive, for example, would match against the project operation in Figure 2 as this node operates on both the **radio** table's **reading** attribute and the **ir** table's **reading** attribute. In node descriptors, "*" is used as a general wildcard for portions of the ternary that the user wishes a given node descriptor to match against any value of. To construct a node descriptor matching any query tree node that operates on radio and infrared readings, for example, the user could instantiate *op* and *p* as "*" while defining *params* as a combination of these two attributes. Finally, the "@" character is used to identify free variables over which conditions can be authored. By stating the *p* part of her node descriptor to be a free variable, and authoring a condition that that free variable should not have the value SU, Alice can inform the optimizer of her constraint that query tree nodes matching her node descriptor are not evaluated by SU. This constraint could be expressed through our `REQUIRING` clause as follows:

```
SELECT radio.reading, ir.reading, radio.elements
  FROM radio, ir
  WHERE radio.coordinates = ir.coordinates
  REQUIRING @p <> SU HOLDS OVER
    <*, {(radio.reading, ir.reading)}, @p>;
```
(2)

Privacy notions are rarely so straightforward, however. User conceptions of privacy are inherently personal and situationally dependent. The `PREFERRING` clause allows our framework to capture such complex privacy notions. While the `PREFERRING` clause is made up of the same basic *constraint* `HOLDS OVER` *node descriptors* building blocks as the `REQUIRING` clause, it makes use of an additional keyword to bind them together. Where the `REQUIRING` clause uses only `AND` to join individual constraints together, constraints in the `PREFERRING` clause can also be joined using `CASCADE`. This second keyword is needed to establish the priority of different constraints relative to one another to form partially ordered preference structures. While two constraints joined by `AND` are considered equally preferred, any constraint before a given `CASCADE` is considered more important by the optimizer than any that are listed after that `CASCADE`.

As an example, let us say that Alice would prefer to keep SU from learning that she is interested in both infrared telescope readings and radio telescope readings. Alice would like it if neither of those pieces of intension is revealed to SU, but if that is not possible, she would prefer that either one or the other is revealed as opposed to revealing her interest in both. This relatively complex notion of query privacy can be succinctly captured in our framework using simply the `AND` keyword (as Alice does not consider the revelation of either her interest in radio readings or her interest in infrared readings to be more important than the other).

```
SELECT radio.reading, ir.reading, radio.elements
  FROM radio, ir
  WHERE radio.coordinates = ir.coordinates
  PREFERRING  @p <> SU HOLDS OVER
    <*, {(radio.reading)}, @p>
  AND @p <> SU HOLDS OVER
    <*, {(ir.reading)}, @p>;
```
(3)

If Alice further wanted all join operations to be performed by PIT's database server, she could add this as a less important constraint using the `CASCADE` keyword:

```
SELECT radio.reading, ir.reading, radio.elements
  FROM radio, ir
  WHERE radio.coordinates = ir.coordinates
  PREFERRING @p <> SU HOLDS OVER
    <*, {(radio.reading)}, @p>
  AND @p <> SU HOLDS OVER
    <*, {(ir.reading)}, @p>
  CASCADE @p == PIT HOLDS OVER
    <Join, *, @p>;
```
(4)

Upon receiving this extended query specification with preferred constraints, the optimizer will attempt to construct a plan that upholds the constraints for keeping **radio.reading** and **ir.reading** from SU (or both). If it can construct a plan that further executes all joins at PIT, all the better. The optimizer will only emit a plan that evaluates all joins at PIT and reveals sensitive information to SU if revealing such information is unavoidable in any plan the optimizer is able to build. Because Alice states that keeping her interests secret from SU is more important to her than executing joins at PIT, the optimizer will never trade off revealing information to SU in favor of executing joins at PIT.

Such an optimization process could result in the query plan shown in Figure 3. This query plan upholds all of the example constraints mentioned in this section.

191

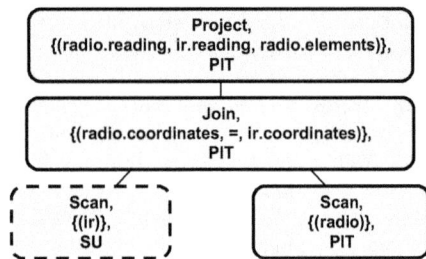

Figure 3: A potential plan for evaluating Alice's query that protects her privacy. The execution location of each node is represented by its border. Nodes with a dashed border are to be executed by SU, while those with a solid border are assigned to PIT.

3.2 Implementation

PostgreSQL is a widely-used, open-source, object-relational database management system [3]. In all, it consists of over 700,000 lines of code. To support our extensions to SQL, we have modified the optimizer contained within PostgreSQL.

As PostgreSQL is not a distributed database management system, the first step in adapting its optimizer to our needs was to modify the optimizer to reason about execution locations of the individual operations that make up an overall query plan. This required modifying all query plan data structures to incorporate execution location state, iterating through possible execution locations of all operations added to a query plan, and revising the plan cost estimator to account for parallel operations occurring at different sites and data transfer times.

Once this was done, we adapted the optimization process to utilize REQUIRING clauses to prune the optimization search space. Any sub-plan that violates a required constraint cannot be emitted as part of a final query plan and can hence be discarded from further consideration during plan construction. To support the PREFERRING clause, we have modified PostgreSQL's dynamic programming approach to query optimization to maintain only the most highly preferred plans over the course of optimization. This heuristic allows us include user preferences and intensional access controls as optimization metrics while offering optimization performance near that of the unmodified optimizer. All together, our modifications to PostgreSQL touched a subset of the code base totaling over 60,000 lines of code.

4. DEMONSTRATION

In this demonstration, we first illustrate the how easily a user with knowledge of SQL can specify constraints on her queries and second, the effect of such constraints on the query optimization process. We show how, when passed into our modified query optimizer alongside a user query, intensional access controls specified through such constraints can drastically change the makeup of the plan devised by the optimizer to protect user privacy with little overhead to optimization time. We present the example scenario and query shown in Section 2, and the different query plans produced by our optimizer when different constraints are issued with the query. In doing so, we present only a small subset of the expressive power available through our framework.

To set up this demonstration, we establish databases sim-

ulating PIT and SU's stores of telescope readings. Specifically, we seed two databases with samples of data gleaned from the Astroshelf project [2], and then adjust their catalog metadata to simulate the optimization of queries over large scale astronomical databases without having to maintain a large scale data store for this demonstration. We assume that SU stores around 4TB of data, while PIT maintains only 1TB, and scale the metadata accordingly.

As we demonstrate only the query optimization process, only the catalog metadata for these databases is accessed in our demonstration. By seeding these databases with sample data from Astroshelf, we can ensure that our demonstration presents realistic examples of query optimization.

We begin our demonstration by presenting the optimization of Alice's query without any constraints on the resulting plan. We present a graphical representation of the resulting evaluation plan, as well as the time required to optimize the query and the estimated run time of the evaluation plan. With this baseline in hand, we then show how the addition of the required constraints shown in Query 1 in Section 3.1 causes the generation of structurally different plans and the minimal effect that the addition of such constraints has on optimization time and estimated runtime. We further demonstrate how our optimizer can detect the presence of conflicting requirements (e.g., Alice requires that all joins happen at PIT and also that no joins happen at PIT), and inform the user of such.

From here, we show the effect of preferred constraints on the optimization process by optimizing Queries 3 and 4 from Section 3.1. We further show how conflicting preferred constraints are of no consequence to our optimizer. If they are separated by a CASCADE, the optimizer will produce a plan upholding the one given before the CASCADE. If they are separated by an AND, the optimizer will support whichever allows for the creation of a faster evaluation plan.

Finally, we demonstrate how other policies idioms can be expressed using our framework. For example, we show how separation of duty controls can be implemented through our constraints (e.g., do not allow any server that scans the infrared readings table to perform any join operations).

Acknowledgments. This work was supported in part by the National Science Foundation under awards CCF–0916015, CNS–0964295, CNS–0914946, CNS–0747247, and OIA-1028162. This work was further partially supported by a gift from EMC/Greenplum.

5. REFERENCES

[1] N. L. Farnan, A. J. Lee, P. K. Chrysanthis, and T. Yu. Don't reveal my intention: Protecting user privacy using declarative preferences during distributed query processing. In *ESORICS*, pages 628–647, 2011.

[2] P. Neophytou, R. Gheorghiu, R. Hachey, T. Luciani, D. Bao, A. Labrinidis, E. G. Marai, and P. K. Chrysanthis. Astroshelf: understanding the universe through scalable navigation of a galaxy of annotations. In *Proceedings of the 2012 ACM SIGMOD International Conference on Management of Data*, SIGMOD '12, pages 713–716, 2012.

[3] The PostgreSQL Global Development Group. Postgresql. http://www.postgresql.org/, Dec. 2012.

RMiner: A Tool Set for Role Mining

Ruixuan Li, Huaqing Li, Wei Wang, Xiaopu Ma, Xiwu Gu

School of Computer Science and Technology
Huazhong University of Science and Technology
Wuhan, Hubei 430074, China
rxli@hust.edu.cn, {lihuaqing, ybwei.wang, xpma}@smail.hust.edu.cn, guxiwu@hust.edu.cn

ABSTRACT

Recently, there are many approaches proposed for mining roles using automated technologies. However, it lacks a tool set that can be used to aid the application of role mining approaches and update role states. In this demonstration, we introduce a tool set, RMiner, which is based on the core of WEKA, an open source data mining tool. RMiner implements most of the classic and latest role mining algorithms and provides interactive tools for administrator to update role states. The running examples of RMiner are presented to demonstrate the effectiveness of the tool set.

Categories and Subject Descriptors

D.4.6 [**Operating Systems**]: Security and Protection—Access

Controls; H.2.8 [**Database Management**]: Database

Application—Data Mining

General Terms

Security, Management.

Keywords

Role-based access control, role engineering, role mining, tool set.

1. INTRODUCTION

The goal of role engineering is to configure a role-based access control (RBAC) system. Usually, role engineering process includes generating roles, assigning roles to users and updating role state. There are two basic approaches for role engineering: top-down approach and bottom-up approach. The top-down approach uses descriptions of business processes, security policies, and other business information to configure an RBAC system. The bottom-up approach uses data mining techniques to discover roles from the existing user-permission assignments and other business information. The bottom-up approach is commonly called role mining.

There are many algorithms have been proposed to mine the roles. The role mining algorithms discover roles from the real world data set that is usually with noise. It is something difficult to

generate a role state that is accurately satisfied with the security needs for an RBAC system. Researches use the ratio of the number of generated roles exactly matching the original role sets to the number of original roles to evaluate a role mining algorithm. If the original role sets are not known, the weighted structural complexity (WSC) [4], which sums up the number of relationships in an RBAC state, is often used to evaluate the performance of the role mining algorithms. Nevertheless, role mining algorithms will not completely solve the role configuration problem. The administrators usually need to correct some improper roles generated by role mining algorithm. Therefore, we need a platform to implement the role mining algorithms and provide a tool set to aid the administrators to update the role state.

WEKA [1] is known as a collection of machine learning algorithms for data mining tasks. However, WEKA workbench platform is not suitable for role mining tasks. The reasons are as follows. Firstly, the input of WEKA is a set of instances that describes the relationship between attributes. An instance means the values on every attributes. In contrast, the input of role mining algorithms contains the user-permission assignments and some business information. If we use instances to indicate the assignments, we must list all the permissions, but their value is just 0 or 1. It is quit redundant and easy to mix assignments and attributes. Secondly, the output of role mining algorithms is a set of associated permissions. This is similar to association rule mining in WEKA, whereas the evaluation criterion in role mining is different from support and confidence that used in association rule mining. The rules with low frequency may be also a role in role mining field. Thirdly, there is lack of a common implementation of role mining algorithms, which makes it hard for researches to do a comparison experiments when designing a new algorithm. Therefore, we need to develop an independent tool set for role mining since the role mining algorithms cannot be migrated to WEKA platform directly.

In this demonstration, we show a role mining platform, namely RMiner. In RMiner, we implement most of the classical role mining algorithms, such as ORCA [2], HierarchicalMiner [3], CompleteMiner [4], FastMiner [4], Anti-apriori [5], GraphOptimization [6], and WeightedRoleMinning [7]. RMiner also provides a role state editor for updating the role state generated by the role mining algorithms. In addition, RMiner offers some abstract interfaces that the users can easily add new role mining algorithms, and discover the difference of the new algorithms compared with others using the visualization tools.

RMiner is implemented by Java. The program for RMiner can be downloaded from http://code.google.com/p/rminer/.

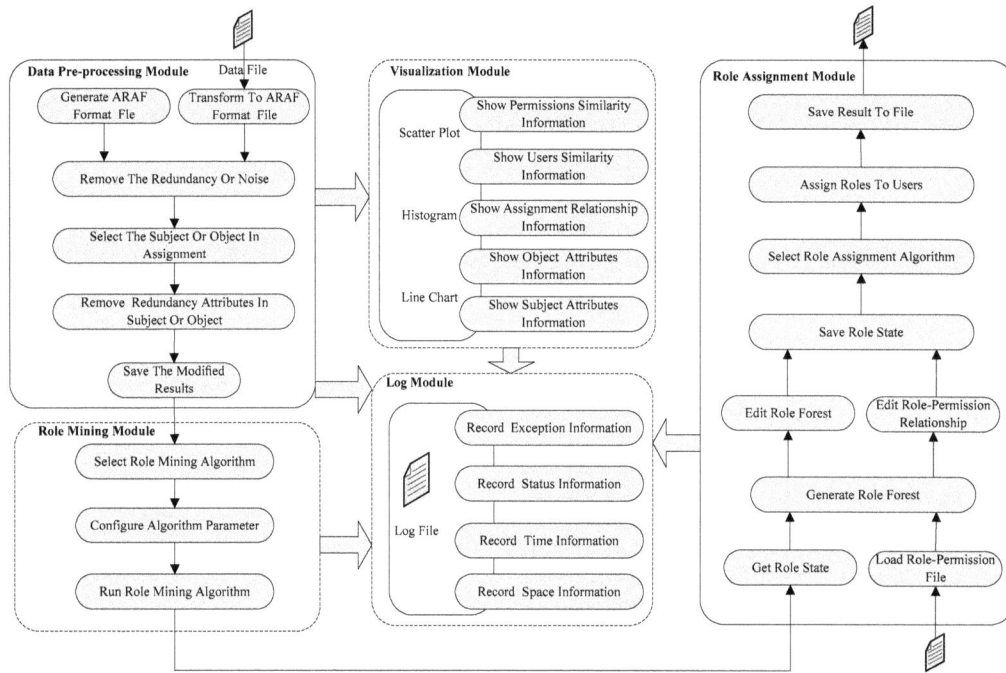

Figure 1. The framework of RMiner.

2. THE FRAMEWORK OF RMINER

In RMiner, we want to provide a tool set to help researchers or administrators do role engineering work. The platform of RMiner can also do some comparison experiments to make them understand the characteristics of the role mining algorithms clearly. The framework of RMiner, as shown in Figure 1, includes five parts: data pre-processing, role mining, role assignment, visualization, and log.

Before using the RMiner, the users must transform the input user-permission relationship to ARAF file format that will be introduced in Section 3.1. The users can also use the artificial user-permission assignments generated by RMiner automatically if they don't offer real user-permission relationships. In general, if the users want to calculate the accuracy of the algorithm, they need to provide the predefined set of roles. After that, the users can remove the redundancy or noise in the input manually. Then the users need to select the subject and object in the assignments and remove the redundant attributes. When the input data are ready, RMiner will use the selected algorithm to generate roles. In the process of role mining, the users can adjust the parameters of the selected algorithm. The output of the selected algorithm contains: ROLES (set of roles), UA (user to role assignments) and PA (role to permission assignments). If these outputs are not satisfied with the users' security needs, the users can update them through a visualization tool, namely role editor. In the stage of role edit, the users can use the role mining result or load the role to permission file for role assignment. If the users want to edit the result, they can edit the role to permission relationship shown in table and edit the role state shown as role forest in RMiner. After editing the role to permission relationship and role state, the users need to select an algorithm for role assignment. The role assignment algorithm builds the Integral UA and PA relationship according to the initial user-permission relationship. The users can save the results into a specified file.

After loading the role to permission assignment relationship and the attributes of the subject and object, the users can view the attribute and assignment relationship information through the visualization module of RMiner. In this module, the users can also know the similarity information of the users and the permissions in the user-permission relationship. RMiner shows the information via scatter plot, histogram or line chart. Through the permission similarity information shown in RMiner, the users can estimate the number of the original roles, which will be useful if they just want to know the number of the roles roughly and don't want to run the role mining algorithms. Besides the above four modules, the log module records the running information, which contains exception, status, time and space information.

3. THE DESIGN OF RMINER

3.1 The Data Structure of RMiner

In order to maintain independence and generality of data set for role mining process, we develop the assignment relationship with attribute file format (ARAF) based on attribute relation file format (ARFF) of WEKA. The only difference between ARAF and ARFF is the concept of latitude. We use latitude to indicate the two assignment sides, and the attributes of a side are described by ARFF format. Figure 2 shows an example of user-permission assignments with user attributes using ARAF format. An ARAF file can be divided into two parts. The first part is the assignment, including assignment name, assignment subject, assignment object and the subject to object assignment relationships which are described by 0/1 matrix. The second part is the attribute information of latitude. This information includes attribute name, attribute data type, such as numeric, string, time and enumerated, and the value of attributes for every instance in latitude.

The latitude of ARAF can be user, role and permission. Thus, we can use ARAF file to indicate the user to permission relationships, role to permission relationships and user to role relationships. In

```
@assignment  upa
@latitude user  {Ann,Bob,Carl}
@latitude permission {rAcc,wAcc,cdAcc,cTrans,rTrans}
@matrix
1,1,0,1,0
1,1,0,1,0
1,0,1,0,1
@attributes of user
@attribute age numeric [10, 80]
@attribute department {HR, BM}
@data
45,HR
20,HR
29,BM
```

Figure 2. An example of ARAF.

general, the assignment in an RBAC system will be relatively sparse. The matrix can be represented using the pressurized reduced storage method. We only record the object labels in every subject assignment.

In the implementation of RMiner, the ARAF file format is corresponding to the data structure for the assignments. It includes sub-structure latitude, matrix, attributes and instances.

3.2 Data Pre-processing Tool

The RMiner interface is shown in Figure 3. We can see that there are five option cards in RMiner: Preprocess, RoleMining, Assignment, Visualize and About. The Preprocess part is to choose and modify the data set used in role mining algorithm. The RoleMining part is to generate roles using the selected algorithm. The Assignment part is to assign the generated roles to users and update the role state. The Visualize part is to provide the interactive 2D display for the role mining process.

Figure 3 also shows the module of data pre-processing interface. The data pre-processing tool in RMiner is to help users clear the noise in the data set. It provides several predefined real data sets and an artificial data generation tool. These will facilitate the use of the RMiner working environment. The users can load the user-permission relationship file, or generate user-permission relationship with RMiner automatically. The users can also edit the user-permission information with the edit button.

3.3 Role Mining Platform

After the preprocessing, the data set is used as the input for role mining algorithm. The users select the role mining algorithm, configure the algorithm parameters, and activate the algorithm. RMiner will automatically execute the selected algorithm, and record the running time, memory space usage and other evaluation information. The users can use the visualization tool to view the generated role set. The same data set can be activated by different role mining algorithms. Thus, we can do the comparison experiments on different algorithms. The generated role set will be formatted as assignment structure ARAF, and their latitudes are role and permission respectively.

In RMiner, we have implemented 13 role mining algorithms, as shown in Figure 4. CompleteMiner, FastMiner and HPRoleMinimization can output role set. ORCA, GraphOptimization, HierarchicalMiner, HPEdgeMinimization, FeatureMiner and YeHRMiner can output role set and role hierarchies. StateMiner and MinimalPerturbation consider perturbation, and WeightedRoleMinning considers the weights of permissions. CCRMimplement and ThesisAlgorithmImplement considers constraints. Anti-apriori mines the constraints in Role-Based Access Control. The users are free to add new role mining algorithms to RMiner platform.

3.4 Role Assignment Tool

The role set generated by role mining algorithm may not fully meet the security needs of the real application. In order to increase the interpretability and generalization ability, the users can manually update the role state in RMiner. As shown in Figure 5, RMiner provides a role editor for users. Role editor uses the partial order of permissions in role sets to build the role forest, which will help user understand the role hierarchy and the weights of roles. The users can use role editor to add, delete or modify the role set. In Figure 5, the left part is the role forest, in which the users can edit every role, and the right part is the role to permission relationship, in which the green part is inherited from parent roles and cannot be edited. After completing modifying the role set, the users can assign the roles to users according to the original user-permission assignments. As we know, this process is a set covering problem. RMiner provides greedy and genetic algorithms to solve the role assignment problem.

3.5 Visualization

Visualization tool in RMiner can assist the users to analysis the mining results more clearly. It translates the data of role mining process into a variety of graphics that indicates the status of the process and reveals the inner nature and regularity. Figure 6 shows the permission similarity information on the university_runningexample dataset. Both X-axis and y-axis represent permissions. The deeper the color of the block is, the bigger the probability of forming a role is. The process of building an RBAC system involves assignment relationships and business information. Visualization tool provides a scatter plot, histogram line and statistical analysis, which facilitates the understanding of the role mining process.

4. CONCLUSIONS AND FUTURE WORK

RMiner provides user a visual role mining and role state updating platform. The design of RMiner is according to the building process of an RBAC system. Users can use the platform to build an RABC system or carry out comparison experiments to analysis the difference between role mining algorithms. RMiner is a unified verification platform that simplifies the process of role mining research and experimental work. However, RMiner only provides a common tool for building an RBAC system. It is not fully adapt to the changes in the RBAC system. At the same time, there is still some inadequate in the data pre-processing and role state updating processes. The data pre-processing almost relies on the manual manipulation. It is hard to apply to large data set. The display of role editor on large data sets is something complex, which will weaken the interaction and the user experience. We will try to improve these in the future work.

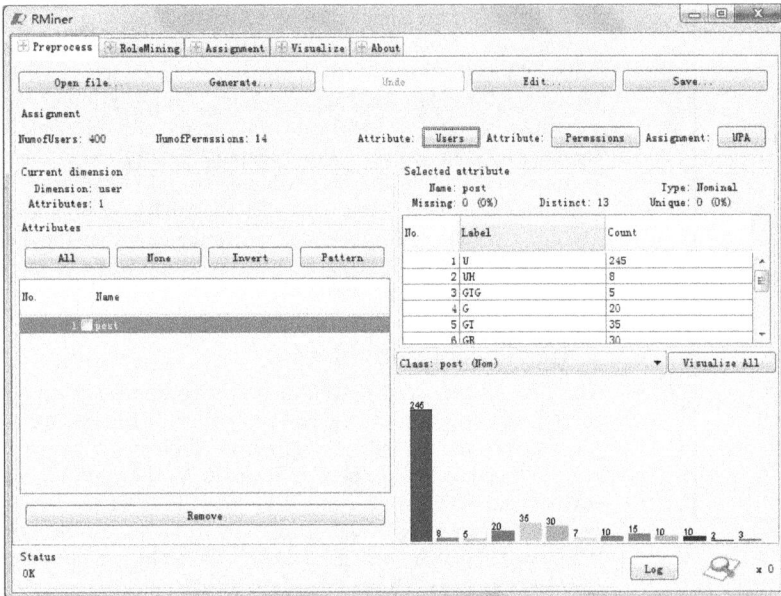

Figure 3. The module of data pre-processing.

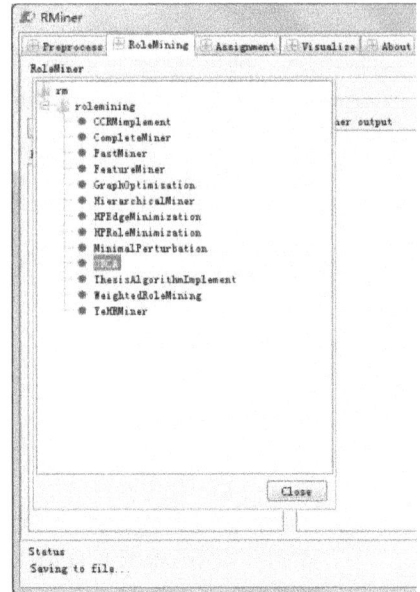

Figure 4. The module of role mining.

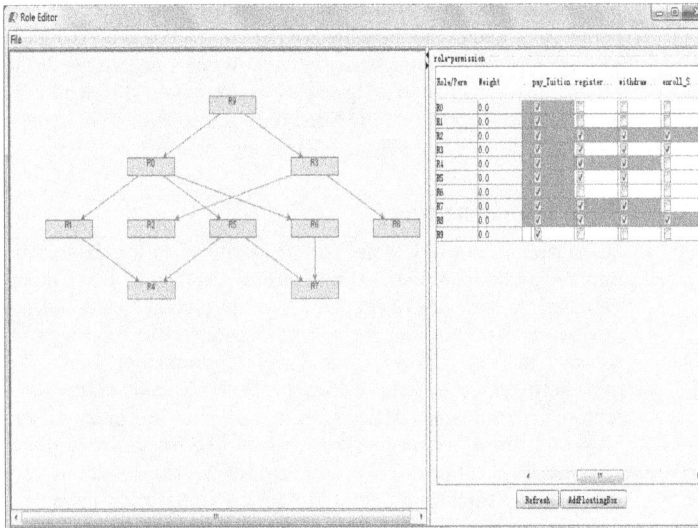

Figure 5. Role editor and assignment in RMiner.

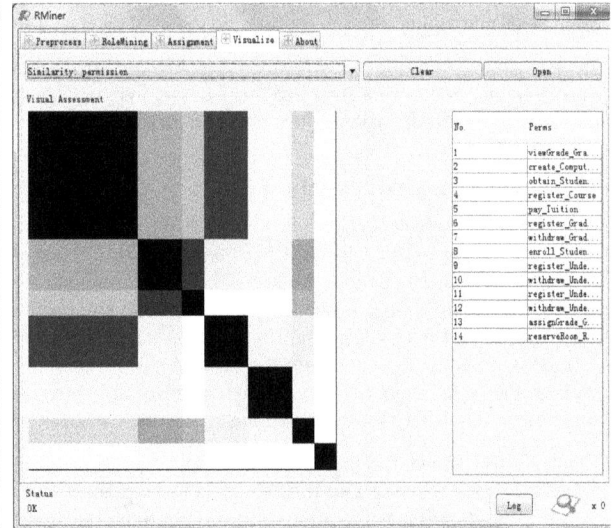

Figure 6. Permission similarity information.

Acknowledgements

This work is supported by National Natural Science Foundation of China under grants 61173170 and 60873225, National High Technology Research and Development Program of China under grant 2007AA01Z403, and Innovation Fund of Huazhong University of Science and Technology under grants 2012TS052 and 2012TS053.

5. REFERENCES

[1] Bouckaert, R., Frank, E., Hall, M., Kirkby, R., Reutemann, P., Seewald, A., and Scuse, D. 2008. *WEKA Manual for Version 3-6-0*. University of Waikato, Hamilton, New Zealand, 2008.

[2] Schlegelmilch, J., and Steffens, U. 2005. Role mining with ORCA. In *Proceedings of the 10th ACM Symposium on Access Control Models and Technologies* (Stockholm, Sweden, June 2005). SACMAT'05, ACM, 168-176.

[3] Molloy, I., Chen, H., Li, T., Wang, Q., Li, N., Bertino, E., Calo, S., and Lobo, J. 2008. Mining roles with semantic meanings. In *Proceedings of the 13th ACM Symposium on Access Control Models and Technologies* (Estes Park, CO, USA, June 2008). SACMAT'08, ACM, 21-30.

[4] Vaidya, J., Atluri, V., and Warner, J. 2006. Roleminer: mining roles using subset enumeration. In *Proceedings of the 13th ACM Conference on Computer and Communications Security* (Alexandria, VA, USA, October 2006). CCS'06. ACM, 144-153.

[5] Ma, X., Li, R., Lu, Z., and Wang, W. 2012. Mining Constraints in Role-Based Access Control. *Mathematical and Computer Modelling*, Elsevier, 55, 1-2 (2012), 87-96.

[6] Zhang, D., Ramamohanarao, K., and Ebringer, T. 2007. Role engineering using graph optimisation. In *Proceedings of the 12th ACM Symposium on Access Control Models and Technologies* (Sophia Antipolis, France, June 2007). SACMAT'07, ACM, 139-144.

[7] Ma, X., Li, R., Lu, Z. 2010. Role Mining Based on Weights. In *Proceedings of the 15th ACM Symposium on Access Control Models and Technologies* (Pittsburgh, PA, USA, June 2010). SACMAT'10, ACM, 65-74.

Secure Benchmarking in the Cloud

Axel Schroepfer, Andreas Schaad,
Florian Kerschbaum
SAP Research Security & Trust
Vincenz-Priessnitz Str. 1
76131 Karlsruhe, Germany
firstname.lastname@sap.com

Heiko Boehm, Joerg Jooss
Microsoft Deutschland GmbH
Konrad-Zuse-Straße 1
85716 Unterschleißheim, Germany
heikob || joerg.jooss@microsoft.com

ABSTRACT

Benchmarking is the comparison of one company's key performance indicators (KPI) to the statistics of the same KPIs of its peer group. A KPI is a statistical quantity measuring the performance of a business process. Privacy by means of controlling access to data is of the utmost importance in benchmarking. Companies are reluctant to share their business performance data due to the risk of losing a competitive advantage or being embarrassed. We present a cryptographic protocol for securely computing benchmarks between multiple parties and describe the technical aspects of a proof of concept implementation of SAP's research prototype Global Benchmarking Service (GBS) on Microsoft's cloud technology Windows Azure.

Categories and Subject Descriptors

H.4 [**Information Systems Applications**]: Miscellaneous

Keywords

Access Control; Privacy; Benchmarking; Cloud

1. INTRODUCTION

Benchmarking is the comparison of one company's key performance indicators (KPI) to the statistics of the same KPIs of its peer group. A KPI is a statistical quantity measuring the performance of a business process. Examples from different company operations are make cycle time (manufacturing) or cash flow (financial). A peer group is a group of (usually competing) companies that are interested in comparing their KPIs based on some similarity of the companies. Examples formed along different characteristics include car manufacturers (industry sector), Fortune 500 companies in the United States (revenue and location), or airline vs. railway vs. haulage (sales market).

Privacy is of the utmost importance in benchmarking. Companies are reluctant to share their business performance data due to the risk of losing a competitive advantage or being embarrassed. As one result of our research work we presented a cryptographic protocol for securely computing benchmarks between multiple parties [1]. We implemented the protocol as a platform for secure benchmarking. The benchmarking platform is not supposed to receive the plain text KPIs from the companies acting as a trusted third party, but rather the KPIs are to be kept entirely private to

the companies. In the security model the benchmarking platform acts as a regular participant without any input. While the privacy protects the confidentiality of the KPIs for the companies, it also alleviates the benchmarking platform from the burden of storing and handling them and protects it from accidental revelation. Another important aspect of the platform is that the subscribed companies only communicate with the service provider, but never amongst each other. Anonymity among the subscribed companies is a required feature and can only be achieved, if they do not need to address messages to each other. The precise requirement for anonymity is that subscribers do not know or refer to any static identifier of other customers (e.g. IP addresses, public keys, etc.). Any static identifier will reveal changes in the composition of the peer group to the subscribers in subsequent executions of the protocol which is undesirable and may break the privacy of the entire system. In many cases, the service provider wants to know the identity of the subscribers for billing purposes, which simplifies communication. In order to keep the proposed protocols practical, they need to be optimized in computation and communication cost. One measure is the number of rounds that are needed to complete the protocol. A round in the service provider model is a step in the protocol that all subscribers need to complete before any subscriber can initiate the next step. The proposed protocols have a constant number of rounds. Another measure is the communication complexity of the protocol. Our protocol has a constant (i.e. linear in the length of the security parameter) communication complexity for each subscriber independent of the number of subscribed companies. Our protocol (cf. [2] for details) presents a practical implementation of privacy-preserving benchmarking for statistics average, median, variance, best-in-class and maximum. It addresses a number of trade-offs in distributed systems (single central platform) and security (key distribution and security assumptions) architecture tuned for performance and economic benefit.

1.1 SAP's Global Benchmarking Service

We have implemented the benchmarking system of [2] in Java. The communication of the cryptographic protocol is based on objects at the service provider side that are called by stubs at the service consumer side. We use Java RMI (Remote Method Invocation) to accomplish the task. Each party of the protocol maintains a local SQL database to store inputs and outputs of the protocol. An adapter allows synchronizing the database with a SAP Business Warehouse system. Both types of parties (service consumer and provider) use a web based GUI (graphical user interface) to alter database information (e.g., settings, peergroup formations, etc.). The GUIs use web services to access the database. This setup runs the mentioned components (except the database) within a web application server. The service provider stack is recommended to be installed on a computational powerful machine while a mobile device is acceptable for the client stack.

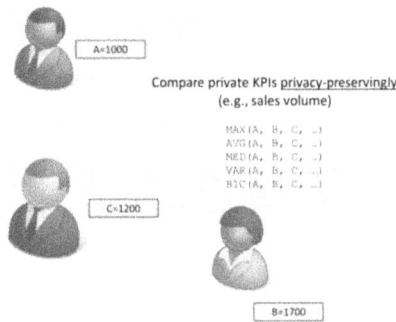

Figure 1: Partners compare KPIs privacy-preservingly.

1.2 Microsoft Azure

Windows Azure is a Microsoft cloud computing platform used to build, deploy and manage applications through a global network of Microsoft-managed data centers. Windows Azure allows for applications to be built using many different languages, tools or frameworks and makes it possible for developers to integrate their public cloud applications in their existing IT environment. Windows Azure provides both Platform as a Service (PaaS) and Infrastructure as a Service (IaaS) services and is classified as the "Public Cloud" in Microsoft's cloud computing strategy, along with its Software as a Service (SaaS) offering, Microsoft Online Services. Windows Azure can be used to build a web application that runs and stores its data in Microsoft data centers. It can connect on-premise applications with each other or map between different sets of identity information.

2. CORE COMPONENTS

The following section describes the relevant architectural components that are involved in the construction of the cloud-based benchmark service, and their Windows Azure specific implementation.

2.1 Entities: Services, Providers &Consumers

We retain the basic platform architecture from our former prototypical construction. That is, we have a service provider (e.g., SAP) that aims to provide a service for secure benchmarking to its customers. Customers will consume the service, respectively subservices, via software running at client side. The service provider has a couple of essential tasks. He has to maintain users; maintain peer groups; schedule benchmarks; store and provide results of performed benchmarks; and act as party within the benchmark protocol in the role of the service provider.

Since most of these tasks can be viewed as management tasks, we decided to group them into one service, the benchmark management service. For the task mentioned last – the participation in the benchmark protocol – we design an independent service. As already mentioned, the protocol is constructed in multiple sections or rounds (five, to be precise). The reason for the separation into multiple services is that each round produces a partial result, i.e., one of the statistics (e.g., the mean that is used in a later round in order to compute the variance). Section 3 discusses another possible separation of rounds into independent services. A fine-grained service separation can be very useful, as it allows to technically and economically optimally use the scaling infrastructure of Windows Azure.

2.2 Communication

The construction of the benchmark platform enables clients to operate within a company network that is protected by a firewall. Access to the outside network may be restricted by a proxy server. Communication from a client is often limited to outbound HTTP (respectively HTTPS) traffic. For this reason the cryptographic protocol is designed as a series of outbound communication calls from the customer to the central service provider.

This basic messaging paradigm hinders native synchronization of clients by the service provider. Synchronization however is a vital aspect and required at several points before and within a run of the protocol. In order to accomplish the desired behavior, we either employ a polling mechanism (on the consumer's side) that is compatible with this communication paradigm (i.e., a client calls a service method iteratively) or we use relative timestamps (on the provider's side).

2.3 Protocol Context - Emulating Stateful Services

Straightforwardly implementing the benchmarking services on Windows Azure leads to a problem: services in Azure are supposed to maintain durable state outside of each individual compute instance. This might be acceptable for the management services exposing methods that would be considered as static from an object oriented programming point of view, but it is a problem for the services of the cryptographic benchmarking protocol. Namely, as already mentioned earlier, the protocol is separated into rounds and each self-contained run of the protocol maintains a context, i.e., intermediate values. From an object oriented programming point of view, a client's call is comparable to a non-static (or instance) method call of an object.

The reasoning behind this design in Azure is, of course, that deployed services are replicated over multiple virtual and physical machines. A client consumes a service using a web service call with an Internet URL endpoint address. This implies that it is practically infeasible for a client to hit the same instance of the object represented by the service in two subsequent calls. Hitting the same instance collides with the objectives of cloud computing – robustness, scalability, and availability through replication, load balancing, et cetera.

We implement the necessary protocol context by using Blob storage in Windows Azure. Blob (Blob stands for binary large object) storage objects are essentially byte arrays addressed via an Internet URL. A service (respectively, a method) can read or write a uniquely named Blob. At the time of this document, the API support of the Windows Azure SDK (software development kit) for locking a Blob (in order to achieve exclusive access) was not available yet (but planned for a future release). We work around this in the following way: We create a Blob on protocol start and attach it to a default name – the ID of the protocol run (which is chosen randomly at the start). We call it the "roundall" Blob. Since the cryptographic protocol is structured, there is always a pre-determined next round and protocol party. We store this information in the Blob (i.e., the first party and the first round on initialization).

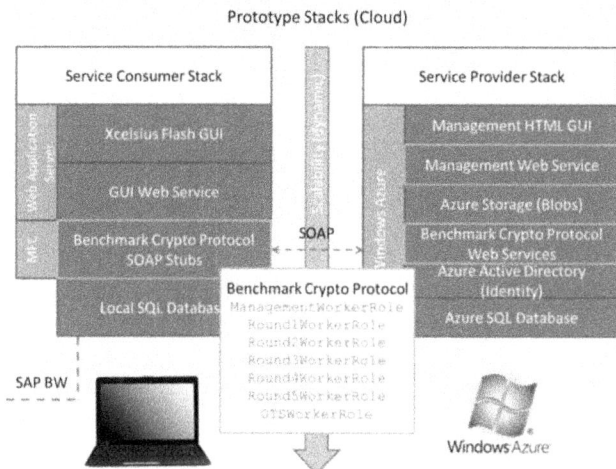

Figure 2: Stack of service consumer and provider (cloud).

Any client's method call to a method will check the Blob and if the respective round ID and party ID matches, the call will be continued (or otherwise be terminated). At the end, the method call will update the Blob. To be precise, it will increment the party ID, and if it is the last party, increment the round ID. Using this lock mechanism, we can handle read and write accesses to other Blobs as well. For instance, we separate the full context of a protocol run into Blobs for each round (round1, ..., round5). Replicating segments of the (benchmark) context (to round contexts) results in an additional performance improvement.

2.4 Data Management

Both entities – the service provider and the service consumer – require data persistence. While the consumer stores its private data either encrypted in the cloud or (potentially not encrypted) locally, the service provider always stores its data in the cloud by design. The following sections describe how we achieve this using Windows Azure technology.

2.4.1 Consumer Side

The consumer needs to store private information, such as his private KPI input that is to be benchmarked, as well as results of executed benchmark runs. We use an SQL database as local storage due to its availability at most clients' sites. However, it is also possible to store the data in the cloud by using the Windows Azure SQL Database. While encryption for local storage does not necessarily need to be handled by the application itself (either because there is no local encryption or the database system encapsulates it), care must be taken when data is stored in the cloud. The application then requires according setup and handling in the application respectively, in order to assure proper encryption (respectively local decryption).

For our prototypical setup, we use a local database system running Microsoft SQL Server because we reuse parts of the Adobe Flash based GUI of the former (not cloud enabled) version of the prototype. It accesses data directly from an SQL connection to a local database. Moreover, this setup also supports the integration with existing SAP Business Warehouse systems, providing aggregated KPIs from live ERP (enterprise resource planning) systems.

2.4.2 Provider Side

The service provider similarly requires data persistency in order to maintain user registrations and peer group settings. Furthermore, the service provider is supposed to store the results of performed benchmark runs. This is in order for the service provider to make this information available to other customers (e.g., to newly joined customers by a purchase or benefit). Intuitively, the benchmarking result data stored at the service provider data is not as confidential as the private KPIs of customers. However, analogously to consumers, the service provider may (want to) store data in encrypted form using encrypted storage services of Windows Azure. In our prototype, we consider it sufficient to only use authorization and access control to unencrypted data. Hence, we store all the service provider's data in the cloud using a Windows Azure SQL database.

2.5 Third Party Identities

The global benchmarking service contains a list of registered users in its database. The registration maps users to peer groups and benchmarks in order to maintain scheduling, as well as to be able to charge users for their service consumption. Identity of consumers is also important in the execution of a benchmark run. It is security critical to ensure that the parties are indeed the ones supposed to be participating in the benchmark run. There are many different protocols to establish the required authenticated channels. The foundational technology of all of them is *identity*. It is cumbersome for service consumers as well as for the service provider to maintain an identity. This is true for the registration as well as for the benchmarking application. For this reason, techniques like single sign on have been constructed which try to hide the complexity of maintaining the identity of a communication or session from users by running standardized protocols in the background. Examples of such protocols are SAML (Security Assertion Markup Language), XACML (eXtensible Access Control Markup Language) and WS-* (web service security protocols). Windows Azure understands these protocols and hence is able to participate in such protocols. That is what enables the usage of third party identity providers. Technically, a third party will issue a (signed) token which asserts a user as a registered user of the third party. An email provider can for instance provide a (signed, temporarily valid) token that a particular user is known to him. In addition the token may provide further information, e.g., the name or email address or facts like that the respective user is logged onto the system. The information (e.g., the name) is, again, standardized. The pieces of information that are provided depend on the respective third party.

For our benchmarking application we require at least a unique identifier (e.g., a constant – possibly random – string). We configured our cloud application to accept tokens issued by the Windows Live ID service that provides a such constant random string as unique identifier. If the service consumer is already logged into Windows Live ID (e.g., by his messenger), then the application is able to directly start to use his identity (a browser component integrated in the application therefore accesses a corresponding cookie). Otherwise, a login screen will appear in order to log into Windows Live ID (and to set the cookie). The final technical effect is that a method call by the client stub will enables the service method of the service provider to access the token (hence the unique identifier) of the caller. Within the method this can be mapped to the service consumer identifier in the service provider database.

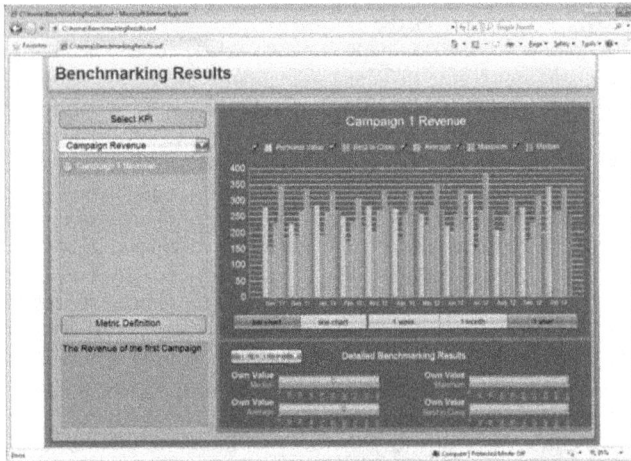

Figure 3: Benchmarking Visualization

3. PERFORMANCE – SCALING ON DEMAND

A Windows Azure subscription includes a set of resources (e.g., number of CPU cores) the subscriber – in our case the benchmarking service provider – can consume. It is up to the subscriber to set the scaling of his cloud application accordingly. The subscriber for instance could decide to double the computational power of his cloud service. He could also decide to only let the service run half of each day to stay with no additional charging. The set of resources is grouped by instances[1], ranging from XS (extra small) to XL (extra-large) and defines contained resources like number of CPU cores, number of SQL databases, number of storage transaction and the like. Windows Azure offers multiple ways to set the instances of a cloud application (to be precise, the instance type of a role), e.g., static or dynamic setting.

3.1 Static Scaling

Naturally, the Windows Azure SDK allows choosing the instance type as an option within the development settings. The deployment utility reads the option and sets the cloud environment accordingly on deployment. This way of setting the instance type is appropriate for cloud applications that know upfront what their demand on resources will be, respectively their economic bounds and that these will not change much over time. Here, static scaling is sufficient.

3.2 Dynamic Scaling

In the case of benchmarking, however, the demand for resources varies. Precisely, it depends on the number of participants. In particular, cryptographic operations, that have a high demand for CPU, are often proportional to the number of participants according to the protocol description in [2]. A valuable feature in that respect is that Windows Azure allows (next to scaling at deployment) also a scaling when the application has already been deployed and is online. This task is accomplished by a REST (representational state transfer) based API that provides access to the service management and thus the configuration of the successfully deployed cloud application. We use this API within the benchmark management service. The benchmark management service is called by the clients, e.g., to figure out whether he is involved in an upcoming benchmark. The method of the service performs a check on the number of all upcoming benchmarks, including a list of participants. Based on these numbers, a dynamic scale-up is performed by calling the formerly mentioned REST API. The construction incorporates the fact, that a change to the configuration will take a certain number of seconds to take effect. Based on the benchmark schedule, the number of participants, the time for up-scaling (respectively down-scaling) and a simplified economic framework (service charges, resource consumption/payment), a dynamic scaling for the benchmarking service has successfully been implemented.

4. CONCLUSION

We successfully implemented a prototype of our benchmarking system for the cloud using Microsoft Windows Azure as platform. We adapted the architecture of our first prototypical (Java based) implementation. The implementation has been done similarly for the consumer side, but been extended to for a richer set of functionality on the provider side. Although the Windows Azure platform would have been able to handle our former Java implementation of the cryptographic protocol, we rather decided to re-implement the cryptographic protocol and respective cryptographic tools in C# and Microsoft .NET. We did so in order to be able to natively access existing API based features of the platform (e.g., scaling). Figure 2 shows the final architecture of our cloud enabled prototype of the secure benchmarking system.

We have the consumer that runs a local database to store his private KPI values that he may have received from a connected SAP Business Warehouse. He takes part in the cryptographic protocol for secure benchmarking by calling cloud service methods of the service provider. That is done within a MFC (Microsoft Foundation Class) client utility. The consumer keeps running a local (tiny) web application server that provides a GUI web service (i.e., a web service that renders the benchmark results from the local database into a format understandable for the GUI) and that hosts the Flash GUI (as depicted in Figure 3).

REFERENCES

[1] Florian Kerschbaum, Practical Privacy-Preserving Benchmarking, Proceedings of the IFIP TC-11 23rd International Information Security Conference, pp. 17-31, 2008.

[2] Florian Kerschbaum, Daniel Dahlmeier, Axel Schröpfer, Debmalya Biswas. On the practical importance of communication complexity for secure multi-party computation protocols. Proceedings of the ACM Symposium on Applied Computing, pp. 2008-2015, 2009.

[3] Brad Calder, Tony Wang, Shane Mainali, and Jason Wu, Windows Azure Blob, May 2009 http://go.microsoft.com/fwlink/?LinkId=153400&clcid=0x409

[4] David Chappell, Introducing Windows Azure, October 2010, http://go.microsoft.com/?linkid=9682907&clcid=0x409

[5] George Huey, Scaling Out with SQL Azure Federation, February 2012, http://msdn.microsoft.com/en-us/magazine/hh848258.aspx

---

[1] cf. http://www.windowsazure.com/en-us/pricing/details/

A Storage-Efficient Cryptography-Based Access Control Solution for Subversion

Dominik Leibenger
University of Paderborn
Warburger Straße 100
33098 Paderborn, Germany
dominik.leibenger@uni-paderborn.de

Christoph Sorge
University of Paderborn
Warburger Straße 100
33098 Paderborn, Germany
christoph.sorge@uni-paderborn.de

ABSTRACT

Version control systems are widely used in software development and document management. Unfortunately, versioning confidential files is not normally supported: Existing solutions encrypt the transport channel, but store data in plaintext within a repository. We come up with an access control solution that allows secure versioning of confidential files even in the presence of a malicious server administrator. Using *convergent encryption* as a building block, we enable space-efficient storage of version histories despite secure encryption. We describe an implementation of our concept for the *Subversion (SVN)* system, and evaluate storage efficiency and runtime of this implementation. Our implementation is compatible with existing SVN versions without requiring changes to the storage backend.

Categories and Subject Descriptors

K.6.5 [**Management of Computing and Information Systems**]: Security and Protection; E.3 [**Data Encryption**]

General Terms

Security, Design, Algorithms, Experimentation, Performance

Keywords

Access control; version control systems; subversion; convergent encryption; confidentiality; efficient storage

1. INTRODUCTION

Version control systems (VCS) have become an invaluable tool for software development and are also used during the creation of all kinds of documents. As their main feature, they allow restoring any previous version of a file. Most VCS also facilitate the collaboration of authors working together on a project. Authors obtain the latest copy from the VCS, work on that copy, and then commit an updated version to the VCS. A VCS will not normally store complete copies of each version of a file: changes might only affect a small fraction of that file, so only differences between two versions are stored.

One of the most common VCS is Subversion (SVN), which relies on a central server to store the history of versioned files. Like other VCS, SVN is not well-suited for working with confidential files. The transport channel is usually protected, e.g. using TLS. However, once on the server, each user with read access to the file system, as well as the server's administrators, can read the file. SVN allows to define access rules, but their enforcement requires a completely trustworthy server. Users can encrypt the content using external applications; unfortunately, this makes it impossible for the VCS to save only space-saving differences between file versions—even with only one byte changed in a long document, the encrypted versions will be completely different. Moreover, key management does not tie in with the versioning system. Even assuming there was a public-key infrastructure (PKI) in place, granting users read access to a file (and revoking that right later on) is a complex and error-prone task. If a user is supposed to get access to more than one file version, access rights must be granted (e.g., the file must be encrypted with the respective user's public key) each time a new version is uploaded to the SVN repository.

Our *contribution* is to define a solution for securing access to files in an SVN repository with the following properties:

- Rights can be managed individually for each file.
- Enforcing read access control through encryption allows protecting the confidentiality of files even against attacks by repository administrators.
- Despite encryption, space-saving differences are stored instead of entire copies of each file version. To achieve this, we allow attackers to see the positions of changes made between different versions of the same file.
- We retain full compatibility with old software versions, though not all features will work if either the client or the server does not support our solution.
- Necessary key exchanges tie in with the SVN architecture. They are authenticated without use of a PKI; a shared secret between a pair of users is sufficient.

The remainder of this paper is structured as follows: We discuss related work in Sec. 2 and outline our goals in Sec. 3. Sec. 4 presents the system design. The encryption scheme that allows for storage efficiency is worked out in Sec. 5; a security analysis follows in Sec. 6. Sec. 7 describes the implementation, which we analyze concerning storage / runtime overhead in Appendix A. Sec. 8 concludes this paper.

2. PRELIMINARIES & RELATED WORK

While the concepts developed in this work might be applied to other VCS, we develop our access control solution for the SVN [19] system. SVN uses a client/server architecture. Each client stores a working copy, which contains both the versions of the files last obtained from the server and the versions edited by the user. After performing changes to files, the client performs a *commit* operation to add the changes to the repository; an *update* gets the latest contents from the repository. Communication with the server can be based on WebDAV [7], or can use a specific SVN protocol [4]. In both cases, the client only sends (or receives) the changes with respect to the previously stored version.

The server stores the whole revision history of the files and folders added to the repository as well as of property lists containing metadata that can be associated to them. After storing a revision, a user cannot change or delete contents of already stored data. Several storage backends exist. The most common one is FSFS [15, 3]; it stores the oldest version of each file completely. Once a file is changed, FSFS only stores the (binary) difference compared to *a* (not necessarily *the latest*) previous version. This way, SVN provides data deduplication between different revisions of individual files. Data deduplication between different files is not provided.

Our goal to develop a secure and storage-efficient access control solution for this system comprises two main challenges: A solution to allow convenient access rights management that includes key distribution, and a concept for data deduplication despite secure encryption. Work on secure file systems faces similar challenges; however, the majority of existing work focusses on the key distribution problem.

The secure file system *SiRiUS* [10] supports per-file access right management by encrypting each file using a randomly-generated key that is encrypted with the authorized users' keys and stored as part of the file's metadata. It supports separate read / write access rights.

Plutus [12] also distinguishes between read and write access rights, but groups files with equal access rights into *file groups* and stores their keys in an encrypted, shared *lockbox* to reduce key distribution costs. The authors introduce a method called *key rotation*: On access rights changes, keys are changed in a way that allows the computation of previous keys from the latest one, which prevents the need for immediate re-encryption of file contents on key changes. *Key regression* [9] fixes some security flaws of *key rotation*.

In contrast, in the *Wuala*[1] distributed file system, Grolimund et al. [11] introduce a data structure called *Cryptree* to explicitly store dependencies between *arbitrary* keys.

We use a simple, SiRiUS-like approach for key distribution as it fits best into the SVN architecture: The other solutions depend on relations between different files which are not guaranteed to be available in SVN setups (for example, a user might check out only a single file or directory).

Despite those systems that focus on key management, few secure file systems provide data deduplication.

Farsite introduces a concept called *convergent encryption (CE)* which we adapt in Section 5: They use a cryptographic hash of a file as a key to encrypt that file, so identical files can be recognized and deduplicated despite secure encryption. Similar to the SiRiUS approach, that key is then encrypted with the authorized users' keys to grant them access rights.

The concept has been extended in [18]: The authors suggest applying CE to chunks of a file, which are determined using a context-sensitive chunking procedure, to allow data deduplication even between similar files. Rashid et al. [17] recently re-used this concept to build a privacy-preserving data deduplication framework for cloud environments. We describe and further extend the procedure of [18] in Sec. 5.

The Tahoe filesystem [20], in contrast, uses CE for deduplication of entire files only. The authors introduce a *convergence secret*, so the equality of files can only be detected by users sharing that secret. This concept is similar to the *obfuscator* we introduce to hide equality of chunks between different files.

None of these approaches have been applied to VCSs. So far, besides using secure channels for communication, existing VCSs only cope with integrity and authenticity. Git[2] and Monotone[3] ensure integrity of the version history (if a trustworthy copy of the current version is available) and integrate the use of signatures. To the best of our knowledge, we are the first to provide a fine-grained, storage-efficient access control solution for a VCS that is resistant to a server compromise and thus able to provide *true* confidentiality.

3. GOALS, THREATS AND ASSUMPTIONS

The *goal* of this work is to protect the *confidentiality*, *integrity* and *authenticity* of specific file versions stored in an SVN repository by providing a fine-grained, user-definable access control solution. In more detail, our goals are:

- *Compatibility:* We limit ourselves to changes that only extend the SVN architecture, without restricting interoperability with existing SVN versions. This especially requires independence of our solution from the used storage backend.
- *Fine-Grained Access Control and Convenient Usability:* Our solution shall allow users of an SVN repository to protect their own files stored in the repository by defining access rights for them. Users shall be able to individually grant read and write permissions for a specific file, as well as permissions to manage the file's access rights, to other specific users. Access rights management shall be convenient insofar as key exchanges between users shall be performed automatically when access rights are managed (we only require a one-time manual key exchange per user for authentication).
- *Integrity and Authenticity:* If access rights have been associated to a file, our solution shall protect the file's integrity and authenticity: every authorized user shall be able to verify if the file's contents have been written by an authorized user according to the currently granted access rights on the file. This shall hold even against active attackers with full read/write access to the repository server. Note that since the SVN architecture expects only the server to store the whole revision history, we cannot provide protection against malicious deletion (including rollbacks that correspond to deleting revisions) by the server administrator.
- *Confidentiality and Storage Efficiency:* We want to provide confidentiality of files whose access rights have been restricted. Thus, attackers with full read/write access to the repository server shall not be able to read those files' contents. This shall be ensured through encryption—using an encryption scheme that is believed to provide IND-CCA-secure encryption.

---

[1] http://www.wuala.com/

[2] http://git-scm.com/about
[3] http://www.monotone.ca/

However, we want to retain storage efficiency, which SVN achieves by deduplicating data between different file revisions. As SVN's storage backend is transparent to the clients, data deduplication has to be done at the server side, i.e. without knowledge of file contents. This leads to a clear conflict with the confidentiality goal. We resolve this conflict by allowing to soften the security requirements when committing further revisions of a specific file. Allowing attackers to see the extent and positions of changes to a file (which includes information about how file contents are moved between revisions) enables generation of ciphertexts suitable for SVN's server-side data deduplication techniques. Users may decide for each file revision if this information leakage is acceptable. For files whose access rights change frequently, users may even decide to allow data deduplication between file revisions with different access rights—again by softening the security requirements. In this case, some additional information is leaked only to users who have or had legitimate rights to read some revision of a file. They are able to decrypt any parts of other revisions of the same file which were contained in an already-known version and might also be able to verify the existence of single plaintext fragments. Further, they are able to derive very limited information from chunk boundaries of other revisions of that file (cf. Section 5).

Note that this information leakage is limited to information leaked between revisions of a single file. We always hide similarities between different *files* as SVN does not perform data deduplication between files anyway.

We achieve these goals under some *assumptions*: As authentication is password-based, we assume that attackers do not know (and cannot break) these passwords. We further assume that no attacker can break the Diffie-Hellman key exchange, and that used hash functions provide resistance against preimage attacks as well as strong collision resistance. Moreover, we assume the existence of a pseudorandom permutation (PRP) which we use as encryption primitive. Users are considered authorized for specific actions w.r.t. a file version if they are granted the corresponding access rights by a user with GRANT rights (i.e. a user allowed to manage access rights) for that file version, as described in Section 4.1. A file owner and other GRANT-authorized users (as well as their SVN clients) are considered trustworthy w.r.t. the specific file.

4. SYSTEM DESIGN

Our access control solution consists of two building blocks: First, we design and integrate a suitable access control concept for the SVN architecture. Second, we adapt an encryption scheme that achieves confidentiality without preventing the use of data deduplication techniques such as SVN's difference calculations. This section deals with the former.

4.1 Overview

The idea of our access control solution is to let the *owner* of a file (i.e. the user adding that file to the SVN) decide on its precise access rights. The following rights can be granted:

- *READ:* Allow to read the contents of the specific file.
- *WRITE:* Allow to modify a specific file's contents.
- *GRANT:* Allow to grant arbitrary rights to and revoke arbitrary rights from other users.

To this point, this definition of access rights seems rather straightforward. However, the semantics of access rights granted for a specific file are not that clear when rights can be changed over time. While *WRITE* and *GRANT* rights can be *granted to* as well as *revoked from* a user effectively at any time, the impact of a *READ* right revocation is less certain: The user could have made copies of the file revisions he had access to, thus revoking the *READ* right would only be effective regarding future but not previous revisions. To make the *effective* rights clear and comprehensible, we tie our access control mechanism to single file *revisions* instead of whole files. In particular, we store all access-rights-related information as metadata for a specific file revision. This leads to minor limitations: According to the revision concept of the SVN architecture, granted rights of archived file revisions are immutable—a user is only able to change these rights for future revisions of the file (so each access right modification requires a commit). However, albeit rights are tied to revisions, modifying a file or its access rights requires the *WRITE* or *GRANT* right for the *latest* revision, thus these rights can be revoked with immediate effect. Solely a *READ* right for an old revision can be exercised by a user even if he does not hold the right for the latest revision.

4.2 Access Rights

As described before, we distinguish between the rights *READ*, *WRITE* and *GRANT*. They are enforced as follows:

- The *READ* right is enforced by encrypting the file contents using a key triple (K_R, K_O, K_I) (for details see Sec. 5) that is generated randomly by the file owner or any *GRANT*-authorized user and only made available to *READ*-authorized users. All cryptographic operations are performed at the client side and the keys are unknown to the repository, so the server can only see the ciphertexts. Thus, access control regarding this right can be resistant to a server compromise. While the repository does not know the file contents, server-side efficient storage of similar file revisions is retained by using a special encryption scheme that is described in Sec. 5.
- *GRANT* access control is performed using a shared secret key K_G (again generated randomly by a *GRANT*-authorized user like the file owner) that is only known to *GRANT*-authorized users. This key is used to prove / verify the integrity / authenticity of access rights, trust relationships and cryptographic keys.
- The *WRITE* right is enforced by a simple server-side ACL, since the repository administrator can modify or delete ciphertexts anyway due to his physical access to the storage.

Whenever access rights are changed, the affected keys are replaced by new keys that are chosen randomly by the *GRANT*-authorized user's client that performs the change.

4.3 Authentication and Key Exchange

To allow a convenient exertion of access rights, we do not require the users to exchange those cryptographic keys manually. Instead, every user u has to remember a single password $CP(u)$ (which *must* differ from the one used to authenticate to the repository) that allows him to exercise all of his access rights. We use the repository as transport channel for communication between users, so we need to minimize the number of communication rounds. This works as follows:

1. An individual key $K_{DH}(f, u)$ is negotiated for every user u of a file f using a Diffie-Hellman key exchange [6]. This key is made available both to the specific user u as well as to every *GRANT*-authorized user of file f. For this, we

regard the group of *GRANT*-authorized users of a specific file f as one party of the DH key exchange and the user u as the other party. The private *DH* value of the *GRANT* group is chosen by any *GRANT*-authorized user (e.g. the file owner); the private *DH* value of u is chosen by u. We store the public DH values in the file's metadata. The private values of the *GRANT* group and of u are stored encrypted with K_G and $CP(u)$, respectively, so that both u and *GRANT*-authorized users are able to determine $K_{DH}(f, u)$ later on.

2. As the DH key exchange does not provide authentication, we authenticate the negotiated DH keys separately. The idea is to build bidirectional trust chains from the owner of file f (who is assumed to be trusted and serves as trust anchor) to every user u—i.e. every user u is authenticated by the file owner over a chain of trusted *GRANT*-authorized users and vice versa. For this, every user u negotiates a secret passphrase with an arbitrary *GRANT*-authorized user using a separate channel (e.g. telephone), which is used by them to authenticate each other. We use a symmetric HMAC-based authentication mechanism; details of this protocol are omitted due to space restrictions.

3. The access rights granted to a user u are stored in the file's metadata and authenticated using an HMAC keyed by K_G so that modifications can be detected by *GRANT*-authorized users. To allow exertion of access rights, the keys associated to an access right are stored within the file's metadata—encrypted with the key $K_{DH}(f, u)$ for every authorized user u. Since $K_{DH}(f, u)$ is known to all *GRANT*-authorized users, changed keys can be distributed easily to the users by simply encrypting the new keys with $K_{DH}(f, u)$.

5. ENCRYPTION SCHEME

In principle, we could use any secure encryption scheme for encrypting file contents. However, traditional schemes would prevent data deduplication between similar file revisions. To achieve storage efficiency, we use a special encryption scheme that we describe in this section.

Unfortunately, data deduplication and secure encryption are conflicting goals as the former has to depend on similarities between contents which the latter requires to hide. This leads to an inevitable trade-off. The benefit of our encryption scheme lies in the fact that it allows to adjust this trade-off: The encryption of single file revisions achieves the same security properties as the underlying encryption function (e.g. AES). However, when further revisions are stored, the user may choose to leak a limited amount of information to allow data deduplication.

Towards this goal, our encryption scheme requires a triple of keys (K_R, K_O, K_I) instead of a single encryption key. K_R corresponds to the classic encryption key that is used to ensure confidentiality. It may be used for an arbitrary amount of encryptions, but has to be changed whenever access rights of the encrypted content change. K_I is used similarly to ensure integrity / authenticity. K_O—the *obfuscator*—serves as a kind of *secret* initialization vector (IV). Using a unique IV for every encryption achieves the strongest security guarantees. However, in contrast to other schemes, using the same IV for multiple file revisions is secure insofar as it only leaks a controlled amount of information: Fixing K_O only results in deterministic encryption—both regarding a whole plaintext as well as variable-length chunks within a plaintext. By revealing which parts have changed between two revisions, this allows data deduplication between ciphertexts of similar

file revisions. Thus, a user may achieve storage efficiency by re-using K_O of an ancestor when creating a new file revision.

To achieve this, we adapt the concept proposed by Storer et al. [18]. Their idea is to split a plaintext m into so-called *chunks* using a context-sensitive chunking procedure before encrypting each chunk deterministically using convergent encryption (see Section 2). This way, identical chunks result in identical ciphertexts. The concatenation of those encrypted chunks forms the ciphertext of m. Unfortunately, this solution would have some shortcomings in our usage scenario: First of all, it would not only leak similarities between different *revisions* of a file, but also between different *files*, as contents are encrypted independent of the encryption key. Furthermore, due to the context-sensitive chunking, chunk boundaries leak some information about the plaintext m. Even worse, deterministic encryption of chunks could also leak information about the structure of m, as repeating contents would lead to repeating chunks and thus to repetitions in the ciphertext.

To overcome these shortcomings, we modify their concept in two points: First, we make the chunking procedure and the computation of chunk-specific keys depend on K_O to limit CE's security implications to the scope of a specific value of K_O. Secondly, we introduce *appearance counters* which are involved in chunk boundary determination and chunk encryption to prevent potential security risks regarding files with repeating contents.

We continue with a formal description of our scheme.

5.1 Formal Description

In this section, we describe our encryption and authentication scheme $\Pi = (\text{GEN}, \text{EncMac}, \text{DEC})$ following the notations defined in [13]. We later analyze our encryption scheme's security in the random oracle model [1], so we assume the existence of a random oracle H. As we focus on the encryption scheme, we refer to the contents of files and file revisions as *messages* in the remainder.

Requirements

We build upon an existing *pseudorandom permutation (PRP)* F (with $F_k(x)$ denoting $F(k, x)$) as defined in [13, Section 3.6.3] analogous to [13, Definition 3.23]:

Definition. *Let* $F : \{0,1\}^* \times \{0,1\}^* \to \{0,1\}^*$ *be an efficient, length-preserving, keyed function. We say that F is a* **pseudorandom permutation** *if for all probabilistic polynomial-time distinguishers D, there exists a negligible function* **negl** *such that:* $\left| Pr[D^{F_k(\cdot)}(1^n) = 1] - Pr[D^{f(\cdot)}(1^n) = 1] \right| \leq negl(n)$, *where $k \leftarrow \{0,1\}^n$ is chosen uniformly at random and f is chosen uniformly at random from the set of permutations mapping n-bit strings to n-bit strings.*

Further, we build upon an existing MAC function $\Pi_M = (\text{GEN}_M, \text{MAC}, \text{VRFY})$ with unique tags. Again, we expect GEN_M to return a uniform random number in $\{0, 1\}^n$.

Utilizing the random oracle H, we define two different hash functions $H_R, H_S : \{0,1\}^n \times \{0,1\}^n \times \{0,1\}^* \to \{0,1\}^n$.

Definition of Π

We construct Π from a to-be-defined private-key encryption scheme $\widehat{\Pi} = (\widehat{\text{GEN}}, \widehat{\text{ENC}}, \widehat{\text{DEC}})$ and the MAC function Π_M according to [13, Construction 4.19]:

- GEN, on input 1^n, runs $\widehat{\text{GEN}}$ and GEN_M to obtain keys K and K_I, respectively.

- ENCMAC, on input key (K, K_I) and message m, computes $c \leftarrow \widehat{\text{ENC}}_K(m)$, $t \leftarrow \text{MAC}_{K_I}(c)$ and outputs (c, t).
- DEC, on input a key (K, K_I) and a ciphertext (c, t), outputs $\widehat{\text{DEC}}_K(c)$ if $\text{VRFY}_{K_I}(c, t) = 1$; otherwise, $\perp$ is returned.

Definition of $\widehat{\Pi}$

The key-generation function $\widehat{\text{GEN}}$ is defined as follows: On input 1^n, it outputs a key tuple (K_R, K_O) with K_R, K_O each being chosen uniformly at random from $\{0, 1\}^n$.

The encryption function $\widehat{\text{ENC}}$ is more complex: When getting a key $K = (K_R, K_O)$ and a message m as input, it first splits the message into chunks, before performing separate encryptions for the individual chunks. The phases of $\widehat{\text{ENC}}$ are now described in detail.

5.1.1 Chunking

Chunking is performed in a similar way as introduced in [14] and presented in the convergent encryption scenario in [18]: A sliding window (fixed size: w bytes) is moved over the message m and the windows' contents $m_{p,w}$ are used as input for the hash function H_R to compute a pseudo-random *fingerprint* at every byte position p (the authors of [14] and [18] use a rolling hash function to compute those fingerprints). The positions whose fingerprints are below a specific threshold T are used as chunk boundaries. We make three changes to the original procedure: First, we calculate the fingerprints using $\text{H}_R(k, i, x)$ with $k := K_O$, so that chunking depends on K_O. Secondly, we prevent repeating window contents from resulting in the same fingerprint by including an appearance counter i in the fingerprint calculation. Thirdly, we introduce a minimum chunk size of l bytes. More formally, we create a chunk boundary at every byte position p that meets the following condition:

$$p - l \geq \max_{p', p' < p}\{p' = 0 \vee p' \text{ is a chunk boundary}\}$$
$$\wedge \ \text{H}_R\left(K_O, \textstyle\sum_{m_{p',w}=m_{p,w}, p'<p} 1, \ m_{p,w}\right) < T \quad (1)$$

By choosing $T = \frac{2^n}{S - l + 1}$ with a to-be-chosen parameter value $S \geq l$, Condition 1—applied to random data—is expected to hold for every S-th byte, resulting in chunks with an average length of S bytes. This is indeed also true for non-random data, as will be discussed in Appendix A.

5.1.2 Chunk encryption

Let $m_1, \ldots, m_q$ be the chunks resulting from the chunking procedure described above, numbered in the order of their appearance. For each chunk m_j, we compute a chunk-specific encryption key K_{m_j} which we use to encrypt the chunk's contents. Instead of using a simple hash value of the chunk contents—as done in [18]—we compute this key as follows:

$$K_{m_j} = \text{H}_S\left(K_O, \textstyle\sum_{m_{j'}=m_j, j'<j} 1, \ m_j\right) \quad (2)$$

Again, the usage of K_O ensures that different keys are computed for equal chunks in different messages, unless the same value K_O was explicitly used for different encryptions—e.g. for different revisions of the same file. To avoid equal encryption of equal chunks within the same message, an appearance counter is used. This counter is 0 for the first and $i - 1$ for the i-th occurrence of the same chunk, thus multiple equal chunks get unique keys.

The key K_{m_j} is then used to encrypt the chunk contents using the pseudorandom permutation F. For technical reasons, we prefix the chunk content with its length before encrypting it[4]. K_{m_j} is then encrypted (using the key K_R) and stored within the encrypted chunk representation. To summarize, every chunk m_j is encrypted as follows (with $\|$ being the concatenation operator):

$$c_j = \left(F_{K_R}(K_{m_j}), F_{K_{m_j}}(\text{LENGTH}(m_j) \| m_j)\right) \quad (3)$$

5.1.3 Finalization

When all chunks have been encrypted, their ciphertexts $c_1, \ldots, c_q$ are concatenated to build the ciphertext c of the whole message:

$$\widehat{\text{ENC}}_{(K_R, K_O)}(m) = \left(\|_{j=1}^q c_j\right) \quad (4)$$

The decryption function $\widehat{\text{DEC}}$ is straightforward: On input a key $K = (K_R, K_O)$ and a ciphertext c, it sequentially decrypts the chunks $c_1, \ldots, c_q$: For every chunk $c_j = (c_j^k, c_j^c)$, it first determines the chunk key $K_{m_j} := F_{K_R}^{-1}(c_j^k)$ and then decrypts the chunk content and length by invoking $l_j \| m_j := F_{K_{m_j}}^{-1}(c_j^c)$. Finally, $\|_{j=1}^q m_j$ is output. Note that decryption depends only on K_R, not on K_O.

5.2 Advantages

If every encryption application uses a random K_O, our scheme achieves CCA-secure encryptions, as we prove in Sec. 6.1. However, it can achieve storage efficiency within the SVN scenario when used as follows:
- Assign random keys K_R, K_O, K_I to every file; change them only on access rights changes.

As long as appearance counters are not affected, using the same K_O for multiple file revisions results in a deterministic, context-sensitive chunking, which achieves identical chunks within unchanged parts between those revisions—even if the positions of those unchanged parts change between revisions (i.e. sth. is inserted or removed). Due to the adaption of convergent encryption, these chunks result in the same ciphertext everytime they are encrypted (both chunk key generation and encryption are deterministic). This way, ciphertexts of similar file revisions overlap, so SVN's storage backend can perform data deduplication while neither requiring knowledge about the file's actual contents nor about the specific encryption scheme. As SVN uses differences during update/commit operations (cf. Sec. 2), this also reduces the network traffic between clients and the repository.

If appearance counters are indeed affected by changes made to a file, different file revisions *might* get slightly different chunkings, thus preventing deduplication of some chunks. Our evaluation results (see Appendix A) suggest that the storage overhead caused by this limitation is negligible.

Note that this only allows data deduplication between different revisions of a specific file as long as its access rights are unchanged. Data deduplication across access rights changes can also be achieved by only changing K_R and K_I on access rights changes (avoiding influences on chunking and encryption of chunk contents). However, this scenario would leak some additional information to attackers with access rights to some other revision of a specific file (see Sec. 6.2.2).

---

[4]When instantiated with a block cipher, this prevents the need for explicit chunk separators in the ciphertext, since decrypting the first few bytes of a chunk allows computing the starting position of the subsequent chunk.

5.3 Implementation Details

While our encryption scheme is independent of its underlying cryptographic functions, its application requires an appropriate choice of these functions. We use SHA-256-HMAC [8] as MAC Π_M and instantiate the random oracle H with SHA-256; queries prefixed by a key are performed using SHA-256-HMAC (with the key used as key instead of a prefix). The pseudorandom permutation F is instantiated with AES-256-CBC [5], with the IVs being chosen as follows to achieve deterministic encryption:

For encryption of the chunk content, we set $IV = 0$. While this is considered to be insecure in general use cases, our content-based key generation guarantees that we never encrypt different data using the same key. This makes the zero vector unique in the scope of the used encryption key.

For encryption of the chunk key, the situation is not that simple: Since the same key K_R is used to encrypt different chunk keys, we cannot use a constant IV here. We solve this by using the first block of the ciphertext of a chunk as IV for the encryption of its corresponding chunk key[5]. Since no two chunks have the same key, these ciphertext blocks differ for different chunks, resulting in a unique IV. Effectively, this makes the first block of the chunk key encryption and the second block of the chunk content encryption depend on the same IV, but since different keys are used for these encryptions, the uniqueness property is retained.

6. SECURITY ANALYSIS

Our encryption scheme's security guarantees depend on its usage: We achieve IND-CCA-secure encryption assuming the existence of a PRP and a random oracle when random values K_O are used for each encryption application[6]. Otherwise, some controlled amount of information is leaked to allow data deduplication. We analyze both variants' security guarantees—regarding attackers that neither know K_R, K_O nor K_I—separately in this section. The security analysis follows the definitions and proofs given in [13].

6.1 IND-CCA with random K_O

To formalize the usage scenario where a random value K_O is used for each encryption application, we consider a slightly modified version Π^* of our encryption and authentication scheme Π, which replaces the encryption part $\widehat{\Pi}$ of the scheme with $\widetilde{\Pi} = (\widetilde{\text{GEN}}, \widetilde{\text{ENC}}, \widetilde{\text{DEC}})$:

- $\widetilde{\text{GEN}}(n)$ invokes $(K_R, K_O) \leftarrow \widehat{\text{GEN}}(n)$ and returns K_R.
- $\widetilde{\text{ENC}}_{K_R}(m)$ invokes $(\_, K_O) \leftarrow \widehat{\text{GEN}}(n)$ to generate a random K_O and returns $\widehat{\text{ENC}}_{(K_R, K_O)}(m)$. (The $\_$ denotes that the first component is ignored.)
- $\widetilde{\text{DEC}}_{K_R}(c)$ simply invokes $m \leftarrow \widehat{\text{DEC}}_{(K_R, \perp)}(c)$ and returns m (note that K_O is not used in decryption).

The only difference between Π and Π^* is that the latter does not include a static value K_O in the key material, but chooses a random value K_O during each encryption.

We want to show that $\widetilde{\Pi}$ and Π^* are CPA-secure and CCA-secure, respectively. For this, we define some variants $\widetilde{\Pi}_i$ of the encryption scheme $\widetilde{\Pi}$. In addition to F, H_R, H_S, we let $\widetilde{\Pi}_i$ have access to 2^n different truly random permutations $f_0(\cdot), \dots, f_{2^n-1}(\cdot)$ (one truly random permutation corresponds to each key of the PRP F), and define it as follows:

- $\widetilde{\text{GEN}}_i = \widetilde{\text{GEN}}, \widetilde{\text{DEC}}_i = \widetilde{\text{DEC}}$
- $\widetilde{\text{ENC}}_i$, on input key K_R and message m, acts like $\widetilde{\text{ENC}}$, but changes the—overall[7]—first i queries to F so that the invocation $F_K(x)$ is replaced by a query $f_K(x)$.

It is easy to see that $\widetilde{\Pi}_0 = \widetilde{\Pi}$. Note that for $i > 0$, $\widetilde{\Pi}_i$ does not represent a correct encryption scheme, as $\widetilde{\text{ENC}}_i$ can produce ciphertexts that $\widetilde{\text{DEC}}_i$ cannot decrypt. We can ignore this since the $\widetilde{\Pi}_i$'s are only auxiliary constructions and our proof does not depend on the existence of $\widetilde{\text{DEC}}_i$.

Theorem. *If H_R, H_S are random oracles, $\widetilde{\Pi}_\infty$ achieves IND-CPA-secure encryption.*

PROOF. Our first goal is to show that $\widetilde{\Pi}$ achieves IND-CPA-secure encryption if *all* PRP invocations are replaced by invocations of truly random functions. We denote this variant by $\widetilde{\Pi}_\infty$ to indicate that $i \to \infty$.

By [13, Definition 3.21], "*a private-key encryption scheme $\widetilde{\Pi}_i$ is IND-CPA-secure if for all probabilistic polynomial-time adversaries $\mathcal{A}$ there exists a negligible function* negl *such that* $\Pr[\text{PrivK}_{\mathcal{A}, \widetilde{\Pi}_i}^{\text{cpa}}(n) = 1] \leq \frac{1}{2} + \text{negl}(n)$, *where the probability is taken over the random coins used by $\mathcal{A}$, as well as the random coins used in the experiment.*" The experiment $\text{PrivK}_{\mathcal{A}, \widetilde{\Pi}_i}^{\text{cpa}}(n)$ is defined as follows in [13, Section 3.5] (for convenience, we adapt the presentation to our notations):

1. A key K is generated by running $\widetilde{\text{GEN}}_i(1^n)$.
2. The adversary $\mathcal{A}$ is given input 1^n and oracle access to $\widetilde{\text{ENC}}_{i_K}(\cdot)$, and outputs a pair of messages m_0, m_1 of the same length.
3. A random bit $b \leftarrow \{0, 1\}$ is chosen, and then a ciphertext $c \leftarrow \widetilde{\text{ENC}}_{i_K}(m_b)$ is computed and given to $\mathcal{A}$. We call c the challenge ciphertext.
4. The adversary $\mathcal{A}$ continues to have oracle access to $\widetilde{\text{ENC}}_{i_K}(\cdot)$, and outputs a bit b'.
5. The output of the experiment is defined to be 1 if $b' = b$, and 0 otherwise. (In case $\text{PrivK}_{\mathcal{A}, \widetilde{\Pi}_i}^{\text{cpa}}(n) = 1$, we say that $\mathcal{A}$ succeeded.)

Now let $\mathcal{A}$ be any adversary solving this experiment in polynomial time $q(n)$ (with $q(n)$ being the number of steps $\mathcal{A}$ may perform—including queries to $\widetilde{\text{ENC}}_{i_K}, H_R, H_S$ and $f_0, \dots, f_{2^n-1}$). The intuition of our proof is as follows: $\mathcal{A}$ can only learn sth. about the challenge, if he sees any of the (random) values output by H_R, H_S, f_k during encryption of m_b at any other point of time. We show that this happens with negligible probability.

Let HQ denote the event that any query to H_R or H_S during encryption of m_b in step 2 is also made at any other point of time during the experiment. Similarly, let FQ denote the event that a specific query $f_k(x)$ during encryption of m_b occurs at any other point of time. If all of those queries are unique (i.e. $\overline{\text{HQ} \vee \text{FQ}}$), $\mathcal{A}$ has never seen any of the values output by H_R (cf. Eq. 1), H_S (cf. Eq. 2) or any f (cf. Eq. 3) that are used to produce the ciphertext of m_b. As H_R, H_S are modelled using a random oracle and as f_k produces truly random outputs, those values are independent from m_0, m_1 in $\mathcal{A}$'s view. Thus, $\mathcal{A}$'s chance to succeed is $\frac{1}{2}$:

$$\Pr[\text{PrivK}_{\mathcal{A}, \widetilde{\Pi}_\infty}^{\text{cpa}}(n) = 1 \mid \overline{\text{HQ} \vee \text{FQ}}] = \frac{1}{2} \tag{5}$$

Repetitions of queries to H_R, H_S within a single encryption are excluded due to the appearance counters. As each

---

[5] This also saves us the need for storing the IV separately.

[6] This always applies to files with only a single revision.

[7] This means the first i queries during $\widetilde{\Pi}_i$'s whole lifetime.

query to H_R and H_S includes the key K_O, which is chosen uniformly at random during encryption, a repetition of some query to H_R or H_S requires that the same value K_O was either chosen by chance during another encryption application or that it was guessed by $\mathcal{A}$ during his runtime. The chance for this to happen within runtime $q(n)$ is:

$$\Pr[\mathsf{HQ}] \leq \frac{q(n)}{2^n} \tag{6}$$

We now analyze the probability of FQ under $\overline{\mathsf{HQ}}$ (i.e. the case where all H_R, H_S queries are unique). A repetition of a query to some f_k during encryption of m_b can occur either during other encryptions or due to direct queries by $\mathcal{A}$. Both cases are analyzed separately in the following paragraphs:

$\widetilde{\mathrm{ENC}}_{i_K}$ queries the truly random permutations by $f_K(j)$ and $f_j(\cdot)$ for every output j produced by H_S (i.e. for each chunk key, cf. Eq. 3). Thus, if all outputs j of H_S are unique, all queries $f_K(j), f_j(\cdot)$ are unique. As we assume $\overline{\mathsf{HQ}}$, no repetition of a query to H_S occurred, so a repetition of a query to any f_k during encryption requires that at least two different queries to H_S produced equal outputs during the experiment. As $\mathcal{A}$ has runtime $q(n)$, he can only query the encryption of messages of length at most $q(n)$. During encryption of a message of length $q(n)$, at most $q(n)$ queries are made to H_S, resulting in a maximum number of $q(n)^2$ queries to H_S during the whole experiment. As H_S generates outputs of length n bits, the collision probability of H_S during the experiment is bounded by $\frac{q(n)^2{}^2}{2 \cdot 2^n}$.

A repetition of a query to f_k might also occur due to an explicit query by $\mathcal{A}$. However, if no repetition of a query to H_S occurred, this requires that $\mathcal{A}$ correctly guesses at least one chunk key j for which a query $f_K(j)$ or $f_j(\cdot)$ is made by $\widetilde{\mathrm{ENC}}_{i_K}$ during encryption of m_b. As $\mathcal{A}$ has runtime $q(n)$ and as there are at most $q(n)$ chunk keys each having a length of n bits, the chance for this to happen is bounded by $\frac{q(n)^2}{2^n}$. We conclude:

$$\Pr[\mathsf{FQ} \mid \overline{\mathsf{HQ}}] \leq \frac{q(n)^2{}^2}{2 \cdot 2^n} + \frac{q(n)^2}{2^n} = \frac{q(n)^4 + 2 \cdot q(n)^2}{2^{n+1}} \tag{7}$$

Combining Equations 5, 6 and 7, we get:

$$\begin{aligned}
& \Pr[\mathsf{PrivK}^{\mathsf{cpa}}_{\mathcal{A},\widetilde{\Pi}_\infty}(n) = 1] \\
=\ & \Pr[\mathsf{PrivK}^{\mathsf{cpa}}_{\mathcal{A},\widetilde{\Pi}_\infty}(n) = 1 \mid \overline{\mathsf{HQ} \vee \mathsf{FQ}}] \cdot \Pr[\overline{\mathsf{HQ} \vee \mathsf{FQ}}] \\
& + \Pr[\mathsf{PrivK}^{\mathsf{cpa}}_{\mathcal{A},\widetilde{\Pi}_\infty}(n) = 1 \mid \mathsf{HQ} \vee \mathsf{FQ}] \cdot \Pr[\mathsf{HQ} \vee \mathsf{FQ}] \\
\leq\ & \Pr[\mathsf{PrivK}^{\mathsf{cpa}}_{\mathcal{A},\widetilde{\Pi}_\infty}(n) = 1 \mid \overline{\mathsf{HQ} \vee \mathsf{FQ}}] + \Pr[\mathsf{HQ} \vee \mathsf{FQ}] \\
\leq\ & \frac{1}{2} + \Pr[\mathsf{HQ}] + \Pr[\mathsf{FQ}] \\
=\ & \frac{1}{2} + \Pr[\mathsf{HQ}] + \Pr[\mathsf{FQ} \mid \mathsf{HQ}] \cdot \Pr[\mathsf{HQ}] + \Pr[\mathsf{FQ} \mid \overline{\mathsf{HQ}}] \cdot \Pr[\overline{\mathsf{HQ}}] \\
\leq\ & \frac{1}{2} + 2\Pr[\mathsf{HQ}] + \Pr[\mathsf{FQ} \mid \overline{\mathsf{HQ}}] \ \leq\ \frac{1}{2} + \frac{2q(n)}{2^n} + \frac{q(n)^4 + 2q(n)^2}{2^{n+1}} \\
=\ & \frac{1}{2} + \frac{q(n)^4 + 2 \cdot q(n)^2 + 4 \cdot q(n)}{2^{n+1}} \ \leq\ \frac{1}{2} + \mathsf{negl}(n) \tag{8}
\end{aligned}$$

This proves that $\widetilde{\Pi}_\infty$ is IND-CPA-secure. $\qquad\square$

Theorem. *If F is a pseudorandom permutation and H_R, H_S are random oracles, $\widetilde{\Pi}$ achieves* CPA-secure *encryption.*

PROOF. We already know that $\widetilde{\Pi}$ achieves CPA-secure encryption if only truly random permutations are used. We will show that $\mathcal{A}$'s advantage is negligible if only single invocations of some truly random permutation are replaced by a

PRP. As there is only a polynomial amount of invocations, we conclude that $\widetilde{\Pi}$ is also CPA-secure using only a PRP.

Regard any polynomially bounded adversary $\mathcal{A}$ with runtime $q(n)$. Our goal is to show that $\Pr[\mathsf{PrivK}^{\mathsf{cpa}}_{\mathcal{A},\widetilde{\Pi}}(n) = 1] \leq \frac{1}{2} + \mathsf{negl}(n)$. We know that $\Pr[\mathsf{PrivK}^{\mathsf{cpa}}_{\mathcal{A},\widetilde{\Pi}_\infty}(n) = 1] \leq \frac{1}{2} + \mathsf{negl}(n)$. Due to his runtime $q(n)$, $\mathcal{A}$ can make at most $q(n)$ queries to $\widetilde{\mathrm{ENC}}_{i_K}$, with each queried message having a maximum length of $q(n)$. As the encryption operation performs at most one query to F_k and f_k, respectively, for every byte of its input, a maximum of $2q(n)^2$ queries to F_k/f_k may occur within the whole experiment. Within this runtime, $\widetilde{\Pi}_\infty$ and $\widetilde{\Pi}_{2q(n)^2}$ behave equally, so we have:

$$\begin{aligned}
\Pr[\mathsf{PrivK}^{\mathsf{cpa}}_{\mathcal{A},\widetilde{\Pi}_{2q(n)^2}}(n) = 1] &= \Pr[\mathsf{PrivK}^{\mathsf{cpa}}_{\mathcal{A},\widetilde{\Pi}_\infty}(n) = 1] \\
&\leq \frac{1}{2} + \mathsf{negl}(n) \tag{9}
\end{aligned}$$

Next we show that $\mathcal{A}$ cannot distinguish the experiments $\mathsf{PrivK}^{\mathsf{cpa}}_{\mathcal{A},\widetilde{\Pi}_i}(n)$ and $\mathsf{PrivK}^{\mathsf{cpa}}_{\mathcal{A},\widetilde{\Pi}_{i-1}}(n)$ with non-negligible probability. We do this by defining a polynomial-time distinguisher $D^{F'(\cdot)}$ as follows:

1. Run $\mathcal{A}(1^n)$ and simulate the oracle $\widetilde{\mathrm{ENC}}_{i_K}(\cdot)$ by executing the algorithm $\widetilde{\mathrm{ENC}}_{i_K}$ to answer $\mathcal{A}$'s oracle queries—with one modification: When the—overall—i-th query to a (pseudo-)random permutation (F or f) is made, use F' instead of $f_K(x)$.
2. When $\mathcal{A}$ outputs messages m_0, m_1, choose $b \leftarrow \{0,1\}$ randomly and return $\widetilde{\mathrm{ENC}}_{i_K}(m_b)$.
3. Continue answering oracle queries by $\mathcal{A}$ as in step 1.
4. When $\mathcal{A}$ outputs b', output 1 if $b' = b$, otherwise 0.

If D is instantiated with the PRP F', the only difference between D and experiment $\mathsf{PrivK}^{\mathsf{cpa}}_{\mathcal{A},\widetilde{\Pi}_{i-1}}(n)$ is that $F'(x)$ is queried instead of $F_j(x)$ at any point of time. As there might be other queries to F_j during the experiment, two situations might lead to inconsistent behavior: $F_j(x)$ might be queried at any other point of time during the experiment and produce different output than $F'(x)$, or $F'(x)$ might produce an output that is also output by $F_j(y), y \neq x$ at any other point of time during the experiment. As the experiment allows at most $2q(n)^2$ invocations of F_j, the probability of the latter is upper-bounded by $\frac{2q(n)^2}{2^n}$. Further, as all invocations $F_j(x)$ done by $\widetilde{\mathrm{ENC}}_{i_K}$ include an n-bit number chosen uniformly at random (cf. Equation 3), a repetition of the invocation $F_j(x)$ requires that this n-bit value has been chosen again by chance or has been guessed by $\mathcal{A}$. The probability for this to happen is upper-bounded by $\frac{2q(n)^2}{2^n}$, too.

If neither of these situations occur, we can think of $D^{F'(\cdot)}$ as using a slightly modified PRP $\widetilde{F}$ (for the whole experiment) that is defined exactly like F, but switches two values so that its outputs are consistent to F': $\widetilde{F}_j(x) = F'(x)$ and $\widetilde{F}_j(F_j^{-1}(F'(x))) = F_j(x)$. As $\widetilde{F}$ is a PRP, the view of $\mathcal{A}$ when run by D is distributed identically to the view of $\mathcal{A}$ in experiment $\mathsf{PrivK}^{\mathsf{cpa}}_{\mathcal{A},\widetilde{\Pi}_{i-1}}(n)$. As the probability for this situation is at least $1 - \frac{4q(n)^2}{2^n}$ and D outputs 1 whenever $\mathcal{A}$ succeeds in the experiment, we know that:

$$\Pr[D^{F'(\cdot)}(1^n) = 1] \geq \left(1 - \frac{4q(n)^2}{2^n}\right) \Pr[\mathsf{PrivK}^{\mathsf{cpa}}_{\mathcal{A},\widetilde{\Pi}_{i-1}}(n) = 1] \tag{10}$$

If D is instantiated with a truly random permutation f', the only difference between D and experiment $\mathsf{PrivK}^{\mathsf{cpa}}_{\mathcal{A},\widetilde{\Pi}_i}(n)$

is that $f'(x)$ is queried instead of $f_j(x)$ at any point of time. We can use the same arguments as before to show that the view of $\mathcal{A}$ when run by D is distributed identically to the view of $\mathcal{A}$ in experiment $\mathsf{PrivK}^{\mathsf{cpa}}_{\mathcal{A},\widetilde{\Pi}_i}(n)$ with probability at least $1 - \frac{4q(n)^2}{2^n}$. Assuming that $\mathcal{A}$ succeeds in any other case, we can give an upper bound:

$$\Pr[D^{f'(\cdot)}(1^n) = 1]$$
$$\leq \left(1 - \frac{4q(n)^2}{2^n}\right)\Pr[\mathsf{PrivK}^{\mathsf{cpa}}_{\mathcal{A},\widetilde{\Pi}_i}(n) = 1] + \frac{4q(n)^2}{2^n} \quad (11)$$

As we know (by assumption) that F' is a PRP, we get:

$$\mathsf{negl}'(n) \geq \Pr[D^{F'(\cdot)}(1^n) = 1] - \Pr[D^{f'(\cdot)}(1^n) = 1]$$
$$\geq \left(1 - \frac{4q(n)^2}{2^n}\right)\Pr[\mathsf{PrivK}^{\mathsf{cpa}}_{\mathcal{A},\widetilde{\Pi}_{i-1}}(n) = 1]$$
$$- \left(1 - \frac{4q(n)^2}{2^n}\right)\Pr[\mathsf{PrivK}^{\mathsf{cpa}}_{\mathcal{A},\widetilde{\Pi}_i}(n) = 1] - \frac{4q(n)^2}{2^n}$$

We can solve this to get:

$$\mathsf{negl}''(n) \geq \left(\mathsf{negl}'(n) + \frac{4q(n)^2}{2^n}\right) \cdot \frac{1}{1 - \frac{4q(n)^2}{2^n}}$$
$$\geq \Pr[\mathsf{PrivK}^{\mathsf{cpa}}_{\mathcal{A},\widetilde{\Pi}_{i-1}}(n) = 1] - \Pr[\mathsf{PrivK}^{\mathsf{cpa}}_{\mathcal{A},\widetilde{\Pi}_i}(n) = 1] \quad (12)$$

Combining Equations 9 and 12, we conclude:

$$\Pr[\mathsf{PrivK}^{\mathsf{cpa}}_{\mathcal{A},\widetilde{\Pi}}(n) = 1] = \Pr[\mathsf{PrivK}^{\mathsf{cpa}}_{\mathcal{A},\widetilde{\Pi}_0}(n) = 1]$$
$$\leq \Pr[\mathsf{PrivK}^{\mathsf{cpa}}_{\mathcal{A},\widetilde{\Pi}_{2q(n)^2}}(n) = 1]$$
$$+ \left|\Pr[\mathsf{PrivK}^{\mathsf{cpa}}_{\mathcal{A},\widetilde{\Pi}_0}(n) = 1] - \Pr[\mathsf{PrivK}^{\mathsf{cpa}}_{\mathcal{A},\widetilde{\Pi}_{2q(n)^2}}(n) = 1]\right|$$
$$\leq \frac{1}{2} + \mathsf{negl}(n)$$
$$+ \sum_{i=1}^{2q(n)^2} \left|\Pr[\mathsf{PrivK}^{\mathsf{cpa}}_{\mathcal{A},\widetilde{\Pi}_{i-1}}(n) = 1] - \Pr[\mathsf{PrivK}^{\mathsf{cpa}}_{\mathcal{A},\widetilde{\Pi}_i}(n) = 1]\right|$$
$$\leq \frac{1}{2} + \mathsf{negl}(n) + 2q(n)^2 \cdot \mathsf{negl}''(n) \leq \frac{1}{2} + \mathsf{negl}'''(n) \quad (13)$$

This proves that $\widetilde{\Pi}$ is CPA-secure. $\qquad\square$

Theorem. *If* $\widetilde{\Pi}$ *achieves IND-CPA-secure encryption,* Π^* *achieves IND-CCA-secure encryption.*

PROOF. As Π^* is an instantiation of [13, Construction 4.19] (see Sec. 5.1), we can apply [13, Theorem 4.20], whose proof can be found in [13, Chapter 4.8]: "*If Π_E is a CPA-secure private-key encryption scheme and Π_M is a secure message authentication code with unique tags, then Construction 4.19 is a CCA-secure private-key encryption scheme.*" Since $\widetilde{\Pi}$ is CPA-secure and Π_M is a secure message authentication code with unique tags, Π^* is CCA-secure. $\qquad\square$

6.2 Security Guarantees with fixed K_O

If K_O is re-used for multiple encryptions (in our system, this can be the case for different revisions of the same file), we intentionally leak some information to allow data deduplication. We allow a possible attacker to see relations between different messages that are encrypted with the same K_O, so he might recognize the positions and the size of plaintext fragments that are identical between different messages. This shall even be true if equal plaintext fragments appear at different positions within different messages.

This is a rather specific use case which prevents the application of classic security properties like ciphertext indistinguishability. However, we want to show that re-using K_O retains some basic notion of security. While we leak information about *identical* contents in different messages, we can prove that we do not leak any information about *different* contents that are encrypted using the same value K_O.

6.2.1 Security Guarantees for Different Plaintexts

To formalize this, we introduce a restricted variant of the $\mathsf{PrivK}^{\mathsf{cpa}}_{\mathcal{A},\widehat{\Pi}}(n)$ experiment seen in the previous section: the *chosen different plaintext attack (CDPA)* experiment. $\mathsf{PrivK}^{\mathsf{cdpa}_d}_{\mathcal{A},\widehat{\Pi}}(n)$ is defined exactly like $\mathsf{PrivK}^{\mathsf{cpa}}_{\mathcal{A},\widehat{\Pi}}(n)$, with the difference that $\mathcal{A}$ is only allowed to ask for encryptions of messages which do not have an overlapping fragment with more than d bytes size. Thus, all substrings occuring in more than one message (including both queries $\mathcal{A}$ makes to $\widehat{\mathrm{ENC}}_K$ as well as the messages m_0, m_1) must have a maximum size of d bytes. If $\mathcal{A}$ does not adhere to these constraints, the output of the experiment is defined to be 0.

Analogous to the previous definition, we say an encryption scheme $\widehat{\Pi}$ is $CDPA_d$-secure if for all probabilistic polynomial-time adversaries $\mathcal{A}$ there exists a negligible function negl such that $\Pr[\mathsf{PrivK}^{\mathsf{cdpa}_d}_{\mathcal{A},\widehat{\Pi}}(n) = 1] \leq \frac{1}{2} + \mathsf{negl}(n)$. Again, the probability is taken over the random coins used by $\mathcal{A}$ and the random coins used in the experiment.

We emphasize that this is a *significantly weaker* security model than CPA security, since we cannot hope to show strong security properties when intentionally leaking information to an attacker. The security proof shall merely provide an intuition that our scheme does not leak information in situations where we do not explicitly require it to do so.

Theorem. *If* $\widetilde{\Pi}$ *achieves CPA-secure encryption,* $\widehat{\Pi}$ *achieves* $CDPA_d$-*secure encryption for* $d = \min\{w, l\} - 1$.

PROOF. To show this, we need to define another variant of our encryption scheme $\widehat{\Pi}$ first. Let $\widehat{\Pi}_i = (\widehat{\mathrm{GEN}}_i, \widehat{\mathrm{ENC}}_i, \widehat{\mathrm{DEC}}_i)$ be defined as follows:

- $\widehat{\mathrm{GEN}}_i = \widehat{\mathrm{GEN}}$, $\widehat{\mathrm{DEC}}_i = \widehat{\mathrm{DEC}}$
- $\widehat{\mathrm{ENC}}_i$, on input key (K_R, K_O), invokes $(\_, K_{O'}) \leftarrow \widehat{\mathrm{GEN}}_i(n)$ to obtain a random $K_{O'}$. Then it acts like $\widehat{\mathrm{ENC}}$, but uses $K_{O'}$ instead of K_O for the—overall—first i queries to $H_X, X \in \{R, S\}$ that it makes during its lifetime.

Now regard the sequence of encryption schemes $\widehat{\Pi}_0, \widehat{\Pi}_1, \ldots$ Surely, $\widehat{\Pi}_0$ behaves exactly like $\widehat{\Pi}$, so we have:

$$\Pr[\mathsf{PrivK}^{\mathsf{cdpa}_d}_{\mathcal{A},\widehat{\Pi}_0}(n) = 1] = \Pr[\mathsf{PrivK}^{\mathsf{cdpa}_d}_{\mathcal{A},\widehat{\Pi}}(n) = 1] \quad (14)$$

We can further see that—up to the i-th oracle query—$\widehat{\mathrm{ENC}}_i$ behaves exactly like $\widehat{\mathrm{ENC}}$, since it uses a fresh, randomly generated key $K_{O'}$ for each encryption application instead of the supplied value K_O.

Now let $q(n)$ be the maximum runtime of $\mathcal{A}$ in experiment $\mathsf{PrivK}^{\mathsf{cdpa}_d}_{\mathcal{A},\widehat{\Pi}}(n)$. In each step, $\mathcal{A}$ can make at most one query to the encryption oracle, so $\widehat{\mathrm{ENC}}$ can be executed at most $q(n)$ times during that experiment. During encryption of a message m, $\widehat{\mathrm{ENC}}$ makes at most $|m|$ queries to H_R and at most $|m|$ queries to H_S, respectively. As—due to its runtime—$\mathcal{A}$ cannot generate plaintexts of length greater than $q(n)$, each encryption query results in at most $2q(n)$ queries to $H_X, X \in \{R, S\}$, resulting in a maximum total number of $2q(n)^2$ queries to H_X during the whole experiment. As $\widehat{\mathrm{ENC}}_i$ and $\widehat{\mathrm{ENC}}$ are identical up to the i-th query to H_X, this implies:

$$\Pr[\mathsf{PrivK}^{\mathsf{cdpa}_d}_{\mathcal{A},\widehat{\Pi}_{2q(n)^2}}(n)=1] = \Pr[\mathsf{PrivK}^{\mathsf{cdpa}_d}_{\mathcal{A},\widehat{\Pi}}(n)=1] \quad (15)$$

We show that an adversary cannot distinguish the experiments $\mathsf{PrivK}^{\mathsf{cdpa}_d}_{\mathcal{A},\widehat{\Pi}_i}(n)$ and $\mathsf{PrivK}^{\mathsf{cdpa}_d}_{\mathcal{A},\widehat{\Pi}_{i-1}}(n)$ with non-negligible probability: The only difference between both experiments is that $H_X(K_{O'},x,y)$ is queried instead of $H_X(K_O,x,y)$ at any point of time within the former experiment.

Per definition, $\mathcal{A}$ can only succeed if all queries made to the encryption oracle during the experiment are different in the sense that no $\min\{w,l\}$-byte window content occurs in more than one query. Thus, different success probabilities for those experiments imply that $\mathcal{A}$ adheres to those constraints. As w-byte window contents are used as input to H_R by the encryption scheme (see Equation 1) and repetitions of the same w-byte window within a single encryption application result in different inputs to H_R due to the appearance counter, this implies that all inputs to H_R during the whole experiment are different. Similarly, as the encryption scheme does not generate chunks smaller than l bytes, all inputs to H_S (see Equation 2) are unique, too.

If $\mathcal{A}$ did not query any of the values $H_X(K_{O'},x,y)$ or $H_X(K_O,x,y)$ directly to the oracle, both values are—due to the random oracle—independent from both all inputs and all other outputs of the random oracle, so $\mathcal{A}$ cannot distinguish between those values. Different success probabilities in both experiments thus require that $\mathcal{A}$ did query any of those values within the experiment. As this requires a correct guess of either K_O or $K_{O'}$ within $\mathcal{A}$'s runtime, the probability for this to happen is at most $\frac{2q(n)}{2^n}$:

$$\left| \Pr[\mathsf{PrivK}^{\mathsf{cdpa}_d}_{\mathcal{A},\widehat{\Pi}_i}(n)=1] - \Pr[\mathsf{PrivK}^{\mathsf{cdpa}_d}_{\mathcal{A},\widehat{\Pi}_{i-1}}(n)=1] \right| \le \frac{2q(n)}{2^n} \quad (16)$$

Combining Equations 14, 15 and 16, we get:

$$\left| \Pr[\mathsf{PrivK}^{\mathsf{cdpa}_d}_{\mathcal{A},\widetilde{\Pi}}(n)=1] - \Pr[\mathsf{PrivK}^{\mathsf{cdpa}_d}_{\mathcal{A},\widehat{\Pi}}(n)=1] \right|$$
$$\le 2q(n)^2 \cdot \frac{2q(n)}{2^n} = \frac{q(n)^3}{2^{n-2}} \quad (17)$$

The only difference between $\mathsf{PrivK}^{\mathsf{cdpa}_d}_{\mathcal{A},\widetilde{\Pi}}(n)$ and $\mathsf{PrivK}^{\mathsf{cpa}}_{\mathcal{A},\widetilde{\Pi}}(n)$ is that $\mathcal{A}$ is less restricted in the latter. We conclude:

$$\Pr[\mathsf{PrivK}^{\mathsf{cdpa}_d}_{\mathcal{A},\widehat{\Pi}}(n)=1] \le \Pr[\mathsf{PrivK}^{\mathsf{cdpa}_d}_{\mathcal{A},\widetilde{\Pi}}(n)=1] + \frac{q(n)^3}{2^{n-2}}$$
$$\le \Pr[\mathsf{PrivK}^{\mathsf{cpa}}_{\mathcal{A},\widetilde{\Pi}}(n)=1] + \frac{q(n)^3}{2^{n-2}} \le \frac{1}{2} + \mathsf{negl}(n) + \frac{q(n)^3}{2^{n-2}}$$
$$\le \frac{1}{2} + \mathsf{negl}'(n) \quad (18)$$

with the last inequality being true because $q(n)$ is polynomially bounded. This shows that $\widehat{\Pi}$ is CDPA_d-secure. $\quad\square$

Theorem. *If $\widehat{\Pi}$ achieves CDPA_d-secure encryption, Π also achieves CDPA_d-secure encryption.*

PROOF. The only difference between $\widehat{\Pi}$, which we have proven to be CDPA_d-secure, and Π is that the latter appends a MAC tag generated by Π_M to each ciphertext. As the calculation of this tag does only depend on the ciphertext and an independent key, its presence surely cannot reduce the security properties provided by $\widehat{\Pi}$. We conclude that Π is CDPA_d-secure, too. $\quad\square$

Combining both theorems, we have proven that Π achieves $\mathrm{CDPA}_{\min\{w,l\}-1}$-secure encryption. Intuitively, this means that an arbitrary amount of plaintexts may be encrypted using the same (K_R, K_O, K_I) key triple without leaking any information to an attacker, as long as none of those plaintexts share a substring of length $\min\{w,l\}$ bytes.

6.2.2 Security Guarantees for Similar Plaintexts

While the model presented in the previous section provides strong security guarantees under certain conditions, we have to intentionally leak some information to achieve storage efficiency. In other words, the conditions required for the proof cannot always be met. We therefore describe what information an attacker can gain in the general case.

It is easy to see that identical plaintexts are always encrypted to the same ciphertext (if K_R, K_O and K_I are unchanged), so in this case, an attacker can see nothing more than *how often* a specific plaintext was encrypted.

The encryption of different, but similar plaintexts (that share a substring of length at least $\min\{w,l\}$ bytes) using the same key is the most common use case. We analyze what information is leaked in this case to provide an intuition that our design decisions are reasonable. The analysis is performed in two steps: First we focus on security implications of our chunk encryption scheme, later we analyze the chunking procedure.

Security Implications of Chunk Encryption

Imagine all chunk boundaries have been determined completely randomly. Let $m^1, \ldots, m^M$ be the list of all messages that have been encrypted with $\widehat{\Pi}$ using the same key and let $c^1, \ldots, c^M$ be their respective ciphertexts. Let further m^j_i denote the i-th chunk of message m^j and let c^j_i denote its encrypted representation. Clearly, our deterministic encryption mechanism leaks information about equality of chunks[8]. But what information is leaked beyond equality?

To analyze this, regard the sequence of all *different* chunks $m'_1, \ldots, m'_r$ that have ever been encrypted using the same key and let C'_i denote the maximum number of occurrences of m'_i within any *single* message. From those chunks, we can build a plaintext $m = \|^r_{i=1}\left(\|^{C'_i}_{j=1} m'_i\right)$. If we apply a modified version of $\widehat{\Pi}$, that achieves exactly that chunking, to m, we get a ciphertext c that contains all encrypted chunks that are contained in $c^1, \ldots, c^M$. Thus, $c^1, \ldots, c^M$ can be reconstructed from c just using knowledge about *which substrings* have to be concatenated in *which order*, so all non-positional information leaked by $c^1, \ldots, c^M$ is leaked by c, too.

In this setup, however, we have only a single application of our encryption scheme that uses a random value K_O, which is CPA-secure as shown in Section 6.1. We conclude that chunk encryptions do not leak information beyond *positions* and *sizes* of contents.

If an attacker knows K_O (e.g. because he has read access to another revision that uses the same K_O), he can encrypt plaintexts (and also determine chunk boundaries) himself, allowing a verification of guessed plaintexts. Therefore, the default behaviour of our implementation is to change K_O on access rights changes.

---

[8]This applies across revisions of the same file with equal K_O, not within one revision due to the appearance counters.

Security Implications of Chunking

We have already seen that an encrypted chunk for itself does not leak any information about its underlying plaintext. However, due to the context-sensitive chunking procedure, we can think of each chunk as being annotated with some information about its plaintext visible to an adversary. To see which information is leaked, regard an arbitrary but fixed chunk c_i. From the chunking mechanism, an attacker gets to know the following facts:

- If c_i occurs within any message at any position other than its beginning, the attacker knows that the first w bytes of the chunk fulfill Condition 1.
- The attacker knows that no w-bytes substring within the last $|c_i| - l$ bytes of c_i fulfill Condition 1 within any yet encrypted message that contains c_i.

We emphasize that an adversary cannot evaluate Condition 1 for any plaintext without knowledge about K_O, so this information does not obviously allow to draw conclusions about the plaintext. However, when two revisions of a file are encrypted using the same K_O, limited structural information about that file might be leaked: Chunking may reveal the positions of changes more precisely than the encryption procedure itself, if a change affects a chunk boundary. In addition, changed chunk boundaries might affect chunk appearance counters and thus the encryption of later equal chunks, so that those chunk ciphertexts might appear to *move* between two revisions. However, both potential issues are in line with our security claims, which allow revealing the positions and extent of changes if K_O is unchanged.

7. SYSTEM IMPLEMENTATION

We have implemented the full concept, as described in the previous sections, into the SVN library source code[9], extended the SVN command line application, and evaluated the performance of our implementation.

We wanted to retain full compatibility to other SVN versions to enable a quick deployment of our extension. We have therefore realized nearly all parts of our solution on the client side—namely the *working copy library*—of the SVN architecture without introducing any new data structures that would have to be handled by the repository. For this, we store all data in so-called *properties*—a versioned file-related meta-data mechanism provided by the SVN architecture. All actions provided by our solution (e.g. encryption/decryption of files, permission administration) are designed to only affect a file's representation or its properties within the user's working copy, while the synchronization between a working copy and the repository (e.g. commit/update operations) stays unchanged.

Key management is implemented as follows: All keys are generated randomly when a confidential file is created or access rights are changed. To allow data deduplication, we do not automatically change a file's K_O when new revisions are generated. A simple command line option allows to achieve stronger security guarantees by explicitly changing K_O.

Regarding compatibility, we support arbitrary combinations between old/new server (repository) versions and old/new client versions. If a client supports our extension, it can securely use our access control solution on some files no matter what other SVN versions are involved at the server

---

[9] We extended revision 1152561 of the repository's trunk (ht tps://svn.apache.org/repos/asf/subversion/trunk)

---

and at the client side. Clients not supporting our solution would just be unable to access confidential files—just like new SVN clients that are not granted rights on those files. If the server runs an old version, only server-side checks like write access control would be disabled, so other clients would be able to delete confidential files. However, such files could still be restored due to the version history provided by SVN.

8. CONCLUSION AND OUTLOOK

We have presented a security solution for the version control system SVN, which enables secure and storage-efficient versioning of documents—even in case of a malicious repository server administrator. The main restrictions of the system are the attacker's capability of seeing the positions of changes in a document, and of verifying whether chunks from a previous version (to which the attacker had been granted access) are still contained in a new version. Both attacks can be prevented by changing the file's *obfuscator*, but this comes at the cost of storage efficiency. Our implementation does not require changes to SVN's storage backend, and is compatible with previous SVN servers (with the exception of write access control) and clients (though old clients cannot access encrypted files). Authentication currently relies on passwords only, as we wanted to avoid the administrative overhead of a PKI. For corporate environments, certificate-based authentication may still be a viable alternative, which we aim at supporting in the future.

9. ACKNOWLEDGMENTS

We thank Gennadij Liske for his valuable comments on the proof (Sec. 6). We further thank Ronald Petrlic, Sebastian Seitz and the anonymous reviewers for their helpful comments. The work is funded by the German Research Foundation (DFG) under GRK 1479.

10. REFERENCES

[1] M. Bellare and P. Rogaway. Random oracles are practical: a paradigm for designing efficient protocols. In *Proceedings of CCS '93*, pages 62–73. ACM, 1993.

[2] B. H. Bloom. Space/time trade-offs in hash coding with allowable errors. *Commun. ACM*, 13(7):422–426, July 1970.

[3] CollabNet, Inc. Skip-Deltas in Subversion. http://svn.apache.org/repos/asf/subversion/tru nk/notes/skip-deltas, Nov. 2005.

[4] CollabNet, Inc. The Subversion protocol. http://svn.apache.org/repos/asf/subversion/tru nk/subversion/libsvn_ra_svn/protocol, Sept. 2011.

[5] J. Daemen and V. Rijmen. AES Proposal: Rijndael. 1999.

[6] W. Diffie and M. Hellman. New directions in cryptography. *IEEE Transactions on Information Theory*, 22(6):644–654, 1976.

[7] L. Dusseault. HTTP Extensions for Web Distributed Authoring and Versioning. RFC 4918, 2007.

[8] D. E. Eastlake 3rd and T. Hansen. US Secure Hash Algorithms (SHA and SHA-based HMAC and HKDF). RFC 6234, 2011.

[9] K. Fu, S. Kamara, and T. Kohno. Key regression: Enabling efficient key distribution for secure distributed storage. In *Proceedings of NDSS*, 2006.

[10] E. Goh, H. Shacham, N. Modadugu, and D. Boneh. Sirius: Securing remote untrusted storage. In *Proceedings of NDSS*, 2003.

[11] D. Grolimund, L. Meisser, S. Schmid, and R. Wattenhofer. Cryptree: A folder tree structure for cryptographic file systems. In *25th IEEE Symposium on Reliable Distributed Systems (SRDS)*, pages 189–198, 2006.

[12] M. Kallahalla, E. Riedel, R. Swaminathan, Q. Wang, and K. Fu. Plutus: Scalable secure file sharing on untrusted storage. In *Proceedings of the 2nd USENIX Conference on File and Storage Technologies*, pages 29–42, 2003.

[13] J. Katz and Y. Lindell. *Introduction to Modern Cryptography: Principles and Protocols*. Chapman & Hall/CRC, 2008.

[14] A. Muthitacharoen, B. Chen, and D. Mazières. A low-bandwidth network file system. In *Proceedings of SOSP '01*, pages 174–187. ACM, 2001.

[15] C. Pilato, B. Collins-Sussman, and B. W. Fitzpatrick. *Version Control with Subversion*. O'Reilly, 2008.

[16] M. O. Rabin. Fingerprinting by Random Polynomials. Technical Report TR-15-81, Department of Computer Science, Harvard University, 1981.

[17] F. Rashid, A. Miri, and I. Woungang. A secure data deduplication framework for cloud environments. In *Tenth Annual International Conference on Privacy, Security and Trust (PST), 2012*, pages 81–87, 2012.

[18] M. W. Storer, K. Greenan, D. D. E. Long, and E. L. Miller. Secure Data Deduplication. In *Proceedings of StorageSS '08*, pages 1–10. ACM, 2008.

[19] The Apache Software Foundation. Apache Subversion. http://subversion.apache.org/, Apr. 2012.

[20] Z. Wilcox-O'Hearn and B. Warner. Tahoe: the least-authority filesystem. In *Proceedings of StorageSS '08*, pages 21–26. ACM, 2008.

APPENDIX

A.   PERFORMANCE EVALUATION

In this section, we evaluate our solution's performance regarding memory and time efficiency. We first discuss an appropriate choice of the parameter values and then analyze their impact on storage efficiency to prove our savings in comparison to usual encryption schemes. Finally, we briefly evaluate our algorithm's memory and time requirements.

A.1   Choice of Parameters

As mentioned in Section 5.1.1, our encryption scheme depends on some parameter values w (window size), l (minimum chunk size) and S (target chunk size). We set $w = 48$ bytes according to the evaluation results provided by Muthitacharoen et al. [14]. For a random file of size z bytes (and with parameter value $l = 1$ byte), we calculated an average encryption overhead of $\frac{43.5z}{S} + 32$ bytes for storing chunk metadata (length and key), padding and the integrity value. We confirmed this formula to be true for non-random data by encrypting the 50 most popular ebooks (47.9 MiB in total) from Project Gutenberg[10], each as UTF8-encoded text file, with randomly chosen keys with values of S in in-

---

[10] http://www.gutenberg.org/ebooks/search.html/?sort_order=downloads, visited on 2012-03-13

---

terval $[32, 4096]$, which resulted in an average deviation of 0.07 percentage points and a maximum deviation of 1.24 percentage points from the expected relative overhead. As our security guarantees depend on $\min\{w, l\}$ (see Sec. 6.2), we set $l = w$, which in addition guarantees a maximum storage overhead of $z + 32$ bytes. With $S \geq 256$, we produce an overhead of $< 20\%$, which we consider an acceptable overhead that we expect to be compensated by the savings due to difference-based efficient storage of multiple file revisions.

A.2   Storage Efficiency

While we have shown that an appropriate parameter choice allows storing single file versions with little overhead, our main goal is the efficient storage of whole repositories containing multiple (and similar) revisions of several files. Our system requires storage overhead at several locations. The main overhead—as described before—is caused by the metadata generated by our encryption scheme and depends on the file's size as well as the parameter value S. In addition, since we store all access-control-relevant information (such as cryptographic material) in the confidential file's properties, every confidential file requires some storage for these properties. The storage requirement for this can be quantified with about 1.5 KiB constant overhead per file and 2 KiB constant overhead per authorized user of this file. Note, however, that thanks to differential storage this is only generated once per access right change (at least once per file), not once per revision. Despite that, we also generate small overhead when storing different file revisions: While for unencrypted files, only the contents that actually changed (+ a negligible overhead) have to be stored, our solution requires storage for each change's full surrounding chunk(s).

To evaluate our achievements regarding storage efficiency of similar file revisions, we first studied our algorithm's performance on a kind of best-case scenario, namely a repository that contains the version history of a single file, with only small changes made between each of its revisions. We simulated this situation by setting up an experiment as follows: At first, we committed an empty, confidential file to a fresh SVN repository. Afterwards, we iterated the following sequence: We chose a position within that file uniformly at random and inserted a random number (chosen uniformly at random in interval $[64, 192]$, i.e. 128 bytes on average) of random bytes there. The resulting extended file version was then committed to the repository, so the file and its version history grew with each iteration. Using the generated repository, we compared our encryption scheme to other solutions: For this purpose, we generated a couple of fresh repositories and re-enacted the previously described repository's version history for each of them with individual configurations. In the first configuration, we achieved confidentiality by encrypting each file revision using a traditional encryption scheme (AES-CBC with a fixed key, but randomly chosen IVs); in the remaining ones, we used our access control solution with different parameter values S.

The results of this experiment are shown in Fig. 1. Each line represents the development of the total storage requirement of a specific repository when storing the first i revisions. The black line (+ markers) shows the unencrypted repository, which unsurprisingly has the least storage consumption. The violet line ($\times$ markers) shows the repository whose content is encrypted with a traditional scheme. As expected, its storage consumption rises rapidly with an in-

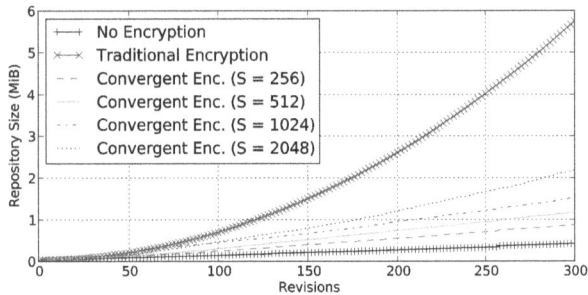

Figure 1: Development of repository size when a versioned confidential file is extended systematically

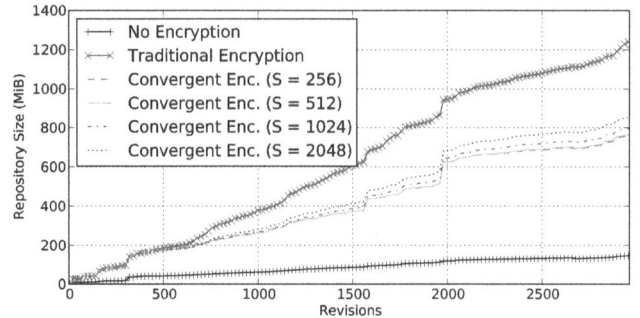

Figure 2: Development of ispCP's repository size

creasing number of revisions due to the need for storing the whole ciphertext of each file version. While the storage efficiency of our encryption scheme varies for different values of S, its savings are significant for either value. $S = 256$ yields the best performance and requires about twice as much storage as the unencrypted configuration. This is in line with our expectation that small (e.g. about-128-byte) changes result in about S bytes of difference in ciphertext on average.

These results could suggest that a lower S results in lower storage consumption in general, so we repeated the experiment with changes of average length 4 096 bytes instead of 128 bytes between revisions. In this setup, our solution produced less overhead and our savings compared to traditional encryption were more significant. However, savings through small chunk sizes (i.e. small differences between ciphertexts) were outweighed by overhead for storing chunk metadata. $S = 512$ yields the best results in that experiment.

While these results show that our encryption scheme allows for efficient storage in some hypothetic best-case scenario, we surely have to verify if these results are transferable into practice. In fact, we identified two problematic situations for our access control solution. The first is a repository consisting of a huge amount of very small files: Since we have to store metadata for each of these files separately, our system would generate a lot of overhead, which might not be compensated by further savings if the file sizes are not considerably greater than our chunk sizes. The second case is a repository consisting of arbitrary files, which do not contain any change history (i.e. each file has only a single revision) or only changes that affect whole file contents. In this case, our encryption scheme would generate chunking-related metadata overhead that is not compensated by space savings due to similar file revisions.

To verify whether these drawbacks are of practical relevance, we evaluated our solution using some real-life data. For this, we re-enacted the version history of the trunk of the open source project $ispCP$[11], which consists of many small ($\approx$ 10 KiB) source code files as well as rarely-changed files such as pictures. Thus, this example combines elements from both problematic scenarios discussed above. Analogously to the previous experiments, the results are shown in Fig. 2. Since the repository starts with a kind of worst-case situation (at the beginning, 2 768 small ($\approx$ 10 KiB) files are added), the storage efficiency of our solution seems to be worse than the one with traditional encryption. With an increasing number of revisions, however, our solution's savings compared to traditional encryption get significant again.

---

[11] http://isp-control.net; repository: http://www.isp-control.net:800/ispcp_svn/trunk, requested on 2012-03-26

A.3 Memory and Time Requirements

We have seen that our access control solution allows efficient storage of encrypted repositories. We now consider the amount of memory and time needed to en-/decrypt confidential files. Besides the specific implementation, there are conceptual aspects critical to memory / time consumption. A trivial implementation has two main drawbacks:

1. Encryption consumes memory in the order of about 48 times the file size as it has to count the appearances of each 48-byte window content (see Sec. 5.1.1).
2. As HMAC computations are time-consuming, computing a rolling HMAC (one computation for every byte of the file size) significantly slows down encryption.

To find a suitable trade-off between memory / time efficiency and security, we evaluated 4 variants of our algorithm:

- *HMAC, no repetitions*: This is a trivial reference implementation of our concept, which implements appearance counters using hash tables. This version is memory-consuming, but adheres strictly to the description in Sec. 5.

- *HMAC, no repetitions, bloom filter*: This variant is similar to the first, but implements the rolling hash appearance counter using a bloom filter [2], achieving memory consumption of about 3 times of the file size by allowing *false positives* (i.e. repetitions could be detected by mistake). As false *negatives* are excluded, this only affects storage efficiency, not security (rolling hash values might change, but repetitions are still excluded).

- *HMAC*: This variant ignores repetitions of rolling hash values, so periodical file contents could lead to periodical chunk boundaries visible in ciphertexts. This has a slightly negative effect on the security properties when applied to files with repeating contents, but—if this limitation is acceptable—significantly reduces memory consumption.

- *Rabin fingerprints*: By using an efficient rolling hash function (i.e. *Rabin fingerprints* [16]) for rolling hash computation (and still ignoring repetitions), encryption is speeded up dramatically. However, while we expect its impact on security to be negligible, we do not recommend this variant as it might leak information about chunk boundaries.

The experiments—performed on an *Intel(R) Core(TM) i5-2500K* machine with 16 GiB RAM—confirmed our expectations: With 3.3 seconds for encrypting a 16 MiB file, the Rabin fingerprint variant performs about 10 times faster than the corresponding HMAC variant—but leads to security drawbacks. The significant decrease (factor 10) of memory consumption achieved by the bloom filter is also done at the expense of computing time (factor 2). When considering only the two provably secure variants, we consider the bloom filter variant the best trade-off. Thus, this variant is our default and has been used for the other experiments.

212

Beyond Accountability: Using Obligations to Reduce Risk Exposure and Deter Insider Attacks

Nathalie Baracaldo
University of Pittsburgh
School of Information Sciences
nab62@pitt.edu

James Joshi
University of Pittsburgh
School of Information Sciences
jjoshi@sis.pitt.edu

ABSTRACT

Recently, the importance of including obligations as part of access control systems for privilege management, for example, in healthcare information systems, has been well recognized. In an access control system, an *a posteriori* obligation states which actions need to be performed by a user after he has accessed a resource. There is no guarantee that a user will fulfill *a posteriori* obligations. Not fulfilling these obligations may incur financial loss, or loss of goodwill and productivity to the organization. In this paper, we propose a trust-and-obligation based framework that reduces the risk exposure of an organization associated with *a posteriori* obligations. We propose a methodology to assign trust values to users to indicate how trustworthy they are with regards to fulfilling their obligations. When access requests that trigger *a posteriori* obligations are evaluated, the requesting users' trust values and the criticality of the associated obligations are used. Our framework detects and mitigates insider attacks and unintentional damages that may result from violating *a posteriori* obligations. Our framework also provides mechanisms to determine misconfigurations of obligation policies. We evaluate our framework through simulations and demonstrate its effectiveness.

Categories and Subject Descriptors

K.6.5 [**Management of Computing and Information Systems**]: Security and Protection; D.4.6 [**Security and Protection**]: Access Controls

Keywords

Risk, obligations, access control, trust, insider threat, RBAC

1. INTRODUCTION

Many application domains, including healthcare information systems, require the inclusion of obligations as part of their access control policies [3, 7, 13]. An obligation is an action that needs to be performed by a user before or after accessing a resource[1]. For instance, systems that need to preserve data privacy may need to impose an obligation to the users after they access a particular resource: e.g., 30 days after a user accesses a patient's record, the user needs to file a report and send a notice of the disclosure to the patient. We refer to an obligation that needs to be carried out after the resource has been accessed as an *a posteriori* obligation.

Managing *a posteriori* obligations is a challenging task, as there is no guarantee that after granting access to a resource, the user will fulfill the imposed obligation. In an ideal world, users are diligent and trusted to perform their tasks provided that they are given all the required resources to do so. Unfortunately, the statistics show a world far from ideal! According to the 2010/2011 CSI survey [12], where an insider is defined as a person that has legitimate access to the resources of an organization, 60.50 % of the respondents reported monetary losses caused by non-malicious insiders. In addition, 40.90% of the respondents said that part of their monetary losses were caused by malicious insiders. Hence, organizations would benefit from a framework that helps mitigate unintentional and intentional damages performed by insiders.

Since organizations assume the risk of having users defaulting on (i.e., ignoring or forgetting to perform) *a posteriori* obligations every time the system imposes them, it is necessary to control such risk exposure. If these obligations are not fulfilled, it may result in fines, penalties, delays, lawsuits, loss of revenue and goodwill, among other negative consequences for the organization. Depending on the criticality of an obligation, the risk exposure may vary from low to severe. Unfortunately, current approaches [7, 14] assign *a posteriori* obligations to users without considering their tendency to fulfill or default on obligations.

In this paper, we propose an obligation-based risk management framework that is able to minimize the risk exposure of an organization caused by *a posteriori* obligations. Our premise is that the risk exposure of the organization can be reduced if we determine how much a user can be trusted to fulfill the obligations assigned to him. We propose an approach to compute how trusted each user is based on his history of fulfillment or defaulting on the obligations assigned to him. The higher the trust value of a user, the more the system trusts him to fulfill *a posteriori* obligations.

---

[1] In this paper we only deal with obligations that are meant to be fulfilled by users. Other types of obligations include those that need to be performed by the system itself.

We use a threshold-based risk management technique in which the criticality of an obligation determines how much a user needs to be trusted in order to assign the obligation to him. When a user requests an access, the user's credentials, his trust value and the criticality of the obligations associated with the requested permissions are used to determine whether he should be granted the requested access and assigned the associated obligations or whether the request should be denied. If the criticality of an obligation is high while the assigned user's trust value is low, granting the requested access would pose a significant risk to the organization, and hence should be denied.

Although the importance of including risk and trust mechanisms in the access control system has been recognized by several researchers, e.g., [5, 2, 16], to the best of our knowledge, none of the existing approaches are designed for the requirements of access control mechanisms that include *a posteriori* obligations. In addition, most of the existing work on obligations [14, 3, 7, 17] has focused on defining obligation properties, languages to express policies that include obligations and providing support for accountability in the system (e.g., establishing who is to blame when an obligation is not fulfilled and making sure that users have all the permissions to perform their assigned obligations). Unlike the proposed approach, existing approaches do not consider the history of users' handling of obligations while making access control decisions –hence, the risk exposure is not mitigated when a user clearly has demonstrated that the obligations assigned to him will most likely be unfulfilled.

The key **contributions** of our work are as follows:

- We emphasize and show that *a posteriori* obligations have an inherent criticality level and propose a comprehensive framework to reduce the risk exposure faced by organizations every time a user is assigned critical obligations. To the best of our knowledge, this is the first work that has integrated the inherent criticality of *a posteriori* obligations and the obligation-based trust value in the authorization decision making process.

- We propose and evaluate a methodology to calculate the obligation-based trust values for each user. The methodology is resilient against users who know how the system computes the trust values and try to exploit this knowledge. Our methodology is also able to discern among users who accidentally do not fulfill an obligation, maliciously avoid the fulfillment of obligations and those who strategically oscillate their behavior to maintain their trust value within an acceptable threshold to launch an attack later.

- We propose a clustering-based methodology to identify policy misconfigurations, users colluding to avoid performing particular obligations and users whose behavior is worse than their peers (e.g., users that systematically avoid fulfilling an *a posteriori* obligation.). This information can be used by the system administrator to take necessary actions, such as updating the policy or monitoring more closely certain users.

- Finally, the proposed framework provides a technique to detect insider threats by monitoring users without invading their privacy (e.g., other methodologies used for this purpose scan users' personal emails) or including subjective measures.

The results of our work can be used to extend access control models that include obligations such as Usage Control (UCON) [20] and role based access control (RBAC) models [8]. Our results can also be integrated with systems that perform situational analysis of users' behavior to identify insider threats such as [4].

The rest of the paper is organized as follows. In Section 2, we present the motivation, threat model and requirements associated with the proposed framework. Our framework is presented in Section 3. In Section 4, we present our methodology to compute the user's trust values. The methodology to find policy misconfigurations and outliers is presented in Section 5. We evaluate our approach in Section 6. The related work is presented in Section 7 and our conclusions in Section 8.

2. MOTIVATION, THREAT MODEL AND REQUIREMENTS

According to [18] some of the insider attacks could be prevented if users were monitored to identify suspicious activities. In particular, insider attack incidents could have been prevented if the system had a monitoring module to evaluate how trusted a user is with respect to *technical* and *psychological* precursors. Some of the *technical precursors* include download and use of hacker tools, failure to create backups, unauthorized access of customers' or coworkers' systems, system access after termination, inappropriate Internet access at work, and the setup or use of backdoor accounts [18]. Among the *psychological precursors*, insider attackers have shown the following symptoms: *disgruntlement, bad attitude towards feedback, anger management issues, disengagement, disregard for authority, performance decrease, stress, confrontational behavior, personal issues, self contentedness, lack of dependability* and *absenteeism* [9].

Although these risk indicators may allow early detection of insider threats, monitoring users can be challenging because of privacy and legal concerns. Several of the indicators proposed in [9] are related to psychological and physical characteristics which are usually seen as private information. For instance, monitoring the health of an individual is not well regarded; indeed, the Health Insurance Portability and Accountability Act (HIPPA) protects individuals' right to medical privacy [19]. Hence including psychological and physical monitoring of a user would breach the HIPPA legislation. Therefore, we need to find an approach to measure these indicators without violating the privacy of the employees. For instance, monitoring employee's performance is a well accepted practice by both employees and employers.

Lets consider the following psychosocial indicators: *disregard of authority* and *lack of dependability* [11]. As part of the *disregard of authority*, the employee disregards rules, authority or policies, and feels above the rules or that they only apply to others. As part of *lack of dependability* an employee is unable to keep commitments and is unworthy of trust. Greitzer *et. al* [11] have tried to find these indicators using human input, which is subjective in nature and may be biased due to interpersonal relationships. For instance, asking an analyst to evaluate these indicators will inevitably lead to a subjective evaluation based on how he sees his coworkers. If an employee is accused unfairly, he may worsen his performance, increase his disgruntlement levels and reduce his trust towards the organization. This may occur if the metrics used in the organization are too subjective.

To address the above problem, we propose to monitor and evaluate the users' behavior towards *a posteriori* obligations as a way to determine these two psychological indicators. When users stop fulfilling their *a posteriori* obligations, they are disregarding authority and they may be less dependable. This may be due to lack of interest and the fact that they may be occupying their time with other activities such as preparing an attack. Monitoring and evaluating users' patterns of fulfilling and violating obligations has several advantages with respect to existing approaches. The rate of fulfilment of obligations can be used as one of the metrics to assess the employees' performance that does not introduce any subjective information in the system. Since employees are being paid to perform their jobs, using performance metrics is a well-accepted practice [9]. An additional advantage of this methodology is its ability to include up-to-date information of a user's behavior. Traditional ways to measure the employee's psychosocial state usually are incorporated slowly into the system (e.g., 360 performance evaluation methodology is usually completed once a year [9]). Therefore, we argue that the obligation-based trust values are an objective measure of the actual, up-to-date performance of the users and hence capture their real behavior.

2.1 Threat Model

The key focus of the proposed framework is to minimize the risk exposure of an organization based on the criticality of *a posteriori* obligations. Our threat model considers the following types of users:

1. *Naïve users:* These are insiders who know the system is monitoring if they have fulfilled or violated a particular obligation. However, they do not know the details of how their trust values and the trust thresholds to access resources are computed by the system.

2. *Strategic users:* These are insiders with knowledge about the system's mechanism to compute trust values. This information gives them the power to try to maintain their trust levels within the expected thresholds to avoid being flagged as suspicious by controlling their behavior in a smart way.

Note that our threat model considers that all the users in the system know that they are being monitored and evaluated, as hiding this information may cause disgruntlement [9]. If employees do not know they are being monitored and the system flags them as suspicious, their disgruntlement may increase making them more prone to become insider attackers.

2.2 Requirements

The proposed access control framework addresses the following requirements for detecting and mitigating the risk exposure of unfulfilled *a posteriori* obligations.

1. The associated access control model should capture the criticality of obligations. The criticality value represents the severity of the impact of not fulfilling the obligation for the organization.

2. Reduce risk of users not fulfilling obligations by considering their trust values and the criticality of *a posteriori* obligations associated with the permissions being

requested. The system should deny access requests to users whose trust value is below a pre-specified threshold associated with *a posteriori* obligations that would be triggered by the access.

3. Compute the obligation related trust value of a user based on the history of fulfilling or defaulting on *a posteriori* obligations as well as his performance with respect to his peers. The trust value should detect when a user is an outlier; e.g., when the user is the only one defaulting on a particular obligation. This trust value should be reliable for the two types of users defined in our threat model.

4. Provide a methodology that allows an administrator to detect policy misconfigurations related to *a posteriori* obligations by identifying patterns of violation of *a posteriori* obligations. The patterns can serve to identify when a particular obligation is not being fulfilled by a large number of users. This may be due to different factors. It is possible that the policy is not updated, but there is a verbal agreement to ignore it or the users that are assigned those obligations are too busy or lazy. The system should also detect when a user is the only one continuously violating an obligation, which may imply he is sabotaging the operation. The knowledge of these patterns can be used to reduce the risk and identify policy misconfigurations.

5. Identify when a user is misbehaving, which in turn indicates that he poses a high risk of becoming an insider attacker, without invading users' privacy.

3. PROPOSED TRUST-AND-OBLIGATION BASED FRAMEWORK

In this section, we present the proposed obligation-based risk management framework. As a key part of the framework, in Section 3.1, we present our Trust-and-oBligation based Core RBAC model (Core TB-RBAC Model) which extends the standard RBAC model [8]. While the methodology we propose to evaluate the trust can be used for any access control system that includes *a posteriori* obligations, in this paper, we choose to extend the RBAC model because of the its extensive adoption and advantages [22]. It encompasses discretionary and mandatory access control models, and supports organization or user-specific requirements. In addition, RBAC uses roles which are a natural abstraction for most organizations, and it provides organizations with economic benefits due to the reduction on the administration cost. In Section 3.2, we present the overall framework architecture.

3.1 The Core TB-RBAC Model

We extend the standard core RBAC model with obligations, risk and trust; it includes the following components.

- U is the set of users, R is the set of roles, P is the set of permissions defined as $P = OPS \times OBJ$, where OPS is the set of operations and OBJ is the set of objects in the system.
- $\mathcal{B}$ is the set of *a posteriori* obligations as defined in Definition 1 below and S is the set of sessions.
- $UA \subseteq U \times R$ is the user to role assignment, as in standard RBAC.

- $\mathcal{BP} \subseteq P \times 2^{\mathcal{B}}$ is *obligation-aware permission* set, where, $bp \in \mathcal{BP}$ is a tuple $\langle p \in P, BS \subseteq \mathcal{B} \rangle$ that indicates that once p has been exercised all the obligations in BS need to be fulfilled.
- $\mathcal{PBA} \subseteq R \times \mathcal{BP}$ is the assignment of obligation-aware permissions to roles. Permissions associated with different roles can have different obligations associated with them. This function replaces permission to role assignment (PA) of traditional RBAC.
- Function $session\_user : S \rightarrow U$ maps a session onto the corresponding user and $session\_roles : S \rightarrow 2^R$ maps a session onto a set of roles.
- Each user $u \in U$ is assigned an obligation-based trust value, $trust(u,t) \in [0,1]$ at time t. If $trust(u,t) = 0$, the user is not trusted. When $trust(u,t) = 1$ the user is completely trusted to perform *a posteriori* obligations. This value is automatically updated by the framework every time the user fulfills or violates an obligation.
- $P_{au} : (r \in R) \rightarrow PS \subseteq P$ is a function that returns the permissions PS assigned to role r. Formally, $P_{au}(r \in R) = \{p \mid (r,\langle p, BS \rangle) \in \mathcal{PBA} \land \langle p, BS \rangle \in \mathcal{BP}\}$.
- $B_{au}(r \in R) \rightarrow B \subseteq \mathcal{B}$ is a function that returns the set of obligations that would be assigned to the user that activates role r. Formally, $B_{au}(r \in R) = \{b \mid (r,\langle p, BS \rangle) \in \mathcal{PBA} \land \langle p, BS \rangle \in \mathcal{BP} \land b \in BS\}$.

We define an *a posteriori* obligation as follows:

DEFINITION 1. *An a posteriori obligation b is defined as a tuple $b = \langle \mathcal{A} \subseteq OPS \times OBJ, D, \varphi \rangle$ where*

1. *$\mathcal{A}$ is a set of actions that need to be performed to fulfil the obligation. The user assigned to b needs to perform all $a \in \mathcal{A}$ in order to fulfill the obligation.*
2. *D specifies how much time a user has to fulfill the obligation after the obligation is assigned to him.*
3. *$0 \leq \varphi \leq 1$ indicates how critical it is for the organization that the obligation is performed in time; where $\varphi = 1$ means that it is very critical and $\varphi = 0$ means that the obligation is not critical at all.*

In order to refer to a particular component of obligation $b \in \mathcal{B}$, we use the dot notation. For instance, $b.\varphi$ returns the criticality value of the obligation.

Obligation Instantiation: Obligations are assigned to users when they activate associated roles, as follows.

DEFINITION 2. *When user u activates role r in a session, for each a posteriori obligation b associated with r, the system instantiates the obligation creating the tuple: $\langle u, b, \tau, \mathcal{S} \rangle$ where:*

1. *u is the user that needs to fulfil the obligation.*
2. *b is the obligation that needs to be fulfilled by u.*
3. *τ is the time when the obligation is acquired by user u.*
4. *$\mathcal{S}$ is the state of the obligation which is initially set to pending.*

Once an *a posteri* obligation has been triggered, it can be in one of the following states: *pending, fulfilled* or *violated*. The interval within which the obligation needs to be fulfilled is $[\tau, \tau + b.D]$. The obligation is *pending* when the user has not perform the actions required by the obligation and the deadline to perform it has not passed. The obligation is

fulfilled when the user performed the required actions within the stipulated time interval. Conversely, the obligation is *violated* when the user does not perform the required actions during the valid interval of time.

Access control decision process: To obtain the permissions authorized for a role, users need to *activate* the role in a *session*. Hence, a user u requesting a permission set $PS \subseteq P$ is granted access to PS if the following conditions hold:

1. $\exists\ RS \subseteq R \land\ PS \subseteq \bigcup_{r \in RS} P_{au}(r) \land (\forall r \in RS : (u,r) \in UA)$, which means that there is a set of roles RS that can provide all the permissions in PS and all of the roles in RS are assigned to user u.

2. The system trusts the user enough to perform all the *a posteriori* obligations that would be acquired by activating the set of roles RS:
$\forall\ r \in RS, BS \subseteq B_{au}(r), b \in BS : trust(u,t) \geq b.\varphi$

In this paper, we do not specify how to select RS so that they respect the least privileged principle, however this can be easily done using one of the algorithms presented in [28].

In the following example, we illustrate how different obligations have different criticality values associated with them.

Example 1: Consider a manufacturing organization. When a new supply container arrives, the employee in charge needs to access the system and register it; this in turn triggers obligation b_1. This obligation corresponds to updating the inventory state after reviewing an order of a component to produce their most sold product. If the user fails to fulfill this obligation on time and the ordered supplies have defects, the entire operation of the organization would be negatively impacted. In case the defect is difficult to notice and nobody recognizes the lack of quality of the supplies, the organization would manufacture defective products. This may lead to a decrease on the goodwill of the organization and may also result in fines and additional product repairing costs for the enterprise. In a second scenario, the defect of the supply is noticed by a different employee during production and the operation is stopped due to the lack of available materials. In this case, the production line is stopped and orders may not be fulfilled on time causing delays, fines and loss of goodwill. Since the entire operation of the organization may be severely affected due to the lack of fulfillment of b_1, its criticality for the organization is *high* so we assign a value of $b_1.\varphi = 0.9$.

Obligation b_2 requires the obliged user to review a report of expenditures by the end of the week. This obligation aims at identifying discrepancies every week. However, an accountant reviews the report at the end of each month, so the discrepancy would be found eventually. The impact of violating this obligation is *medium* because not performing the obligation does not have long term repercussions for the organization. Only in the short term the discrepancy would exist. Hence, we assign $b_2.\varphi = 0.5$. Finally, when a user registers a new sale, obligation b_3 is triggered requiring the user to update the internal review file with comments regarding the interaction with the client. This obligation has *low* impact because not updating the file does not affect the operations of the organization. Thus, we can assign $b_3.\varphi = 0.3$. ∎

The above example shows that the criticality of an obligation depends on the impact of its violation. The risk expo-

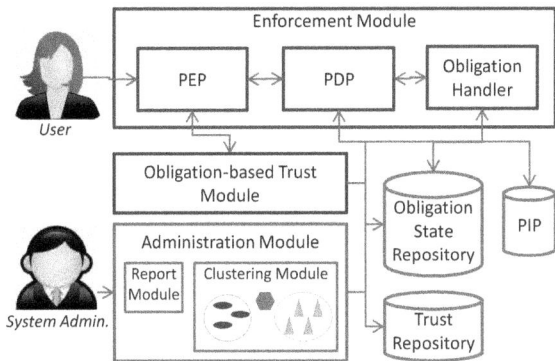

Figure 1: Architecture of the framework.

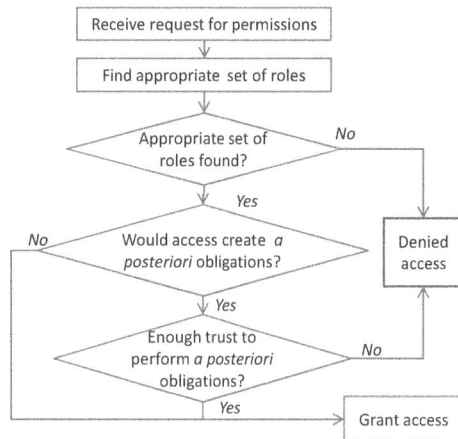

Figure 2: Processing flow of an access request.

sure an organization faces when an *a posteriori* obligation is assigned to a user is a function of the criticality of that obligation and the likelihood that the user will default on it. The larger the trust value of the user, the less likely he would default on an obligation. We use the criticality value of an obligation as a threshold that indicates how trusted a user needs to be in order to be assigned to a particular *a posteriori* obligation. Note that the criticality of the obligations can be expressed qualitatively and later mapped to a quantitative measure. Hence, the policy specifier can use any of the existing risk assessment methodologies (e.g., [27, 1]) to assign these values.

3.2 Framework Architecture

Figure 1 presents the architecture of our framework. First, we describe the functionality of each of the modules in the system and then we show the steps followed when a user's access request arrives at the system. The *Obligation-based Trust Module* monitors the users of the system and is in charge of determining the trust values associated with all of them. The trust values are stored in the Trust Repository.

The *Administration Module* generates alerts of possible policy misconfigurations related to *a posteriori* obligations and suspicious users. The *Clustering Module* finds the patterns of misbehavior and the *Report Module* generates the corresponding alert reports for the administrator. This process is explained in Section 5.

In addition, the framework contains the *Enforcement Module* which consists of the Policy Enforcement Point (PEP), the Policy Decision Point (PDP) and the Obligation Handler. The *Obligation Handler* is responsible for maintaining the state (*pending, fulfilled* or *violated*) of the instantiated obligations in the system up-to-date. This information is stored in the *Obligation State Repository*. Every time an obligation changes its state to *fulfilled* or *violated*, the system informs the *Obligation-based Trust Module* of the new information, which in turn updates the trust value of the corresponding user. The PEP is in charge of intercepting all the access requests of the users in the system and it passes them to the PDP, which evaluates the request according to the policy stored at the Policy Information Point (PIP). The PDP returns the grant or deny decision to the PEP, which enforces the decision.

Figure 2 presents the process that is followed by the system to determine whether an access request is granted or denied. When a request is received by the PEP, it forwards the request to the PDP which retrieves the set of roles that need to be activated in order to grant the access. If the system cannot find such a set, the request is denied as the user is not authorized for roles that provide the requested permissions. If the roles that provide the privileges are found, the system evaluates whether activating them would create any *a posteriori* obligations for the user. If so, the PDP retrieves the trust value of the user and determines whether the value offsets the criticality of the obligations that would be assigned to the user. When the user is trusted enough to complete successfully such obligations, the access is granted and the *Obligation Handler* instantiates them according to Definition 2. In case the user is not trustworthy enough to fulfill one or more of the obligations that would be assigned to him, the system denies the access request.

4. TRUST COMPUTATION

In this section, we present the methodology to compute the trust of a user. As noted by Greitzer *et. al* [10], one of the limitations of threshold-based approaches is the fact that smart attackers would try to stay within the threshold to avoid being detected. Hence, the trust computation mechanism needs to account for strategically controlled variations on the user's behavior. Strategic changes in behavior occur when a user first constructs a good level of trust and then starts misbehaving. In addition, the trust value should provide a way to discern when the user accidentally does not perform an obligation. We want to reduce the trust value to account to the bad behavior, but give the opportunity to users to redeem themselves if they have defaulted obligations by mistake. In addition, the trust value should include a group factor to determine whether the evaluated user is the only one among the users assigned to a particular obligation, who is repetitively violating the obligation.

Our trust model considers the following aspects to find the obligation-based trust value ($trust(u, t)$):

1. His recent behavior.
2. His historical behavior, which shows how many times he has fulfilled or defaulted on assigned obligations.
3. His sudden changes in the behavior, which allows the system to penalize the user for negative changes in behavior.
4. His performance with respect to other users.

Our trust model is inspired by that of Srivatsa *et. al* pre-

Table 1: Notation

$m(M, b)$	Function that returns the multiplicity (number of elements of type b) contained in multiset M.
$\mathcal{B}$	Set of obligations in the system
GB_u^T	Multiset that contains the obligations fulfilled by user u in observation group T
BB_u^T	Multiset that contains the obligations violated by user u in observation group T
TGB^T	Multiset that contains the obligations fulfilled by all users in observation group T
TBB^T	Multiset that contains the obligations violated by all users in observation group T
$totalRisk(u, T)$	Function that returns the total risk of the obligations fulfilled and violated in observation group T by user u

sented in [26], where the first three components are included; however, we compute the trust values differently. In addition, to capture the overall group behavior and its relation to that of an individual user, we include the drift from the group. In Section 7, we discuss in further detail the differences between our approach and the one presented in [26].

4.1 Trust Methodology

An observation o of a user's behavior consists of a *fulfilled* or *violated* obligation ($o = \langle u \in U, b \in \mathcal{B}, final\_status \rangle$). We assume a user's observations are ordered based on their generation timestamps and that they are grouped in what we call *observation groups*. Each observation group contains a fixed maximum number of observations x. If at a particular time instant there are m logged observations, there would be $n = \lceil m/x \rceil$ groups. We denote observation groups as $T_1, ..., T_i, ...T_n$, where, group T_n contains the most recently logged observations and T_1 contains the oldest observations. Each group T_i for $2 \leq i \leq n$ is guaranteed to contain x observations while T_1 may contain less than x observations. The groups are recalculated every time a new observation is logged to the system. For instance, suppose that the fixed maximum number of observations per group is set to three ($x = 3$), and that, at time t_{19}, the system has logged six observations $o_1, ..., o_6$, where o_1 is the first and o_6 the last observation logged, respectively. At t_{19} there are two groups T_1 and T_2, where T_1 contains $[o_1, o_2, o_3]$ and T_2 contains observations $[o_4, o_5, o_6]$. Suppose that at t_{22} another observation o_7 is generated; it causes a re-grouping of observations as follows: a new group T_3 is created containing the most recent observations $[o_5, o_6, o_7]$, T_2 contains $[o_2, o_3, o_4]$ and T_1 contains the oldest observation o_1. Hence, T_3 contains the most recent beharvior of the user. In this way, at time instant t the observation groups are created according to the observations available and each group represents the behavior of a user in a period of time.

Table 1 contains the notation that we use in the rest of the paper. We use multisets to refer to the observations in each group. A *multiset* is a collection in which each element may appear more than once. For instance, a multiset of obligations $M = \{b_1, b_2, b_3, b_1\}$ contains obligation b_1 twice. The *multiplicity* is a function that returns the number of times an element appears in a multiset and is defined as

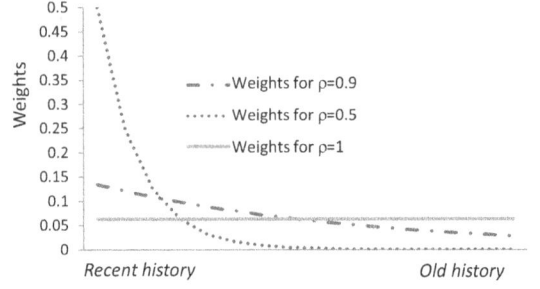

Figure 3: Effect of ρ on the historic trust (Definition 4) considering that all the obligations have the same criticality.

$m : Multiset \times element \rightarrow int$. In the previous example $m(M, b_1) = 2$ as obligation b_1 appears two times.

DEFINITION 3. *The raw trust $RT_u[T]$ of user u in observation group T is calculated using the following expression:*

$$RT_u[T] = \frac{\sum\limits_{b \in \mathcal{B}} b.\varphi * m(GB_u^T, b)}{\sum\limits_{b \in \mathcal{B}} b.\varphi * m(GB_u^T, b) + \sum\limits_{b \in \mathcal{B}} b.\varphi * m(BB_u^T, b)}$$

The raw trust captures the behavior of user u in period defined by the observation group T and it is a weighted average of the number of obligations fulfilled over the total number of obligations assumed by the user. The weights are determined by the importance of the obligations themselves (φ). In this fashion, an obligation that is very critical to the organization has a heavier impact on the raw trust, than one that is not so critical. A user that has violated all his acquired obligations has a raw trust equal to zero. In contrast, when the user has promptly fulfilled all his assigned obligations, his raw trust is equal to one.

DEFINITION 4. *The historical trust of user u for observation group T_n, $H_u[T_n]$, is computed as follows:*

$$H_u[T_n] = \sum_{k=1}^{n-1} RT_u[T_{n-k}] * w_k$$

where w_k is the weight of observation group T_{n-k} which is calculated as follows:

$$w_k = \frac{\rho^{k-1} + totalRisk(u, T_{n-k})}{\sum_{i=1}^{n-1}(\rho^{i-1} + totalRisk(u, T_{n-i}))}$$

where $0 \leq \rho \leq 1$.

When the weight for recent events is much higher than those of previous observations, the system allows the users to improve their trust values rather quickly because it prioritizes the most recent behavior. The weight w_k has two components, decay of historical information and the criticality of the observation groups. The first one is provided by ρ^{k-1} and allows the system administrator to change the importance of each historical observation group. Figure 3 depicts the effect of ρ on w_k. When $\rho = 1$, all the observation groups have the same weight; hence all the periods that contribute to the historical trust have the same importance. In this case, the historical trust is equivalent to the average of the raw trust. When $\rho = 0.5$, some of the older observations do not have much weight and we would be losing some information. In contrast, when $\rho = 0.9$ there is a desirable effect in which all the historical observations are considered, but the more recent ones have more weight than the older ones. We prefer to have ρ nearby 0.9 to maintain freshness of the observations while considering all the historical information available.

The second component of the weight w_k corresponds to the total criticality of the obligations that are included in observation group T_{n-k}. This component allows us to provide a higher weights to observation groups that contain obligations with higher criticality values and inhibits *strategic users* from improving their trust values by fulfilling only low criticality obligations.

DEFINITION 5. *The trust fluctuation $D_u[T]$ of user u in observation group T is defined as follows:*

$$D_u[T] = RT_u[T] - H_u[T]$$

which represents the variation of the current trust with respect to the historical trust.

When $D_u[T] \geq 0$, the user has improved or maintained his behavior with respect to his historical trust. In contrast, when $D_u[T] < 0$, the user behavior has worsened.

It is also desirable to discover when a user does not fulfill a particular obligation more frequently than his peers, which may represent attempts to sabotage the operation. We capture it using the notion of *group drift*.

DEFINITION 6. *The group drift, $G_u^b[T]$, of obligation $b \in \mathcal{B}$ for user u in observation group T is defined as follows: If $m(BB_u^T, b) = 0$, then $G_u^b[T] = 0$. Otherwise:*

$$G_u^b[T] = \frac{m(BB_u^T, b)}{m(TBB^T, b)} - \frac{m(BB_u^T, b) + m(GB_u^T, b)}{m(TBB^T, b) + m(TGB^T, b)}$$

Here, $0 \leq G_u^b[T] \leq 1$. If the user has not violated any obligation of type b, his group drift is zero. In addition, the group drift is zero if user u is the only one that has been assigned to obligation b, as there is no evidence that shows his behavior is drifting from the group (in fact, there is no group). When the number of users assigned to b increases, there is more evidence as to how far apart from the group the user is. When $G_u^b[T] = 0.5$, it means that half of the total assigned obligations (fulfilled and violated in observation group T) were violated by u. A $G_u^b[T]$ close to one implies that user u is the only person in a large group that has violated the obligation.

A big drift from the average may actually predict attempts to **sabotage** the operation. This is specially relevant when a constantly violated obligation has a large criticality value (φ). This behavior is suspicious and is penalized as follows.

DEFINITION 7. *The benchmark penalization of user u in observation group T, $PG_u[T]$, is calculated as follows:*

$$PG_u[T] = \sum_{\forall b: G_u^b[T] > \chi_b} \delta_b$$

where $0 \leq \chi_b \leq 1$ is a threshold for obligation $b \in \mathcal{B}$ that specifies how far apart from the group a user needs to be in order to be penalized and δ_b is the penalization received for drifting from the group substantially.

In the previous definition, when $G_u^b[T] > \chi_b$, user u is an outlier that does not fulfill obligation b, and should be penalized by an amount of δ_b. Note that the penalization and the threshold of each violated obligation $b \in \mathcal{B}$ (δ_b and χ_b) may have different values in the system depending on the importance of the obligation ($b.\varphi$). Finally, we compute the total obligation-based trust values for user u at time t, which is equivalent to finding the trust value for observation group T_n (remember that the most recent observation group is denoted by T_n).

DEFINITION 8. *The individual obligation-based trust $trust(u, T_n)$ of user u in observation group T_n is calculated as follows:*

$$trust(u, T_n) = \begin{cases} trust(u, T_{n-1}) & \text{if } \gamma(D_u[T_n]) = 0 \\ 0 & \text{if } \mathcal{T} \leq 0 \\ \mathcal{T} & \text{otherwise} \end{cases}$$

where
$\mathcal{T} = \alpha \times RT_u[T_n] + \beta \times H_u[T_n] + \gamma \times (D_u[T_n]) - PG_u[T_n]$
and $\alpha + \beta + \gamma = 1$.

Here, α represents the weight of the current behavior, β represents the weight of the historical information and γ the weight of sudden changes of behavior. We use two possible values for this latter weight, γ_1 and γ_2, to be able to penalize heavily negative changes in behavior while allowing users to regain trust slowly for positive changes. Letting $\gamma_1 < \gamma_2$, when $D_u[T_n] \geq 0$, we use γ_1 and when $D_u[T_n] < 0$ (the user behavior has worsened), we use γ_2. In this way, the user takes longer to regain trust than to lose it. We show the effect of these weights in Section 6.

In Definition 8, if the user does not change his behavior his trust value remains unchanged with respect to the previous interval of time. When the $\gamma * D_u[T_n] - PG_u[T_n]$ is too small making $\mathcal{T}$ negative (recall that $\gamma * D_u[T_n]$ is negative when a negative change of behavior occurs), the new trust value is zero, which is the minimum possible. Finally, when none of these two cases happen, the trust is updated according to the current and historical behavior, the behavior fluctuations and the benchmark penalization.

We evaluate our trust methodology in Section 6. In the following section, we present the *Administration Module* which is in charge of detecting policy misconfigurations.

5. ADMINISTRATION MODULE

An important consideration for monitoring systems is the fact that some of the suspicious behaviors may in fact be due to factors other than insider attacks and incompetence. For instance, if it is informally agreed that an obligation is no longer required, but the policy is not up-to-date, users may be ignoring that particular obligation in accordance with the informal agreement. To find the patterns of misbehavior, we incorporate clustering techniques within the administrative module. These patterns can be used by the policy administrator to review whether a particular obligation should cease to exist or to see why those employees are not performing them (e.g., the reasons could include: the obligations may no longer be necessary for the business process, users are too busy, the obligation should be assigned to other roles, etc.). In addition, during this process, users that are not fulfilling a particular obligation more often than their peers are also

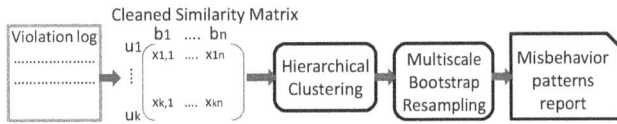

Figure 4: Procedure to find the patterns of misbehavior.

identified. In what follows we explain the process followed by this module, but first we provide some background on clustering algorithms.

5.1 Clustering Algorithms

Clustering is an unsupervised machine learning technique that aims to discover similar groups and outliers in datasets with unknown characteristics. We refer to [15] for a comprehensive review. Each observation being compared is represented by a vector that contains information about different characteristics. Clustering algorithms use a distance measure to identify how far apart the observations being clustered are. Different distance metrics exist in the literature, e.g., Euclidian, Manhattan distances. There are two types of clustering algorithms: *hierarchical* and *partitional*. *Partitional* methods require the specification of the number of clusters to be found; given this number, they output a solution with that number of clusters. In contrast, *hierarchical* algorithms do not need as input the number of clusters to be found and output several possible clusters. The hierarchical clustering algorithms begin by placing each observation into a separate cluster. Then, they verify the distances between all the observations and put together the two most similar ones in a new cluster. Existing methods to perform hierarchical clustering mainly vary on the way they compute the similarity between clusters; among them are *Ward, single-link* and *mean/average* methods. A detailed discussion on the differences among them can be found in [15].

The output of hierarchical clustering algorithms is a set of possible clusters, however, they do not assess the strength of the relation between the grouped observations. *Multiscale bootstrapping resampling* [25] is a methodology that allows us to overcome this downside by computing p-values for each of the clusters found by the hierarchical clustering algorithm. The methodology indicates the clusters that have high cohesion, which allows the data analyst to focus his attention in those relevant patterns.

5.2 Process to Find Patterns of Misbehavior

The process to find patterns of misbehavior is illustrated in Figure 4 and should be performed periodically. We use a clustering technique to detect patterns of misbehavior and outliers. We utilize hierarchical clustering, as it does not require the specification of the number of clusters to be found. This is appropriate since administrators do not know whether the users in the system have similar misbehaviors, whether they can be grouped or how many groups would result. The only parameter that needs to be specified is the distance metric to compare individuals and clusters. We use Ward hierarchical algorithm with Manhattan distance, as it finds better clusters for our purpose. We evaluate different algorithms in Section 6.

In order to use the algorithm, the logged information is set up in a *similarity matrix* $M_{|U| \times |\mathcal{B}|}$, which has one row for each of the users and one column for each obligation of the system. Each cell $x_{i,j}$ in the matrix contains the total

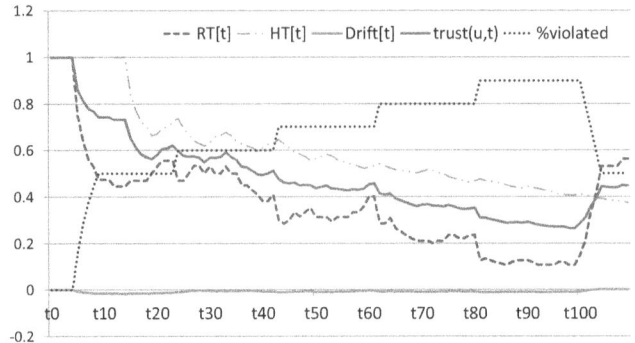

Figure 5: Evolution of trust values when the percentage of violated obligations increases, with $\alpha = 0.4$, $\gamma_1 = 0.01$, $\gamma_2 = 0.03$ and $\rho = 0.9$.

number of obligations of type b_j that user u_i has violated. The information included can have as much historical information as the administrator desires. Then, the matrix is cleaned by removing users that have not misbehaved, as there is no point in trying to find patterns of misbehavior for them.

The cleaned similarity matrix is used as input for the clustering algorithm, which outputs a set of possible clusters. Then, the system performs a multiscale bootstrapping resampling that establishes which of the clusters are cohesive. *Cohesive clusters* may represent policy misconfiguration or users colluding not to perform an obligation. This information can be used by the administrator to take corrective measures. For instance, he may decide to investigate why a cluster of users is not fulfilling an obligation and if appropriate, he may remove the obligation from the policy. On the other hand, *outliers* with a high number of obligation(s) violated may represent lazy, absent users or employees that may have higher risk of becoming insider attackers. This information can be used to further monitor their performance. Figure 8a presents an example. The dendogram was generated by the clustering algorithm and it shows all the possible clusters. The multiscale bootstraping resampling method created the rectangles that show the cohesive clusters that represent different patterns of misbehavior. Note that u_{10} is an outlier; if the number of obligations violated is high, he is flagged as suspicious.

6. EVALUATION

In this section, we begin by evaluating our proposed trust methodology presented in Section 4. Then, we present the assessment of the procedure to find patterns of misbehavior presented in Section 5.

Evaluation of the trust methodology: We evaluated our system under different users' behaviors. We generated synthetic data to test our approach. In each iteration, a user could fulfill or violate one of 15 *a posteriori* obligations. The criticality values of the obligations were assigned using the following distribution: 10% of obligations were set to high (0.9), 60% were set to medium (0.6) and the remaining were set to low (0.3) criticality. The number of observations in each period was set to 10. Each of the points in the following experiments was found every time a new observation was generated. In our experiments, we used $\rho = 0.9$ to compute

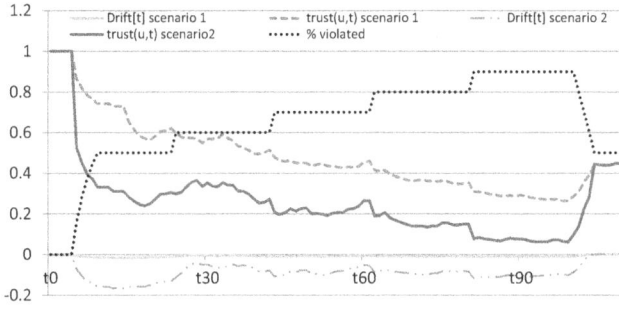

Figure 6: Trust values comparison for: *scenario 1*: $\alpha = 0.4$, $\gamma_1 = 0.01$ and $\gamma_2 = 0.03$ and *scenario 2*: $\alpha = 0.4$, $\gamma_1 = 0.01$ and $\gamma_2 = 0.3$.

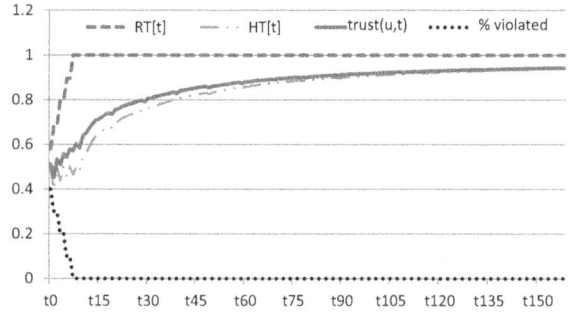

Figure 7: User redemption after having a trust value of 0.5. Parameters used: $\alpha = 0.4$, $\gamma_1 = 0.01$, $\gamma_2 = 0.03$ and $\rho = 0.9$.

the historical trust (Definition 4), for the reasons explained in Section 4. Our implementations was done in java.

Misbehaving users: To verify that our methodology is able to identify when a user is misbehaving, we examined three different cases. Figure 5 presents the results for a user that initially was completely trusted $trust(u, t_0) = 1$, but later starts misbehaving, as it is shown by the percentage of violated obligations per period. As the number of violated obligations increases, the obligation trust value, $trust(u, t)$, of the user is reduced. In addition, the historical and raw trust values also decrease as the misbehavior continuous. Consider an obligation with a high criticality of 0.9. If the user attempts to access a permission that would require the fulfillment of that particular obligation, he would not be able to obtain the privilege after t_5. Around t_{17}, he would lose accesses that require a trust value higher than 0.6.

If the administrator desires the system to react faster to unfavourable changes in behavior, the weight γ_2 can be set up higher to increase the punishment for negative drifts on user's behavior. For the same user we presented in the previous experiment, Figure 6 shows how the system increases its sensitivity to negative behaviors. Scenario 1 presents a conservative γ_2 weight while scenario 2 shows the results for a bigger γ_2 value. The obligation trust value of the user decreases faster for scenario 2 than for scenario 1 resulting in a faster revocation of highly critical privileges. This is due to the amplified effect of a negative drift, which is also shown in the figure. For scenario 1, the drift is almost zero, while for scenario 2, the negative effect is substantially smaller, which according to Definition 5 results in a smaller obligation-based trust value. Hence, the larger γ_2, the faster the system reacts to negative behaviors.

Redemption: We also evaluated the results of the system when a user improves his behavior. This is relevant, as it is possible that the user was not able to fulfill his obligations due to legitimate reasons (e.g., absence caused by sickness), hence, the system should allow the user to improve his trust value based on his new behavior. At the same time, it is important that the trust increases slowly, otherwise attackers would be able to increase their trust value too fast. Figure 7 shows the results of a scenario in which the user's initial trust values are set to 0.5, but after t_7 he starts fulfilling all the assigned obligations. Since the user fulfills all the obligations (from t_7 onwards), $RT[T]$ is always equal to one and the drift is always zero. The user requires twenty periods of spotless behavior before he improves his trust to 0.8 (with the parameters of scenario 1). Because the good

behavior continues, the user's trust value also continues the improvement trend.

Evaluation of the methodology to find patterns of misbehavior: We created several logs with different patterns of misbehavior, outliers and noise. A *misbehaving pattern* consists of several users not fulfilling a particular obligation, as if there was a legitimate informal agreement not to perform that obligation. *Outliers* are users who did not fulfill continuously a particular obligation and hence had a larger number of violations for that obligation than the average of the users. In addition, we included random *accidents* which represented obligations not fulfilled, unintentionally e.g., once someone missed a deadline. These observations can be considered as noise. The maximum number of obligations in the system was set to 15, the maximum number of users to 30 and we generated a total of 10 logs. We used R [21] to run cluster algorithms and the bootstrapping sampling method (with a significance level of 0.95) on the data and verified how many of the expected observations were classified correctly. We compared three hierarchical clustering algorithms: *Ward, single-link* and *mean* with two distances *Euclidean* and *Manhattan*. Since we know the existing patterns in the data tested, we can compare the solutions of the algorithms. The expected patterns in the data, are referred to as *classes*; they represent the ground truth. For example, $class_1 = \{u_0, u_1\}$ represents the users that violated obligation b_4, $class_2 = \{u_2, u_3\}$ represents the users who violated obligation b_6, $class_3 = \{u_4, u_5\}$ represents the users violating b_8 and $class_4 = \{u_6, u_7, u_8, u_9\}$ represents those violating obligation b_{12}. Figure 8 presents two solutions; one found by *Ward with Manhattan* and the other by *Single-link with Euclidean*. The rectangles around the users represent cohesive clusters. For the Ward output, the four expected classes were found. In contrast, the Single-link algorithm created one cluster for all the elements in classes 3 and 4, failing to identify the existing misbehaving pattern. In this case, Ward with Manhattan outperformed Single-link with Euclidean.

To compare clustering algorithms *purity* and *entropy* are typically used [30]. *Entropy* is a function of the distribution of classes in the resulting clusters and *purity* is a function of the relative size of the largest class in the resulting clusters. The details of how to calculate these metrics are provided in Appendix A. Both entropy and purity are in the interval [0,1]. Solutions with higher purity are preferred, while solutions with small entropies are preferred.

Table 2 presents the comparisons among the algorithms. Ward in combination with Manhattan distance provides the

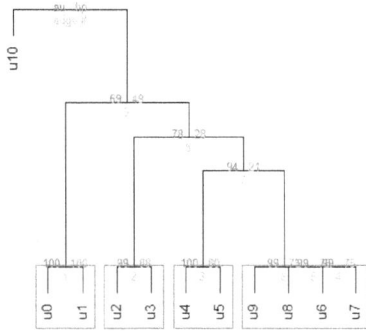

(a) Ward with Manhattan

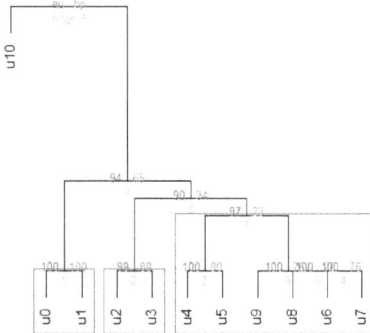

(b) Single-link with Euclidean

Figure 8: Example. The boxes in the dendongram represent cohesive clusters.

Table 2: Comparison between clustering algorithms

Method	Average Entropy	Average Purity
Ward Eucledian	0.28	0.68
Ward Manhattan	0.19	0.70
Average Eucledian	0.32	0.64
Average Manhattan	0.28	0.67
Single Eucledian	0.33	0.62
Single Manhattan	0.26	0.67

most reliable results according to both of the metrics used, as clusters found most of the time represented the existing classes. The worst results were found for single-link in combination with euclidean distance. In addition, when the algorithms used euclidean distance to measure difference among users, the results were consistently worse than when they used Manhattan distance. The empirical validation shows that the best option is to use Ward with Manhattan.

7. RELATED WORK

Obligations: The work closest to ours is [3], where Bettini *et. al* propose calculating a reliability value based on the history of fulfillment of obligations. However the work limits itself to providing a syntax to include this value into the obligation policy and does not provide a methodology to calculate it. In contrast, we have provided a threat model, a comprehensive methodology to calculate the obligation based trust value of each user and a methodology to find policy misconfigurations, colluding and suspicious users.

Most existing work related to obligations focus on providing accountability in the system [7, 14]. The idea is to assign *a posteriori* obligations to the users in such a way that the only reason for the obligation to fall into a *violated* state is user's incompetence. Li *et. al* [17] propose a XACML extension specify obligations as state machines. None of these works include risk management as part of the decision making process to assign an *a posteriori* obligation to a user. In addition, we could integrate the algorithm proposed in [7] with our approach to support cascading obligations.

Our policy definition augmented RBAC with obligations, obligation criticality and user's trust. In [29], an RBAC policy augmented with obligations was presented. The way in which obligations and permissions are integrated is the same as in our policy. However, their obligations do not contain a criticality value as ours, and they do not perform a trust analysis when assigning *a posteriori* obligations.

Other approaches have tried to reduce the risk exposure through the use of *system* obligations (e.g., [5]), which are obligations performed by the system itself. These obligations are meant to mitigate the risk, e.g., an obligation may consist of having the system close a file after a low trusted user has accessed it. These approaches differ from ours in that they not consider the inherent risk of *a posteriori* obligations. Hence, our approach and theirs are complementary.

Risk and trust access control models: Although several approaches combine access control with risk and trust [16, 24, 2, 23], to the best of our knowledge this is the first one that considers risk when assigning *a posteriori* obligations to users and provides a trust based methodology to do so. In [16] an abstract model for incorporating the concept of risk in UCON was presented. They consider risk coming from components such as the user, object, operations, connection used and the trust provenance of the attribute certificates. However, they do not include the obligations as part of the risk components. We believe that it is relevant to incorporate *a posteriori* obligations in the risk assessment as they are inherently risky. In [24] a methodology that considers the history of usage of a particular resource by a user to decide whether to grant or deny him access was presented. Their system gives positive points for good interactions and penalties when the interaction is inadequate. Based on these values a security clearance is calculated for the user. If the clearance does not dominate the object's level the access is denied. In [23], the authors propose a risk based approach in which each user has a budget assigned. Every time the user accesses an object some of its budget is spent. The cost to access each object varies depending on whether the user is authorized for it or not. Non authorized objects are more expensive. If the user runs out of budget, he will no longer be able to access the system's objects. These works were not designed to manage the risk of *a posteriori* obligations.

Baracaldo *et. al* [2] propose a trust and risk access control model to deter insider attacks. Each user is assigned a trust value for the current context and behavior, and each permission is assigned a risk value. Based on the risk of the permissions that a role is authorized for, a trust threshold is found for it. The user can activate in a session a role if he is authorized for it and if his trust value is greater than the trust threshold of the role. This work does not include obligations and can be integrated with ours. In [4], Buford *et. al* present a system to perform situational analysis of users' behavior to identify insider threats. Our work is complementary, as the obligation-based trust values can be used to increment the knowledge base of their system.

Trust: Several approaches for calculating trust in different domains have been proposed, yet, none of them are directly applicable for obligation-based risk management. Due to space limitations, we cannot discuss all of them; a comprehensive survey can be found in [6]. We built our trust approach based in the one presented by Srivatsa *et. al* in [26]. Their trust module was designed for decentralized overlay networks. In their work, the final trust value of a node is based on its current and historical behavior and sudden changes of behavior. Our methodology is different from theirs in several ways. i) In [26], all the failures or good behaviors have the same weights. In the case of obligations, this assumption is not valid as each obligation has its own criticality value. ii) Our historical value includes the criticality of the obligations to prevent strategic users from manipulating the trust computation by fulfilling only low-criticality obligations. iii) We include the group drift as part of our trust computation which allow us to identify users trying to sabotage particular operations by avoiding the fulfilment of one or more obligations. Since the application scenario for which [26] was designed does not have this requirement, group behaviors are not considered there. In addition, we propose a methodology to identify policy misconfigurations.

8. CONCLUSIONS

In this paper, we have proposed a framework to control the risk exposure caused by *a posteriori* obligations. As part of this framework, we proposed and evaluated a methodology to identify how trustworthy a user is to fulfill *a posteriori* obligations. Our methodology considers the latest, historical and sudden changes on users' behavior as well as users' behavior compared to his peers. The obligation-based trust value associated with each user is used to decide whether to grant or deny accesses that create *a posteriori* obligations. When a user is not considered trusted enough to fulfil *a postoriori* obligations, accesses that require the assignment of highly critical obligations are denied. In this way, our framework reduces the risk exposure caused by *a posteriori* obligations and identifies and deters insider threats without compromising the privacy of the users. In addition, we propose a clustering-based methodology to find patterns of misbehavior and outliers in the system. Our methodology can serve to identify policy misconfigurations and suspicious users. This information allows the system administrator to take appropriate measures.

Our work can be integrated into any access control model that includes *a posteriori* obligations (e.g., UCON) and risk aware role activation mechanisms (e.g., [2]). We believe that considering the inherent risk of *a posteriori* obligations can help the systems better understand a user's intentions and mood as well as reduce the risk exposure of an organization. As future work, we plan to extend our approach to include cascading obligations which are obligations whose fulfillment creates additional obligations.

Acknowledgments

This research has been partly supported by the U.S. National Science Foundation awards IIS-0545912 and DUE-0621274.

9. REFERENCES

[1] C. Alberts, S. Behrens, R. Pethia, and W. Wilson. Operationally critical threat, asset, and vulnerability evaluation (octave), 1999.

[2] N. Baracaldo and J. Joshi. A trust-and-risk aware rbac framework: tackling insider threat. In *Proc. of the 17th ACM symposium on Access Control Models and Technologies*, SACMAT '12, pp. 167–176, 2012.

[3] C. Bettini, S. Jajodia, X. Wang, and D. Wijesekera. Obligation monitoring in policy management. In *Policies for Distributed Systems and Networks, 2002. Proc. 3rd International Workshop on*, pp. 2–12, 2002.

[4] J. Buford, L. Lewis, and G. Jakobson. Insider threat detection using situation-aware mas. In *Information Fusion, 2008 11th International Conf. on*, pp. 1–8, 2008.

[5] L. Chen and J. Crampton. Risk-aware role-based access control. In *Proc. of the 7th International Workshop on Security and Trust Management.*, 2011.

[6] J.-H. Cho, A. Swami, and I.-R. Chen. A survey on trust management for mobile ad hoc networks. *Communications Surveys Tutorials, IEEE*, 13(4):562–583, 2011.

[7] O. Chowdhury, M. Pontual, W. H. Winsborough, T. Yu, K. Irwin, and J. Niu. Ensuring authorization privileges for cascading user obligations. In *Proc. of the 17th ACM symposium on Access Control Models and Technologies*, SACMAT '12, pp. 33–44, 2012.

[8] D. F. Ferraiolo, R. Sandhu, S. Gavrila, D. R. Kuhn, and R. Chandramouli. Proposed nist standard for role-based access control. *ACM Trans. Inf. Syst. Secur.*, 4:224–274, 2001.

[9] F. Greitzer, D. Frincke, and Z. M. Social/ethical issues in predictive insider threat monitoring, 2011.

[10] F. Greitzer and R. Hohimer. Modeling human behavior to anticipate insider attacks, 2011.

[11] F. Greitzer, P. Paulson, K. L., L. Franklin, T. Edgar, and F. D. Predictive modeling for insider threat mitigation, 2009.

[12] C. S. Institute. 2010/2011csi computer crime and security survey, 2010.

[13] K. Irwin, T. Yu, and W. Winsborough. Assigning responsibility for failed obligations. In *Trust Management II*, pp. 327–342, 2008.

[14] K. Irwin, T. Yu, and W. H. Winsborough. On the modeling and analysis of obligations. In *Proc. of the 13th ACM conf. on Computer and communications security*, CCS '06, pp. 134–143, 2006.

[15] A. K. Jain, M. N. Murty, and P. J. Flynn. Data clustering: a review. *ACM Comput. Surv.*, 31(3):264–323, 1999.

[16] S. Kandala, R. Sandhu, and V. Bhamidipati. An attribute based framework for risk-adaptive access control models. In *Proc. of 6th International Conf. on Availability, Reliability and Security*, ARES '11, 2011.

[17] N. Li, H. Chen, and E. Bertino. On practical specification and enforcement of obligations. In *Proc. of the 2nd ACM conf. on Data and Application Security and Privacy*, CODASPY '12, pp. 71–82, 2012.

[18] A. Moore, D. Cappelli, and T. R. The "big picture" of insider it sabotage across u.s. critical infrastructures, 2008. CERT, http://www.cert.org/insider_threat.

[19] U. D. of Health and H. Services. The health insurance portability and accountability act (hipaa), 1996.

[20] J. Park and R. Sandhu. The uconabc usage control model. *ACM Trans. Inf. Syst. Secur.*, pp. 128–174, 2004.

[21] R. Project. Package for hierarchical clustering with p-values (pvclust), 2012.

[22] Q. M. S. Osborn, R. Sandhu. Configuring role-based

access control to enforce mandatory and discretionary access control policies. 2000.

[23] F. Salim, J. Reid, U. Dulleck, and E. Dawson. Budget-aware role based access control. *Computers and Security*, 2012.

[24] R. Shaikh, K. Adi, and L. Logrippo. Dynamic risk-based decision methods for access control systems. *Computers and Security*, 31(4):447–464, 2012.

[25] H. Shimodaira. Approximately unbiased tests of regions using multistep-multiscale bootstrap resampling, 2004.

[26] M. Srivatsa, L. Xiong, and L. Liu. Trustguard: countering vulnerabilities in reputation management for decentralized overlay networks. In *Proc. of the 14th international conf. on World Wide Web*, WWW '05, pp. 422–431, 2005.

[27] G. Stoneburner, A. Goguen, and A. Feringa. Risk management guide for information technology systems, recommendations of the national institute of standards and technology, 2002.

[28] Y. Zhang and J. B. D. Joshi. Uaq: a framework for user authorization query processing in rbac extended with hybrid hierarchy and constraints. In *Proc. of the 13th ACM SACMAT*, SACMAT '08, pp. 83–92, 2008.

[29] G. Zhao, D. Chadwick, and S. Otenko. Obligations for role based access control. In *Proc. of the 21st International Conf. on Advanced Information Networking and Applications Workshops - Vol. 01*, AINAW '07, 2007.

[30] Y. Zhao and G. Karypis. Criterion functions for document clustering experiments and analysis. *Mach. Learn.*, 55(3), 2002.

APPENDIX

A. ENTROPY AND PURITY OF CLUSTERING SOLUTIONS

Entropy and Purity are two measures typically used to evaluate the quality of clustering solutions when the ground truth (classes) are known [30]. *Entropy* is a function of the distribution of classes in the resulting clusters. The entropy for each cluster S_r of size n_r is defined as:

$$E(S_r) = -\frac{1}{log(q)} \sum_{i=1}^{q} \frac{n_r^i}{n_r} log \frac{n_r^i}{n_r}$$

where q is the number of classes in the data set, and n_r^i is the number of users of the class ith that were assigned to the rth cluster. The entropy of the entire solution is computed as follows:

$$Entropy = \sum_{r=1}^{k} \frac{n_r}{n} E(S_r)$$

where n is the total number of users in each cluster and k is the number of found clusters. An algorithm that provides a perfect solution, according to the entropy metric, will result in clusters that contain users from a single class, in which case $Entropy = 0$. The smaller the entropy the better.

Purity is a function of the relative size of the largest class in the resulting clusters. The purity of cluster S_r is defined as

$$P(S_r) = \frac{1}{n_r} max_i(n_r^i)$$

which is the number of users of the largest class in a cluster divided by the cluster size. The total purity of a clustering solution is the weighted average of the clusters' purities:

$$Purity = \sum_{r=1}^{k} \frac{n_r}{n} P(S_r)$$

A higher purity represents a better solution.

Property-Testing Real-World Authorization Systems

Alireza Sharifi[*]
a9sharif@uwaterloo.ca

Paul Bottinelli[†]
paul.bottinelli@epfl.ch

Mahesh V. Tripunitara[*]
tripunit@uwaterloo.ca

[*]ECE, University of Waterloo, Canada   [†]IC, EPFL, Switzerland

ABSTRACT

We motivate and address the problem of testing for properties of interest in real-world implementations of authorization systems. We adopt a 4-stage process: (1) express a property precisely using existential second-order logic, (2) establish types of traces that are necessary and sufficient to establish a property, (3) adopt finitizing assumptions and show that under those assumptions, verifying a property is in **PSPACE**, and, (4) use a model-checker as a trace-generator to generate instances of traces, and exercise the implementation to check for those traces. We discuss our design of a corresponding testing-system, and its use to test for qualitatively different kinds of properties in two commercial authorization systems. One is a database system that we call the $\mathcal{D}$ System, and the other is a file-sharing system that we call the $\mathcal{I}$ System. (We use pseudonyms at the request of the respective vendors.) In the context of the $\mathcal{D}$ System, our testing has uncovered several issues with its authorization system in the context of procedures that aggregate SQL statements that, to our knowledge, are new to the research literature. For the $\mathcal{I}$ System, we have established that it possesses several properties of interest.

Categories and Subject Descriptors

D.4.6 [**Operating Systems**]: Security and Protection—*Access controls*; D.2.5 [**Software Engineering**]: Testing and Debugging—*Testing tools (e.g., data generators, coverage testing)*

General Terms

Security

Keywords

Testing, Model Checking, Properties

[†]The second author's contributions to this work were made as an exchange student at the University of Waterloo.

1. INTRODUCTION

Authorization deals with the specification and management of accesses principals have to resources. It is an important aspect of security. We address the problem of testing implementations of authorization systems for properties that are of interest.

Authorization systems can be complex; this is the underlying technical challenge in our work. The complexity arises from a feature that realistic authorization systems have: it is possible to not only directly authorize a principal to a resource, but also to do so indirectly. For example, a principal may acquire some rights via membership in groups or roles. Similarly, if the principal is authorized to execute a program, in the context of that program she may have some additional rights.

The reason such indirect ways are allowed is to balance the scalability needs of enterprise authorization systems, and security. Enterprise authorization systems must typically support large numbers of principals (e.g., users) and resources (e.g., files and documents). Providing indirect authorizations eases administrative burden. Granting a right to a group, for example, is less burdensome than granting it to each member of the group.

Given an implementation of an authorization system, one may want to test it. The objective is to ascertain whether the implementation has certain security and availability properties of interest. For example, in an authorization system that supports the notion of groups, we may want to ask, "if Alice is a member of the group G at the time G is authorized to read file f, she should be authorized to read file f at that time." The two direct authorizations in the example refer to Alice's membership in G, and G's authorization to f. (This is a special case of what we call the forward availability property — see Section 4.1).

Prior foundational work suggests that the problem of verifying that an authorization system has such a property may be intractable or even undecidable [12, 16, 17]. This is the case even if we want to carry out such verification "on paper," i.e., considering only the design of the system, and not any implementation. Clearly, such limits on the tractability of verification apply to testing as well. Nonetheless, we argue that the problem we address is an important one. If an implementation does not have a property we seek, we either need to redesign it, or address some implementation bug that causes it to not have the property.

Furthermore, in testing, it is customary to make the *small-scopes assumption* [10], with which we bound the scope of the system that is tested. The manner in which we apply the small-scopes assumption is to limit the system under test to contain only a few entities (e.g., principals, resources, and groups). The mindset behind the small-scopes assumption is that a system has a property we seek if and only if it has the property under the small-scopes assumption.

We argue that customary software testing is not geared to the kinds of properties we address in this work, that are specialized to authorization systems. This is not surprising — a similar observation has been made in other contexts in security, for example, testing for bugs in cryptographic implementations [2].

However, we do borrow ideas from software testing, for example, the small-scopes assumption which we discuss above. Similarly, the use of model-checking for software testing [15] and the use of traces to verify models "on paper" [19, 20] have been explored in recent work. Our work also has similarities to penetration testing in the context of security, in particular, the flaw-hypothesis methodology [13]. We discuss these in Section 5 on related work.

Our work We first propose and adopt a 4-stage process for property-testing an implementation of an authorization system. We show the stages in Figure 1.

1. In the first stage, we articulate properties of interest. A property typically balances generality and specificity. The specificity comes from the authorization features that the system under test supports. For example, one of the systems to which we have applied our methodology, the $\mathcal{I}$ System (see Section 4), does not have notions of executable programs or scripts via which a principal acquires rights. Consequently, some of the properties we articulate for the $\mathcal{D}$ System (see Section 3.1) are not meaningful for the $\mathcal{I}$ System.

   Particularly from a research-standpoint, properties that we anticipate are relevant not only to the two systems we discuss in this work, but to large classes of authorization systems.

   Another issue regards the syntax in which we express properties. We have adopted existential second-order temporal logic[‡][9] in this work. The reason is that it gives us an elegant syntax and an associated precise semantics that is sufficient for us to succinctly express the properties we consider. It is conceivable that a different syntax is more natural to express other properties.

2. A property is a declarative specification. A system under test can be more naturally seen as a procedural entity. To test for a property, therefore, we introduce the notion of a trace. A trace is a sequence of authorization states and the state-change from one to the next.

   We relate properties to traces: we identify traces that should exist, or should not exist in the system for a property to hold. That is, we establish assertions of the form, "property p holds if and only if no trace of type t is generated by the system."

3. We make finitizing (i.e., small-scopes) assumptions that are realistic. That is, we assume that certain parameters are bounded by constants. This assumption is crucial to the practicality of our approach. In Theorem 1, we establish that verifying a property under the kind of finitizing and other assumptions about predicates and their arity that we make, is in **PSPACE**.

   This implies that we can employ an approach similar to model-checking [6]. We point out that for a particular property, the problem is not necessarily **PSPACE**-complete. For example, the verification problem for all the three properties we consider for the $\mathcal{D}$ System are in co-**NP**. **PSPACE** is an upper-bound only.

4. Based on the finitization, we identify instances of traces for which we need to check in the system under test. We then exercise an implementation and check whether the instances of traces are generated, or not generated by the implementation. We use a model-checker as the trace-instance-generator (see Section 2.2).

We have designed a testing system based on the four stages above, and built portions of it. We discuss it in Section 2.2. We have used it to apply the above methodology to two real-world systems. One, which we call the $\mathcal{D}$ System, comprises components of the authorization system built into a commercial database system. The other comprises portions of the authorization system that underlies a commercial system for controlled file sharing that we call the $\mathcal{I}$ System. We have been in communication with the vendors of both systems, and both have requested us to use pseudonyms for their systems.

In the $\mathcal{D}$ System, we have discovered flaws in the authorization system related to procedures that aggregate SQL statements, and make calls to other procedures. To our knowledge, these have not been presented before in the literature. We have discussed our findings with the vendor, and discuss their response in Section 3.5.

The kinds of issues we identify are very different from well-known SQL injection and buffer overflow vulnerablities that have plagued database systems [3, 8]. We discuss the properties and our findings in Section 3.4.

For the $\mathcal{I}$ System, we have verified that it has several properties. The vendor has confirmed that the establishment of these properties is indeed of interest to them, and consistent with their intended design. The kinds of properties we discuss for the systems are qualitatively different. We choose to present these properties in this paper to demonstrate that a good range of properties of interest can be tested for.

Layout The remainder of this paper is organized as follows. In the next section, we discuss our methodology and the system we have designed based on it in more detail. In Section 3, we discuss our application to the $\mathcal{D}$ System. In Section 4, we discuss our application to the $\mathcal{I}$ System. We discuss related work in Section 5 and conclude with Section 6.

2. MORE DETAILS ON THE TESTING METHODOLOGY

In this section, we discuss our methodology in more detail, and also discuss the testing system we have put together based on it. The first stage in our methodology is to articulate properties. Our choice of syntax is existential second-order temporal logic [9].

Authorization system To articulate properties of interest, we first need an abstraction for an authorization system. We discuss the basic elements of such an abstraction here. Particular systems may extend these, as we need in the $\mathcal{D}$ System (Section 3). As is customary in temporal logic, the system progresses in what are called *time steps*. A system is as follows.

- Time progresses only as a consequence of actions.

- In a time step, exactly one action occurs.

- There are two possible actions:

  - "x is directly authorized to y" and,

  - "x is directly unauthorized from y".

[‡]We recognize that "temporal" is redundant once we specify "existential second-order." We include that term to emphasize that some of the properties we consider have temporal aspects.

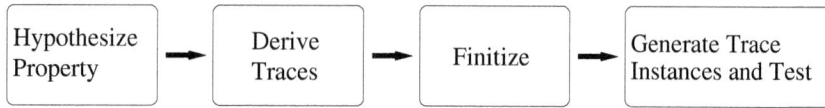

Figure 1: The four stages in our testing methodology.

Operator	Read as	Explanation
X	Next	(X p) means that formula p will hold in the next state.
F	Eventually	(F p) means that formula p will eventually hold in the future.

Table 1: Temporal operators that we use.

- With each action, we associate a predicate. We call such predicates *action-predicates*. We have the following two kinds of action-predicates that correspond to the above two kinds of actions, respectively.

  – Authorization action: $\mathsf{dAuth}(x, y)$

  – Unauthorization action: $\mathsf{dUnauth}(x, y)$

The argument x is the entity being authorized or unauthorized, and y is the entity to which it is authorized or from which it is unauthorized. A direct authorization of x to y may be, for example, a group x being authorized to a file y, or a principal x being added to the group y.

It may seem surprising that we consider only an authorization action, and do not qualify it as, for example, an authorization to read or write. For the properties we consider, it turns out that this suffices. As we mention earlier, we can extend our basic abstraction if necessary.

- An action predicate is true in a particular time step if the particular action is effected in that time step. Consequently, we adopt the following rule with regards to the above predicates. We use "→" for implication and "¬" for negation.

  $$\mathsf{dAuth}(x, y) \longleftrightarrow \neg \mathsf{dUnauth}(x, y)$$

- In addition to action predicates, we have the following *non-action predicate*: $\mathsf{auth}(x, y)$, which indicates that x is authorized to y.

Semantics We endow a semantics to auth, dAuth and $\mathsf{dUnauth}$ by specifying a model [9]. We omit the details here and use a somewhat informal notation. To indicate that an authorization of x to y is part of the authorization state, we simply write $\mathsf{auth}(x, y)$; we write $\neg \mathsf{auth}(x, y)$ to indicate that it is not. Whether x and y are abstract arguments or concrete values is clear from context (e.g. x is a group of users and y is a file). A state-change is associated with a predicate dAuth or $\mathsf{dUnauth}$ that becomes true as a consequence of the action. To denote a state-change on x to y, we simply write $\mathsf{dAuth}(x, y)$ or $\mathsf{dUnauth}(x, y)$ respectively.

Authorization state An authorization state is a family of sets, one for each predicate p. The set that corresponds to a particular predicate p contains those tuples $\langle x_1, \ldots, x_k \rangle$ for which $p(x_1, \ldots, x_k)$ is true, where we assume that p's arity is k. For example, in an authorization system that has the $\mathsf{auth}, \mathsf{dAuth}$ and $\mathsf{dUnauth}$ pred-

icates only, a state is a collection of $\mathsf{auth}(x, y)$, $\mathsf{dAuth}(x, y)$ and $\mathsf{dUnauth}(x, y)$ that are true.

Properties and Traces A property is a formula that is specified in existential second-order temporal logic using the predicates we mention above. The temporal operators we use for the properties we consider in this work are shown in Table 1. A property is typically an implication of the form "$F_1 \rightarrow F_2$," where F_1, F_2 are formulas, and F_2 is typically an assertion regarding the auth predicate. We defer a discussion on specific properties to Sections 3 and 4 in which we discuss our two applications.

As we discuss in Section 1, we need traces as procedural specifications that relate declarative properties to the system under test. A trace is a three tuple: a start authorization state, a sequence of state changes, and a final authorization state. A trace may be parameterized. For example, we may use a parameter for a user or group that is authorized to a resource in the specification of a trace. In our third stage, we concretize traces to what we call instances of traces. In theory, a parameter could take on one of infinitely many values, and therefore there may be an infinite number of trace instances that we may associate with a trace. We finitize the trace instances that we need to consider by making assumptions about the real system.

2.1 Relationship to Model-Checking

We can perceive testing as a verification problem. The question then is whether we can place an upper-bound on the computational complexity of the problem. We point out that for the logic we adopt, verification of a property is undecidable in general. However, under assumptions that we argue are realistic for the kind of testing we do, this is not the case, as the following theorem asserts.

Theorem 1. *Let an authorization system and a property of interest be expressed using at most p predicates, each of at most constant arity, a. Also let n be the number of entities (user, groups, resources, etc.) that can exist in an authorization system. Then, whether the system has the property is decidable in **PSPACE**.*

All the assumptions in the statement of the above theorem can be thought of as finitizing assumptions. The proof of the theorem relies on the observation that to maintain the truth value of each predicate for each tuple of entities, we need $O(n^a)$ bits, because each predicate has arity at most a[§]. Therefore, each authorization state can be encoded with $O(pn^a)$ bits, which is polynomial in the size of the input, given the assumption that a is a constant.

The above theorem tells us that we can reduce our testing problem under the assumptions stated in the theorem to model-checking

---

[§]We use $O(\cdot)$ as is customary in computing: $f(x) = O(g(x))$ means that $g(x)$ is an asymptotic upper-bound for $f(x)$ [7].

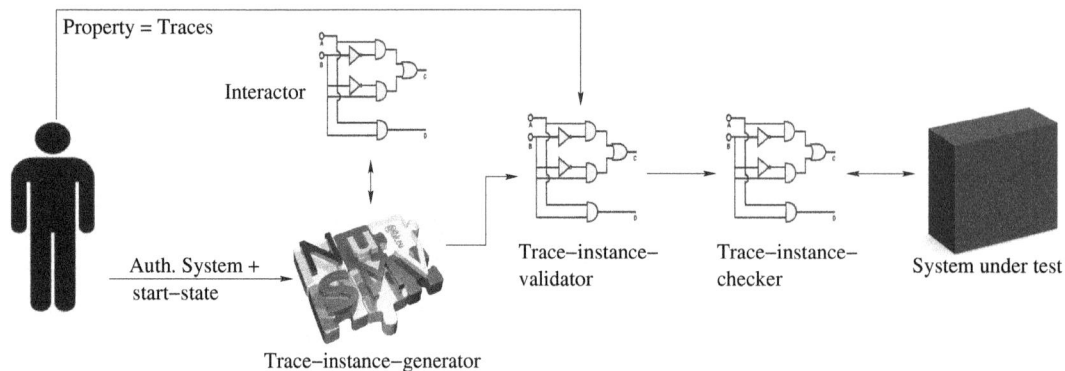

Figure 2: Our testing system. The "interactor," "trace-instance-validator," and "trace-instance-checker" are automata (programs or humans). In our current implementation, the interactor and the trace-instance-validator are human-driven. We discuss the components in Section 2.2.

[6]. Indeed, our testing methodology can be seen as model-checking under those assumptions. We point out that we use a model-checker as part of our process, but in a somewhat non-standard way, as a trace-generator. We discuss this in the next section on our testing system.

2.2 A Testing System

We have designed a testing system based on the methodology we discuss in Section 1 and above. We show it in Figure 2 and discuss it in this section. Our implementation of it is not complete; however, we have implemented it sufficiently for us to carry out the applications we discuss in the next two sections.

As the figure indicates, a human user specifies the authorization system and a start-state for it. She specifies also the property of interest. The property of interest is specified as a set of traces that are sufficient and necessary for the property to hold. We derive these for particular properties for our applications in Sections 3 and 4. We use a model-checker, specifically NuSMV [1], as a generator of trace-instances. The input to NuSMV is a model (a "program," in NuSMV parlance), which encodes the authorization system and a start-state for it. The finitization assumptions are built into the model we input to NuSMV.

We then ask NuSMV to generate trace-instances for that model ("simulate," in NuSMV parlance). We do this in what NuSMV calls "interactive mode." The interactive mode guarantees that every possible trace-instance is generated. As its name suggests, its intent is for a human user to interact with NuSMV as the trace-instances are generated. This part is realized in what we call the Interactor in Figure 2.

One may wonder why we do not provide the property of interest also as input to NuSMV. The reason is that we want to exercise every trace-instance that pertains to the property against the system under test. NuSMV can only tell us whether the (abstract) model we provide it satisfies the property.

Each trace-instance generated by NuSMV is then validated against the traces that correspond to the property by the Trace-instance-validator in Figure 2. That is, we check whether a particular trace-instance that NuSMV generates is indeed an instance of a trace that pertains to the property. We then check whether each validated trace-instance is generated by the system under test. This is done by the Trace-instance-checker.

We have not yet fully automated the entire process in Figure 2. In particular, interaction with NuSMV and the validation done by the

trace-instance-validator are performed by humans. We recognize that without fully automating the entire process, our testing system cannot scale. However, even with the current level of automation, we have been able to apply our system meaningfully (Sections 3 and 4).

The Trace-instance-checker exercises a trace on the system under test in one of two ways. For the $\mathcal{D}$ System, we can exercise a trace either programmatically, via an Application Programmer Interface (API), or by simulating the keystrokes and mouse-clicks of a human user. For the $\mathcal{I}$ System, the only interface we have been provided is the latter. To simulate a human user, we use the Robot class in Java.

3. APPLICATION 1: THE $\mathcal{D}$ System

In this section, we discuss our application of our testing methodology to the system that we call the $\mathcal{D}$ System. The $\mathcal{D}$ System comprises components of the authorization system contained within a commercial database system. The components of the authorization system with which we deal are discretionary permissions to database tables, and permissions to procedures.

The Structured Query Language (SQL) is a command-line syntax for querying and manipulating relational database tables. An example of a SQL command is "select * from book_table where price > 100." This is the equivalent of exercising a read permission on particular entries in the table called book_table.

A procedure may be used to aggregate multiple SQL statements. For example, a user Alice may create a procedure that takes as argument a new entry for a table, first checks some condition on existing entries in the table, and inserts the new entry only if the condition is met. A procedure may also invoke other procedures. In these aspects, procedures are like executable programs.

Authorization Every table is associated with an owner. Customarily, the owner is the user that creates the table. The owner may then, at her discretion, grant permissions over the table to other users. In Figure 3, for example, a user Alice grants Bob the right to insert entries into the table t that she owns.

Similarly, every procedure is associated with a definer, who is its creating user. That user may then give other users the permission to execute that procedure. In Figure 3, for example, Bob grants Carl the right to execute Bob's procedure def, and Carl grants Dan the right to execute Carl's procedure inv.

228

```
Alice: grant insert on table t to Bob          Carl: procedure inv(x), invoker's rights
                                                        invoke Bob's procedure def(x)
Bob:    procedure def(x), definer's rights
            insert x into Alice's table t             grant execute on procedure inv to Dan

        grant execute on procedure def to Carl   Dan:  invoke Carl's procedure inv(23)
```

Figure 3: An example with four users in the $\mathcal{D}$ System, Alice, Bob, Carl and Dan. Alice owns the table t, and grants insert privilege over it to Bob. Bob defines the procedure def to be definer's rights and grants Carl execute privilege to it. The procedure def inserts a row into Alice's table. Carl creates an invoker's rights procedure inv and grants Dan execute privilege to it. The procedure inv invokes Bob's procedure def. Finally, Dan attempts to execute Carl's procedure inv.

A procedure may be annotated to run with invoker's rights or definer's rights. As one may expect, when a procedure is invoked, an invoker's rights procedure runs with the privileges of the invoker of the procedure, and a definer's rights procedure runs with the privileges of the definer. For example, in Figure 3, Bob's procedure def is specified to be definer's rights. (It is annotated as neither definer's nor invoker's rights; the former is the default.) So, if Carl were to invoke Bob.def, the "insert into alice.t..." statement within it should run with the privileges of Bob.

The $\mathcal{D}$ authorization system We refer to the subsystem within the database system that comprises discretionary permissions to tables, and permissions to procedures as the $\mathcal{D}$ System. In particular, we focus on the co-existence of the two. We focus on nested procedures — procedures that invoke other procedures, that ultimately issue a SQL statement. Figure 3 is an example — inv invokes def, which in turn issues a SQL statement.

Specifically, we constrain the $\mathcal{D}$ System as follows. We have m procedures $p_1, \ldots, p_m$. Each p_i is owned by a user u_i where $u_i \neq u_j$ for any $i \neq j$. For $i > 1$, the procedure p_i invokes the procedure p_{i-1} only. Only one table exists in the $\mathcal{D}$ System, which we denote as p_0. We consider only one kind of privilege to the table p_0 in the $\mathcal{D}$ System, the privilege to insert into it. The procedure p_1 attempts to exercise the insert privilege to p_0. The table p_0 is owned by a user u_0. We also have a user u_{m+1} that owns no procedure. The properties we care about address whether the user u_{m+1} can exercise the insert privilege over the table p_0 via the procedures $p_m, \ldots, p_1$.

An example of the $\mathcal{D}$ System is the system shown in Figure 3. In the figure, u_0 is Alice, u_1 is Bob, u_2 is Carl and u_3 is Dan. The table t is p_0, the procedure def is p_1, and inv is p_2. We seek to know whether Dan can exercise the insert privilege over the table Alice.t by executing Carl.inv.

The $\mathcal{D}$ System in our syntax We adopt the predicates auth, dAuth and dUnauth as we discuss in Section 2. Each is 2-ary. We discuss their semantics in the $\mathcal{D}$ System below.

We adopt a predicate $\mathsf{def}(p)$ to indicate whether a procedure p is definer's rights. We adopt also a function $\mathsf{eff}(p)$ that outputs the effective user of p and is defined inductively using the def predicate as follows:

$$\mathsf{def}(p_i) \rightarrow \mathsf{eff}(p_i) = u_i \quad \text{for all } i$$
$$\neg\mathsf{def}(p_i) \rightarrow \mathsf{eff}(p_i) = \mathsf{eff}(p_{i+1}) \quad \text{for all } i < m$$
$$\neg\mathsf{def}(p_m) \rightarrow \mathsf{eff}(p_m) = u_{m+1}$$

Unix Our above rules for defining the eff function in the $\mathcal{D}$ System come from Unix systems. We observe the similarity between executing procedures in the $\mathcal{D}$ System, and executing programs in Unix systems.

In Unix systems, a program typically runs with invoker's rights. However, it is possible to use the setuid bit [5] to cause a program to run with definer's rights. Given this similarity and the somewhat long history of the setuid bit, we adopt the way Unix systems handle indirect authorization via running programs as correct.

Our definition of the eff function above captures the manner in which Unix systems define what they call the effective user in a program that is running. If a program does not have the setuid bit set, then the effective user is the invoker; otherwise, it is the definer. (Of course, we do not consider programs that change the effective user within themselves, as those scenarios are not pertinent to the $\mathcal{D}$ System.)

Semantics of auth and dAuth The predicate $\mathsf{dAuth}(x, y)$ has to do with whether x is directly authorized to y. In the $\mathcal{D}$ System, $\mathsf{dAuth}(x, y)$ becomes true if we issue the SQL command to (directly) authorize x to y. For example, in Figure 3, after Alice issues the grant command, for $u_1 =$ Bob and p_0 the table, $\mathsf{dAuth}(u_1, p_0)$ is true. In the start-state, $\neg\mathsf{dAuth}(x, y)$ for all x, y.

As we mention above, our properties of interest deal with whether u_{m+1} can acquire the privilege to p_0 via his authorization to p_m. Consequently, the semantics of $\mathsf{auth}(u_i, p_j)$ is whether u_i has access to p_j via his right to execute p_{i-1}, in the case that $i > 1$. Of course, if $j \geq i$, then $\neg\mathsf{auth}(u_i, p_j)$ in all states. If $i = 1$, then $\mathsf{auth}(u_1, p_0) = \mathsf{dAuth}(u_1, p_0)$.

In the testing system that we discuss in Section 2.2 and show in Figure 2, these semantics translate to the following for the trace-instance-checker. The truth-value of $\mathsf{dAuth}(x, y)$ and $\mathsf{dUnauth}(x, y)$ is assumed based on the commands we issue. We ascertain the truth value of $\mathsf{auth}(u_i, p_j)$ in a state by checking whether u_i is able to successfully execute p_j via p_{i-1}.

3.1 Properties of interest

We now articulate the three properties we consider for the $\mathcal{D}$ System. We call them necessity, security and temporal consistency.

Necessity With the necessity property, we intuitively seek to answer the following question: is there a situation that a user is required to have more privileges than should be necessary to gain access? If yes, then we say that the system does not possess the necessity property; otherwise we say it does. The opposite of necessity is redundancy — that the system requires more privileges than should be necessary.

What we mean by "more" privileges in this context comes from the scenario that corresponds to the $\mathcal{D}$ System in Unix, as we discuss in the previous paragraph.

DEFINITION 1 (NECESSITY). *the $\mathcal{D}$ System has the Necessity property if and only if the following is true for all u_i, p_j, $0 \leq j < i$ in all states of the system.*

229

$$(\mathsf{dAuth}(u_i, p_{i-1}) \wedge_{k=j+1}^{i-1} \mathsf{dAuth}(\mathsf{eff}(p_k), p_{k-1})) \rightarrow$$
$$\mathsf{auth}(u_i, p_j)$$

To explain the above property, it may be easier to consider its contrapositive. What it says if is if u_i is not authorized to p_j, then u_i is not directly authorized to p_{i-1}, or for some k, the effective user of p_k is not authorized to p_{k-1}. As we mention above, this comes directly from the notion of effective user in the context of Unix programs. For u_i to be authorized to p_j via the "chain" of programs $p_{i-1}, \ldots, p_{j+1}$, the effective user for each of those programs must be authorized to the program at the next level. We recall from the previous section that the only thing p_k does is attempt to exercise the privilege over p_{k-1}.

Security The security property asks whether there is a situation in which a user is able to gain access with too few privileges.

DEFINITION 2 (SECURITY). *The $\mathcal{D}$ System has the security property if and only if the following is true for all u_i, p_j, $0 \leq j < i$ in all states of the system.*

$$\mathsf{auth}(u_i, p_j) \rightarrow (\mathsf{dAuth}(u_i, p_{i-1})$$
$$\wedge_{k=j+1}^{i-1} \mathsf{dAuth}(\mathsf{eff}(p_k), p_{k-1}))$$

The security property can be seen as the complement of the necessity property. It states that if u_i is authorized to p_j, then u_i must be authorized to p_{i-1}, and for every p_k, the effective user for p_k must be authorized to p_{k-1}.

Temporal Consistency Temporal consistency captures the following intuition. Suppose, at a given time, a certain set of privileges is necessary and sufficient to gain some access. Then, at any time in future, that set should be exactly the set of privileges needed to gain the same access. We expect the $\mathcal{D}$ System to have temporal consistency — the set of privileges to gain access should not change over time.

DEFINITION 3 (TEMPORAL CONSISTENCY). *The $\mathcal{D}$ System has the temporal consistency property if and only if the following is true for all u_i, p_j, p_l, $0 \leq j < l < i$ in all states of the system.*

$$(\mathsf{auth}(u_i, p_j) \wedge \mathsf{dAuth}(\mathsf{eff}(p_l), p_l))$$
$$\rightarrow \mathsf{X}(\mathsf{dUnauth}(\mathsf{eff}(p_l), p_l)$$
$$\rightarrow \mathsf{X}(\mathsf{dAuth}(\mathsf{eff}(p_l), p_l) \rightarrow \mathsf{auth}(u_i, p_j)))$$

3.2 Traces

We now discuss the traces that are necessary and sufficient to verify the properties from the previous section. As we mention in Section 1, properties are declarative assertions and it is not possible to show that a system has or does not have a property directly. To relate properties and systems, we introduce the notion of a trace. A trace is an imperative (or procedural) specification of states that an authorization system can reach or cannot reach.

DEFINITION 4 (TRACE). *A trace is a tuple $\langle s_{init}, t, s_{fin} \rangle$, where s_{init} is an initial authorization state, t is a sequence of state-changes, and s_{fin} is a final authorization state.*

As notation, we write "$\mathsf{auth}(a, b)$ in the state s" to indicate an authorization, and "$\neg\mathsf{auth}(a, b)$ in ..." to indicate a lack of authorization. For the state-changes, we know that each causes a dAuth or $\mathsf{dUnauth}$ to become true. Therefore, we represent a sequence of state changes with those predicates. For example, the sequence $\mathsf{dAuth}(a, b), \mathsf{dUnauth}(b, c)$ indicates that a is first authorized to b, and then, b is unauthorized from c.

To express traces of interest to us, we make the following syntactic assumptions about any trace. These assumptions pertain to dAuth and $\mathsf{dUnauth}$. As we mention in Section 2, those predicates have to do with whether we issue commands for authorization or unauthorization. Therefore, it is easy to ensure that these assumptions are indeed true — we do not cause the actions that correspond to dAuth and $\mathsf{dUnauth}$ to occur in violation of these assumptions.

One of our assumptions is that we cannot have two instances of $\mathsf{dAuth}(a, b)$ in a sequence of state-changes unless there is a $\mathsf{dUnauth}(a, b)$ somewhere between them. Similarly, we cannot have two instances of $\mathsf{dUnauth}(a, b)$ unless we have a $\mathsf{dAuth}(a, b)$ between them. Another assumption is that an instance $\mathsf{dUnauth}(a, b)$ cannot occur in a sequence when the number of $\mathsf{dAuth}(a, b)$ and $\mathsf{dUnauth}(a, b)$ that occur before is even.

DEFINITION 5 (REDUNDANCY TRACE). *A trace in the $\mathcal{D}$ System is redundant if and only if the entries s_{init}, t and s_{fin} are as follows.*

- *In the initial state s_{init}, for every x, y, $\neg\mathsf{auth}(x, y)$ and $\mathsf{dUnauth}(x, y)$.*

- *Let $t = \langle t_1, \ldots, t_n \rangle$ for $n \geq 1$ and $i, j \geq 0$:*
  - *$\mathsf{dUnauth}(\mathsf{eff}(p_k), p_{k-1}) \rightarrow \mathsf{F}(\mathsf{dAuth}(\mathsf{eff}(p_k), p_{k-1}))$ for $0 \leq j < k < i \leq n$ in t, and,*
  - *$\mathsf{dUnauth}(u_i, p_{i-1}) \rightarrow \mathsf{F}(\mathsf{dAuth}(u_i, p_{i-1}))$ in t.*

- *In the final state s_{fin}, $\neg\mathsf{auth}(u_i, p_j)$.*

The initial state, s_{init} has no authorizations. For the trace t between s_{init} and the final state s_{fin} above, the first condition states that the effective user of p_k is eventually authorized directly to p_{k-1}. The second condition states that u_i is eventually authorized directly to p_{i-1}. The point behind these conditions are clarified in the next section, in which we relate traces to properties.

DEFINITION 6 (INSECURE TRACE). *A trace in the $\mathcal{D}$ System is insecure if and only if The entries s_{init}, t and s_{fin} are as follows.*

- *In the initial state s_{init}, for every x, y, $\neg\mathsf{auth}(x, y)$ and $\mathsf{dUnauth}(x, y)$.*

- *Let $t = \langle t_1, \ldots, t_{n-1}, t_n \rangle$ and $t' = \langle t_1, \ldots, t_{n-1} \rangle$ for $n \geq 1$ and $i, j \geq 0$:*
  - *$\mathsf{dUnauth}(\mathsf{eff}(p_k), p_{k-1}) \rightarrow \mathsf{F}(\mathsf{dAuth}(\mathsf{eff}(p_k), p_{k-1}))$ for $0 \leq j < k < i \leq n$ in t'.*
  - *$\mathsf{dUnauth}(u_i, p_{i-1}) \rightarrow \mathsf{F}(\mathsf{dAuth}(u_i, p_{i-1}))$ in t'.*
  - *Either $t_n = \mathsf{dUnauth}(\mathsf{eff}(p_{k'}), p_{k'-1})$ for some k', $0 \leq j < k' < i$, or $t_n = \mathsf{dUnauth}(u_i, p_j)$.*

- *In the final state s_{fin}, $\mathsf{auth}(u_i, p_i)$.*

DEFINITION 7 (TEMPORALLY INCONSISTENT TRACE). *A trace in the $\mathcal{D}$ System is temporally inconsistent if and only if the entries s_{init}, t and s_{fin} are as follows.*

- *In the initial state s_{init}, for every x, y, $\neg\mathsf{auth}(x, y)$ and $\mathsf{dUnauth}(x, y)$.*

- *Let $t = \langle t_1, \ldots, t_{n-2}, t_{n-1}, t_n \rangle$ and $t' = \langle t_1, \ldots, t_{n-2} \rangle$ for $n \geq 1$ and $i, j \geq 0$:*

- $\mathsf{dUnauth}(\mathsf{eff}(p_k), p_{k-1}) \to \mathsf{F}(dauth(\mathsf{eff}(p_k), p_{k-1}))$ *for $0 \leq j < k < i \leq n$ in t'.*

- $\mathsf{dUnauth}(u_i, p_{i-1}) \to \mathsf{F}(dauth(u_i, p_{i-1}))$ *in t'.*

- $t_{n-1} = \mathsf{dUnauth}(actv(p_l), p_{l-1})$ *for some l, $0 \leq j < l < i$.*

- $t_n = \mathsf{dAuth}(actv(p_l), p_{l-1})$ *for the same l as the previous state change.*

- *In the final state s_{fin}, $\neg\mathsf{auth}(u_i, p_j)$.*

3.3 Relating Properties and Traces

We now relate the properties from Section 3.1 with the traces from the previous section in Theorems 2–4.

Theorem 2 (Necessity). *The $\mathcal{D}$ System has the necessity property if and only if it produces no redundancy trace.*

PROOF. Only if: By contradiction. Assume that the system has the necessity property, but produces a redundancy trace $\langle s_{init}, t, s_{fin} \rangle$. Then we know that, in the final state s_{fin}, $\neg\mathsf{auth}(u_i, p_j)$ from Definition 5. We immediately have a contradiction because we assume that the system has the necessity property, and therefore, the formula from Definition 1 should be true in all states, but it is false in the state s_{fin}.

If: Assume that the system does not have the necessity property. This means that there exists a state in which the formula from Definition 1 is not true. The only way for it to be not true is with $\neg\mathsf{auth}(u_i, p_j)$ and $(\mathsf{dAuth}(u_i, p_{i-1}) \wedge_{k=j+1}^{i-1} \mathsf{dAuth}(\mathsf{eff}(p_k), p_{k-1})$ true. So, the system can produce the following redundancy trace: starting from s_{init}, in which there are no authorizations, we start performing state changes of the form $0 \leq j < k < i$, $\mathsf{dAuth}(\mathsf{eff}(p_k), p_{k-1})$ and $\mathsf{dAuth}(u_i, p_{i-1})$ for a specific i and j. Then we enter the state in which all the predicates related to the exercised state changes are true. From the state in our initial assumption, we know that there exists such a state in the system. So we have a state in which $\mathsf{auth}(u_i, p_j)$ is not true. The produced trace is a redundancy trace. $\square$

Theorem 3 (Security). *The $\mathcal{D}$ System has the security property if and only if it produces no insecure trace.*

PROOF. The proof is straightforward and similar to the proof for the Theorem 2. In the "if" part, we only need to do one more state change in the trace to be sure that at least one of the unauthorization state changes is true. $\square$

Theorem 4 (Temporal consistency). *The $\mathcal{D}$ System has the temporal consistency property if and only if it produces no temporally inconsistent trace.*

PROOF. Only if: By contradiction. Assume that the system has the temporal consistency property, but produces a temporally inconsistent trace $\langle s_{init}, t, s_{fin} \rangle$. Then we know that, in the final state s_{fin}, $\neg\mathsf{auth}(u_i, p_j)$ from Definition 7. We immediately have a contradiction.

If: Assume that the system is not temporally consistent. It means that there exists a state in which the formula from Definition 3 is not true. The only way for it to be false is when $(\mathsf{auth}(u_i, p_j) \wedge \mathsf{dAuth}(\mathsf{eff}(p_l), p_l))$, in the next state $\mathsf{dUnauth}(\mathsf{eff}(p_l), p_l)$ and in the following next state $\neg\mathsf{auth}(u_i, p_j) \wedge \mathsf{dAuth}(\mathsf{eff}(p_l), p_l)$ are true. So there is a trace that can be produced by the system as follows: from the empty state we do state changes to enter the state in which we have $\mathsf{auth}(u_i, p_j) \wedge \mathsf{dAuth}(\mathsf{eff}(p_l), p_l)$. To enter such a state we do the direct authorizations that the necessity property

proposes. If the system does not have the necessity property we do more state changes to give the objects inside the sequence of access of user u_i to procedure p_j to grant access of p_j to u_i indirectly via other procedures inside the sequence. Then we do a sequence of state changes $\mathsf{dUnauth}(u_k, p_l)$, and $\mathsf{dAuth}(u_k, p_l)$. In the following state s_{fin}, $\mathsf{auth}(u_i, p_j)$ is false. The produced trace is a temporally inconsistent trace. $\square$

3.4 Results for the $\mathcal{D}$ system

We have used our testing-system with different values for m (number of procedures and corresponding users) to exercise the $\mathcal{D}$ System with the traces we discuss in the previous section to determine whether it has the necessity, security and temporal consistency properties. We have discovered that the $\mathcal{D}$ System does not have the necessity, security or temporal consistency properties. To our knowledge, these flaws in the $\mathcal{D}$ System have not been presented before in the literature.

The lack of the necessity property means that some extra privileges than what we would consider meaningful are needed before a user has access. The lack of the security property means that with only seemingly insufficient privileges, a user is able to gain access. And the lack of temporal consistency means that the set of privileges that is needed changes over time.

We now present the results for the smallest m for which the $\mathcal{D}$ System displays these problems. This was for $m = 3$. That is, we have five users, $u_0, \ldots, u_4$. We have a table p_0, and three procedures $p_1, \ldots, p_3$. The user u_i owns the procedure/table p_i.

Correctness is specified in our necessity, security and temporal consistency properties in Section 3.1. We have verified that our Linux system has all of these properties. In the Linux system p_0 is a data file that the user u_4 attempts to write to, by invoking the program p_3. The program p_3, in turn, attempts to execute the program p_2 and so on.

We explain one of the cases in detail, and present all the results in Table 2. We summarize our findings after our discussions of the case that we present in detail.

Consider that case that $\mathsf{def}(p_1), \neg\mathsf{def}(p_2), \neg\mathsf{def}(p_3)$. That is, the case that p_1 is definer's rights, and p_2 and p_3 are invoker's rights. Correct authorizations are shown in the following table.

	Correct			
	p_0	p_1	p_2	p_3
u_0	0	0	0	0
u_1	1	0	0	0
u_2	0	0	0	0
u_3	0	0	0	0
u_4	0	1	1	1

The above table expresses the authorizations for the necessity and security properties to hold. What we require for this case is that u_4 is authorized to p_1, p_2 and p_3, and u_1 is authorized to p_0. To intuit why this makes sense, consider the following.

The procedure p_3 requires u_4 to have execute privilege over it. As it is invoker's rights, when p_3 invokes p_2 within it, the effective user is u_4. The procedure p_2 is also invoker's rights. Therefore, the effective user is still u_4, and u_4 needs have the execute privilege to p_1. Finally, p_1 is definer's rights. Therefore, the effective user is its definer, u_1, who needs to have the insert privilege to p_0.

The $\mathcal{D}$ System's table differs from the above. At the time that the procedures are defined, the following is the table for the $\mathcal{D}$ System. We associate it with the subscript 1 to indicate that this is at the time that the procedures are defined.

$\mathcal{D}_1$				
	p_0	p_1	p_2	p_3
u_0	0	0	0	0
u_1	1	0	0	0
u_2	0	1	0	0
u_3	0	0	1	0
u_4	0	0	0	1

The above table demonstrates that for this case, the $\mathcal{D}$ System does not satisfy the security or necessity properties. For the security property to be satisfied, we require a 1 to appear in the same cells as the Correct table above. The fact that u_4 is not required to have the execute privilege over p_2 is an example of something that causes the security property to be violated.

For the necessity property to be satisfied, we require no 1's to appear where there is a 0 in the corresponding cell in the Correct table. The fact that u_3 is required to have execute privilege to p_2 is an example of something that causes the necessity property to be violated.

Once the procedures have been defined, it turns out that u_4 is authorized to p_0 (via $p_3, \ldots, p_1$) even if some rights are revoked, as indicated by the following table. This demonstrates its lack of the security property as we have only three 1's, as opposed to four in the Correct table above. We associate this table with the subscript 2 to indicate that this is some time-period after the procedures are defined.

$\mathcal{D}_2$				
	p_0	p_1	p_2	p_3
u_0	0	0	0	0
u_1	1	0	0	0
u_2	0	0	0	0
u_3	0	0	1	0
u_4	0	0	0	1

3.5 Summary of results

Table 2 demonstrates that co-existence of procedure authorizations and discretionary authorizations to tables are flawed in the $\mathcal{D}$ System. In only one case does $\mathcal{D}_1$ (the $\mathcal{D}$ System at the time of defining the procedures) match the Correct table — this is when all three of p_1, p_2 and p_3 are definer's rights. However, even for this case, we have a temporal consistency problem, as we are able to revoke u_2's authorization to execute p_1 once the procedures have been defined, and still, u_4 is able to exercise the insert privilege over the table p_0 via the procedure p_3.

In one other case, specifically $\neg\mathsf{def}(p_1), \mathsf{def}(p_2), \mathsf{def}(p_3)$, $\mathcal{D}_1$ does not have a security problem. However, it has a necessity problem: the user u_1 is redundantly required to have the insert privilege to p_0. In this case as well, we have a temporal consistency problem. Furthermore, $\mathcal{D}_2$ in this case has a security issue — two of the privileges can be revoked after defining the procedures, and u_4 still has access.

Vendor's response We have communicated our findings to the vendor of the $\mathcal{D}$ System, and helped them reproduce these issues. Their response is the following. They acknowledge all three of the security, redundancy and temporal-inconsistency issues. For the first two issues (security and redundancy), they clarified to us that these exist by design.

That is, the default privilege mode when one invokes a procedure p_2 from within a procedure p_1 is for p_2 to run with definer's rights, immaterial of whether p_1 is defined to run with invoker's or definer's rights. They have a different (and somewhat less natural)

syntax by which a programmer can cause p_2 to run with invoker's rights instead. To us, this default choice suggests poor design; however, that is a subjective assessment on our part.

As for temporal-inconsistency, the vendor has acknowledged that this is a bug in their implementation. They are working on what they call a critical patch, and requested that we not publish this paper till their customers have had a chance to apply that patch. They like to give their customers up to 1 year to apply the patch. Instead, we offered to use a pseudonym to refer to their system and abstract some syntactic details so we could go ahead and publish now, but still be sensitive to any security implications to their customers. They tell us that we will be credited when their patch is released.

4. APPLICATION 2: THE $\mathcal{I}$ System

Our other application has been to a commercial file-sharing system that we call the $\mathcal{I}$ System. The properties that we discuss for the $\mathcal{I}$ System are somewhat different than for the $\mathcal{D}$ System. The reason is that the $\mathcal{I}$ System's features that we seek to exercise are different from those of the $\mathcal{D}$ System. For example, the $\mathcal{I}$ System does not have the equivalent of procedures.

The $\mathcal{I}$ System In the $\mathcal{I}$ System, a resource is a file. Authorization is discretionary — there is the notion of users, who own files. The owner of a file may grant access to the resource to other users. Such users must first be designated as what are called contacts of the owner. A user may create groups and add contacts to groups.

There is only one kind of access, which is called sharing. A user may authorize either a contact or a group access to a particular file he owns. The software provides two interfaces to a user for authorization management. We show redacted screen-shots of each in Figures 4 and 5 in Appendix A.

If an owner authorizes a user u to a group or file x and the interface says that that is successful, then we assume that u is authorized to x. For indirect authorizations, we can check whether a user in question indeed has an access, or does not have access with a file-access test outside of the $\mathcal{I}$ system.

We are able to model the $\mathcal{I}$ System in our syntax using only the 2-ary predicates auth, dAuth and dUnauth. There is only one kind of authorization in the $\mathcal{I}$ System, which is to share a file.

4.1 Properties of interest

We defined six properties for the $\mathcal{I}$ System: necessity, security, forward availability, backward availability, forward safety and backward safety. We define these below. The first two, necessity and security, are somewhat simpler versions compared to those for the $\mathcal{D}$ System.

DEFINITION 8 (NECESSITY). *$\mathcal{I}$ System has the necessity property if and only if the following is true for all a, b in all states of the system.*

$$\mathsf{dAuth}(a, b) \longrightarrow \mathsf{auth}(a, b)$$

The property defined in Definition 8 expresses that if a is directly authorized to b, then it is authorized to b.

DEFINITION 9 (SECURITY). *$\mathcal{I}$ System has the security property if and only if the following is true for all a, b in all states of the system.*

$$(\mathsf{dUnauth}(a, b) \wedge \neg(\exists l \geq 1, x_1, \ldots, x_l. \mathsf{dAuth}(a, x_1)$$
$$\wedge \mathsf{dAuth}(x_1, x_2) \wedge \ldots \mathsf{dAuth}(x_l, b))) \longrightarrow \neg\mathsf{auth}(a, b)$$

232

def(p_1), ¬def(p_2), ¬def(p_3)			def(p_1), ¬def(p_2), def(p_3)		
Correct	$\mathcal{D}_1$	$\mathcal{D}_2$	Correct	$\mathcal{D}_1$	$\mathcal{D}_2$
0 0 0 0	0 0 0 0	0 0 0 0	0 0 0 0	0 0 0 0	0 0 0 0
1 0 0 0	1 0 0 0	1 0 0 0	1 0 0 0	1 0 0 0	1 0 0 0
0 0 0 0	0 1 0 0	0 0 0 0	0 0 0 0	0 1 0 0	0 0 0 0
0 0 0 0	0 0 1 0	0 0 1 0	0 1 1 0	0 0 1 0	0 0 1 0
0 1 1 1	0 0 0 1	0 0 0 1	0 0 0 1	0 0 0 1	0 0 0 1
def(p_1), def(p_2), ¬def(p_3)			def(p_1), def(p_2), def(p_3)		
0 0 0 0	0 0 0 0	0 0 0 0	0 0 0 0	0 0 0 0	0 0 0 0
1 0 0 0	1 0 0 0	1 0 0 0	1 0 0 0	1 0 0 0	1 0 0 0
0 1 0 0	0 1 0 0	0 0 0 0	0 1 0 0	0 1 0 0	0 0 0 0
0 0 0 0	0 0 1 0	0 0 1 0	0 0 1 0	0 0 1 0	0 0 1 0
0 0 1 1	0 0 0 1	0 0 0 1	0 0 0 1	0 0 0 1	0 0 0 1
¬def(p_1), ¬def(p_2), def(p_3)			¬def(p_1), ¬def(p_2), ¬def(p_3)		
0 0 0 0	0 0 0 0	0 0 0 0	0 0 0 0	0 0 0 0	0 0 0 0
0 0 0 0	1 0 0 0	0 0 0 0	0 0 0 0	1 0 0 0	0 0 0 0
0 0 0 0	0 1 0 0	0 0 0 0	0 0 0 0	0 1 0 0	0 0 0 0
1 1 1 0	1 0 1 0	1 0 1 0	0 0 0 0	0 0 1 0	0 0 1 0
0 0 0 1	0 0 0 1	0 0 0 1	1 1 1 1	1 0 0 1	1 0 0 1
¬def(p_1), def(p_2), ¬def(p_3)			¬def(p_1), def(p_2), def(p_3)		
0 0 0 0	0 0 0 0	0 0 0 0	0 0 0 0	0 0 0 0	0 0 0 0
0 0 0 0	1 0 0 0	0 0 0 0	0 0 0 0	1 0 0 0	0 0 0 0
1 1 0 0	1 1 0 0	1 0 0 0	1 1 0 0	1 1 0 0	1 0 0 0
0 0 0 0	0 0 1 0	0 0 1 0	0 0 1 0	0 0 1 0	0 0 1 0
0 0 1 1	0 0 0 1	0 0 0 1	0 0 0 1	0 0 0 1	0 0 0 1

Table 2: Our complete results for our tests for the $\mathcal{D}$ System with $m = 3$. For each case (e.g., def(p_1), def(p_2), ¬def(p_3)), we have five rows that correspond to the rights of the users $u_0, \ldots, u_4$, respectively. We have four columns, that correspond to the table p_0, and procedures $p_1, \ldots, p_3$. A "1" indicates that that user needs to have the privilege to that procedure/table so the necessity and security properties are satisfied. $\mathcal{D}_1$ corresponds to the system immediately after we create all the procedures, and $\mathcal{D}_2$ corresponds to the system at a later time, after we perform some actions on it.

The property defined in Definition 9 expresses that if a is directly unauthorized from b, and there is no "chain" of direct authorizations from a to b, then a is not authorized to b.

With the following forward-availability property, we seek to capture what is customarily seen as a natural semantics for authorization via groups and roles. When a has access to b, and in future b has access to c, then a has access to c.

DEFINITION 10 (FORWARD AVAILABILITY). $\mathcal{I}$ *System is forward available if and only if, for all a, b, c.*

$$(\mathsf{auth}(a,b) \wedge \neg\mathsf{auth}(b,c)) \rightarrow \mathsf{X}(\mathsf{auth}(b,c) \rightarrow \mathsf{auth}(a,c))$$

An intuition behind forward availability above is provided by the example of a user u being authorized to a resource r via membership in a group g. We require that u must be a member of g before g is authorized to r for u to be authorized to r. With backward availability, we change the order of the two direct authorizations from that example. That is, for u to be authorized to r, we require that g be authorized to r before u is authorized to g.

DEFINITION 11 (BACKWARD AVAILABILITY). $\mathcal{I}$ *System has the backward availability property if and only if the following is true for all a, b, c.*

$$(\mathsf{auth}(b,c) \wedge \neg\mathsf{auth}(a,b)) \rightarrow \mathsf{X}(\mathsf{auth}(a,b) \rightarrow \mathsf{auth}(a,c))$$

A system may have one or both of the forward and backward availability properties, or neither. In our example from above of u being authorized to f via g, a system has both properties when the

ordering of the two direct authorizations does not matter. This is the case, for example, for groups in Unix systems. In other systems such as secure multicast [11], forward availability is desirable, but not backward availability.

The above availability properties are two example properties where we want authorization to hold. With forward and backward safety, we have two example properties where we want authorization to not hold.

With forward safety below we express that unless a is already authorized to c, authorizing b to c after a is authorized to b does not grant a authorization to c. From the standpoint of intuitive appeal, we see forward safety as the natural counterpart of forward availability. That is, simply because b is now authorized to c should not give a authorization to c via b. To us, this captures the notion of the "leakage" of a privilege that was originally proposed by Harrison et al. [16].

DEFINITION 12 (FORWARD SAFETY). $\mathcal{I}$ *System has the forward safety property if and only if the following is true for all a, b, c.*

$$(\mathsf{auth}(a,b) \wedge \neg\mathsf{auth}(b,c) \wedge \neg\mathsf{auth}(a,c))$$
$$\rightarrow \mathsf{X}(\mathsf{auth}(b,c) \rightarrow \neg\mathsf{auth}(a,c))$$

The following backward-safety property is the safety counterpart of backward availability. The difference from forward safety is the temporal ordering of the authorizations of a to b, and b to c.

DEFINITION 13 (BACKWARD SAFETY). $\mathcal{I}$ *System has the backward safety property if and only if the following is true for* *all a, b, c.*

$$(\mathsf{auth}(b,c) \land \neg\mathsf{auth}(a,b) \land \neg\mathsf{auth}(a,c))$$
$$\rightarrow \mathsf{X}(\mathsf{auth}(a,b) \rightarrow \neg\mathsf{auth}(a,c))$$

Relationship between properties A natural question that arises is whether one of the recent four properties is related to another even before we consider them in the context of a given authorization system. And indeed, we have the following relationships between availability and safety that we fully expect. In the following, a "non-empty system" means a system in which we can create some entity that can take the place of a, b and c in Definitions 10–13.

Theorem 5. *If a non-empty system is forward available, then it is not forward safe. If a non-empty system is backward available, then it is not backward safe.*

It is easy to prove the above theorem. To show the first assertion, for example, we pick an a, b, c and a state such that in that state the left-hand side of the formula in Definition 10 is true and the formula is satisfied. This choice now serves as a counterexample to Definition 12. The contrapositives of the two assertions in the theorem may also be of interest. That is, a forward (backward) safe system is not forward (backward) available. We point out also that these assertions are not "if and only if" – a system may be neither forward (backward) available nor forward (backward) safe.

4.2 Traces

We now define traces that correspond to properties in the previous section. Recall the definition for a trace from Section 3.2.

DEFINITION 14 (REDUNDANCY TRACE). *A trace in the $\mathcal{I}$ System is redundant if and only if the entries s_{init}, t and s_{fin} are as follows.*

- *In the initial state s_{init}, for every x, y, $\neg\mathsf{auth}(x,y)$ and $\mathsf{dUnauth}(x,y)$.*

- *Let $t = \langle t_1, \ldots, t_n \rangle$ for $n \geq 1$:*

    - $\mathsf{dAuth}(a,b) \rightarrow \mathsf{F}(dunauth(a,b))$
    - $t_n = \mathsf{dAuth}(a,b)$.

- *In the final state s_{fin}, $\neg\mathsf{auth}(a,b)$.*

DEFINITION 15 (INSECURE TRACE). *A trace in $\mathcal{I}$ System is insecure if and only if the entries s_{init}, t and s_{fin} are as follows.*

- *In the initial state s_{init}, for every x, y, $\neg\mathsf{auth}(x,y)$ and $\mathsf{dUnauth}(x,y)$.*

- *Let $t = \langle t_1, \ldots, t_n \rangle$ for $n \geq 1$:*

    - *Pick a set $\{x_1, \ldots, x_k\}$ for some $k > 1$.*
    - $\mathsf{dUnauth}(x_i, x_{i+1}) \rightarrow \mathsf{F}(dauth(x_i, x_{i+1}))$ *for $1 \leq i < k$ in t*
    - $t_n = \mathsf{dUnauth}(x_j, x_{j+1})$ *for a j, $1 \leq j < k$.*

- *In the final state s_{fin}, $\mathsf{auth}(x_1, x_k)$.*

We use the forward availability property from definition 10 for the following definition of a forward available trace. We denote that except necessity and security properties, other properties only concern the non action predicate. To check these properties using traces we need to assume that the system has necessity property. fortunately $\mathcal{I}$ System has the necessity property.

DEFINITION 16 (FORWARD AVAILABLE TRACE). *A trace in $\mathcal{I}$ System is forward available if and only if the entries s_{init}, t and s_{fin} are as follows.*

- *In the initial state s_{init}, $\mathsf{auth}(a,b)$, $\mathsf{dAuth}(a,b)$ and for every x, y except a, b, $\neg\mathsf{auth}(x,y)$ and $\mathsf{dUnauth}(x,y)$.*

- *Let $t = \langle t_1, \ldots, t_n \rangle$ for $n \geq 1$:*

    - $\mathsf{dUnauth}(a,b) \rightarrow \mathsf{F}(\mathsf{dAuth}(a,b))$ *in t.*
    - $\mathsf{dAuth}(a,c) \rightarrow \mathsf{F}(\mathsf{dUnauth}(a,c))$ *in t.*
    - $t_n = \mathsf{dAuth}(b,c)$.

- *In the final state s_{fin}, $\mathsf{auth}(a,c)$.*

We define the following three kinds of traces similarly, relying on the corresponding properties from Section 4.1.

DEFINITION 17 (BACKWARD AVAILABLE TRACE). *A trace in $\mathcal{I}$ System is backward available if and only if the entries s_{init}, t and s_{fin} are as follows.*

- *In the initial state s_{init}, $\mathsf{auth}(b,c)$, $\mathsf{dAuth}(b,c)$ and for every x, y except b, c, $\neg\mathsf{auth}(x,y)$ and $\mathsf{dUnauth}(x,y)$.*

- *Let $t = \langle t_1, \ldots, t_n \rangle$ for $n \geq 1$:*

    - $\mathsf{dUnauth}(b,c) \rightarrow \mathsf{F}(\mathsf{dAuth}(b,c))$ *in t.*
    - $\mathsf{dAuth}(a,c) \rightarrow \mathsf{F}(\mathsf{dUnauth}(a,c))$ *in t.*
    - $t_n = \mathsf{dAuth}(a,b)$.

- *In the final state s_{fin}, $\mathsf{auth}(a,c)$.*

DEFINITION 18 (FORWARD SAFE TRACE). *A forward safe trace is the same as a forward available trace (see Definition 16), with the only exception that in the final state s_{fin}, $\neg\mathsf{auth}(a,c)$ is true.*

DEFINITION 19 (BACKWARD SAFE TRACE). *A backward safe trace is the same as a backward available trace (see Definition 17), with the only exception that in the final state s_{fin}, $\neg\mathsf{auth}(a,c)$ is true.*

4.3 Relating Properties and Traces

We now relate properties and traces via Theorems 8–11. We omit the proofs — they are similar to those for the theorems in Section 3.3.

Theorem 6 (Necessity). *The $\mathcal{I}$ System has the necessity property if and only if it produces no redundant trace.*

Theorem 7 (Security). *The $\mathcal{I}$ System has the security property if and only if it produces no insecure trace.*

Theorem 8 (Forward availability). *The $\mathcal{I}$ System has the forward availability property if and only if it produces no forward safe trace.*

Theorem 9 (Backward availability). *The $\mathcal{I}$ System has the backward availability property if and only if it produces no backward safe trace.*

Theorem 10 (Forward safety). *The $\mathcal{I}$ System has the forward safety property if and only if it produces no forward available trace.*

Theorem 11 (Backward safety). *The $\mathcal{I}$ System has the backward safety property if and only if it produces no backward available trace.*

4.4 Results for the $\mathcal{I}$ System

We established the following results for the $\mathcal{I}$ System using our testing methodology and system. The $\mathcal{I}$ System satisfies the necessity, security, and forward and backward availability properties. It does not possess the forward and backward safety properties.

Vendor's response The vendor of the $\mathcal{I}$ System has confirmed that our results are consistent with their intended design.

5. RELATED WORK

We are aware of only three uses of state-space exploration in the context of access control. In safety and security analysis [12, 16, 17], one provides as input a start-state and a specification of how states can change. One then asks whether a state with certain properties is reachable, or whether all reachable states have a certain property. In more recent work [14], state-space exploration has been used to verify that the design of particular authorization schemes is sound. What this means is that a particular syntax is specified for the specification of authorization schemes. A new authorization scheme may be specified with the syntax, but the question remains as to whether any scheme that is syntactically valid is also semantically valid. State-space exploration may be used for this purpose. The third use is in information flow, for example, the work of Souza et al. [18]. Our work is different from such existing work related to state-space exploration in access control. Our goal is to determine whether an implemented access control system has properties that were determined to be desirable in its design. In other words, does the "real world" access control system have a property of interest?

There is also a large amount of research in checking for vulnerabilities in software. A comprehensive discussion is well beyond this paper. However, there is relatively little work for real-world access control systems that targets concrete implementations. The work of Bauer et al. [4] is relevant in this context. That work proposes a framework to apply misconfiguration-prediction to access control policies. They predict misconfiguration might happen in the system, based on the visible accesses in the system so far. Our work is on property-testing an implementation of an authorization system rather than the detection of misconfigurations in policies.

Our work borrows ideas from software testing, in particular the small-scopes hypothesis [10]. It also has similarities to recent work that proposes the use of model-checking for software testing [15]. However, such work focuses on aspects such as white-box testing of software (i.e., with access to the source-code) and achieving coverage. Our focus is in testing for properties related to authorization, which to our knowledge, conventional software testing does not cover.

There has also been recent work in the use of traces to verify access control models that are specified in UML [19, 20]. However, such work does not consider testing actual systems, and considers only "on paper" verification. Furthermore, the models tested do not consider administrative changes, which, for example, the $\mathcal{I}$ System that is one of our application contexts incorporates.

Finally, our work also has similarities to flaw-hypothesis or penetration testing [13]. A major difference, however, is that we hypothesize somewhat sophisticated properties that are specific to authorization systems.

6. CONCLUSION

We have addressed the problem of testing an implementation of an authorization system for properties of interest. We have proposed a 4-stage approach: articulation of properties, construction of traces, finitization and a model-checking based approach to testing a system. We have considered several properties in the context of two commercial systems: the $\mathcal{D}$ System and the $\mathcal{I}$ System. We have discovered flaws in the $\mathcal{D}$ System related to the co-existence of authorizations to procedures and discretionary rights to tables that, to our knowledge, have not appeared before in the literature.

There is considerable scope for future work. One avenue is the articulation of a larger set of properties of interest, and abstracting those properties into a "meta-property." This would be similar to the notion of a query in prior work [12]. Completing the implementation of our testing system is also interesting future work.

7. REFERENCES

[1] Nusmv. http://nusmv.fbk.eu/.

[2] Mihhail Aizatulin, Andrew D. Gordon, and Jan Jürjens. Extracting and verifying cryptographic models from c protocol code by symbolic execution. In *Proceedings of the 18th ACM conference on Computer and communications security*, CCS '11, pages 331–340, New York, NY, USA, 2011. ACM.

[3] Chris Anley. Advanced sql injection in sql server applications. *White paper, Next Generation Security Software Ltd*, 2002.

[4] Lujo Bauer, Yuan Liang, Michael K. Reiter, and Chad Spensky. Discovering access-control misconfigurations: New approaches and evaluation methodologies. In *CODASPY'12: Proceedings of the Second ACM Conference on Data and Application Security and Privacy*, February 2012. To appear.

[5] Hao Chen, David Wagner, and Drew Dean. Setuid demystified. In *USENIX Security Symposium*, pages 171–190, 2002.

[6] Edmund M. Clarke, Orna Grumberg, and Doron Peled. *Model checking*. MIT Press, 2001.

[7] Thomas H. Cormen, Charles E. Leiserson, Ronald L. Rivest, and Clifford Stein. *Introduction to Algorithms (3. ed.)*. MIT Press, 2009.

[8] E. M. Fayo. Advanced sql injection in oracle databases. *Technical report, Argeniss Information Security, Black Hat Briefings*, 2005.

[9] Michael Huth and Mark Dermot Ryan. *Logic in computer science - modelling and reasoning about systems (2. ed.)*. Cambridge University Press, 2004.

[10] D. Jackson and C.A. Damon. Elements of style: analyzing a software design feature with a counterexample detector. *Software Engineering, IEEE Transactions on*, 22(7):484–495, jul 1996.

[11] Yongdae Kim, Adrian Perrig, and Gene Tsudik. Simple and fault-tolerant key agreement for dynamic collaborative groups. In *Proceedings of the 7th ACM Conference on Computer and Communications Security (CCS 2000)*, pages 235–244, November 2000.

[12] Ninghui Li and Mahesh V. Tripunitara. Security analysis in role-based access control. *ACM Transactions on Information and Systems Security (TISSEC)*, 9(4):391–420, November 2006.

[13] Richard R. Linde. Operating system penetration. In *Proceedings of the May 19-22, 1975, national computer conference and exposition*, AFIPS '75, pages 361–368, New York, NY, USA, 1975. ACM.

[14] Jianwei Niu, Ravi Sandhu, Ram Krishnan, and William H. Winsborough. Group-centric secure information sharing models for isolated groups. *ACM Transactions on*

Information and System Security, 14(3):1–29, November 2011.

[15] Corina S. Pasareanu. Combining model checking and symbolic execution for software testing. In Achim D. Brucker and Jacques Julliand, editors, *TAP*, volume 7305 of *Lecture Notes in Computer Science*, page 2. Springer, 2012.

[16] Walter L. Ruzzo, Michael A. Harrison, and Jeffrey D. Ullman. Protection in operating systems. *Communications of the ACM*, 19(8):461–471, August 1976.

[17] Ravi S. Sandhu. Undecidability of the safety problem for the schematic protection model with cyclic creates. *Journal of Computer and System Sciences*, 44(1):141–159, February 1992.

[18] Deepak D. Souza, Raveendra Holla, K. R. Raghavendra, and Barbara Sprick. Model-checking trace-based information flow properties. *Journal of Computer Security*, 19(1):101–138, January 2011.

[19] Wuliang Sun, Robert B. France, and Indrakshi Ray. Rigorous analysis of uml access control policy models. In *POLICY*, pages 9–16. IEEE Computer Society, 2011.

[20] Lijun Yu, Robert B. France, Indrakshi Ray, and Wuliang Sun. Systematic scenario-based analysis of uml design class models. In Isabelle Perseil, Karin Breitman, and Marc Pouzet, editors, *ICECCS*, pages 86–95. IEEE Computer Society, 2012.

APPENDIX

A. SCREEN-SHOTS FOR THE $\mathcal{I}$ System

Figure 4 shows the list of a groups a user has created to the left (i.e., "Managers", "Developers", etc.), and the sharing of a file with the group named Developers to the right, under "Recipients." Figure 5 shows how memberships in groups are managed using the other interface.

Figure 4: Sharing a file with a group named "Developers" using one of the $\mathcal{I}$ system's interfaces.

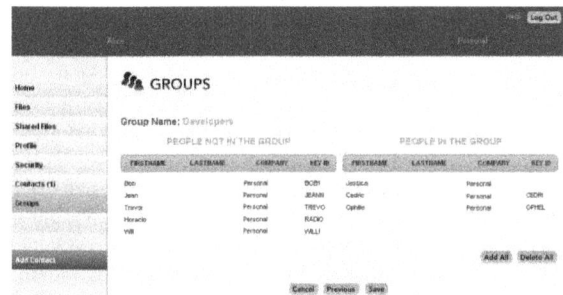

Figure 5: Group-membership management in the $\mathcal{I}$ system.

User-Centric Management of Distributed Credential Repositories: Balancing Availability and Vulnerability

Jens Köhler
Karlsruhe Institute of
Technology (KIT) - Steinbuch
Centre for Computing (SCC) &
Institute of Telematics
Karlsruhe, Germany
jens.koehler@kit.edu

Jens Mittag
Karlsruhe Institute of
Technology (KIT) - Steinbuch
Centre for Computing (SCC) &
Institute of Telematics
Karlsruhe, Germany
jens.mittag@kit.edu

Hannes Hartenstein
Karlsruhe Institute of
Technology (KIT) - Steinbuch
Centre for Computing (SCC) &
Institute of Telematics
Karlsruhe, Germany
hartenstein@kit.edu

ABSTRACT

To relieve users of the burden to memorize and manage their credentials while allowing for seamless roaming between various end devices, the idea of so-called credential repositories that store credentials for users came to attention. Both the risk of the credential repository being unavailable and the risk of the credentials becoming compromised are managed by the party that hosts the credential repository and that has to be trusted by the user. Removing the need for a trust relationship to a single party implies that users have to manage the risks themselves, for instance, by splitting the credentials across multiple systems/parties. However, if the systems differ in terms of availability and vulnerability, determining a suitable splitting strategy to manage the tradeoff between credential availability and vulnerability constitutes a complex problem. In this paper we present CREDIS, an approach that supports the user in building a credential repository based on heterogeneous systems that differ in terms of vulnerability and availability. CREDIS enables users to specify requirements on the availability and the vulnerability of the distributed credential repository and determines an optimal strategy on how to split secrets across the heterogeneous systems. We prove the NP-hardness of finding an optimal strategy, introduce an approach based on Integer Linear Programming to find optimal strategies for medium sized scenarios and propose heuristics for larger ones. We show that the CREDIS approach yields a reasonably secure and available credential repository even when the distributed repository is built based on low-grade devices or systems.

Categories and Subject Descriptors

K.6.5 [**Management of computing and information systems**]: Security and Protection; D.4.6 [**Operating Systems**]: Security and Protection

General Terms

algorithms, management, performance, security, reliability

Keywords

credential management, user-centric risk management, distributed credential repository

1. INTRODUCTION

The service landscape in the world wide web requires users to keep track of a multitude of credentials such as passwords. Furthermore, especially when facing the cloud computing paradigm or outsourcing scenarios in general, stronger secrets like cryptographic keys for encryption [14] or authentication [17,18,29] need to be managed. From a user's perspective it is hard to keep track of those secrets because of the quantity of password credentials and due to cryptographic keys not being made for being memorable.

Storing the secrets on user devices is a common approach to solve this problem (Figure 1a)). However, as modern users tend to roam between devices, the secrets have to be stored on each device to be accessible. To simplify this process, several synchronization solutions exist (e.g., Firefox Sync, Chrome Password Sync,...). Using these, the accumulated stored secrets are typically only protected by a weak password that could be attacked using offline dictionary attacks in case of a single device being compromised. Furthermore, users have to plan ahead on which devices they want to use and initialize the synchronization beforehand.

Another approach is to store secrets using so-called credential repository services (Figure 1b)). Users can contact the credential repository service from arbitrary devices and get access to the stored secrets upon providing the correct memorable password. While this approach remedies the shortcomings of synchronization solutions and enables seamless roaming between devices, the user has to trust the system/party hosting the credential repository. Furthermore, the credential repository constitutes a single point of failure, both in terms of availability and vulnerability: When the credential repository is offline, the user no-longer has access to his secrets. When it is compromised, the secrets of the users are compromised as well.

To address the vulnerability issue of credential repositories, cryptographic protocols that can be used to split secrets across multiple servers have been proposed [3,6,9,13]. Using the protocols, a certain number of servers have to be avail-

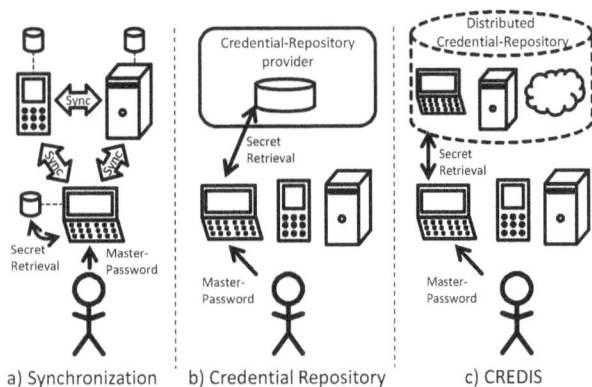

Figure 1: Approaches for credential management

able to retrieve secrets and the same number of servers have to be compromised to compromise the secrets. While inducing a tradeoff between secret availability and vulnerability, we believe that splitting up secrets across multiple servers to enhance security is a seminal idea. However, the user still has to trust a single party that hosts the servers. To remove the requisite for a trust relationship, users can use the mentioned protocols to split their secrets across multiple parties or even their own devices (e.g., desktop computers, notebooks, mobile phones) (Figure 1c)). Thus, managing the risk of storing secrets in terms of their availability and their vulnerability is no longer a task of a trusted party, but of the users themselves. Users have to assess the availability and the vulnerability of each provider/device and develop a strategy on how to distribute the secrets. In particular, the tradeoff between the availability and the vulnerability of the secrets has to be balanced according to the user's needs. Developing an optimal strategy is a complex problem that will be proven to be NP-hard in this paper.

In this paper we propose CREDIS (**C**redential **RE**pository **D**istributed on **I**nhomogeneous **S**ystems), a concept that allows a user to specify the properties of the systems at hand as well as requirements on availability and vulnerability of the credential repository. CREDIS then uses this information to find a suitable strategy on how to split the secrets across the specified systems, taking the individual properties of each system into account. In order to retrieve a secret, the user retrieves parts of the secret by authenticating to the systems via password and reconstructs the secret from the parts. As the user accesses the secrets on his/her terminal, our approach assumes that the terminal of the user is trusted. The systems hosting the credential repository, however, are not regarded to be entirely trustworthy.

The main contributions of this papers are:

- A **concept to split secrets across semi-trusted systems that are heterogeneous** in terms of availability and vulnerability.

- An **NP-hardness proof** for the problem of finding an optimal strategy on how to split the secrets.

- An **approach based on Integer Linear Programming** to determine an optimal strategy for medium sized scenarios and **heuristics** to approximate the optimal strategy for larger scenarios.

- A **performance evaluation** of the proposed approaches and a **quality evaluation** of the solutions produced by the heuristics.

The paper is structured as follows: In Section 2 related work is presented. In Section 3 the problem statement is clarified and terms that are used in the paper are introduced. Section 4 shows how the user can define the scenario and specify his requirements. This information can than be used by the approaches presented in Section 5 to derive a strategy on how to split the key. The approaches will be evaluated in Section 6 before Section 7 concludes the paper.

2. RELATED WORK

A practiced approach to address the problem of storing secrets while allowing the user to roam between devices is to synchronize the stored secrets between the devices [7,12,27]. However, users have to know beforehand which devices they plan to use and have to initialize the synchronization accordingly. Furthermore, once a device of the user is compromised, the stored secrets might become compromised as well if they are only protected by a weak password vulnerable to offline dictionary attacks.

Other approaches tackle the problem of storing credentials while allowing for roaming users by hardware tokens such as SmartCards or USB-tokens [10]. Whereas using hardware tokens does not require the user to memorize secrets, not all devices support them. Furthermore, the users have to bring the token whenever they plan to access the secrets and not all applications justify the costs of acquiring such a token.

The approach to store the credentials in a central credential repository to enable seamless roaming [11,28] has been implemented by multiple commercial solutions [10]. Furthermore, credential repositories like MyProxy [4,5,25] and SafeBox [1] received much attention in the grid community and are actively used. However, credential repositories commonly rely on the security/trustworthiness of a central component. Besides the fact that this component constitutes an attractive target for attackers, not all users have access to such a trusted central component.

To address the issue of central credential repositories being an attractive target and of high risk system components, several mechanisms for hardening the security of these central components exist [21, 24]. However, even fewer users have access to *such* a hardened server or fully trust providers that offer hardened servers. Furthermore, recently compromised certificate authorities show that even highly secured central components can be vulnerable to attacks [20].

Cryptographic protocols proposed in [3,6,9,13,16,22,23] allow to split secrets across multiple servers so that the secret only becomes compromised if a given subset of these servers is compromised. These protocols are already used to establish credential repositories that are split across several servers [10] (e.g., in the VeriSign Personal Trust Service [15]). However, splitting up the secrets reduces their availability, as to retrieve a secret multiple servers need to be online. An adaptive deployment of secret parts that takes availability and vulnerability properties of the servers into account remains an open problem.

RAID concepts [26] have been studied in particular for enhancing data availability by redundantly storing data. However, RAID concepts do not address data confidentiality. While CREDIS uses similar mechanisms to achieve the availability of secrets, it considers the secrets' vulnerability, too. Thus, CREDIS combines both concepts, cryptographic protocols to enhance the confidentiality of the secrets and redundancy to enhance the availability of the secrets.

Key escrow systems constitute a remotely related topic. Key escrow systems encrypt the keys used to encrypt messages with a master key and append the encrypted keys to the ciphertext [8]. Thus, the ciphertext is accessible without knowledge of the actually used encryption key, if the master key is known. However, as the escrowed keys are potentially accessible by anybody, key escrow systems require a cryptographically strong master key. As such a key is not memorable, the primary focus of key escrow systems lies on the recovery of lost keys or governmental surveillance rather than usability. While our approach also uses a cryptographically strong key to encrypt the user's secrets, the user can get access to this key by providing a common, low-entropy password, as the systems storing the secrets blacklist users after a certain number of wrong password guesses.

CREDIS reduces the problem of finding an optimal secret distribution strategy on an *Integer Linear Programming* (ILP) problem. This methodology is also applied in other publications [14, 19]. However, the application domains differ significantly from the problem at hand. Furthermore, the reduction of the problem to an ILP problem is not trivial in itself and constitutes a major contribution of this paper.

3. GENERAL CONCEPT AND TERMINOLOGY

To build a credential repository based on systems that have individual degrees of availability and vulnerability, the question that needs to be answered is: "Given a number of heterogeneous systems, how can secrets be stored on them in such a way that the user's requirements concerning the availability and the vulnerability of the secrets are fulfilled?".

We denote the systems used to store the secrets on as *stores* (S). First of all, the problem of securely storing multiple secrets can be simplified by encrypting the secrets with a single cryptographic *key* and replicating the ciphertext on all stores. Thus, it suffices to develop a strategy for securely storing the key on the stores. Any secret can be obtained by retrieving the key as well as the encrypted secrets from the stores and decrypting the secrets. As the encrypted secrets are stored on every store, the availability and the vulnerability of secrets only depend on the availability/vulnerability of the key. Thus, only the strategy to store the key has to adhere to the user's requirements on the credential store.

In the following we will use the term *key-availability* for the probability of the key being available at a given point in time. The term *key-vulnerability* will be used for the probability of the key becoming compromised between the instant of being provisioned on the devices and the planned point in time when the key becomes deprovisioned/renewed.

Cryptographic protocols [3, 6, 9, 13] can be utilized to split the key across multiple stores to lower the key-vulnerability. This is achieved by splitting the key into multiple *fragments* that can be stored on different stores. The set of these fragments is denoted as a fragment *bundle* (B). To retrieve the key, the user has to retrieve all fragments of the bundle by authenticating against each store that stores a fragment of the bundle via password[1]. After successful authentication, each store transmits the stored fragments to the user. Once all fragments of the bundle are obtained, the user can re-

---

[1] This is simplified. Most protocols employ sophisticated mechanisms that prevent offline dictionary attacks on the password in case a subset of the stores is compromised.

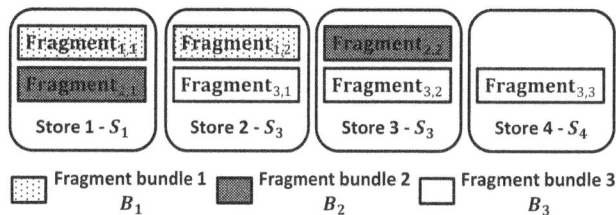

Figure 2: Exemplary key fragments distribution

construct the key from the fragments. The protocols ensure that the key retrieval process does not affect the security of the key as long as the user's terminal is not compromised and only a subset of stores is compromised. Thus, as long as only a subset of fragments in the bundle is compromised, the key remains uncompromised. However, if one or more stores are not available, even legitimate users cannot reconstruct the key, as the fragments stored by the unavailable stores cannot be retrieved.

In the following the notation $B_1 = \{S_1, S_2, \dots\}$ expresses that on each store S_i resides a fragment of bundle B_1. The key can be fragmented multiple times, creating multiple independent bundles. While the key can be deduced from each complete bundle, bundles are independent of each other, i.e., all fragments of at least one bundle have to be known to deduce the key. The fragments of different bundles can be distributed on the stores arbitrarily. The bundles along with the assignment of the contained fragments to the stores is denoted as the *key fragments distribution* in the following.

By generating multiple independent bundles from the key, a fine grained balancing of key-availability and key-vulnerability can be performed. For instance, consider the exemplary key fragments distribution shown in Figure 2 with the bundles $B_1 = \{S_1, S_2\}$, $B_2 = \{S_1, S_3\}$, $B_3 = \{S_2, S_3, S_4\}$. The key would be considered compromised if S_1 and S_3 are compromised, as the attacker would have access to both fragments of B_2. Removing B_2 from the key fragments distribution would result in a lower overall key-vulnerability, as the event of S_1 and S_3 being compromised would not imply a compromised key (the attacker would only know subsets of B_1 and B_3). However, removing B_2 would also reduce key-availability since a legitimate user would not be able to retrieve the key anymore if S_2 was not available.

Thus, a tradeoff is implied by storing multiple bundles:

- The key is **available** as long as all fragments of at least one bundle are available, i.e., all stores hosting those fragments are available.

- The key is **compromised** once all fragments of at least one bundle are compromised, i.e., all stores hosting those fragments are compromised.

Utilizing the introduced notions, the question to be answered can be reformulated as: "Given a number of (heterogeneous) stores, how can a key fragments distribution be found that adheres to the user's requirements concerning the key-availability and the key-vulnerability?"

4. SCENARIO DEFINITION AND POLICY PROFILE

Before an optimal key fragments distribution can be generated, the user has to specify the properties of the stores at hand (*scenario*) and the requirements the key fragments distribution needs to fulfill (*policy profile*).

4.1 Scenario Definition

For each store at hand, the user specifies the probability of the store being available (*store-availability*) and the probability of the store being compromised (*store-vulnerability*). In the following, $V(S_1)$ denotes the vulnerability of store S_1 and $A(S_1)$ denotes its availability. We define store-availability as the probability of a store being available at a given point in time and store-vulnerability as the estimated probability that a store is compromised unnoticedly during the timespan between key deployment and key deletion. The aspect of finding meaningful values for both store-availability and store-vulnerability will be discussed in Section 6.2.

4.2 Policy Profile Definition

The scenario being defined, the user has to specify policies a suitable key fragments distribution has to fulfill. These policies can be sub-divided into *boundary conditions* and the *optimization criterion*. While the boundary conditions have to hold for a feasible key fragments distribution, the optimization criterion specifies which of the feasible key fragments distributions is considered optimal by the user.

The user may specify all or just a subset of the following **boundary conditions**:

- **Maximum key-vulnerability**: Defines the upper acceptable bound for the probability of the key becoming compromised.

- **Minimum key-availability**: Defines the lower acceptable bound for the probability of the key being available.

- **Maximum number of bundles**: Defines the upper acceptable bound for the number of bundles to prevent online dictionary attacks. Depending on the "wrong-password" policy of the stores, the number of bundles directly affects the number of possible password guesses an attacker can make before being blacklisted by the stores (e.g., with 3 bundles and 5 password tries before being blacklisted, an attacker can make 15 guesses on the password before being locked out).

The user may choose the property that is most important to him by specifying the **optimization criterion**:

- **Key-availability maximization**: Requests the feasible key fragments distribution with maximum probability of the key being available.

- **Key-vulnerability minimization**: Requests the feasible key fragments distribution with minimum probability of the key becoming compromised.

- **Composite optimization**: Key-availability and key-vulnerability can also be weighted to optimize for a ratio of the two properties (e.g., 1*key-availability - 5*key-vulnerability).

In the following, a key fragments distribution that adheres to the optimization criterion is denoted the *optimal key fragments distribution*. The scenario setup and the specified policy profile constitutes an optimization problem. Methods to solve this problem will be presented in Section 5.

5. FINDING THE OPTIMAL KEY FRAGMENTS DISTRIBUTION STRATEGY

In the following we will show that the problem of determining an optimal key fragments distribution is NP-hard and how it can be linearized to an *Integer Linear Programming* (ILP) problem that can be solved by standard ILP solvers. Furthermore, we will propose a heuristic with a better performance to obtain close-to-optimal solutions for large problem instances that cannot be optimally solved in feasible time. An evaluation of both approaches will be presented in Section 6.

5.1 NP-hardness proof

To prove the NP-hardness of finding an optimal key fragments distribution, the NP-hard *KNAPSACK* problem can be reduced to finding an optimal key fragments distribution for a specific scenario that is build by transforming the *KNAPSACK* problem:

Given: A *KNAPSACK* problem instance: A set of items $I = \{i_1, i_2, \ldots, i_n\}$ with values $c_1, c_2, \ldots, c_n$ and weights $w_1, w_2, \ldots, w_n$ assigned to each of them is given. Furthermore, a weight capacity W of the knapsack exists.
Wanted: A subset of items $K \subseteq I$ so that $\sum_{i_j \in K} w_j \leq W$ holds and $V = \sum_{i_j \in K} c_j$ is maximized.
Reduction:

1. Define the policy profile as:

   - Stores: $\mathcal{S} = \{S_1, S_2, \ldots, S_n\}$
   - Minimum key-availability boundary condition: A
   - Maximal number of fragment bundles: 1
   - Optimization criterion: Key-vulnerability minimization

   Choose the minimal key-availability as $A = 2^{-W}$, store-availability of each S_j as $a_j = 2^{-w_j}$ and the store-vulnerability as $v_j = 2^{-c_j}$.

2. Find the optimal solution for the policy profile. This will result in one fragment bundle B_1.

3. Solution transformation: For each S_j in the fragment bundle B_1 put item i_j in the knapsack.

PROOF. **Correctness:** As according to the policy profile B_1 is the only fragment bundle, the availability of the key can be calculated as $\prod_{S_j \in B_1} a_j$. Due to the minimum key-availability boundary condition policy it holds that:

$$\prod_{S_j \in B_1} a_j \geq A$$
$$\Leftrightarrow \prod_{i_j \in K} 2^{-w_j} \geq 2^{-W}$$
$$\Leftrightarrow \sum_{i_j \in K} w_j \leq W$$

Thus, the weight of all items in the knapsack does not exceed the knapsacks capacity. Consequently, each feasible bundle choice can be mapped on a feasible subset of items in the knapsack and vice versa. □

PROOF. **Optimality:** According to the policy profile, B_1 is the only fragment bundle. Thus, the vulnerability of the key can be calculated as $\prod_{S_j \in B_1} v_j$. As the solution for the policy profile is optimal, it holds that the vulnerability of other feasible fragment bundle choices ($\mathcal{B}^{feas}$) is bigger or equal to that of B_1:

$$\forall B' \subseteq \mathcal{B}^{feas} : \prod_{S_j \in B'} v_j \geq \prod_{S_j \in B_1} v_j$$

$$\stackrel{Correctness}{\Leftrightarrow} \forall K' \subseteq \mathcal{K}^{feas} : \prod_{i_j \in K'} 2^{-c_j} \geq \prod_{i_j \in K} 2^{-c_j}$$

$$\Leftrightarrow \forall K' \subseteq \mathcal{K}^{feas} : \sum_{i_j \in K'} c_j \leq \sum_{i_j \in K} c_j$$

Thus, as all other valid item choices ($\mathcal{K}^{feas}$) that fit in the knapsack are less or equally valuable, K is the optimal solution of the *KNAPSACK* problem instance. $\square$

The reduction and the transformation of the solution is doable in polynomial time. Thus, the optimization problem at hand has been proven to be NP-hard.

While the proof only shows the NP-hardness of finding solutions for policy profiles with the key-vulnerability minimization optimization criterion set, it can be shown analogously that key-availability maximization problems are also NP hard. To do so, the dual knapsack problem (i.e., minimizing the total value of the items while reaching a least a certain knapsack weight) can be reduced on a policy profile with a key-availability maximization optimization criterion.

5.2 Mapping on an ILP problem

For mapping the problem of finding the optimal key fragments distribution on an ILP problem, we need to be able to determine the key-availability and the key-vulnerability of given key fragments distributions. Bundles can overlap in the sense that one or more stores store fragments of each bundle. Therefore, the stochastic event of a bundle being compromised is not independent of the stochastic event of another bundle being compromised if both bundles overlap.

Example: *Let us consider an exemplary key fragments distribution consisting of two bundles $B_1 = \{S_1, S_2\}$ and $B_2 = \{S_2, S_3\}$ as a running example in this section with store-vulnerabilities of $V(S_1)=0.1$, $V(S_2)=0.2$, $V(S_3)=0.15$ and store-availabilities $A(S_1)=0.7$, $A(S_2)=0.8$, $A(S_3)=0.9$. While it holds that $V(B_1) = V(S_1) * V(S_2) = 0.02$ and $V(B_2) = V(S_2) * V(S_3) = 0.015$, the probability of the key becoming compromised (i.e., at least one bundle becoming compromised) does not amount to $1 - (1 - V(B_1)) * (1 - V(B_2)) = 0.0494$ as the vulnerabilities $V(B_1)$ and $V(B_2)$ both depend on the vulnerability of S_1.$\square$*

In the following we will denote stochastic events as *relevant*, if their occurrence implies a compromised or available bundle (and therefore key).

Example: *$B_1 = \{S_1, S_2\}$ makes both events, "S_1, S_2 and S_3 being compromised" as well as "S_1, S_2 being compromised and S_3 not being compromised" relevant, as in both cases all fragments of B_1 are compromised. Concerning key-availability, B_1 makes the events of "S_1, S_2 and S_3 being available" as well as "S_1, S_2 being available and S_3 being not available" relevant, as in both cases the fragments of B_1 can be retrieved.$\square$*

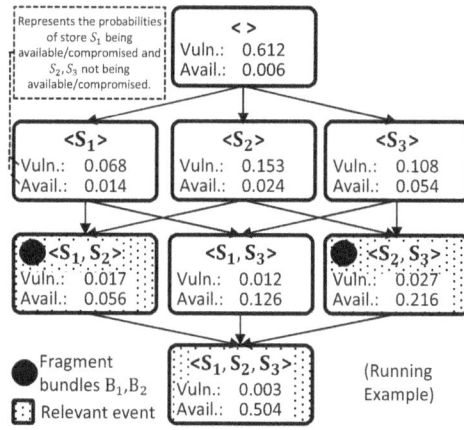

Figure 3: Rating of an exemplary key fragments distribution (with exemplary Vuln. & Avail. rates)

The relevant events concerning key-availability are exactly those events in which the key would be available, the relevant events concerning key-vulnerability are exactly those events in which the key would be compromised. Thus, the sum of the occurrence probabilities of relevant events concerning key-availability equals the key-availability of the key fragments distribution. Analogously, the sum of the occurrence probabilities of relevant events concerning the key-vulnerability equals the key-vulnerability.

To make the problem of rating key fragments distributions more explicit, we modeled it as a graph that will be denoted as *event relevance graph* in the following. The event relevance graph for our exemplary key-fragments distribution is depicted in Figure 3. Event relevance graphs can be interpreted as follows: Each node $<S_{i_1}, S_{i_2}, \ldots>$ can be interpreted as the event of the stores $S_{i_1}, S_{i_2}, \ldots$ being available and all remaining stores not being available. The occurrence probability of these events is denoted by "Avail." in Figure 3. Each node can also be interpreted as the event of the stores $S_{i_1}, S_{i_2}, \ldots$ being compromised and all remaining stores not being compromised. The occurrence probability of these events is denoted by "Vuln." in Figure 3.

Example: *In Figure 3, node $<S_1>$ corresponds to the event of S_1 being compromised while S_2 and S_3 are not compromised (occurrence probability: $V(S_1) * (1 - V(S_2)) * (1 - V(S_3)) = 0.068$). Node $<S_1>$ also corresponds to the event of S_1 being available while S_2 and S_3 are not available (occurrence probability: $A(S_1) * (1 - A(S_2)) * (1 - A(S_3)) = 0.014$).$\square$*

Each directed edge from an event e_1 to an event e_2 in the graph expresses that if a bundle is compromised/available in case of occurrence of the event e_1 it would also be compromised/available if event e_2 occurs. In particular, these semantics of the edges imply that, if an event is relevant, all events that can be reached from this event in the graph have to be relevant, too.

Example: *A bundle that is compromised if S_1 is compromised and S_2, S_3 are not compromised (node $<S_1>$), it would also be compromised if S_1 and S_2 are compromised and S_3 is not compromised (node $<S_1, S_2>$). Analogously, a bundle that is available if S_1 is available and S_2, S_3 are not available (node $<S_1>$), it would also be available if S_1 and*

S_2 are available and S_3 is not available (node $<S_1, S_2>$). Thus, the event relevance graph contains an edge from node $<S_1>$ to node $<S_1, S_2>$. Our exemplary key fragments distribution that consists of the bundles $B_1 = \{S_1, S_2\}$ and $B_2 = \{S_2, S_3\}$ is expressed in Figure 3 by black circles. Node $<S_1, S_2>$ is relevant, as B_1 would be compromised/available in the event of S_1 and S_2 being compromised/available and S_3 not being compromised/available. The same applies for node $<S_2, S_3>$ and B_2. Furthermore, all nodes that can be reached from $<S_1, S_2>$ and $<S_2, S_3>$ are relevant as well due to the semantics of the edges.$\square$

Rating key fragment distributions: Both the probability of at least one of the bundles being compromised and at least one of the bundles being available can be calculated by summing up the "Vuln." and "Avail." occurrence probabilities of the relevant nodes respectively. Thus, the policy transformation problem is reduced to finding a choice of bundles so that both the sum of the "Avail." property and the sum of the "Vuln." property of the relevant nodes fulfill the policy profile.

Example: *The key-availability of the key fragments distribution shown in Figure 3 amounts to $0.056 + 0.504 + 0.216 = 0.776$. The key-vulnerability amounts to $0.017 + 0.003 + 0.027 = 0.047$.$\square$*

This resulting problem is a linear problem and can be formulated as an ILP problem as follows:

Constants:

N: Set of nodes in the event relevance graph.
V: Max. key-vulnerability defined in the policy profile.
V_i: Vuln. of node n_i.
A: Min. key-availability defined in the policy profile.
A_i: Avail. of node n_i.
$maxBdls$: Max. number of bundles constraint.
$E(n)$: Set of (child) nodes that are reachable from node n.
$I(n)$: Set of (parent) nodes that can reach node n.

Variables:

x_i: Node n_i is relevant.
y_i: Node n_i represents a bundle.

ILP: $\max \sum_{n_i \in N} A_i * x_i$ **or** $\min \sum_{n_i \in N} V_i * x_i$ $\quad$ (0)

s.t.

$$\sum_{n_i \in N} V_i * x_i \leq V \qquad (1)$$

$$\sum_{n_i \in N} A_i * x_i \geq A \qquad (2)$$

$$\forall n_j \in N : \frac{1}{|E(n_j)|} * \sum_{n_i \in E(n_j)} x_i \geq x_j \qquad (3)$$

$$\forall n_j \in N : x_j \geq y_j \qquad (4)$$

$$\forall n_j \in N : \sum_{n_i \in I(n_j)} x_i + y_j \geq x_j \qquad (5)$$

$$\forall n_j \in N : 1 - \frac{\sum_{n_i \in I(n_j)} x_i}{|I(n_j)|} \geq y_j \qquad (6)$$

$$\sum_{n_i \in N} y_i \leq maxBdls \qquad (7)$$

$$\forall n_j \in N : x_i \in \{0, 1\} \qquad (8)$$

$$\forall n_j \in N : y_i \in \{0, 1\} \qquad (9)$$

The target function can be defined depending on the policy profile's optimization criterion. In the listed ILP problem, target functions for maximizing the key-availability or minimizing the key-vulnerability are shown in equation (0). However, arbitrary (linear) target functions can be specified (e.g., for a composite optimization criterion).

Constraints (1) and (2) limit the key-vulnerability and the key-availability of the feasible solutions according to the policy profile. Constraint (3) assures, that nodes can only be marked as relevant, if all their child nodes are relevant. While each node that represents a bundle needs to be relevant (4), each relevant node has to represent a bundle or a parent node has to be relevant (5). Constraint (6) is optional and enforces that a node may only represent a bundle if no parent node is relevant. Without (6), the solution of the ILP might contain redundant bundles that neither affect key-availability nor key-vulnerability and can be purged, i.e., bundles containing other bundles can be eliminated. The number of bundles has to be limited according to the specified policy profile (7). Furthermore, nodes can either be relevant ($x_i = 1$) or not relevant ($x_i = 0$)(8). The same has to hold for nodes representing a bundle (9).

Solving the ILP problem yields the optimal choice of bundles. Solving ILP problems is NP-hard and the number of nodes that have to be taken into account depends exponentially on the number of stores ($N = 2^{|stores|}$). However, we will show in Section 6 that the approach is feasible for problems with up to 9 stores. For larger problem instances we will propose heuristics in Section 5.3.

5.3 A heuristic approach

To address large problem instances with more than 9 stores as they may occur with the advent of ubiquitous computing [2], more efficient heuristics may be employed that approximate the optimal solution. We propose heuristics for both key-availability maximization (*MaxAvail*) and key-vulnerability minimization (*MinVuln*) problems.

5.3.1 MaxAvail heuristic

The pseudocode algorithm of the **MaxAvail** greedy heuristic is listed in Algorithm 1. The basic principle consists of adding stores to a bundle until the maximum key-vulnerability boundary condition is satisfied (cf. line 7). The choice which store to add in each step depends on the benefit for adding the store (cf. line 8-24). The store's benefit is calculated by dividing the gain in key-availability Δa by the gain in key-vulnerability Δv that would result from adding the current bundle including the store to the solution. Once the maximum key-vulnerability boundary condition is satisfied, the bundle is committed to the solution (cf. line 26-27) and the process is repeated for a new bundle. This is done until adding additional bundles does not yield any availability gain (cf. line 20) or the maximum number of bundles as specified in the policy profile is reached (cf. line 4).

Example: *An exemplary run of the MaxAvail heuristic on the example introduced in Section 5.2 is shown in Figure 4 for a maximum key-vulnerability boundary condition of 0.05. The algorithm starts with an empty fragment bundle set that does not induce any vulnerability ($vuln_{total} = 0$). In the first step, the benefit of adding each store to an empty bundle is calculated by dividing the gain in key-availability by the gain in key-vulnerability. For instance, by adding store S_1 to the bundle, the events of $<S_1>$, $<S_1, S_2>$, $<S_1, S_3>$,*

Algorithm 1 MaxAvail heuristic

```
 1: procedure MAXAVAIL(stores, vuln_max, maxBdls)
 2:     bundles ← ∅
 3:     vuln_total ← 0
 4:     while |bundles| ≤ maxBdls do
 5:         B_cur ← ∅
 6:         vuln_cur ← 1
 7:         while vuln_total + vuln_cur > vuln_max do
 8:             benefit_best ← −1
 9:             for S ∈ stores do
10:                 Δv, Δa ← Rate(B_cur ⋃{S}, bundles)
11:                 if Δv ≠ 0 then
12:                     benefit_cur ← Δa/Δv
13:                     if benefit_cur > benefit_best then
14:                         benefit_best ← benefit_cur
15:                         bestS ← S
16:                         bestVLoss ← Δv
17:                     end if
18:                 end if
19:             end for
20:             if benefit_best = −1 then
21:                 return bundles
22:             end if
23:             B_cur ← B_cur ⋃{bestS}
24:             vuln_cur ← bestVLoss
25:         end while
26:         bundles ← bundles ⋃{B_cur}
27:         vuln_total ← vuln_total + vuln_cur
28:     end while
29:     return bundles
30: end procedure
```

$<S_1, S_2, S_3>$ (cf. Figure 3) become relevant. Their summed up key-vulnerability values amount to 0.1 and their summed up key-availability values amount to 0.7. Thus, the benefit of adding S_1 is 7. As the benefits of adding S_2 or S_3 are less than that, S_1 is added to the bundle. The key-vulnerability induced by the bundle ($vuln_{cur} = 0.1$) is bigger than the maximum key-vulnerability 0.05. Thus, another store has to be added to the current bundle (cf. line 7 in Algorithm 1). The process of rating the benefits of the remaining stores is repeated and the best one (S_3) is added to the bundle. As the key-vulnerability induced by the bundle $vuln_{cur} = 0.015$ is less than the maximum key-vulnerability, the bundle $\{S_1, S_3\}$ can be added to the fragment bundle set.

After the first bundle is submitted to the fragment bundle set, the algorithm checks whether additional bundles can be added to improve the solution (cf. Step 2 in Figure 4). The heuristic starts with an empty bundle and rates the benefit of adding each store, taking the already submitted bundles into account: For instance, by adding store S_3 to the bundle, only the events of $<S_3>$ and $<S_2, S_3>$ additionally become relevant, as $<S_1, S_3>$ and $<S_1, S_2, S_3>$ are already relevant due to the submitted bundle of Step 1. Again, stores are added until the sum of the induced key-vulnerability of the submitted bundles ($vuln_{total}$) and of the current bundle ($vuln_{cur}$) is less than the maximum key-vulnerability. If this is not possible, the heuristic terminates and returns the submitted bundles. The procedure of creating bundles and adding them to the fragment bundle set is repeated until the maximum number of bundles as specified by the user is reached and the fragment bundle set is returned as the solution.

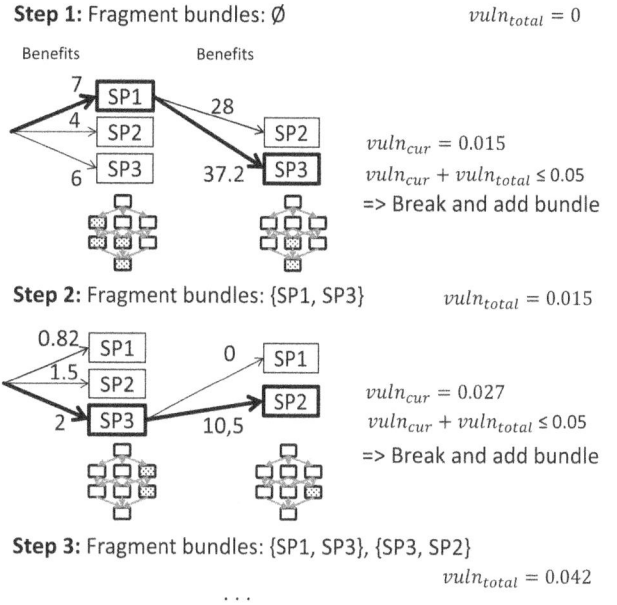

Step 1: Fragment bundles: ∅ $vuln_{total} = 0$

$vuln_{cur} = 0.015$

$vuln_{cur} + vuln_{total} \le 0.05$

=> Break and add bundle

Step 2: Fragment bundles: {SP1, SP3} $vuln_{total} = 0.015$

$vuln_{cur} = 0.027$

$vuln_{cur} + vuln_{total} \le 0.05$

=> Break and add bundle

Step 3: Fragment bundles: {SP1, SP3}, {SP3, SP2}

$vuln_{total} = 0.042$

. . .

Figure 4: Exemplary run of the MaxAvail heuristic

5.3.2 Rate algorithm

The pseudocode procedure makes use of another procedure listed in Algorithm 2 to determine the gain in availability Δa and the gain in vulnerability Δv that would result from adding a bundle B_{cur} to the bundles that are already contained in the solution. The steps the algorithm performs are exemplarily shown in Figure 5. The depicted graphs can be interpreted as described in Section 5.2. In Figure 5 the events that are relevant due to B_{cur} and the events that are relevant due to other bundles B_1 and B_2 that are already contained in the solution are shown. When adding B_{cur} to the solution one event will be additionally relevant, influencing both key-availability and key-vulnerability. However, the naive approach of keeping track of all relevant events and calculating the influence of B_{cur} by only considering the *additionally* relevant events does not scale well, due to the fact that $2^{|stores|}$ nodes would have to be tracked.

Algorithm 2 Rate algorithm

```
 1: procedure RATE(B_cur, bundles)
 2:     Δv ← 0
 3:     Δa ← 0
 4:     for all bundleCombination ∈ 2^bundles do
 5:         curIntersection ← B_cur
 6:         for all B ∈ bundleCombination do
 7:             curIntersection ← curIntersection ⋃ B
 8:         end for
 9:         if |bundleCombination| is uneven then
10:             Δv ← Δv − ∏_{S∈curIntersection} V(S)
11:             Δa ← Δa − ∏_{S∈curIntersection} A(S)
12:         else
13:             Δv ← Δv + ∏_{S∈curIntersection} V(S)
14:             Δa ← Δa + ∏_{S∈curIntersection} A(S)
15:         end if
16:     end for
17:     return Δv, Δa
18: end procedure
```

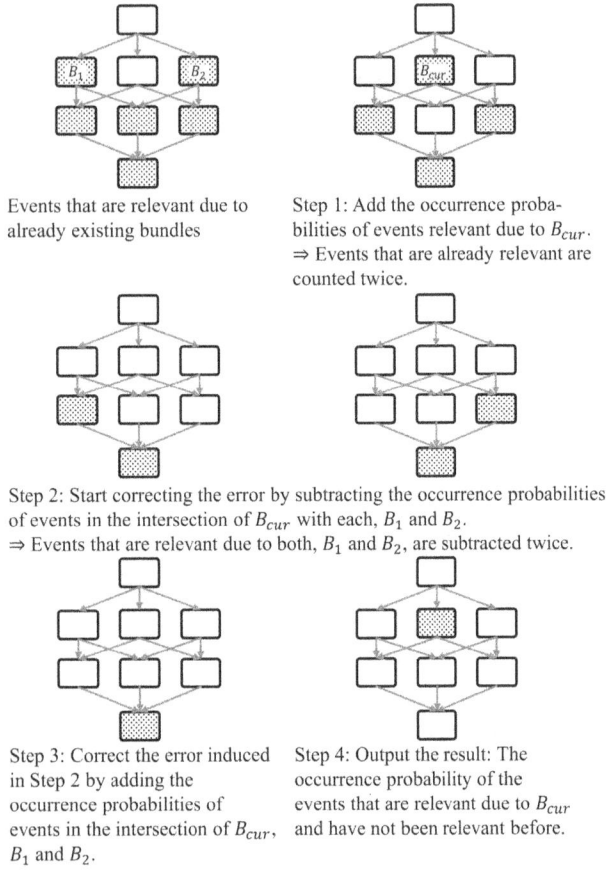

Events that are relevant due to already existing bundles

Step 1: Add the occurrence probabilities of events relevant due to B_{cur}. ⇒ Events that are already relevant are counted twice.

Step 2: Start correcting the error by subtracting the occurrence probabilities of events in the intersection of B_{cur} with each, B_1 and B_2. ⇒ Events that are relevant due to both, B_1 and B_2, are subtracted twice.

Step 3: Correct the error induced in Step 2 by adding the occurrence probabilities of events in the intersection of B_{cur}, B_1 and B_2.

Step 4: Output the result: The occurrence probability of the events that are relevant due to B_{cur} and have not been relevant before.

Figure 5: Process of rating an additional bundle

To work around that, our algorithm initially naively determines the vulnerability of B_{cur} by calculating the product of the store-vulnerabilities of all stores in B_{cur}[2]. Probabilistic theory dictates that this product equals the sum of the events that are relevant because of B_{cur} (cf. Figure 5, Step 1). In order to correct the error of including events that are already relevant because of existing bundles, our algorithm subtracts the occurrence probabilities of the events in the intersection of B_{cur} and each existing bundle (line 10-11 in Algorithm 2). For instance, the summed up probabilities of the events in the intersection of B_{cur} and B_1 can be easily determined by calculating the vulnerability of the imaginary bundle $B_{cur} \bigcup B_1$ (cf. Figure 5, Step 2). Subtracting both the summed up probabilities of $B_{cur} \bigcup B_1$ and $B_{cur} \bigcup B_2$, another error is induced, as the event contained in both $B_{cur} \bigcup B_1$ and $B_{cur} \bigcup B_2$ is subtracted two times. To remedy that, the summed up probabilities of the events in the intersection of B_{cur}, B_1 and B_2 (cf. Figure 5, Step 3) are computed as explained and readded to the result (line 13-14 in Algorithm 2).

Taking the *Rate* procedure into account, the asymptotic execution time of the MaxAvail algorithm amounts to $O(m * n^2 * 2^m)$, where n constitutes the number of stores and m the maximum number of bundles defined in the policy profile. Therefore, it does not depend exponentially on the num-

---

[2]For the sake of simplicity, we only address vulnerability in the explanation. However, all steps can be analogously performed for availability.

ber of stores but only on the number of maximum bundles specified in the policy profile. We argue, that in realistic scenarios, this parameter will not be chosen exceptionally large to prevent online dictionary attacks performed by external attackers.

5.3.3 MinVuln heuristic

The **MinVuln** binary search heuristic to solve key-vulnerability minimization problems can be constructed by using the MaxAvail heuristic presented in Section 5.3. MinVuln approximates the solution of MaxAvail that offers the required key-availability and a minimum key-vulnerability. A target precision has to be specified that describes the tolerable absolute deviation from this minimum key-vulnerability. The pseudocode of MinVuln is shown in Algorithm 3.

Algorithm 3 MinVuln heuristic

1: **procedure** MINVULN($stores, avail_{min}, maxBdls, prec$)
2:     $vuln_{max} \leftarrow 0.5$
3:     $curPrec \leftarrow 0.5$
4:     **while** $curPrec > prec$ **do**
5:         $curSol = MaxAvail(stores, vuln_{max}, maxBdls)$
6:         $curPrec \leftarrow \frac{curPrec}{2}$
7:         **if** $avail_{min} \leq Availability(curSol)$ **then**
8:           $sol \leftarrow curSol$
9:           $vuln_{max} \leftarrow vuln_{max} - curPrec$
10:       **else**
11:         $vuln_{max} \leftarrow vuln_{max} + curPrec$
12:       **end if**
13:     **end while**
14:     **return** sol
15: **end procedure**

The algorithm starts by using the MaxAvail heuristic to solve a key-availability maximization problem that has been constructed by copying the scenario definition and the maximum number of bundles from the actual problem that has to be solved (line 5). The maximum key-vulnerability boundary condition is initially set to 0.5 ($vuln_{max}$, line 2). If the key-availability of the solution satisfies the key-availability boundary condition of the original problem, the $vuln_{max}$ parameter is tightened by subtracting the current precision parameter ($curPrec$, line 7-9) to check if a feasible solution with a lower key-vulnerability exists. Otherwise $vuln_{max}$ is loosened by adding $curPrec$ (line 10-12) to find a feasible solution. Afterward, another key-maximization problem with the new $vuln_{max}$ boundary condition parameter is solved and the precision parameter is halved (line 6). This process is repeated until $curPrec$ falls below the required precision $prec$ (line 4). Once the algorithm terminates, the last key fragments distribution that adhered to the key-availability boundary condition of the original problem is returned (lines 8, 14).

Example: *An exemplary run of the MinVuln heuristic is shown in Figure 6 for a scenario with a required min. key-availability ($avail_{min}$) of 0.85 and a target precision of $\frac{1}{30}$. The precision variable $curPrec$ is initially set to 0.5. In the first step, the min. key-availability requirement is substituted by a max. key-vulnerability requirement of 0.5 ($vuln_{max}$). Solving this problem using the MaxAvail heuristic results in a solution with a key-availability of 0.99 which is higher than the requested $avail_{min}$. In Step 2, the precision variable $curPrec$ is halved and to find potential solu-*

curPrec | vuln_max | Availability(curSol)

(Figure 6 diagram:)

	curPrec	$vuln_{max}$ (0.75 0.5 0.25 0)	Availability(curSol)
Step 1	$\frac{1}{2}$	⊢————————⊣	$0.99 > avail_{min}$
Step 2	$\frac{1}{4}$	⊢————⊣	$0.95 > avail_{min}$
Step 3	$\frac{1}{8}$	curPrec ⊢—⊣	$0.84 \leq avail_{min}$
Step 4	$\frac{1}{16}$	⊢——⊣	$0.86 > avail_{min}$
Step 5	$\frac{1}{32}$	⊢—⊣	$0.845 \leq avail_{min}$

$curPrec = \frac{1}{32} < prec \rightarrow$ **Break**

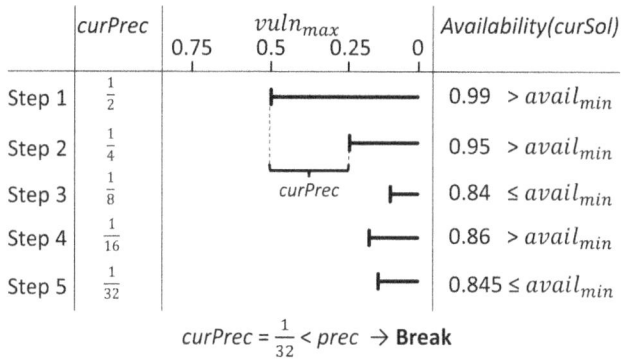

Figure 6: Exemplary run of the MinVuln heuristic ($avail_{min} = 0.85$, $prec = \frac{1}{30}$)

	S_1	S_2	S_3	S_4	S_5	S_6	Min. Avail.	Vuln.
Vuln.	0.25	0.25	0.05	0.1	0.2	0.05		
Avail.	0.7	0.7	0.95	0.9	0.9999	0.99		
Scen.1	x	x	x	x	x	x	0.99	0.0016875
Scen.2	x	x	x	x	x	x	0.95	0.0003063
Scen.3	x	x	x	x	x		0.99	0.0183125
Scen.4	x	x	x	x	x		0.95	0.0061250
Scen.5	x	x	x	x			0.99	0.0915625
Scen.6	x	x	x	x			0.95	0.0306250

Table 1: Vulnerability of solutions for different scenarios with a key-availability boundary condition.

tions with a smaller key-vulnerability, $vuln_{max}$ is tightened by subtracting $curPrec$. Solving this problem results in a solution with a key-availability of 0.95. Thus, ($vuln_{max}$) is tightened again in Step 3. The solution of Step 3, however, results in a key-availability of 0.84 which violates the min. key-availability requirement of the original scenario. Thus, $vuln_{max}$ is loosened by adding $curPrec$ in Step 4. This procedure is repeated until the precision variable is below $\frac{1}{30}$, the threshold defined by the passed prec parameter. Once this happens, the last feasible solution is returned as a result which would be the solution of Step 4 in this example.

The asymptotic execution time of MinVuln amounts to $O(log(p) * m * n^2 * 2^m)$, where p constitutes the precision parameter, n constitutes the number of stores and m the maximum number of bundles defined in the policy profile. A more detailed performance evaluation of the heuristic will be presented in Section 6.3.

6. EVALUATION & DISCUSSION

6.1 Benefit of adaptively fragmenting keys

To evaluate the benefit of adaptively fragmenting keys on multiple systems, we analyzed the optimal solutions generated by CREDIS for specific scenarios. We investigated scenarios including up to six stores (S_1: notebook, S_2: mobile phone, S_3: home server, S_4: entertainment system, S_5: cloud provider, S_6: home organization). While the store-availability and store-vulnerability values have been estimated, the calculated solutions provide an idea of the scenario's influence on the properties of the optimal solution.

The results of our analysis are shown in Table 1. The stores included in each scenario are marked with an "x". The policy profile contained a minimum key-availability boundary condition of either 95% or 99% and the optimization criterion was key-vulnerability minimization. The vulnerability of the key fragments distributions produced by CREDIS is shown in the column "Vuln.". The values illustrate the tradeoff between availability and vulnerability. For instance, comparing scen. 1 with scen. 2 shows that relaxing the availability requirement by 4 percentage points results in a key-vulnerability that is an order of magnitude smaller. Furthermore, scen. 5 and scen. 6 show that even without the highly available stores S_5 and S_6, a high degree of availability can be reached at the cost of vulnerability. However

notice that the vulnerability of scen. 5's and scen. 6's solution is still better than that of every store in scen. 6 and better than that of S_1, S_2 and S_4 in scen. 5 respectively.

To provide a more general impression of the benefit CREDIS achieves compared to traditional approaches to store keys on single or multiple systems, we compared the key-availability and key-vulnerability of the solutions provided by three static strategies with those provided by CREDIS. Those three strategies constitute: Storing the key on a single device (*Single system*), replicating the key over all stores (*Replicated*) and fragmenting the key on all stores (*Partitioned*). We investigated scenarios with a varying number of stores with a fixed store-availability of 0.85 and a fixed store-vulnerability of 0.1. The results of the computations are shown in Figure 7. The connected points in the plot constitute the key-vulnerability of CREDIS-solutions for varying minimum key-availability policies (x-axis) and a varying number of stores. Furthermore, the key-vulnerability and key-availability of solutions provided by the static strategies are plotted as points labeled by the number of stores used.

While the number of stores does not affect the solution if the key is only stored on a single system (*Single system* in Figure 7), it is affected when partitioning or replicating the key on all stores at hand. In case of partitioning the key, the key-vulnerability *and* the key-availability decrease by orders of magnitude the more stores are used (*Partitioned* in Figure 7). In case of replicating the key, both key-availability and key-vulnerability increase by orders of magnitude (*Replicated* in Figure 7). Thus, the *Replicated* and the *Partitioned* strategy are both extreme strategies. In fact their solutions constitute upper/lower bounds for reachable key-availability and key-vulnerability values respectively.

However, in realistic scenarios, often a good balance between key-availability and key-vulnerability is demanded. Highly available keys that are highly vulnerable are as unfavorable as securely stored keys that are rarely available. CREDIS balances key-availability and key-vulnerability as much as possible, taking into account the user-defined minimum key-availability or maximum key-vulnerability boundary conditions in the policy profile. For instance, Figure 7 illustrates that CREDIS minimizes the key-vulnerability as much as possible without violating the minimum key-availability boundary condition. This results in a solution that is – depending on the number of stores – by orders of magnitude better than the naive approach of storing the key on a single system without neglecting either key-availability or key-vulnerability. Furthermore, notice that CREDIS can in fact reach the extreme solutions if it is necessary to fulfill the policy profile (e.g., *Partitioned* with 2 stores vs. CREDIS with 2 stores and minimum availability of 0.7225).

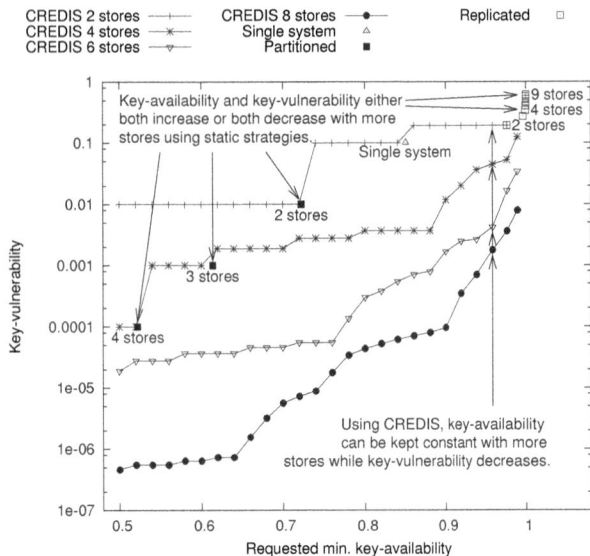

Figure 7: Simple strategies vs. CREDIS assuming store-availability 0.85 and store-vulnerability 0.1, optimization criterion: minimize key-vulnerability.

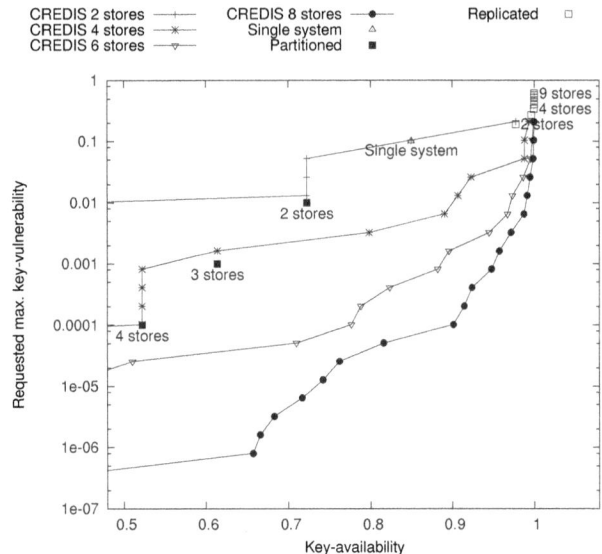

Figure 8: Simple strategies vs. CREDIS assuming store-availability 0.85 and store-vulnerability 0.1, optimization criterion: maximize key-availability.

We additionally measured CREDIS solutions for key-availability maximization scenarios with varying maximum key-vulnerability policies. The results are shown in Figure 8 and are very similar to those for key-vulnerability minimization scenarios with varying minimum key-availability in Figure 7. The slight differences can be explained as follows: In Figure 7 the key-vulnerabilities of the optimal solutions are depicted in on the y-axis and the x-axis depicts the *requested* minimum key-availabilities. Thus, the actual key-availability of each solution is greater or equal to that depicted on the x-axis. Analogously, in Figure 8, the key-availability of the optimal solutions are depicted on the x-axis and the *requested* maximum key-vulnerabilities on the y-axis. The actual key-vulnerability of each solution is less or equal to that.

6.2 Discussion: Usability and Limitations

Having evaluated the benefits of adaptively managing risk, the usability of user-centric risk management in general and of CREDIS in particular has to be discussed. Before risk can be managed, it needs to be assessed. While providing methodologies on how to derive meaningful values for both store-availability and store-vulnerability of a store is out of the scope of this paper, we provide ideas on how to initially determine store-availability and store-vulnerability: The store-availability of a system can be measured by monitoring the system over a certain period of time. To determine suitable value for the store-vulnerability parameter, studies can be employed to create guidelines (e.g., "the probability of a mobile phone becoming unnoticedly compromised in a timespan of 1 year amounts to 10%"). We believe that the quantification of the risk that comes with systems like user devices or cloud providers in a more fine grained manner constitutes a promising future research direction.

Regarding the specification of the requirements, it is possible to aid the user by presenting the range of valid values for the minimum key-availability and the maximum key-vulnerability that result in a solvable problem. The maximum reachable key-availability (and the maximum key-vul-

nerability) is determined by the key fragments distribution that *replicates* the key on *all* STs. The minimum key-availability (and the maximum key-vulnerability) is determined by the key fragments distribution that *fragments* the key on *all* STs. The user may choose a minimum key-availability and/or a maximum key-vulnerability from these ranges.

In terms of CREDIS's usability, the initial deployment of the secrets induces a certain overhead for the users, as the properties of all stores and the requirements on the credential repository have to be specified. However, these initial steps only have to performed to determine a suitable key fragments distribution. To retrieve the stored secrets, only a password has to be submitted. The lookup of the used systems' network addresses is independent of CREDIS and part of the implementation. For instance, distributed hash tables (DHTs) can be utilized for this purpose.

In the scope of this paper, we assume that the store-availability and the store-vulnerability of a store is independent from the store-availability and the store-vulnerability of other stores. Whereas this assumption does not hold in some cases, it constitutes an acceptable simplification for a first approach to the problem. We will take inter-dependencies of the parameters into account in future work.

An inherent problem of credential repositories (and other approaches such as synchronization) is constituted by the fact that a single password can be used to access multiple credentials. This especially constitutes a security issue if credentials require different protection levels (e.g., credit card PINs vs. chat messenger passwords). While this security issue is inherent to the problem setting of simplifying the credential management itself, CREDIS allows to categorize credentials by their required protection level. For instance, it is possible to define distinct credential repositories for "high-risk" credentials and "low-risk" credentials. Thus, the user may enter his password for the "low-risk" repository at a terminal and access the according credentials without the risk of the "high-risk" credentials becoming compromised.

Figure 9: Execution time: ILP-approach vs. Max-Avail heuristic (95% confidence interval)

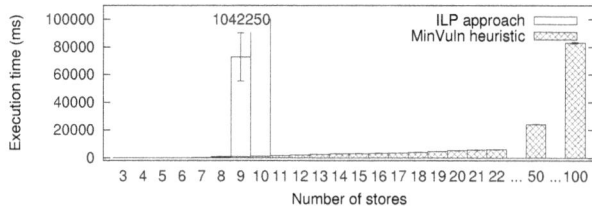

Figure 10: Execution time: ILP-approach vs. Min-Vuln heuristic (95% confidence interval)

6.3 ILP approach vs. heuristics

To evaluate the quality of the proposed heuristics we investigated both the *execution time* and the *solution quality* of the heuristics.

To evaluate the **execution time** of the heuristics, we compared the average execution time of the heuristics with the average execution time of the ILP approach. For each number of stores depicted in Figure 9 we generated 1000 random scenarios and measured the average solving time of both the heuristics and the ILP approach. For each scenario, the store-availability was independently and uniformly chosen from the range $(0.7, 1]$ for each store. The store-vulnerability was independently and uniformly chosen from the range $(0, 0.2]$. In case of the MaxAvail heuristic the policy profile contained a max. key-vulnerability boundary condition that was uniformly chosen from the range $(0, 0.1]$. In case of the MinVuln heuristic a min. key-availability boundary condition was uniformly chosen from the range $[0.7, 1)$ and the precision parameter was set to 2^{-15}. The maximum amount of bundles was limited to 10 in the policy profile. The experiment has been run on a machine with 4GB RAM and a 2.93GHz dual core CPU. To solve the ILP problems, the ILP solver Gurobi[3] was utilized. Our heuristics ran single-threaded, so only one CPU core was utilized in the measurements of the heuristic's execution time.

The results of our execution time measurements for the MaxAvail heuristic are shown in Figure 9. Notice that solving the problem by using the ILP approach is possible in reasonable time up to around 9 stores (avg. execution time: 302 seconds, not shown in the graph). The execution time of the ILP approach inclines exponentially the more stores are used. This is due to the size of the event relevance graph introduced in Section 5.2 that depends exponentially on the number of stores and the fact that solving ILP problems in general cannot be done in polynomial time. The execution time of the MaxAvail heuristic remains below 1 second even for problem instances with more than 20 stores and does not incline exponentially. Furthermore, even for large sce-

---

[3]http://www.gurobi.com

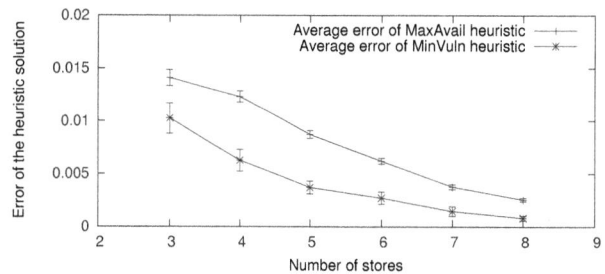

Figure 11: Absolute error: ILP-approach vs. greedy heuristics (95% confidence interval)

narios with 100 stores, the execution time of the MaxAvail heuristic remained feasible at an average of 5 seconds.

The execution time measurements of the MaxAvail heuristic are shown in Figure 10. While the MinVuln heuristic certainly performs worse than the MaxAvail heuristic, large problem instances still can be solved in acceptable time. Furthermore, the ILP approach does not perform well for large key-vulnerability minimization problems either. The MinVuln heuristic could solve scenarios with 100 stores on average in 83 seconds. We assume that even bigger scenarios can be solved in feasible time, even if as of today we cannot imagine such scenarios.

To evaluate the **solution quality** of the proposed heuristics, we determined the optimal solutions of small and medium sized problem instances using the ILP algorithm and compared the solutions of the greedy algorithms to them. We measured 10000 random scenarios for each number of stores shown in Figure 11. The random scenarios and policy profiles have been generated as described in Section 6.3.

The average error of the greedy heuristic's solution from the optimal solutions is shown in Figure 11 on the y-axis. The error has to be interpreted as the error in terms of key-availability for the MaxAvail and the error in terms of key-vulnerability for the MinVuln heuristic. The graph indicates that the induced errors are reasonably low for boundary conditions that are specified with the granularity of 10^{-2} rather than 10^{-3} or more. Furthermore, we argue that the induced error is acceptable, considering that the availability and vulnerability properties of the stores cannot be specified in a more fine grained manner in most cases.

The measurements indicate that the error declines with a rising number of stores. Based on the assumption that this trend continues for larger problem instances (which obviously cannot be proven without calculating the optimal solution for larger problem instances), we believe that for large problem instances the heuristics produce solutions that are even closer to the ILP optimum.

7. CONCLUSION

In this paper we presented CREDIS, an approach to optimally balance the vulnerability and the availability of secrets by fragmenting them on multiple systems that are heterogeneous in terms of availability and vulnerability. CREDIS enables users to freely specify what they consider an optimal fragmenting strategy by allowing them to define their needs in a policy profile. We showed that the approach can yield a reasonably secure and available credential repository even if only low-grade stores in terms of availability and vulnerability are at hand. Furthermore, we proved that the problem of determining an optimal strategy is NP-hard. However, the problem can be solved in feasible time for scenarios with up to 9 stores by Integer Linear Programming. For larger scenarios, we proposed heuristics and showed that they scale well for scenarios with up to 100 stores. We evaluated the quality of the heuristic's solutions to be acceptable for regular requirements. In future work, we will address the challenge of interdependent store availability and vulnerability properties.

8. REFERENCES

[1] J. H. Abawajy. An online credential management service for intergrid computing. In *Proc. of the IEEE Asia-Pacific Services Computing Conf. (APSCC)*, pages 101–106, 2008.

[2] L. Atzori, A. Iera, and G. Morabito. The internet of things: A survey. *Computer Networks*, 54(15):2787–2805, Oct. 2010.

[3] A. Bagherzandi, S. Jarecki, N. Saxena, and Y. Lu. Password-protected secret sharing. In *Proc. of the 18th ACM Conf. on Computer and Communications Security (CCS)*, pages 433–444, 2011.

[4] J. Basney, M. Humphrey, and V. Welch. The myproxy online credential repository. *Software: Practice and Experience*, 35(9):801–816, July 2005.

[5] J. Basney, W. Yurcik, R. Bonilla, and A. Slagell. Credential wallets: A classification of credential repositories highlighting myproxy. In *Proc. of the 31st Research Conf. on Communication, Information and Internet Policy (TPRC)*, 2003.

[6] X. Boyen. Hidden credential retrieval from a reusable password. In *Proc. of the 4th Int. Symp. on Information, Computer, and Communications Security (ASIACCS)*, pages 228–238, 2009.

[7] L. L. Burch, D. G. Earl, and S. R. Carter. Techniques for establishing and managing a distributed credential store. Patent EP1560100, August 2005.

[8] D. E. Denning and D. K. Branstad. A taxonomy for key escrow encryption systems. *Communications of the ACM*, 39(3):34–40, Mar. 1996.

[9] W. Ford and J. Kaliski, B.S. Server-assisted generation of a strong secret from a password. In *Proc. of the 9th IEEE Int. Workshops on Enabling Technologies: Infrastructure for Collaborative Enterprises (WET ICE)*, pages 176–180, 2000.

[10] S. Gupta. Security characteristics of cryptographic mobility solutions. In *Proc. of the Annual PKI Research Workshop*, pages 117–126, 2002.

[11] D. Gustafson, M. Just, and M. Nystrom. Securely available credentials (SACRED) - credential server framework - RfC 3760, 2004.

[12] D. Huynh, M. Robshaw, A. Juels, and B. Kaliski. Password synchronization. Patent US6240184, May 2001.

[13] D. P. Jablon. Password authentication using multiple servers. In *Proc. of the Conf. on Topics in Cryptology: The Cryptographer's Track at RSA (CT-RSA)*, pages 344–360, 2001.

[14] K. Jünemann, J. Köhler, and H. Hartenstein. Data outsourcing simplified: Generating data connectors from confidentiality and access policies. In *Proc. of the Workshop on Data-intensive Process Management in Large-Scale Sensor Systems (CCGrid-DPMSS)*, pages 923–930, 2012.

[15] J. Kim, H. Kwon, H. Park, S. Kim, and D. Won. An improvement of VeriSign's key roaming service protocol. In *Proc. of the Int. Conf. on Web engineering (ICWE)*, pages 281–288, 2003.

[16] T. Kwon. Virtual software tokens - a practical way to secure PKI roaming. In *Proc. of the Int. Conf. on Infrastructure Security (InfraSec)*, pages 288–302, 2002.

[17] J. Köhler and H. Hartenstein. Occasio: an operable concept for confidential and secure identity outsourcing. In *Proc. of the IFIP/IEEE Int. Symp. on Integrated Network Management (IM)*, 2013.

[18] J. Köhler, S. Labitzke, M. Simon, M. Nussbaumer, and H. Hartenstein. Facius: An easy-to-deploy saml-based approach to federate non web-based services. In *Proc. of the 11th IEEE Int. Conf. on Trust, Security and Privacy in Computing and Communications (TrustCom)*, 2012.

[19] F. Larumbe and B. Sansò. Optimal location of data centers and software components in cloud computing network design. In *Proc. of the 12th IEEE/ACM Int. Symp. on Cluster, Cloud and Grid Computing (CCGrid)*, pages 841–844, 2012.

[20] N. Leavitt. Internet security under attack: The undermining of digital certificates. *Computer*, 44(12):17–20, Dec. 2011.

[21] M. Lorch, J. Basney, and D. Kafura. A hardware-secured credential repository for grid PKIs. In *Proc. of the 4th IEEE/ACM Int. Symp. on Cluster, Cloud and Grid Computing (CCGrid)*, pages 640–647, 2004.

[22] P. D. MacKenzie and M. K. Reiter. Networked cryptographic devices resilient to capture. In *Proc. of the IEEE Symp. on Security and Privacy (SP)*, 2001.

[23] P. D. MacKenzie, T. Shrimpton, and M. Jakobsson. Threshold password-authenticated key exchange. In *Proc. of the 22nd Int. Cryptology Conf. on Advances in Cryptology (CRYPTO)*, pages 385–400, 2002.

[24] J. P. McGregor and R. B. Lee. Protecting cryptographic keys and computations via virtual secure coprocessing. In *Proc. of the Workshop on Architectural Support for Security and Anti-virus (WASSA)*, pages 11–21, 2004.

[25] J. Novotny, S. Tuecke, and V. Welch. An online credential repository for the grid: Myproxy. In *Proc. of the 10th IEEE Int. Symp. on High Performance Distributed Computing (HPDC)*, pages 104–111, 2001.

[26] D. A. Patterson, G. Gibson, and R. H. Katz. A case for redundant arrays of inexpensive disks (RAID). In *Proc. of the ACM Int. Conf. on Management of Data (SIGMOD)*, pages 109–116, 1988.

[27] T. R. Pesola. System and method for automatic synchronization of managed data. Patent US 2003/0125057 A1, Dec 2001.

[28] R. Sandhu, M. Bellare, and R. Ganesan. Password-enabled PKI: Virtual smartcards versus virtual soft tokens. In *Proc. of the Annual PKI Research Workshop*, 2002.

[29] T. Ylonen and C. Lonvick. The secure shell (SSH) authentication protocol - RfC 4252, 2006.

A Versatile Access Control Implementation: Secure Box

Bruno Alves Pereira Botelho
Fundação CPqD
Rod. Campinas-Mogi-Mirim km 118,5
13086-902 Campinas – SP – Brazil
+55(19) 3705-7140
bpereira@cpqd.com.br

Dennis Guimarães Pelluzi
Fundação CPqD
Rod. Campinas-Mogi-Mirim km 118,5
13086-902 Campinas – SP – Brazil
+55(19) 3705-4936
dpelluzi@cpqd.com.br

Emilio Tissato Nakamura
Fundação CPqD
Rod. Campinas-Mogi-Mirim km 118,5
13086-902 Campinas – SP – Brazil
+55(19) 3705-6857
nakamura@cpqd.com.br

ABSTRACT

In this demonstration paper, we describe the implementation of a versatile access control prototype based on multimodal biometrics and graphical passwords that had been designed and developed aligned with the current mobile, multichannel, multiservice, and usability demanding world. The BYOD scenario had also been considered to address the challenges related to protect both corporate and personal information that exist in mobile devices with no more boundaries.

Categories and Subject Descriptors

D.4.6 [**Security and Protection** (K.6.5)]: *Access controls, Authentication, Cryptographic controls, Information flow control.*

General Terms

Experimentation, Security, Human Factors.

Keywords

Versatile access control, multimodal biometric authentications, iconographic password, authentication.

1. INTRODUCTION

The present-day reality, where the access to multiple services is provided by wide-ranging channels and performed through an increasing variety of devices, shows that the traditional password-based authentication methods are very limited. In this multichannel and multiservice context, users are forced to deal with an increasing number of passwords and fraudsters are taking advantages of this, focusing more commonly in password hacking to obtain non-authorized access to services and information, both personal and corporate.

An intrinsic security and usability dilemma lies between a strong password, which is difficult to crack but difficult to memorize and very likely to be re-used in several services; and a weak password, which is easy to remember but also easy to crack. In the multiservice environment, where a unique password is required for each service, this dilemma becomes more evident, as multiple passwords need to be chosen, memorized and used by the user.

Besides that, the multichannel and multi-device environments face another challenge which is mainly involved with usability: the difficult to typing strong passwords on the smartphones' virtual keyboards, and the dilemma to create a distinct password for this new channel, which forces the user to define an additional password to be memorized.

In addition, in the BYOD (Bring Your Own Device) scenario, where personal information blends with corporate data in the same device, the challenge to protect the access becomes even greater. Threats include the loss of the personal mobile device containing corporate data, as well as the dangerousness of gaining access to corporate services using a combination of corporate password security policies and personal passwords.

Furthermore, the mobile device becomes a new attack vector for obtaining access to several services, as observed in an increasing security incidents related to mobile [1] and in the image based brute-force attacks against touchscreen devices [2].

To sum up, there is a need for a set of authentication methods that fits in the current mobile, multichannel, multiservice and usability demanding world.

This demonstration shows a prototype that implements a versatile access control, conceived and developed within that context, which considers that traditional passwords are no longer suitable to the current reality. This prototype, named Secure Box, implements multimodal biometric authentication, using both facial and voice recognition, additionally with iconographic authentication [3], in order to provide a versatile access control to specific services.

Secure Box emerged from the *BIOMODAL* research and development project. The objective is to develop technologies for voice and facial multimodal biometric and iconographic authentication for mobile devices. Secure Box prototype uses authentication technologies originally developed for the project.

The following sections are organized as follow: section 2 introduces the concept and architecture of the Secure Box, including its access levels, security and the implemented authentication methods, as well as some screenshots. Section 3 describes how the demonstration will be performed during SACMAT 2013.

2. SECURE BOX PROTOTYPE
2.1 Concept

Secure Box is a secure area in smartphones, initially developed for Android, designed to protect services and information in two different access control levels:

1. Access to Secure Box;

2. Access to services protected by Secure Box.

The access to both levels is obtained by selecting one of the following options:

    a) Facial biometric authentication;

    b) Voice biometric authentication;

    c) Iconographic authentication.

The concept of Secure Box is to protect the access to services and their respective sensitive data in a way that they can only be accessed by the authenticated user. Access control is versatile as the user is able to select the combination of multiple authentication methods to access the Secure Box in a multi-factor and/or multimodal biometric authentication. This versatility can also be found in the second level of the Secure Box access control, where any combination of the provided authentication methods can be used individually for each service. For some services that require low security levels, protection can be directed only to the first level of access control, discarding the second level.

In this regard, for instance, a user may use solely facial biometric authentication to access Secure Box in the first level of access. Inside the Secure Box, user may configure the prototype to use the iconographic authentication to access the corporate e-mail in the second level of access. The access to the other service, such as the ERP system, can be configured to be secured by the combination of the voice biometric authentication and the iconographic authentication.

Secure Box can be used to segregate corporate services and data from the personal data in order to be only accessible via intrinsic user authentication. On the other hand, personal data could be accessible in the traditional way. In the case of the loss of the mobile device, corporate data will still have two additional access control levels, while personal services, such as the access to pictures or personal email (password not required during each access because it is stored in the device), for instance, can be granted directly when the device is unlocked or compromised.

Another usage scenario for Secure Box is for personal purposes, where access to pictures, emails and contacts, for instance, can be performed only through Secure Box access controls.

2.2 Architecture

The features of the Secure Box prototype were defined to suit the device usage in the context of multiservice, multichannel, multi-device and BYOD. In addition, Secure Box architecture considers the balance between security and usability, an ever-increasing demand of mobile users.

The versatile access control mechanism is individual as it focuses on the mobile device, which is independent and personal. Thus, the prototype defined an offline architecture, which required that the iconographic password and the both voice and facial biometric references to be stored within the device. This offline operation required establishing a series of security controls, such as the encryption using dynamic generated keys, as discussed in Section 2.3.

The Secure Box architecture can be divided in four main elements: User Services, Application Manager, Access Control and BioAPI Service (see Figure 1), as we can see in the following sections.

2.2.1 User Services

Services accessed exclusively by Secure Box. Users can see the services after the first authentication to access Secure Box and use them after the second level of individually defined authentication methods. The implemented services in the prototype are: password repository, expense management and e-mail reader.

2.2.2 Secure Box Application Manager

Responsible for starting Secure Box services after successful second authentication level for the correspondent service. The *Secure Box Application Manager* module activates the *Access Control* module for authentication.

2.2.3 Access Control

Performs authentication and authorizes access to both levels: access to the Secure Box and access to the specific services. These accesses follow the rules established in the authentication methods: facial biometric, voice biometric and iconographic password.

2.2.4 BioAPI Service

Provides functions calls to enrollment, verification and storage of biometrics references and also for the iconographic authentication. The *BioAPI Service* is based on the BioAPI Framework, which is a set of function interfaces established by the BioAPI Consortium [4]. This service is loaded when starting Secure Box and unloaded when closing the application. Despite being part of the Secure Box solution, the *BioAPI Service* is a stand-alone application and can be used by other applications. BioAPI uses Biometric Service Provider (BSP) libraries that enable the use of operations required in the verification process. These operations use the mobile device biometric sensors (camera and microphone) to capture and process user data. Each authentication method has a specific BSP. Secure Box uses BSP for voice, facial and graphic password verification. It also uses *Access Control* components to communicate with *BioAPI Service*.

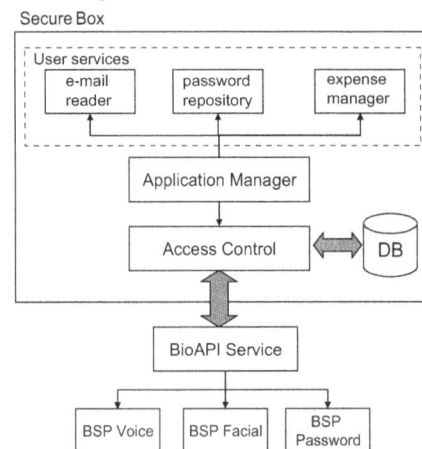

Figure 1: Secure Box architecture.

2.3 Security

The Secure Box prototype considers fifteen security points (see Figure 2) where a biometric system can be compromised. These points are being considered to be secured in the project, especially during the implementation of biometric algorithms. Particularly, the prototype had implemented a method to protect the biometric references, complemented by cryptographic mechanisms to secure the storage and to check the integrity of the prototype components.

Secure Box operates on a virtual file system specially designed to store all services and their respective data in a secure way. This virtual file system is based on the File Allocation Table (FAT) design/architecture, which uses a table to locate each file data on the disk. This allows the file to be divided in a similar data clusters and scattered around the disk. These data clusters are encrypted using the Advanced Encryption Standards (AES), which is a 128-bits data encryption block and key size of 128, 192 and 256-bits. The proposed operation mode is the XTS, which is based on the Xor-Encrypt-Xor (XEX) that allows an efficient processing of data clusters. This mode is compatible with the proposed secure file system and provides support to the storage units with dimensions indivisible by the size of data clusters.

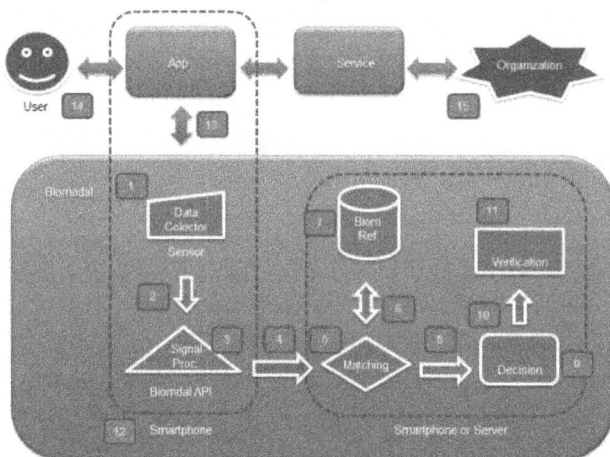

Figure 2: Security aware points in biometric systems

An important aspect of the architecture and the security mechanisms is related to the services included in Secure Box. One option was to use the existing services and incorporate them to Secure Box, while the other was to use only validated services. Aspects such as service integrity and vulnerability resulting from each implementation method were analyzed. The greatest challenge was to ensuring an appropriate security level, in which services and data would only be accessible through Secure Box.

In this way, Secure Box requires a bi-directional verification of components and services. Services to be included in Secure Box must be digitally signed using mechanisms established by ECPVS (Elliptic Curve Pinstov Vanstone Signature) standard. When the user accesses the service, Secure Box validates the components with the digital certificate together with its access control.

2.4 Authentication Methods

The Secure Box prototype specifies and implements three authentication methods that can be used in a versatile way and combined in both existing access control levels (access to Secure Box and access to services): facial biometric authentication, voice biometric authentication and iconographic authentication.

The authentication libraries had been implemented in C language, whereas authentication module encapsulation fits the BioAPI basic architecture specification (ISO/IEC 19784), including an adaptation to the iconographic authentication.

The three methods are described in the following sections:

2.4.1 Facial Biometric Authentication

Facial biometric algorithms are being implemented according to the mobile devices usage scenario, considering substantial variations of use, including illumination, position and natural day-to-day changes. There are still many aspects in this usage scenario to be resolved by the entire scientific community. The major differential related to the authentication method in Secure Box lies in the development through simulation and training using a biometric database with samples of Brazilian individuals, which tends to improve the algorithm results and optimize its evolution.

In general, facial biometric algorithms can be divided in four parts:

- Preprocessing.
- Facial feature extraction.
- User biometric reference generation.
- Verification.

A crucial aspect in the biometric authentication is its robustness against spoofing attacks, where a picture or video, for instance, can be used to forge the user to get the access. Because of the area's continuous evolution, the facial biometric algorithms used by Secure Box prototype are in constant development.

2.4.2 Voice Biometric Authentication

Similar to facial biometric authentication, voice biometric algorithms are being developed using the biometric database with Brazilian individuals. In Brazil, this is an important aspect as the algorithms under development include typical variations of the local language (Portuguese).

The technology related to voice biometric authentication implements the following basic modules:

- Parameter extraction.
- User biometric reference training.
- Verification.

2.4.3 Iconographic Authentication

Iconographic passwords take advantage of touchscreen technology on mobile devices through use of icons and images instead of the virtual keyboard. This combination of security with usability allows the use of images and icons instead of the characters represented on virtual keyboards. This can be translated into a greater facility to memorize passwords [5], more usability [6] and less correlation with passwords that can be guessed or be listed in dictionaries.

One of the main features in the iconographic authentication is the ability to use a collection of flexible icons, both in size and type of icons. This flexibility leads to a new perspective to evaluate security and usability, once the collection of items included in the iconographic authentication system can be broader than the alphanumeric keyboard, and icons can be replaced or optimized, what is something impossible when using a keyboard. Besides the size of the collection and the icons included in it, the iconographic authentication system tested in this analysis enables users to configure the size of the iconographic password, the order (position) and the number of icons presented, the arrangement or non-arrangement of the iconographic password, in addition to the possibility to use the same icon twice in a password.

The analyzed iconographic authentication represents an implementation with established parameters that consist of selecting, no matter the order, a previously chosen subset of the twenty icons, which are randomly distributed in a 5x4 grid.

2.5 Screenshots

Figure 3 shows the Secure Box prototype screenshots: starting Secure Box; iconographic authentication and facial biometric authentication. Figure 4 shows the voice biometric authentication and authentication methods for each service in Secure Box.

Figure 3: Secure Box first level of access, iconographic authentication and facial biometric authentication.

Figure 4: Secure Box voice biometric authentication and authentication methods for each particular service.

3. DEMONSTRATION PROPOSAL

The objective of this demonstration is to present a versatile access control mechanism implemented in the Secure Box prototype, which provides flexibility in selecting the best authentication methods for each specific case. The purpose is not to evaluate the effectiveness of biometric algorithms and iconographic authentication, as these technologies are constantly evolving in the scientific community and the project is under development. The demonstration will be performed in two stages:

1. Demonstration of Secure Box prototype operation emphasizing authentication methods.

2. Enrollment of biometric records and definition of iconographic passwords to be used by the versatile access control mechanism (volunteers required).

The demonstration will be performed on Android smartphone, but the screen can be displayed on a larger screen by using a video projector. There is a limitation regarding the screen projection for facial recognition. However, during the second stage of the demonstration, volunteers will be able to evaluate it by in-hand usage of the prototype.

In the demonstration scenario, the first stage intends to demonstrate the first level of access control to Secure Box prototype. This will be performed through a unique authentication mechanism (iconographic authentication). The focus will be to show how the user can choose another authentication method, or combine them.

In the second stage, a set of services (e-mail, expense management, password repository) will be configured using the corresponding authentication method, according to the required security level. In this regard, the email service will be configured using facial biometric authentication, whereas the password repository will be configured with all three authentication methods: facial biometric authentication, voice biometric authentication and iconographic authentication. In addition, the expense management service will not use an authentication method. This service will be accessed directly from Secure Box.

During the demonstration, Secure Box will be reset and volunteers will be able to set an iconographic password and enroll their biometric information. They will also be able to test the versatile access control and configure the authentication methods to be used in every service available in Secure Box.

4. ACKNOWLEDGMENTS

The authors acknowledge the financial support given to this work, under the project "Biometric Multimodal and Iconographic Authentication for Mobile Devices – BIOMODAL", granted by the Fund for Technological Development of Telecommunications – FUNTTEL – of the Brazilian Ministry of Communications, through Agreements Nr. 01.09.0627.00 with the Financier of Studies and Projects - FINEP / MCTI..

5. REFERENCES

[1] Tech World, "Top security threats in 2013: Mobile attacks", accessed on March 28, 2013, http://features.techworld.com/security/3420126/top-security-threats-in-2013-mobile-attacks/.

[2] B. Botelho, E. Nakamura, N. Uto, "Implementation of Tools for Brute Forcing Touch Inputted Passwords", in The 7th International Conference for Internet Technology and Secured Transactions - ICITST-2012, December, 2012.

[3] X. Suo, Y. Zhu, and G. Owen, "Graphical passwords: a survey", in ACSAC '05 Proceedings of the 21st Annual Computer Security Applications Conf., 2005, pp. 463-472.

[4] ISO/IEC JTC 1/SC 37. Information technology - Biometric application programming interface – Part 1: BioAPI specification, ISO/IEC 19784-1:2006. Genebra, 2006. 167 p.

[5] I. Ávila, E. Menezes, A. Braga, "Memorization Techniques in Iconic Passwords", in IHCI 2012 (Interfaces and Human Computer Interaction 2012), July 2012.

[6] C. Tambascia, A. Braga, E. Menezes, F. Negrão, "User Experience Evaluation In The Creation And Use Of Iconographic Passwords For Authentication In Mobile Devices", in The Second International Conference on Mobile Services, Resources, and Users - MOBILITY 2012, October 2012.

Permission Path Analysis Based on Access Intelligence

Detlef Sturm
Beta Systems Software AG
Alt-Moabit 90d
D-10559 Berlin
detlef.sturm@betasystems.com

Axel Kern
Beta Systems Software AG
Josef-Lammertings-Allee 14
D-50933 Köln
axel.kern@betasystems.com

ABSTRACT

The current Idintity and Access Management (IAM) landscape mainly consists of classic Identity Management (IdM) and business-oriented Access Governance. IdM focuses more on providing a single point of administration and provisioning users with the needed access rights. In contrast, Access Governance concentrates on integrating business departments in the assignment and controlling of access rights in the organisation. It therefore provides functions like access request and approval workflows and access certification processes. In addition, the demand to analyse access right structures to cover compliance requirements increases. We therefore use a business intelligence (BI) based approach to complement the current IAM landscape with comprehensive and powerful analysis capabilities.

We see the following additional values in providing a separate Access Intelligence system:

- Using a BI system allows us to convert the access data into a format which allows flexible and fast analytics.

- We can fulfil the demand of many organisations to separate their operative access control systems and the analytics system.

Using the well-known capabilities of a BI system, new analyses are provided. One example is the permission path analysis. It divides complex access structures into single paths and thereby lays the foundation for effective access right analyses. In this paper we present the permission path analysis and describe two evaluations based on it.

Categories and Subject Descriptors

K.6.5 [**Management of Computing and Information Systems**]: Security and Protection

Keywords

Access Intelligence, Identity Management, Access Governance, Role-Based Access Control

1. INTRODUCTION

Many organisations have a heterogeneous system landscape which uses a number of different access right concepts. The goal of all these concepts is to provide users with those access rights on resources they need to fulfil their work. Based on the high number of users and resources to protect in large organisations, the administration of these access rights can be quite complex and time consuming. Depending on the particular system, a number of different techniques using quite a number of diverse security objects like roles, user groups, authorisation profiles and resource groups. The rationale behind these security objects is always encapsulation: Instead of assigning single access rights some kind of grouping is used allowing easier administration. The drawback is a higher complexity of access right structures due to the higher number of object types and the multitude of connections.

For the analysis of the resulting access right structures, new questions arise which can be answered using our Access Intelligence system. Besides the basic question "Who has which access right on what resource?" the widely ramified structure leads to "How (i.e. via which security objects) did a user get his access rights?". In our Access Intelligence system we have developed a method which divides the complete access right structure into single paths as a base for powerful analysis capabilities. The above question can thus be concretised as "Via which access right paths does a user get his access rights?" This approach allows a multitude of novel analyses which we cover under the term "permission path analysis".

2. ACCESS INTELLIGENCE

Governance in access management also called "Identity and Access Governance" (IAG) means that the business departments take on more responsibility for safeguarding resources and restricting activities. In consequence, the assignment of access rights must be controlled more tightly, and existing rights must be confirmed (recertified) at regular intervals. One of the main challenges of Access Governance is presented by the need to handle huge quantities of data and their extremely complex structures. A solution is achieved by aggregating and visualizing these data in a business understandable form.

Established procedures and methods in Business Intelligence (BI) have become the cornerstone for achieving this. The use of BI methods to prepare authorisation structures leads the way to Access Intelligence. The basic, mature principles that make business intelligence successful for business

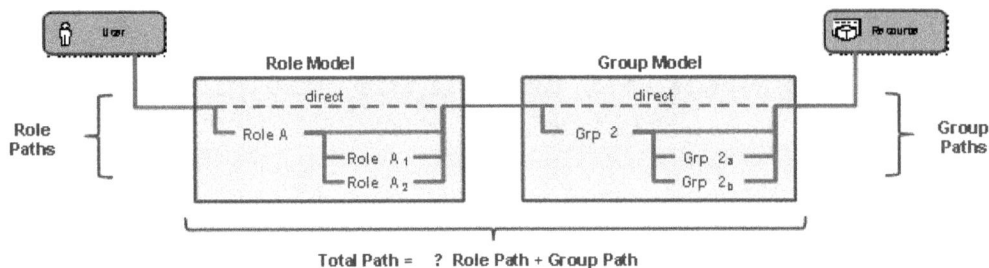

Figure 1: Role and Group Paths

decisions can be applied in IAG to achieve real transparency of activities involving access in the enterprise. As a result, well-proven methods are finding their way into new areas of application.

Access Intelligence provides powerful and comprehensive analysis features. These include access rights reports and activities like:

- Ready-to-use and pre-configured standard reports which will be distributed either via scheduler/email notification or on demand. Moreover, the on-demand reports can also be adapted manually by filtering, sorting and sizing.

- Ad-hoc reports: self-service Business Intelligence that allows the easy, efficient creation of individual reports according to specific needs, based on a business understandable data model.

3. PERMISSION PATH ANALYSIS

The major part of access right assignments normally occurs using additional security objects like roles and groups. Roles are mostly used as organisation-wide objects and often reflect business responsibilities. Groups are mostly used in specific access control systems like Windows Active Directory or IBM RACF. In addition, role and group concepts often use (separate) hierarchies. In terms of the permission path analysis, role and group models build separate collections of paths. The overall path of an authorisation (e.g. the assignment of a resource to a user via roles and groups) results in the addition of all single paths (see fig. 1).

For clarification, we show a simple authorisation structure. The example in fig. 2 consists of three users which are assigned to several resources using different paths. We use role hierarchies as well as group hierarchies. As a result, the following paths from users to resources occur:

1. User 1 → RoleA → RoleA1 → Grp1 → Resource I (Path Length: 3)

2. User 1 → RoleA → RoleA2 → Grp2 → Grp2a → Resource II (Path Length: 4)

3. User 1 → RoleA → RoleA2 → Grp2 → Grp2b → Resource III (Path Length: 4)

4. User 2 → RoleA2 → Grp2 → Grp2a → Resource II (Path Length: 3)

5. User 2 → RoleA2 → Grp2 → Grp2b → Resource III (Path Length: 3)

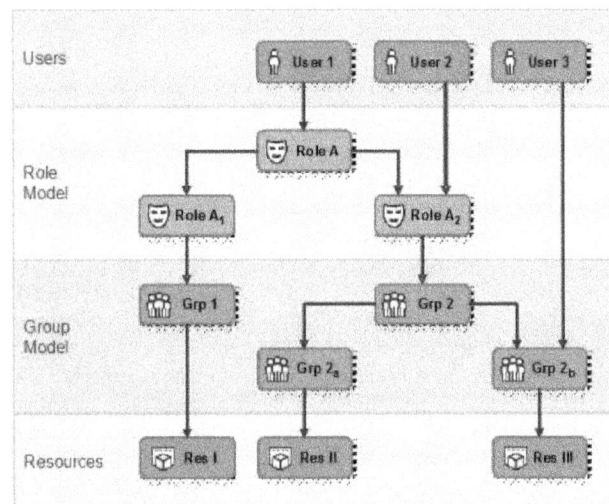

Figure 2: Example of a simple access right structure

6. User 3 → Grp2b → Resource III (Path Length: 1)

Besides the user-resource view, other connections exist:

- user-role, user-group,

- role-role, role-group, role-resource,

- group-group, group-resource.

An organisation could, for example, be interested in analysing its roles and groups including the relevant permission paths. The analysis for role A produces four connected groups using the following paths:

- Group1:   via RoleA1

- Group2:   via RoleA2

- Group2a: via RoleA2 Grp2

- Group2b: via RoleA2 Grp2

The concept of permission paths allows novel analyses like redundancy analysis or path length analysis.

3.1 Redundancy Analysis

The redundancy analysis examines redundant paths in access right structures. Redundant paths are multiple access right assignments which occur when security objects with

254

overlapping assignments are connected. For overlapping role or group models, the following scenarios exist:

Role and group model in itself do not show overlaps. By connecting both structures, redundancies occur. In fig. 3, group 3 is connected to role A via two different paths.

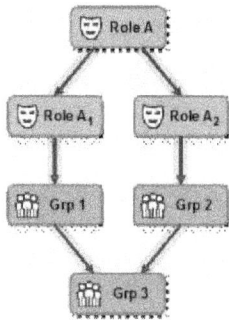

Figure 3: Redundancy Scenario 1

In the role model, a group is assigned to more than one role. Via the role hierarchy, a redundancy occurs in fig. 4.

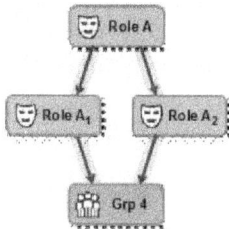

Figure 4: Redundancy Scenario 2

Fig. 5 shows an example, where redundant paths exist inside the role model.

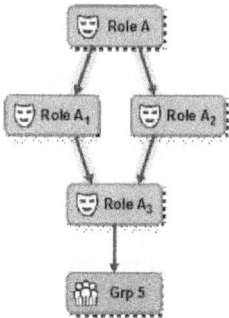

Figure 5: Redundancy Scenario 3

The role and group model in fig. 6 are free of redundancies. However, overlaps can occur when assigning roles to users. The example shows that User 5 is connected to group 2 via two different paths. The assessment whether specific redundancies are intended or not is dependent on the access right models of an organisation. Our Access Intelligence system provides comprehensive reports to analyse path structures so that unwanted redundancies can be detected. In the last chapter we describe two use cases to illustrate this.

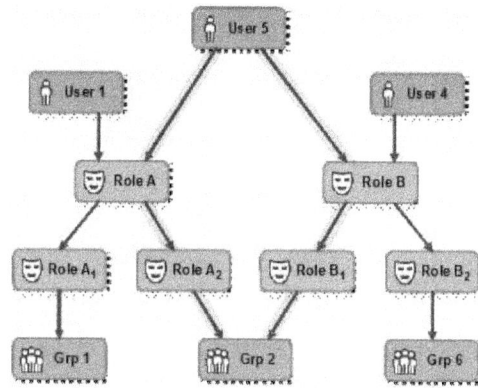

Figure 6: Redundancy Scenario 4

3.2 Path Length Analysis

The redundancy analysis examines the length of paths in access right structures. The path length is defined as the number of security objects between two end points of a connection, e.g. a user and a resource. Organisations often have comparable average path lengths due to the implemented access right models. E.g., a typical role model has two or three hierarchy levels. There may also be specific policies like "critical resources should always be directly connected". Deviations of path lengths from the average can imply security risks and are therefore highlighted in the Access Intelligence system.

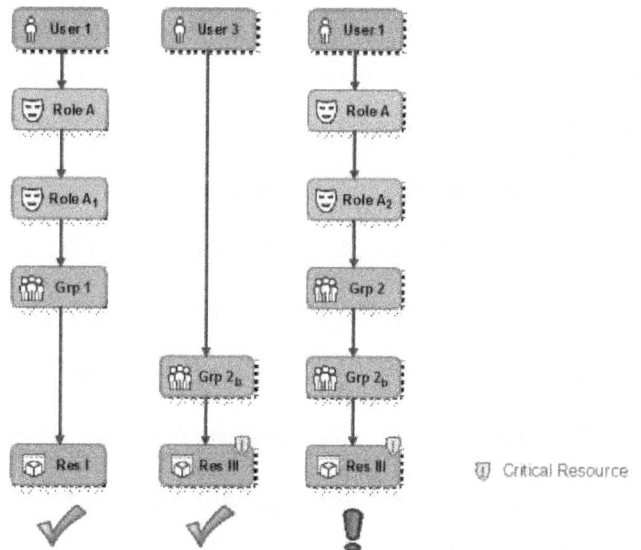

Figure 7: Access Right Paths and Critical Resources

The example in fig. 7 shows the path length analysis for the access to resources I and III where Resource III is marked as "high risk". The assignment of Resource I has the average path length of 3 and therefore is OK. The assignment of the critical Resource III to User 3 has path length 1 and complies with the company policy "Critical resources have to be directly connected to users". The last connection, however, does not comply with this policy. It is therefore highlighted. This finding should possibly lead to a correction of the access right structure for this resource.

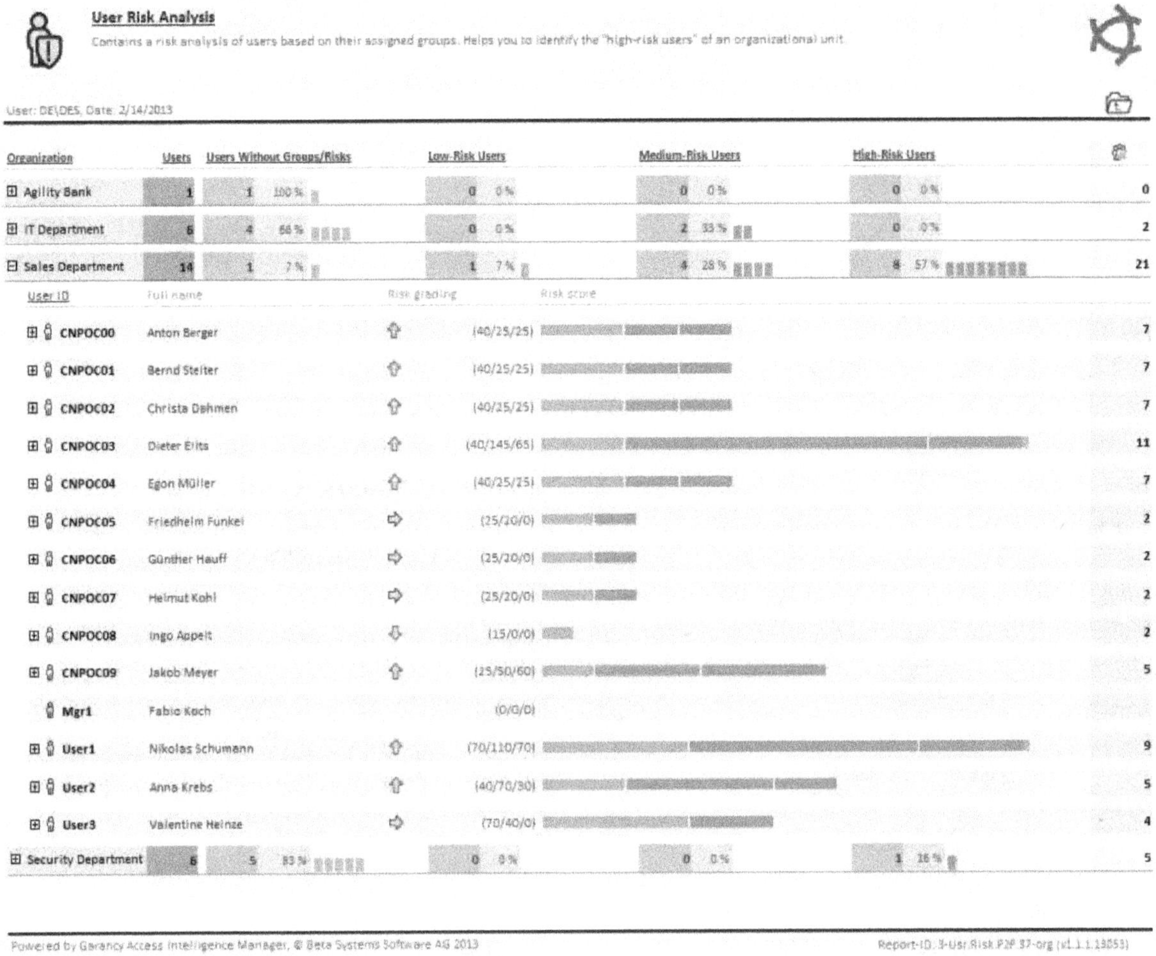

Figure 8: User Risk Analysis Report

Using the path length analysis in our Access Intelligence system allows easy checking of specific organisational policies and detecting flaws in the access right structures. Consequent use of these analyses and adaptation of the concerned assignments lead to a higher quality of the access model.

4. USE CASES

4.1 Use Case 1: Role Modelling

Every security object (e.g. a role) which encapsulates a number of access rights should have a clear and understandable semantic. Thus the usage and control of the access control model is much simpler and less error-prone for administrators, auditors etc. One criterion for a clear semantic is the strict separation of functions between roles. This can be achieved by minimising redundancy between roles.

4.2 Use Case 2: Direct Control of Critical Resources

Every organisation has access rights with high risks assigned to their users (e.g. which allow paying high sums of money). Controlling these critical authorisations is one of the most important aspects of access governance. Access

Intelligence supports organisations for this task in two ways:

- Access rights with high risks are highlighted to allow risk scoring. Fig. 8 shows a corresponding user risk analysis report.

- Policies can be checked. As mentioned earlier, one policy could be that critical resources should always be directly assigned. This policy can easily be verified using the path length analysis.

4.3 Use Case 3: Depth of Role Hierarchies

With increasing depth, the complexity of a role hierarchy goes up. Normally, organisations use a somehow fixed structure of roles. Often access rights are collected in so-called IT roles which in turn are assigned to business roles which comprise the rights for an organisational unit or function. Sometimes a second level for business roles exists to allow further structuring. Thus, average role path lengths of 2 or 3 occur. Via path length analysis in Access Intelligence, deviations can easily be detected, analysed and corrected if necessary.

Sticky Policies for Mobile Devices

Francesco Di Cerbo
Applied Research
Security & Trust
SAP Labs France
805, av. Donat
06250 Mougins, France
francesco.di.cerbo@sap.com

Slim Trabelsi
Applied Research
Security & Trust
SAP Labs France
805, av. Donat
06250 Mougins, France
slim.trabelsi@sap.com

Thomas Steingruber
Free University of
Bozen-Bolzano
Piazza Universitá 1
39100 Bolzano-Bozen, Italy
thomas.steingruber@gmail.com

Gabriella Dodero
Free University of
Bozen-Bolzano
Piazza Universitá 1
39100 Bolzano-Bozen, Italy
gabriella.dodero@unibz.it

Michele Bezzi
Applied Research
Security & Trust
SAP Labs France
805, av. Donat
06250 Mougins, France
michele.bezzi@sap.com

ABSTRACT

Mobile devices consume significant amounts of information, from different sources. Thus they often deal also with sensitive or confidential data, in places or situations that could be not appropriate, or not compliant with a corporate policy: context-aware access/usage control solutions can counter such situations. We propose a prototype, called *ProtectMe*, that exploits "Sticky Policies" (SP) that are attached to resources and prescribe usage conditions.

Since mobile devices cannot foresee usage conditions of collected data, ProtectMe integrates SPs within any information consumable by mobile devices, and dynamically enforces their usage constraints. It assists users in attaching access and usage control conditions stated by resource-specific SPs, and it enforces them by making use of contextual information collected by mobile devices.

The aim of the prototype is to show the feasibility of the SP approach, merging security functionalities within a concept for expressing SPs in a user-friendly manner.

Categories and Subject Descriptors

D.4.6 [**Security and privacy**]: Security services—*access controls, information flow controls*

General Terms

Security

Keywords

Context-Aware Access Control, Context-Aware Usage Control

1. INTRODUCTION

Exploiting the diffusion of Internet connections all around the world, advanced smartphones or tablets can make use anywhere of professional data and information; yet such devices quite often are not secured , as phenomena like "Bring Your Own Device" [2] seem to suggest. Despite interesting opportunities provided by mobility, inconveniences may arise, for instance by interacting in mobility with sensitive data, in insecure locations or when connected to public networks. Mobile corporate users are responsible for using information appropriately, so they can take advantage of *access and usage control systems*, to avoid insecure situations or prevent data leakages.

A usage control system [1, 5] protects resources, by allowing or preventing operations on them, according to specific policies, that can be different for each resource. We claim that context-aware access and usage control systems can be a significant support for users in mobility, and to validate this approach, we developed a prototype, *ProtectMe*.

ProtectMe adopts the "Sticky Policy"(SP) paradigm in order to specify access and usage control directives for data created, consumed or exchanged, with an Android mobile device. ProtectMe evaluates such conditions, taking advantage of mobile device's embedded services, like the GPS position system. The SP concept binds specific control metadata to a resource, then deals with the resulting entity as a single piece of information. In this way, once a resource is annotated by a sticky policy, it can only be processed according to the latter. We assume that resources can be located anywhere (i.e. cloud servers, QR Codes, RFID, photos, 3G network, wifi proxy, etc.) and that for each environmental container a sticky policy can be attached. ProtectMe extends the approach presented by Trabelsi et al. [7], thus supporting SPs written with XACML v3 [4] and PPL languages, to express access and usage control directives, like authorizations, obligations and conditions on Android devices.

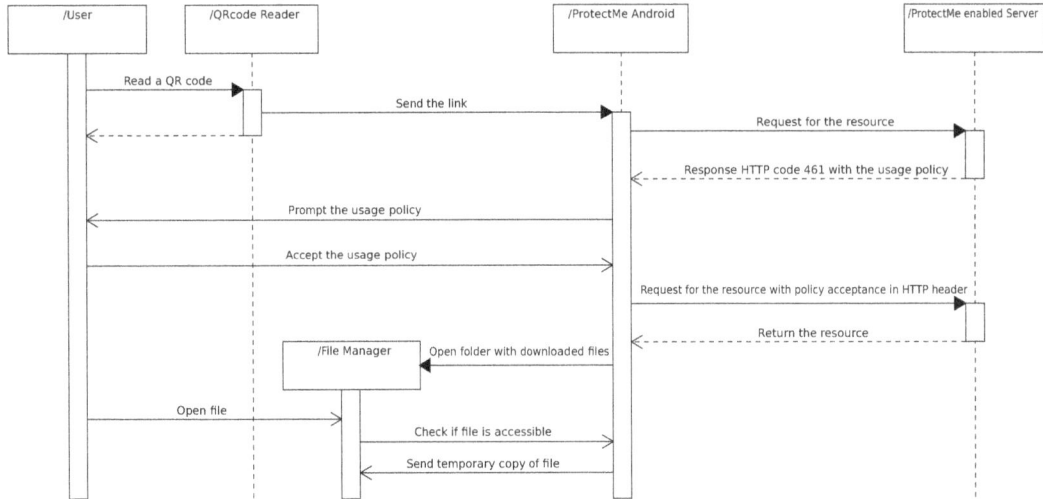

Figure 1: Demo Sequence Diagram

2. DEMONSTRATION SCENARIO

A company organizes a convention for its business partners, who are likely to attend the convention bringing their mobile devices. Conference materials can be exchanged even if they are confidential, as business partnerships imply specific NDA to be in place. However, how to state restrictions on data in a clear and user-friendly manner? and how to enforce that confidential data are not further shared? ProtectMe can help with these issues, allowing data access and usage on mobile devices. The demonstration scenario is depicted in Fig.1.

ProtectMe-protected resources can be retrieved through specific links, that are embedded in QR codes for user's convenience. QR embedded links refer to a particular interaction protocol (identified by the *protectme://* prefix), that is handled by the ProtectMe Android service, rather than by the web browser. The service contacts a ProtectMe-enabled cloud service in order to retrieve the resources; but, downloading them, it is provided with a resource-specific SP.

ProtectMe service renders the SP in a user-friendly manner (Fig. 2), so that such user can accept the policy terms. Then, it contacts the server again, this time notifying about user acceptance, and retrieves the requested resource.

ProtectMe service encrypts the resource with a secret key (unavailable to the user, and unique per-device, stored on a secure storage area [6]), and then stores the encrypted file in the mobile device's storage. Only ProtectMe-aware applications can now open the file, through the ProtectMe service; in this scenario, we are considering one of such applications, a file manager, that attempts to open the resource, with a declared purpose (reading, sharing, writing, deleting): the request is managed by ProtectMe service, that verifies the compliance to the SP (possibly using contextual information, like location). If conditions are met, then ProtectMe creates a temporary copy of the requested file, and deletes it just after having passed it to the File Manager. In this way, a low-level Linux kernel functionality prevents any further access to the resource, and no further operation shall be possible.

3. PROTOTYPE DESCRIPTION

ProtectMe is implemented as an Android service, that can be invoked by third-party applications through a standard Android inter-application communication interface (AIDL [1]). In particular, ProtectMe: **a)** manages the association between a resource and its SP, that expresses the allowed access control directives and usage purposes, as well as conditions and obligations associated to the resource exploitation; **b)**prevents arbitrary usages of SP-protected resources, through the usage of encryption techniques as described in Sec. 2; **c)** enforces the associated usage policies for a resource; i.e., to allow or to deny any specific usage request for a resource, deciding whether it is allowed or not according to the previously established policy: this decision considers also contextual information provided or received by the mobile phone like the actual physical location, active network connection and so on; **d)** interacts with remote resource providers, from which resources can be retrieved together with their associated SP.

ProtectMe provides also a user-friendly SP rendering functionality; as SP can be hard ho understand, ProtectMe embeds a concept for describing SP terms in a simple way, organized on three different elements (see Fig. 2): *Overview*, that shows a list of protected resources, together with complementary information about like authorship and others; *Restrictions*, that presents all restrictions on resources, in particular with respect to usage purposes, allowed locations (rendered on a map as well) or network connections; *Conditions*, that refers to obligations like "erase the data after 7 days" or "notify per email at each use", that will be executed automatically by ProtectMe when requested.

ProtectMe architecture is composed by a number of components, that follows to a certain extent XACML architecture for access control, extending it with usage control directives proposed by [1]. In particular, ProtectMe is composed by: *Policy Enforcement Point* (PEP), that exposed methods to access protected resources; *Policy Decision Point* (PDP), that is responsible for evaluating requests received by PEP, interacting with other modules like SPP and PIP; *SP management Point* (SPP), that mostly handles resource-policy associations, as well as SP retrieval: in fact, it parses SPs

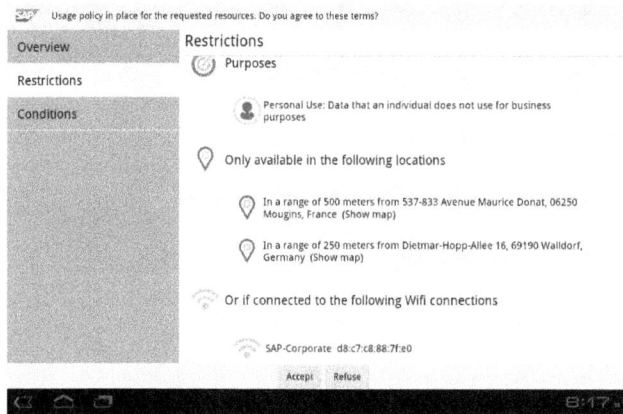

Figure 2: ProtectMe Policy Rendering

and stores them in the Android SQLite DB, to optimize performances; *Policy Information Point* (PIP), responsible for gathering data from mobile device sensors; and a *façade*, that exposes the publicly available functionalities, in the form of an Android service interface.

4. ACKNOLEDGEMENTS

This paper was partially supported by the EU FI-PPP FI-WARE project [Grant no. 285248].

5. REFERENCES

[1] Android Developer Guide. Android interface definition language (AIDL). http://goo.gl/itg7a. accessed on 2013-02-15.

[2] J. Drew. Managing cybersecurity risks. http://goo.gl/5krAZ. accessed on 2012-12-14.

[3] OASIS. eXtensible access control markup language (XACML).

[4] J. Park and R. Sandhu. The UCON ABC usage control model. *ACM Transactions on Information and System Security (TISSEC)*, 7(1):128–174, 2004.

[5] A. Pretschner, M. Hilty, and D. Basin. Distributed usage control. *Communications of the ACM*, 49(9):39–44, 2006.

[6] SAP AG. Sybase unwired platform 2.1 - data vault API references. http://goo.gl/53siE. accessed on 2013-02-15.

[7] S. Trabelsi, A. Njeh, L. Bussard, and G. Neven. The ppl engine: A symmetric architecture for privacy policy handling. In *W3C Workshop on Privacy and data usage control*, volume 4, 2010.

Content-based Information Protection and Release in NATO Operations*

Alessandro Armando
DIBRIS, U. of Genova, Italy
and
Security and Trust Unit,
FBK-Irst, Trento, Italy
armando@fbk.eu

Matteo Grasso
Security and Trust Unit,
FBK-Irst, Trento, Italy
mgrasso@fbk.eu

Sander Oudkerk
Agent Sierra Consultancy
Services
Amsterdam, Netherlands
sander.oudkerk@agentsierra.nl

Silvio Ranise
Security and Trust Unit,
FBK-Irst, Trento, Italy
ranise@fbk.eu

Konrad Wrona
NATO Communications and
Information Agency
The Hague, Netherlands
konrad.wrona@ncia.nato.int

ABSTRACT

The successful operation of NATO missions requires effective and secure sharing of information among coalition partners and external organizations, while avoiding the disclosure of sensitive information to untrusted users. To resolve the conflict between confidentiality and availability, NATO is developing a new information sharing infrastructure, called Content-based Protection and Release.

We describe the architecture of access control in NATO operations, which is designed to be easily built on top of available (service-oriented) infrastructures for identity and access control management. We then present a use case scenario drawn from the NATO Passive Missile Defence system for simulating the consequences of intercepting missile attacks. In the system demonstration, we show how maps annotated with the findings of the system are filtered by the access control module to produce appropriate views for users with different clearances and terminals under given release and protection policies.

Categories and Subject Descriptors

D.4.6 [**Security and Protection**]: Access controls

---

*The work of the first, second, and fourth authors was partly supported by NCI Agency TCA 2012:02 and the "Automated Security Analysis of Identity and Access Management Systems (SIAM)" project funded by Provincia Autonoma di Trento in the context of the "team 2009 - Incoming" CO-FUND action of the European Commission (FP7).

Keywords

NATO information sharing infrastructure, Attribute-based Access Control, XACML

1. INTRODUCTION

The successful operation of NATO missions requires effective and secure sharing of information among not only partners of the coalition, but also with external organizations (e.g. the International Committee of the Red Cross). While making as much information as possible available to the various participants involved in a mission, it is crucial to avoid the disclosure of sensitive details to users with insufficient clearance. Of course, the conflict between confidentiality and availability of information greatly complicates the task of information sharing. On the one hand, some pieces of information must be disclosed to external partners in order to ensure their effective involvement in a NATO mission. On the other hand, the disclosure of certain other pieces of information may negatively affect the outcome of the mission and should clearly be avoided.

In current NATO operations, timely sharing of information is hampered as a result of a number of limitations that are inherent to the traditional use of security markings, the two most important of which are the following. First, a security marking reflects the protection requirements and release conditions of a resource at the time of creation. Only manual (time-consuming) intervention can be used to update the markings to accommodate changes in security constraints, following strict information management procedures that may involve consultation with the resource originator (when possible). Second, owing to subjective interpretations of the security policy, resource originators may derive different security markings for resources with similar content. This leads to a situation in which similar resources are protected in different ways, leading to under- or over-restricted information sharing.

To overcome these limitations, NATO is developing a new information sharing infrastructure [5] that uses (XML-based) content metadata to enable decisions about the release of information according to *Content-based Protection and Release* (*CPR*) policies. Access control decisions are taken by considering the attributes (e.g. the clearance) of the user requesting the resource, the content metadata associated with the various pieces of information in the requested resource (e.g. the paragraphs comprising a text), and the capabilities of the *terminal* (i.e. the device and connection used by the requester to access the resource) that are related to processing, storing, and transmitting data. CPR policies aim to overcome the limitations introduced by the use of security markings discussed above by separating the association of attributes with resources from the process of determining their protection requirements and release conditions. The attributes of a resource are content properties used to derive access decisions by taking into consideration also the attributes of users, those of terminals, the protection requirements and the release conditions specified in appropriate policies by NATO security experts. This greatly reduces errors due to subjective interpretations of security directives, ensures the homogeneous protection of resources with similar content, and permits timely changes in release or protection policies to reflect evolving security requirements.

In this paper, we focus on the access control component of the NATO information sharing infrastructure. We first review the access control model of CPR policies (Section 2). We then present the enforcement architecture for CPR policies, which are designed to be easily built on top of available (service-oriented) infrastructures for identity and access control management (Section 3). Finally (Section 4), we describe a demonstration of the enforcement of CPR policies for use case scenarios drawn from the NATO Passive Missile Defence (PMD) system (see e.g. [5]), which simulates the consequences of intercepting missile attacks. The demonstration shows how maps generated by the PMD system are filtered to produce appropriate views for users of both NATO and civilian organizations, and prevent the disclosure of sensitive information to untrusted users.

2. OVERVIEW OF THE CPR ACCESS CONTROL SYSTEM

Modern joint military missions rely on network-centric operations. The NATO information sharing infrastructure [5] is built around an access control component that operates in an open and distributed environment. It has been observed that traditional access control models—such as discretionary (DAC), Mandatory (MAC), and role-based (RBAC) models—are not always adequate in this environment [2]. The Attribute-Based Access Control (ABAC) model (see e.g. [3]) offers a powerful and unifying extension to these well-known models.

In ABAC, requesters are granted or denied access to a resource based on the properties, called attributes, that may be associated to users, resources, and the context. Examples of attributes are identity, role, and military rank of users; identity, precision, and sensitivity of resources; time of day and (some part of) the system state for the context. In ABAC, suitably defined attributes can represent security labels, clearances and classifications (for encoding MAC), identities and access control lists (for DAC), and roles (for RBAC). In this sense, ABAC supplements traditional access control models rather than supplanting them [3]. Policies in ABAC can be seen as conditions on the attribute values of the entities involved in an access decision or, in other words, they are Boolean functions that map the attribute values of

the user u, the resource r, and the context c to true ("permit") when u is entitled to get access to r in the context c, and false ("deny") otherwise.

The model underlying CPR policies can be seen as a refinement of ABAC in three respects. First, in addition to the attributes of users, resources, and the context, those of terminals are considered, i.e. the capabilities of the device through which a user is trying to access a resource. Examples of terminal attributes are the hardware model, the type of encryption used to locally store data, and the type of connection to the terminal (e.g. SSL).

Second, the CPR (access control) policies are structured in two distinct sub-policies:

- a *release policy*, taking into account user, resource, and contextual attributes

- a *protection policy*, taking into account resource, terminal, and contextual attributes.

This enables separation of policy management roles and reflects the current procedures used within international and governmental organizations, including NATO. For example, consider the situation in which a user wants to access NATO classified information. This requires, on the one hand, connecting to a network infrastructure used for processing NATO classified information. To do this, a terminal must satisfy a number of technical requirements related to hardware and software configuration that are precisely defined in NATO technical directives and guidance documents. On the other hand, the security policy governing user access to the documents stored in the network is defined in a separate set of directives and guidance documents.

Third, access in CPR is content-based, i.e. decisions about the release of information are derived from content metadata. (For simplicity, a read-only mode for accessing information is considered in this paper.) Depending on the granularity with which content metadata is associated to (pieces of) a resource, access requests are then answered with *permitted views*, i.e. selected pieces of a resource that the user is allowed to access, and not with a simple "permit/deny" answer. Granular association of content metadata to information is particularly suited when resources are structured as containers of information that may recursively contain other structured or atomic resources, each one with its own content metadata. A mechanism for the fine-grained association of attributes to selected pieces of information in structured resources is NATO XML-labelling [4], which allows for the binding of extensive content-metadata structures to subsets of an XML node set. In general, a typical structured resource is an XML document in which content metadata is captured in XML attributes for each of the elements in the document. Access control systems for XML documents have already been proposed in the literature. While we believe that some of the techniques used in these works (e.g. [1]) can be adapted to enhance the performance of the CPR access control system when mediating access to XML documents, our work is more general as it aims to mediate access to a variety of structured resources (ranging from PDF files to military documents in proprietary formats) in a way that is transparent to the user.

Abstractly, the CPR access control system mediates the request to read the content of a structured resource r submitted by a user u with a terminal t in two phases. First, it retrieves the attributes of u and t together with those of all the (sub-)resources contained in r; let $R(r)$ be their set. Second, it builds the permitted view of the resource derived from r, which is composed of only those resources in $R(r)$ that u is permitted to view by using t according to the given release and protection policies. When none of the resources in $R(r)$ can be accessed by u, "deny" is returned.

3. ARCHITECTURE OF THE CPR ACCESS CONTROL SYSTEM

The OASIS standard XACML (eXtensible Access Control Markup Language)[1] is an ABAC framework, in which attributes associated with requesters, resources, and the context are used to decide whether a given user may access a resource in a particular context. The XACML standard defines, in addition to a declarative access control policy language implemented in XML, an architecture for the enforcement of policies describing how to evaluate authorization requests according to the rules defined in policies. Since CPR policies can be seen as a refinement of ABAC policies (as argued in Section 2), we propose an architecture for the CPR access control system that can be easily integrated with the XACML framework. Figure 1 shows the architecture of the CPR access control system. Readers familiar with XACML can easily recognize the use of four modules (PEP, PDP, PIP, and PAP, whose role is explained below) that are part of the XACML architecture for policy enforcement defined in the OASIS standard. The integration of these components in the CPR access control system has been designed to solve three main issues that are specific to information sharing in NATO missions.

First, CPR policies take into considerations terminal attributes in addition to users, resources, and contextual information (as is standard in ABAC). In XACML 3.0, the `AttributeDesignator` construct allows for the addition of attributes to pre-defined categories (i.e. `subject`, `resource`, `environment`, and `action`) and the definition of attributes for custom categories, such as one for terminals in CPR. In the architecture of Figure 1 (upper left corner), user and terminal attributes are encapsulated in credentials that are stored in two databases, managed by an Identity Provider (IdP). This offers support for the authentication of users via, e.g., Single-Sign-On (SSO) solutions, and of terminals (devices) by using, e.g., Trusted Platform Modules (TPM). When the condition of a rule in an XACML policy involving users or terminals needs to be evaluated, their credentials are retrieved from the appropriate database. Second, CPR policies base authorization decisions on the various pieces of information contained in a resource. Since NATO missions involve several types of resource, the role of the Resource Mediator (bottom of Figure 1) is to maintain the association between identifiers (e.g. URIs) of composed and atomic resources with their attributes. For this, it is assumed that dedicated sub-modules that are capable of retrieving both the identifiers and the attribute-value pairs of atomic resources are available. Indeed, the design and implementation of these sub-modules depend on the types of resources. There are some general approaches that can be taken to address this task. For example, the XACML 3.0 Hierarchical

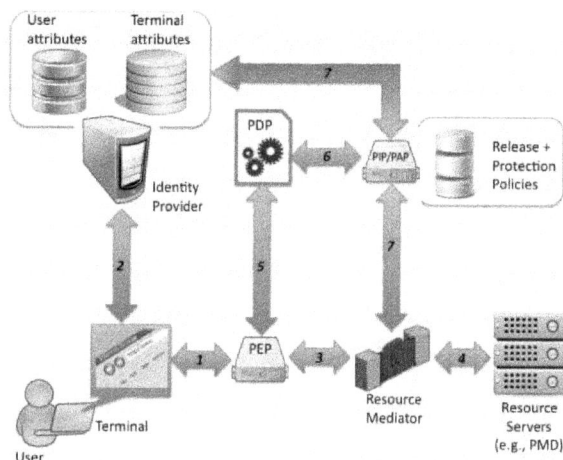

Figure 1: CPR Access Control System Architecture

Resource Profile[2] may be used to handle resources organized as hierarchies. Another approach could be the use of the NATO XML-labelling specification [4] that permits the association of content labels to a variety of resources.

Third, access decisions are not simply "permit" or "deny" but consist of permitted views of the requested resource, containing only that information that can be accessed by the requester. This implies that a request to access a composed resource r must be expanded into several access requests, one per resource contained in r. This is made possible by the Resource Mediator, which is capable of extracting both the identifiers of each resource in r and their associated attributes. In this way, a set of multiple resource access control requests can be formed, once the attributes of users, terminals, and environment have also been obtained. XACML 3.0 offers support for multiple requests via the so-called Multiple Decision Profile, which allows performance improvements by packing multiple access queries into one XACML request.

We now describe the data flow underlying the architecture in Figure 1, where the double arrows stand for request-response interactions. A user u, via a terminal t, makes a request to the available *Resource Servers* (RS) using a browser. The request is intercepted (arrow *1*) by a *Policy Enforcement Point* (PEP). If u and t are not yet authenticated, the browser is redirected (arrow *2*) to the IdP, which is responsible for authentication. Then the PEP forwards (arrow *3*) the request to the *Resource Mediator* (RM), which selects the appropriate RS and forwards (arrow *4*) the request to it. The RS retrieves the resource from a database or performs some computation to build it. Once available, the resource is passed back to the RM, which assigns it an identifier r and extracts the set $IAV(r)$ of pairs $(r', A_{r'})$ where r' is the identifier of a resource in r and $A_{r'}$ is the associated set of attribute-value pairs (if r is atomic, then $IAV(r)$ contains just one pair (r, A_r)). At this point, the RM sends to the PEP (arrow *3*) the set $R(r) = \{r'|(r', A_{r'}) \in IAV(r)\}$ of resource identifiers in r. In turn, the PEP sends to the *Policy Decision Point* (PDP) (arrow *5*) a tuple composed of the identifiers of u and t (e.g. the tokens obtained from the IdP during authentication) together with the set $R(r)$;

[1] http://docs.oasis-open.org/xacml/3.0/

[2] http://docs.oasis-open.org/xacml/3.0/xacml-3.0-hierarchical-v1-spec-cd-03-en.html

such a tuple encodes the (multiple) request of the user u to get access to all those resources in $R(r)$ that he/she is allowed to view using terminal t. The *Policy Information Point* (*PIP*) is asked (arrow **6**) to retrieve the attributes of u and t from the databases (right-angled arrow **7**) together with the attributes of the resources in $R(r)$ from the RM (vertical arrow **7**). The latter can be easily extracted from the set $IAV(r)$ that is stored in the RM. At this point, the PDP returns to the PEP (arrow **5**) the collection of decisions for the multiple resource request under the pre-defined CPR policy (obtained as a combination of release and protection policies), which has also been retrieved by the PIP, which also acts as a *Policy Administration Point* (*PAP*) in our architecture. (The reason to merge the PIP and the PAP is to provide the possibility to pre-process policies so that only those constraining the attribute values of u, t, and (most importantly, because of the variety of the type of resources and potentially large number of associated attributes) r are included, as those that do not mention them are certainly not applicable.) In this way, a "permit" or a "deny" decision is associated to each resource identifier in $R(r)$ and the PEP can ask the RM to compute the permitted view r' of r by including only those resources in $R(r)$ for which the PDP has returned "permit." Finally, the PEP sends r' back to the browser (arrow **1**).

We have implemented the architecture in Figure 1 on top of the WSO2 Security & Identity Gateway Solution[3] that supports authentication based on SAML 2.0[4] and authorization through XACML.

4. THE NATO PASSIVE MISSILE DEFENCE DEMONSTRATION

The goal of the NATO Passive Missile Defence (PMD) system is to minimize the effects of missile attacks. The PMD system runs simulations of a missile attack in a given geographic area by taking into account several parameters, such as the type of missile employed in the attack and weather conditions. As a result of the simulation, a map of the predicted missile impact area is calculated, enriched with annotations about a description of the consequences of the impact at several locations, hazard areas with risk analysis, the trajectories of the threatening and intercepting missiles, sub-munition locations and descriptions, etc. The maps are represented in the XML-based Keyhole Markup Language (KML) so that, e.g., Google Earth can be used to visualize them (see e.g. Figure 2).

The PMD system is an important component of NATO missions for crisis-response planning and disaster preparation. In this context, missions require the coordination of coalition partners with civilian organizations (e.g. for rescue and medical operations). Thus, sharing (selected parts of) the content stored in KML maps created by the PMD system is crucial for the success of a mission. When we demonstrate the system, we show that the CPR access control system of Figure 1 can support the disclosure of information depending on suitably defined CPR policies, such as (a) a soldier may see sub-munition locations and descriptions while a civilian cannot (this depends on the clearance of the user and is part of the release policy), (b) a soldier taking part in the opera-

Figure 2: A KML map generated by the PMD system with missile trajectories and hazard areas

tions in the area of the PMD simulation can access the map, but a soldier not involved in the mission—even one with a high rank—cannot (this is an instance of the need-to-know principle and is again part of the release policy), and (c) to access the description of the consequences of intercepting the missile, the terminal should have an enhanced configuration guaranteeing a secure connection and local encryption of data (this condition depends on the capabilities of terminals and is part of the protection policy).

The system demonstration is structured as follows. First, we illustrate the CPR policies and some sets of attribute values that characterize typical users and terminal profiles in military and civilian organizations. We show a complete KML map that the PMD system has generated as the result of running a certain simulation; for an example, see Figure 2. We then consider the map as a KML file and its graphic rendering by Google Earth. We make explicit the relationship between the graphical objects and the corresponding KML resources together with their identifiers and attributes (content metadata). This concludes the overview of the attributes and allows us to present excerpts of the XACML file containing the CPR policy sketched above: the evaluation of some conditions on the attributes will be demonstrated on the users, terminals, and resources previously considered. The demo is concluded with a step-by-step execution (cf. the data-flow in Figure 1) of some resource requests and a comparison of the permitted views of the same map accessed by different users and terminals.

5. REFERENCES

[1] E. Damiani, S. De Capitani di Vimercati, S. Paraboschi, and P. Samarati. A fine-grained access control system for XML documents. *ACM Trans. Inf. Syst. Secur.*, 5(2):169–202, May 2002.

[2] S. De Capitani di Vimercati, S. Foresti, S. Jajodia, and P. Samarati. Access control policies and languages in open environments. In *Secure Data Management in Decentralized Systems*, 2007.

[3] X. Jin, R. Krishnan, and R. Sandhu. A Unified Attribute-Based Access Control Model Covering DAC, MAC and RBAC. In *DBSec*, 2012.

[4] S. Oudkerk. NATO Profile for the 'Binding of Metadata to Data Objects' - version 1.0. Technical Note 1455, NC3A, The Hague, Netherlands, 2011.

[5] K. Wrona and G. Hallingstad. Development of High Assurance Guards for NATO. In *Military Comm. and Info. Sys. Conf. (MCC)*, 2012.

---

[3] http://wso2.com/solutions/security-and-identity-gateway/
[4] http://docs.oasis-open.org/security/saml/v2.0/

Author Index

www.ingramcontent.com/pod-product-compliance
Lightning Source LLC
Chambersburg PA
CBHW061352210326
41598CB00035B/5961